Theorising the Legitimacy of EU Regulatory Agencies

Natalia Kohtamäki

Theorising the Legitimacy of EU Regulatory Agencies

PETER LANG

Bibliographic Information published by the Deutsche Nationalbibliothek
The Deutsche Nationalbibliothek lists this publication in the Deutsche Nationalbibliografie; detailed bibliographic data is available online at http://dnb.d-nb.de.

Library of Congress Cataloging-in-Publication Data
A CIP catalog record for this book has been applied for at the Library of Congress.

Project financed with the resources from the National Science Centre, Poland
Decision number: DEC-2013/09/D/HS5/01277

Cover Design: © Olaf Gloeckler, Atelier Platen, Friedberg
Cover image: © Emilia Skowrońska

ISBN 978-3-631-74861-9 (Print) · E-ISBN 978-3-631-78535-5 (E-PDF)
E-ISBN 978-3-631-78536-2 (EPUB) · E-ISBN 978-3-631-78537-9 (MOBI)
DOI 10.3726/b15422

Peter Lang – Berlin · Bern · Bruxelles · New York · Oxford · Warszawa · Wien

Reviewed by Profesor Adam Łazowski, School of Law, University of Westminster
Language editing: Radosław Alf, Andrew Dobson

www.peterlang.com

Acknowledgements

When referring to the fundamental idea that drove the creation of the EU regulatory agencies, which have become platforms for the coordination of exchanges of opinions and information in specific areas of the European internal market, it should be emphasised that for a scholarly work to be created, intellectual discourse and opportunities for dialogue with other researchers are of fundamental importance. While working on this publication, I experienced the kindness of many people whose constructive criticism and useful comments influenced the final shape of the analysis I conducted.

In particular, I would like to thank the authorities of the Faculty of Law and Administration at the Cardinal Stefan Wyszyński University in Warsaw, including, first of all, the Dean, Professor Marek Michalski, and secondly, the Director of the Institute of International Law, the European Union and International Relations, Professor Elżbieta Karska, for their support and encouragement while completing the book.

In addition, I would like to thank the publishing reviewer, Professor Adam Łazowski, for his many valuable substantive comments. I am also grateful for the feedback which I received from the discussions with Professors of my "home" Faculty of Law and Administration at the Cardinal Stefan Wyszyński University in Warsaw, as well as for the support of my colleagues from this Faculty and from Law Faculties of the Universities in Jena, Berlin, Bonn and Helsinki.

My special thanks go to the Director of the Walter Hallstein Institute for European Constitutional Law at the Law Faculty of the Humboldt University of Berlin, Professor Matthias Ruffert, whose valuable suggestions were reflected in the clarification of the research scope of this treatise. I also wish to express my gratitude to the employees of the Chair for Public Law and European Law, headed by Professor Ruffert, for their assistance with a library query at the Humboldt University of Berlin and the Berlin State Library.

This monograph also owes much of its existence to the magnificent collection of publications in the Library of the German Bundestag in Berlin. I would like to express my gratitude to Ms Renate Körber and the Library's employees for making it possible for me to make use of it. I also wish to thank Director Aleksandra Deptuła and the employees of the Library of the Faculty of Law and Administration at the Cardinal Stefan Wyszyński University in Warsaw for helping me to make use of their Polish collections.

This book could not have been completed without the financial support granted by the National Science Centre Poland. As part of the research grant financed by this institution (Decision number: DEC-2013/09/D/HS5/01277), I was able to purchase specialised foreign-language literature on regulatory agencies, complete a research internship in Berlin in May 2016, participate in nationwide congresses on European issues and most importantly publish this work in English with a publishing house possessing international reach. I cordially thank them for providing this support to me.

It would not have been possible to carry out my research project, which culminated in this publication, without the commitment of the employees of the Bureau of Scientific Research at the Cardinal Stefan Wyszyński University. My special thanks go to the Director of this unit, Dr. Tomasz Janus.

Finally, I would like to thank my closest family, without whose continuous support and understanding this work could not have been accomplished.

I dedicate this book to my beloved son, Karol, whose boundless enthusiasm caused all the obstacles and doubts on the way to vanish without a trace.

Natalia Kohtamäki
Warsaw, December 2018

Contents

List of Abbreviations

ACER	Agency for the Cooperation of Energy Regulators
AEK	Akademia Ekonomiczna w Krakowie (Cracow University of Economics)
AFSJ	Area of Freedom, Security and Justice
AG	Advocate General
AHAW	Panel on Animal Health and Welfare
approx.	approximately
BEREC	Office of the Body of European Regulators for Electronic Communications
BPC	Biocidal Products Committee
BSE	bovine spongiform encephalopathy
c.	*circa* (Latin): approximately
CdT	Translation Centre for the Bodies of the European Union
CHMP	Committee for Medicinal Products for Human Use
CEBS	Committee of European Banking Supervisors
Cedefop	European Centre for the Development of Vocational Training
CEIOPS	Committee of European Insurance and Occupational Pensions Supervisors
CEPOL	European Union Agency for Law Enforcement Training (European Police College)
CEPS	Centre of European Policy Studies
CESR	Committee of European Securities Regulators
Cf.	*confer* (Latin): compare
CFSP	Common Foreign and Security Policy
CJEU	Court of Justice of the European Union
CONTAM	Panel on Contaminants in the Food Chain
CoRAP	Community Rolling Action Plan
CORINE	Coordination of Information on the Environment
CPMP	Committee for Proprietary Medicinal Products
CPVO	Community Plant Variety Office
CSDP	Common Security and Defence Policy
CVMP	Committee for Veterinary Medicinal Products
DG(s)	Directorate(s)-General
EASA	European Aviation Safety Agency
EASO	European Asylum Support Office

EBA	European Banking Authority
ECB	European Central Bank
ECDC	European Centre for Disease Prevention and Control
ECHA	European Chemicals Agency
ECN	European Competition Network
ECPR	European Consortium for Political Research
ed.	edited
EDA	European Defence Agency
EEA	European Environment Agency
EFCA	European Fisheries Control Agency
EFSA	European Food Safety Authority
e.g.	*exempli gratia* (Latin): for example
EHEC	enterohemorrhagic *Escherichia coli*
EIGE	European Institute for Gender Equality
EIOPA	European Insurance and Occupational Pensions Authority
EIT	European Institute of Innovation and Technology
EMA	European Medicines Agency
EMCDDA	European Monitoring Centre for Drugs and Drug Addiction
EMSA	European Maritime Safety Agency
ENISA	European Network and Information Security Agency
EPIN	European Policy Institutes Network
EPO	European Patent Office
EPSO	European Personnel Selection Office
ERA	European Union Agency for Railways
ESA	European Space Agency
ESA(s)	European Supervisory Authority/-ies
ESCB	European System of Central Banks
ESFS	European System of Financial Supervision
ESIL	European Society of International Law
ESMA	European Securities and Markets Authority
ESRB	European Systemic Risk Board
et al.	*et alii* (Latin): and (the) others
etc.	*et cetera* (Latin): and the remaining things
ETF	European Training Foundation
EU	European Union
EUAN	EU Agencies Network
EUI	European University Institute
eu-LISA	European Agency for the Operational Management of Large-Scale IT Systems in the Area of Freedom, Security and Justice

EUIPO	European Union Intellectual Property Office
EUISS	European Union Institute for Security Studies
EUMC	European Monitoring Centre for Racism and Xenophobia in the European Union
EU-OSHA	European Agency for Safety and Health at Work
Eurofound	European Foundation for the Improvement of Living and Working Conditions
Eurojust	European Union's Judicial Cooperation Unit
Europol	European Police Office
ED	Executive Director
f. (ff.)	and the following page(s) or paragraph(s)
FDA	Food and Drug Administration
FIIA	Finnish Institute of International Affairs
Fn.	footnote
FNI	Fridtjof Nansen Institute
Forum	Forum for Exchange of Information on Enforcement
FRA	European Union Agency for Fundamental Rights
FRAN	Frontex Risk Analysis Network
Frontex	European Border and Coast Guard Agency
IBEI	Institut Barcelona d'Estudis Internacionals (Barcelona Institute of International Studies)
ibid.	*ibidem* (Latin): at the same place
i.e.	*id est* (Latin): that is
IHCP	Institute for Health and Consumer Protection
ISP	Instytut Spraw Publicznych (Institute of Public Affairs)
JAA	Joint Aviation Authorities
JRC	Joint Research Centre
GSA	European Global Navigation Satellite Systems Agency
GMO	Panel on Genetically Modified Organisms
lit.	*littera* (Latin): letter
LSE	London School of Economics
MEP(s)	Member(s) of European Parliament
MB(s)	Management Board(s)
MSC	Member State Committee
MZES	Mannheim Centre for European Social Research
NCCR	National Centres of Competence in Research
NDA	Panel on Dietetic Products, Nutrition and Allergies
NewGov	New Modes of Governance Project
NGOs	non-governmental organisations

No(s).	*numero(s)* (Latin): number(s)
OJ	Official Journal of the European Communities/Union
OHIM	Office for Harmonization in the Internal Market
p. (pp.)	page(s)
para(s)	paragraph(s)
PCU	External Border Practitioners Common Unit
Ph.D.	*Philosophiae doctor* (Latin): doctor
PMO	Office for Administration and Payment of Individual Entitlements
RAC	Committee for Risk Assessment
RASFF	Rapid Alert System for Food and Feed Safety
REACH	Registration, Evaluation and Authorisation of Chemicals (EU Regulation No. 1907/2006)
RECON	Project 'Reconstituting Democracy in Europe'
SatCen	European Union Satellite Centre
SCIFA	Strategic Committee on Immigration, Frontiers and Asylum
SEAC	Committee for Socio-Economic Analysis
SIEF	Substance Information Exchange Forum
SRB	Single Resolution Board
SRM	Single Resolution Mechanism
SSM	Single Supervisory Mechanism
SVHC	Substances of Very High Concern
SWP	Stiftung Wissenschaft und Politik (German Institute for International and Security Affairs)
TARN	Academic Research Network on Agencification of EU Executive Governance
TCE	Treaty establishing a Constitution for Europe
TEC	Treaty establishing the European Community
TEU	Treaty on European Union
TFEU	Treaty on the Functioning of the European Union
transl.	translated
UK	United Kingdom
U.S.	United States of America
v.	*versus* (Latin): against/in contrast to
Vol.	volume
WUJ	Wydawnictwo Uniwersytetu Jagiellońskiego (Jagiellonian University Press)
WUŁ	Wydwawnictwo Uniwersytetu Łódzkiego (Lodz University Press)
WUW	Wydawnictwo Uniwersytetu Warszawskiego (Warsaw University Press)

WUWr	Wydawnictwo Uniwersytetu Wrocławskiego (Wroclaw University Press)
Wyd. KUL	Wydawnictwo Katolickiego Uniwersytetu Lubelskiego (Catholic University of Lublin Press)
Wyd. PŁ	Wydawnictwo Politechniki Łódzkiej (Lodz University of Technology Press)
Wyd. UKSW	Wydawnictwo Uniwersytetu Kardynała Stefana Wyszyńskiego (Cardinal Stefan Wyszyński University Press)
Wyd. UMCS	Wydawnictwo Uniwersytetu Marii Curie-Skłodowskiej (Maria Curie-Skłodowska University Press)
Wyd. UR	Wydawnictwo Uniwersytetu Rzeszowskiego (Rzeszow University Press)

Introduction

For years, EU regulatory agencies aroused little emotion among practitioners and scholars in the field of European governance. Although the first bodies of this kind emerged back in the mid-1970s, they truly took hold in the landscape of European institutions in the 1990s. At first, they simply played an informational and advisory role. After the year 2000, however, a significant change occurred in the way that they were perceived. The publication of the "White Paper on European Governance" of 25 July 2001 marked the transformation of the European Commission's strategy for regulatory agencies. Since then they have become a useful instrument for streamlining regulatory processes and strengthening the position of the Commission, which stands at the forefront of expanding the apparatus of the European administration.

The number of agencies has been steadily rising since the early 2000s. Before 2000, there were approximately ten of them; now there are more than thirty. It is even difficult to put an exact number on them due to varying classifications found in the literature that concerns them, and the use of changing criteria, which include or exclude particular bodies from the assemblage that can be tagged under the name "EU regulatory agencies". According to European nomenclature, these agencies are also called decentralised agencies[1]. Firstly, this is meant to reflect the split of competencies in various sectors of the internal market: from issues related to e.g. food safety, trade in medicines and chemicals, to issues related to air and rail transport, quality of professional life, environmental protection and financial supervision. Secondly, the adjective "decentralised" refers to the geographical dispersion of agencies, which have their seats in the different member states. The seats of these bodies are the subject of intensive negotiations between the member states, which want to host as many institutions of this kind as possible, mainly due to the prestige involved and the growing importance of these agencies. That is because they have gained wider and wider powers, thus becoming a permanent feature of the EU legislative and decision-making system.

Agencies that have been established in recent years, such as the European Supervisory Authorities, operating in the area of financial supervision, can be considered a new type of institution compared to the existing bodies. This is

1 See information on EU websites: https://europa.eu/european-union/about-eu/agencies/decentralised-agencies_en; http://europa.eu/european-union/about-eu/agencies/overhaul_en (20.3.2018).

due to their greatly broadened catalogue of competencies in comparison with the already existing EU regulatory agencies, and, admittedly, they undoubtedly reflect a significant deepening of the integration process. EU regulatory agencies of this new type are gradually beginning to resemble national agencies or ministries, primarily when one considers the direct influence that they can exert on natural and legal persons in the member states.

However, the expanding powers of regulatory agencies raise much controversy. On the one hand, the advisability of establishing costly expert bodies, whose activities may not always provide tangible results, has been questioned[2] and, on the other hand, doubts of a legal nature have emerged over the status of regulatory agencies in the European governance system, their growing institutional autonomy and their vague level of democratic legitimacy. A particularly controversial matter concerns the issues that arise when regulatory agencies are established, as well as those involved with holding them accountable for the actions they undertake. These are not regulated in primary law. These agencies have been created under varying Treaty norms, often through a "compulsory" search for a provision that can be used, and they mostly operate on the basis of their founding regulations, i.e. acts of secondary law.

Despite the growing interest in the topic of EU regulatory agencies in the past twenty years, their legal position and actual activities still remain in a hazy sphere of ambiguity. The demand for the professional opinions that agencies provide in major sectors of the market appears to be an effective justification for any legal deficiencies. And yet precisely on account of the agencies' involvement in decision-making and regulatory processes in various areas, such as air and rail transport safety, trade in chemicals and medicines, food safety, or financial supervision, the powers of these institutions are undergoing thorough analysis.

In order for expert support to meet the expectations placed on it by EU institutions and individual member states, it is important to guarantee regulatory agencies broad autonomy of action. This autonomy is safeguarded through different mechanisms that ensure that agencies have a relatively wide scope of organisational and functional independence. Such guarantees, which determine the rules of procedure for drafting various expert documents influencing

2 Although as recently as the early 2000s there were voices full of enthusiasm in the context of the idea of creating regulatory agencies. Authors such as Xénophon A. Yataganas expressed the view that regulatory agencies were the only effective response to the expansion of the bureaucratic machine in Brussels. See X.A. Yataganas, 'Delegation of Regulatory Authority in the European Union. The Relevance of the American Model of Independent Agencies', *Jean Monnet Working Paper*, No. 3, 2001, pp. 7 ff.

the shape and the implementation of sector-specific legal acts, are specified in the founding regulations establishing particular agencies. These guarantees raise diverse doubts in the context of these sorts of technocratic expert bodies "breaking away" from democratic control. This generates the following questions, which the Author attempts to answer in the context of legitimisation theories:

(1) Is it possible to apply the classic understanding of democratic legitimacy to regulatory agencies, or should we rather search for other methods of legitimising the activities of such bodies?
(2) What is their place in the European regulatory space?
(3) What is their role in the processes shaping the European executive order?
(4) How autonomous can agencies remain in reference to the European Union's institutions?
(5) What does the issue of their accountability before the European Commission, the European Parliament and the Council look like?
(6) Does the involvement of regulatory agencies in shaping politically determined solutions for many sectors of the internal market deepen the democratic deficit mentioned in the context of how the European Union functions?

There are several reasons for the rise in the number of regulatory agencies in recent years. One of the most important ones is a change in the approach of EU authorities, primarily the European Commission, in relation to the status and tasks of these institutions. As it is nowadays crucial to prepare legal solutions on various, often very detailed, matters which require expertise, the European Commission, in order to maintain its position of a "credible regulator", needs to have expert backup ready to provide it with specialised support when necessary. The intensification of the European legislative process has not only been a result of deepening European integration, but also reflects the overall trends of "tightening the regulatory spiral" at the national level as well. At a time of new hazards and crises threatening the economic stability of different sectors, certain member states have made efforts to create so-called safety networks, which include institutional and normative mechanisms for preventing crises and ensuring effective crisis management. Among such mechanisms, an important role is played by regulatory agencies, which have emerged, not only in most administrative systems of Western countries, but also at the EU-wide level. This has been part of the process of "agencification" of the administrative space – a process that has taken place over the last few decades.

EU regulatory agencies have become an important feature of the multilevel security network, acting in many cases as platforms for coordinating the activities of the individual member states at the European level. Over the years, in parallel with the integration processes, various forums have been developed to support the joint activities of national authorities. As mutual contacts continued to intensify within the internal market, loose committees and commissions bringing together the national officials were no longer enough. The EU bureaucratic apparatus got to a phase when it needed continuous support from established institutions for an indefinite period of time in order to draw up increasingly complicated legal acts in individual sectors. The committees or other consultative bodies that preceded the agencies may be considered the first step in the process of the rapidly developing institutionalisation of cooperation between the member states.

Therefore, the emergence of agencies also stemmed from the actual demand for independent expert institutions, which, particularly in the case of bodies created after 2000, were supposed to fill the "regulation gap". The rivalry between EU institutions has also been important. The Commission, initially wary of regulatory agencies, in the twenty-first century came to see them as useful allies in the strengthening of its own position.

As the process of creating such bodies has intensified, the interest in them has grown as well. In the past twenty years, the agencies have become one of the most popular research topics, both among lawyers and political scientists. The background and legal basis for their establishment, competencies, autonomy, control mechanisms, and also their place in the EU institutional system have all been subject to analysis. There are so many publications that one can get lost in a thicket of analyses that are often very specialised and usually incomprehensible to a layman. The vastness of the literature dedicated to EU agencies is best evidenced by the fact that articles are written about publications that already exist in this field[3]. The spectrum of issues discussed is quite broad: from very specific matters related to the functioning of selected agencies, to more general issues with agencies treated as part of multilevel European governance mechanisms.

Interestingly, as recently as in the 1990s, regulatory agencies were shrouded in mystery and did not evoke much interest among researchers. One of the few examples of interest in these topics was the 1997 special issue of the *Journal of European Public Policy* edited by Alexander Kreher and Yves Mény. Recent years have seen a real explosion of various publications dedicated to agencies, primarily

---

3 M. Egeberg, J. Trondal, 'Researching European Union Agencies: What Have We Learnt (and Where Do We Go from Here)?', *Journal of Common Market Studies*, Vol. 55, No. 4, 2017, pp. 675–690; J. Jordana, J.C. Triviño-Salazar, 'European Union Agencies: A Transnational Logic?', *IBEI Working Papers*, No. 54, 2017.

in English and to a lesser extent also in other languages, mainly German. These are usually works by lawyers or political scientists. Those that particularly deserve attention include studies by Matthias Ruffert, Michelle Everson, Ellen Vos, Deirdre Curtin, Renaud Dehousse, Madalina Busuioc, Merijn Chamon, Martijn Groenleer, Andreas Orator, Thomas Groß, Miroslava Scholten, Herwig C.H. Hofmann, Damien Geradin, Johannes Saurer, Mark Thatcher, Jarle Trondal and Morten Egeberg. These lawyers and political scientists do not exhaust the long list of European authors dealing with the agency system.

Works by lawyers concern various aspects of how regulatory agencies function: from panoramic presentations of all agencies to analyses of the problems associated with control mechanisms applied to agencies, the legal responsibility of these bodies compared with similar mechanisms applied for U.S. regulatory agencies, or the role of their expert advice in the European regulatory and decision-making process. Political science studies, in turn, focus on the role of agencies in the evolution of the European governance system. Analyses combining the legal and political science perspectives can be seen quite frequently, both in collective works and authorial monographs. The main reason for this practice is the complexity of these issues, which should be understood in an interdisciplinary manner by employing research methods from legal and administrative sciences, the theory of politics, management, and even philosophy as well as the theory of law.

An interesting phenomenon in this context is the meagre interest of researchers in developing a comprehensive theoretical approach to the legitimacy of the activities of EU regulatory agencies. Most studies include only sketchy references to this problem. In the context of the large number of analyses concerning the practical aspects of holding agencies accountable, this gap associated with the limited interest among researchers in the theoretical conceptualisation of the functioning of those agencies is striking. In the studies that comprehensively analyse different aspects of the existence of these bodies, we can even find explicit references stating that this aspect of understanding the agency system is deliberately omitted[4].

The Author's academic background resulting from her research interests in theory of law and theory of international relations prompted her to take up the challenge and write a treatise on these issues. The main purpose of the

---

4 D. Curtin, R. Dehousse, 'European Union Agencies: Tipping the Balance?', in: M. Busuioc *et al.* (ed.), *The Agency Phenomenon in the European Union. Emergence, Institutionalisation and Everyday Decision-Making*, Manchester/New York 2014, p. 200.

research was an in-depth analysis of the legal status and the place of regulatory agencies in the EU institutional structure in the context of the legitimacy of these bodies. The book focuses on theoretical aspects of the subject matter. Intentionally, it cites a number of concepts of legitimacy developed in the context of the European Union's institutional structures. Most of the theoretical models analysed have been created by lawyers. The proposal by the German law theoretician Fritz Scharpf, whose dichotomous division into input- and output-oriented legitimacy has become the starting point for most deliberations on the EU regulatory agencies' theoretical justification, is particularly noteworthy in these considerations. Apart from that, it is also the starting point in this book, for a broader critical overview of numerous, more or less mature theoretical concepts, useful for the sake of explaining and justifying the activities of regulatory agencies in the rapidly evolving European institutional system.

The theoretical perspective has been illustrated with practical examples regarding the powers of the agencies selected. The practical research involved an in-depth interpretation of statuses, competencies and control mechanisms contained in the founding regulations and other legal acts, primarily with regards to four agencies: EFSA, ECHA, Frontex and EBA. Their evolving powers make it possible to form a thesis about the gradual emergence of a new type of EU agency with real regulatory competencies.

This publication is a contribution to research in the field of European law. Due to its emphasis on theoretical considerations, it also uses research instruments from the theory and philosophy of law. A necessary addition was also to make use of the methodology from the field of politics and theories of international relations. This is not unheard of in the case of the legitimacy of international organisations, including the institutional system of the European Union. Researchers increasingly enrich strictly legal analysis with conceptual elements from other scholarly domains, e.g. political science, international relations, sociology, or philosophy. In this case, the intention is to show the broadest possible spectrum of the process of theorising about the legitimacy of the regulatory agencies' activities. This book compiles the most important theoretical models, in the Author's view, and subjects them to critical analysis. It cannot be denied that in many cases a peculiar artificiality of justifications constructed with regard to the functioning of European administration is evident.

The book consists of three basic parts, divided into chapters. The first part includes a presentation of the EU agency system, drawing attention in Chapter 1 to terminological difficulties, the development of these bodies in a historical perspective, their tasks, and the legal framework determining their functioning as well as their organisational structure. Chapter 2 constitutes a presentation of four selected agencies (EFSA, ECHA, Frontex and EBA) in the context of their special regulatory powers and their impact on the evolution of the European governance system through agency mechanisms. The closing Chapter 3 is intended to introduce the reader to the issue of regulatory agencies and it cites the most important rulings of the EU Court of Justice modifying the understanding of these bodies and their status in the EU institutional system.

The seminal section of this book is the second part, which analyses major theories of legitimisation formulated with respect to the EU institutions. A critical analysis of these theories is conducted in this part, considering e.g. their adequacy in the face of the rapidly changing European governance mechanisms. Chapter 4 deals with terminological issues. It juxtaposes basic terms in the discourse about the empowerment of the public institutions' activities, such as legitimacy, autonomy and accountability. The very issue of the book's title is also addressed in this chapter as it appears that there are not any mature theories of legitimacy that fully explain the issues associated with the legitimacy of the special EU administrative bodies and, due to the specific character of the agency system, there will not be any for a long time. Thus, it intentionally discusses "theorising" on this topic, referring to the numerous efforts of researchers from different disciplines focusing on the issues of the empowerment of the EU administrative apparatus. Regulatory agencies often play only a marginal role in these theoretical discussions, hence the efforts to juxtapose their tasks and status with the existing catalogue of theoretical concepts.

Chapter 5 analyses theoretical explanations focusing on classically understood democratic legitimacy, i.e. legitimacy associated with "democratic input" where there is active citizen influence on the functioning of the public administration. For understandable reasons, in the case of international organisations, particularly as specific as the European Union, the remoteness from direct electoral mechanisms makes it largely impossible to create a "chain of legitimisation" pointing to a direct civic mandate which empowers action. Chapter 6 includes an assessment of alternative concepts of legitimacy, which, as intended by the researchers who developed them, are supposed to constitute a kind of remedy to the weakness of a strictly democratic type of justification. It focuses on the issues associated with functional empowerment, involving e.g. the expert background of the official personnel of EU regulatory agencies, transparency and the effectiveness of the agencies' activities as well as mechanisms of inclusion and participation of the various social groups consulted in the decision-making processes coordinated by the agencies. What brings Chapter 6 to a close is a critical reflection on normative legitimacy in the context of agency activity. In the case of such administrative bodies, this kind of legitimacy is not entirely clear due to their weak "anchoring" (Germ. *Verankerung*) in the Treaties. Organising the rather chaotically expanding agency system takes place in the form of legally non-binding declarations of the EU institutions. Specific powers and detailed tasks, in turn, are laid down in the founding regulations and other legal acts, often modified in order to broaden the competency catalogue of a particular agency in accordance with changes taking place in the internal market.

An important, closing section of these considerations is presented in the third part of the book where a practical analysis of specific mechanisms falling within theoretical concepts is conducted. Chapter 7 deals with direct democratic legitimacy associated with the so-called input, or the involvement of citizens in shaping agencies themselves as well as their tasks. It identifies determining factors in the democratic legitimacy of public institutions such as authorisation, safeguards and accountability. In the case of regulatory agencies, these mechanisms are complex and there are separate publications dedicated to them in the relevant literature. As part of these considerations, they deserve attention with regard to practical solutions used in the founding regulations of the agencies discussed in the first part: EFSA, ECHA, Frontex and EBA, as they are an empirical illustration of the theoretical assumptions discussed at length in the second part. This is complemented with Chapter 8 where technocratic legitimacy (so-called output legitimacy) and procedural legitimacy (so-called throughput legitimacy), which fall within the alternative models of empowerment of public administration, are assessed from an empirical perspective.

Part I The Evolution of EU Regulatory Agencies

1 Regulatory Agencies in the Administrative System of the European Union

1. The Origins

a) Understanding the Term "Regulatory Agency"

aa) The Phenomenon of Regulation in the Context of "Agencification"

Defining "Regulation"

When one attempts to explain the term "regulatory agency", initially it is worth considering the term "regulation" which is defined in different ways depending on the field of inquiry[1]. Apart from economists, who analyse state interference in economic processes[2], regulation is a subject of interest for lawyers, political scientists and sociologists. As for the following deliberations, what is of importance is the legal perspective, which in a broad sense envisages the state's legislative involvement in specific sectors of the economy as it pursues socially important objectives such as the protection of public goods. Most often, this involves regulating the infrastructural sectors of the economy, which primarily includes network industries such as telecommunications, power, engineering, gas industry, postal services, transport, etc.[3]

The etymology of the term "regulation" can be derived from the Latin noun *regula* meaning line, measure but also norm; as well as the verb *regere*, which means to lead, rule, but also regulate and standardise[4]. Therefore the original meaning is associated with the regulating activity of the state, which shapes social

---

1 For an overview of definitions of the term "regulation" used in various academic disciplines, see C. Koop, M. Lodge, 'What is Regulation? An Interdisciplinary Concept Analysis', *Regulation & Governance*, Vol. 11, No. 1, 2017, pp. 97 ff.

2 In short, economists understand the term regulation as any state interventions aimed at preventing irregularities in the functioning of the markets. See M. Leschke, 'Regulierungstheorie aus ökonomischer Sicht', in: M. Fehling, M. Ruffert (ed.), *Regulierungsrecht*, Tübingen 2010, pp. 290 ff.; R.U. Fülbier, 'Regulierung. Ökonomische Betrachtung eines allgegenwärtigen Phänomens', *Wirtschaftswissenschaftliches Studium*, Vol. 28, No. 9, 1999, pp. 468 ff.

3 More M. Szydło, *Regulacja sektorów infrastrukturalnych jako rodzaj funkcji państwa wobec gospodarki*, Warszawa 2005, pp. 31 ff.

4 See K. Kumaniecki (ed.), *Słownik łacińsko-polski*, Warszawa 1983.

relations by means of legal acts[5]. In German-language literature, such interventionist involvement of the state is also equated with a special form of state supervision in economically important sectors of the market (Germ. *staatliche Wirtschaftsaufsicht*). The legislative activity of a state institution is connected with its capability to control[6]. Hence, regulating means shaping certain normative patterns of behaviour, but also enforcing them. These actions are primarily aimed at supporting free competition as well as protecting public goods in a specific sector of the market[7].

In most European languages "regulation" in a broad sense corresponds to the English meaning of the term which, in the American tradition, encompasses all the legislative and administrative instruments used by the state in order to solve specific problems in the social and economic domain. In this context, four groups of tasks are usually identified: (1) collecting information, (2) law making, (3) formulating principles and rules of conduct as well as implementing standards, and (4) monitoring or controlling their execution. In order for these tasks to be carried out effectively, a system was developed in the United States consisting of special independent institutions entrusted with regulatory powers in thematically defined administrative areas. These bodies were called agencies. They constitute an important element in the evolution of public governance processes and are marked by three key characteristics in the American model: (1) participation in law making as well as shaping and enforcing certain patterns of behaviour, (2) the possession of decision-making autonomy, and (3) being subject to limited judicial review[8]. These bodies, due to their strong position and wide-ranging powers, have become a subject of scholarly analysis and an inspiration for similar solutions in other parts of the globe.

---

5 See M. Ruffert, 'Begriff', in: Fehling, Ruffert (ed.), *Regulierungsrecht*, pp. 336, 359; T. Nieborak, *Aspekty prawne funkcjonowania rynku finansowego Unii Europejskiej*, Warszawa 2008, p. 18.

6 In this context regulation is understood according to the classic definition by Philip Selznick: "In its central meaning *regulation* refers to sustained and focused control exercised by a public agency over activities that are valued by the community", P. Selznick, 'Focusing Organizational Research and Regulation', in: R.G. Noll (ed.), *Regulatory Policy and the Social Sciences*, Berkeley 1985, p. 363.

7 See T. von Danwitz, 'Was ist eigentlich Regulierung?', *Die öffentliche Verwaltung. Zeitschrift für öffentliches Recht und Verwaltungswissenschaft*, Vol. 57, No. 23, 2004, p. 977; H.-W. Laubinger, 'Regulierungsrecht: Gibt's das – und wenn ja: wie viele?', *Verwaltungsblätter für Baden-Württemberg*, Vol. 31, No. 8, 2010, pp. 307 ff.

8 Danwitz, 'Was ist eigentlich', p. 978.

One of the best known scholars on the topic, the Italian political scientist Giandomenico Majone, wrote in the mid-1990s that by transferring the American models onto European ground a "regulatory state" was born, which has been active in important sectors of the economy through autonomous expert bodies vested with quasi-legislative powers[9]. Within this concept typical state activities involving redistribution of wealth need to be distinguished from tasks of a regulatory nature. Regulation is understood in this context as a technical task that can be entrusted to experts and that requires simplified legitimisation mechanisms[10]. In such an approach "regulating" will mean any activity of public authorities that influences the behaviour of citizens[11].

The "New Public Management" Concept and the Regulatory Agencies

The term "regulatory agency" should be understood in the broader context of the changes taking place in the structures of public administration in the Western world. The creation of bodies of this kind was an expression of the pursuit of new modes of governance developed as part of the strong liberalisation and deregulation trends which appeared in the 1980s and 1990s. Reforms of the organisational structures of public administration were built into a concept called New Public Management. It envisioned the reorganisation of institutional structures and governance methods in the public sector accompanied by technological changes and rapid growth of market economies in order to make administrative bodies capable of providing a quick response to the needs of the recipients of public services. It became important to align governance techniques used by public authorities with those practised in the private sector. In view of this concept, public institutions were primarily supposed to be effective and efficient, i.e. achieve the best possible results at the lowest possible costs. One of the ideas

9 See G. Majone, 'The Rise of the Regulatory State in Western Europe', *West European Politics*, Vol. 17, No. 3, 1994, pp. 77 ff.; M. Lodge, 'Regulation, the Regulatory State and European Politics', *West European Politics*, Vol. 31, Nos. 1–2, 2008, pp. 280 ff.; J.G. Christensen, V. Lehmann Nielsen, 'Administrative Capacity, Structural Choice and the Creation of EU Agencies', *Journal of European Public Policy*, Vol. 17, No. 2, 2010, p. 179.

10 See M. Jachtenfuchs, 'Der Wandel des regulativen Mehrebenensystems der EU', *DMS – Der moderne Staat. Zeitschrift für Public Policy, Recht und Management*, No. 1, 2010, p. 111.

11 For a comparison of the concept by Majone with the conclusions of other researchers analysing the phenomenon of "regulation" in the EU context, see Koop, Lodge, 'What is Regulation?', p. 98.

concerning how to reach this objective was to create regulatory agencies, which were autonomously managed and made flexible use of market mechanisms[12].

The performance of such institutions, regulating important market sectors, was to be, first and foremost, credibly independent, i.e. free of any pressure from policymakers, or determined e.g. by the electoral calendar. This ascribed significance to the idea of the institutional autonomy of regulatory agencies, which were from their outset created with emphasis primarily put on their effectiveness, professionalism and the wide range of tasks that they were supposed to perform. Hence, in the literature on the subject, the intensive process of creating regulatory agencies described, perhaps a bit awkwardly, as "agencification", has been perceived as a functional solution[13]. The idea of creating regulatory agencies, first developed in state systems and only later in supranational structures, was a consequence of technological progress and the development of certain economic sectors that resulted from it. These processes necessitated far-reaching specialisation of administrative bodies. This, in turn, gave rise to the idea of delegating tasks that required a sufficient level of expertise to institutions which were specifically prepared for executing them[14].

One of the key objectives of New Public Management was decentralisation, i.e. diverting the management process from the centre to an array of specialised, independent and effective entities. Hence, terms such as deconcentration, fragmentation or vertical specialisation of the hitherto-existing institutional system come up in this context[15]. The guaranteeing of broad institutional autonomy for

---

12 See T. Christensen, P. Lægreid, 'Introduction – Theoretical Approach and Research Questions', in: T. Christensen, P. Lægreid (ed.), *Transcending New Public Management: The Transformation of Public Sector Reforms*, Aldershot 2007, pp. 4 ff.; F. Shirvani, 'New Public Management und europäische Agenturen: Transparenzfragen bei der Modernisierung der Verwaltungsorganisation', *Die öffentliche Verwaltung. Zeitschrift für öffentliches Recht und Verwaltungswissenschaft*, Vol. 61, No. 1, 2008, pp. 1–4; E. Młodzik, 'Założenia koncepcji New Public Management', *Zeszyty Naukowe Uniwersytetu Szczecińskiego. Współczesne Problemy Ekonomiczne*, Vol. 858, No. 11, 2015, pp. 187 ff.

13 See B. Rittberger, A. Wonka, 'Introduction: Agency Governance in the European Union', in: B. Rittberger, A. Wonka (ed.), *Agency Governance in the EU*, London/New York 2012, p. 3; F. Gilardi, 'Policy Credibility and Delegation to Independent Regulatory Agencies: A Comparative Empirical Analysis', *Journal of European Public Policy*, Vol. 9, No. 6, 2002, pp. 877–883.

14 More C. Pollitt *et al.*, *Agencies. How Governments Do Things Through Semi-Autonomous Organizations*, Basingstoke/Hampshire 2005, pp. 3 ff.

15 See Shirvani, 'New Public Management', pp. 6 ff.

the newly created offices was, however, to be balanced by appropriate control mechanisms[16]. Maintaining a balance between control and independence is not easy and often entails the need for top-down coordination of the offices' activities and that is just a step away from the re-centralisation of tasks and competencies[17].

From the perspective of political science, developments associated with public administration reforms are perceived as an echo of the globalisation processes that are modifying traditional governance methods both domestically and internationally. New ideas on how to solve problems are emerging as well as ways of coordinating cooperation between diverse entities within dispersed, multilevel, multidimensional, or multilateral structures[18]. The global internationalisation of social life, on the one hand, leads to the removal of various administrative and legal barriers in the flow of resources between countries, but, on the other hand, along with technological development, it necessitates the creation of institutions capable of coordinating the interactions of a variety of actors within complex integration processes.

In this context, researchers dealing with the evolution of public administration go as far as to talk about "regulatory capitalism", paradoxically considering the expansion of regulatory networks to be a permanent component of the neoliberal vision of the world. In the view of David Levi-Faur, one of the authors of the concept of "regulatory capitalism", deregulation constitutes an important ideological element of neoliberalism. On the other hand, regulatory actions on a national level are in a natural way complementary to such a vision and constitute a response to a practical need[19]. Therefore, periods of intense deregulation

---

16 Most often national agencies have their autonomy guaranteed in a formal way (*de jure* autonomy), which is complemented by the authority's actions to maintain its independent position (*de facto* autonomy). See L. Ennser-Jedenastik, 'The Politization of Regulatory Agencies: Between Partisan Influence and Formal Independence', *Journal of Public Administration Research and Theory*, Vol. 26, No. 3, 2016, pp. 509–516.

17 See Christensen, Lægreid, 'Introduction', p. 8; T. Christensen *et al.*, *Still Fragmented Government or Reassertion of the Centre?*, in: Christensen, Lægreid (ed.), *Transcending*, pp. 18 ff.

18 See S. Bieleń, *Polityka w stosunkach międzynarodowych*, Warszawa 2010, p. 197.

19 See D. Levi-Faur, 'The Global Diffusion of a Regulatory Capitalism', *Annals of the American Academy of Political and Social Science*, Vol. 598, No. 1, 2005, p. 14; J. Jordana *et al.*, 'The Global Diffusion of Regulatory Agencies: Channels of Transfer and Stages of Diffusion', *Comparative Political Studies*, Vol. 44, No. 10, 2011, pp. 1361 ff.; T. Christensen, P. Lægreid, 'Regulatory Agencies – The Challenges of Balancing Agency Autonomy and Political Control', *Governance. An International Journal of Policy, Administration, and Institutions*, Vol. 20, No. 3, 2007, p. 502.

are usually followed by a period of time necessary to modify the existing regulatory solutions or introduce new ones. The growth of contemporary markets, partly associated with state-of-the-art technologies, requires state intervention. Moreover, strong transnational interdependencies that mark relations between different entities in the modern world render autarkic solutions impossible. It is necessary for countries to cooperate in the pursuit of common ideas to fight systemic threats that, in a crisis situation, affect the integrated economies of many countries virtually simultaneously. In the face of the changes taking place in the world, the idea of *laissez-faire*, characteristic for the nineteenth-century liberalism (from Fr. *laissez faire*, "let [them] act") which implied absolute individual freedom, most of all in the economic and social sphere, has lost its *raison d'être*. The state in liberal democracies has returned to the function of a regulator that cares about economic stability and maintaining civil trust, delegating a significant portion of specific tasks to regulatory agencies.

While the intensity of creating such bodies in Europe significantly increased in the late twentieth century, the origins of these processes can be traced back to the 1920s, to the establishment of offices that were supposed to regulate national financial markets[20]. What is noteworthy here is the diffusivity of regulatory trends. This means that we can see a "fashion" for creating institutions of a particular type in a given economic sector or for introducing particular normative solutions. Agencies have been launched in the last thirty years as part of government programmes in many countries worldwide, including the United Kingdom, the Netherlands, Japan, South Korea, Thailand, or New Zealand. The regulatory trend made it to the United States even earlier, where, as already mentioned, the model of a regulatory agency, which has been copied in other corners of the globe, was created, as well as in Nordic states such as Finland and Sweden[21].

Both domestically and internationally the creation of a particular office does not always stem from an actual need. It is quite often driven by an "infatuation" with solutions implemented elsewhere[22]. As a result of such regulatory enthusiasm, special offices in different corners of the world have been entrusted with tasks in the fields of public utilities, consumer protection, telecommunications,

---

20 Levi-Faur, 'The Global Diffusion', p. 16.

21 Pollitt *et al.*, *Agencies*, p. 7; C. Talbot, 'The Agency Idea. Sometimes Old, Sometimes New, Sometimes Borrowed, Sometimes Untrue', in: C. Pollitt, C. Talbot (ed.), *Unbundled Government: A Critical Analysis of the Global Trend to Agencies, Quangos and Contractualisation*, London/New York 2004, pp. 3 ff.; M. Everson, 'Independent Agencies: Hierarchy Beaters?', *European Law Journal*, Vol. 1, No. 2, 1995, p. 182.

22 Levi-Faur, 'The Global Diffusion', pp. 22–27; Christensen, Lægreid, 'Introduction', p. 7.

transport, environmental protection, etc. The spreading institutional and normative models, whenever implemented into the national legal systems, are subject to local interpretations, i.e. adaptation to the national legal culture, tradition and existing practices.

Despite national differences, it is possible to construct a general definition of an agency functioning in the domestic legal system of a country. It is an institution, operating under the provisions of public law[23] as well as performing public tasks, while maintaining its financial, personnel and organisational independence from its "parent" ministry[24] Full institutional autonomy is not possible due to control mechanisms, such as the influence of a given ministry on the budgeting of a particular agency and its involvement in the shaping of its main objectives and tasks[25]. Among many different types of agencies established on the wave of "agencification" processes, e.g. agencies focused on security and defence, paying agencies, agencies managing public funds (e.g. pension reserve funds, or state investment funds), there are also regulatory agencies whose primary, though not exclusive, task involves improving the quality of regulations introduced in a particular market sector[26]. This is supposed to be possible chiefly on account of high qualifications and knowledge of sectoral specifics[27], including technical and economic issues.

Agencies contribute to the fulfilment of one of the key assumptions of New Public Management, i.e. the increased effectiveness of administrative instruments. The pursuit of the ideal of microeconomic efficiency, achieved thanks to the use of free-market mechanisms, has led to a departure from the principle of majoritarianism. This attitude implies that decisions in democratic systems are taken by majorities. The choice of the majority from a set of equal citizens legitimises the actions of relevant authorities, especially when they are involved in redistribution of wealth[28]. The call for administrative efficiency has led to the evolution

23 Although in different legal systems a mixed, public and private legal status is also possible. See Pollitt *et al.*, *Agencies*, pp. 8 ff.

24 Talbot, 'The Agency Idea', pp. 7–12.

25 See C. Pollitt *et al.*, 'Agency Fever? Analysis of an International Policy Fashion', *Journal of Comparative Policy Analysis. Research and Practice*, Vol. 3, No. 3, 2001, pp. 271–275.

26 Christensen, Lægreid, 'Regulatory Agencies', p. 503; K. Marchewka-Bartkowiak, 'Agencje wykonawcze', *Biuro Analiz Sejmowych. Infos. Zagadnienia społeczno-gospodarcze*, No. 17, 2011, p. 2.

27 The term "sectoral" will be used in this treatise in relation to the various economic sectors of the EU internal market.

28 For more information about the concept see S. Macedo, 'Against Majoritarianism: Democratic Values and Institutional Design', *Boston University Law*

of this classic understanding of the issue of public institutions' democratic legitimacy. Agencies have obtained their powers by way of having them delegated from above as part of the processes of externalising competences. Their staff are not elected in democratic elections. Neither are they managed in a way that reflects the "will of the people". Thus, in Anglo-Saxon literature they are called non-majoritarian institutions. Therefore, their actions are legitimised in other ways, primarily by referring to well-developed mechanisms of control that also involve the participation of different social groups that have an interest in the regulatory activity of particular agencies[29]. A distinct weakness of these bodies, which is detrimental to the quality of the regulations they prepare, is their vulnerability to political pressure related to the influence of a specific ministry (the problem of principal-agent relations)[30] or so-called regulatory capture, i.e. acting in support of regulated entities rather than in the public interest[31]. Interestingly, in the EU directives that liberalise different sectors of the internal market, greater stress is put on protecting national agencies from the influence of the business community and industry than protecting them from political pressure[32]. In the context of agencies, there are also allegations of excessive growth of administrations in order to create lucrative positions for current decision-makers, the susceptibility of agency experts to the influence of their own community as well as the risk associated with the possibility of corrupt conduct[33].

Review, Vol. 90, No. 2, 2010, pp. 1031–1034; A. Sulikowski, 'Prawa a ideologia. Prawa jednostki z perspektywy krytycznej myśli prawniczej i socjologicznej', *Roczniki Nauk Społecznych*, Vol. 7(43), No. 4, 2015, p. 28.

29 See M. Thatcher, A. Stone Sweet, 'Theory and Practice of Delegation to Non-Majoritarian Institutions', *West European Politics*, Vol. 25, No. 1, 2002, p. 2; M. Thatcher, 'The Third Force? Independent Regulatory Agencies and Elected Politicians in Europe', *Governance. An International Journal of Policy, Administration, and Institutions*, Vol. 18, No. 3, 2005, pp. 348 ff.; G. Majone, 'Temporal Consistency and Policy Credibility: Why Democracies Need Non-Majoritarian Institutions', *EUI Working Paper RSC*, No. 96/57, 1996, pp. 2 ff.

30 See A.R. Zito, 'European Agencies as Agents of Governance and EU Learning', *Journal of European Public Policy*, Vol. 16, No. 8, 2009, p. 1225.

31 See M. Szydło, *Prawo konkurencji a regulacja sektorowa*, Warszawa 2010, pp. 269 ff.; M. Ugur, 'Regulatory Quality and Performance in EU Network Industries: Evidence on Telecommunications, Gas and Electricity', *Journal of Public Policy*, Vol. 29, No. 3, 2009, pp. 348, 356 ff.

32 D. Geradin, N. Petit, 'The Development of Agencies at EU and National Levels: Conceptual Analysis and Proposals for Reform', *Jean Monnet Working Paper*, No. 1, 2004, p. 25.

33 Pollitt *et al.*, *Agencies*, p. 4; R.U. Fülbier, 'Regulierung', p. 472.

bb) EU Regulatory Agencies

The regulatory agencies of the European Union differ significantly from corresponding institutions within the particular member states. This arises from the distinct character of these institutions which, first of all, function in an international environment, meaning they are not nation-state institutions, and, secondly, they receive concrete tasks that are delegated to them, and which are formulated in the legislation that established them, i.e. usually regulations which are acts of secondary law. They are not European Union authorities that are directly included in Treaty law. Nonetheless, they act as a support for EU institutions, including first and foremost the European Commission. Granting them specific competencies, therefore, is limited in many ways. The most important limitations are of a legal nature and result from primary law as well as the case law of the Court of Justice of the European Union (CJEU)[34].

In addition to formal barriers, there are also equally important political determinants that make it impossible to create "fully-fledged" regulatory agencies at the EU level. Firstly, the member states jealously protect their regulatory powers, primarily in sectors of vital importance for their national economies. Hence, ideas for deepened integration in such areas as, for example, the provision of public services, supervision of financial markets, protecting competition and pro-competitive sectoral regulation, are met with limited enthusiasm on the part of the member states. This is expressed, for example, in the reluctance of national regulatory authorities to strengthen cooperation, mainly in the context of delegating specific powers. On the other hand, it is acceptable to have loose consultative bodies whose role is limited to coordinating the flow of information, or acting as discussion clubs. This is particularly true for European regulatory agencies since the 1990s, the establishment of which should be perceived similarly to that of their counterparts on a national level as an expression of liberalisation trends modernising public governance processes. The agencies created within the European Community at the time fitted the concept of a multi-layered regulation system where they were supposed to play an integrative role, as well as a coordinating one, in the process of developing regulatory strategies in the supranational dimension[35].

---

34 They will be described to a greater extent in Chapter 3.

35 See D. Coen, C. Doyle, 'Liberalisation of Utilities and Evolving European Regulation', *Economic Outlook*, Vol. 24, No. 3, 2000, pp. 23–25; M. Busuioc *et al.*, 'The Phenomenon of European Union Agencies: Setting the Scene', in: Busuioc *et al.* (ed.), *The Agency Phenomenon*, p. 3.

Secondly, the intra-EU backdrop and the struggle for influence between EU authorities have also been significant. For a long time the European Commission was sceptical about the concept of delegating powers to subsidiary institutions. A transfer of any regulatory, decision-making powers or those related to policy-making in a given market sector seemed inadmissible. In the second half of the 1990s, however, the Commission came to see agencies not just as effective tools for preparing drafts of normative acts in a professional manner, a task for which on its own it did not have enough administrative capacity, but also as important allies in the process of strengthening its position against the European Parliament in the European institutional system[36].

The scandals that plagued the Commission at the time were not without significance for these developments. They culminated in the resignation of the entire European Commission chaired by Jacques Santer in March 1999. At the time it was recognised that the Commission's capacity as a credible institution, able to draft normative acts in specialised, rapidly changing economic sectors, such as civil aviation, food safety, telecommunications or financial supervision, had come to an end[37]. Santer's successor, Romano Prodi, was an advocate of restoring the authority of the Commission as an effective regulatory body based on agency support[38]. A pretext for strengthening the position of regulatory agencies came with the crises of the 1990s, for example in the agricultural market there was one case involving epidemics of diseases affecting livestock (bovine spongiform encephalopathy, BSE), and another affecting cloven-hoofed animals (foot-and-mouth disease). On top of this there was contamination of animal feed with dioxins. A regulatory agency endowed with discretionary powers, including regulatory competences, modelled on the U.S. Food and Drug Administration (FDA), was designed as a solution for this case[39].

---

36 See A. Musa, 'Reforming the European Union Agency Governance: More Control, Greater Accountability', *Croatian and Comparative Public Administration*, Vol. 14, No. 2, 2014, pp. 320 ff.

37 The argument of credibility of drafted regulations is a central one for the establishment of both national and European agencies. See G. Majone, 'The Credibility Crisis of Community Regulation', *Journal of Common Market Studies*, Vol. 38, No. 2, 2000, pp. 276–284; Ennser-Jedenastik, 'The Politization', pp. 508 ff.

38 At the time there were even voices calling for the creation of a European "service culture" implemented within a transparent and effective agency system. See M.H. Koch, 'Mittelbare Gemeinschaftsverwaltung in der Praxis', *Europäische Zeitschrift für Wirtschaftsrecht*, Vol. 16, No. 15, 2005, pp. 455 ff.

39 See G. Majone, 'Delegation of Regulatory Powers in a Mixed Polity', *European Law Journal*, Vol. 8, No. 3, 2002, pp. 328–330.

Following objections coming from the Legal Service within the administrative structures of the Commission and as a consequence of the reluctance of the member states to transfer broader powers to the agency level, the European Food Safety Authority (EFSA), which was established in 2002, did not become a European equivalent of the U.S. agency. This agency was to be responsible for monitoring and forecasting threats to the European food market, rather than for managing crises involving a politically determined decision-making process or else drafting legal acts relevant to food safety[40]. In the view of Majone, who described the situation as it was developing in 2002, it was a temporary victory of traditionalists over the supporters of entrusting EU agencies with broader powers[41]. His hypothesis was confirmed less than ten years later when the global financial crisis forced more decisive action which led, among other things, to the establishment of three European Supervisory Authorities (ESAs)[42] endowed with decision-making and quasi-regulatory powers in the field of financial supervision.

It is worth taking a broader look at the processes of EU "agencification". Undoubtedly, European integration in particular sectors of the economy has shifted legislative regulatory competencies to the EU level. Nonetheless, the implementation of individual provisions takes place at the national level, whereas the European Commission maintains a monitoring role. The member states, therefore, have some freedom regarding the transposition of EU law into the legislation of individual countries[43]. This leads to significant differences both in the legislation itself as well as its interpretation and enforcement by particular authorities[44]. A good example of this can be found in the implementation of financial law regulations. The shortcomings of this process were pinpointed

---

40 See Speech by Prodi, Plenary Session of European Parliament, Strasbourg, 5.10.1999, http://europa.eu/rapid/press-release_SPEECH-99-121_en.htm (20.3.2018); European Commission, *White Paper on Food Safety*, COM(1999) 719 final, 12.1.2000.

41 Majone, 'Delegation', p. 329.

42 ESAs: European Banking Authority (EBA), European Securities and Markets Authority (ESMA) and European Insurance and Occupational Pensions Authority (EIOPA).

43 *Cf.* M. Scholten, 'Mind the Trend! Enforcement of EU Law Has Been Moving to "Brussels"', *Journal of European Public Policy*, Vol. 24, No. 9, 2017, pp. 1350 ff.; E. Mastenbroek *et al.*, 'Clawing Back Lost Powers? Parliamentary Scrutiny of the Transposition of EU Social Policy Directives in the Netherlands', *West European Politics*, Vol. 37, No. 4, 2014, pp. 755 ff.

44 See M. Egeberg, J. Trondal, 'National Agencies in the European Administrative Space: Government Driven, Commission Driven or Networked?', *Public Administration*, Vol. 87, No. 4, 2009, p. 779.

in the context of the 2008–2010 financial crisis. These include such endeavours as "gold plating" and a "deregulation race". The former involves "refining" EU directives by overly rigorous implementation into national legal systems; the latter, competition between the member states in order to create the best possible legal framework to attract investors in various sectors of the economy in the process of transposing EU law. This action results in regulatory arbitrage, which means that businesses choose those markets that guarantee them as much freedom as possible in terms of the normative framework[45]. The patchy implementation of EU directives frequently leads to inconsistencies in the formulation of specific requirements and a dilution of the objectives defined in EU legal acts.

In such a situation it is important to have a coordinating body to allow the elaboration of a common interpretation of regulations and a specific standard for practice in a given sector. In order to carry out these tasks, it is necessary to attain a high level of professionalism within a particular institution, formulate a common regulatory philosophy and achieve trust between regulatory bodies at various levels[46]. Such an integrative role is performed by EU regulatory agencies; this should be perceived as a more limited solution that uses different institutional models to those used by national authorities. In most cases they can be seen as a part of the reform of the European administrative system towards the creation of a complex institutional and normative framework, which makes use of supranational, international and national mechanisms of cooperation. Thus, the establishment of European agencies does not result from fighting within the traditionally understood ministerial bureaucracy, as in the case of national agencies, nor from partisan games or calculations related to the efficiency of the administrative apparatus. The evolution of European regulatory agencies is also hindered by the framework of multilevel international cooperation. Networking, or the coexistence of many different entities in the process of public governance, prevents the transformation of European regulatory authorities into agencies similar to, for example, the U.S. model. Therefore, some researchers draw the conclusion that the term "regulatory agency" in relation to the EU bodies in

---

45 The "deregulation race" involves actions designed to increase the attractiveness of a particular market for investors that results in a significant decline in regulatory standards and control mechanisms. The phenomenon is described by such terms as "competition in laxity", "race to the bottom", "rush to the bottom of regulation mentality". More about "gold plating" and "deregulation race" in the context of the banking market N. Kohtamäki, *Die Reform der Bankenaufsicht in der Europäischen Union*, Tübingen 2012, pp. 64 ff.

46 Majone, 'Delegation', p. 336.

question does not correspond to reality and is quite far-fetched[47]. We should recognise, however, that the European environment has a specific nature and it is difficult to apply solutions characteristic for the U.S. government administration to it[48].

The intensification of the integration process in Europe seen since the 1990s has triggered a "regulatory revolution" in line with the assumptions of New Public Management. The revolution has primarily meant harmonising the market through directives implemented with varied commitment by the member states. An important effect of these processes was also the development of a "regulatory state" mentioned at the beginning of the chapter, and the establishment of regulatory agencies at the national level, often in accordance with recommendations included in EU directives[49]. However, national agencies are not always in favour of creating a coordinating agency at the EU level. They often see it as a rival institution that usurps their powers and prevents the development of their own competences. Moreover, European regulatory agencies, as they coordinate the process of the homogenous implementation of EU directives, can be perceived as intruders limiting the freedom of the member states in the process of transposing law. Their reluctance to transfer even limited powers to the supranational level also results from the creation of regulatory agencies in sectors that until recently were dominated by state monopolies, i.e. fully controlled by the member states[50].

Regardless of mutual animosities, both types of agencies together with many other entities, such as executive agencies, expert committees under the comitology procedure[51], high-level groups, working groups, regulatory networks

---

47 Majone, 'The Credibility', p. 290; Lodge, 'Regulation', p. 286; T. Groß, 'Die Kooperation zwischen europäischen Agenturen und nationalen Behörden', *Europarecht*, No. 1, 2005, p. 57.

48 Damien Geradin had a different look at the possibility of implementing U.S. models in Europe, seeing U.S. solutions as a useful inspiration for European institutions. See D. Geradin, 'The Development of European Regulatory Agencies: What the EU Should Learn from American Experience', *Columbia Journal of European Law*, Vol. 11, No. 1, 2004, pp. 2 ff. See also M. Chamon, 'Agencification in the United States and Germany and What the EU Might Learn From It', *German Law Journal*, Vol. 17, No. 2, 2016, pp. 122 ff.

49 Gilardi, 'Policy Credibility', pp. 874 ff.

50 See M. Thatcher, 'The Creation of European Regulatory Agencies and its Limits: A Comparative Analysis of European Delegation', in: Rittberger, Wonka (ed.), *Agency Governance*, pp. 12, 17; Geradin, 'The Development', p. 12.

51 The comitology procedure is a specific consultation procedure for implementing acts. Special committees of experts from the member states review, in a non-binding way,

as well as the Directorates General of the Commission (DGs) make up a structure within the internal market that scholars tend to call the Single European Regulatory Space. This term implies a multilevel system where specific rules of conduct are established, legal acts are adopted and implemented as well as where data from certain economic sectors is collected and distributed[52].

b) EU Regulatory Agencies in a Historical Perspective

aa) Institutional Placement

The Four-Level Model of the EU Organisational Structure

Changes in the European administrative space primarily involve a gradual evolution of the process of implementing European law. In principle, the member states are responsible for this. In practice, however, an increasingly significant role is played by European institutions, especially by the European Commission, which stands at the top of the European administration. Entities, whose existence is not sufficiently regulated in primary law, also play a significant role. In German academic literature they are called "non-Treaty" institutions (institutions "outside the Treaties") or bodies that were "unforeseen on the grounds of the Treaties" (Germ. *vertragsfremd*). They constitute the middle level of the European administration – between EU authorities and governmental institutions in the member states[53].

The classic model of the European organisational structure created by Meinhard Hilf in the 1980s should be referenced here[54]. It assumed that the first

---

drafts of implementing acts which are prepared by European Commission. On the basis of their review the Commission decides about the final version of an implementing act. For the comitology procedure in detail see *EU Monitor*: https://eumonitor.eu/9353000/1/j9vvik7m1c3gyxp/vha0t8afc0ya (20.3.2018).

52 More D. Levi-Faur, 'Regulatory Networks and Regulatory Agencification: Towards a Single European Regulatory Space', in: Rittberger, Wonka (ed.), *Agency Governance*, pp. 32–51. The German-language literature mentions complex regulatory structures in this context (Germ. *Regelungs-/Regulierungsstrukturen*), Ruffert, 'Begriff', pp. 351 ff.

53 See Steger, *Zur Verselbständigung von Unionsagenturen. Eine Untersuchung am Beispiel der Energie-Agentur ACER und ihrer Mitwirkung beim Erlass tertiären Unionsrechts*, Baden-Baden 2015, pp. 33 ff.; D. Fischer-Appelt, *Agenturen der Europäischen Gemeinschaft. Eine Studie zu Rechtsproblemen, Legitimation und Kontrolle europäischer Agenturen mit interdisziplinären und rechtsvergleichenden Bezügen*, Berlin 1999, p. 173; Groß, 'Die Kooperation', p. 54.

54 This division has become a permanent part of the canon of the German legal literature and is repeated, also on a polemical basis, whenever the European institutional structure is discussed. See M. Hilf, *Die Organisationsstruktur der Europäischen Gemeinschaften.*

level of this structure is shaped by institutions whose existence is clearly defined in primary law. According to the current legal situation, these are the seven main EU institutions listed in Article 13(1) TEU: the European Parliament, the European Council, the Council, the European Commission, the Court of Justice of the European Union, the European Central Bank and the Court of Auditors as well as the two supporting bodies described in Article 13(4) TEU: the Economic and Social Committee and the Committee of Regions. The second level consists of bodies, the creation of which, is underpinned by an explicit Treaty basis. This involves institutions that are part of the administrative apparatus of the main and subsidiary authorities as well as advisory institutions established on the basis of Articles 99, 134, 141, 162, 207(3), 228 and 240 TFEU[55].

The third level consists of bodies without any explicit reference to them in primary law that would indicate their tasks, organisational character and the conditions for establishing them. These entities are created under the general provisions of the Treaty and they are known as "non-Treaty" bodies[56]. They can be established by the main EU institutions on the basis of their general legislative competences as defined in Treaty provisions. These bodies can have legal personality, wide institutional autonomy and an extensive catalogue of tasks[57]. At the fourth level in Hilf's ranking there are institutions whose actions cause direct legal effects predominantly within the member states. The organisational arrangements and powers of those institutions are regulated in secondary law[58].

In the light of considerations discussed in the subsequent parts of this book, the third level involving regulatory agencies deserves particular attention. These

---

Rechtliche Gestaltungsmöglichkeiten und Grenzen, Berlin 1982, pp. 13 ff. About the importance of Hilf's model see C. Görisch, *Demokratische Verwaltung durch Unionsagenturen*, Tübingen 2009, pp. 188 ff.; Steger, *Zur Verselbständigung*, pp. 33 ff.

55 See K. Weißgärber, *Die Legitimation unabhängiger europäischer und nationaler Agenturen*, Baden-Baden 2016, p. 196.

56 Hilf, *Die Organisationsstruktur*, pp. 109 ff.; C. Calliess, 'Art. 13 EUV', in: C. Calliess, M. Ruffert (ed.), *EUV/AEUV. Das Verfassungsrecht der Europäischen Union mit Europäischer Grundrechtecharta. Kommentar*, München 2011, pp. 214, 220 ff.

57 For more discussions on defining agencies, see *Detailed Analytical Fiches*: Papers Produced During Inter-Institutional Dialogue, 2010, https://europa.eu/european-union/about-eu/agencies/overhaul_en (20.3.2018): European Commission's Analytical Fiche No. 1, 2010, *Definition and Classification of "European Regulatory Agency"*.

58 Examples of such organisations include the European Judicial Network. See Calliess, 'Art. 13 EUV', p. 214.

institutions are independent entities with legal personality[59], established under secondary legislation, usually regulations[60], for an indefinite period of time[61], endowed with their own powers as well as enjoying wide institutional autonomy, which is expressed e.g. in having their own budget and administrative structure[62]. Despite a long-lasting debate on this topic, no coherent definition of these bodies that would be reflected in the Treaty law has yet been elaborated. There have been ideas to modify the old Article 7 TEC and to include regulatory agencies in the catalogue of community institutions contained there. After the changes introduced by the Treaty of Lisbon, Article 13 TEU refers to that provision. It defines the EU institutional framework as consisting of the abovementioned seven main authorities and two subsidiary ones. But there is no place for regulatory agencies in that provision. Including them in the list found in Article 13 TEU would mean their formal integration into the existing institutional structure. This would, therefore, solve the problem of the required institutional checks and balances in the system of EU authorities. There was also no decision on a

59 The issue of legal personality of regulatory agencies is governed by regulations which establish them. The only exceptions are the initial agencies, Cedefop and Eurofound. Although in their case the issue was not explicitly regulated, it is assumed that they also have legal personality. See R. Uerpmann, 'Mittelbare Gemeinschaftsverwaltung durch gemeinschaftsgeschaffene juristische Personen des öffentlichen Rechts', *Archiv des öffentlichen Rechts*, Vol. 125, No. 4, 2000, p. 557.

60 Although some authors, like Martijn Groenleer, also point to older-generation agencies, classified in the old II and III pillar, which were provided for in primary law. This view, however, has become subject to criticism, since a reference to a particular agency in the Treaty law does not in itself mean that it was automatically established on this legal basis. See M. Groenleer, *The Autonomy of European Union Agencies. A Comparative Study of Institutional Development*, Delft 2009, p. 19; M. Chamon, *EU Agencies. Legal and Political Limits to the Transformation of the EU Administration*, Oxford/New York 2016, pp. 9, 12.

61 The European Union Agency for Network and Information Security (ENISA), which was established for a definite period is an example. Its mandate has been extended three times so far. Currently, according to Article 36 of Regulation (EU) No. 526/2013 of 21.5.2013 on the European Union Agency for Network and Information Security, OJ 2013, L 165/41, it is scheduled to operate until 2020.

62 This definition has functioned for two decades in academic literature and the Commission's documents. See J. Barcz, M. Górka, A. Wyrozumska, *Instytucje i prawo Unii Europejskiej*, Warszawa 2012, p. 180; M. Górka, 'Instytucje i organy UE', in: A. Łazowski, A. Zawidzka-Łojek (ed.), *Instytucje i porządek prawny UE*, Warszawa 2015, p. 94; Fischer-Appelt, *Agenturen*, p. 38; European Commission's Analytical Fiche No. 1, 2010.

separate provision that would make an explicit reference to the possibilities and conditions permitting the creation of regulatory agencies[63].

The absence of a definition of an agency in primary law as well as the lack of provisions defining their status and operational framework demonstrate the chaos that accompanies the evolution of these institutions. It is also reflected in the nomenclature used in reference to the agencies included at the Hilf's third level. In the literature the term "regulatory agencies" is usually used to describe these EU bodies, as a parallel to the U.S. model[64]. The adjective "regulatory" also accompanies agencies in most documents of the European Commission, where they are, for example, defined as entities actively engaged in the performance of executive tasks as well as the creation of instruments designed to regulate a specific sector[65].

EU Regulatory Agencies as a Result of the Decentralised Integration

Some researchers point out that not all agencies have an influence on the shaping of specific regulatory policies in the EU, hence the term "decentralised" would be more accurate; this was the version that the European Parliament advocated in the process of developing a common position of the EU institutions towards agencies[66].

This adjective is also ambiguous. On the one hand, it is about so-called functional decentralisation, i.e. distributing administrative tasks between different committees, commissions and agencies that support the Treaty bodies in

---

63 Geradin, 'The Development', p. 15.

64 It is a prevailing term both in the English-language (regulatory agencies) and German-language literature (Germ. *Regulierungsagenturen*), e.g. B. Saerbeck, *Unabhängige europäische Regulierungsagenturen. Ihr Einflusspotenzial am Beispiel der Europäischen Umweltagentur*, Wiesbaden 2014, pp. 40 ff. For the European Commission's direct reference to the U.S. model, see Chamon, *EU Agencies*, pp. 6 ff.

65 "Regulatory agencies are required to be actively involved in the executive function by enacting instruments which help to regulate a specific sector. The majority of them are intended to make such regulation more consistent and effective by combining and networking at Community level activities which are initially a matter for the member states". See the European Commission's Communication: *The Operating Framework for the European Regulatory Agencies*, COM(2002) 718 final, 11.12.2002, p. 4. See also the Communication issued by the European Commission, the European Parliament and the Council: *European Agencies – The Way Forward*, COM(2008) 135 final, 11.3.2008.

66 See *Resolution of the European Parliament on Financial Management and Control of EU Agencies*, 23.4.2009, OJ 2009, L 255/206. *Cf.* e.g. A.C. Hansen-Nootbaar, *Unabhängigkeit und Legitimation europäischer Agenturen*, Frankfurt am Main 2013, pp. 25 ff.

decision-making processes, technical expertise, data collection and coordinating cooperation between EU-level and national level institutions[67]. Cooperation between different administrative bodies organised this way is called "decentralised integration"[68]. On the other hand, "decentralisation" means the geographical dispersion of the bureaucratic apparatus and "going outside" Brussels. In this case it is possible to adapt solutions dedicated to specific, local needs more efficiently, although such a solution also entails reduced efficiency and increased costs due to an excessive rise in the number of institutions involved. In practice, in the case of agencies that are analysed, we can only talk about geographical decentralisation, i.e. locating their headquarters outside Brussels. This is not a favourable solution for economic reasons, but it is supposed to guarantee greater independence from the influence of the European Commission[69]. As for the substantive dimension of decentralisation, an opposite phenomenon can be noticed in the context of EU regulatory agencies. This involves, at the supranational level, the centralisation of tasks that did not exist before, or remained in the domain of national authorities.

Both dimensions of decentralisation are part of the phenomenon of "deconcentration" which, in official EU documents, is connected with the policy of "externalising" the tasks of the European Commission. This policy has been developed since the early 2000s[70]. It transfers some of the Commission's responsibilities to independent external institutions in order to focus on its

---

67 See E. Vos, 'Reforming the European Commission: What Role to Play for EU Agencies?', *Common Market Law Review*, Vol. 37, No. 5, 2000, pp. 1116 ff.

68 Groß, 'Die Kooperation', p. 55.

69 Geradin, Petit, 'The Development of Agencies', pp. 18–22; C. Scott, 'Agencies for European Regulatory Governance: A Regimes Approach', in: D. Geradin *et al.* (ed.), *Regulation through Agencies in the EU: A New Paradigm of European Governance*, Cheltenham 2005, pp. 70 ff.; N. Kohtamäki, 'Kultura organizacyjna w agencjach regulacyjnych Unii Europejskiej', *Polski Przegląd Stosunków Międzynarodowych*, No. 5, 2015, p. 84.

70 The term "deconcentration" appears e.g. in the Commission's communication on the creation of the so-called executive agencies, more about them in the later part of this chapter. See the European Commission's Communication, *Externalisation of the Management of Community Programmes Including Presentation of a Framework Regulation for a New Type of Executive Agency*, COM(2000) 788 final, 13.12.2000, pp. 4 ff. For detailed information about "deconcentration" see also Michael H. Koch's monograph devoted to the phenomenon of externalising the tasks of the Commission, *Externalisierungspolitik der Kommission. Zulässigkeit und Grenzen mittelbarer Gemeinschaftsverwaltung*, Baden-Baden 2004, pp. 56 ff.

core functions involving the legislative process. The Commission is, therefore, the central authority coordinating the agency system. This was reflected in the nomenclature accompanying its expansion back in the 1990s when working documents referred to the Commission's "satellite bodies", rather than regulatory agencies[71]. Admittedly, they were not seen as the main element of the Community Method, which is the basic instrument of supranational management in the EU. It involves a transfer of certain competences and decision-making mechanisms by the member states to the level of the EU institutions. Over time, however, regulatory agencies have become a significant backup for the Commission, strengthening its "technocratic ethos" as a key institution in the EU's supranational institutional system, engaged in the process of European legislation and implementation as well as monitoring compliance of the member states with it[72]. Despite their growing importance in the European executive order, agencies have remained, with some exceptions, in principle "non-Treaty" bodies.

Although there is no consistency and coherence in EU documents when it comes to defining these bodies, the term "regulatory agencies" will be used in the following deliberations, primarily due to its widespread use in specialised literature, both legal and in the field of political science, but also because it reflects the idea that originally drove the European Commission into the process of delegating a number of norm-setting tasks to agencies[73]. The adjective "regulatory" also corresponds to modern developmental trends in the European institutional system. These indicate a desire to establish new agencies and transform the existing ones into bodies actively involved in the process of European legislation, as well as implementing the law in specialised sectors of the internal market. Therefore, although most agencies do not have regulatory powers, all

---

71 See A. Kreher, 'Agencies in the European Community – A Step Towards Administrative Integration in Europe', *Journal of European Public Policy*, Vol. 4, No. 2, 1997, p. 227.

72 See M. Busuioc *et al.*, 'Agency Growth Between Autonomy and Accountability: The European Police Office as a "Living Institution"', in: Rittberger, Wonka (ed.), *Agency Governance*, pp. 70 ff.; J. Ruszkowski, *Ponadnarodowość w systemie politycznym Unii Europejskiej*, Warszawa 2010, pp. 282 ff.

73 See a report by an expert group established by the then President of the European Commission, Prodi, headed by André Sapir: *An Agenda for a Growing Europe. Making the EU Economic System Deliver*, July 2003, pp. 152 ff. The report assumed that deepened economic integration must be accompanied by better and more efficient management. See Scott, 'Agencies', p. 67; J. Supernat, 'Agencje europejskie', in: E. Ura *et al.* (ed.), *Rola i znaczenie zarządzania kryzysowego w systemie bezpieczeństwa państwa*, Rzeszów 2013, pp. 80 ff.

of them, regardless of their task catalogue, actively participate in the shaping of the European legal system or, more broadly, what is called the "EU's regulatory output" in the literature[74]. It is conventional to use the term "EU regulatory agencies", despite the specific character of these institutions, which is different from that of their national counterparts.

Regulatory Agencies versus *Other Bodies in the EU Institutional Structure*

In the absence of a formal definition, regulatory agencies are often described with the use of negative definitions. This means that internal organisational units of the European Commission, such as EU Statistical Office (Eurostat) or DGs, are not among such bodies. Executive agencies, which are established by Commission decisions for a definite period of time to perform specific tasks associated with EU programmes, are also not among them[75]. Executive agencies are dependent on the Commission, report to particular DGs, and are based in Brussels. Regulatory agencies also formulate part of a specific policy shaped by a given DG within the Commission's administrative apparatus, but the relationship between these entities is not one of hierarchical subordination. Instead, they resemble relations between ministries and independent agencies from a certain economic sector within legal systems at a national level. Thus, in the case of regulatory agencies, we can speak of "parent" DGs, which have their "contact address" in the European Commission, as taking part in joint policymaking in a specific market sector[76].

---

74 See A. Wonka, B. Rittberger, 'Credibility, Complexity and Uncertainty: Explaining the Institutional Independence of 29 EU Agencies', *West European Politics*, Vol. 33, No. 4, 2010, p. 733.

75 See Council Regulation (EC) No. 58/2003 of 19.12.2002 laying down the statute for executive agencies to be entrusted with certain tasks in the management of Community programmes, OJ 2003, L 11/1. The list of executive agencies see http://ec.europa.eu/info/departments/education-and-culture_pl (20.3.2018). More M. Zieliński, 'Agencje wykonawcze UE', *Europejski Przegląd Sądowy*, No. 6, 2014, pp. 15 ff. Distinguishing between executive and regulatory agencies does not pose much difficulty due to their different status and capabilities. But some researchers are critical towards the naming of these bodies, pointing out that both the types of agencies are of executive nature, see Groß, 'Die Kooperation', p. 57; W. Weiß, 'Agencies *versus* Networks: From Divide to Convergence in the Administrative Governance in the EU', *Administrative Law Review*, Vol. 61, Special Edition, 2009, pp. 48 ff.

76 Besides "parent" DGs, which are close to regulatory agencies due to their area of activity, they too usually contact the Directorate-General for Budget, the Directorate-General for Human Resources and Security and the Internal Audit Service. See W. Jann

Institutions, the existence of which has been specified explicitly in the Treaties, such as the European Central Bank, are not regulatory agencies either. Moreover, regulatory agencies should not be confused with organisations established under intergovernmental agreements outside the EU institutional structure, e.g. the European University Institute (EUI) in Florence[77]. Despite nomenclatural similarity, they are not autonomous intergovernmental organisations, such as the European Space Agency (ESA) or the European Patent Office (EPO)[78], nor are they internal organisational units in the EU's administrative system, such as the European Personnel Selection Office (EPSO), the Joint Research Centre (JRC) or the Office for Administration and Payment of Individual Entitlements (PMO). This last category involves intra-EU subsidiary bodies that do not have institutional autonomy or legal personality[79].

Regulatory agencies differ from the agencies for the Common Security and Defence Policy (CSDP) as well as for the Area of Freedom, Security and Justice (AFSJ), i.e. those that were classified in the so-called II and III pillars before the changes introduced by the Treaty of Lisbon. The first group includes the EU Institute for Security Studies (EUISS), the EU Satellite Centre (SatCen) and the European Defence Agency (EDA). The latter includes the European Police Office (Europol), the EU's Judicial Cooperation Unit (Eurojust) and the EU Agency for Law Enforcement Training (CEPOL). The abovementioned agencies of the former II and III pillar show many similarities to the regulatory agencies that were generally included in the old I pillar. One of the basic differences is the authority that initiates the establishment of those bodies. For agencies involved in the issues of security, defence and justice – it is the Council. But for regulatory agencies – it is the European Commission. To distinguish them, the agencies of the former II and III pillar are called Union agencies or intergovernmental agencies[80]. This formal division has been maintained in EU documents that

---

et al., 'Best Practice in Governance of Agencies – A Comparative Study in View of Identifying Best Practice for Governing Agencies Carrying out Activities on Behalf of the European Union', *Study. Policy Department on Budgetary Affairs*, January 2008, p. 156.

77 See D. Barbieri, E. Ongaro, 'EU Agencies: What is Common and What is Distinctive Compared with National-Level Public Agencies', *International Review of Administrative Science*, Vol. 74, No. 3, 2008, p. 400; Kreher, 'Agencies', p. 228.

78 Groenleer, *The Autonomy*, p. 20.

79 See T. Hustedt *et al.*, *Verwaltungsstrukturen in der Europäischen Union. Kommission, Komitologie, Agenturen und Verwaltungsnetzwerke*, Wiesbaden 2014, p. 146.

80 Jann *et al.*, 'Best Practice', p. 96.

arrange the status of regulatory agencies in the EU institutional system. For this reason, the abovementioned agencies, which according to the Joint Statement of the Commission, the Council and the Parliament of July 2012, form part of the Common Foreign and Security Policy (CFSP) or the Common policy in the area of Justice and Home Affairs, will not be a subject of this analysis[81].

Regulatory agencies, despite some similarities, are also not identical to the so-called regulatory networks that constitute parallel solutions designed to streamline the European administration. Networks are supranational or intergovernmental structures consisting of representatives of regulatory authorities at a national level established for the purpose of formalising, organising and coordinating mutual cooperation as well as harmonising the practices applied in a given sector[82]. They are created on the initiative of the European Commission or regulatory authorities at the level of the member states. Their stage of institutionalisation is significantly lower than in the case of EU regulatory agencies. As a rule, they are not hierarchically organised institutions with their own budgets and independent personnel[83]. They are typically open, collective bodies, the purpose of which is the exchange of views and the elaboration of a common position, based on voluntary participation. Regulatory networks can coexist alongside regulatory agencies, complement their tasks and also constitute an initial phase before cooperation is deepened and an appropriate EU regulatory agency is established[84]. Networks, which primarily constitute a form

81 *Joint Statement and Common Approach*, 19.7.2012, https://europa.eu/european-union/sites/europaeu/files/docs/body/joint_statement_and_common_approach_2012_en.pdf (20.3.2018). See Chamon, *EU Agencies*, p. 20; Groenleer, *The Autonomy*, p. 116.

82 The European Competition Network (ECN) is an example of such a network, bringing together representatives of competition protection offices from all member states. See S. Wilks, 'Agencies, Networks, Discourses and the Trajectory of European Competition Enforcement', *European Competition Journal*, Vol. 3, No. 2, 2007, pp. 438 ff.

83 Their work is usually coordinated by the board assisted by the secretariat as well as committees and working groups comprising professionals from a given market sector. Networks have different degrees of institutionalisation. The leading role is often played by the European Commission, thus some regulatory networks are even described as "steered" or "directed" networks. See *ibid.*, p. 448.

84 Due to the possibility of such an evolution, intermediate forms between an agency and a regulatory network (networked agency/agencified network) are also identified. Regulatory agencies have evolved from existing networks of cooperation e.g. in the aviation sector. The European Aviation Safety Agency (EASA) replaced the network of Joint Aviation Authorities (JAA). About regulatory networks: M. Maggetti, F. Gilardi, 'The Policy-Making Structure of European Regulatory Networks and the Domestic Adoption of Standards', in: Rittberger, Wonka (ed.), *Agency Governance*, pp. 52 ff.;

of cooperation between national regulatory bodies, are useful instruments for the member states to employ in order to exercise influence on the European Commission in the process of shaping policies in significant market sectors. EU regulatory agencies, on the other hand, usually perform the opposite role and they are seen as entities used by the Commission in the process of modelling the activities of the member states[85].

bb) Development over Time

The Beginnings

In the academic literature there have been frequent attempts to arrange agencies according to various criteria. The simplest one is the chronological criterion. This assumes that there have been several phases of agency growth. The first, original, phase, involved two agencies created in 1975: the European Centre for the Development of Vocational Training (Cedefop) and the European Foundation for the Improvement of Living and Working Conditions (Eurofound). The establishment of those two agencies did not yet herald a transformation in the shaping of European administrative mechanisms. Due to the rigid understanding of the principles of institutional balance in the Community, delegation of powers to institutions that are not regulated in primary law was then nothing more than a unique step, possible in those two cases because of the limited powers and special area of activity of Cedefop and Eurofound[86]. Both the agencies fitted into the community programme to improve living and working conditions in the member states, for example by supporting vocational training. Despite the fact that none of the first agencies had decision-making powers, they should be seen as typical instruments of "soft influence"[87], the justification cited in the regulation that established Eurofound reflects the assumptions that guided the Commission in the subsequent stages of the growth of the agency system. The creation of this agency was deemed necessary partly because the European Community was not in a position to "carry out analyses, and studies, as well as to conduct research

D. Coen, M. Thatcher, 'Network Governance and Multi-Level Delegation: European Networks of Regulatory Agencies', *Journal of Public Policy*, Vol. 28, No. 1, 2008, pp. 49 ff.

85 See Christensen, Lehmann Nielsen, 'Administrative Capacity', p. 179.

86 Geradin, 'The Development', p. 8.

87 See M. Everson, G. Majone, 'European Agencies within the Treaties of the European Union', in: G. Majone *et al.* (ed.), *The Role of Specialised Agencies in Decentralising EU Governance. Report presented to the Commission*, Brussel 1999, p. 67.

systematically and scientifically"[88]. Therefore, from the outset, agencies were supposed to support the Commission in specialised tasks which other Community institutions were unable to handle. Their main asset is technical expertise that other institutions at the supranational level do not have. The first two agencies were conceived as simple advisory bodies. Thus, they were in tune with the specific character of that stage of European integration, when the competencies of Community bodies were limited, in comparison to the current state of affairs[89]. No one suspected at the time that an entire agency system would be established, contributing to a rapid evolution of EU governance and leaving a significant mark on the institutional structure of the whole European integration process.

The second, more intensive, stage took place just fifteen years later, in the 1990s. A great deal of information and monitoring agencies were then created, e.g. the European Environment Agency (EEA) in 1990, the European Monitoring Centre for Drugs and Drug Addiction (EMCDDA) in 1993 as well as the Community Plant Variety Office (CPVO) in 1994. A decision made by representatives of the member state governments at the level of the heads of state and government on the location of the headquarters of some of the institutions and departments of the Community as well as Europol confirmed the existence of decentralisation trends in European governance. It officially designated headquarters for several agencies that were established in the 1990s[90].

The "White Paper" of 25 July 2001

The third phase involved agencies created in the early 2000s and this period was the most dynamic. A breakthrough moment occurred when the "White Paper on European Governance" was published by the European Commission on 25 July 2001[91] followed by two Communications: in June and in December of

---

88 See the preamble of Council Regulation (EEC) No. 1365/75 of 26.5.1975 on the creation of a European Foundation for the Improvement of Living and Working Conditions, OJ 1975, L 139/1.

89 Hustedt *et al.*, *Verwaltungsstrukturen*, p. 148.

90 *Decision Taken by Common Agreement between the Representatives of the Governments of the Member States, Meeting at Head of State and Government Level, on the Location of the Seats of Certain Bodies and Departments of the European Communities and of Europol*, OJ 1993, C 323/01. See P. Sander, 'Europäische Agenturen: Rechtsgrundlagen in und sonstige Berührungspunkte mit dem primären Unionsrecht', in: N. Raschauer (ed.), *Europäische Agenturen*, Salzburg 2012, pp. 3 ff.

91 *European Governance. A White Paper*, COM(2001) 428 final, 25.7.2001, OJ 2001, C 287/1.

2002 on better legislation,[92] along with a framework on regulatory agencies[93]. These were programming documents designed to show a desire to find a way out of the deadlock in which the European Union was entangled, for numerous reasons, at the dawn of the twenty first century[94]. They complemented the administrative reform that also involved the Commission which, being weakened by corruption scandals, set out to redefine and update the understanding of its tasks when Prodi was appointed as its chairman in 1999[95].

In the face of various crises, voices were raised in support of the re-evaluation of the existing way of thinking about European governance[96]. The process of creating an increasingly integrated internal market, for which the road was paved by the 1986 Single European Act and the 1992 Treaty of Maastricht, forced debate on the need to introduce uniform standards, patents, permits, and technical guidelines on manufacturing, operating and using, for example, certain devices, safety rules, consumer protection rules, and more, within the EU. The legal framework was expected to respond to the challenges posed by intensifying cooperation. This would have been impossible to accomplish within the existing institutional structures, which were based on the Commission's bureaucratic framework[97]. In the early 2000s Monika Niedźwiedź rightly pointed out that: "the casuistry and detailed nature of largely technical regulations influenced

92 *European Governance. Better Law Making*, Brussels, COM(2002) 275 final, 5.6.2002.

93 *The Operating Framework*, COM(2002) 718 final.

94 *Cf.* Yataganas, 'Delegation', pp. 4 ff.

95 The programme of the European Commission's "renewal" was also presented in a "White Paper": *Reforming the Commission. A White Paper. Part I*, COM(2000) 0200 final, 5.3.2000. The European Commission, established in its current shape in 1967, is considered by many scholars in the field of administrative science to be a relatively young, constantly evolving institution in comparison to those in the member states. Therefore, proposals to reform it, which are repeated over the decades, are not surprising. See T. Balint *et al.*, 'Bureaucratic Change in the European Administrative Space: The Case of European Commission', in: D. Curtin, M. Egeberg (ed.), *Towards a New Executive Order in Europe*, London/New York 2015, p. 39.

96 This partly relates to the crisis in the food market. The breakdown of trust in European institutions was also amplified by the corruption scandal that led to the resignation of the entire European Commission chaired by Santer in 1999 (mentioned above).

97 Unless the apparatus would have been expanded towards becoming a completely opaque structure employing tens of thousands of workers; this solution was unlikely due to political objections which partly resulted from the high costs such a procedure would carry. See Yataganas, 'Delegation', p. 7.

the emergence of a new governance model defined in the literature as technocratic governance"[98].

In the 2001 "White Paper" this idea was expressed explicitly by emphasising the necessity of transferring national models of entrusting regulatory tasks to agencies at the European level. It was recognised that such an institutional model guarantees effective implementation of European law and provides greater possibilities of controlling the manner in which it is applied[99]. The "White Paper" opened a new period in the perception of regulatory agencies as a significant, effective and sustainable element in the European governance system, based on such core values as openness, participation, responsibility, effectiveness and coherence[100]. In order to put the agencies in line with these assumptions, the necessity to delegate greater powers to them was emphasised, including the power to make decisions, particularly in the context of verifying the implementation and application of regulations requiring technical expertise.

According to the wording of the "White Paper", however, agencies should not have powers delegated to them which: (1) lead to the creation of general regulations, (2) are based on provisions in Treaty law requiring the direct involvement of the Commission, (3) involve settling disputes associated with public interest, (4) are politically determined and require the discretionary power of the decision-making authority and those that (5) entail comprehensive economic analysis. These bodies should keep high institutional autonomy, but operate within a clearly defined legal framework while at the same time maintaining high transparency and clear mechanisms of control[101]. The "White Paper" also expressed a view which confirmed the actual situation and, in practice, it

98 M. Niedźwiedź, 'Rola agencji europejskich w strukturze instytucjonalnej Unii Europejskiej a postanowienia traktatu ustanawiającego Konstytucję dla Europy', in: S. Dudzik (ed.), *Konstytucja dla Europy. Przyszły fundament Unii Europejskiej*, Kraków 2005, p. 302. See also M. Zieliński, 'Agencje Unii Europejskiej', in: R. Grzeszczak, A. Szczerba-Zawada (ed.), *Prawo administracyjne Unii Europejskiej*, Warszawa 2016, pp. 164 ff.

99 *European Governance*, COM(2001) 428 final. See K.A. Wojtaszczyk, 'Agencje w systemie UE. Typologia oraz podstawy teoretyczno-metodologiczne prowadzenia badań', in: M. Witkowska, K.A. Wojtaszczyk (ed.), *Agencje, komitety i inne jednostki organizacyjne UE*, Warszawa 2015, pp. 11 ff.

100 See M. Höreth, 'The European Commission's White Paper on Governance: A "Tool-kit" for Closing the Legitimacy Gap of EU Policymaking?', *ZEI Discussion Paper*, No. 94, 2001, p. 10.

101 For more about this issue, see E. Vos, 'Independence, Accountability and Transparency of European Regulatory Agencies', in: Geradin *et al.* (ed.), *Regulation*, pp. 121 ff.

became something of a curse in the process of establishing agencies. Namely, it was confirmed that institutions of this type would be established after a separate evaluation of each case of this type[102]. Therefore, the chaos that accompanied the creation of agencies was legitimised, as well as the high level of discretion involved in formulating the demand for such bodies[103].

Searching for an Inter-Institutional Agreement

Regardless of that unfortunate statement, the Commission announced, in the "White Paper", the necessity to regulate the legal framework for the establishment and functioning of regulatory agencies. This announcement was reflected in the abovementioned Communication of December 2002 entitled "The Operating Framework for the European Regulatory Agencies"[104]. These bodies were meant to "relieve" the European Union of performing technical and expert tasks so that it could focus on its core responsibilities, related to European legislation. Agencies were classified as entities participating in the formulation of the European executive order, while simultaneously maintaining the institutional balance and the appropriate transparency of the system, based primarily on supervision by the European Commission[105]. Agencies were supposed to carry out precisely defined tasks that required expertise and that were created on the initiative of the Commission when it wanted to solve a specific problem. In the Communication, agencies were divided into those that had decision-making powers in specific cases, and those endowed mainly with executive powers which supported the work of the European Commission[106]. The December Communication also repeated the Commission's earlier announcement of June 2002 emphasising the urgency of reaching an inter-institutional agreement between the Commission, the Council and the European Parliament on the issue of settling the legal status of regulatory agencies[107].

---

102 *European Governance*, COM(2001) 428 final.

103 See M. Wieloński, 'Prawny wymiar funkcjonowania agencji, komitetów i innych jednostek organizacyjnych. Wnioski na przyszłość', in: Witkowska, Wojtaszczyk (ed.), *Agencje*, p. 50.

104 *The Operating Framework*, COM(2002) 718 final.

105 "Agencies as an executive instrument", see *ibid.*, p. 5. See also Busuioc *et al.*, 'The Phenomenon', pp. 7 ff.

106 The European Commission made it particularly clear in the Communication that agencies had no right to adopt universally applicable legal acts that are general by design. See *The Operating Framework*, COM(2002) 718 final, pp. 8, 11.

107 *Ibid.*, pp. 3 ff.; *European Governance*, COM(2002) 275 final, p. 5.

A draft of such an agreement presented in 2005 was an attempt to respond to the need expressed in the Commission's Communications[108]. In the draft, the Commission proposed the creation of a framework to arrange the process of establishing agencies, assigning them specific tasks and controlling them. In the enclosed definition of the term "regulatory agencies", it also stated that when performing regulatory activities, agencies in fact do not need to have powers to adopt norms or legal acts. This did not help in any way to determine the status of these bodies in a clearer way[109].

In the course of events, the 2005 draft agreement did not come into force. But the reason for that was not the weakness of its substance, but rather the political climate. The Council prevented debate concerning the matter, arguing that an inter-institutional agreement is not an appropriate instrument to build a coherent normative framework for regulatory agencies. The Commission's proposal was also considered to be too detailed, not leaving enough room for creative discussion. The Council's resistance stemmed from concerns about excessive strengthening of the Commission's position in the European institutional system. Such a change in the balance of power could mean a gradual reduction in the political role of the Council and the influence of the individual member states over important sectors of the internal market when taking into account the perspective of national economies[110]. The European Commission officially withdrew the draft only in March 2009, when it became clear that an agreement of that kind would not obtain the Council's approval[111].

The withdrawal of the draft agreement was preceded by the Commission's Communication of March 2008, where it attempted to outline a plan to find a way out of the deadlock in the debate on regulatory agencies. Agencies were

---

108 *Interinstitutional Agreement on the Operating Framework for the European Regulatory Agencies. Draft*, COM(2005) 59 final, 25.2.2005.

109 *Ibid.*, p. 4.

110 See S. Andoura, P. Timmerman, 'Governance of the EU: The Reform Debate on European Agencies Reignited', *EPIN Working Paper*, No. 19, 2008, p. 25; Groenleer, *The Autonomy*, p. 110; M. Wittinger, '"Europäische Satelliten": Anmerkungen zum Europäischen Agentur(un)wesen und zur Vereinbarkeit Europäischer Agenturen mit dem Gemeinschaftsrecht', *Europarecht*, No. 5, 2008, p. 611; M. Everson *et al.*, 'European Agencies in between Institutions and Member States', in: M. Everson *et al.* (ed.), *European Agencies in between Institutions and Member States*, Alphen aan den Rijn 2014, p. 5.

111 *Withdrawal of Obsolete Commission Proposal*, 2009/C71/07, 25.3.2009, OJ 2009, C 71/17.

officially recognised as a part of the EU's "institutional machine" which required urgent clarification and regulation in terms of their functioning and supervision over them[112]. It was acknowledged that, despite holding talks aimed at reaching an agreement on agencies, the problems associated with them had not gone away. The March Communication primarily highlighted the issues related to the poor transparency of the agency system, as well as the vague mechanisms for legitimising the actions of these bodies and holding them accountable[113]. It was concluded that since the prepared draft agreement from 2005 did not secure the political approval of the member states, it was necessary to open a new debate on agencies, including all three EU institutions from the start, in order to reach a common understanding of the role of these bodies and their relationship with the European Commission, the European Parliament and the Council[114]. An inter-institutional dialogue on the topic of agencies was undertaken by a special Working Group set up in March 2009. During its work, in line with the call included in the 2008 Communication, the Commission was to refrain from establishing new regulatory agencies. This recommendation, however, was not upheld, partly because of the emergency situation associated with the financial crisis in the European markets. This created a unique opportunity to establish powerful supervisory agencies in the financial sector (EBA, ESMA and EIOPA)[115].

The "Common Approach" of 19 July 2012

The Inter-institutional Working Group carried out an in-depth review of regulatory agencies, taking into account their structure, functioning, control mechanisms, financing, etc. The effects of this work were included in more than thirty detailed analytical papers[116]. As a result of debate, an agreement was reached in June 2012, followed by a Joint Statement from the three EU institutions on decentralised agencies and the "Common Approach" which accompanied it[117]. Those documents were of a declarative nature; as such they

---

112 *European Agencies – The Way Forward*, COM(2008) 135 final, 11.3.2008, p. 1.

113 *Ibid.*, p. 6.

114 *Ibid.*, p. 8.

115 *Ibid.*, p. 9. See Weißgärber, *Die Legitimation*, p. 33.

116 *Detailed Analytical Fiches*: Papers Produced During Inter-Institutional Dialogue, 2010, https://europa.eu/european-union/about-eu/agencies/overhaul_en (20.3.2018).

117 *Joint Statement and Common Approach*, 19.7.2012. See also M. Šefčovič, 'Ein Ordnungsrahmen für die dezentralisierten Agenturen der EU', *Europäische Zeitschrift für Wirtschaftsrecht*, Vol. 23, No. 21, 2012, pp. 801 f.

were a kind of political manifesto, and they were not legally binding[118]. Yet they marked an important breakthrough in understanding the role and place of regulatory agencies in the European institutional system. The documents, one could say, effectively sanctioned the existing *status quo*. Therefore, agencies are no longer a subject of discussion in terms of whether entities of this sort should be created. Nevertheless, they became the leitmotif of debate on how to shape their tasks in order to prevent primary law and the institutional balance in the EU from being compromised[119].

The "Common Approach" introduced consistent standards for the creation and functioning of regulatory agencies, which from then on were officially called decentralised, in line with a recommendation by the European Parliament[120]. Many of the elements proposed in the document were only a confirmation of existing practices. Criticism in the debate was primarily focused on the limited involvement of EU institutions in developing mechanisms to monitor the work of agencies and improving the system of holding them accountable[121]. Regardless of its weaknesses, the "Common Approach" reflected a change in the political atmosphere around regulatory agencies. A "Roadmap", i.e. a plan for a staged implementation of the arrangements set out in the "Common Approach" was unveiled in December 2012. It included ninety detailed tasks to be carried out in order to achieve the objectives delineated in the "Common Approach"[122]. An assessment of the performance of these tasks was made by the Commission twice: in December 2013 and in April 2015[123]. The provisions of the "Common Approach" relate to future agencies, although in practice it can be seen that

118 For more, see M. Scholten, 'The Newly Released "Common Approach" on EU Agencies: Going Forward or Standing Still?', *The Columbia Journal of European Law Online*, Vol. 19, No. 1, 2012, p. 3.

119 Hustedt *et al.*, *Verwaltungsstrukturen*, p. 157.

120 On the position of the European Parliament on the naming of agencies, see Weißgärber, *Die Legitimation*, p. 34.

121 *Cf.* Everson *et al.*, 'European Agencies', p. 5.

122 The text of the "Roadmap" is available at: https://europa.eu/european-union/sites/europaeu/files/docs/body/2012-12-18_roadmap_on_the_follow_up_to_the_common_approach_on_eu_decentralised_agencies_en.pdf (20.3.2018).

123 *Commission Progress Report on the Implementation of the Common Approach*, 10.12.2013; *Report from the Commission: Progress Report on the Implementation of the Common Approach on EU Decentralised Agencies*, COM(2015) 179 final, 24.4.2015.

reviews of regulations relating to the agencies that already exist have taken many of the postulates into account[124].

Fifteen years of efforts have failed to integrate the assumptions related to regulatory agencies into a regulation that would arrange the status and activities of these institutions in a legally binding way, like in the case of executive agencies[125]. The "Common Approach" only contains recommendations. These are usually followed, but need not be in cases where this is justified in the context of particular agencies. Reports on the implementation of the recommendations proposed in 2012, however, indicate adherence to the deadlines set out in the "Roadmap" with regard to harmonising the naming of agencies and their offices, legal issues related to the establishment of agency seats, and also regarding the methods of reporting on the tasks performed or financing mechanisms[126].

The programming documents of the early 2000s opened the era of the so-called third generation agencies, which was marked by much higher "delegational enthusiasm" than in the previous decades. This meant a gradual reconstruction of the European administrative system towards structuring it according to the sectoral divisions of the internal market[127]. Agencies with increasing decision-making, operational, or even semi-legislative authority began to emerge alongside agencies intended merely to support and assist. In the second decade of the twenty first century it also became common to expand the mandate of the existing agencies by modifying their powers: mainly through increasingly detailed sector-specific regulations. Agencies classified in the so-called third generation category include e.g. EFSA as well as the transport agencies: the European Maritime Safety Agency (EMSA), the European Aviation Safety Agency (EASA) and the EU Agency for Railways (ERA). With

124 ERA is a good example. For changes related to it, see M. Będkowski-Kozioł, 'Status i zadania Europejskiej Agencji Kolejowej – stan obecny i perspektywy w świetle projektu IV pakietu kolejowego UE', *Internetowy Kwartalnik Antymonopolowy i Regulacyjny*, No. 7(3), 2014, pp. 54–56.

125 Regulation (EC) No. 58/2003.

126 Chamon, *EU Agencies*, pp. 97–100.

127 German authors write about the European Commission's friendly attitude towards delegating competences (Germ. *Delegationsfreundlichkeit*). See Hustedt *et al.*, *Verwaltungsstrukturen*, p. 150; J. Fleischer, 'Die europäischen Agenturen als Diener Vieler Herren? Zur Steuerung und Rolle von EU-Agenturen', in: W. Jann, M. Döhler (ed.), *Agencies in Westeuropa*, Wiesbaden 2007, p. 224.

the establishment of agencies dedicated to financial supervision (EBA, ESMA and EIOPA) in 2011, we can speak of a further evolution of the agency system (fourth generation) which is signified by the emergence of institutions with increasing independence and powers, not previously seen at the European or national levels[128].

The chronological breakdown has an organisational nature, but it does not contribute much when it comes to defining agencies as such, since it is to a great extent arbitrary and mainly based on the criterion of time. Therefore, this division is sometimes modified in a variety of ways: through the flexible combination of particular phases or moving individual agencies to one group or another. Such discretion stems from the lack of a clear profile of the agencies that were established at a particular stage. The only long-term trend that makes it possible to identify a fourth phase is the trend to endow agencies with even broader powers[129]. Despite the artificiality of such chronological classifications, a tabular presentation of all the agencies in the order of their creation will facilitate further analysis of the subject. The table includes the current full names of agencies – in some cases, over the years, they have undergone changes[130]. In later discussions particular agencies will usually be called by their English abbreviations. The date of the establishment of an agency is considered to be the year when the regulation to establish it was issued[131], although in some cases the actual functioning of an agency may have begun at a later stage[132].

128 See M. Greta, J. Otto, *Proces decyzyjny i zarządczy w UE. Znaczenie systemu agencyjnego*, Łódź 2016, pp. 44 ff.; A. Dumała (ed.), *Agencje Unii Europejskiej*, Warszawa 2002, pp. 6 ff.

129 Hustedt *et al.*, *Verwaltungsstrukturen*, p. 150.

130 For instance, the Office for Harmonization in the Internal Market (OHIM) in 2016 had its name changed to the European Union Intellectual Property Office.

131 Even when it was later replaced by other legal acts, like in the case of the European Aviation Safety Agency, established by Regulation (EC) No. 1592/2002 of 15.7.2002 (OJ 2002, L 240/1) replaced by Regulation (EC) No. 216/2008 of 20.2.2008 on common rules in the field of civil aviation and establishing a European Aviation Safety Agency, OJ 2008, L 79/1.

132 For instance, the European Training Foundation (ETF) was actually launched in 1994, even though the regulation establishing it was issued in 1990.

The historical development of regulatory agencies of the European Union

I generation	II generation	III generation	IV generation
1975: – Centre for the Development of Vocational Training, Cedefop – European Foundation for the Improvement of Living and Working Conditions, Eurofound	**1990:** – European Environment Agency, EEA – European Training Foundation, ETF **1993:** – European Monitoring Centre for Drugs and Drug Addiction, EMCDDA – European Medicines Agency, EMA – European Union Intellectual Property Office, EUIPO **1994:** – European Agency for Safety and Health at Work, EU-OSHA – Community Plant Variety Office, CPVO – Translation Centre for the Bodies of the European Union, CdT	**2002:** – European Food Safety Authority, EFSA – European Maritime Safety Agency, EMSA – European Aviation Safety Agency, EASA **2004:** – European Union Agency for Railways, ERA – European Network and Information Security Agency, ENISA – European Centre for Disease Prevention and Control, ECDC – European Global Navigation Satellite Systems Agency, GSA – European Border and Coast Guard Agency, Frontex **2005:** – European Fisheries Control Agency, EFCA **2006:** – European Chemicals Agency, ECHA – European Institute for Gender Equality, EIGE	**2009:** – Agency for the Cooperation of Energy Regulators, ACER – Office of the Body of European Regulators for Electronic Communications, BEREC[a] **2010:** – European Asylum Support Office, EASO – European Banking Authority, EBA – European Securities and Markets Authority, ESMA – European Insurance and Occupational Pensions Authority, EIOPA

(*continued on next page*)

The historical development of regulatory agencies of the European Union		
	2007: – European Union Agency for Fundamental Rights, FRA (replaced the European Monitoring Centre for Racism and Xenophobia, EUMC, created in 1997) **2008:** – European Institute of Innovation and Technology, EIT	**2011:** – European Agency for the Operational Management of Large-Scale IT Systems in the Area of Freedom, Security and Justice, eu-LISA **2014:** – Single Resolution Board, SRB

[a] Not all authors agree that BEREC is an agency. See Chamon, *EU Agencies*, p. 67; R.M. Pal, 'The Body of European Regulators for Electronic Communications and Its Influence on Polish Telecommunications Law', *Review of Comparative Law*, Vol. XXII, 2015, pp. 89 ff.

c) Motives for the Creation of Regulatory Agencies within the EU Institutional Structure

aa) Functionality

Nowadays, in the European Union, regulatory agencies are an irremovable, permanent element of the institutional landscape. They perform an important role in integration processes and it is impossible to imagine harmonisation of the law and actions of the individual member states in specific market sectors without the coordinating role that they play. They have become a symbol of the capabilities of the European administration in terms of its flexibility and effectiveness[133]. Such premises were also at the root of the concept of developing the European agency system. Therefore, the main motive for the creation of EU regulatory agencies can be described as a functional one. Since the 1990s, when the European Commission was charged with responsibilities associated with the preparation of normative

133 Everson *et al.*, 'European Agencies', p. 3.

acts in specialised sectors of the internal market, there has been a growing awareness of the necessity to establish expert bodies of a technical nature, supporting the Commission and, at least in theory, enjoying independence from political influence, both on the part of the Commission, and on the part of other EU and national entities[134]. Thanks to independent expertise, the credibility of EU law was supposed to increase, while agencies were to be primarily associated with the performance of the function understood as the provision of information[135]. The trend was in line with the concept developed by researchers specialising in administrative sciences from the late 1980s[136]. It envisaged the functional adaptation of administrative bodies to new challenges and problems. According to the assumptions of this concept, institutional reforms in the administration will, therefore, constitute a response to emergency situations and the emergence of previously non-existing tasks, as well as changes in the supervised market sector[137].

Empirical research has found that a European regulatory agency is most likely to be established when demand arises in a certain market sector, due to its dynamic growth, for regulatory institutions which can respond quickly and flexibly to an emerging situation, and that are capable of guaranteeing the reliability of opinions, guidelines and recommendations which they prepare. Moreover, due to the presence of an array of various participants engaged in a given sector, there is a need to create a platform for coordinating their activities. In addition, within the existing structure, at the European level, so far there is no appropriate expert background that would make it possible to work out positions based on expertise[138]. Agencies are meant to facilitate the resolution of problems resulting from the phenomenon of information asymmetry as well as the uneven distribution of specialised knowledge between administrative bodies and entities active in a specific market sector. The air and maritime transport

---

134 Advocates of the reform emphasised at the time the "gap" between the capabilities of the Commission's administrative apparatus and the expectations it faced in connection with the development of the internal market and the intensification of integration processes in Europe. See Majone, 'The Credibility', pp. 279 ff.

135 On the concept of "regulation through information", see G. Majone, 'The New European Agencies: Regulation by Information', *Journal of European Public Policy*, Vol. 4, No. 2, 1997, pp. 264–267.

136 For more, see J.G. March, J.P. Olsen, *Rediscovering Institutions: The Organizational Basis of Politics*, New York/London 1989, pp. 53–117.

137 See Balint *et al.*, 'Bureaucratic Change', pp. 50 ff.

138 See Thatcher, 'The Creation', p. 14; A. Surdej, 'Rola wyspecjalizowanych agencji w funkcjonowaniu UE: Stan obecny i kierunki rozwoju', *Zeszyty Naukowe AEK*, No. 654, 2004, pp. 90 ff.

sector is a good example with which to illustrate the assumptions above. One of the main arguments advanced in the context of the necessity to create appropriate European regulatory agencies in those areas were: major difficulties and delays in the process of implementing directives into national legal systems, the lack of a proper flow of information between relevant national authorities as well as significant divergences in regulatory and supervisory practices applied in the member states[139].

The creation of EU regulatory agencies was also expected to lead, at least in theory, to a reduction in transaction costs, and the provision of opportunities for shaping positions within specific EU policies that would be neutral in relation to national interests. Economic calculation was supposed to be one of the basic arguments for an intensification of the integration process through its enhanced institutionalisation, understood as harmonising law and creating supranational bodies working for the standardisation of the practices in a specific market sector[140]. These processes occur while adhering to the principle of subsidiarity, which implies, in simple terms, that every level of government is responsible for the performance of only those tasks that cannot be properly carried out at lower levels[141]. Such assumptions are consistent with the economic theory of federalism, developed in the context of European integration. Institutional and normative solutions are taken into account, which are supposed to ensure the highest efficiency from the economic point of view. Balancing takes place at various levels of governance. Those which are the most effective, from the profit and loss perspective, are selected[142]. In the case of regulatory agencies at the EU level,

139 See M. Groenleer *et al.*, 'Regulatory Governance Through Agencies of the European Union? The Role of the European Agencies for Maritime and Aviation Safety in the Implementation of European Transport Legislation', *Journal of European Public Policy*, Vol. 17, No. 8, 2010, p. 1214.

140 See Geradin, Petit, 'The Development of Agencies', p. 6.

141 More M.M. Kenig-Witkowska, A. Łazowski, R. Ostrihansky, *Prawo instytucjonalne Unii Europejskiej*, Warszawa 2017, pp. 178 ff.; A. Kuś (ed.), *Prawo instytucjonalne Unii Europejskiej*, Lublin 2012, pp.114 ff.; R. Grzeszczak, 'Podział kompetencji w UE', in: Łazowski, Zawidzka-Łojek (ed.), *Instytucje*, pp. 20 ff.

142 Such profit and loss calculation was seen in the case of the European Regulatory Authority that was planned in the second half of the 1990s for the sake of the telecommunications sector. Following a negative assessment by the stakeholders representing that sector, the Commission issued a communication rejecting the need to establish such an agency at the time. See the European Commission's Communication, *Towards a New Framework for Electronic Communications Infrastructure and Associated Services. The 1999 Review*, COM(1999) 539 final, 10.11.1999, p. 9. For more on

assumptions involving transaction cost calculations are, however, secondary in relation to political determinants. This means that a bigger role is played by political pressures related to, for example, a desire to create an EU agency in a specific member state, rather than the actual efficiency or operational costs of such a body[143]. The establishment of three financial supervisory agencies (EBA, EIOPA and ESMA) in 2011 was a prime example of this. The headquarters of these agencies were placed in the United Kingdom, Germany and France, instead of just one agency headquarters that would probably have been less costly and perhaps more effective thanks to the concentration of tasks in one place. This would have greatly facilitated direct flows of information that are particularly important for maintaining financial stability in the European markets.

Regulatory agencies are also supposed to improve the level of transparency of the European administrative system through a clear division of tasks between them and the European Commission[144]. In practice the meetings of their collective decision-making bodies, which will be discussed in the context of the organisational structure of particular agencies, are often playing fields for different groups lobbying for vested interests. Due to the specific character of most EU agencies, usually acting as platforms to coordinate the actions of national authorities but without replacing them, it is also difficult to reduce the transaction costs for entities operating in a certain market sector. There is also no single transparent outline to reflect the distribution of powers between EU regulatory agencies, the Commission, and national authorities. In every sector of the internal market, due to its specific character, distinct development over time, and current political situation, there may be some differences in emphasis.

bb) Institutional Isomorphism

There are also sociological concepts that assume the mechanical reproduction of institutional frameworks in multilevel management structures. This is referred to as institutional isomorphism. It can occur in two variants: copying an agency model at the EU level, i.e. either adopting a certain institutional model from one sector of the internal market to other ones or reproducing national-level solutions at the EU

---

the economic theory of federalism, see R.P. Inman, D.L. Rubinfeld, 'Economics of Federalism', in: F. Parisi (ed.), *The Oxford Handbook of Law and Economics. Public Law and Legal Institutions*, Vol. 3, Oxford/New York 2017, pp. 84 ff.

143 See W. Kilb, 'Europäische Agenturen und ihr Personal – die großen Unbekannten?', *Europäische Zeitschrift für Wirtschaftsrecht*, Vol. 17, No. 9, 2006, p. 273.

144 Geradin, Petit, 'The Development', p. 8; F. Shirvani, 'New Public Management', pp. 6–9.

level. The latter variant fits into the isomorphism model also seen within national frameworks, when many bodies, similar as far as their structure is concerned, are created in a particular economic sector[145].

Interestingly, the processes of "homogenisation", i.e. various authorities and institutions becoming very similar to each other, can also be considered as being one of the ways to legitimise their actions. Such a type of institutional isomorphism is called mimetics. In this case the resemblance is a protective, defensive mechanism. Similar competencies as well as an analogous institutional structure are designed to validate the existence and operation of another regulatory body in the common activity field. Isomorphism can also be coercive, i.e. resulting from the use of coercion where a stronger, hierarchically superior institution, directly or indirectly, by virtue of its authority influences the institutional shape and actions of the subordinate body. Another variant of institutional isomorphism is called normative. In this context, the adjective "normative" means that the processes of the creation and the evolution of institutions are dependent on social norms and are subordinated to them. The shape of a certain body is influenced by such factors as the level of staff education, their nationality, status, social background as well as recruitment practices and organisational culture. Institutions that employ staff of a similar profile and operate in a system of comparable symbols, values, norms and rituals will look increasingly more alike[146].

Within the multilevel system of European governance all of the abovementioned variants of institutional isomorphism can be observed with various intensity. One characteristic issue is the adaptation of organisational solutions to ones already in existence that have been accepted and legitimised. This refers to models that have had their worth proven in practice, e.g. the German institutional model of shaping and conducting monetary policy, or the French and Irish models of food safety management, which have inspired European-wide solutions[147].

---

145 Christensen, Lehmann Nielsen, 'Administrative Capacity', pp. 178, 184.

146 C.M. Radaelli, 'Policy Transfer in the European Union: Institutional Isomorphism as a Source of Legitimacy', *Governance. An International Journal of Policy, Administration, and Institutions*, Vol. 13, No. 1, 2000, pp. 27 ff.; P.J. DiMaggio, W.W. Powell, 'The Iron Cage Revisited: Institutional Isomorphism and Collective Rationality in Organizational Fields', in: W.W. Powell, P.J. DiMaggio (ed.), *The New Institutionalism in Organizational Analysis*, Chicago 1991, pp. 63 ff.

147 J. Fleischer, 'European Agencies as Engines of Regulation? On Different Architectural Strategies of the Regulatory State', Paper Prepared for the 3rd ECPR Annual Conference, 8.–10.9.2005, pp. 8, 23.

cc) *Political Reasons*

Reforming the European administrative system with the use of regulatory agencies can be also analysed from the historical perspective. So-called historical institutionalism perceives the motives for the establishment of agencies as an expression of the development of the existing structures. Thus, agencies become successors to comitology committees, mechanisms that previously existed to facilitate cooperation within the European Parliament and the European Commission, Community programmes as well as other forms of collaboration developed at the intergovernmental level[148]. The limitations of existing institutions necessitate the creation of new ones. The establishment of agencies is, in this case, interpreted from a certain historical context, i.e. the current balance of power in the constellation of EU institutions with alliances formed by the member states[149]. In the historical approach, political decisions aimed at working out new institutional solutions are analysed in sequential summaries, taking into account the specific political situation as well as the time that is necessary to reach a compromise. Institutional development is treated from this perspective as a process rather than a single episode involving the establishment of a particular body[150].

Another motive that is brought up as an important issue, in the process of transforming the European administrative system, is the European Commission's desire to extend its influence. The Commission is undoubtedly a key EU authority when it comes to the establishing of regulatory agencies, and supervision of how

148 For example, two committees preceded the creation of the European Medicines Agency (EMA): the Committee for Proprietary Medicinal Products (CPMP) and the Committee for Veterinary Medicinal Products (CVMP); committees coordinating cooperation in the area of financial services preceded the creation of European financial supervisory agencies: the Committee of European Banking Supervisors (CEBS) – EBA, the Committee of European Securities Regulators (CESR) – ESMA, the Committee of European Insurance and Occupational Pensions Supervisors (CEIOPS) – EIOPA. The Committee of Inquiry into the Drug Problem that existed within the European Parliament was transformed into the European Monitoring Centre for Drugs and Drug Addiction (EMCDDA). The CORINE program (Coordination of Information on the Environment) was replaced e.g. by the European Environment Agency (EEA). See Kreher, 'Agencies', p. 233.

149 See D. Coen, M. Thatcher, 'Reshaping European Regulatory Space', *NewGov Policy Brief*, No. 28, 2008, p. 3.

150 See V.A. Schmidt, C.M. Radaelli, 'Policy Change and Discourse in Europe: Conceptual and Methodological Issues', *West European Politics*, Vol. 27, No. 2, 2004, p. 191.

they function. It plays a decisive role at the stage of initiating debate on the advisability of setting up a specific agency. In every such case it also presents a proposal for such an institution's founding regulation. However, the Commission itself is not a monolith and there are often disputes within its bureaucratic apparatus over the acceptance of ideas related to agency creation. Entities that block such developments are usually the Legal Service and the Directorate-General for Competition. On the other hand, DGs that deal with rapidly developing markets, such as the Directorate-General for Energy and Transport, or the Directorate-General for Financial Stability, Financial Services and Capital Markets Union, are interested in establishing such bodies[151].

The shape of an agency is rarely exclusively an outcome of functional or practical considerations. It usually results directly from the political determinants related to struggles between the European Commission, the European Parliament and the member states[152]. The latter play an important role, often preferring to maintain the *status quo*, i.e. for the Commission to coordinate actions in a given market sector in cooperation with national authorities. The member states can lobby the specific agency in order to strengthen their influence. The role of regulatory agencies at the national level is not without importance. They often fight with great dedication to strengthen their independent position in the national institutional system. Bringing representatives of such an agency into cooperation with partner agencies from other member states at the supranational level within a European regulatory agency leads to the increased importance of a given regulatory authority in the intra-state dimension. Therefore, it turns out that national regulatory agencies are indeed the entities that provide an incentive to strengthen and institutionalise sectoral cooperation[153]. Usually, though not always, they then seek to secure the seat of such a body for one of their cities[154]. This is accompanied by great prestige, hence a fierce fight for an agency is often played out between the member states, overshadowing the substantive issues involving its future tasks[155].

---

151 Majone, 'Delegation', pp. 328 ff.

152 Rittberger, Wonka, 'Introduction', p. 4.

153 There is even talk about "sectoral solidarity" in the supranational dimension, see Wilks, 'Agencies', p. 450.

154 François Mitterand was actively involved in the process of creating the EMCDDA, although the seat of this agency is located in Lisbon. See Kreher, 'Agencies', p. 232.

155 Difficulties in reaching a compromise on the headquarters of a particular agency often led to delays in its launch and necessitated the introduction of costly temporary

The Commission reluctantly delegates powers that are already effectively exercised within its administrative apparatus, a prime example of which is policy-making in the realm of competition, e.g. efforts to fight cartels or to ban mergers and acquisitions of companies. There is no chance, therefore, of establishing a European Cartel Office, which has been called for since the 1960s, due to the resistance of the Directorate-General for Competition[156]. The situation looks different in sectors where the Commission has not yet been active or has not had meaningful powers. Rail transport, trade in pharmaceuticals or financial supervision are good examples of these. Under the "guise" of delegating competencies, in such cases, the Commission transfers powers that it had not previously had to the newly established regulatory agencies. Thus in practice, for several years it has not followed the legislative doctrine that is still formally in place and mandates that EU institutions delegate only the powers which they themselves have been guaranteed in Treaty law[157]. In the case of regulatory agencies this involves the takeover of powers previously exercised by regulatory authorities in the member states or ones that did not exist before at all.

The Commission, particularly thanks to agencies created in the 2000s, has in this way strengthened its position in comparison with other EU institutions, including, above all, the European Parliament and the member states[158]. Regarding the rivalry between EU institutions, efforts to "parliamentarise" the

---

solutions, such as the creation of a provisional seat in Brussels. Haggling over the seat of a specific agency often looks quite pathetic. This was the case, for example, with then-Italian Prime Minister Silvio Berlusconi's critical remarks about Finnish cuisine, made in the context of the Finnish-Italian competition for the seat of the EFSA in 2005. It has been increasingly stated in recent years that a desire to "host" an agency on one's territory was the leitmotif in the process of establishing it. See W. Hummer, 'Von der "Agentur" zum "interinstitutionellen Amt"', in: S. Hammer *et al.* (ed.), *Demokratie und sozialer Rechtsstaat in Europa. Festschrift für Theo Öhlinger*, Wien 2004, p. 105. This has been subject to widespread criticism, e.g. in the context of the competition for two agencies, EMA and EBA which have had their headquarters in London and need to move to the territory of other member states as Britain exits the EU. See C.B. Schiltz, 'Die verrückte Behördenschwemme in der EU', *Die Welt* of 3.6.2010; C.B. Schiltz, 'Wer profitiert vom Brexit?', *Die Welt* of 22.6.2017; R. Höltschi, 'Das Rennen um die Brexit-Beute ist eröffnet', *Neue Züricher Zeitung* of 23.6.2017.

156 See S. Wilks, L. McGowan, 'Disarming the Commission: The Debate over a European Cartel Office', *Journal of Common Market Studies*, Vol. 32, No. 2, 1995, pp. 260 ff.

157 It is the so-called *Meroni* doctrine. See Chapter 3.

158 See U. Häde, 'Jenseits der Effizienz: Wer kontrolliert die Kontrolleure? Demokratische Verantwortlichkeit und rechtsstaatliche Kontrolle der europäischen

Commission, i.e. for the Parliament to expand its control mechanisms over the Commission, have been discussed for several years[159]. The expansion of its complex administrative system, also consisting of regulatory agencies, is an attempt to counterbalance those projects. On this issue too, however, the Parliament has tried to offset the Commission's efforts with its own proposals for new agencies, e.g. for promoting European linguistic diversity or solving specific problems of the island regions[160]. These attempts have been unsuccessful and regulatory agencies have remained an effective instrument of influence assigned mainly to the European Commission[161].

The last significant motive, connected with those discussed earlier, is the desire on the part of the Commission, as well as the member states, to seize an arising opportunity to reform the existing state of affairs. This explanation refers to a concept that has developed in relation to management processes in large organisations that was popularised by the American political scientist John Kingdon[162]. He wrote about "policy windows" in the context of analysing mechanisms used in public policy. A policy window is a temporary convergence of several factors that allows for radical change. Among those factors, Kingdon first singled out the problem stream, which means that an issue that is significant for many actors needs to emerge, which draws their attention and prompts the search for new solutions. It is often a sudden event, disaster, crisis or tragedy that focuses the attention of the public and politicians, motivating the latter to remedy the situation quickly. Secondly, Kingdon pointed to the policy stream. The entities interested in a change need to include those that are capable of modifying the existing state of affairs. Thirdly, he identified the political stream, which involves the use of certain pre-existing political strategies, proposals and draft reforms that already function in the realm of public debate and which could be applied in a given situation. These three elements have to be synchronised for a

---

Finanzaufsichtsbehörden', *Europäische Zeitschrift für Wirtschaftsrecht*, Vol. 22, No. 17, 2011, p. 663.

159 Majone, 'The Credibility', pp. 284 ff.

160 Andoura, Timmerman, 'Governance', p. 3.

161 See also Chapter 8.

162 Kingdon's work was first published in 1984 and sparked a heated discussion. It has been recently republished: J. Kingdon, *Agendas, Alternatives and Public Policies*, Boston 2014, pp. 165 ff., which reopened the debate. An issue of the *European Journal of Political Research* dedicated in full to Kingdon's concept was an expression of this. See one of the articles published in that issue: M. Howlett *et al.*, 'Streams and Stages: Reconciling Kingdon an Policy Process Theory', *European Journal of Political Research*, Vol. 54, No. 3, 2015, pp. 422 ff.

transformation of the existing solutions to take place. Oftentimes, the establishment of a new regulatory agency is, indeed, reflected by the concurrence of the various circumstances analysed by Kingdon. Prime examples include the establishment of such bodies in response to crises in the food market (EFSA), the financial market (EBA, ESMA, EIOPA, SRB) or in response to the *Erica* tanker accident and the sinking of the tanker, *Prestige* (EMSA)[163].

2. The Profile of EU Regulatory Agencies

a) The Legal Basis for Their Establishment

aa) The Need of an Adequate Legal Basis

Despite intensive expansion of the agency system, the member states have opted not to make changes in the primary law regulating the status of agencies in the Treaties. Such regulations were not included in the Treaty of Amsterdam or the Treaty of Nice in spite of debates, and announcements that the factual situation would be regulated. Neither did the Treaty which established the Constitution for Europe – although it, admittedly, did not come into force – envisage provisions concerning regulatory agencies[164]. The Treaty of Lisbon did not contribute to a radical change of the existing situation either – it also failed to introduce any provision that would authorise the EU *expressis verbis* to create bodies of this kind. No longer can they be considered "not foreseen under the Treaties" entities ("non-Treaty" institutions), because they have been recognised in numerous articles dealing with the EU's administrative structure, e.g.: Article 263(1) and (5) TFEU, Article 265(1) and (3) TFEU, Article 267(1) lit. b TFEU, Article 277 TFEU, Article 287(1) TFEU and Article 298(1) TFEU. The last one deserves special attention, because it sanctions the existence of the so-called European administration. Article 298(1) TFEU stipulates that "in carrying out their missions, the institutions, bodies, offices and agencies of the Union shall have the support of an open, efficient and independent European administration". Article 298(2) TFEU specifies that the European Parliament and the Council, acting by means

163 More A. Boin *et al.*, 'Building European Union Capacity to Manage Transboundary Crises: Network or Lead-Agency Model', *Regulation & Governance*, Vol. 8, No. 4, 2014, pp. 419 ff.

164 See Wittinger, 'Europäische Satelliten', p. 611; J. Saurer, 'EU Agencies 2.0 – The New Constitution of Supranational Administration beyond the EU Commission', Paper Presented by the Comparative Administrative Law Conference, Yale Law School, April 2016.

of regulations in accordance with the ordinary legislative procedure, can create relevant provisions to put such a European administration in place[165].

The term "organisational units" appeared in Article 298(1) TFEU in most of the EU language versions of the Treaty of Lisbon[166]. In the English version the term was replaced with "bodies/offices" and "agencies"[167]. There are no doubts in legal doctrine[168] that by "organisational units" we should indeed understand agencies that, together with the national authorities, are supposed to jointly provide modern European administration. The adjectives that describe it are noteworthy – it is supposed to be "open", "efficient" and "independent". Enshrining these requirements in primary law constitutes a Treaty commitment to fulfil them. In legal doctrine there are various interpretations of the independence of the EU administration. On the one hand, it can be seen in the functional perspective, this means that administrative activity should be impartial and justified, free of pressure and external influence. On the other hand, it can be viewed in the vertical perspective, i.e. in the context of the EU's institutional structure. Such a provision would, therefore, mean an independent position for the EU's administrative bodies in relation to the European Commission. Such autonomy would be expressed in the administrative bodies – including, above all, regulatory agencies – not being subject to instructions from the European Commission[169]. It is, nonetheless, doubtful whether their autonomy should be understood so broadly. The autonomy of the European Central Bank, established in detail in the Treaties, is a case in point – it was guaranteed organisational, functional and financial independence[170]. There are no such detailed provisions for the bodies, offices and agencies of the European administration.

---

165 Chamon, *EU Agencies*, p. 47.

166 E.g. in Polish: "jednostki organizacyjne" and in German: "sonstige Stellen".

167 The word "agencies" also appears in the Bulgarian, Danish, Estonian, Greek, Irish, Slovenian, Slovak, Romanian and Swedish versions. *Cf.* A. Nowak-Far, 'Jednolitość prawa unijnego a jego wielojęzyczność', in: C. Mik (ed.), *Unia Europejska. Zjednoczeni w różnorodności*, Warszawa 2012, pp. 74 ff.

168 According to Aleksander Peczenik the term "legal doctrine" refers to the activity of legal scholars as well as to the products of this activity. See A. Peczenik, *A Treatise of Legal Philosophy and General Jurisprudence. Scientia Juris: Legal Doctrine as Knowledge of Law and as a Source of Law*, Vol. 4, New York 2005, pp. 2 ff.

169 See K. Michel, *Institutionelles Gleichgewicht und EU-Agenturen. Eine Analyse unter besonderer Berücksichtigung der European Banking Authority*, Berlin 2015, pp. 43 ff.

170 Article 130 TFEU and Article 282(3) sentence 3 and 4 TFEU. See *ibid.*, p. 44.

It is worth noting here that Article 298 TFEU accidentally became a "foothold" to justify the independent position of regulatory agencies. The original idea that accompanied its inclusion in the Treaty of Lisbon was related to an initiative by Sweden, advocated already during the drafting of the Treaty, which was supposed to establish a Constitution for Europe[171]. The initiative, which involved the creation of a standard that was supposed to guarantee the existence of "good administrative culture" in the pan-European dimension, followed Sweden's years-long efforts to promote its own "good governance" models[172]. Article 298 TFEU should be interpreted in reference to Article 41 of the Charter of Fundamental Rights, which guarantees the right to good administration. According to the first section of the Article, "every person has the right to have his or her affairs handled impartially, fairly, and within a reasonable time by the institutions, bodies, offices and agencies of the Union". In this sense, the requirement for the European administration to be independent constitutes a starting point for the more detailed provisions of Article 41(1) of the Charter of Fundamental Rights. Autonomy, therefore, primarily means the impartiality of administrative bodies as well as equal and fair treatment of the parties involved. In this sense it refers to both citizens and entities subject to control or supervision[173], but from the three requirements – openness, efficiency and independence – expressed in Article 298(1) TFEU, it does not follow how the European administration should look in terms of institutions and competences. Neither does this provision address the question of how EU institutions can establish the bodies, offices and agencies that make up this administration.

According to Article 5(1) sentence 1 and (2) TEU, the Union acts solely within the competences conferred upon it in the Treaties in order to achieve the objectives specified therein. It is the so-called principle of conferred or attributed powers, according to which the EU acts only within the scope that it has been granted within primary law[174]. Consequently, since the issue of establishing and functioning of regulatory agencies was not directly stated in the Treaties, the establishment of each body of this type requires that the founding regulation cites a specific and relevant Treaty rule, on the basis of which, the new institution

171 The equivalent of Article 298 TFEU was Article III-398 TCE.

172 *Cf.* Saurer, 'EU Agencies', p. 5.

173 See Michel, *Institutionelles Gleichgewicht*, p. 46.

174 More Z. Hurej, 'Zasada kompetencji przyznanych w prawie wspólnotowym a suwerenność państw członkowskich', *Acta Universitatis Wratislaviensis. Przegląd Prawa i Administracji*, Vol. 77, No. 3052, 2008, pp. 135 ff.

is to operate[175]. It should be stressed here that since regulatory agencies are autonomous and independent entities with legal personality, it is not possible to create them under Article 249(1) TFEU. This provision guarantees the statutory autonomy of the European Commission, which is expressed in the formal aspect, meaning the ability to determine its rules of procedure, as well as the material aspect, involving the ability to establish internal operational procedures and the internal organisational structure. Regulatory agencies, though closely linked to the Commission and perceived as an important part of the surrounding administrative system, are not part of its internal organisational structure[176]. Their establishment thus requires a separate legal basis.

bb) Residual Competence Clause of Article 352 TFEU

Initially, until the late 1990s, the old Article 308 TEC, which was replaced by Article 352 TFEU after the changes introduced by the Treaty of Lisbon, was used for this purpose. That provision introduced legislative competences that were defined in legal doctrine as "residual" or "complementary" (Germ. *Abrundungskomptenz, Flexibilitätklausel*)[177]. It stipulated that "if action by the Community should prove necessary to attain, in the course of the operation of the common market, one of the objectives of the Community and this Treaty has not provided the necessary powers, the Council shall, acting unanimously on a proposal from the Commission and after consulting the European Parliament, take the appropriate measures". As agencies acted within the common market and served the purpose of accomplishing it, the requirements of Article 308 TEC were considered to have been met[178].

Currently, Article 352(1) TFEU stipulates that "if action by the Union should prove necessary, within the framework of the policies defined in the Treaties, to attain one of the objectives set out in the Treaties, and the Treaties have not provided the necessary powers, the Council, acting unanimously on a proposal from the Commission and after obtaining the consent of the European Parliament,

175 C. Calliess, 'Art. 5 AEUV', in: Calliess, Ruffert (ed.), *EUV/AEUV*, pp. 515 ff.

176 More S. Kirste, 'Das System der Europäischen Agenturen. Erläutert am Beispiel des Europäischen Innovations- und Technlogieinstituts', *Verwaltungsarchiv. Zeitschrift für Verwaltungslehre, Verwaltungsrecht und Verwaltungspolitik*, Vol. 102, No. 2, 2011, p. 273; M. Ruffert, 'Art. 249 AEUV', in: Calliess, Ruffert (ed.), *EUV/AEUV*, p. 2236; Görisch, *Demokratische Verwaltung*, pp. 233–235.

177 *Cf.* M. Rossi, 'Art. 352 AEUV', in: Calliess, Ruffert (ed.), *EUV/AEUV*, p. 2733.

178 Kirste, 'Das System', p. 273.

shall adopt the appropriate measures. Where the measures in question are adopted by the Council in accordance with a special legislative procedure, it shall also act unanimously on a proposal from the Commission and after obtaining the consent of the European Parliament". The main provision of Article 308 TEC – to facilitate the attainment of the objectives defined in the Treaty when it does not provide the necessary powers for the Community's institutions or when they are insufficient – was transferred to Article 352 TFEU. This provision means that a source of competences of EU institutions can be a Treaty provision that sets out an obligation to carry out a specific task, e.g. to accomplish the common market.

The doctrine of implied powers is limited by a number of safeguards. The primary one is the rule of law, which holds that competences should not be presumed. EU institutions can only act on the basis of, and within, the law. Since the European Union is not a state, it does not have so-called competence-competence, meaning it cannot grant itself any competences beyond those conferred on in the Treaties by the member states. Regulations introduced into the European legal system under Article 352 TFEU have to fall within the powers conferred on EU institutions by the member states. They must not be a disguised attempt to change Treaty provisions or to upset the balance in the division of administrative tasks between the EU and its member states guaranteed in primary law[179].

In the face of the rapid growth of the agency system Article 308 TEC, which had been used for the first, relatively "weak" agencies, was no longer a convenient instrument for the EU institutions, including above all the European Parliament[180]. Two arguments mattered. First, it required unanimity in the Council. This requirement was transferred to Article 352(1) TFEU. Second, it provided for a consultation procedure with the European Parliament, which meant that the position of this body was limited in the process of creating new agencies. This element was modified by the Treaty of Lisbon. Currently Article 352(1) TFEU mentions the Parliament's consent. Therefore, the Parliament's position was strengthened. This brought it close to the conditions guaranteed

179 Opinion of the Court of Justice of 26.3.1996, No. 2/94 on the Accession by the Communities to the European Convention for the Protection of Human Rights and Fundamental Freedoms, OJ C 1996, p. 1759. See R. Vetter, 'Die Kompetenzen der Gemeinschaft zur Gründung von unabhängigen europäischen Agenturen', *Die Öffentliche Verwaltung. Zeitschrift für öffentliches Recht und Verwaltungswissenschaft*, Vol. 58, No. 17, 2005, pp. 730 ff.

180 *Ibid.*, p. 724.

within the ordinary legislative procedure[181]. In the enlarged EU, the creation of regulatory agencies under Article 352(1) TFEU, which provides for unanimity in the Council, is virtually impossible due to the risk of veto by the individual member states. The second requirement - consultations with the European Parliament - led to the marginalisation of this body in the process of creating the EU agencies. The decisive voice belonged to the Council, which conducted behind-the-door consultations in working groups with representatives of the European Parliament. Consequently, negotiations on the institutional shape and tasks of agencies were driven by the member states, practically excluding the public[182].

Moreover, in line with what was emphasised above, Article 352 TFEU is a norm that makes it possible to introduce certain detailed solutions that are consistent with the general Treaty framework, in special cases, when there is no specific authorisation. It is a norm of an auxiliary nature. Establishing information agencies on this legal basis in several cases was not, therefore, a violation of the wording of this provision. But it is not a norm that meets the requirements for a permanent justification for creating new EU agencies. Especially when their competences may appear controversial from the point of view of the competence balance defined in primary law[183]. Hence, as the agency system kept growing, there were increasingly frequent references to detailed provisions that were introduced by the Treaty of Maastricht within sector-specific policies, recognising Article 308 TEC as the appropriate legal basis only in special cases[184]. This was

181 See Michel, *Institutionelles Gleichgewicht*, p. 121.

182 Merijn Chamon writes in this context about the full control of the member states over the process of "agencification", *EU Agencies*, pp. 119, 139. See also D. Curtin, 'Delegation to EU Non-Majoritarian Agencies and Emerging Practices of Public Accountability', in: Geradin *et al.* (ed.), *Regulation*, pp. 98 ff.

183 Hansen-Nootbaar, *Unabhängigkeit*, pp. 119 ff.; Weißgärber, *Die Legitimation*, p. 266.

184 See S. Griller, A. Orator, '"Mapping the Jungle": A Legal Attempt to Classify European Agencies', *NewGov. New Modes of Governance Project*, No. 4, 2006, p. 12. The Commission's recommendation expressed in the Communication, *The Operating Framework*, COM(2002) 718 final, p. 7, provided an indication: "Since the regulatory agency is an instrument of implementation of a specific Community policy, it follows that the legal instrument creating it must be based on the provision of the Treaty which constitutes the specific legal basis for that policy. This was the approach adopted when creating the most recent regulatory agencies in the fields of food safety and transport, which represented a break with the previous system of automatically using Article 308 TEC as the legal basis. Of course, in the current institutional framework, when

the case, for example, with the Fundamental Rights Agency (FRA) in 2007[185]. It was an exception proving the rule, i.e. the search for a specific legal basis for most of the so-called third and fourth generation agencies since the early 2000s among norms indicated the development of EU policies for significant market sectors. These provisions, called "material norms" in legal doctrine[186], would allow for the creation of "appropriate measures" contributing to this development. Such a "measure" could be, for example, a regulatory agency. By choosing a new legal basis, the Commission opted to change the procedure for the establishment of new agencies. Specific competence norms provide for the co-decision procedure or the ordinary legislative procedure and, consequently, the role of the Parliament in the process of creating these bodies increased.

A good example of a "material" justification of the regulatory agencies' existence is given by the norms under which the European transport authorities were created. EASA and EMSA were established under Article 80(2) TEC (currently Article 100(2) TFEU) and ERA under Article 71(1) TEC (currently Article 91(1) TFEU). Other examples of third generation agencies for which specific legal bases were sought include the European Centre for Disease Prevention and Control (ECDC) – established under Article 152(4) TEC (currently Article 168(4) TFEU) or the European Institute of Innovation and Technology (EIT) created under Article 157(3) TEC (currently Article 173(3) TFEU)[187]. It is assumed that, in principle, norms of this kind are a permissible legal basis for the establishment of regulatory agencies, if those bodies are consistent with the sectoral policy regulated by that norm, by way of a "close relationship", and constitute an appropriate and necessary "measure" to achieve the objectives defined in this norm[188].

---

the legal basis for a specific action is Article 308 itself, the instrument setting up the agency must also be based on this provision".

185 The choice of this legal basis resulted from a lack of an appropriate provision in the Treaties referring to fundamental rights. See A. von Bogdandy, J. von Bernstorff, 'The EU Fundemantal Rights Agency within the European and International Human Rights Architecture: The Legal Framework and Some Unsettled Issues in a New Field of Administrative Law', *Common Market Law Review*, Vol. 46, No. 4, 2009, p. 1048; A.M. Kosińska, 'The Role of the Fundamental Rights Agency in Irregular Migrant's Rights Protection', *Review of Comparative Law*, Vol. XVIII, 2013, pp. 93 ff.

186 Germ. *materielle Normen*, see Hansen-Nootbaar, *Unabhängigkeit*, p. 120.

187 More about individual legal bases for regulatory agencies N. Sölter, *Rechtsgrundlagen europäischer Agenturen im Verhältnis vertikaler Gewaltenteilung*, Berlin 2017, pp. 197–212.

188 Hansen-Nootbaar, *Unabhängigkeit*, p. 122.

cc) Validity of Article 114 TFEU as a Legal Basis

Developing the Harmonisation Model under Article 114 TFEU

Most third and fourth generation agencies refer, however, to another norm, which is supposed to authorise EU institutions to establish specialised EU regulatory agencies, i.e. Article 95 TEC (currently Article 114 TFEU) which is controversial in this context. This provision deals with the creation of measures that are supposed to harmonise national legal systems. It is of a functional character, meaning it does not involve a specific sector of the internal market, but its establishment and functioning as a whole. Similarly to Article 352 TFEU, it is used when more detailed Treaty provisions prove to be insufficient. But this norm cannot become a symbolic "lifeline" in every situation when there is no appropriate sector-specific legislation for designing a new regulatory agency[189].

The controversies around Article 114 TFEU involve the question of whether it is an appropriate legal basis for establishing agencies as well as equipping them with particular competences. The problem comes up in the context of recognising an institutional solution – e.g. regulatory agencies – as a measure to harmonise law in the member states. EU regulatory agencies primarily perform administrative tasks. In legal doctrine, there have long been critical voices raised regarding the broad interpretation of Article 114 TFEU and the use of this legal basis to draw conclusions about the EU's implied powers covering matters of an administrative nature[190]. The evolving perception of this provision was partly a result of the changing attitude of the EU institutions' legal services, including above all the Council. In the 1990s, lawyers within these services assumed that the establishment of institutions such as agencies was an action that went beyond the formula of harmonising the national law, because it was not related in any way to the obligation to implement specific provisions by the member states at the national level. This stance changed over time as the European institutional system developed. It was recognised that it did not directly refer to the harmonisation of law, but rather it constituted broad

189 More E. Fahey, 'Does the Emperor Have Financial Crisis Clothes. Reflections on the Legal Basis of the European Banking Authority', *Modern Law Review*, Vol. 74, No. 4, 2011, pp. 581 ff.

190 C. Ohler, 'Rechtmäßige Errichtung der Gemeinschaftsagentur ENISA', *Europäische Zeitschrift für Wirtschaftsrecht*, Vol. 17, No. 12, 2006, p. 373; Vos, 'Reforming', p. 1122.

support for a process which can also take the form of institutional solutions, not just normative ones[191].

The practical reason accompanying the selection of this legal basis for designing many agencies equipped with broad competences, e.g. EBA, ESMA and EIOPA, like in the case of the abovementioned "material norms", was connected with the choice of a legislative procedure that allowed a compromise to be reached. Article 114 TFEU provides for the ordinary legislative procedure, so it does not require, like e.g. Article 352 TFEU, a unanimous position in the Council to be reached – a qualified majority is enough. In the face of growing animosities between the individual member states, particularly in the context of creating institutions such as regulatory agencies, which have important powers intensifying the integration process, undoubtedly, it was an important argument for this provision. As for the financial supervision agencies, the UK lobbied for choosing Article 352 TFEU as the legal basis. This position stemmed from British scepticism towards the idea of institutionalised supervisory cooperation in the European Union. The idea was rejected, therefore, due to a possible veto in the Council and the potential paralysis of the entire EU financial market reform[192].

The ENISA Case

British scepticism towards Article 114 TFEU (then Article 95 TEC) as the appropriate legal basis for the establishment of EU agencies had already been expressed, in 2006, in the context of challenging the legal basis used to set up the ENISA two years earlier. The United Kingdom then filed a complaint to the CJEU urging for the annulment of the regulation (EC) No. 460/2004 of 10 March 2004 establishing the agency[193]. The proceedings were conducted according to the procedure provided for in Article 263 TFEU and concerned the possibility of using Article 95 TEC as the appropriate provision for the creation of a regulatory agency which would support the Commission on technical matters.

The UK, which was the complainant in this case, argued that Article 114 TFEU was not a legal basis that allowed the adoption of a regulation in order to establish a regulatory agency[194]. The British pointed out that the appropriate legal basis for the establishment of advisory bodies to the Commission

---

191 Chamon, *EU Agencies*, p. 143; I. Maletić, *The Law and Policy of Harmonisation in Europe's Internal Market*, Cheltenham/Northhampton 2013, pp. 147–150.

192 See Kohtamäki, *Die Reform*, p. 157.

193 OJ 2004, L 77/1. Changed by Regulation (EU) No. 526/2013.

194 Case C-217/04, *United Kingdom v. Parliament and Council*, [2.5.2006] ECR I-3771, para 11.

was Article 308 TEC (currently Article 352 TFEU)[195]. ENISA was to serve as specialised technical support of an institutional nature[196]. It was not organised as an office to replace national regulatory authorities. According to the case made by the British, it is difficult to recognise it as a measure facilitating convergence between laws, regulations and administrative provisions in the member states[197]. Therefore, none of the articles of the regulation constituting the legal act establishing the agency, contributed, according to the case set out in the complaint, even indirectly and in a limited manner, to the harmonisation of national laws[198]. Summing up the position elaborated in the complaint, one can say that there were two arguments against the use of Article 114 TFEU as an appropriate legal basis. Firstly, the norm does not provide for the establishment of auxiliary bodies of advisory nature, and secondly, the tasks set out in the founding regulation of the ENISA are not of a harmonising nature[199].

The CJEU disagreed with that position and rejected the complaint. Their argumentation cited an earlier Court ruling from 2005 on the *Smoke flavourings* case[200]. The United Kingdom was also the complainant then, requesting the annulment of Regulation (EC) No. 2065/2003 of 10 November 2003 on the issue of smoke flavourings used or intended for use in foods or on their surfaces[201]. The complainant challenged the possibility of using Article 95 TEC as a legal basis for this regulation, claiming it did not bring national legislations closer[202]. On the other hand, it established a centralised procedure at Community level for issuing smoke flavourings permits, in which another regulatory agency – the EFSA – cooperated closely with the European Commission[203]. In the complainant's view, the state of affairs fell outside of the competence defined in Article 95 TEC, which concerns harmonising national legal systems[204]. The Court ruled then that the norm could be used if "it is actually apparent from the legal act, in a

195 *Ibid.*, para 21.
196 *Ibid.*, para 17.
197 *Ibid.*, para 16.
198 *Ibid.*, paras 14,15.
199 Extensively about the case: Ohler, 'Rechtmäßige Errichtung', p. 369; V. Randazzo, 'Case C-217/04, United Kingom *v.* European Parlament and Council of the European Union', *Common Market Law Review*, Vol. 44, No. 1, 2007, pp. 156 ff.
200 Case C-66/04, *United Kingdom v. Parliament and Council*, [6.12.2005] ECR I-10553.
201 OJ 2003, L 309/1.
202 Case C-66/04, para 18.
203 *Ibid.*, para 11.
204 *Ibid.*, paras 18–26.

way which is objectively reviewable, that its purpose is to improve the conditions for the establishment and functioning of the internal market"[205]. The Court pointed out in this case that the Community legislature, depending on the general situation and the circumstances of a particular case within a domain subject to harmonisation, has a certain margin of discretion regarding the technique used to bring legislation closer, and that would be the most appropriate way of achieving the intended result[206].

In its ruling on the *ENISA* case, the Court formulated a position that was a logical consequence of the 2005 ruling. It stated e.g. that as part of forming harmonisation measures, it may be "necessary to provide for the establishment of a Community body responsible for contributing to the implementation of a process of harmonisation", but provided that such a body would deal with the adoption of non-binding support or framework measures facilitating the uniform implementation and application of harmonisation acts. The Court therefore recognised that Article 114 TFEU does not contain limitations regarding addressees of legal acts issued on its basis[207]. It emphasised at the same time, however, that tasks conferred on such an agency should be "closely linked to the subject matter of the acts approximating the laws, regulations and administrative provisions of the member states"[208]. This is particularly the case when an agency, established this way, provides services to third parties, for example national authorities or entities that affect the homogenous implementation of harmonising provisions and that facilitate their application[209]. The Court ruled that the EU legislature has significant discretion regarding methods of harmonising law, because it took into consideration the claim that none of the provisions of the founding regulation for ENISA even indirectly approximate to the laws of the member states and the agency should, in principle, restrict itself to providing non-binding advice and not to interfere with the competences of national authorities[210]. The Court could therefore conclude that non-binding opinions of subsidiary authorities, such as ENISA, created as part of technical support for the Commission and the member states, can make it easier

205 *Ibid.*, para 44.

206 *Ibid.*, paras. 45, 46, 52.

207 Case C-217/04, para 44.

208 *Ibid.*

209 *Ibid.*, para. 45. See M. Skowron, 'Agencje i urzędy europejskie w orzecznictwie TS', *Europejski Przegląd Sądowy*, No. 9, 2014, p. 44; Sölter, *Rechtsgrundlagen*, p. 109.

210 It is about "free assessment" in the understanding stated in: Case C-66/04, para 45. See Case C-217/04, paras 14,43; Skowron, 'Agencje', p. 44.

to transpose EU directives into national law and contribute to their implementation at the national level[211]. According to this reasoning, Article 114 TFEU constitutes an appropriate basis both for the establishment of an agency as well as entrusting it with advisory powers.

The *ENISA* ruling is considered to be a landmark as far as the process of creating European administration in the context of the existing "constitutional" framework is concerned[212]. It paved the way for intensive "agencification" of the European administrative space and it was also the beginning of a new perception of these institutions in the Court's case law. Nicolas Sölter, the author of a monograph on the legal bases used for the establishment of regulatory agencies, described the Court's attitude in relation to agencies as a specific kind of *laissez-faire* approach, giving permission to assign specific powers, significant for the development of the internal market, to agencies[213]. There is no doubt that the 2006 ruling made it possible to create more agencies under Article 114 TFEU. This was important, for example, in a crisis situation when the EU was faced with a collapse in financial markets. The necessity to search for institutional solutions in 2011 took the form of the financial supervisory agencies (EBA, ESMA and EIOPA).

The ESMA Case

The powers of the ESMA triggered another complaint by the United Kingdom at the CJEU that was filed in 2012[214]. Apart from the creation of a supervisory institutional structure with financial supervisory agencies, one of the most important efforts to restore financial stability in the European markets after the 2008–2010 collapse and to ensure their safety in the future included intensified attempts to harmonise financial market regulations. Such efforts included a reform of the legal framework regulating so-called short selling, an investment strategy that makes it possible to profit from price declines in securities. In simplified terms, it can be characterised as follows. The investor sells securities that are not on his investment account at the time of the transaction. Therefore, he or

211 Case C-217/04, para 64.

212 Vinzenzo Randazzo even wrote in a comment on this ruling about its "constitutional significance", 'Case C-217/04', p. 155, and Christoph Ohler about the necessity to make re-evaluations in the European constitutional law in the context of understanding the administrative institutional system, 'Rechtmäßige Errichtung', p. 372.

213 Sölter, *Rechtsgrundlagen*, p. 27.

214 ESMA was created under Regulation (EU) No. 1095/2010 of 24.11.2010 on the establishment of the European Securities and Markets Authority, OJ 2010, L 331/84.

she must obtain them and deliver them to the buyer by the settlement date. The investor reckons here that he or she will buy the securities more cheaply than he has sold them[215]. Transactions of this kind carry various risks and they can undermine financial market stability, for example, by causing individual financial institutions to collapse and posing a systemic risk[216]. Due to their speculative potential, it is believed that short selling transactions contributed to the global financial crisis and problems in the euro zone.

The member states have therefore taken appropriate steps at the national level to regulate short selling. Measures restricting or prohibiting short selling of some or all securities have been adopted[217]. These scattered efforts in the integrated EU financial market have proven to be insufficient, hence the idea of harmonising legislation in this area at the EU level. The regulation on short selling and selected aspects of credit risk swaps came into force on 25 March 2012 and has been applied since 1 November 2012. It includes Article 28, controversial from the British point of view, conferring "intervention powers in special circumstances" on the ESMA[218]. These powers include the possibility of obliging natural or legal persons holding net short positions to submit information on them to a competent authority or to disclose them to the public[219]. Moreover, ESMA can ban or restrict short selling transactions by legal or natural persons[220]. The UK rejected the possibility of introducing such competences at the supranational level, fearing attempts to check or weaken London as a global financial centre. These fears related to an outlook resulting from the experiences of the

215 The legal definition of short selling see Article 2(1) lit. b of Regulation (EU) No. 236/2012 of 14.3.2012 on short selling and certain aspects of credit default swaps, OJ 2012, L 86/1. See J. Payne, 'The Regulation of Short Selling and Its Reform in Europe', *European Business Organization Law Review*, Vol. 13, No. 3, 2012, pp. 413 ff.

216 More I.H.-Y. Chiu, 'Macroprudential Supervision: Critically Examining the Developments in the UK, EU and Internationally', *Law and Financial Markets Review*, Vol. 6, No. 3, 2012, pp. 186 ff.

217 European Commission, *Proposal of a Regulation of the European Parliament and of the Council on Short Selling and Certain Aspects of Credit Default Swaps*, COM(2010) 482 final, 15.9.2010, pp. 2 ff.

218 The powers are consistent with the ESMA's competences guaranteed already in the founding Regulation No. 1095/2010 in Article 9(5). The provision states, among other things, that in certain situations "the Authority should also be able to temporarily prohibit or restrict certain financial activities". About the controversies related to Article 9(5) of Regulation No. 1095/2010 see Kohtamäki, *Die Reform*, pp. 195–197.

219 Article 28(1) lit. a of Regulation No. 236/2012.

220 Article 28(1) lit. b of Regulation No. 236/2012.

2008–2010 financial crisis, holding that interventionist decisions in the face of a threat are seldom exclusively of a technical, objective or specialised nature. They usually involve political considerations and, due to the fierce rivalry between Europe's major financial centres, such as London, Paris and Frankfurt am Main, the UK's concerns were not unjustified[221].

In its complaint filed on 1 June 2012[222], the United Kingdom argued that Article 28 of Regulation No. 236/2012 was unlawful for four reasons – the last, fourth argument referred to the issue of an appropriate legal basis[223]. In the complainant's view, by recognising that Article 28 entrusts the ESMA with the power to adopt individual measures concerning natural and legal persons, it should be concluded that the provision infringes the provisions of Article 114 TFEU[224].

Advocate General, Niilo Jääskinen supported the complainant's arguments on this issue, stating that Article 114 TFEU is not an appropriate legal basis for delegating interventionist powers within the meaning of Article 28 of Regulation No. 236/2012[225]. In his view, while Article 114 TFEU can be considered, in line with the existing case law[226], as appropriate when establishing new regulatory agencies and granting decision-making powers to the ESMA under Article 28, in substitution of the assessment made by competent national authorities, it falls outside the common understanding of Article 114 TFEU[227].

---

221 See N. Sowels, 'The Role of Finance in the UK's Relationship with the European Union', in: K. Tournier-Sol, C. Gifford (ed.), *The UK Challenge to Europeanization: The Persistence of British Euroscepticism*, Basingstoke/Hampshire 2015, pp. 210 ff., 218; R. van Gestel, 'European Regulatory Agencies Adrift? Case-270/12 United Kingdom of Great Britain and Northern Irland *v.* European Parliament and Council of the European Union, Judgment of 22 January 2014', *Maastricht Journal of European and Comparative Law* , Vol. 21, No. 1, 2014, p. 189.

222 Action brought on 1.6.2012, OJ 2012, C 273/3.

223 The other arguments will be described in Chapter 3.

224 *Ibid.*

225 The opinion of Advocate General Niilo Jääskinen presented on 12.9.2013, ECLI:EU:C:2013:562 (hereinafter: Opinion of AG Jääskinen). More on his stance: H. Marjosola, 'Case C-270/12 – Stress Testing Constitutional Resilience of the Powers of EU Supervisory Authorities – A Critical Assessment of the AG's Opinion', *EUI Working Papers LAW*, No. 2, 2014, pp. 8 ff.; H. von Livonius, 'EuGH: Generalanwalt halt Art. 28 der EU-Leerverkauf-Verordnung für nichtig', *Recht der Finanzinstrumente*, No. 4, 2013, p. 339.

226 It is primarily the ruling in the *ENISA* case, Case C-217/04.

227 Opinion of AG Jääskinen, paras 27–59.

Contrary to the Advocate General's arguments, the CJEU stated in its ruling that Article 114 TFEU is an appropriate legal basis for delegating interventionist powers to a regulatory supervisory agency[228]. The Court recalled that a legislative act adopted under Article 114 TFEU should meet two requirements: it should include measures for approximating the laws, regulations and administrative provisions of the member states, and have as its objective the establishment and the functioning of the internal market[229]. The Court – citing the motives on the basis of which Regulation No. 236/2012 was adopted, emphasised in its judgment of the 22 January 2014 concerning the specific character of Article 28 and its harmonising importance – argued that in the face of serious threats to the orderly functioning and integrity of the financial markets, emergency measures performed by the individual national supervisory authorities are insufficient. It is advisable, however, to introduce an EU-wide mechanism that would also include the possibility of issuing individual decisions addressed to specific entities in the financial markets[230]. Therefore, the objective of Article 28 is to approximate laws to the regulations and administrative provisions of the member states, as provided for in Article 114 TFEU[231]. The other premise – the establishment and functioning of the internal market – is also met thanks to the creation of a common regulatory framework for requirements and powers concerning short selling and credit risk swaps as well as ensuring greater coherence and coordination in appropriate measures taken by the member states in a crisis situation[232].

This argumentation implies a rather broad interpretation of Article 114 TFEU. The motive that justifies the Court's approach is ensuring financial stability through the creation of common regulatory frameworks and an intervention system at the EU level, including the possibility of formulating individual decisions addressed to private entities. The liberal attitude of the CJEU on the issue of "adapting" the legal basis for the establishment of new regulatory

228 Case C-270/12, *United Kingdom v. Parliament and Council (Short-Selling)*, [22.1.2014], EU:C:2014:18.

229 *Ibid.*, para 100. More about the harmonisation of EU law in order to establish and improve the internal market in the context of the ruling by the CJEU of 22.1.2014, see I. Maletić, 'Delegating Harmonization of the Internal Market in Case C-270/12 United Kingom of Great Britaing and Northern Irland *v*. European Parliament and Council of the EU (Short Selling Ban)', Judgment of 22 January 2014, *Yearbook of European Law*, Vol. 33, No. 1, 2014, pp. 511 ff.

230 Case C-270/12, paras 108–109.

231 *Ibid.*, para 112.

232 *Ibid.*, paras 113–115.

agencies has been repeatedly criticised in legal literature[233]. The main argument relates to the creation of a European executive order with the use of agencies, which violates the principle of subsidiarity and the primacy of the member states in the process of implementing European law into national legal systems[234].

Longstanding Practice as an Answer to the Weak Legal Basis

The expansion of the European administrative system, signified by the emergence of new agencies with increasingly broad powers and relatively weak foundations in the Treaties, is sometimes even described with the use of quite dramatic metaphors. German authors have written about the danger of developing "administrative ulcers", an "organisational and legal curse" or the creation of a "democracy-breaking Leviathan"[235]. The latter comparison refers to the Hobbesian concept of a Leviathan, a "massive state mechanism" identified with absolute monarchy[236]. In the EU institutional system, the role of an absolute monarch is assumed by an increasingly influential technocracy, in which complex legal justifications are sought instead of introducing the seemingly simplest solution in the form of direct provisions in primary law that would justify the creation and functioning of the agency system.

Sölter was right to conclude that, despite the absence of clear regulations in Treaty law regarding the procedure for the creation of the agency system, thanks to longstanding and established practice (Lat. *longa consuetudo*) developed over forty years in the EU's institutional structures, we can speak of the customary permissibility of the functioning of such bodies[237]. The very existence of regulatory agencies has not aroused any great emotions for a long time, and an agency system consisting of several dozen entities is a permanent part of the European administrative space. The chances of reversing the course of history

233 See Wittinger, 'Europäische Satelliten', pp. 617, 626; M. Brenner, 'Die Agenturen im Recht der Europäischen Union – Segen oder Fluch?', in: J. Ipsen, B. Stüer (ed.), *Europa im Wandel. Festschrift für Hans-Werner Rengeling*, Köln/München 2008, pp. 203 ff.; G. Hermes, 'Legitimationsprobleme unabhängiger Behörden', in: H. Bauer *et al.* (ed.), *Demokratie in Europa*, Tübingen 2005, p. 488.

234 *Cf.* A. Nowak-Far, A. Michoński, *Krajowa administracja w unijnym procesie podejmowania decyzji*, Warszawa 2004, pp. 20 ff.

235 See Sölter, *Rechtsgrundlagen*, p. 27; Brenner, 'Die Agenturen', p. 195.

236 See A. Utzinger, 'Thomas Hobbes' "Leviathan". Anatomie eines Staats-Wesens', in: P. Michel (ed.), *Spinnenfuß und Krötenbauch. Genese und Symbolik von Kompositwesen*, Zürich 2013, pp. 279 ff.

237 Sölter, *Rechtsgrundlagen*, p. 97.

and moving away from the agency model of EU administration are, as Wolfgang Kilb aptly put it more than ten years ago, illusory[238]. Hence the consistent inclusion of the concept of institutional evolution in the existing legal framework. In this context, the assertion, expressed by Robert Uerpmann in 2000, that the open question about the legal basis for the existence and functioning of agencies is shrouded in a peculiar sort of shame and a "conspiracy of silence", has remained unchanged[239]. Their existence is tacitly accepted, their growing powers are taken for granted, and they do not require any further explanation.

Undoubtedly, a step forward was the inclusion of numerous provisions in primary law after the changes introduced by the Treaty of Lisbon, in which attention was drawn to the existence of agencies in the European institutional system. Along with the abovementioned longstanding practice relating to their establishment, as well as a trend seen for more than ten years in CJEU case law, which involved the acceptance of new, powerful agencies in the EU institutional system, a situation that until recently had seemed impossible, was perpetuated. Contrary to the expectations from more than a decade ago, the Commission is able to transfer ever-wider powers to independent and powerful regulatory agencies without them having a clear legal basis in primary law[240]. The ideas that came up during the work of the European Convention in 2002, in this respect did not translate into actual modifications of primary law[241]. An appropriate vehicle would be an article similar to Article 298 TFEU. Sölter proposed Article 298a TFEU, which would explicitly provide for the possibility of creating specialised advisory bodies with legal personality and specific powers regulated in appropriate founding regulations[242]. Yet a provision like that is unlikely to be included in the Treaties. The reason is obvious and it results from the lack of political will to modify the existing legal situation. Significant regulatory changes should not be expected, since the EU institutions and the member states, which are able, when necessary, to impose the establishment of a particular agency and broaden the powers of the existing ones, have met with the Court's approval in this regard.

---

238 Kilb, 'Europäische Agenturen', p. 273.

239 Uerpmann, 'Mittelbare Gemeinschaftsverwaltung', p. 557.

240 In the early 2000s, it seemed impossible that the agency system would be able to develop without introducing appropriate changes in the Treaties. See Scott, 'Agencies', pp. 74 ff.; Curtin, 'Delegation', p. 94.

241 Final Report of Working Group V, 'Complementary Competencies', 4.11.2002, CONV 375/1/02.

242 Sölter, *Rechtsgrundlagen*, p. 301.

b) Tasks

aa) Classifying EU Regulatory Agencies

Emphasis is often put on the heterogeneity of regulatory agencies, i.e. their diversity stemming from the variety of tasks they undertake. We can speak them having a broad spectrum of roles, from that of an "advisor" or "consultant", to a "leading player" in shaping a particular policy in a specific market sector[243]. That diversity results from the historic developments described above. Political determinants at a specific time have influenced how the position, tasks or status of a particular agency were shaped. Hence the lack of homogeneity in this institutional system, the casuistic nature of the solutions used in the context of regulatory agencies and difficulties in their systematisation[244]. Some go as far as to write in this context about agency "disorder" (Germ. *Agenturunwesen*) and a lack of a well-thought-out strategy for supervising the activities of agencies[245].

Agencies, due to their sectoral specificities, narrow specialisation and diversity of tasks performed, have long remained distant, unknown and somewhat mysterious entities, not only for those not in the know. This was reflected in a comparison made by the then-President of the European Commission, Jose Manuel Barroso, who said that they were like peculiar EU satellites the purpose of which, just like real satellites, is to provide information and observations from remote galaxies[246]. In the internal market, such galaxies would be specialised areas, unexplored by EU bureaucracy, like detailed issues related to equipment for passenger aircraft, genetically modified food or short selling mechanisms in the capital markets. Agencies, admittedly, do not deal with abstract consulting, but rather with detailed issues that require expertise which, however, affects the daily lives of millions of citizens of the EU member states who are by no means aware of the impact the agencies have on specific legal regulations that are relevant to them, or even of their existence[247].

---

243 See *The Operating Framework*, COM(2002) 718 final, pp. 7 ff.

244 Griller, Orator, 'Mapping the Jungle', p. 2.

245 Wittinger, 'Europäische Satelliten', pp. 609 ff.

246 See G.N. Toggenburg, 'Die EU-Grundrechteagentur: Satellit oder Leitstern?', *SWP-Aktuell*, No. 8, 2007, p. 3.

247 Image campaigns run for the past ten years with the intent to familiarise EU citizens with the activity of regulatory agencies have been of little help. See e.g. a video promoting the agencies: https://www.youtube.com/watch?v=r5uTJZ6JVoY (20.3.2018), or the brochure with the slogan "Whatever You Do We Work For You",

Taking into account the lack of coherence and consistency in agency making, the simplest organising criterion is the functional one. It was used in the classification proposed by the European Commission, the European Parliament and the Council in the 2008 Communication. It identified: (1) agencies authorised to issue binding individual decisions, (2) agencies that support the Commission and, when necessary, the member states by drawing up technical and scientific expert opinions and inspection reports, (3) operational agencies, (4) agencies participating in collecting, analysing and forwarding objective, reliable and clear information as well as building networking links between different entities operating in a given sector of the market and finally (5) agencies performing a servicing role for other EU institutions[248].

There are many classifications in academic literature of regulatory agencies. In most cases, they are similar to one another, although individual authors assign particular agencies to different groups in spite of their being in similar categories. Such categorisations are thus largely of a conventional nature and are used to "familiarise" the readers with the opaque maze of institutions.

Among many suggestions, the classifications proposed by a pair of Austrian lawyers deserve attention. Stefan Griller and Andreas Orator identified agencies without decision-making powers, agencies with actual decision-making powers and agencies with a formally guaranteed catalogue of decision-making powers[249]. In the first group, they included agencies engaged in a variety of tasks, but with a lack of decision-making powers, whether formally guaranteed or implied in relation to third parties. These are agencies supporting EU institutions in carrying out specific programmes (e.g. ETF, CdT, GSA), monitoring agencies (e.g. EEA, EU-OSHA), agencies facilitating cooperation between the member states, international organisations and any other stakeholders in a given market sector (e.g. Cedefop, Eurofound, Frontex) as well as agencies collecting important information for developing the internal market (e.g. ENISA, ECDC). In the second group, the researchers included agencies with actual decision-making powers, which in practice are in a position to directly influence the legislative actions of the European Commission and the process of implementing European law in the member states with the aid of their expertise (e.g. EMA, EFSA, EMSA)[250].

---

available in three languages: https://publications.europa.eu/en/publication-detail/-/publication/8c134ef0-8907-11e5-b8b7-01aa75ed71a1 (20.3.2018).

248 *European Agencies – The Way Forward*, COM(2008) 135 final, p. 7.

249 Griller, Orator, 'Mapping the Jungle', pp. 13–27.

250 This category is also identified by other authors, see e.g. Geradin, Petit, 'The Development of Agencies', p. 48 ; E. Chiti, 'An Important Part of the EU's Institutional

The third group, according to Griller and Orator, includes agencies with formally guaranteed decision-making powers. This means that such decision-making powers are conferred on regulatory agencies in founding regulations and sector-specific regulations that also affect third parties, such as businesses, financial institutions, regulatory authorities in the member states and even individuals. This is the most rapidly growing group of agencies. In addition to agencies such as EUIPO, CPVO, ECHA, EASA, financial supervisory agencies – EBA, ESMA and EIOPA – created in recent years can be included in this group as well as previously existing agencies, the competences of which have been gradually expanded. A good example of the latter is ERA – its powers were greatly increased when the fourth railway package was implemented[251].

A simplified division was proposed by yet another Austrian lawyer, Arno Kahl, who singled out two main groups of agencies – those of an informational nature and those acting to strengthen the internal market[252]. The informational activities of agencies can be divided into instrumental activities, meaning those that serve specific administrative tasks, e.g. make it possible to prepare decisions or draft legal acts, and the so-called final activities, meaning they only serve to obtain specific data about entities operating in a particular sector[253]. Advisory and informational bodies notably include the EIT, which unlike other agencies does not draw up its own opinions for the professional preparation of decisions issued by EU institutions. Its actions are addressed e.g. to universities and scientific centres[254]. Waldemar Hummer builds on Kahl's classification, identifying agencies that facilitate the functioning of the internal market (e.g. EFSA, EMSA, EASA, ECHA, ENISA), agencies with monitoring functions (e.g. EEA, EMCDDA), agencies supporting social dialogue at the EU-wide level (e.g. EU-OSHA, Cedefop) and agencies supporting the EU in the performance of its tasks (e.g. CdT)[255].

Machinery: Features, Problems and Perspectives of European Agencies', *Common Market Law Review*, Vol. 46, No. 5, 2009, p. 1405.

251 Będkowski-Kozioł, 'Status', pp. 54–56; K. Barrow, 'EU Agency for Railways Prepares for New Role', *International Railway Journal* of 6.9.2016.

252 A. Kahl, 'Europäische Agenturen im Lichte der dynamischen Verwaltungslehre', in: K. Arnold *et al.* (ed.), *Recht, Politik, Wirtschaft. Dynamische Perspektiven. Festschrift für Norbert Wimmer*, Wien/New York 2008, pp. 253 ff.

253 See E. Chiti, 'The Emergence of a Community Administration: The Case of European Agencies', *Common Market Law Review*, Vol. 37, No. 2, 2000, p. 317.

254 It influences their activities through special "advisory partnerships" called Knowledge and Innovation Communities. See Kirste, 'Das System', p. 271.

255 Hummer, 'Von der Agentur', p. 111.

Agencies with management, operational, decision-making and quasi-regulatory tasks can be included in the group of agencies strengthening the development of the internal market. Such agencies, alongside informational bodies, were singled out by Madalina Busuioc, who built her classification on the criterion of the power of individual agencies. Agencies with advisory and informational powers are the weakest. On the scale proposed by Busuioc, the influence of agencies grows towards the strongest ones, endowed with decision-making and quasi-regulatory competences. In practice, such a theoretical scheme does not always apply. Advisory and informational agencies can be influential[256]. It should be taken into account that information is rarely politically neutral and it easily becomes a significant vessel in political skirmishes. Obtaining specific data cannot be separated from creating a political agenda and implementing sector-specific policies[257]. Individual agencies have different powers and, therefore, the abovementioned categories should be seen as overlapping rather than mutually exclusive subsets[258]. Busuioc mentions the EASA as an example of an agency with a variety of competences. It is an operational cooperation agency, i.e. it acts as a coordinator of activities in the domain of aviation safety on the territory of the member states. It also has decision-making and quasi-regulatory powers[259].

The classifications outlined above, have been modified by Martijn Groenleer, Michael Kaeding and Esther Versluis, who identified agencies of informational-advisory and semi-regulatory nature[260]. Bodies included in the latter group have decision-making powers, i.e. they can make decisions in specific cases that also affect private parties; they also have inspection powers entailing control over the actions of national regulatory authorities as well as entities operating within the regulated sector (e.g. financial institutions); competences involving national training of officials and other people engaged in the inspection process and monitoring a specific area in the EU internal market. The German lawyer Thomas Groß also follows this route, expanding the division proposed in the abovementioned Communication by the Commission of December 2002, naming agencies with

256 *Cf.* Saerbeck, *Unabhängige europäische Regulierungsagenturen*, pp. 60 ff.

257 See M. Shapiro, 'The Problems of Independent Agencies in the United States and the European Union', *Journal of European Public Policy*, Vol. 4, No. 2, 1997, Vol. 4, pp. 284 ff.

258 M. Busuioc, *European Agencies. Law and Practices of Accountability*, Oxford 2013, p. 38.

259 N. Kohtamäki, 'Autonomia instytucjonalna urzędów regulacyjnych Unii Europejskiej: przykład Europejskiej Agencji Bezpieczeństwa Lotniczego', *Internetowy Kwartalnik Antymonopolowy i Regulacyjny*, No. 2(5), 2016, pp. 63–65.

260 Groenleer *et al.*,'Regulatory Governance', pp. 1215 ff.

supporting powers and those with limited decision-making capabilities in relation to third parties, i.e. natural and legal persons[261]. Supporting powers in this context should be understood in a broad sense as any competences that can help improve the Commission's legislative actions in a given sector. Thus, they will be mostly technical, expert and scientific tasks associated with the drafting of opinions, recommendations and reports, consisting of collecting and compiling important data shared with the stakeholders, involving conducting research and inspections and also coordinating cooperation with countries outside the EU and other actors in international relations interested in cooperation in a particular area[262].

bb) Critical Assessment

Opponents of regulatory agencies put forward many critical arguments in the context of their tasks, which can be divided into two groups in reference to the abovementioned classifications. On the one hand, these bodies can be seen as an inflationary growth of European bureaucracy, which contributes little to actual management in a specific sector of the internal market. This argument is usually applied to "weak" agencies, i.e. those with advisory, informational, monitoring, supporting, operational, or coordinating powers. In this case, the focus is typically put on the unnecessary proliferation of "Eurocratic" institutions, the only task of which is to duplicate the activities of national-level institutions or already existing international organisations[263]. On the other hand, in the case of "strong" agencies which have decision-making powers, meaning that they can make decisions in specific cases, while also having quasi-regulatory or semi-legislative competences, critics of the "agencification" of the European administrative space talk about a stealthy "interception" of sectorally important functions and tasks carried out by EU institutions that are contrary to the wording of the Treaties[264]. In this context, the absence of democratic legitimacy in the case of these bodies is a particularly important problem. According to this critical vision, they have

261 *The Operating Framework*, COM(2002) 718 final, p. 4.

262 *Cf.* Groß, 'Die Kooperation', pp. 57 ff.

263 The problem of duplicating tasks has been discussed with regard to many agencies. The high-profile debate over the EU Agency for Fundamental Rights deserves attention. See Toggenburg, 'Die EU-Grundrechteagentur', pp. 3–5.

264 In literature this thought has repeatedly been expressed e.g. by Groenleer who is writing about "placing too much power in the hands of appointed 'Eurocrats' within the agencies who cannot easily be held accountable for their actions", *The Autonomy*, p. 17.

become one of the many elements of European technocracy which are unaccountable, and in a way they function simply for their own sake, in isolation from the real "maladies" of ordinary mortals[265].

Regardless of the criticism, which in many specific cases is often justified, the classifications presented above serve mainly as an illustration of the subject matter. It constitutes an attempt to reflect the spectrum of competences conferred on the agencies. The scope of the tasks that are assigned to them is growing ever broader and becomes ever more detailed with each passing decade. We can thus speak of a departure from the main idea that guided the initiators of these agencies in the 1990s. The point was to create institutions whose character would reflect the pluralism of the internal market. For this reason, one of the primary tasks of EU regulatory agencies is to coordinate cooperation in a specific area and monitor consistent implementation of regulatory policies in a certain market sector[266]. The key thing is not just a common understanding of specific problems, but also the homogenous interpretation of the proposed solutions. Hence, some of these bodies have, for example, inspection powers (e.g. EASA, EMSA or EFCA). Agencies also work towards the standardisation of regulatory practices applied by national authorities, including e.g. supervisory practices. They constitute a kind of a "conveyor belt" when it comes to the collection and forwarding of information within a specific area that they are involved in. Institutionalisation of sectoral cooperation and mediation between different governance levels are the main operational pillar of regulatory agencies.

As Groenleer rightly noted, over time regulatory agencies have become something more than a technical instrument in the process of implementing EU law and harmonising regulatory practices[267]. Some agencies achieve an autonomous position, becoming a "key player" in a specific economic sector – not just in the European dimension, but also internationally. They gain autonomy, and recognition of their performance, not thanks to formal provisions that guarantee their independence or commit the member states to cooperate closely with them, but mainly thanks to the high degree of professionalism and expertise of their actions. Through becoming empowered to issue decisions that are binding for natural and legal persons, they have obtained the status of specific administrative

265 Curtin, 'Delegation', p. 88.

266 Management agencies and operational cooperation agencies identified by Busuioc should be perceived within these functions. Management agencies include CdT, GSA, or ETF, and operational ones –EMSA, Frontex, or ECDC. See Busuioc, *European Agencies*, p. 39.

267 Groenleer, *The Autonomy*, p. 20.

bodies at a supranational level[268]. As they gain independence, often greater than that formally guaranteed in their founding regulations, agencies move away from their clear relationship of subordination to EU institutions as well as to the member states.

The traditional, rationalist currents in the theory of international relations – neorealism and neoliberalism – assume that countries engage in international cooperation are motivated not by altruistic considerations, but by the desire to make a profit and obtain maximum benefit[269]. Just as liberal currents emphasise the absolute gains of all participants in cooperation, realistic currents work on the assumption that it is necessary to compile and compare the relative gains of individual actors[270]. In both cases the forms of international cooperation that include regulatory agencies are a means to achieve one's own objectives. The theoretically clear principal-agent relationship, i.e. direct or indirect, subordination to "principals", or the member states (through EU institutions), especially in the case of agencies created in recent years, is gradually, yet consistently, evolving as their decision-making and semi-legislative powers keep expanding.

c) Organisational Structure

aa) The Board

The Board Composition

All agencies have a limited mandate to act that is defined in the acts of secondary law that establish them. The character of any agency's powers is associated with the expertise that allows it to support the Commission in the regulatory process. In order to keep up with the priorities for sector-specific policies defined by the Commission, agencies shape their own programmes and action plans. An important role in this process is played by agency bodies. The organisational structure of the agencies is, in most cases, similar and does not directly depend on the size or specific tasks of the institution. In the literature it is described as dual, because two bodies play a central role: a collegial decision-making body which is usually the board, as well as a monocratic executive body – a director

268 Hansen-Nootbaar, *Unabhängigkeit*, p. 19.

269 More M. Herdegen, *Der Kampf um die Weltordung. Eine strategische Betrachtung*, München 2019, pp. 53–64.

270 See S.L. Lamy, 'Contemporary Mainstream Approaches: Neo-Realism and Neo-Liberalism', in: J. Baylis *et al.* (ed.), *The Globalization of World Politics. An Introduction to International Relations*, New York 2011, p. 120.

who is responsible for performing administrative, operational and management tasks related to the agency's daily functioning[271].

Agency boards can be of diverse natures. No agency is autonomous enough to shape its personal make-up completely on its own, separately from the member states and EU institutions. Boards have decision-making, steering and controlling functions. Therefore, they form the core of an agency's institutional structure. Agency boards are composed of representatives from various institutions. There is no single, one-size-fits-all model. They usually consist of representatives with voting rights representing the member states and the European Commission[272], but they can also be bodies made up of independent experts, e.g. the EFSA. National representatives can also be rotating members of the board, just as in the case of the European Institute for Gender Equality (EIGE)[273]. The board of that agency consists of a representative of the Commission and eighteen representatives of member states appointed by the Council on the basis of proposals from the member states concerned, in an order compliant with the rotation of the Presidencies[274].

However, the Commission as a rule has its own representatives, numbering between one and six, usually with voting rights[275]. Their presence is meant to ensure control over the work of the agencies and also to guarantee institutional balance in the EU system[276]. The member states' representatives are in most cases appointed by national regulatory authorities and they are usually the senior executives of these authorities. In many cases, the Council appoints representatives from the member states[277], often together with their alternates. The basic principle, specified

---

271 Kirste, 'Das System', p. 272; Andoura, Timmerman, 'Governance', pp. 10 ff.

272 The Commission's representatives do not have voting rights in EUIPO and CPVO. See M. Buess, 'Accountable and Under Control? Explaining Governments' Selection of Management Board Representatives', *Journal of Common Market Studies*, Vol. 53, No. 3, 2015, pp. 497 ff.

273 *Cf.* M. Półtorak, 'EIGE jako przykład działalności wspierającej równe traktowanie kobiet i mężczyzn w UE', *Roczniki Administracji i Prawa*, Vol. XIV, 2014, pp. 59 ff.

274 See Article 10(1) and (3) of Regulation (EC) No. 1922/2006 of 20.12.2006 establishing the European Institute for Gender Equality, OJ 2006, L 403/9.

275 See European Commission's Analytical Fiche No. 5, 2010, *Composition and Designation of the Management Board.*

276 Some authors interpret participation of the Commission's representatives as an echo of the provisions of the anti-delegation *Meroni* doctrine. More about this issue Chamon, *EU Agencies*, pp. 67 ff.

277 Cedefop, Eurofound, EU-OSHA. More about the Council's involvement in the election and appointment of board members at individual agencies, see Analytical Fiche No. 5, 2010.

in most founding regulations, is adequate experience and expertise in the area which is important for the activity of a particular agency[278]. The terms of office of agency boards range from two-and-a-half years to five years which can be considered a short period of time in comparison with national regulatory authorities[279].

A variant of parallel bodies – one with management and administration tasks, the other acting as a platform of cooperation between national regulatory authorities – is also possible. This is the case e.g. with the Agency for the Cooperation of Energy Regulators (ACER) where members of the Administrative Board are appointed by the Council, the Parliament and the Commission, and members of the Board of Regulators are dispatched by national regulatory authorities[280]. The former body adopts a multi-year programme as well as a work plan for the next year. It also appoints the agency director and exercises budgetary powers. In the case of the latter, the Commission has a representative without voting rights alongside the national representatives. The Board of Regulators issues opinions e.g. about a candidate who is supposed to be appointed as the director, it also approves a yearly work plan and a part of an annual report on its regulatory activity as well as delivering opinions on guidelines and recommendations issued by the agency[281].

In most of the agencies, board members can be assisted by representatives of many EU and external entities which act as non-voting members or observers[282].

---

278 An exception is ECHA, where an additional *explicite* requirement to have "relevant expertise in the fields of general, financial and legal matters" was included. See Article 79(2) of Regulation (EC) No. 1907/2006 of 18.12.2006 on the Registration, Evaluation, Authorisation and Restriction of Chemicals (REACH) and the establishment of a European Chemicals Agency, OJ 2006, L 396/1. About competences of board members, see M. Mayrhofer, 'Europäische Agenturen: Organisation und Verfahren', in: Raschauer, *Europäische Agenturen*, pp. 50 ff.

279 More Groenleer, *The Autonomy*, pp. 120 ff.

280 A similar system was introduced in the three financial supervisory agencies: EBA, ESMA and EIOPA, where the main decision-making body is the Board of Supervisors, comprising the heads of national financial supervisory authorities. In organisational and administrative tasks it is supported by the Management Board. See Articles 40, 43, 45 and 47 of Regulations Nos. 1093/2010, 1094/2010 and 1095/2010. More Kohtamäki, *Die Reform*, pp. 164–168.

281 See Articles 12–15 of Regulation (EC) No. 713/2009 of 13.7.2009 establishing the Agency for the Cooperation of Energy Regulators, OJ 2009, L 211/1. See Steger, *Zur Verselbstständigung*, pp. 439–452.

282 E.g. stakeholders have voting rights in Cedefop and Eurofound. Representatives of the European Parliament as a rule have voting rights, with the exception of the boards at ETF and GSA.

They can be, for example, representatives of: the European Parliament, regulatory agencies from "sister" market sectors or authorities from third-party states and states seeking accession. In order to reflect their desire to increase the transparency of agency work and to provide them with broad social legitimacy, members of the boards also increasingly include e.g. representatives of private and public organisations, i.e. the businesses and scientific communities who are interested in participating in decision-making process[283]. There is no rule regarding the procedure for electing them. All three EU institutions are sometimes involved. In such a case the Council, after consultations with the European Parliament, usually elects such representatives on the basis of a list prepared by the Commission. In the cases of other agencies, the Commission autonomously participates in the process of selecting stakeholders.

As is indicated by this brief overview, the composition of the boards can vary greatly between individual agencies. The boards also differ in size: from several to several dozen members[284]. There is also no consistency as far as naming is considered[285]. The 2012 "Common Approach" attempted to harmonise this diversity. Just as was mentioned above, the recommendations it contains are in essence guidelines that should be applied to future agencies and possibly respected in the case of a reform of the existing agencies. In a board, which, within the "Common Approach", functions as a Management Board (MB), all the member states should be represented[286] along with two representatives of the Commission, possibly a representative of the European Parliament and, as part

283 For example, the board of the EMA is composed of two representatives of an organisation of patients and one representative of an organisation of veterinarians. See Article 65(1) of Regulation (EC) No. 726/2004 of 31.3.2004 establishing community procedures for issuing permits for medicinal products for human and veterinary use and supervision over them, as well as establishing the European Medicines Agency, OJ 2004, L 136/1. More on this topic Mayrhofer, 'Europäische Agenturen', p. 50.

284 The boards at Cedefop and Eurofound are the biggest, with *c.* ninety members. EFSA and EIGE have the smallest boards, with fourteen and eighteen members respectively, assisted by representatives of the Commission. See N. Font, 'Informal Rules and Institutional Balances on the Boards of EU Agencies', *Administration & Society*, Published Online in June 2015, p. 9.

285 They can be e.g. Management Boards (e.g. ECHA, EEA, ENISA), Administrative Boards (e.g. ACER, EMSA, EFCA), or Governing Boards (e.g. Cedefop, EIT, EU-OSHA).

286 Unless a state voluntarily gives up activity in the area where the agency is involved. More about the exceptions such as eu-LISA: Chamon, *EU Agencies*, p. 67.

of an outreach towards various entities operating in a given sector – representatives of the broadly understood stakeholders[287].

Due to the participation of the European Parliament in control and supervisory tasks over regulatory agencies, there are voices suggesting that the involvement of its representatives in the work of the agency board can generate conflicts of interest. Merijn Chamon even writes about an anomaly in reference to this state of affairs, pointing to the incomprehensibility of the fact that the Parliament, a legislative body, is active in agency boards that are executive bodies[288]. In most cases, this is a result of the Parliament's efforts to obtain more influence over the decision-making process in the European agency system. But a reverse trend has been observed for several years that involves the Parliament's desire to strengthen its role, not as an entity directly participating in agency tasks, but an institution controlling them. Representatives of this body, therefore, have not sat on the MBs of agencies created in recent years[289].

The Board Decision Making

Voting MB members elect a chairperson – usually one of the representatives of the member states – for a two-year term with the possibility of re-election from among its members. EFCA, ETF and CdT are exceptions where the chairperson is one of the Commission's representatives. On the other hand, in the case of Eurofund its representative acts as vice-chairperson[290]. As for the voting procedure, the "Common Approach" proposed that current business matters should be decided by an absolute majority, while for matters of special importance, such as appointing and dismissing the director or adopting the budget' a two-thirds qualified majority would suffice. At present, there are many different voting procedures in individual agencies: from simple majority to various types of qualified majorities (of all board members or those present) and unanimity in special cases [291].

---

287 *Joint Statement and Common Approach*, 19.7.2012, p. 5.

288 Representatives of the European Parliament sit on boards of seven agencies (with voting rights in six of them, e.g. in ECHA, EMA, ACER). See Analytical Fiche No. 5.

289 M. Egeberg *et al.*, 'Building Executive Power at the European Level: On the Role of European Union Agencies', in: Busuioc *et al.* (ed.), *The Agency Phenomenon*, p. 28. There are no representatives of the Parliament e.g. in eu-LISA created in 2011. See Article 13 of Regulation (EU) No. 1077/2011 of 25.10.2011 establishing the eu-LISA, OJ 2011, L 281/1.

290 See European Commission's Analytical Fiche No. 6, 2010, *Role and Functioning of the Management Board.*

291 E.g. Article 12(8) in connection with Article 25(2) of Regulation (EC) No. 168/2007 of 15.2.2007 establishing the Agency for Fundamental Rights, OJ 2007, L 53/1.

Regardless of formal provisions in founding regulations, in many regulatory agencies, which are – not without reason – considered to be model examples of European deliberative institutionalism, a substantial portion of decisions is made by consensus. However, it may sometimes be the case that a particular voting procedure serves to strengthen the position and leverage of specific actors on the board of an agency[292]. Most often, the aim is to be able to effectively pursue national interests[293]. The balances of power and networks of interdependencies in boards are a good illustration of the famous concept of the U.S. political scientist, Andrew Moravcsik, a representative of neoliberalism in the theory of international relations. He assumed that interactions between subjects of international relations are shaped on the foundation of their preferences. They underpin strategies developed by policymakers. The behaviour of states, on the other hand, is determined by their evolving preferences as well as the preferences of other actors in the international environment. The neoliberal current perceives states as interdependent entities whose interests are restricted by the interests of other players, including international organisations[294]. There is no doubt that, particularly in MBs of more influential agencies with semi-regulatory powers, states seek to build coalitions in order to secure favourable outcomes in those market sectors that are important for them[295].

It is worth noting here that despite the theoretically equal status of all board members, particularly voting actors, the actual impact of individual representatives varies[296]. Apart from the special role of the Commission's representative and the board chairperson, representatives of the individual member states also have various opportunities to influence agency decisions. Interdependencies between different entities, understood as mutual dependencies, are not without importance. We are discussing here a specific type of interaction that could be compared to the

292 Empirical research on this issue: Font, 'Informal Rules', pp. 11 ff.

293 In many agencies representatives of member states receive instructions on how to vote on particular issues. See M. Buess, 'European Union Agencies and Their Management Boards: An Assessment of Accountability and Demoi-Cratic Legitimacy', *Journal of European Public Policy*, Vol. 22, No. 1, 2015, p. 103.

294 See A. Moravcisk, 'Taking Preferences Seriously: A Liberal Theory of International Politics', *International Organization*, Vol. 51, No. 4, 1997, pp. 518–521.

295 More N. Kohtamäki, 'Realizacja interesu narodowego w strukturach Unii Europejskiej na przykładzie autonomicznych agencji regulacyjnych', *Annales Universitatis Paedagogicae Cracoviensis. Studia Politologica*, Vol. XVII, No. 214, 2016, pp. 135–142.

296 See M. Martens, 'Voice or Loyalty? The Evolution of the European Environment Agency (EEA)', *Journal of Common Market Studies*, Vol. 48, No. 4, 2010, p. 883.

feedback loops that develop in multilevel networks of national regulatory authorities[297]. Individual entities mobilise goal-oriented coalitions in those networks to pursue certain priorities significant from the point of view of national interests. The effectiveness of these coalitions directly results from their ability to create and navigate such a specific "network environment". Those who have such abilities are primarily officials from the so-called old member states, which is not only due to their more extensive experience as a result of the longer presence of these states in the integrated European system, but often also from their bigger economic potential as well as the cultural determinants related to that. It is associated, for example, with the greater management abilities of representatives of Anglo-Saxon and Nordic countries and greater confidence in presenting their cases among representatives from Western Europe as well as their better substantive and linguistic preparation[298].

When decisions are taken by way of voting, the voice of the Commission is less significant due to the typically small number of representatives of this body in relation to the number of representatives of national regulatory authorities[299]. Taking that into consideration, in order to guarantee a special role for the Commission in the agency decision-making process, the "Common Approach" introduced a safeguarding solution, which has the nature of a recommendation, at least for the time being. If the Commission finds that an agency board has made a decision exceeding the mandate of that agency, or which violates EU law or EU policy objectives, then it can appeal to the board with a demand for it to refrain from issuing a decision. Should the Commission's demand be overruled by the board, it can formally notify the European Parliament and the Council[300].

Boards are central, strategic bodies of agencies, therefore, they constitute a significant element of the European administrative system. As if through a lens, they show the multitude of actors involved in the European system of deliberative management. They also provide a mechanism for individual players to influence the decision-making processes within agencies. The key role is played here by the member states and the European Commission. The election of MB

297 See Bieleń, *Polityka*, pp. 16, 185 ff. In this context, Jarle Trondal and Lene Jeppesen write about mult-level epistemic networks. See J. Trondal, L. Jeppesen, 'Images of Agency Governance in the European Union', *West European Politics*, Vol. 31, No. 3, 2008, pp. 418, 424 ff.

298 More M. Busuioc, 'European Agencies and Their Boards: Promises and Pitfalls of Accountability Beyond Design', *Journal of European Public Policy*, Vol. 19, No. 5, 2012, pp. 726 ff., 730; Egeberg *et al.*, 'Building Executive Power', pp. 34, 36.

299 See Wonka, Rittberger, 'Credibility', p. 745.

300 *Joint Statement and Common Approach*, 19.7.2012, p. 13.

members, the selection of participants in their meetings and the voting procedure in particular cases, all reflect the impact of particular entities, including above all the member states and EU institutions. That is often already apparent at the stage of making a decision to create an agency[301]. Agency boards consist altogether of a total of more than a thousand members, including approx. nine hundred representatives of the member states and approx. seventy representatives of the Commission[302]. They constitute a crucial link in defining the lines of action for agencies, including their activity in shaping sector-specific policies.

The Influence of the European Commission

Apart from the formal provisions contained in the regulations founding the particular agencies, the informal rules developed over years of practice that determine specific behaviours of the board members at individual agencies are often significant. In this context a prime example is how the positions of the Commission's representatives are shaped in particular agencies. Their status comes not just from formal provisions in founding acts. It is determined by particular habits, customs or what constitutes the significant core of the so-called organisational culture of every institution[303]. The representative of the Commission can, for example, modify the priorities in the agency task plan submitted for discussion at board meetings[304] or influence how customary solutions are developed when it comes to conducting a debate, e.g. by interrupting it and presenting its own position between speeches delivered by the member state representatives as well as closing the meetings at a convenient time for the Commission. On the other hand, one of the basic, informal operation rules in most agencies is to work out specific compromise positions in a smaller group than the MB and submitting them for discussion or directly for formal approval in the broader forum. If the Commission expresses its objection on a given issue at such a "backstage meeting" which precedes official arrangements, then an agreement on this issue is usually blocked during board meetings[305].

---

301 On the example of EEA: Martens, 'Voice or Loyalty?', pp. 884 ff., 887.

302 Font, 'Informal Rules', p. 2.

303 See N. Kohtamäki, 'Kultura organizacyjna', pp. 69–75.

304 And also actively participate in formulating the priorities included in the annual task plan of a given agency. There is often strong pressure from the DG concerned which can force the inclusion or removal of particular tasks from the programme. See on the example of EEA Martens, 'Voice or Loyalty?', p. 888.

305 Nuria Font, on the basis of surveys carried out among representatives of selected agencies, emphasises the special role of the Commission which is even described by

In some agencies there are smaller bodies called executive bureaus, committees or boards, composed of a few people, including usually the representative of the Commission and the board chairperson. They constitute an important element of such a multi-stage shaping of decisions and arrangements. The "Common Approach" justified the existence of such bodies, officially describing them using the term Executive Boards and stressing their role in monitoring and controlling the activity of agencies[306]. They are in charge of drawing up a detailed agenda submitted for discussion at board meetings, which usually take place a few times a year[307]. They are particularly useful in large boards, which, due to their size, are unable to perform tasks relating to management or operations effectively[308].

In many bodies of this sort, the Commission's representative, together with the chairperson of the board and the agency director, constitute, by informal arrangement, a specific triumvirate that decides about the agency's lines of action. These persons are most deeply involved in the work of the agency and also have the greatest knowledge about its activities. This partly results from the fact that they participate in the administrative tasks of these bodies on an ongoing basis and follow the developments that are important from the point of view of the agency in its day-to-day practice. The Commission's representatives or agency directors are full-time EU officials. Representatives of the member states in agency boards, on the other hand, are usually heads of national regulatory authorities, ministries and agencies, i.e. officials from the member states. Their activity in the work of an agency is sporadic. It is an additional professional duty, often – little liked. Thus, knowledge of, as well as interest in, specific tasks and problems of an agency on the part of national representatives may be limited[309].

Regardless of this state of affairs, the member state representatives play an important role in the democratic legitimisation of agency activities. According to Michael Buess, their participation in the work of the board legitimises the

---

one of the respondents as the leading actor, 'Informal Rules', pp. 10–12. Although, it can happen that an agency's persistence in pushing a particular issue can change the Commission's attitude and force it to get interested in the issue, see Martens, 'Voice or Loyalty?', p. 892.

306 See European Commission's Analytical Fiches Nos. 5, 6, 31 (*Commission Role*), 2010; *Joint Statement and Common Approach*, 19.7.2012, p. 5.

307 M. Busuioc, M. Groenleer, 'Wielders of Supranational Power? The Administrative Behaviour of the Heads of European Union Agencies', in: Busuioc *et al.* (ed.), *The Agency Phenomenon*, p. 142.

308 Busuioc, 'European Agencies and Their Boards', p. 727.

309 *Ibid.*, p. 730; Busuioc, *European Agencies*, p. 88 ff.; Martens, 'Voice or Loyalty?', p. 893.

activities of an agency both vertically, through reference to their "parent" institutions which have legitimacy associated with the election of particular decision-makers by the citizens of the given member states, and, to a lesser extent, horizontally, that is to say transnationally, where the legitimising role is played by control mechanisms as part of network interactions with "sister" institutions in other member states[310].

bb) The Director

The Commission, which plays an important role in the board, strives to indirectly influence other agency bodies. One of these ways is the MB's involvement in the appointment of agency directors, which is regulated in the "Common Approach", as well as control over the proper performance of the responsibilities assigned to them[311]. The MB's supervision over the activity of the director constitutes an important element of balancing powers in the institutional structure of the EU's regulatory agencies. Checks and balances, such as the board's participation in the selection and appointment of the director, his or her disciplinary liability, or the presence of the director in board meetings, constitute a hedge against the "free rein" of the particular bodies, and are one of the major elements of an agency's accountability[312].

Directors act as leaders in the regulatory agencies and represent them independently in external contacts. They become the "face" of the institution. They actively participate in shaping the identity of their agencies, making efforts to boost their prestige, authority or status, not only in the European environment. Directors also seek to justify the purpose of a given agency and its importance in the European institutional system. They become advocates of its legitimacy as well as promoting the validity of its existence[313]. Their role increases if the agency is active in the international environment. Many of the EU's regulatory agencies are present in various international forums that work to intensify cooperation in a particular area and they also establish partnerships with third-party countries

---

310 Buess, 'European Union Agencies', pp. 95, 98 ff. See also Chapter 7.

311 Analytical Fiche No. 6; *Joint Statement and Common Approach*, 19.7.2012, p. 6.

312 Busuioc, *European Agencies*, pp. 78 ff. The "Common Approach" particularly emphasised the need to strengthen control mechanisms over agency directors: *Joint Statement and Common Approach*, 19.7.2012, p. 6.

313 More about the role of the leader in public administration: M. Husar Holmes, 'Validating the Relevance of Leadership in Public Administration', *International Journal of Organization Theory and Behavior*, Vol. 12, No. 2, 2009, pp. 257 ff.

and international organisations, in cooperation with the board and often after prior approval by the Commission. This is partly reflected in memorandums and agreements reached with those entities[314].

Directors are usually appointed by boards in accordance with proposals put forward by the Commission[315]. It is not uncommon that after being elected by the board, they are often obliged to appear before the European Parliament and answer questions from MEPs and they can also request the board to appoint their deputies[316]. The main tasks of agency directors include preparing the draft budget plan, the annual work programme and the annual report on its activities. They coordinate the day-to-day work of their agencies, supervise the implementation of the work programme and budget and strive to maintain the operational capability of the managed entity[317]. They often cooperate with the agency's secretariat to prepare documents that are then debated at board meetings. They also make decisions on matters referring to staff, including the organisational structure of the agency. As far as they are concerned, there is also no consistency when it comes to the naming of the function they perform; the most common names of the function include: the Director, the Executive Director, the Administrative Director, the Administrative Manager, or the President[318].

Candidates for this position are mainly expected to have appropriate qualifications in a given field as well as management skills[319]. They are usually

314 These documents are of different nature and they are described with terms such as "agreement", "working arrangement", "administrative arrangement", "memorandum of understanding", or "memorandum of cooperation". In the literature dedicated to the issue of international activity of regulatory agencies, it is considered to be a special form of EU external administrative action which is permissible and does not upset the institutional balance. See F. Coman-Kund, 'The International Dimension of the EU Agencies. Charting a Legal-Institutional "Twilight Zone"', *TARN Working Paper*, No. 5, 2017, pp. 2–13.

315 The full list of procedures dedicated to the appointment of directors of individual agencies: Analytical Fiche No. 7; *Joint Statement and Common Approach*, 19.7.2012, p. 6.

316 It is like that, for example, in EASA. The Executive Director can request the appointment of Directors supporting them in administrative tasks. See Articles 33(2) and 39 of Regulation (EC) No. 216/2008.

317 See Busuioc, Groenleer, 'Wielders of Supranational Power?', p. 128.

318 European Commission's Analytical Fiche No. 8, 2010, *Tasks, Duties and Responsibilietes of the Director*. The "Common Approach" did not include a suggestion for a common name of this body, unlike in the case of the board.

319 See Groenleer, *The Autonomy*, p. 123.

officials who have built their experience within their national administrative structure or in the structures of the European Commission. They can also have experience stemming from the private sector or scientific and academic communities. Directors, being officials at the supranational level, do not represent the interests of their own countries. Geographical criteria do not play a part in their selection, so the distribution of directorial positions between the member states in the several dozen European agencies is uneven[320]. The term of a director is usually five years with a possible one-time renewal or extension. There are also no clear, consistent procedures regarding the dismissal of a director. It is accepted, in principle, that it is a solution used by the board, with the possible involvement of the Commission only in particularly blatant cases[321].

In the regulations which have founded agencies in recent years, the independence of directors in carrying out their tasks has been regulated explicitly. In the case of older agencies, where there are no such *de jure* provisions, achieving an independent position in managing an agency largely depends on the interpersonal skills of a director and his or her ambitions. In practice, it is a problematic thing for directors to "set themselves free" from the influence of the Commission. An overly independent position of a director can result in loss of support from the Commission and consequently the director being forced to leave the agency after their first term[322].

Specialists in organisation management believe that one of the determining factors influencing an institution's actions and ways of responding is the director's personality, i.e. his or her psychological features or charisma. He or she is the one who motivates employees, ensures the proper flow of information, and strives to resolve internal conflicts and alleviate tensions with the external environment[323]. Directors of EU agencies succeed in this respect to various degrees, due to numerous safeguards both formally included in the founding regulations as well as those resulting from established, non-formal practices.

Undoubtedly, though, taking into account the specific character of the EU institutional system, agency directors in most cases correspond to this theoretical framework, becoming an important link in consolidating the activities of the bodies that they represent. This is reflected in the joint efforts of directors seeking

320 Leaders from Western European countries outnumber others. See Busuioc, Groenleer, 'Wielders of Supranational Power?', pp. 135–138.

321 *Ibid.*, pp. 136, 144 ff.

322 Font, 'Informal Rules', p. 14.

323 See R. Mead, T.G. Andrews, *International Management. Culture and Beyond*, Chichester/Hoboken 2009, pp. 4, 111 ff.

to enhance inter-agency cooperation and the flow of information about the functioning of the agencies. Their efforts led to the creation of the EU Agencies Network (EUAN) which works to develop common practices, strengthen the position of agencies in the European administrative space, promote good governance and implement more effectively the mandate shared by these bodies, e.g. acting as highly specialised expert institutions. Agency directors play a special role within this network, pursuing effective management e.g. by sharing services and resources between agencies or improving the information flow. The agency network is governed by the so-called troika: the previous, the current and the next director of individual agencies holding the one-year presidency in the network. All the directors meet regularly to discuss the issues related to financing agencies, recruitment procedures as well as common strategies for informing the outside world about the work of agencies in the European administrative system[324].

cc) Other Bodies

Parallel to the administrative section, dominated by the board and the director, in many agencies there is a scientific and research section consisting of different types of committees and advisory platforms that bring together highly qualified specialists in a given field. They can be professionals dispatched by national regulatory authorities or specialists selected in open recruitment procedures. They are responsible for substantive preparation of expert documents, such as opinions or recommendations[325]. Founding regulations usually guarantee the independent position of expert committees, whose members should be free from political influence and should not accept any instructions or guidelines from EU institutions, the member states or other entities. The expert structure is often supplemented by the involvement of bodies consisting of stakeholders from a particular market sector. They have the right to express their opinions as part of the agency's decision-making process[326].

Boards of appeal function in agencies equipped with decision-making powers[327]. Specialists in the domains of the particular agencies are on most of

---

324 More https://euagencies.eu/ (20.3.2018).

325 See Groenleer, *The Autonomy*, pp. 124 ff.

326 E.g. in EASA or ETF, more about the activity of stakeholders in EU agencies: I. Pérez-Durán, 'Political and Stakeholder's Ties in European Union Agencies', *Journal of European Public Policy*, Published Online in September 2017, pp. 2 ff.

327 They can be found in ECHA, EASA, ACER, EUIPO, CPVO and SRB. The three financial supervisory agencies – ESMA, EBA and EIOPA – have a joint Board of Appeal.

these boards alongside lawyers. They are appointed by the board from a list of candidates, who are initially selected and proposed by the Commission after open recruitment takes place[328]. In all the founding regulations for agencies that have boards of appeal there are provisions regarding the independence of their members. Decisions that can be appealed in these boards are explicitly listed in the founding regulations of their respective agencies. Complaints against decisions of boards of appeal, or in such cases when decisions of the regulatory agencies cannot be subject to their appeal, can be brought to the CJEU under Article 263 TFEU[329].

The organisational structure of agencies in the schematic understanding outlined above, may be considered to be relatively simple. Yet one needs to remember that it comes in many significantly different variants. In spite of the efforts to systematise and harmonise institutional solutions in individual agencies, they remain diverse in many ways, stemming from sectoral specifics, informal rules and practices developed in a given area over the years, which determine the character and tasks of individual agency bodies, as well as the provisions in their founding regulations that were formulated, as was mentioned before, under the influence of various political pressures.

328 This is so in the case of ECHA, EASA, ACER, EBA, ESMA, EIOPA and SRB. A slightly different procedure, involving the Council, is provided for in the founding regulations of EUIPO and CPVO. See T. Groß, *Die Legitimation der polyzentralen EU-Verwaltung*, Tübingen 2015, pp. 74 ff.

329 More P. Chirulli, L. de Lucia, 'Specialised Adjudication in EU Administrative Law: The Boards of Appeal of EU Agencies', *European Law Review*, Vol. 40, No. 6, 2015, pp. 835 ff.; Busuioc, *European Agencies*, pp. 198 ff.

2 The Transformation of the Classic EU Regulatory Agency Model

1. The Specific Character of Selected Agencies

Out of more than thirty regulatory agencies, the following four will be analysed in this chapter: the European Food Safety Authority (EFSA), based in Parma; the European Chemicals Agency (ECHA), based in Helsinki; the European Border and Coast Guard Agency (Frontex), based in Warsaw, and the European Banking Authority (EBA), formerly based in London, now in Paris after Britain's decision to exit the EU[1]. They have been selected primarily due to their strong position in the EU agency system. They owe their high standing in the EU institutional structures to the broad powers which have been entrusted to them, including decision-making competencies (ECHA, EBA), as well as their considerable authority obtained thanks to providing informational, advisory and operational support (EFSA, Frontex).

The intention of this detailed analysis of the primary tasks of the agencies selected and their institutional structure is to exemplify the deepening problem of their weak or insufficient democratic legitimacy as the agency model undergoes transformation. This problem is emphasised by their ever broader

---

1 In June 2017, the European Council adopted a special procedure to move the seats of European institutions, including EBA and EMA, in connection with Britain's exit from the EU. The decision to move those agencies was made on 20.11.2017. The member states decided to move the seat of the EBA to Paris and that of the EMA to Amsterdam. See F. Landscheidt, 'Der Sitzwechsel europäischer Agenturen am Beispiel der Europäischen Arzneimitelagentur im Rahmen des "Brexit"', *Zeitschrift für europarechtliche Studien*, Vol. 20, No. 1, 2017, pp. 3 ff. The relocation is scheduled to be finalised in 2019. A fierce battle had been fought for the seats of both these powerful and important agencies, not only due to the prestige that comes with hosting EU institutions, but also due to tangible economic benefits for the city concerned. Agencies organise several hundred expert meetings a year, attended e.g. in the case of the European Medicines Agency by approx. thirty-five thousand specialists from Europe and across the world. The importance of both of these agencies is best demonstrated by Britain's efforts to keep them in London. The European Commission categorically rejected this solution: see V. Miller, 'EU Agencies and Post-Brexit Options', *House of Commons Briefing Papers*, No. 7957, 2017, pp. 10–15; see also in the broad context of the Brexit: A. Łazowski, R.A. Wessel, 'The External Dimension of Withdrawal from the European Union', *Revue des Affaires Européennes*, No. 4, 2016, pp. 623 ff.

competencies not being backed up by adequate empowerment in order for these institutions to take actions interfering not just with the proprietary prerogatives so far guaranteed solely for sovereign states (e.g. in the area of financial supervision or managing borders), but also the rights and obligations of private entities, including individuals.

At first glance, these bodies have little in common. They operate under mandates defined in their founding regulations in diverse sectors of the internal market. Taking into account the tasks assigned, we would also need to classify them into various groups[2]. ECHA and EBA are agencies endowed with decision-making powers with the possibility of issuing binding decisions for addressees, which can include national regulatory authorities and third parties[3]. EFSA, on the other hand, is a typical advisory agency with supporting powers, aiming to provide expert opinions to the EU institutions and the member states although it is also often classified in one group together with the ECHA and EMA. This not only due to them having similar areas of specialisation. They also have similar institutional structures[4]. They can be grouped together as agencies with instrumental powers[5]. In this context, their functions are explicitly understood as supporting ones, i.e. EFSA, EMA, and partly also ECHA, act as professional backup for market authorisation procedures, with the European Commission remaining the final decision-maker[6]. Frontex, in turn, is classified as an operational agency, i.e. one that performs a range of practical tasks to put EU policies into practice[7]. In this specific case it mainly means operational and intervention tasks at the EU's external borders. As was mentioned above, these divisions are of a conventional nature. All four agencies play an important coordinating

---

2 For more on the specific character of these powers in the context of the phenomenon of European internal market regulation see E. Chiti, 'European Agencies' Rulemaking: Powers, Procedures and Assessment', *European Law Journal*, Vol. 19, No. 1, 2013, pp. 95–100.

3 See Curtin, Dehousse, 'European Union Agencies', p. 197.

4 See S. Krapohl, 'Credible Commitment in Non-Independent Regulatory Agencies: A Comparative Analysis of the European Agencies for Pharmaceuticals and Foodstuffs', *European Law Journal*, Vol. 10, No. 5, 2004, p. 519; Buess, 'European Union Agencies', p. 100.

5 See Chiti, 'An Important Part', p. 1403.

6 See M. Busuioc, 'Blurred Areas of Responsibility: European Agencies' Scientific "Opinions" under Scrutiny', in: M. Ambrus *et al.* (ed.), *The Role of "Experts" in International and European Decision-Making Processes. Advisors, Decision Makers or Irrelevant Actors*, Cambridge 2014, p. 384.

7 Hansen-Nootbar, *Unabhängigkeit*, p. 53.

role with regard to the activities of the member states, monitor threats in their areas of competency, which arise in the internal market, and also perform expert functions to meet the needs of the EU institutions as well as the member states[8].

Their selection is not accidental. EFSA and ECHA are agencies with strong technocratic legitimacy. This means that apart from the powers formally guaranteed in the regulations, their role in the EU administrative system stems from the authority they have built up over the years. Therefore, their influence is also a result of informal interactions based on the trust placed in the agencies by the EU institutions, including above all the European Commission, but also national regulatory authorities as well as entrepreneurs and consumers. These agencies prepare documents of a scientific nature, such as opinions, guidelines or recommendations, based on expertise, available neither to an average consumer, nor to qualified officials at the EU or national level. On account of the fact that these agencies have access to expertise provided by professionals from narrow specialisations, we can speak of the phenomenon of information asymmetry in their case. Economists associate it with an advantage, concerning information, that one party to a transaction enjoys over the other. In the case of agencies, this means that they have a privileged position in terms of the overview and understanding of a problem or situation, precisely on account of their expertise. Although the European Commission is the EU executive authority with sole legislative initiative in the field of EU law, it often remains only a formal decision-maker when it comes to specialised issues, fully incorporating agency proposals into its draft legislation[9].

Madalina Busuioc has accurately diagnosed this state of affairs by emphasising the vagueness of the division between tasks associated with risk analysis and limited to the role of an opinion former, and tasks described as risk management that entail decision-making competencies. In the case of certain agencies it frequently turns out that an expert body becomes informally, in an implicit manner, the actual decision-maker[10]. This is caused not only due to the lack of personnel in the Commission's administrative apparatus who are specialised in every area important for the dynamic internal market, but also because the creation of a specific regulatory agency leads to the gradual reduction in importance

---

8 More G. Permanand, E. Vos, 'Between Health and the Market: The Roles of the European Medicines Agency and European Food Safety Authority', *Maastricht Faculty of Law Working Paper*, No. 4, 2008, pp. 8–12.

9 See e.g. Font, 'Informal Rules', pp. 5 ff.

10 Busuioc, 'Blurred Areas', pp. 384, 389 ff.

of the roles of the existing structures dealing with similar subject matter within the Commission[11]. The complexity of the internal market, on the one hand, is signified by a multitude of problems that have to be subjected to broadly understood regulation; on the other hand, due to the rapid growth of this market, ever more narrow specialisation is required as well as the necessity to have, and continuously improve expertise in a particular area. The Commission's attachment to the agencies' opinions and other expert documents is also grounded in the authority that these bodies have, the desire to maintain their independent position as well as the necessity to comply with procedural requirements defined in many founding regulations and detailed sectoral regulations that explicitly regulate the need to abide by agency recommendations[12]. The authority of regulatory agencies largely depends on policymakers. If the documents that they prepare were not respected by the EU institutions and the member states, one of the main elements of legitimising their existence would disappear. This is because the legitimacy of agency activities is derived primarily from their "expert input" into the development of the European integration process[13].

Frontex, in the face of the refugee crisis that has severely affected Europe for the past several years, is an agency that in 2016 underwent a profound transformation. Criticism of its previous actions prompted reforms that resulted in the broadening of the catalogue of its competencies as well as its institutional reorganisation. EBA, on the other hand, is an agency that, just like EFSA, was created as a direct response to a particular crisis. Despite many earlier proposals to establish an EU financial supervisory agency, all of them were rejected over the years as unrealistic due to a lack of political will on the part of the member

---

11 Paradoxically this does not mean a reduction in the Commission's bureaucratic apparatus. Quite the contrary, it has been expanding in parallel to the growth of the agency system. See empirical studies Egeberg *et al.*, 'Building Executive Power', pp. 25–28.

12 It is so, for example, in the case of technical standards issued by EBA, ESMA and EIOPA which the Commission cannot change without prior consultation with the relevant agency. See R. van Gestel, T. van Golen, 'Enforcement by the New European Supervisory Agencies: Quis Custodiet Ipsos Custodes?', in: K.P. Purnhagen, P. Rott (ed.), *Varieties of European Economic Law and Regulation: Liber Amicorum for Hans Micklitz*, New York 2014, p. 772; C. Ohler, 'Die Einheitlichkeit der europäischen Aufsichtsarchitektur und die Besonderheit der Versicherungswirtschaft', *Zeitschrift für die gesamte Versicherungswissenschaft*, Vol. 101, No. 4, 2012, p. 444.

13 More T. Gehring, S. Krapohl, 'Supranational Regulatory Agencies between Independence and Control: The EMEA and the Authorization of Pharmaceuticals in the European Single Market', *Journal of European Public Policy*, Vol. 14, No. 2, 2007, pp. 209, 215.

states. The 2008–2010 financial crisis radically changed their attitude, forcing decisive steps in the shape of a reform of the normative and institutional system within the integrated European financial market[14]. EBA was established together with its twin agencies: ESMA and EIOPA. All three are considered to be the most powerful among the existing regulatory agencies. They are the best example of transforming the agency model, primarily due to the catalogue of semi-regulatory and decision-making tasks that have been assigned to them. EBA was chosen from among the three financial supervision agencies due to its special role in the so-called Banking Union, a network created to ensure stability in the European banking market[15].

All the four agencies selected as examples of the evolution of these bodies are marked by a strong mandate, whether conferred immediately in their founding regulations (EBA), strengthened along the way just as their competencies actually expanded (EFSA, ECHA) or modified *de jure* by the provisions of a new founding regulation (Frontex). They are good examples confirming the claim, debated for several years in the literature dedicated to the agency system, that the role of such bodies, due to a change in the attitude of the EU institutions as well as the member states towards them, will constantly and systematically evolve[16]. There is a great demand for including agencies – which theoretically are neutral, professional entities – more decisively into the process of creating robust sector-specific policies. Agencies are elevated from the role of an advisor or an assistant in the implementation of European law to the role of a "co-decision maker"[17] and they are gradually becoming entities with an actual capacity for action in a particular sector of the market at the EU level. This is possible thanks to

---

14 See E. Chiti, 'In the Aftermath of the Crisis – The EU Administrative System between Impediments and Momentum', *Cambridge Yearbook of European Legal Studies*, Vol. 17, No. 1, 2015, pp. 313 ff.

15 More J.J. Węc, 'Proces konstytuowania Unii Bankowej. Geneza, podstawy prawna, cele i zasady działania', *Rocznik Integracji Europejskiej*, No. 8, 2014, pp. 33 ff.

16 See M. Everson, 'European Agencies: Barely Legal?', in: Everson *et al.* (ed.), *European Agencies*, pp. 62 ff.; H.C.H. Hofmann, 'A European Regulatory Union? The Role of Agencies and Standards', in: P. Koutrakos, J. Snell (ed.), *Research Handbook on the Law of the EU's Internal Market*, Cheltenham 2017, pp. 462 ff.; M. Egeberg, J. Trondal, 'Agencification of the European Union Administration. Connecting the Dots', *TARN Working Paper*, No. 1, 2016, pp. 5 ff.; S. Augsberg, 'Agencification der Kommissionsverwaltung', *Europarecht*, Beiheft, No. 1, 2016, pp. 134 ff.

17 Busuioc *et al.*, 'The Phenomenon', p. 6.

an increasing number of tasks being transferred directly to agencies. This peculiar "task expansion" has a direct functional foundation, i.e. it results from the demand that emerges e.g. in crisis situations and forces the member states to search for long-term solutions while taking into account the common interests of many markets, not just vested national interests[18].

2. The European Food Safety Authority – EFSA

a) Creation and Design

The European Food Safety Authority was created in 2002 as a reaction to the food crises of the 1990s[19], which caused a sharp drop in consumer trust both towards governmental authorities as well as the legal and institutional mechanisms designed to ensure food safety[20]. It turned out that, in the face of rapidly spreading threats throughout the internal market, authorities of the individual member states were powerless, and instruments at the disposal of those at the supranational, pan-European level were insufficient. This prompted a search for effective solutions to find a way out of the deadlock, both in the institutional dimension – i.e. better coordination of actions performed both by European and nation-state level bodies – and in the normative dimension, in order to achieve greater coherence in applicable legislation[21]. A programming document was published in 2000, outlining changes in both of these dimensions, entitled the "White Paper on Food Safety"[22]. It announced the establishment of a regulatory agency involved primarily in the formulation of independent scientific opinions on risk assessment and risk communication in the food market. Risk management, as well as taking decisions and actions to ensure and restore stability in

18 Egeberg *et al.*, 'Building Executive Power', p. 21.

19 BSE and the foot-and-mouth disease as well as contamination of food in the European market with dangerous dioxins.

20 The legal basis for the creation of the Agency are Article 114 TFEU (former Article 95 TEC) and Article 168(4) lit. b TFEU (former Article 152(4) lit. b TEC).

21 For more about the circumstances surrounding the creation of EFSA see C. Roederer-Rynning, C. Daugbjerg, 'Power Learning or Path Dependency? Investigating the Roots of the European Food Safety Authority', *Public Administration*, Vol. 88, No. 2, 2010, pp. 320 ff.; L. Hellebø Rykkja, 'Independent Food Agencies – Restoring Confidence', *Policy and Society. An Interdisciplinary Journal of Policy Research*, Vol. 23, No. 4, 2004, pp. 127 ff.

22 European Commission, *White Paper on Food Safety*, COM(2000) 719 final, 12.1.2000.

the food market in a crisis situation, remained the responsibility of the European Commission[23].

The idea that inspired such a clear distinction between risk assessment and risk management was a reflection of the fears related to the possibility of regulatory agencies snatching "sovereign" competencies, or those directly associated with political action. In simple terms, risk management is the art of controlling and reconciling various interests, it involves the allocation of resources, defining and accomplishing objectives as well as searching for pragmatic compromises based on the initial assumptions made[24]. Management associated with the political decision-making process was supposed to form part of the competencies of the European Commission and other institutions engaged in legislative action at the EU level. Interestingly, this division of tasks was determined by a desire to ensure appropriate democratic legitimacy for the EU institutions' activities. Entrusting broad political powers to independent regulatory agencies would mean, according to the opponents of that solution – including the then European Commissioner for Health and Consumer Protection, David Byrne – that the democratic accountability of European decision-makers would be diluted[25]. The "White Paper on Food Safety" cited the arguments relating to the position of the Commission enshrined in primary law, which is supposed to perform specific legislative and controlling functions. A transfer of such powers outside of the Commission would entail making necessary changes in the Treaty law[26].

---

23 *Ibid.*, p. 14 ff. See Permanand, Vos, 'Between Health', pp. 20, 25.

24 See an overview of the definitions in: Bieleń, *Polityka*, p. 13.

25 See D. Byrne, 'The Genesis of EFSA and the First 10 Years of EU Food Law', in: A. Alemanno, S. Gabbi (ed.), *Foundations of EU Food Law and Policy. Ten Years of the European Food Safety Authority*, Farnham/Burlington 2014, p. 18.

26 See Point 32, *White Paper on Food Safety*, COM(2000) 719 final, p. 14: "The inclusion of risk management in the mandate of the Authority would raise three very serious issues. Firstly, there is a serious concern that a transfer of regulatory powers to an independent Authority could lead to an unwarranted dilution of democratic accountability. The current decision-making process provides a high degree of accountability and transparency, which could be difficult to replicate in a decentralised structure. Secondly, the control function must be at the heart of the Commission's risk management process if it is to act effectively on behalf of the consumer, notably in ensuring that recommendations for action arising from control are properly followed up. The Commission must retain both regulation and control if it is to discharge the responsibilities placed upon it under the Treaties. Thirdly, an Authority with regulatory power could not be created under the current institutional arrangements of the European Union, and would require modification of the existing provisions of the EC

EFSA is a typical assistance agency, or pre-decision-making agency, which actively participates in the phase preceding the issuance of specific legal instruments by the Commission[27]. It is assumed, based on the concepts described above which analyse institutional isomorphism, that EFSA was modelled on the regulatory authorities in France and Ireland, which were created as expert bodies rather than strictly regulatory ones[28]. EFSA was the first EU agency whose unique position was so strongly emphasised, on account of the distinguished importance of the expert opinions that it issued. This thought was first expressed in the 2000 "White Paper" and later formulated in Article 22(2) of Regulation No. 178/2002 which oversees the issues related to the Europeanisation of food law, and established the EFSA[29]. According to that provision, "the Authority shall provide scientific advice and scientific and technical support for the Community's legislation and policies in all fields which have a direct or indirect impact on food and feed safety".

EFSA was thus conceived as an agency, the expert opinions of which, as well as its professional advice were to constitute a scientific foundation for legal acts developed by EU institutions[30]. EFSA has no power to issue general, legally binding and effective *erga omnes* legal acts[31]. The specialised documents it elaborates, however, are considered to be so-called soft law acts, which, although formally are not binding, often play a crucial role when it comes to the wording of EU regulations or directives. The starting point for the establishment of the agency was the idea that the high quality of expert documents developed by this body would directly correspond with its greater level of independence from political influence and pressures. According to Article 22(7) of Regulation No. 178/2002, EFSA is supposed to be an "independent advisor" that acts in a reliable and transparent way, in close cooperation with competent institutions in

---

Treaty. For these reasons, it is not proposed to transfer risk management competencies to the Authority".

27 See J. Molinier, 'L'élaboration d'un cadre commun aux agences de l'Union', in: J. Molinier (ed.), *Les agences de l'Union européenne. Collection droit de l'Union européenne dirigée par Fabrice Picod*, Bruxelles 2011, p. 227; Hansen-Nootbaar, *Unabhängigkeit*, p. 68.

28 *Cf.* Roederer-Rynning, Daugbjerg, 'Power Learning', pp. 322, 325 ff.

29 Regulation (EC) No. 178/2002 of 28.1.2002 laying down the general principles and requirements of food law, establishing the European Food Safety Authority and laying down procedures in matters of food safety, OJ 2002, L 31/1.

30 Busuioc, 'Blurred Areas', p. 383.

31 See C. Pintado, 'A Taxonomy of EFSA's Scientific Outputs', in: Alemanno, Gabbi (ed.), *Foundations*, p. 29.

the member states. The idea that inspired the initiators of the agency was primarily connected with the desire to restore consumer trust in the European food market. The agency was expected to earn that trust with its special role as a coordinator of the national regulatory authorities with its high-quality expertise.

EFSA did not obtain equivalent powers to those conferred on EMA, which issues opinions on business licenses for medicinal products in accordance with a centralised, pan-European procedure[32]. EMA also has the power to charge pharmaceutical companies fees, thanks to which it is financially more independent than agencies that only have resources allocated in the EU budget, as is the case with EFSA[33]. This body has a budget of approx. eighty million euros, which is smaller than the budget of Frontex, but much bigger than that of EBA. The agency employs approx. four hundred and forty people. This ranks it as one of the biggest EU agencies[34].

The position of the EFSA, which is slightly weaker than was originally envisaged, resulted from a compromise between the EU institutions and the member states. The Commission and the European Parliament advocated the broadening of the new body's powers and adopting Anglo-Saxon models. However, the member states considered food safety issues to be particularly sensitive and were reluctant to shift tasks from the national to the EU level, even if they were to take a similar form to that of the EMA rather than those in powerful national authorities, such as the FDA in the U.S.[35]. Yet the creation of a body to stimulate existing cooperation seemed not only a natural, but also a necessary solution. In the face of the cross-border food crises, it became clear that nation states were unable to cope with such threats on their own. The food crises were one of

---

32 Regulation (EC) No. 726/2004. See Gehring, Krapohl, 'Supranational Regulatory Agencies', pp. 209 ff.

33 For a comparison of the competencies of EFSA and EMA see Krapohl, 'Credible Commitment', pp. 530 ff.; Permanand, Vos, 'Between Health', pp. 17 ff. For a comparison of their autonomous position see M. Groenleer, 'Agency Autonomy Actually: Managerial Strategies, Legitimacy, and the Early Development of the European Union's Agencies for Drug and Food Safety Regulation', *International Public Management Journal*, Vol. 17, No. 2, 2014, pp. 265–276.

34 European Court of Auditors, 'Report on the Annual Accounts of the European Food Safety Authority for the Financial Year 2016 Together with the Agency's Reply', OJ 2017, C 417/115.

35 See Roederer-Rynning, Daugbjerg, 'Power Learning', pp. 320, 327; A. Alemanno, 'The European Food Safety Authority at Five', *European Food and Feed Law Review*, Vol. 3, No. 1, 2008, pp. 3 ff.

the first events that simultaneously affected many European markets with huge destructive force[36].

Globalisation processes understood as liberalisation, deregulation, and dismantling barriers to the flow of resources between countries, not only involved economic benefits for the cooperating parties, but also generated more risks and increased the vulnerability of the entire system globally and regionally. In economic literature the term "systemic risk" was coined in this context, this meant the possibility that a largely unpredictable event could destabilise the functioning of the entire economic system[37]. It is a sudden threat that can trigger a cross-border crisis destabilising the economies of many countries. Therefore, a debate started in the mid-1990s, in the context of food regulations, about the need to create a pan-European system that would enable more effective risk assessment, demonstrate higher levels of transparency than the hitherto existing forms of cooperation and create clear-cut control mechanisms[38].

Attempts to overcome a crisis are usually accompanied by the conviction that only the "brightest minds" can find the right solution in a difficult situation. Hence, tasks related to risk assessment and information management in a specific sector are entrusted to expert bodies. These experts, specialists, and professionals are supposed to have almost supernatural abilities enabling them to deal with complex challenges such as threats in the agricultural market, the collapse of financial markets, the debt crisis in the particular member states or the refugee crisis. EFSA was one of the first EU regulatory agencies created distinctly as a direct – "expert" – response to a crisis[39].

---

36 Permanand, Vos, 'Between Health', pp. 14 ff.

37 Concerning systemic risk in the context of the EU market, see C. Ohler, 'Back in Balance? The EU and the Challenges of International Financial Regulation', in: D. Kochenov, F. Amtenbrink (ed.), *European Union's Shaping of the International Legal Order*, New York 2014, pp. 298–300.

38 See K.T. Paul, 'The Europeanization of Food Safety: A Discourse-Analytical Approach', *Journal of European Public Policy*, Vol. 19, No. 4, 2012, pp. 553 ff.; E. Vos, 'Responding the Catastrophe: Towards a New Architecture for EU Food Safety Regulation', in: C.F. Sabel, J. Zeitlin (ed.), *Experimentalist Governance in the European Union: Towards a New Architecture*, Oxford 2010, pp. 152 ff.

39 It was also one of the first agencies to be assigned emerging risk tasks. See A. Kocharov, 'EFSA and Identification of Emerging Risks', *European Food and Feed Law Review*, Vol. 5, No. 3, 2010, p. 144.

b) Structure and Tasks

The mandate of the EFSA was defined in detail in Articles 29 and 31 of Regulation No. 178/2002, which specified when it can issue scientific opinions as well as provide scientific and technical assistance. It can issue opinions on its own initiative or at the request of the Commission, the European Parliament and every member state[40]. It also provides scientific and technical assistance at the request of the European Commission within any domain in the scope of its mission. Such assistance includes, for example, supporting the Commission in the establishment and evaluation of technical criteria as well as the development of technical guidelines. In order to ensure professional advice for the EU institutions and the member states, EFSA draws support from an extensive body of experts. The structure of the agency includes a scientific and research division consisting of a Scientific Committee and ten permanent Scientific Panels. They are a continuation of the structures that existed before EFSA was created. The first part of the regulatory reform in the European food market involved the establishment of eight Scientific Committees and one Multidisciplinary Scientific Committee at the then General Directorate for Consumer Policy and Fisheries which were to provide expert assistance to the Commission in the legislative process. It turned out, however, that the capacity of such bodies embedded within the Commission itself was insufficient[41].

The structure of EFSA reflects this evolution. The Scientific Committee acts as a body coordinating the work of permanent Scientific Panels. This ensures the procedural consistency of scientific opinions, particularly in the context of implementing working procedures and harmonising working methods in individual panels. It also delivers opinions on multi-sectoral issues falling within the competence of more than one Scientific Panel. In special cases it can also set up working groups that can be composed of external experts. Among the Committee

40 It cannot issue documents of this kind at the request of other entities from outside the EU. The idea that led to its creation involved risk management within the EU, hence the agency performs "service functions" for entities within the EU system. See M. Groenleer, S. Gabbi, 'Regulatory Agencies of the European Union as International Actors. Legal Framework, Development over Time and Strategic Motives in the Case of the European Food Safety Authority', *European Journal of Risk Regulation*, Vol. 4, No. 4, 2013, p. 484.

41 See D. Chalmers, '"Food for Thought": Reconciling European Risks and Traditional Ways of Life', *Modern Law Review*, Vol. 66, No. 4, 2003, p. 535; V. Silano, 'EFSA's Science Strategy: Taking Stock and Looking Ahead', in: Alemanno, Gabbi (ed.), *Foundations*, p. 23.

members there are chairpersons of the panels and six independent scientific experts[42]. The scientific panels include e.g. the Panel on Dietetic Products, Nutrition and Allergies (NDA), the Panel on Animal Health and Welfare (AHAW) and the Panel on Contaminants in the Food Chain (CONTAM)[43].

According to Article 28 of Regulation No. 178/2002, the Scientific Committee and the permanent Scientific Panels submit opinions on issues and they can organise public hearings if necessary. Scientific opinions constitute the main expression of the agency's advisory activity. In addition to these, there is other scientific output, such as statements, guidance, conclusions and reports[44]. Expert studies prepared by the agency are made public in accordance with the assumptions of the abovementioned concept of New Public Management. The founding regulation repeatedly stressed the independence and objectivity, as well as the transparency, of risk analysis and assessment activities for the European food market[45]. The transparency of activities was explicitly guaranteed in Article 38(1) of Regulation No. 178/2002 which provides for immediate publication of agendas and minutes, protocols from meetings of bodies that constitute the scientific division, as well as their opinions and information on which they are based, reports on the agency's activities, results of scientific studies, rejected requests for issuing opinions, etc. In the case of public consultations, some documents are even published by the agency in a draft version[46].

Transparency also applies to the work of the agency's administrative bodies, including EFSA's main decision-making body – the Management Board, the meetings of which are in principle open[47]. The MB consists of a representative of the European Commission and fourteen highly qualified members, appointed by the Council after consultations with the Parliament from among candidates put forward by the Commission, while ensuring broad geographical distribution

42 The number and names of permanent Scientific Panels can be changed by the Commission at EFSA's request. See Article 28(4) of Regulation No. 178/2002.

43 All the specialists in the bodies of the scientific and research division are appointed by the Management Board upon a proposal from the Executive Director on the basis of a list of candidates put forward after the publication of a relevant call on the EFSA website, in the EU's Official Journal and in renowned scientific publications. See Article 28(5) of Regulation No. 178/2002.

44 For a comment on these documents see Pintado, 'A Taxonomy', pp. 31–39.

45 Articles 6(2), 9, 22(7), 32, 38 and 55(2) of Regulation No. 178/2002. Such postulates were also contained in the *White Paper on Food Safety*, COM(2000) 719 final, p. 9.

46 See Pintado, 'A Taxonomy', p. 31.

47 Article 38(2) of Regulation No. 178/2002.

of the member states and taking into account the experience of candidates in institutions operating in the food market, including consumer organisations[48]. Such a solution reinforces the agency's expert character as it means that its own professionals are selected for the decision-making body. The Executive Director, assisted by the Secretariat, oversees the coordination of the agency's work[49]. He or she is appointed by the MB from a number of candidates proposed by the Commission after being selected through open competition. Before appointment, the candidate nominated by the MB is promptly summoned before the European Parliament to make a statement and answer questions submitted by MEPs[50].

A day-to-day exchange of views with national authorities dealing with food security is made within the Advisory Forum, which is composed of representatives of the relevant national-level institutions in the member states. The Forum is an important platform of collaboration between the EU and national regulatory authorities. Within its framework, early-warning mechanisms are developed. The flow of information on scientific research is carried out in such a way that the duplication of its results is avoided[51]. In addition, EFSA has created so-called focal points enhancing cooperation at the national level and constituting the core of expert domestic networks[52].

The agency also acts as a platform that strengthens cooperation between authorities through the search for data, and its collection and collation. This involves e.g. information on the extent and prevalence of biological risks or the contamination of food and feed. EFSA obtains data, for example, from national institutions and it shares the results of such research with the EU institutions as well as the member states.[53] It is also the authority which controls the consistency of scientific opinions in the field of food safety within the internal market. In a case where discrepancies are identified between its opinions and the documents issued by national regulatory authorities, the Commission's scientific committees or EU agencies, EFSA undertakes action to eliminate them[54]. EFSA is also a

48 Article 25(1) of Regulation No. 178/2002.

49 A graphic illustration of the structure of EFSA's administrative division is available on the EFSA's website: https://www.efsa.europa.eu/sites/default/files/assets/orgchart.pdf (20.3.2018).

50 Article 26(1) of Regulation No. 178/2002.

51 Article 27 of Regulation No. 178/2002.

52 A network of such points was launched in 2007. Their full list is available on the EFSA's website: https://www.efsa.europa.eu/en/people/fpmembers (20.3.2018).

53 Article 33 of Regulation No. 178/2002.

54 Article 30(3) and (4) of Regulation No. 178/2002.

member of the Rapid Alert System for Food and Feed Safety (RASFF), a network created for reporting direct or indirect food-related threats to human health. Besides EFSA, it also includes the member states and the Commission. The latter manages the network, but EFSA is the authority that analyses the data collected through RASFF and issues guidance in specific cases[55]. In a crisis situation that involves a risk to food safety, the Commission sets up a crisis unit in which EFSA also participates as an entity providing scientific and technical assistance[56].

c) Legitimacy

The EFSA is one of the agencies with the strongest technocratic legitimacy which is built, not only on the foundation of the high quality of the expert documents it draws up, but also on the broad participation of the entities involved in the work in the food chain[57]. The concept of food safety in the EU is based on the idea of controlling the entire manufacturing process in accordance with the principle of "from farm to table". EFSA makes use of numerous opportunities for consultations with food producers, non-governmental organisations, research centres and consumers. The participation of the parties interested in the consultation process is supposed to additionally legitimise EFSA's expert activity, allowing the agency to tap into a wider range of data and ensure the transparency of food policy-making[58].

Over more than fifteen years of its existence, EFSA has consistently strengthened its position, becoming one of the most influential regulatory agencies in

---

55 This was so, e.g. in the case of the threat involving the spread of the EHEC virus in 2011. See B. Appel *et al.* (ed.), 'EHEC-Ausbruch 2011. Aufklärung des Ausbruchs entlang der Lebensmittelkette', *Bundesinstitut für Riskobewertung. Wissenschaft*, No. 4, 2011, pp. 15 ff. The issues related to the early-warning system are also regulated in Article 50 of Regulation No. 178/2002. For more about EFSA's activity in RASFF see J. Lawless, 'EFSA under Pressure: Emerging Risks, Emergencies and Crises', in: Alemmano, Gabbi (ed.), *Foundations*, pp. 95 ff.; S. Parisi *et al.*, *Chemistry and Food Safety in the EU. The Rapid Alert System for Food and Feed (RASFF)*, Cham 2016, pp. 19 ff.

56 Article 56(2) of Regulation No. 178/2002.

57 This view is shared by many authors who point to the agency's involvement also in cooperation with international organisations and third countries in the area of food safety. See Groenleer, Gabbi, 'Regulatory Agencies', p. 480.

58 See EFSA's stakeholders: https://www.efsa.europa.eu/en/partnersnetworks/stakeholder (20.3.2018). In the context of stakeholders' engagement, we can talk about social values of legitimacy. See Hellebø Rykkja, 'Independent Food Agencies', p. 126.

the internal market[59]. Although it has no formal decision-making powers, it has built its strong position on the foundation of expert knowledge and the high quality of the opinions it draws up. In this context, it is even called a "normative authority" that influences indirectly, through the opinions of its experts, the activities of the Commission, the member states, private entities, and even national courts[60]. Its mandate has been developed thanks to the Commission, which, using the provisions of Articles 29 and 31 of Regulation No. 178/2002, makes active use of the agency's expert assistance on all the food safety issues in accordance with a broad understanding of the EFSA's mission mentioned in its founding regulation[61]. The mandate of the EFSA has also been strengthened thanks to provisions included in sector-specific legal acts such as regulations and directives shaping the EU legal framework in the field of genetically modified food[62].

3. The European Chemicals Agency - ECHA

a) Creation and Design

The European Chemicals Agency is a "sister" agency of the EFSA, but unlike the latter, it is able to issue general and abstract decisions that are binding on entities from outside the EU institutional system[63]. ECHA was officially launched in June 2007[64] and from the very beginning of its functioning it has been perceived

---

59 Empirical research indicates that EFSA, along with ECHA, is one of the most independent agencies in the EU system. See Wonka, Rittberger, 'Credibility', p. 740. Groenleer holds a different opinion, claiming that EFSA is less independent than its founding regulations suggests, 'Agency Autonomy', p. 257.

60 *Cf.* Chalmers, 'Food for Thought', pp. 538–542; Vos, 'Responding', pp. 156 ff.

61 Pintado, 'A Taxonomy', p. 30; T. Riesz, 'Europäische Gesundheitsagenturen - zugleich ein Beitrag zum Europäischen Arzneimittelzulassungssystem', in: Raschauer (ed.), *Europäische Agenturen*, p. 160.

62 E.g. Regulation (EC) No. 1829/2003 of 22.9.2003 on genetically modified food and feed, OJ 2003, L 268/1; Commission Implementing Regulation (EU) No. 503/2013 of 3.4.2013 on applications for the authorisation of genetically modified food and feed, OJ 2013, L 157/1; Directive No. 2001/18/EC of 12.3.2001 on the deliberate release into the environment of genetically modified organisms, OJ 2001, L 106/1.

63 See A. Orator, *Möglichkeiten und Grenzen der Einrichtung von Unionsagenturen*, Tübingen 2017, p. 173.

64 ECHA in fact became operational a year later. See J. Wettestad, 'Do New EU Agencies Mean Decreased National Powers? The Case of Chemicals and Norway', *FNI Report*, No. 14, 2014, p. 7.

as an expression of the EU's expanding executive capacity obtained with the aid of the agency system[65]. It has become one of the more important symbols of the centralisation of regulatory powers in a given market sector at the EU level. It was introduced as a controversial institutional solution as part of the reform of the European law on chemicals, which involved the establishment of the REACH system. The document that modernised its existing legal status was Regulation (EC) No. 1907/2006 of 18 December 2006 concerning the Registration, Evaluation, Authorisation and Restriction of Chemicals (REACH) as well as the establishment of the ECHA[66]. The terms included in the name of the system, that is Registration, Evaluation, Authorisation and Restriction of Chemicals, constitute the core of the EU's strategy for the safe production and use of chemicals in the European markets.

The idea of establishing an agency engaged, not just in informational, preparatory or coordinating, but also decision-making tasks in the area of European chemicals trade triggered a lengthy, heated debate which exposed the aspirations of, and tensions between, the EU institutions and the member states which had different opinions on the reform of the regulatory framework in this field[67]. The system for chemical trading in the European markets that preceded the introduction of REACH was dominated by the activity of national regulatory authorities that cooperated with the Commission. The European Chemicals Bureau operated under its auspices. It constituted part of the Institute for Health and Consumer Protection (IHCP), operating along with other research institutes

---

65 See M. Martens, 'Executive Power in the Making: The Establishment of the European Chemicals Agency', in: Busuioc *et al.* (ed.), *The Agency Phenomenon*, pp. 42 ff.; T. Ehnert, *The European Chemicals Agency. Beyond the Scope of the Meroni Doctrine?*, Maastricht 2008, pp. 7 ff.

66 OJ 2006, L 396/1. The legal basis for this regulation and thus for the ECHA was Article 114 TFEU. Plans to create the REACH system were outlined in the Commission's 2001 "White Paper": *White Paper. Strategy for a Future Chemicals Policy*, COM(2001) 88 final, 27.2.2001. The proposal set out in this document did not provide for the establishment of a regulatory agency. It was only proposed that the coordinating powers of the European Chemicals Bureau should be expanded. See Martens, 'Executive Power', pp. 49 ff.

67 See E. Rehbinder, 'Die REACH-Verordnung – Entstehungsgeschichte, Zielsetzung, Anwendungsbereich, Hauptinhalte', in: R. Hendler *et al.*, *Neues europäisches Chemikalienrecht (REACH)*, Berlin 2008, pp. 36 ff.

within the JRC established by the Commission[68]. These bodies were primarily responsible for collecting and evaluating data. As integration advanced, the existing normative and institutional solutions appeared to be insufficient. Hence the idea of intensifying harmonisation efforts in the field of the European law on chemicals e.g. by introducing mechanisms for information flow and decision making within REACH with regard to all the chemicals available in the internal market.

The main innovation was a general obligation to register all the substances produced in, or imported into, the EU in quantities of one tonne or more per year[69]. The objective of REACH is to ensure a high level of human health and protection of the natural environment as well as the free movement of substances in their original form, such as components in mixtures and in products, while enhancing the competitiveness and innovativeness of the European chemical industry. The provisions of Regulation No. 1907/2006 apply in various degrees to virtually all companies, not just businesses from the chemical sector. Producers and importers have the most obligations, mainly involving registration, while distributors have the least, since their activities are limited to providing information within the supply chain[70].

The REACH system comprehensively regulates the safety assessment of chemical substances in the entire supply chain, since downstream users have also been included in the performance of control obligations. The wording of the regulation that introduced new arrangements in the field of chemical safety was the subject of fierce debates in 2003–2006. The primary objective was to maintain the consistency of the proposed solutions and the widest possible control scope of chemical substances in the European markets. The guiding principle was to introduce a registration requirement for all manufactured and traded substances as well as to shift risk assessment obligations from the remit of administrative entities to the level of businesses operating in the chemical industry as it is broadly understood[71]. The eventual effect was described by commentators as, "the biggest EU regulation ever undertaken"[72].

---

68 *Cf.* M. Bronckers, Y. van Gerven, 'Legal Remedies under the EC's New Chemicals Legislation REACH: Testing a New Model of European Governance', *Common Market Law Review*, Vol. 46, No. 6, 2009, p. 1826; Martens, 'Executive Power', p. 46.

69 Article 6(1) of Regulation No. 1907/2006.

70 See G. Mielczarek, 'Rola systemu REACH w zarządzaniu chemikaliami', in: A. Lesiuk (ed.), *Praktyka ochrony środowiska*, Lublin 2015, p. 80.

71 Recital 18 of Regulation No. 1907/2006.

72 I. Gubbels-van Hal, J. Pelkmans, 'Is REACH Going Well?', *CEPS Policy Brief*, No. 198, 2009, pp. 1 ff.; E. Stokes, S. Vaughan, 'Great Expectations: Reviewing 50 Years of

The main authority within REACH is the ECHA, which "should be central to ensuring that chemical legislation and the decision-making processes and scientific basis underlying it have credibility with all of the stakeholders and the public"[73]. In order to bring this about, the agency needs to earn the trust of the EU institutions, the member states and the public with regard to its activities. Therefore, according to the assumptions of Regulation No. 1907/2006, it is vital to ensure that ECHA has an independent position as well as high scientific, technical and regulatory capacities and that it operates in a transparent and efficient way[74]. This became particularly important in light of the political background during the ECHA's establishment[75].

b) Structure

Implementation of these assumptions is supposed to be partly facilitated by a clear division of tasks in the organisational structure of the agency. The Management Board is composed of representatives of the member states, who are formally appointed by the Council, as well as up to six representatives appointed by the Commission, including three non-voting representatives from the interested parties, and two independent persons appointed by the European Parliament. Board members are nominated on the basis of their experience and expertise in the field of chemical safety or chemical regulations[76]. The agency's

Chemicals Legislation in the EU', *Journal of Environmental Law*, Vol. 25, No. 3, 2013, pp. 416 ff. There are also opinions in academic literature that describe it as a "flagship regulation" or "milestone in the EC's legislative activities", see Bronckers, van Gerven, "Legal Remedies", p. 1870.

73 Recital 95 of Regulation No. 1907/2006.

74 *Ibid.*

75 In addition to disputes over the scope of its competences, the member states actively competed for the seats of the newly created bodies. Finland lost a fierce rivalry with Italy for the seat of the EFSA and, in compensation, was given the right to host the ECHA. Due to this agency's importance in the development of sectoral regulations, it was considered to be a major achievement of Finnish diplomacy. *Cf.* I. Jasinskaja-Lahti, M. Laine (ed.), 'Founding the European Chemicals Agency: The Perspectives of the Employees and the Authorities of the City of Helsinki', *City of Helsinki Urban Facts. Research Series*, No. 7, 2009, pp. 13 ff. Despite the advantages of locating the agency in Helsinki outlined in the report, surveys carried out by Groenleer pointed to problems associated with placing the seat of one of the most important EU agencies for the internal market in "peripheral" Helsinki according to some EU officials, *The Autonomy*, p. 125. For more about the difficulties with finding experts willing to relocate and start work in Helsinki see Stokes, Vaughan, 'Great Expectations', p. 428.

76 Article 79(1) and (2) of Regulation No. 1907/2006.

legal representative is the Executive Director, designated by the MB on the basis of a list of candidates drawn up by the Commission following an open call for expressions of interest. Before his or her appointment, the selected candidate makes a statement before the European Parliament and answers questions from MEPs. The ED is chosen on the grounds of his or her expertise and experience in the field of chemical safety or law on chemicals[77]. He or she is assisted in his or her work by the Secretariat, which mainly performs technical and administrative tasks[78].

The ECHA, similarly to the EFSA, has an extensive scientific division that includes the Member State Committee (MSC), the Committee for Risk Assessment (RAC), the Committee for Socio-Economic Analysis (SEAC) and the Biocidal Products Committee (BPC). Members of MSC and BPC are directly designated by the member states, whereas members of RAC and SEAC are selected by the MB from a number of candidates proposed by the member states. The committees can add five more members to their composition, who are chosen on the basis of their specific qualifications. The term of office for all of them is three years and can be renewed. The committees can create working groups and also make use of support from external experts. Committee members are supported with the aid of scientific and technical resources available to the member states as well as competent national regulatory authorities that are supposed to facilitate the activities of the ECHA's scientific committees and their working groups[79].

The MSC is a platform designed to facilitate agreement between the member states[80]. It participates in several REACH processes, such as evaluation and authorisation. Compromise solutions are worked out at its meetings with the

---

77 Article 84 of Regulation No. 1907/2006.

78 Articles 76(1) lit. g and 77(2) of Regulation No. 1907/2006.

79 Article 85 of Regulation No. 1907/2006 and Article 75 of Regulation (EU) No. 528/2012 of 22.5.2012 concerning the making available on the market and use of biocidal products, OJ 2012, L 167/1. See information on the commitees on the ECHA's website: https://echa.europa.eu/about-us/who-we-are/member-state-committee; https://echa.europa.eu/about-us/who-we-are/committee-for-risk-assessment; https://echa.europa.eu/about-us/who-we-are/committee-for-socio-economic-analysis; https://echa.europa.eu/about-us/who-we-are/biocidal-products-committee (20.3.2018).

80 The MSC is an important control mechanism which is particularly significant in the context of ECHA's decision-making powers. Therefore, one can rightly agree with the statement that "the influence of the member states in the governance of ECHA is more substantial than in regard to other European agencies, such as EFSA", Bronckers, van Gerven, 'Legal Remedies', p. 1829.

aim of eliminating any potential discrepancies of opinions between the member states and divergences regarding requests for the identification of substances of very high concern. Moreover, the Committee issues opinions on guidance, drafted by the ECHA, concerning the list of substances subject to the procedure of authorisation[81]. In cases where no agreement is reached in the MSC, the issue is passed on to the discretion of the European Commission. The three remaining committees, in turn, draft expert opinions on behalf of ECHA within their areas of responsibility. Apart from that, they are concerned with e.g. the risk posed by specific substances to human health and the environment as well as the socio-economic impact of legislative actions referring to chemicals or issues related to the availability and use of biocidal products. The final decisions, on the basis of ECHA opinions, which are drafted by individual committees, are made by the Commission. Proposals are elaborated by the committees on the basis of consensus, but if it is not possible for this to be attained, then decisions are made by a voting majority. Both the justification for the particular position of the ECHA committee and the explanations for minority positions are disclosed[82].

An important coordinating body is the Forum for Exchange of Information on Enforcement (Forum). It supervises the network of national regulatory authorities responsible for enforcing compliance with REACH legislation. The Forum's main objective is to ensure consistent harmonisation in the field of the law on chemicals. Its tasks, therefore, include the dissemination of good practices, coordination of the implementation of law into national legal systems, improving information flow processes and coordinating the exchange of inspectors. The Forum is composed of national representatives and the European Commission, as well as, optionally, invited experts and representatives of interested parties organisations accredited to ECHA. Specific solutions for enforcing certain legal standards are developed within ten working groups. The Forum only uses "soft measures", it cannot formulate binding guidance on enforcing REACH provisions[83].

c) Tasks within the REACH System

The REACH system, in accordance with its name, has created several groups of tasks where ECHA plays a central role in their implementation. Among

81 *Ibid.*, p. 1825. See Article 77(3) of Regulation No. 1907/2006.

82 Article 85(8) of Regulation No. 1907/2006. See information on the tasks of all the committees on the ECHA website: https://echa.europa.eu/about-us (20.3.2018).

83 Article 86 of Regulation No. 1907/2006.

those there are: registration, evaluation, authorisation and relevant restrictions as far as chemicals are concerned. The remit of ECHA has also been broadened by adding detailed legal acts, such as regulations of biocidal products, making them available for use in the market, and the regulation referring to the classification, labelling and packaging of substances and mixtures[84]. The agency's mandate was broadly formulated in Article 77(1) of Regulation No. 1907/2006. According to that provision, ECHA is supposed to provide the member states and the EU institutions with "the best possible scientific and technical advice on questions relating to chemicals which fall within its remit and which are referred to it".

Several changes have been adopted within REACH with the purpose of improving the management and control of the trade of chemicals on EU territory. The division between "new" and "existing" chemical substances was abandoned, with all substances and mixtures being subjected to control mechanisms[85]. The most important of them is the obligation to register relevant activities. Without meeting this requirement, substances on their own and as components of preparations or products, cannot be produced or placed on the market on EU territory. Implementation of the obligation to register products, following the principle "no data, no market", is linked to entrusting a range of tasks to ECHA which replaced national regulatory authorities in this regard[86]. Registration documents are submitted to the agency by all producers and importers of substances that are placed on the market in a quantity of at least one tonne per year. The obligation to register was also imposed regarding substances already "existing" in the market and those introduced before 1981. They are described as Phase-in Substances[87]. Regulation No. 1907/2006 specified registration deadlines for them, understood

---

84 See Regulation No. 528/2012 and Regulation (EC) No. 1272/2008 of 16.12.2008 on classification, labelling and packaging of substances and mixtures, OJ 2008, L 353/1. For more about the characteristics of the ECHA's tasks, see M. Schlögl, 'Europäische Agenturen im Umweltrecht. EUA und ECHA', in: Raschauer (ed.), *Europäische Agenturen*, pp. 200–207.

85 "Existing" chemicals are those that were placed on the European market before 18.9.1981 while the "new" ones are those placed after that date. More *ibid.*, p. 200.

86 Article 5 of Regulation No. 1907/2006.

87 It was estimated that in 2010–2018 about thirty thousand Phase-in Substances would be subjected to registration in the ECHA procedure. But the first phases of registration already signified that these estimates were too low. See Gubbels-van Hal, Pelkmans, 'Is REACH', p. 5.

as dates by which registration dossiers should be sent to the ECHA-run system[88]. The agency manages all registration dossiers.

The REACH regulation specified in detail what information they should include: for example, data on production and safe use of a substance[89]. In the case of substances subject to registration placed on a quantity of at least ten tonnes per registrant, a chemical safety assessment and report are additionally required[90]. ECHA verifies the completeness of the registration dossier and assigns a number to every registration[91]. If data is missing, the agency can refuse registration if the registrant fails to provide the missing data necessary to complete the registration dossier within a prescribed period[92]. It is a binding decision for third parties, i.e. manufacturers or importers, which can be appealed with the ECHA's Board of Appeal[93]. The agency notifies the competent regulatory authority of the relevant member state on whose territory the substance is manufactured or where the importer's headquarters are located[94]. If the information obtained in the registration procedure is not classified, it is made public in ECHA's online database[95]. The obligation to register, transferred by Regulation No. 1907/2006

88 For a list of the deadlines see Mielczarek, 'Rola systemu REACH', pp. 83 ff.; D.J. Knight, 'Chemicals in the European Union. The European Chemicals Agency Experience', *Chemistry International*, Vol. 34, No. 6, 2012, pp. 6 ff.

89 Article 10 and Annex VI of Regulation No. 1907/2006. In the phase preceding final registration, entities approaching ECHA can participate in the Substance Information Exchange Forum (SIEF) which allows for the exchange of information with co-registrants on the submitted substances. See Gubbels-van Hal, Pelkmans, 'Is REACH', p. 6; Bronckers, van Gerven, 'Legal Remedies', pp. 1830 ff.

90 Article 14(1) of Regulation No. 1907/2006.

91 Verification of completeness ("completeness check") does not include assessment of the adequacy or relevance of the submitted data. See Articles 20, 23 and 28 of Regulation No. 1907/2006. About five per cent of applications in each tonnage category is randomly subjected to more detailed control ("compliance check"). See T. Siegel, *Entscheidungsfindung im Verwaltungsverbund*, Tübingen 2009, p. 350; E. Korkea-aho, *Adjudicating New Governance: Deliberative Democracy in the European Union*, Abingdon/New York 2015, p. 118.

92 A characteristics of these powers: Siegel, *Entscheidungsfindung*, p. 313.

93 Articles 20(2) and (5), 91–93 of Regulation No. 1907/2006. The Board of Appeal is a quasi-judicial body that makes it possible to appeal ECHA's decisions in accordance with Article 76(1) lit. h of Regulation No. 1907/2006. More about this body M. Navin-Jones, 'A Legal Review of EU Boards of Appeal in Particular the European Chemicals Agency Board of Appeal', *European Public Law*, Vol. 21, No. 1, 2015, pp. 146 ff.

94 Article 20(4) of Regulation No. 1907/2006.

95 See https://echa.europa.eu/information-on-chemicals (20.3.2018).

to the EU level, made ECHA the entity which entrepreneurs have to initially approach when placing a substance on the internal market. It is, therefore, like other agencies (e.g. EMA), an important link in ensuring so-called pre-market control, before certain products obtain marketing authorisation[96].

The second major group of ECHA's tasks involves the evaluation of registration dossiers. The REACH regulation specifies that verification can include information contained in the technical dossiers, and the assessment and report on chemical safety as well as the registrant's clarifications submitted in specific cases. The agency checks whether all the requirements included in Regulation No. 1907/2006 have been met and whether all the information has been submitted properly[97]. On the basis of document analysis, ECHA may prepare a draft decision requiring the registrants to submit additional information within a specified time limit[98]. ECHA also examines proposals on testing set out in registration documents or downstream user reports. Priority is given to testing of substances of particular relevance for the environment[99]. On the basis of the examination conducted, ECHA makes a decision requiring that a test be carried out and that sets a deadline for the submission of its results. The agency enjoys a broad margin of discretion here, although draft decisions should be made in consultation with the competent national authorities and the MSC according to the procedure specified in Articles 50 and 51 of Regulation No. 1907/2006[100]. In its final decisions, ECHA can e.g. change the testing conditions in relation to the proposal submitted by the registrant. It can also require additional tests or reject the registrant's proposal altogether[101].

As mentioned above, the requirement to assess chemical safety rests with entities registering a substance. One exception is substances that pose a particular risk to human health and the environment. ECHA identifies such priority substances on the basis of registration dossier assessments and compiles a draft Community Rolling Action Plan (CoRAP)[102]. The final plan is adopted on the basis of an MSC's opinion. It includes information such as which substances

---

96 *Cf.* Martens, 'Executive Power', pp. 48 ff.

97 A detailed procedure for verifying documentation was set out in Article 41 of Regulation No. 1907/2006.

98 Article 41(3) of Regulation No. 1907/2006.

99 These can be, for example, substances which are carcinogenic, mutagenic or toxic. See Article 40(1) of Regulation No. 1907/2006.

100 More Siegel, *Entscheidungsfindung*, p. 351.

101 Article 40(3) of Regulation No. 1907/2006.

102 Article 44(1) and (2) of Regulation No. 1907/2006.

require an annual evaluation and which member states are responsible for evaluating certain substances[103]. ECHA coordinates the assessment of priority substances. In the event that two or more member states express an interest in evaluating the same substance and they cannot come to an agreement, the MSC decides which national authority will be competent. In special cases, when this body also fails to reach an agreement, the Commission decides which member state's authorities will be assigned the task[104]. The member states can also submit proposals of priority substances to ECHA at any time, thus requesting their inclusion in CoRAP, which is published on the agency's website[105].

The third major group of the ECHA's tasks involves issuing permits. Particularly dangerous substances, such as toxic, carcinogenic, mutagenic, and those that adversely affect fertility, etc. are "candidates" for inclusion on the list of substances found in Annex XIV[106]. They are described as Substances of Very High Concern (SVHC) and require permits due to their properties[107]. A central procedure for granting permits introduced by the REACH regulation is designed, not only to ensure stringent control over these hazardous agents, but also to lead to their gradual substitution with alternative, less harmful substances or technologies[108]. Requests for permits are filed with the agency and opinions about particular substances are drafted within its structure. A leading role in the process is played by the scientific committees, RAC and SEAC. The final decision on granting authorisation is taken by the European Commission on the basis of the agency's opinion[109]. Permits are, as a rule valid, until the Commission makes

103 Article 44(2) and Article 45(1) of Regulation No. 1907/2006.

104 Article 45(2) and (3) of Regulation No. 1907/2006.

105 Article 45(5) of Regulation No. 1907/2006.

106 Article 57 of Regulation No. 1907/2006. See E. Korkea-aho, 'Effects of the EU Chemicals Regulation REACH in a Globalized Internal Market: FCD and FMB', *Common Market Law Review*, Vol. 53, No. 3, 2016, pp. 766 ff. A list of "candidate" substances is published on ECHA's website: https://echa.europa.eu/candidate-list-table (20.3.2018). Placing a substance on the candidacy list results in a range of information obligations for manufacturers of products containing these substances. See Articles 31 and 33 of Regulation No. 1907/2006.

107 More C. Klika, 'The Implementation of the REACH Authorisation Procedure on Chemical Substances of Concern: What Kind of Legitimacy?', *Politics and Governance*, Vol. 3, No. 1, 2015, pp. 129–133.

108 Article 55 of Regulation No. 1907/2006. See Bronckers, van Gerven, 'Legal Remedies', p. 1833.

109 Articles 60 and 64 of Regulation No. 1907/2006.

a decision to change or withdraw them[110]. The Commission's decisions depend on the level of risk to human health posed by a substance and any possible socio-economic benefits[111]. In addition, when there is "unacceptable" risk posed by a substance to human health or the environment, ECHA can participate in the procedure to adopt or amend current restrictions[112]. An important role in the process is played by the RAC and SEAC, which issue opinions on restrictions for particular substances due to the need to reduce the risk[113].

d) Legitimacy

ECHA is the central authority in the European system. It is the only one of its kind in the world. The authority is designed to ensure chemical safety in European markets[114]and is, therefore, one of the biggest EU agencies. The institution coordinates the flow of information about chemical substances. It employs nearly six hundred workers and has an annual budget of more than one hundred and ten million euros[115]. Due to its special role, particularly in the registration procedure, it is considered to be a pilot entity in the "European informational network" in the field of data on chemical substances[116]. A wide range of entities involved in chemical regulation and supervision as well as manufacturing, use, import

---

110 Article 61(1) of Regulation No. 1907/2006.

111 Article 60(2) and 4 of Regulation No. 1907/2006. Thorsten Siegel calls it a two-step procedure. Risk to human health is evaluated and in case permits cannot be granted on this basis, also economic and social benefits are evaluated, *Entscheidungsfindung*, pp. 319, 353 ff.

112 Articles 68 and 69 of Regulation No. 1907/2006. See Schlögl, 'Europäische Agenturen', p. 206.

113 Articles 70 and 71 of Regulation No. 1907/2006.

114 M. de Morprugo, 'The European Union as a Global Producer of Transnational Law of Risk Regulation: A Case Study on Chemical Regulation', *European Law Journal*, Vol. 19, No. 6, 2013, pp. 789–793.

115 European Court of Auditors, 'Report on the Annual Accounts of the European Chemicals Agency for the Financial Year 2016 Together with the Agency's Reply', OJ 2017, C 417/98. The agency's budget consists not only of the EU funds, but also of its own resources e.g. in the form of registration fees. See e.g. Articles 6(4), 7(5) and 9(2) of Regulation No. 1907/2006.

116 "ECHA als Informationslotse", see Siegel, *Entscheidungsfindung*, p. 356; Stokes, Vaughan, 'Great Expectations', pp. 426 ff. Article 64(2) of Regulation No. 1907/2006 deserves attention in this context as it establishes an obligation for the agency to provide a wide range of information on chemical substances (in accordance with the procedure set out in Articles 118 and 119 of Regulation No. 1907/2006).

and consumption of products containing chemical substances are included in the relevant cooperation mechanisms. Hence, terms such as a well-developed "European Composite Administration" or "inclusive governance" are used in the context of the REACH system[117].

ECHA is also a platform for communication between the member states and the Commission, playing an important role particularly in risk management tasks for the SVHC[118]. Due to its broad powers, ECHA is considered to be a chief administrator in the institutional and normative framework regulating trade in chemicals in the internal market[119]. The involvement of many entities operating in the European chemical market in the regulatory process under the auspices of the agency strengthens the legitimacy of the entire REACH system, also contributing indirectly to greater efficiency of the instruments used within its framework[120]. Due to the shift of regulatory responsibility to non-state actors and the inclusion of various stakeholders, including primarily small and medium sized enterprises as well as the public in the consultation processes, it can be said that it has a kind of social legitimacy. It distinguishes the REACH system both from solutions used before its introduction and the European regulatory systems in other sectors[121].

4. The European Border and Coast Guard Agency - Frontex

a) Creation

EFSA and ECHA are similar to each other in terms of the area of their activity and are important due to the weight of their specialised expert body of knowledge,

---

117 V. Heyvaert, 'The EU Chemicals Policy: Towards Inclusive Governance?', *LSE Law, Society and Economy Working Papers*, No. 7, 2008, pp. 5 ff.; M. Pawlik, *Das REACH-System und die Meroni-Doktrin. Ein imperfekter Quantensprung im Europäischen Verwaltungsverbund*, Baden-Baden 2013, pp. 16–22. Such a system also allows for more active participation of interested non-EU countries. Concerning the opportunities that REACH and ECHA offer for Norway see Wettestad, 'Do New EU Agencies', p. 10.

118 Knight, 'Chemicals', p. 6.

119 Martens, 'Executive Power', p. 48.

120 Heyvaert, 'The EU Chemicals Policy', pp. 4, 12 ff.

121 Stokes, Vaughan, 'Great Expectations', pp. 413, 429, 433; Klika, 'The Implementation', p. 134; M. Whyte, 'REACH Regulation. Last Tango in Helsinki', *ICIS Chemical Business* of 29.10–4.11.2007.

whereas the European Border and Coast Guard Agency is one of the EU's largest and most powerful operational agencies[122]. Its importance has increased in recent years due to the migration crisis involving a rapidly growing number of refugees and economic migrants who have arrived in Europe since 2015. Frontex was created in October 2004 as the European Agency for the Management of Operational Cooperation at the External Borders of the Member States of the European Union[123]. A major reform, or, indeed, a rebirth of the agency, as some commentators saw it, took place exactly twelve years later[124]. Not only was the name of the institution modified, a decision was also taken to broaden its operational capabilities[125]. Previous modifications of the agency's mandate, carried out through changes to the existing founding regulation, had proven to be insufficient in the face of the enormous challenges associated with the huge migration wave[126]. In particular, the member states situated along migration routes, such as Italy, Greece or Hungary, were unable to cope with the challenges connected with the massive influx of migrants. As a result of the weakness of national systems for managing EU borders, thousands of third-country nationals made it into the

---

122 See Hansen-Nootbar, *Unabhängigkeit*, p. 53; S. Léonard, 'EU Border Security and Migration into the European Union: Frontex and Securitisation through Practices', *European Security*, Vol. 19, No. 2, 2010, pp. 238 ff. Orator classifies Frontex in the group of agencies strengthening cooperation between the member states in a particular area (Germ. *Agenturen zur Kooperations- und Koordinationsförderung*), *Möglichkeiten*, p. 93.

123 Regulation (EC) No. 2007/2004 of 26.12.2004 establishing a European Agency for the Management of Operational Cooperation at the External Borders of the Member States of the European Union, OJ 2004, L 349/1. The legal basis for the establishment of this agency are Article 77(2) lit. b and Article 79(2) lit. c TFEU which concern measures adopted in accordance with the ordinary legislative procedure in the area of controls on persons crossing the EU's external borders and illegal immigration and unauthorised residence. See M. Rossi, 'Art. 77 AEUV', in: Calliess, Ruffert (ed.), *EUV/AEUV*, p. 1094.

124 See the EurActiv comment of 13.10.2016, https://www.euractiv.com/section/justice-home-affairs/news/leggeri-revamped-frontex-will-be-game-changer/ (20.3.2018).

125 Regulation (EC) No. 2016/1624 of 14.9.2016 on the European Border and Coast Guard, OJ 2016, L251/1.

126 They were introduced into Regulation No. 2007/2004 twice: on 11.7.2007 by Regulation (EC) No. 863/2007 (OJ 2007, L 199/30) and on 25.10.2011 by Regulation (EU) No. 1168/2011 (OJ 2011, L 304/1). It was stated in Recital 1 to the new Regulation No. 2016/1624 that radical changes were needed since it was necessary to create a "comprehensive" solution to resolve the problem of "unprecedented migratory flows".

Schengen zone[127]. Frontex in its existing shape turned out to be an inefficient mechanism for cooperation. Therefore, the agency's mandate was broadened in a new founding regulation, elevating its status in the European agency system[128].

b) Structure

The design of Frontex, unlike its most important tasks, did not change much and still has a classic, dual character[129]. The main decision-making body is the Management Board, composed of representatives of member states and two voting representatives of the Commission[130]. Countries associated with the implementation, application and development of the Schengen "acquis" can participate in the work of the MB. Details of such participation are specified in association agreements concluded with these countries[131]. The agency is managed by the Executive Director, independent in the performance of his or her duties, who is appointed by the MB from among candidates proposed by the Commission and selected in a recruitment process announced in the Official Journal of the EU[132].

Due to many concerns over human rights violations by Frontex since the beginning of its existence, several safeguards were introduced after the reform[133].

---

127 T. Tammikko, 'The New Frontex and the Future of Schengen. A Brick Fortress, or a Castle Made of Sand?', *FIIA Briefing Paper*, No. 219, 2017, pp. 3 ff.; S.A. Vasile, 'The European Union Refugee Crisis. A General Description of the Phenomenon and Its Implications on Long-Term Architecture of the European Legislation', *Journal of Criminal Investigations*, No. 2, 2015, pp. 121 ff.

128 The announcement that the position of Frontex would be strengthened and a new founding regulation would be presented came as one of the European Commission's first steps towards the migration crisis: Communication from the Commission to the European Parliament, the Council, the European Economic and Social Committee and the Committee of the Regions, 'A European Agenda on Migration', COM(2015) 240 final, 13.5.2015, pp. 3, 10.

129 See a detailed presentation of the existing institutional structure: E. Barner-Gaedicke, *FRONTEX – Ohne Kontrolle zur europäischen Grenzschutztruppe? Demokratische Kontrolle der Agentur FRONTEX*, Hamburg 2017, pp. 45–53.

130 Articles 62 and 63(1) of Regulation No. 2016/1624.

131 Article 63(3) of Regulation No. 2016/1624.

132 Articles 68 and 69(1) and (2) of Regulation No. 2016/1624.

133 About the weakness of the existing system see E. Papastavridis, '"Fortress Europe" and Frontex: Within or Without International Law?', *Nordic Journal of International Law*, Vol. 79, No. 1, 2010, pp. 81 ff.; J. Santos Vara, S.R. Sánchez-Tabernero, 'In Deep Water: Towards a Greater Commitment for Human Rights in Sea Operations Coordinated by Frontex?', *European Journal of Migration and Law*, Vol. 18, No. 1, 2016,

Firstly, there is the Consultative Forum that supports the MB and the ED on matters involving fundamental rights. Representatives of the two regulatory agencies concerned - EASO and FRA - participate in its work, as well as representatives of the United Nations High Commissioner for Refugees and other organisations that are involved. The Consultative Forum has access to information related to the agency's respect for fundamental rights and has the right to conduct on-the-spot visits to joint operations and rapid interventions, with the consent of the host member state, and return to carry out follow-up inspections[134]. Secondly, an atypical institutional solution within the agency is the appointment of the Fundamental Rights Officer (FRO) who contributes to the elaboration of Frontex's strategy for respecting fundamental rights and then monitors its observance[135]. The third safeguard is the introduction of the so-called complaints mechanism that allows people directly affected by the actions of staff involved in Frontex operations to file complaints about specific breaches of fundamental rights. The complaints are then handled by the FRO[136].

Since its launch in 2005, the agency has carried out its tasks in Warsaw, but for more than a decade of its existence no agreement governing the issue of where the agency should be based has been concluded with the host state. Although a memorandum between the Polish Minister of the Interior and Administration and the agency's Executive Director on the headquarters and other issues related to its functioning was concluded in 2007, the document did not meet the requirements for the sorts of legal acts that are observed in the case of other agencies[137]. It also raised reasonable doubts as to its legal nature, the procedure for concluding it and its consistency with the Polish Constitution[138]. In accordance with the assumptions set out in the 2012 "Common Approach", provisions on the need for an appropriate formal regulation of the issues related to the seats

---

pp. 67 ff. For the broader perspective, see E. Karska (ed.), *Globalne problemy ochrony praw człowieka*, Warszawa 2015.

134 Article 70 of Regulation No. 2016/1624.

135 Article 71 of Regulation No. 2016/1624.

136 Article 72 of Regulation No. 2016/1624.

137 Memorandum of Understanding between the Executive Director of Frontex and the Minister of the Interior and Administration of the Republic of Poland on the Headquarters and Certain other Issues Related to the Functioning of Frontex in the Republic of Poland, Warsaw, 26.3.2007. The document has not been published.

138 See M. Zieliński, 'Porozumienie dotyczące siedziby agencji Unii Europejskiej Frontex w Polsce. Aspekty konstytucyjne', *Przegląd Sejmowy*, Vol. XXIV, No. 1(132), 2016, pp. 54 ff.

of individual agencies appeared both in the changes to Regulation No. 2007/2004 introduced in 2011 and extensively in the new founding Regulation No. 2016/1624[139]. In contrast to the agencies described earlier (EFSA and ECHA), where relevant agreements were signed soon after their creation[140], the negotiating process on the appropriate agreement between Poland and Frontex was arduous and lengthy. It was brought to a successful conclusion with the March 2017 signing of the relevant agreement pursuant to the provisions of the new founding regulation and its ratification by Poland in July 2017[141].

c) Tasks

aa) Background

Frontex is a good example of the weakness of the nomenclature used in relation to EU agencies. In the new regulation, the institution did not obtain decision-making powers similar to those of ECHA, such as authorisation, registration or evaluation powers. Neither is it an agency of normative nature, like EFSA, which may not adopt its own legislative acts, but plays a leading role in how the European regulatory space is shaped in the area of food safety[142]. Hence, the adjective "regulatory" can be questioned in the case of Frontex[143]. The term "decentralised agency" also does not fully reflect the nature of its powers. The

139 Chamon points out that in the "Common Approach", a relatively short, twelve-page document, no less than one page was devoted to the issues related to regulating agency seats. The issues have also been discussed in the EU institutions, primarily the European Parliament, since 2008. *Cf.* Chamon, *EU Agencies*, pp. 93–97. See 'Joint Statement and Common Approach', 19.7.2012, p. 4; Article 15 of Regulation No. 2007/2004 and Article 57 of Regulation No. 2016/1624.

140 EFSA: Accordo di Sede tra La Republica Italiana e l'Autorità Europea per la Sicurezza Alimentare, *Gazetta Ufficiale delle Republica Italiana*, No. 21, 26.1.2006, pp. 5–19; ECHA: Seat Agreement between the Government of the Republic of Finland and the European Chemicals Agency, *Suomen Säädöskokoelman Sopimussarja*, No. 11, 25.1.2008, p. 90.

141 Frontex: Act of 20.7.2017 on the Ratification of the Agreement on the Seat between the Republic of Poland and the European Border and Coast Guard Agency (Frontex), signed in Warsaw on 9.3.2017, *Dziennik Ustaw*, No. 1501, 4.8.2017.

142 See Korkea-aho, *Adjudicating*, p. 126; Chalmers, 'Food for Thought', p. 538.

143 Although, like other agencies, it is often described as such: H. Rosenfeldt, 'The European Order and Coast Guard Rising: Recent Developments in the Light of EU Accountability Standards and Mechanisms', Paper Presented at the Refugee Law Initiative 2nd Annual Conference, London, June 2017, p. 2.

EU institutions, including above all the Council and the Commission, do not have competencies in the field of coordinating or supporting border management processes[144]. Frontex reflects the efforts undertaken by the member states for the past decade to strengthen practical cooperation between their border authorities[145]. Therefore, instead of decentralising specific competencies, we should rather talk in its case about long-term attempts to harmonise administrative practices for ensuring border security.

One can, nonetheless, consider why these efforts actually took on an institutionalised form and ended in the establishment of an agency, given that most member states were wary of the need to create an operationally autonomous EU institution in this particular area of competence[146]. In the literature on regulatory agencies, critical voices have been raised for several years about the point of establishing new bodies of this kind in areas where cooperation mechanisms are already effective and a new agency contributes little to the existing structures of network cooperation[147]. These issues have also been raised specifically in the context of Frontex, pointing out that acting as a focal point for Community discussions on practical management and also as an entity coordinating information exchange in this field does not necessarily constitute a significant enough change to justify the use of the agency instrument[148].

---

144 See J. Pollak, P. Slominski, 'Experimentalist but not Accountable Governance? The Role of Frontex in Managing the EU's External Borders', *West European Politics*, Vol. 32, No. 5, 2009, p. 905; D. Kietz, N. von Ondarza, 'Sicherheit delegieren. EU-Agenturen in der inneren und äußeren Sicherheit', *SWP-Studie*, April 2016, pp. 9, 18.

145 *Cf.* J. Rijpma, 'Hybrid Agencification in the Area of Freedom, Security and Justice and Its Inherent Tensions: The Case of Frontex', in: Busuioc *et al.* (ed.), *The Agency Phenomenon*, p. 85; S.A. Vasile, A. Călugăriță, 'European Agencies, Institutions and Bodies Engaged in Border Security in the Face of Illegal Migration Flows', *Journal of Criminal Investigations*, No. 1, 2012, pp. 193 ff.

146 Besides the European Commission, Germany called for a strong agency and centralisation of powers at the EU level. Such ideas were openly opposed by e.g. UK and Denmark. See S. Wolff, A. Schout, 'Frontex as Agency: More of the Same?', *Perspectives on European Politics and Society*, Vol. 14, No. 3, 2013, p. 315.

147 More extensively about the mildly successful evolution of network structures in the area of aviation safety that led to the establishment of EASA in 2003 see A. Schout, 'Inspecting Aviation Safety in the EU: EASA as Administrative Innovation?', in: E. Vos (ed.), *European Risk Governance – Its Science, Its Inclusiveness and Its Effectiveness*, Mannheim 2008, pp. 266 ff.; A. Schout, 'Assessing the Added Value of an EU Agency for Aviation Safety', *Journal of Public Policy*, Vol. 31, No. 3, 2011, pp. 366 ff.

148 See Wolff, Schout, 'Frontex', p. 307.

Frontex was created as a result of efforts focused on "communitarising" the policy of external border management undertaken after the changes introduced by the Treaty of Amsterdam. The primary aim was to shift emphasis from the existing forms of intergovernmental cooperation, carried out under the auspices of the Council, towards a new agenda to develop a Community-based approach. There are voices claiming that it was a deliberate effort designed to create an institution bearing responsibility on a European scale for any failures in managing the waves of migrants arriving in Europe[149]. In addition it was more about responsibility in the eyes of the media, because Frontex, according to the mandate contained in the original founding regulation of 2004, had no real executive, decision-making or legislative powers.

Frontex replaced previously existing coordination structures. As a result of the changes introduced by the Treaty of Amsterdam, the Strategic Committee on Immigration, Frontiers and Asylum (SCIFA) was created. It was a Council working group consisting of high-level officials from the member states and drafting recommendations on immigration, borders and asylum issues. The SCIFA+ group, which was separately created within it, was the direct predecessor of Frontex. It managed the operational network in which border guard officials from the member states participated. It also monitored and approved joint operations and pilot projects. SCIFA+ did not have, however, its own resources to effectively perform operational tasks. Therefore, the External Border Practitioners Common Unit (PCU), a parallel, auxiliary forum intended to facilitate more intense cooperation in this area, was created in 2002. That entity was supposed to play a leading role in coordinating and controlling operational projects[150]. SCIFA+/PCU constituted a typical form of the cooperation between national authorities that had been developed over several decades in other market sectors. Activity within such a network is derived from the mandates of individual authorities, the competencies of which are regulated in national legal systems[151]. Frontex, in its original form, fitted into the concepts of already existing cooperation mechanisms primarily in the context of increasing efficiency

149 J. Rijpma, 'Frontex: Successful Blame Shifting of the Member States', *Analyses of the Elcano Royal Institute*, No. 69, 2010, p. 2.

150 See F. Coman-Kund, *European Union Agencies as Global Actors. A Legal Study of the EASA, Frontex and Europol*, Oxon/New York 2018, pp. 172 ff.

151 See Wolff, Schout, 'Frontex', pp. 314 ff.

and effectiveness in the field of organising joint operations and the exchange of information[152].

The 2016 reform of the agency primarily meant an increase in personnel and financial resources and thus a greater capacity to act[153]. The agency's budget is supposed to rise from two hundred and fifty million euros in 2016 to approx. three hundred and twenty million euros in 2020. Also, the number of personnel will more than double over that period – from three hundred and sixty employed in 2016 to approx. one thousand[154]. This increase results from additional powers associated with the protection of the EU's external borders, assigned to Frontex in its new founding regulation. The main idea behind these changes was connected with the harmonisation of European practices in this field. The aim was to increase the influence of EU institutions on the behaviour of the individual member states in the context of tackling the effects of the refugee crisis[155]. Such calls had been made for years[156], but concrete steps were undertaken only in the face of the "dramatic situation at the external borders"[157].

bb) Integrated Border Management

The problem of protecting the EU's external borders comes not only from their length, but also their vulnerability, which is related to the location of the routes

---

152 See H. Ekelund, 'The Establishment of Frontex: A New Institutionalist Approach', *Journal of European Integration*, Vol. 36, No. 2, 2014, pp. 103 ff.

153 It was carried out in a short time. The characteristics of the process of changes: F. Ferraro, E. de Capitani, 'The New European Border and Coast Guard: Yet Another "Half Way" EU Reform?', *ERA Forum*, Vol. 17, No. 3, 2016, pp. 385 ff.

154 See the European Commission, 'Proposal for a Regulation (EU) on the European Border and Coast Guard and Repealing Regulation (EC) No. 2007/2004, Regulation (EC) No. 863/2007 and Council Decision 2005/267/EC', COM(2015) 671 final, 15.12.2015, p. 8; European Court of Auditors, 'Report on the Annual Accounts of the European Border and Coast Guard Agency for the Financial Year 2016 Together with the Agency's Reply', OJ 2017, C 417/233.

155 Comments on the reform, especially on the German side, included voices about the need to eliminate individual actions, out of sync with the EU-wide policy, such as e.g. Hungary's construction of a fence along its border with Serbia and Croatia in 2015. See K. Bensch, 'Mehr Macht für Frontex 2.0', *Tagesschau* of 6.10.2016.

156 Jorrit Rijpma wrote back in 2010: "The Agency could and indeed should play a role in improving national border-guard sensitivity towards protection issues and improve awareness of these services' obligations under Community and international law", 'Frontex', p. 5.

157 Recital 1 of Regulation No. 2016/1624.

for illegal mass migration, mainly from North Africa[158]. On account of these factors, since the beginning of the agency, there have been calls to intensify activities towards more effective controls at the EU's external borders. Since external borders are an expression of a country's sovereignty, efforts to develop cooperation mechanisms in this field have run into resistance from the member states. In legal terms, sovereignty is an attributive and idealising feature of a state. This means it determines the formal side of a state's relationship with its external environment and is associated with its legal distinctness and independence[159]. The competence to regulate any relations inside the state, regardless of external factors, is connected with a defined territory enclosed in defined borders. Integration processes force a redefinition of the traditionally understood concept of sovereignty as some competences are transferred to shared institutions. In the case of administrative tasks involving border protection, cooperation between the member states is described as networked governance. This type of management means shaping interdependencies between cooperating entities, sharing resources within cooperation structures and shifting various powers, including powers of control, to a common level involving consultations with all the parties involved[160]. The main assumption accompanying the creation of administrative networks, such as links between border services of the member states "under the umbrella" of Frontex[161], is to increase the capacity of the cooperating institutions

---

158 See J. Trubalska, 'Wielowymiarowe zarządzanie granicami zewnętrznymi Unii Europejskiej', *Przegląd Geopolityczny*, Vol. 19, 2017, pp. 104 ff.

159 See Bieleń, *Polityka*, p. 98; J. Kranz, 'Kilka uwag o federalizmie i suwerenności w kontekście UE', *Sprawy Międzynarodowe*, No. 1, 2012, pp. 109 ff.; J. Czaputowicz, 'Sovereignty in Theories of European Integration and the Perspective of the Polish Constitutional Tribunal', *Yearbook of Polish European Studies*, Vol. 17, 2014, pp. 15 ff.

160 A. Schout, A. Jordan, 'The European Union's Governance Ambitions and Its Administrative Capacities', *Journal of European Public Policy*, Vol. 15, No. 7, 2008, p. 958.

161 Apart from coordinating the activities of border management institutions, cooperation between specialised networks is developed within Frontex. Frontex Risk Analysis Network (FRAN) is the most developed one of them. It brings together experts dealing with broadly understood border risk analysis. Various strategic reports which diagnose the current security situation are created there. A subnetwork of FRAN is the European Document Fraud Risk Analysis Network (EDF-RAN) that coordinates exchange of information between interested institutions in the field of providing false data, statements and documents by persons crossing the borders. Moreover, Frontex also coordinates cooperation in the field of risk analysis in four networks with non-EU countries (Western Balkans Risk Analysis Network, WB-RAN; Eastern European Borders Risk Analysis Network, EB-RAN; Turkey-Frontex Risk Analysis Network,

to effectively solve problems which are difficult to tackle alone. An additional factor is the possibility of jointly performing executive tasks and also creating a forum where individual actors can, not only in a formal way, influence jointly made decisions[162].

Frontex is a platform whose purpose is to coordinate cooperation between the member states in the field of border management. This primarily means an institutional and procedural framework for collaboration between national border services. The main assumption behind the creation of this agency did not change even after the 2016 reform. Thus, fears that the member states would lose their sovereign powers in managing their borders have proven to be groundless[163]. The change involves an intensification of the common mechanisms, which is reflected e.g. in the establishment of an EU-wide technical and operational strategy for integrated border management ("European Integrated Border Management Strategy"). The very concept of joint management had for years just been a political declaration in its nature, reproduced in documents such as the 2001 Laeken Declaration.[164] It obtained a binding character after it was included in the Treaty of Lisbon. Solutions that are part of the integrated management of the EU's external borders stem from legal regulations stipulated in Title V Part III TFEU – "Area of Freedom, Security and Justice", particularly Articles 67 and 77 TFEU. These provisions point to the need to maintain solidarity with the actions of the EU member states. Additionally, they set policy objectives in the field of border controls, asylum and immigration, stating that the policy is expected to lead to the elimination of restrictions at EU internal borders while maintaining control of persons and the supervision at the external borders as well as a gradual implementation of an integrated management system for the EU's external borders[165]. Strategies of national authorities responsible for border management

---

TU-RAN and Africa-Frontex Intelligence Community, AFIC). See http://frontex.europa.eu/intelligence/strategic-analysis/ (20.3.2018). More also Vasile, Călugăriță, 'European Agencies', p. 194.

162 Since its establishment, Frontex has been seen as a network agency: "Frontex can be understood as [...] a network agency, since it introduces and develops coherence, durability and stability among formal as well as informal network activities, thus reducing the transaction costs of coordination. [It is] supposed to support and link national and supranational authorities", Pollak, Slominski, 'Experimentalist', pp. 906 ff.

163 See Tammikko, 'The New Frontex', pp. 2 ff.

164 See Presidency Conclusions. European Council Meeting in Laeken, 14–15.12.2001, Annex I: 'Laeken Declaration on the Future of the European Union', SN 300/1/01 REV1.

165 Article 77(1) TFEU. See Trubalska, 'Wielowymiarowe zarządzanie', p. 107; Ferraro, de Capitani, 'The New', pp. 388 ff.

must be, according to Article 3 of Regulation No. 2016/1624, consistent with the abovementioned EU-wide technical and operational strategy.

Integrated border management is implemented through the so-called shared responsibility of Frontex and authorities in the member states, which "still retain primary responsibility for the management of their sections of the external borders"[166]. The constituent parts of the European integrated border management were listed in Article 4 of Regulation No. 2016/1624, but it is rightly pointed out in the literature that those provisions did not regulate the competences of the EU institutions to define the strategy for European integrated border management which was explicitly set out in the preamble of Regulation No. 2016/1624[167]. In the regulation itself, it was only stated in Article 3(2) that "technical and operational strategy" is elaborated by the Management Board of Frontex at the request of the Executive Director. Frontex, therefore, has become the entity that defines strategic objectives in the field of integrated border management and coordinates the process of implementing these strategic decisions. Similarly to the decision-making powers of ECHA and EBA, such a state of affairs causes legitimate concerns about maintaining the principle of institutional balance[168].

Unlike in the previous Regulation No. 2007/2004, after the reform Frontex was assigned competences for shaping specific assumptions of a political nature[169]. The leading argumentation of the EU institutions in such cases emphasises, however, the specialised, technical nature of their activities, which is meant to exclude any decision-making autonomy of a particular agency. In practice, on the other hand, especially in crisis circumstances, when a rapid and firm response is required, there is a high risk of theoretically politically neutral agencies becoming an arena for rivalry between individual entities, including above all the European Commission and the member states[170]. As is mentioned

---

166 "Member States shall retain primary responsibility for the management of their sections of the external borders", Article 5(1) of Regulation No. 2016/1624.

167 Recital 8 of Regulation No. 2016/1624: "The development of policy and legislation on external border control and return, including the development of a European integrated border management strategy, remains a responsibility of the Union institutions". See Ferraro, de Capitani, 'The New', p. 390.

168 See Pawlik, *Das REACH-System*, pp. 145–151; M. Busuioc, 'Rule-Making by the European Financial Supervisory Authorities: Walking a Tight Rope', *European Law Journal*, Vol. 19, No. 1, 2013, pp. 113 ff.

169 See T. Groß, 'Unabhängige EU-Agenturen – eine Gefahr für die Demokratie?', *JuristenZeitung*, Vol. 67, No. 22, 2012, p. 1088.

170 See Kietz, von Ondarza, 'Sicherheit', p. 13.

in Chapter 1, the individual member states participate in the work of particular agencies with varying commitment and the shape of the most important documents, such as the abovementioned EU-wide technical and operational strategy, is decided by backstage negotiations where the Commission officials are the most influential. With that in mind, it would be desirable for national parliaments to be more greatly involved in the process of shaping the normative framework of European integrated border management. However, the European Parliament failed to play its expected role in this matter, just as it did not push for the formal guarantees of such an involvement within the legislative process for the renewed Frontex founding regulation. Its silence, in the view of Francesca Ferraro and Emilio de Capitani, expresses the suggestion "that the spirit, if not the letter, of the Treaties has been ignored and that the democratic principle in the current EU construction is weakening faced with the increasing role of executives and unelected bureaucracies such as, in the case of [...] the Management Board of the "new" European agency (Frontex)"[171].

cc) Supportive Tasks

The agency's role as its part of the abovementioned "shared responsibility" primarily involves carrying out supporting tasks, meaning "reinforcing, assessing and coordinating the actions of member states"[172]. Such tasks of the agency include monitoring migratory flows, carrying out risk analysis with regard to integrated border management, making "vulnerability assessments", including assessments of the capacity and readiness of the member states to combat threats at the borders, organisation of joint operations, providing technical and operational assistance, developing technical standards and setting up and deploying European Border and Coast Guard teams. Moreover, Frontex carries out operations to return illegal immigrants; it trains national border guards and participates in research activities relevant for the control of external borders[173]. Frontex is also an important body coordinating cooperation between the member states and external entities, such as third countries, as well as international organisations in the area of migration-related challenges. It also works to prevent cross-border crime[174]. While it had some powers in this field even before the reform, in the 2016

171 Ferraro, de Capitani, 'The New', p. 392.
172 Article 5(3) of Regulation No. 2016/1624.
173 For the full catalogue of tasks, see Article 8 of Regulation No. 2016/1624.
174 Articles 52–54 of Regulation No. 2016/1624. See also Coman-Kund, 'The International Dimension', pp. 12, 18 ff.

regulation it obtained more responsibility for concluding working arrangements with third country authorities[175]. This prompted concerns in some member states in the context of the possible restriction of their freedom in shaping bilateral border policies with their neighbours[176]. These concerns seem to be slightly exaggerated in the context of well-developed safeguards against any arbitrariness of the agency in this field. Draft working arrangements for cooperation with third country authorities require prior approval by the Commission. Before they are concluded, Frontex should also inform the European Parliament[177].

After the reform, the agency became responsible for initiating so-called rapid border interventions. These constitute particularly difficult challenges due to the recent massive influx of third country nationals. Rapid interventions are launched by Frontex for a specified time period at the request of a member state[178]. The member states can also request that Frontex launch joint operations "to face upcoming challenges" related to border protection[179]. Both "rapid interventions" and "joint operations" are preceded by a thorough, reliable and up-to-date risk analysis. This makes it possible to rank these tasks in order of their importance and urgency[180]. Plans for "joint operations" are created in close cooperation between the host member state and the agency[181]. They are binding both for

175 Previously, the issue of working arrangements was narrowly defined. It was emphasised in Article 14(2) of Regulation No. 2007/2004 that the "framework of working arrangements [is] concluded with […] authorities [of third countries], in accordance with the relevant provisions of the TFEU [and] those working arrangements shall be purely related to the management of operational cooperation". Consequently, safeguards were weaker. There was no mention of prior approval of draft arrangements by the Commission, only its prior opinion. See Article 14(8) of Regulation No. 2007/2004. Even before its reform, Frontex developed operational cooperation with third countries, e.g. Turkey, Egypt, Libya or Senegal. More Vasile, Călugărită, 'European Agencies', p. 194.

176 Such concerns were voiced in the public debate, for example, in Finland, particularly with regard to this country's independence in shaping its border cooperation with the Russian Federation. See Tammikko, 'The New Frontex', p. 5. For the broader perspective, see N. Zaun, *EU Asylum Policies. The Strong Regulating States*, Cham 2017, pp. 19 ff.

177 Article 54(2) of Regulation No. 2016/1624.

178 Article 15(2) of Regulation No. 2016/1624. In Regulation No. 2007/2004, the mandate of Frontex for the so-called rapid interventions was limited. See Article 8 of this regulation.

179 Article 15(1) of Regulation No. 2016/1624.

180 Article 15(3) of Regulation No. 2016/1624.

181 Article 16(1) and (2) of Regulation No. 2016/1624.

them and the other participating member states[182]. In the case of a "rapid intervention", the agency's Executive Director requests the member states to immediately deploy border guards or other staff from the so-called rapid reaction pool at the borders specified in the operational plan, which is drawn up together with the member states[183]. Staff from the "rapid reaction pool" can be moved to places "where strengthened deployment is most needed" in response to shifting priorities for ongoing and planned operations. The ED makes decisions concerning such actions after consulting the Management Board[184]. The Frontex intervention corps numbers one thousand five hundred staff dispatched by the member states in accordance with their contributions specified in Annex I to Regulation No. 2016/1624[185].

Even if the burden of ensuring border security rests on the member states that directly manage the EU external border, in a situation that requires urgent action and when external border controls become ineffective to such an extent that it risks jeopardising the functioning of the Schengen Area, it is possible for EU institutions to take action without a request from a member state. This scenario can be initiated in the following situations: (1) if a member state fails to implement a recommendation issued by Frontex within the specified time limit which defines the measures necessary to be taken in accordance with the vulnerability assessment carried out and aimed at eliminating vulnerabilities in border protection[186]; (2) if a member state that faces special and disproportionate challenges at the external borders has failed to request "sufficient support" from the agency in accordance with the procedure provided for in the founding regulation[187], and (3) when a member state is not taking the necessary steps to implement actions under Articles 15, 17 and 18 of Regulation No. 2016/1624[188]. In such cases the Council, acting by a qualified majority on the basis of a proposal from the Commission, can immediately adopt a decision by means of an implementing act that sets out measures that are supposed to be implemented

182 Article 16(3) of Regulation No. 2016/1624.

183 Article 17(7) of Regulation No. 2016/1624.

184 Article 17(1) of Regulation No. 2016/1624.

185 Article 20(5) of Regulation No. 2016/1624.

186 Articles 13(6–8) and 19(1) lit. a of Regulation No. 2016/1624.

187 Article 19(1) lit. b of Regulation No. 2016/1624.

188 Those provisions provide for initiating joint operations and rapid interventions at the external borders (Article 15 of Regulation No. 2016/1624), the procedure for launching rapid border interventions (Article 17 of Regulation No. 2016/1624) and the use of migration management support teams (Article 18 of Regulation No. 2016/1624).

by Frontex in order to mitigate the risk that has emerged at the border. In its decision the Council obliges the member state concerned to cooperate with the agency in the implementation of the proposed measures[189].

This procedure means that common mechanisms are developed in special emergency situations. Frontex plays an important, but not decisive role in their implementation. The Commission consults the agency before making its proposal and it can be assumed that, similarly to other documents of this kind produced by regulatory agencies, the expert opinion of this body will have a significant influence on the wording of the document prepared by the Commission. In the abovementioned urgent situations, when a decision about an intervention is taken by the Council, the host state and Frontex have to agree on the operational plan before a corps, mostly consisting of border guards, is deployed[190].

In a case when the level of external border protection is insufficient or when a member state fails to comply with a decision by the Council, it is possible to reintroduce border controls inside the Schengen zone. This takes place under the procedure set out in Article 29 of the Regulation of the EU code on the rules governing the movement of persons across borders (Schengen border code)[191]. It concerns "exceptional circumstances where the overall functioning of the area without internal border control is put at risk", so e.g. a situation when a member state fails to comply with a decision made by the Council like the one that was described above. The procedure to reintroduce controls is used "as a last resort and as a measure to protect the common interests"[192]. It is an element of pressure on those member states that can be considered frontline countries due to their geographical location at the EU borders. When they are unable to defuse an identified, serious threat, the Council, at the request of the Commission, can recommend that one or more member states reintroduce border controls along the entire border or parts of it. Such a reintroduction can remain in force for a period of up to six months and it can be prolonged three times for a further period of up to six months[193]. Such solutions have already been applied by Germany, Austria, Sweden, Denmark and Norway. In 2016 and 2017 they temporarily reintroduced controls at their borders in the face of the mass influx of migrants and refugees[194].

---

189 Article 19(1) sentence 2 of Regulation No. 2016/1624.

190 Article 19(4) and 5 of Regulation No. 2016/1624.

191 Regulation (EU) No. 2016/399 of 9.3.2016, OJ 2016 L 77/1.

192 Article 29(2) of Regulation No. 2016/399.

193 Article 29(1) of Regulation No. 2016/399.

194 See Tammikko, 'The New Frontex', p. 5.

Frontex's new mandate also includes the possibility of dispatching liaison officers to third countries. It can use them to carry out activities there and this is expected to enhance the agency's cooperation with, for example, countries in the Western Balkans. Liaison officers are experts appointed by the Executive Officer from Frontex personnel. They act as intermediaries between the agency and authorities in the member states who are responsible for border management. One of their most important duties is to submit reports to the Frontex Executive Director on the situation at the external borders and the capacity of the particular member state to take effective action in border administration. Liaison officers also report on the progress of return operations[195] to third countries from which the illegal migrants have come[196].

d) Legitimacy

In the case of Frontex, the literature often mentions functional empowerment. Legitimacy in this case stems from the performance of specific tasks. Frontex at the time of its creation was a response to repeated calls starting from the mid-1990s to strengthen cooperation between the member states in the area of border protection. According to Helena Ekelund, who has analysed the creation of the agency from the perspective of historical institutionalism, certain social processes legitimise the choice of concrete institutional solutions[197]. The demand for a more effective operational cooperation between border guards than had taken place previously, was not only an impulse for the creation of the agency, but also its reform in 2016. In the case of Frontex, the historical context was therefore of crucial importance. When it was created, the substantial EU enlargement of 2004 was a challenge, i.e. a significant expansion of the area requiring integrated control. The 2016 reform, on the other hand, was a response to the failing mechanisms of cooperation and exchange of information in the face of the refugee crisis of 2015. Frontex is a typical supporting agency with distinctive know-how. But its main role, unlike in the case of EFSA and ECHA, is not to provide technical or scientific expertise[198]. Legitimacy in this case is outcome-based.

---

195 "Return operations" are connected with returns of non-EU-nationals who have exhausted all legal avenues to legitimise their stay within the EU. Frontex coordinates such operations at a technical and operational level. See https://frontex.europa.eu/operations/return/ (20.3.2018).

196 Article 12(2) and(3) lit. h of Regulation No. 2016/1624.

197 Ekelund, 'The Establishment', p. 110.

198 *Ibid.*, p. 113.

Frontex constitutes a response to a specific demand associated with the necessity to improve border management within the EU area. Nonetheless, despite high-sounding pronouncements, post-2016 Frontex does not stand at the top of a fully-fledged European Border and Coast Guard system that would make it possible to achieve the ideals of solidarity and shared responsibility on the issues involving border security and solving migration problems[199]. Similarly, as in the case of other EU agencies operating in network structures, this agency continues to be more of an intergovernmental cooperation forum than a supranational body.

5. The European Banking Authority – EBA

a) Creation

The European Banking Authority (EBA) is one of the most powerful agencies in the EU system[200]. Some have even claimed that together with its "sister" bodies – the European Insurance and Occupational Pensions Authority (EIOPA) and the European Securities and Markets Authority (ESMA) – it forms a new type of regulatory agency[201]. They were created, just like EFSA and the "new" Frontex, as a direct response to a crisis in a particular sector of the integrated European market[202].

---

199 See Ferraro, de Capitani, 'The New', p. 387.

200 The legal basis for the creation of all the three European financial supervisory agencies is Article 114 TFEU. Due to their special powers, the issue has been analysed in depth in the literature. Interest particularly increased in the context of the ruling by the CJEU concerning the ESMA competencies, cited earlier in Chapter 1, Case C-270/12 [22.1.2014]. See H. van Meerten, A. Ottow, 'The Proposals for the European Supervisory Authorities (ESAs): The Right (Legal) Way Forward?', *Tijdschrift voor Financieel Recht*, No. 1/2, 2010, pp. 9 ff.; P. van Cleynenbreugel, '*Meroni* Circumvented? Article 114 TFEU and EU Regulatory Agencies', *Maastricht Journal of European and Comparative* Law, Vol. 21, No. 1, 2014, pp. 66 ff.; M. Chamon, 'The Empowerment of Agencies under *Meroni* Doctrine and Article 114 TFEU: Comment on United Kingdom *v.* Parliament and Council (*Short selling*) and the Proposed Single Resolution Mechanism', *European Law Review*, Vol. 39, No. 3, 2014, pp. 384 ff.

201 See Chiti, 'An Important Part', pp. 1427 ff.; Busuioc *et al.*, 'The Phenomenon', p. 3; N. Moloney, 'EU Financial Market Regulation after the Global Financial Crisis: "More Europe" or More Risks?', *Common Market Law Review*, Vol. 47, No. 5, 2010, p. 1344; E. Howell, 'The Evolution of ESMA and Direct Supervision: Are There Implications for EU Supervisory Governance?', *Common Market Law Review*, Vol. 54, No. 4, 2017, p. 1028.

202 For more about anti-crisis activities in Europe in the context of democratic legitimacy see W. Weidenfeld, 'Europa in der Krise – die strategischen Perspektiven', in: P. Hilpold,

In the face of the financial crisis that affected the European markets in 2008–2010, one of the first steps in reforming the European financial security system was the creation of a new structure to coordinate supervisory mechanisms in the macro- and micro-prudential dimension within the internal financial market in January 2011. A plan for changes to strengthen coherent supervisory solutions at the EU-wide level was inspired by the High-Level Group on Financial Supervision, which had been established by the European Commission under the chairmanship of Jacques de Larosière. A report prepared by the group in 2009 identified many problems that paralysed cooperation between national financial supervision authorities, particularly in a crisis situation, requiring swift and decisive steps[203]. The primary concerns about the existing security system included[204]: (1) heterogeneous implementation of EU financial directives, (2) diverse supervisory practices in the member states as a consequence of non-homogenous implementation of EU legislation, (3) institutional chaos resulting from a multitude of various systems of supervisory authorities in the member states, (4) poor flow of information between national authorities, particularly concerning big financial institutions which operated across borders, (5) a lack of established procedures for solving conflicts between national supervisors, and (6) the inefficiency of the existing bodies coordinating cooperation in the field of financial supervision at the EU level[205].

Attention is drawn among scholars to the special role of these kinds of high-level expert groups, usually established *ad hoc* by the Commission to solve specific problems. Their ideas can be seen by referring to the main assumptions of social constructivism, a current that has rapidly developed since the 1980s as part of the theoretical deliberations of specialists in international relations

W. Steinmair (ed.), *Neue europäische Finanzarchitektur. Die Reform der WWU*, Berlin/Heidelberg 2014, pp. 83–87.

203 See The High-Level Group on Financial Supervision in the EU Chaired by Jacques de Larosière, *Report*, Brussels, 25 February 2009, pp. 39 ff.

204 Extensively about the shortcomings of the existing structure, see Nieborak, *Aspekty prawne*, pp. 149 ff.

205 It is a reference to the so-called Lamfalussy procedure level three committees, which no longer exist: CEBS, CESR and CEIOPS. See Kohtamäki, *Die Reform*, pp. 40–44, 72–77; F. Amtenbrink, 'Institutionelle Aspekte der neuen europäischen Finanzmarktregulierung und -aufsicht', in: L. Gramlich, C. Manger-Nestler (ed.), *Europäisierte Regulierungsstrukturen und -netzwerke. Basis einer künftigen Infrastrukturvorsorge*, Baden-Baden 2011, pp. 120 ff.

studies[206]. Constructivism, is one of the few research approaches in the theory of international relations which is useful in the analysis of the international legal system, primarily in the context of understanding the rules and norms governing social relations. They are perceived as collective understanding of phenomena and processes. Assigning certain meanings to a particular phenomenon and formulating them in the form of a specific norm not only influences the behaviour of specific entities, but also modifies their identity and shapes interests. Rules and regulations, as understood in constructivism, are not an "external structure" dependent on the material potential of entities. According to constructivists, they are generated by complex interactions between various actors at the state and international level while simultaneously co-shaping them[207]. It can therefore be concluded, referring to constructivist assumptions, that the vision for an institutional system in the area of European financial supervision created by the High-Level Group imposed certain notions as to the development of these structures within the EU.

Karim Knio, who analysed the financial supervision reform from the constructivist perspective, rightly pointed out that we are dealing in this context with an "ideational turn" which means that an "ideational analysis" of individual actors interests, e.g. the member states, the EU institutions or financial institutions, is not a direct reflection of reality, but rather a kind of perception, a capturing of reality and events by a given addressee, in this case the expert group led by de Larosière. In this understanding, it is the ideas, notions, specific visions that create the interests of actors, and not the other way round[208].

This argumentation can be accepted if we analyse the institutional evolution of the European supervisory structures, which have become a true reflection of the vision outlined by experts in 2009. A qualitative change in the existing situation was introduced by the European System of Financial Supervision (ESFS) which constitutes an institutionalised network of European and national supervisory authorities[209]. The European Systemic Risk Board (ESRB) operates at the macroprudential level

---

206 See M. Barnett, 'Social Constructivism', in: Baylis *et al.* (ed.), *The Globalization*, pp. 148 ff.; J. Czaputowicz, 'Wprowadzenie. Potencjał konstruktywizmu w wyjaśnianiu integracji europejskiej', in: J. Czaputowicz (ed.), *Zastosowanie konstruktywizmu w studiach europejskich*, Warszawa 2016, pp. 7 ff.

207 J.T. Checkel, 'The Constructivist Turn in International Relations Theory', *World Politics*, Vol. 50, No. 2, 1998, pp. 327 ff.

208 K. Knio, 'The Role of Experts and Financial Supervision in the European Union: The de Larosière Commission', in: Ambrus *et al.* (ed.), *The Role*, pp. 344 ff.

209 There is an extensive literature on the new EU supervisory system. See e.g. B. Hagen, *Ist die EU für eine zentrale Versicherungsaufsicht bereit? Kompetenzrechtliche Untersuchung*

and is responsible for identifying systemic risk and countering related threats[210]. The three abovementioned European Supervisory Authorities coordinate activities in the area of microprudential supervision at the EU level[211].

ESFS is an integrated network of national and EU supervisory authorities where day-to-day supervision is, as a rule, exercised by national financial supervision authorities[212]. This system is often compared to the European System of Central Banks created in 1998[213], but it is a more complex solution. It can be considered as a realisation of the "European Composite Administration", i.e. a close connection between the member states' administrative structures and EU level institutions, whose aim is the same as that found in the other market sectors, i.e. increasing the effectiveness and coherence of the process of implementing EU legal norms and facilitating the information flow between individual entities engaged in multilevel management[214].

The creation of ESFS triggered a heated debate in the legal literature on the fundamental dilemma in this context, i.e. whether it is more important for supervisory

der institutionellen Dimension der Europäisierung der Versicherungsaufsicht, Zürich/St. Gallen 2014; F. Hänle, *Die neue Europäische Finanzaufsicht. Kompetenzen der neuen Europäischen Wertpapier- und Marktaufsichtsbehörde (ESMA)*, Hamburg 2012; M. Fedorowicz, *Nadzór nad rynkiem finansowym Unii Europejskiej*, Warszawa 2013.

210 Regulation (EU) No. 1092/2010 of 24.11.2010 on European Union macro-prudential oversight of the financial system and establishing a European Systemic Risk Board, OJ 2010, L 331/1. For more about this institution see T. Myklebust, 'Form and Function of the ESRB. A Critical Analysis', in: M. Andenas, G. Deipenbrock (ed.), *Regulating and Supervising European Financial Markets. More Risks than Achievements*, Cham 2016, pp. 44 ff.

211 ESAs were established under three founding regulations formulated using a similar model: Regulation (EU) No. 1093/2010 of 24.11.2010 establishing a European Banking Authority, OJ 2010, L 331/12; Regulation (EU) No. 1094/2010 of 24.11.2010 establishing a European Insurance and Occupational Pensions Authority, OJ 2010, L 331/48; Regulation (EU) No. 1095/2010 of 24.11.2010 establishing a European Securities and Markets Authority, OJ 2010, L 331/84.

212 With the exception of the so-called significant banks which are supervised by the ECB.

213 See e.g. M. Fedorowicz, 'Porównanie koncepcji normatywnych nowego europejskiego nadzoru finansowego oraz Europejskiego Systemu Banków Centralnych - wybrane zagadnienia', *Studia Europejskie*, No. 2, 2011, pp. 49 ff. About the federal structure of the ESFS: R. Bismuth, 'The Federalisation of Financial Supervision in the US and the EU: A Historical Comparative Perspective', in: Andenas, Deipenbrock (ed.), *Regulating*, pp. 241 ff.

214 The metaphor of "European Composite Administration" (Germ. *Europäischer Verwaltungsverbund*) is connected with a comprehensive look at the EU governance mechanisms. According to such a view: national, intergovernmental and supranational

institutions ensuring financial market security to act effectively in a situation where the member state markets are closely intertwined, and instability in one of them may quickly destabilise the others, or whether the priority lies with democratic mechanisms involving an appropriate legal basis and the broad legitimacy of the bodies to be established[215]. The three European financial supervisory agencies, led by the European Banking Authority, to a certain degree sprang out of this dilemma. The effectiveness and efficiency of EU bureaucratic structures, equated with so-called output legitimacy, needed to be balanced with appropriate control safeguards as part of a specific European input legitimacy which involves the ability of member state nationals to directly express their preferences and expectations[216].

The primary objective of the ESFS, set out by the EU legislature in the regulations establishing the ESAs, was to ensure the adequate implementation of financial sector regulations in such a way as to preserve financial stability and ensure confidence in the financial system as a whole, as well as provide sufficient protection for consumers of financial services[217]. It soon turned out, however, as critics of the 2011 reform had predicted, that the proposed coordination mechanisms in the banking sector, particularly in relation to the biggest financial institutions, were insufficient[218]. The next step towards the creation of structures resembling national security networks was the formation of the so-called Banking Union[219]. The Banking Union was designed by the Commission to place the banking sector "on a firmer foundation" and restore confidence in the common currency[220]. It consists of two, now fully operational, main

institutions are understood as entities collaborating in the decision-making, informational, or supervisory levels. See Kahl, 'Europäische Agenturen', p. 246.

215 See A. Spendzharova, 'Becoming a Powerful Regulator. ESMA in European Financial Sector Governance', *TARN Working Paper*, No. 8, 2017, pp. 6 ff.; Howell, 'The Evolution of ESMA', pp. 1049 ff.

216 See M. Everson, 'The European System of Financial Supervision: A Technology of Expertise', in: Ambrus *et al.* (ed.), *The Role*, pp. 315–319.

217 Article 2 of Regulations Nos. 1093/2010, 1094/2010 and 1095/2010.

218 Kohtamäki, *Die Reform*, p. 101, Amtenbrink, 'Institutionelle Aspekte', pp. 121, 125.

219 The starting point for implementing this concept were the Communications published by the European Commission in autumn of 2012: Communication from the Commission to the European Parliament and the Council, 'A Roadmap towards a Banking Union', COM(2012) 510 final, 12.9.2012; Communication from the Commission, 'A Blueprint for a Deep and Genuine Economic and Monetary Union Launching a European Debate', COM(2012) 777 final/2, 30.11.2012.

220 'A Roadmap towards a Banking Union', COM(2012) 510 final, p. 2.

pillars[221]: the Single Supervisory Mechanism (SSM) and the Single Resolution Mechanism (SRM)[222]. The Single Supervisory Mechanism, which is crucial for the EBA tasks, means the far-reaching Europeanisation of financial supervision, hence it is sometimes even described by the media as centralised European supervision. It is run by the ECB in cooperation with supervisory authorities of the participating member states. The transfer of supervisory competencies over credit institutions in the euro zone, and other countries participating in the Banking Union, to the ECB was set out in detail in the 2013 regulation[223]. According to the provisions of that legal act, the ECB began performing supervisory tasks in November 2014[224].

The eurozone countries were supposed to be the main group of countries covered by the mechanisms of the Banking Union. From the beginning, efforts were also undertaken to integrate the already existing structure in the form of the ESFS with the planned Banking Union, also described as the integrated financial framework[225]. The main link between both of these structures is EBA, a

221 The European Deposit Insurance Scheme, still under construction, is supposed to become the third pillar. See A. Jurkowska-Zeidler, 'Europejski System Gwarantowania Depozytów: Trzeci brakujący filar do dokończenia Unii Bankowej', *Annales Universitatis Mariae Curie-Skłodowska. Lublin – Polonia. Sectio H*, Vol. L, No. 4, 2016, pp. 173 ff.

222 In SRM, a special role is played by an unusual regulatory agency, the Single Resolution Board, which has a slightly different organisational structure than other EU agencies. See also M.B. Beroš, 'Some Reflections on the Governance and Accountability of the Single Resolution Board', *TARN Working Paper*, No. 3, 2017.

223 Regulation (EU) No. 1024/2013 of 15.10.2013 conferring specific tasks on the ECB concerning policies relating to the prudential supervision of credit institutions, OJ 2013, L 287/63.

224 There is already extensive literature on the Banking Union and the role of the EBC in SSM. See e.g.: K. Alexander, 'European Banking Union: A Legal and Institutional Analysis of the Single Supervisory Mechanism and the Single Resolution Mechanism', *European Law Review*, Vol. 40, No. 2, 2015, pp. 154 ff.; N. Moloney, 'European Banking Union: Assessing Its Risks and Resilience', *Common Market Law Review*, Vol. 51, No. 6, 2014, pp. 1616 ff.; K. Peters, 'Die geplante europäische Bankenunion – eine kritische Würdigung', *WM. Zeitschrift für Wirtschafts- und Bankrecht*, No. 9, 2014, pp. 396 ff.; J.A. Kämmerer, P. Starski, 'Die Europäische Zentralbank in der Bankenunion oder: Vor Risiken und Nebenwirkungen wird gewarnt', *Zeitschrift für Gesetzgebung*, Vol. 28, No. 4, 2013, pp. 323 ff.; T. Tuominen, 'The European Banking Union: A Shift in the Internal Market Paradigm?', *Common Market Law Review*, Vol. 54, No. 5, 2017, pp. 1359 ff.

225 An integrated financial framework is, alongside integrated budgetary framework and integrated economic policy framework, a part of the deeper Economic and Monetary Union. See D. Schoenmaker, 'An Integrated Financial Framework for the Banking

supervisory regulatory agency responsible for the banking sector. Its tasks were defined as a mission "to build a common legal framework and supervisory culture across the whole Union"[226].

b) Structure

The EBA, like many agencies created in recent years, has a more complicated institutional structure than its predecessors from the second half of the 1990s[227]. It is built in a similar fashion to EIOPA and ESMA. There are two managing collective bodies in the financial supervision agencies. The main decision-making body is the Board of Supervisors, which is composed of: voting members – heads of national supervisory authorities; and non-voting members – the Executive Director and one representative from the European Commission, the ECB, the ESRB and the "sister" financial supervision agencies (EIOPA and ESMA) respectively. Board meetings can be attended by invited observers, representatives of national central banks, and, in appropriate cases, representatives of national authorities that administer deposit guarantee schemes as well as additional representatives of national supervisory authorities if more than one institution is involved in banking supervision in a particular country[228]. It is therefore a body whose meetings can be attended by several dozen people, which makes it difficult to make binding decisions quickly. The work of the Board of Supervisors is, thus, facilitated by committees and panels that can be set up e.g. to settle cross-border disputes between individual banking supervision authorities in the member states[229].

The close relationship between the EBA and the ECB is reflected, for example, in their participation in meetings of decision-making bodies. Not only does a representative of the ECB participate in the meetings of the Board of Supervisors, but invited representatives of EBA can participate as observers in meetings of the Supervisory Board, the ECB's main body on banking supervision matters[230].

Union: Don't Forget Macro-Prudential Supervision', *European Commission Economic Papers*, No. 495, 2013.

226 'A Roadmap towards a Banking Union', COM(2012) 510 final, p. 5. The synchronising legal act was the Regulation (EU) No. 1022/2013 of 22.10.2013 amending the regulation on the establishment of the EBA with regard to entrusting special tasks to the ECB, OJ 2013 L 287/5.

227 See Michel, *Institutionelles Gleichgewicht*, pp. 207 ff.

228 Article 40 of Regulation No. 1093/2010.

229 Articles 19 and 41 of Regulation No. 1093/2010.

230 Recital 70 of Regulation No. 1024/2013.

Institutional ties translate into exchanges of information and synchronisation of actions. This is significant e.g. when the ECB establishes international relations in the field of banking supervision. When administrative agreements are concluded in this field or other initiatives are developed e.g. with third-country supervisory authorities, the ECB has to take the EBA's international activity into account[231]. Agreements concluded by the ECB and EBA do not create legal obligations for the EU or the member states. The ECB's cooperation with the banking supervisory agency is subject to monitoring. Every three years, the European Commission is required to publish a report on the ECB's supervisory activity which must include information about cooperation with EBA[232].

The normal decision-making procedure in the Board of Supervisors provides for the adoption of agency decisions by a simple majority. Exceptions to this rule include decisions on drafts of the so-called regulatory and implementing technical standards, on issuing guidelines and recommendations, and on reconsidering decisions to ban or restrict financial activities[233]. Due to the multitude of exceptions from the "classic" decision-making procedure, we can only agree with the view expressed in the legal literature that the "rule-exception" juxtaposition found in Article 44(1) of Regulation No. 1093/2010 is superficial, and the most important decisions are made by qualified majority[234]. This solution is not accidental and results partly from the importance of the agency's quasi-legislative powers over the wording of legal norms in the field of EU banking law, and the desire of the member states to control these decision-making processes. The introduction of different voting procedures was a compromise between the smaller member states, which only host subsidiaries and branches of large financial institutions, and the bigger member states where the biggest transnational financial institutions have their headquarters. The former preferred simple majority voting, the latter aimed to strengthen their position through qualified majority voting[235].

The Chairperson is responsible for preparing the work of the Board of Supervisors, chairing the meetings not only of the Board, but also of the

---

231 Article 8 of Regulation No. 1024/2013 and Article 33 of Regulation No. 1093/2010.

232 Article 32 lit. f of Regulation No. 1024/2013.

233 Article 44 of Regulation No. 1093/2010.

234 See M. Lehmann, C. Manger-Nestler, 'Das neue europäische Finanzaufsichtssystem', *Zeitschrift für Bankrecht und Bankwirtschaft*, Vol. 23, No.1, 2011, p. 7; A. Ottow, 'The New Supervisory Architecture of the Financial Markets', in: Everson *et al.* (ed.), *European Agencies*, p. 134.

235 See van Gestel, van Golen, 'Enforcement', pp. 764 ff.

Management Board[236]. This is the agency's other collective body. It carries out administrative tasks associated e.g. with budgetary matters, the EBA's annual and multi-annual work programme, and the staff policy plan[237]. The Management Board, in addition to the Chairperson, is composed of six other members of the Board of Supervisors, elected by it for a two-and-a-half year term, with representation reflecting the Union as a whole. The Commission's representative acts as an observer without the right to vote, except on budgetary matters[238].

The distribution of administrative tasks and those related to the agency's involvement in shaping the sector-specific policy between the Board of Supervisors and the Management Board was an intentional move designed to improve its work. A similar assumption was behind the splitting of the agency leader's tasks between two officials. EBA is represented by a Chairperson appointed by the Board of Supervisors following an open selection procedure. As in most other agencies, management tasks are carried out by the Executive Director who is appointed, just like the Chairperson, by the Board following an open selection procedure. The appointment requires confirmation by the European Parliament[239]. Unlike the procedure used in most agencies, the Commission is not involved in the process of appointing the EBA's Executive Director.

Close cooperation between all the EU financial supervisory agencies (EBA, EIOPA and ESMA) is ensured by the Joint Committee of European Supervisory Authorities, which deals with cross-sectoral matters, particularly with regard to financial conglomerates and information exchange with the ESRB[240]. Legal protection, in turn, is provided by the Board of Appeal, which is also common for the three supervisory agencies. Natural and legal persons, including national supervisory authorities, can appeal decisions of individual supervisory agencies to it. According to Article 263 TFEU, natural and legal persons and the EU institutions can file complaints against decisions taken by the Board of Appeal, also when they cannot be appealed[241], to the CJEU[242].

---

236 Article 48(1) of Regulation No. 1093/2010.

237 Article 47 of Regulation No. 1093/2010.

238 Article 45 of Regulation No. 1093/2010.

239 Article 51(2) of Regulation No. 1093/2010.

240 Article 54 of Regulation No. 1093/2010.

241 In the case of complaints about other measures than decisions, e.g. complaints about provisions of the so-called technical standards.

242 EU institutions do not have the right to appeal to the Board of Appeal, thus, they can immediately lodge complaints under Article 263 TFEU. Natural and legal persons first have to lodge an appeal if possible. See Article 61 of Regulation No. 1093/2010. See Lehmann, Manger-Nestler, 'Das neue', p. 19; S. Storr, 'Rechtsschutz

An important role in controlling the agency's activities is played by the Banking Stakeholder Group composed of thirty members representing the interests of credit and investment institutions, their employees, consumer organisations and small and medium-sized enterprises. The control mechanism involves at least the theoretical possibility of EBA's activities being influenced by representatives of different interest groups constituting this body[243]. EBA is obliged to consult it e.g. when developing regulatory and implementing technical standards. The agency should also provide it with all the necessary information and the Stakeholder Group itself can also, on its own initiative, submit opinions and offer advice on issues related to the EBA's tasks[244].

c) Tasks

aa) Regulatory Powers

The complexity of the institutional structure in the case of the European Banking Authority is a result of its broad competencies. As it was mentioned in Chapter 1, only a few EU agencies can truly be described as "regulatory". This adjective describes the powers of the European Banking Authority, which basically has all the types of competencies that are generally attributed to European agencies[245]. These include coordinating, analytical, monitoring, mediation, harmonisation and finally regulating as well as decision-making powers. It is impossible to refer in detail to the entire catalogue of the agency's tasks, which is very extensive compared to other EU agencies[246]. The uniqueness of the financial supervision agencies has aroused growing interest among researchers since the moment of

---

gegen Regulierungsmaßnahmen in der Europäischen Union', in: Gramlich, Manger-Nestler (ed.), *Europäisierte Regulierungsstrukturen*, pp. 110–112.

243 About the problems associated with adequate representation of interested parties in this body and the difficulties in its functioning, see M. Simoncini, 'Legal Boundaries of European Supervisory Authorities in the Financial Markets: Tensions in the Development of True Regulatory Agencies', *Yearbook of European Law*, Vol. 34, No. 1, 2015, p. 345.

244 Article 37 of Regulation No. 1093/2010. See Pérez-Durán, 'Political and Stakeholder's Ties', p. 13.

245 T. Wörner, *Rechtlich weiche Verhaltenssteuerungsformen Europäischer Agenturen als Bewährungsprobe der Rechtsunion*, Tübingen 2017, pp. 45 ff., 86; G. Tsagas, 'The Regulatory Powers of the European Supervisory Authorities: Constitutional, Political and Functional Considerations', in: Andenas, Deipenbrock (ed.), *Regulating*, pp. 116 ff.; Simoncini, 'Legal Boundaries', pp. 323 ff.

246 Article 8 of Regulation No. 1093/2010.

their creation. There is already, therefore, extensive literature on the specific issues related to the functioning of these bodies, with particular focus on the EBA[247].

At this point, it is worth briefly relating the EBA's most important competencies, because they constitute a kind of breakthrough in the understanding of the agencies' role in the European institutional system. These competences have become a barometer of change in the perception of EU agencies and the possibility of assigning ever-greater powers to them. EBA is an institution that develops drafts of technical standards as well as guidelines and recommendations. These powers can be considered to be of a quasi-legislative nature. Hence, Andreas Orator, in a comprehensive classification of all the EU agencies, placed EBA in the category of "agencies empowered to legislate" (Germ. *rechtsetzungsbefugte Unionsagenturen*)[248].

The founding regulation singled out regulatory technical standards approved by the Commission by means of delegated acts in order to give them binding legal effect according to Article 290 TFEU as well as implementing technical standards adopted by the Commission by means of implementing acts according to Article 291 TFEU[249]. Technical standards are meant to be a direct reflection of the expert knowledge amassed in the EBA decision-making bodies. Without doubt, they also constitute the strongest mechanism for harmonisation of European financial law. Partly due to the anti-delegation *Meroni* doctrine[250], a safeguard formula was created in the founding regulations that emphasised that technical standards, as the name of this legal instrument indicates, "shall be technical, shall not imply strategic decisions or policy choices"[251]. Such a clause opened the way for all the three ESAs to be active in the creation of legally binding acts significantly changing the existing shape of the European financial market. The cases in which they have the right to create technical standards are set out in detail in key EU financial directives[252].

247 See e.g. P. Weismann, *European Agencies and Risk Governance in EU Financial Market Law*, Oxon 2016, pp. 119 ff.; E. Ferran, 'The Existential Search of the European Banking Authority', *European Business Organization Law Review*, Vol. 17, No. 3, 2016, pp. 286 ff.; G. Lo Schiavo, 'The European Supervisory Authorities: A True Evolutionary Step along the Process of European Financial Integration?', Conference Papers. Vilnius University, 2013, pp. 297 ff.

248 Orator, *Möglichkeiten*, pp. 174 ff.

249 Recitals 22 and 24 of Regulation No. 1093/2010. See Chiti, 'European Agencies', p. 100.

250 See Chapter 3.

251 Articles 10(1) and 15(1) of Regulation No. 1093/2010.

252 See Kohtamäki, *Die Reform*, p. 179; Hagen, *Ist die EU*, p. 221.

Technical standards are adopted by the Commission by means of regulations or decisions, so that they do not require implementation into national legal systems[253]. Unlike directives governing the scope of activity of individual financial supervision agencies, technical standards apply directly, creating specific rights and obligations for individual financial institutions, national supervisory authorities and other entities. EBA drafts technical standards in a complicated procedure set out in Articles 10 and 15 of the founding regulation. The agency is their actual author, although formally they are issued by the European Commission. The Commission's role basically comes down to approving them[254]. If the Commission decides to reject an agency draft or to change it, it needs to provide a detailed explanation for this. Any changes in the draft without prior consultation with the competent financial supervisory agency (e.g. EBA) are inadmissible. Only in the case of the agency's inactivity or when it fails to submit draft standards within the time limit specified in appropriate directives, does the Commission have the right to adopt such a legal instrument without its participation. It is particularly controversial when compared to the Treaty understanding of delegated and implementing acts according to Articles 290 and 291 TFEU. Primary law in this context does not provide, however, for limiting the role of the Commission in favour of other bodies[255].

Quasi-regulatory competences are complemented by the ability of the EBA to issue guidelines and recommendations. Practitioners and experts from the banking sector participate in their preparation, which is supposed to legitimise the impact of these legal instruments. They are recognised as so-called soft law, similarly e.g. as in the case of EFSA. Although they formally do not have binding force, they, in fact, shape many detailed regulations and practices, because they are usually accepted by the addressees, while maintaining the wording proposed by the agency[256]. Guidelines and recommendations, according to Article 16(1) of Regulation No. 1093/2010, are designed to establish "consistent, efficient and effective supervisory practices" and also to ensure "common, uniform and consistent application of Union law". Similarly to drafting technical standards, before

---

253 This solution was adopted in the legislative process. The original idea envisaged the possibility that technical standards would be issued by the ESAs. See Ottow, 'The New Supervisory Architecture', p.132.

254 See Weismann, *European Agencies*, pp. 126, 129; J. Schemmel, *Europäische Finanzmarktverwaltung. Dogmatik und Legitimation der Handlungsinstrumente von EBA, EIOPA und ESMA*, Tübingen 2018, pp. 207–237.

255 See Busuioc, 'Rule-Making', p. 117.

256 See Wörner, *Rechtlich weiche Verhaltenssteuerungsformen*, pp. 8 ff., 17; Chiti, 'European Agencies', p. 96.

issuing a guideline or a recommendation, EBA can conduct open consultations, perform a cost and benefit analysis related to the application of these measures and also request opinions from the Stakeholder Group. It is worth noting here that the Commission's approval is not needed for them to be issued. The addressees of guidelines and recommendations, i.e. national authorities and particular financial institutions, are obliged to comply with them. National supervisory authorities publicly declare whether they have complied with a guideline or recommendation. If they do not comply with these instruments, they are required to inform the agency and provide a justification for their failure to do so[257].

The EBA publishes information on non-compliance with its instruments by competent administrative authorities in the member states. The possibility of identifying the authorities that do not apply guidelines and recommendations (strengthened by exposing these entities also in the annual report) is meant to increase the motivation of national authorities to comply with these soft-law instruments. This approach is described as "naming and shaming". The financial community builds mutual relations primarily on a foundation of trust and reputation. Exposing an entity directly as "insubordinate" can drastically reduce its prestige and consequently its leverage in the specific "web of dependencies" in the milieus of European financial institutions[258]. Interestingly, in their case, the mechanism "act or explain", or in other words "comply or explain", used to strengthen the legal force of guidelines and recommendations, is slightly weaker than the one intended for national supervisory authorities. Financial institutions are obliged to provide detailed information on their intentions regarding compliance with a guideline or recommendation only when it is clearly specified in these measures[259].

bb) Coordinating Powers

Among the many tasks of the EBA, Article 29 of Regulation No. 1093/2010 includes a call for building a common financial supervision culture. It reflects the idea of supervisory convergence repeatedly expressed in these documents in different contexts. According to Article 29(1) of Regulation No. 1093/2010, this means consistent supervisory practices and approaches as well as uniform

---

257 Article 16(2–4) of Regulation No. 1093/2010.

258 Concerning the strong position of "soft measures" in the banking sector, see L. Dragomir, *European Prudential Banking Regulation and Supervision: The Legal Dimension*, London/New York 2010, pp. 222 ff.

259 See van Gestel, van Golen, 'Enforcement', pp. 766–768.

procedures in the field of financial supervision on EU territory. In order to fulfil these assumptions, EU supervisory agencies, including EBA, provide specialised opinions to competent national authorities on any issue related to financial supervision. It is a new, previously unseen soft-law instrument, used on the sole initiative of the agency. The possibility of drafting similar expert opinions for the Commission, the Parliament and the Council for the sake of fostering supervisory convergence was additionally guaranteed in Article 1(5) of Regulation No. 1093/2010[260].

Supervisory agencies constitute a specific platform coordinating the activities of national financial supervision authorities and European institutions. Therefore, Article 29(1) lit. e of Regulation No. 1093/2010 provides for organising sectoral and cross-sectoral training and supporting personnel exchange mechanisms between different types of supervisory bodies. The rotation of clerks within the multilevel administrative structure is meant to strengthen and disseminate the broadly understood (i.e. understood in the normative and institutional dimension) European financial supervisory culture. This term only found use in the regulations which established the ESAs. While the CEBS, CEIOPS and CESR committees, which were predecessors of EBA, EIOPA and ESMA, also performed many coordinating and harmonising tasks, they mostly operated in an informal way, based on the goodwill of clerks from supervisory institutions in the member states. In this context, the role of EBA is clearly stronger, which is reflected in Article 29(2) of its founding regulation, which opens the way for it to develop "new practical instruments and convergence tools" in the area of financial supervision[261].

The abovementioned activities intended to shape a European supervisory culture are complemented by the so-called single rule book: a uniform set of rules addressed to all financial institutions in the internal market. The idea, formulated by the European Council in June 2009, was picked up as an important element on the path towards a consistent understanding of European financial supervision. This means collecting all the supervisory legislation in a single, transparent set that includes a range of legal instruments such as directives, technical standards or guidelines and recommendations[262].

---

260 Michel, *Institutionelles Gleichgewicht*, pp. 192 ff.; Moloney, 'European Banking Union', pp. 1610 ff.

261 Ferran, 'The Existential Search', p. 309.

262 See EBA's activity in the development of the single rule book: http://www.eba.europa.eu/regulation-and-policy/single-rulebook (20.3.2018). See also I.H.-Y. Chiu, 'Power and Accountability in the EU Financial Regulatory Architecture: Examining

cc) Decision-Making Powers

Yet the most controversial matter in the process of creating the EBA was its decision-making powers, which are directly addressed to particular entities and, as a rule, do not require the involvement of EU institutions. If there is a breach of Union law, in emergency situations and in the case of settling disagreements between competent authorities in cross-border situations, EBA is empowered to formulate decisions obliging national supervisory authorities and individual financial institutions to take concrete action, including even the cessation of some practices. These three cases are governed by Articles 17, 18 and 19 of Regulation No. 1093/2010. They provide for complicated, multi-stage procedures that constitute a hedge against any arbitrary and spontaneous action by the agency. Decisions on a case-by-case basis, addressed to national supervisory authorities, or private entities are made according to the provisions of the regulation only when national authorities fail to respond to earlier recommendations[263].

If there is a breach of EU law, according to Article 17 of Regulation No. 1093/2010, EBA carries out an investigation and after that it can address a recommendation to the national authority setting out the action to be taken to ensure compliance with EU norms. When the supervisory institution fails to respond, the European Commission issues a formal opinion taking into account the agency's recommendations. If there is still no response from the national supervisor and also in the case that it is necessary to "remedy such non-compliance in a timely manner", EBA is empowered to adopt an individual decision addressed to a particular participant in the financial market. This requires necessary action to be taken by the market participant to comply with its obligations resulting from EU law and this may involve the necessity to cease certain practices[264].

In the case of threats to the orderly functioning, integrity and stability of the financial markets, according to Article 18 of Regulation No. 1093/2010, EBA "actively facilitates and coordinates" any actions undertaken by relevant authorities in the member states. Moreover, when the Council, on the basis of Article 18(2) of Regulation No. 1093/2010, declares an emergency situation, EBA is empowered,

Inter-Agency Relations, Agency Independence and Accountability', in: Andenas, Deipenbrock (ed.), *Regulating*, pp. 77 ff., 99.

263 See Weismann, *European Agencies*, pp. 132–146; P. Schammo, 'Actions and Inactions in the Investigation of Breaches of Union Law by the European Supervisory Authorities', *Common Market Law Review*, Vol. 55, No. 5, 2018, pp. 1424–1429.

264 Article 17(6) of Regulation No. 1093/2010. See M. Scholten, A. Ottow, 'Institutional Design of Enforcement in the EU: The Case of Financial Markets', *Utrecht Law Review*, Vol. 10, No. 5, 2014, p. 83.

after meeting the conditions set out in Article 18(3) of Regulation No. 1093/2010, to adopt individual decisions requiring competent authorities to undertake specific action. If the national authorities fail to respond, EBA can adopt an individual decision addressed to a market participant, i.e. a specific financial institution[265].

Article 19 of Regulation No. 1093/2010 sets out the procedure for binding mediation in the case of disputes between competent supervisory authorities in cross-border situations. If they fail to reach an agreement in a conciliation phase, EBA may require the national supervisory institutions to take, or refrain from undertaking, specific action. If the competent authority does not comply with the decision of the EU supervisory agency, it can issue an individual decision addressed to a market participant.

It is worth noting that decisions issued by the EBA under Articles 17, 18 and 19 of Regulation No. 1093/2010 take precedence over all the other decisions on a given issue adopted by competent national authorities. Due to a number of conditions that have to be met before they are made, issuing them can be considered a unique competency. None of the three situations listed in the regulation occurs frequently. Countries seek to prevent breaches of EU law in this particularly sensitive area of financial law. A declaration of an emergency situation by the Council, on account of their related costs and far-reaching political consequences, is a solution designed only for extreme cases. On the issue of cross-border disputes, in turn, authorities in the member states seek to keep things discrete and to solve their problems between themselves without involving the higher, EU level[266].

d) Legitimacy

In conclusion, we can say that while EBA, with an annual budget of thirty-six million euros and approx. one hundred and fifty employees, is a medium-sized agency[267], it clearly stands out in the agency system with its special competencies. In particular, its regulatory or rulemaking powers are considered to be controversial[268]. Lawyers that have analysed the agencies point out that,

---

265 See Ferran, 'The Existential Search', pp. 305 ff.

266 Articles 17(6), 18(4) and 19(4) of Regulation No. 1093/2010. See Weißgärber, *Die Legitimation*, p. 54.

267 European Court of Auditors, *Report on the Annual Accounts of the European Banking Authority for the Financial Year 2016 Together with the Agency's Reply*, OJ 2017, C 417/87.

268 See van Gestel, van Golen, 'Enforcement', p. 766.

as agency activity increases, they can be considered a "powerful innovation in uncharted territory", even a "Copernican revolution", meaning in practice a significant advantage of the ESAs over the Commission in shaping European financial law[269]. It can change proposals for technical standards put forward by EBA "only in very restricted and extraordinary circumstances, since the Authority is the actor in close contact with knowing best the daily functioning of financial markets"[270]. The special position of the agency in the process of creating regulations in the field of banking supervision is, therefore, a result of, as in the case of the aforementioned agencies (EFSA and ECHA), the specialised preparation of its employees and experts that constitute its main decision-making bodies. The European Commission's staff does not have this kind of expert knowledge. The emerging information asymmetry gives EBA an "advantage" which, however, should be balanced by adequate control mechanisms that are in line with the concept of accountability of public administration institutions. Yet do such control mechanisms guarantee enough empowerment or proper legitimacy for a bureaucracy that is "drifting away" from citizens and, to quote the words of Michelle Everson, "usurps democratic process and sovereign will"[271]?

The European financial supervisory agencies, which enjoy the broadest powers yet conferred onto such bodies, represent the phenomenon called "technocratisation" or "scientification" of the European administrative space in the most complete way. By shifting particular supervisory competences in such a sensitive area for national economies as financial market security, countries contribute to the consolidation of the European executive order. Its existence, in turn, can be seen in the context of the eroding sovereignty of the state, which continues to lose some of its important powers and thus control over its own executive power[272]. Therefore, it is particularly important in this case to find an adequate legitimising theory as an essential complement to the practical control mechanisms provided for in the founding regulations of the particular

269 See M. de Bellis, 'Procedural Rule-Making of European Supervisory Agencies (ESAs). An Effective Tool for Legitimacy?', *TARN Working Paper*, No. 12, 2017, p. 1; Schemmel, *Europäische Finanzmarktverwaltung*, pp. 359 ff.

270 Recital 22 of Regulation No. 1093/2010.

271 Everson, 'The European System', p. 318. See also J. Barcz, 'Pojęcie suwerenności w świetle współzależności między sferą ponadnarodową a państwową', in: J. Kranz (ed.), *Suwerenność i ponadnarodowość a integracja europejska*, Warszawa 2006, pp. 70 ff.

272 I. Lipowicz, 'Europeizacja administracji publicznej', *Ruch Prawniczy, Ekonomiczny i Socjologiczny*, Vol. LXX, No. 1, 2008, p. 6.

agencies. The existing schemes for legitimising the activity of regulatory agencies by attributing special functions to them, and including them in public consultation processes or embedding their tasks in a specific procedural framework, seem unconvincing in the context of the complex tasks of the European Banking Authority[273].

273 See the critical overview of theoretical concepts developed in the context of EU regulatory agencies, Part II.

3 Regulatory Agencies and the Principle of Institutional Balance in the European Union

1. The Principle of Institutional Balance in the European Union

a) The Absence of the Traditional Tripartite Separation of Powers

The problem of institutional balance is usually examined through the prism of the tripartite separation of powers in the political systems of particular countries. The European Union is not a country and, therefore, it is difficult to apply the classic concepts of separation of powers to it. According to the legal situation after the Treaty of Lisbon entered into force in 2009, the Union is a single international organisation which, nonetheless, maintains its specific character. Due to the supranationality of its institutional structures, the European Union is called a *sui generis*, i.e. one of kind, entity[1]. The member states have transferred a range of sovereign powers to this organisation, primarily involving legislation and, to a lesser extent, implementation of law as well as judicial control of compliance with the law. Each of the EU institutions explicitly defined in Article 13(1) TEU is an exponent of specific national and supranational interests. For this reason, the issue of the relationships between them is an important subject, which has been debated in legal scholarship for decades[2]. Despite the absence of Montesquieu's traditional tripartite separation of powers between the legislative, the executive and the judicial branches (Lat. *trias politica*), the European Communities were, from the outset, organised on the foundation of the rule of law. This was partly reflected in the principle of institutional balance, which is of a systemic nature for the EU structure and, as some authors claim, constitutes an equivalent of the

---

1 G. Conway, 'Recovering a Separation of Powers in the European Union', *European Law Journal*, Vol. 17, No. 3, 2011, pp. 304, 315 ff.; T. Dubowski, *Zasada równowagi instytucjonalnej w prawie Unii Europejskiej*, Warszawa 2010, pp. 15 ff.; B. Smulders, K. Eisele, 'Reflections on the Institutional Balance, the Community Method and the Interplay between Jurisdictions after the Lisbon', *Yearbook of European Law*, Vol. 31, No. 1, 2012, pp. 113 ff. See also A. Łazowski, 'Charakter prawny i cele UE', in: Łazowski, Zawidzka-Łojek (ed.), *Instytucje*, pp. 3 ff.; T.G. Grosse, 'Kryzys integracji europejskiej w świetle koncepcji Arnolda Toynbee'go', *Przegląd Zachodni*, No. 4(365), 2017, pp. 25 ff.

2 See J.-P. Jacqué, 'The Principle of Institutional Balance', *Common Market Law Review*, Vol. 41, No. 2, 2004, pp. 383 ff.

traditional tripartite separation of powers[3]. An analysis of Treaty prerogatives does not allow for the definition of clear boundaries between the legislative power and the executive power at the EU level, as in nation state systems[4]. We can only agree with Koen Lenaerts that this does not mean, however, "that the separation-of-powers focus is meaningless in the case of Community. It rather suggests that tracing the separation of powers in the Community is a somewhat more subtle undertaking than the mere identification of the three basic organs of public authority"[5].

b) Judicial Activism of the European Court of Justice

The case law of the Court of Justice has been of fundamental importance for the development of this principle[6]. Much has been said in this context about the Court's activism with its creative interpretation of Treaty law which led to the formulation of the concept of institutional balance in relation to the integrated European system[7]. The Court's efforts to consolidate the principle of institutional balance are an important element in the processes of conceptualising the democratic principles underpinning the functioning of the European Union. Institutional balance reinforces the legal legitimacy of the activities of EU bodies[8]. The beginnings of the evolution of this principle in the Court's case law date back to 1958 and involve the judgments in the *Meroni* case[9]. It was the first time the Court addressed the issue of delegating competences between

---

3 *Ibid.*, p. 384; Conway, 'Recovering', p. 319; Smulders, Eisele, 'Reflections', p. 114; Kenig-Witkowska, Łazowski, Ostrihansky, *Prawo*, pp.146–150.

4 See J. Galster, O. Łachacz, 'Kilka uwag o podziale władzy w Unii Europejskiej', *Studia Prawnoustrojowe*, No. 26, 2014, p. 69; K. Lenaerts, 'Some Reflections on the Separation of Powers in the European Community', *Common Market Law Review*, Vol. 28, No. 1, 1991, pp. 12 ff.

5 Lenaerts, 'Some Reflections', p. 13.

6 See R. Grzeszczak, 'Prawo pierwotne UE', in: Łazowski, Zawidzka-Łojek (ed.), *Instytucje*, pp. 122–124.

7 See also J. Galster, 'Zasada równowagi instytucjonalnej w orzecznictwie Trybunału Sprawiedliwości Unii Europejskiej', *Gdańskie Studia Prawnicze*, Vol. XXXI, 2014, p. 110.

8 See D. Yuratich, 'Article 13(2) TEU: Institutional Balance, Sincere Co-operation, and Non-Domination During Lawmaking', *German Law Journal*, Vol. 18, No. 1, 2017, p. 101.

9 Cases 9/56 and 10/56, *Meroni & Co. v. High Authority of the European Coal and Steel Community*, [13.6.1958] ECR 133 and 157. For more on this issue see pt. 2 of this chapter.

Community institutions. In its 1958 ruling, which will be described in the next point, on the *Meroni* doctrine, the Court concluded that institutional balance is a significant normative criterion on the basis of which the admissibility of certain competence shifts can be decided[10], but it defined the principle more broadly more than it did thirty years later in its 1990 *Chernobyl* ruling[11].

According to the Court, the Treaties created an institutional balance based on the division of competencies between individual bodies. Observance of the principle means that each institution exercises its powers with due regard for the powers of other institutions. Breaches of this rule are subject to sanctions. The Court of Justice was obliged in the Treaties to ensure that the law, in its interpretation and application is observed. Therefore, it acts as a guardian of the institutional balance, making sure that the competencies of EU institutions are not infringed. This is to be achieved through judicial control of the competencies of individual bodies, carried out through the right to file complaints to the Court of Justice[12]. The Court, with its systemic interpretation, granted the European Parliament the right to bring an action for annulment, recognising that the absence of an appropriate Treaty provision in the legal system at the time was a procedural gap[13].

Taking into account the current development of the Court's case law, this was a special, precedent-making ruling. As Michelle Everson rightly pointed out at the time, "not even the immediate threat of radioactive contamination of foodstuffs within Europe was held to relieve the Council of its legislative duty to consult Parliament under the principle of institutional balance. Functionality, or a speedy and effective response to an emerging situation, was not, in the Court's opinion, a sufficient justification for the negation of the principle of institutional balance"[14]. That remark should be interpreted through the prism of the CJEU's position regarding the steps undertaken by the EU institutions to overcome the

10 Dubowski, *Zasada*, p. 106.

11 Case 70/88, *European Parliament v. Council* ('Chernobyl'), [22.5.1990] ECR I-2041.

12 *Ibid.*, paras 22–23. See G. Winter, 'Kompetenzverteilung und Legitimation in der Europäischen Mehrebenenverwaltung', *Europarecht*, No. 2, 2005, p. 262; Galster, 'Zasada równowagi', p. 117; M. Jaśkowski, 'Miejsce podstawowych zasad ogólnych prawa wspólnotowego w hierarchii wspólnotowych źródeł prawa', in: C. Mik (ed.), *Zasady ogólne prawa wspólnotowego*, Toruń 2007, pp. 72 ff.

13 Case 70/88, para 26. See G. Bebr, 'Case C-70/88, European Parliament *v.* Council, Judgment of the Court of Justice of 22 May 1990', *Common Market Law Review*, Vol. 28, No. 3, 1991, pp. 674 ff.

14 Everson, 'European Agencies', p. 50.

financial crisis of 2008–2010. In this case, however, which will be discussed in the context of the 2014 ruling on the European Securities and Markets Authority[15], the CJEU opted for a more flexible stance in the name of restoring and ensuring future financial stability in the European markets, reinterpreting the traditionally understood principle of institutional balance[16].

c) The Treaty Provisions

Regardless of the Court's case law, Article 7 TEC was the normative inspiration to formulate the principle of institutional balance before the Treaty of Lisbon came into force. The Article listed the Community institutions, specifying how they were to carry out their competences. Institutional balance was a result of the organisational structure of the Communities and a clear division of competencies between particular Treaty institutions[17]. After the changes introduced by the Treaty of Lisbon, the legal basis for the division of competencies between EU institutions became Article 13(2) TEU, which states that "each institution shall act within the limits of the powers conferred on it in the Treaties, and in conformity with the procedures, conditions and objectives set out in them. The institutions shall practice mutual sincere cooperation". This provision expands the formula from Article 7 TEC, which only mentioned acting "within the limits of the powers conferred […] by this Treaty". This means that institutions are bound not only by the limits established in primary law, but also by the particular procedures considered in the light of Treaty determinants and objectives[18]. Institutional balance should, therefore, be considered more broadly than only through the prism of Article 13(2) TEU. Other Treaty provisions defining the scope of competencies of particular institutions and indicating the form of their mutual relationships are also important.

It is assumed that a violation of institutional balance involves breaching the system of the division of competencies between the EU institutions. This division is considered to be binding, therefore the EU institutions are obliged to confine themselves to their areas of activity and should not interfere in the tasks of others. Nonetheless, this assumption does not preclude close cooperation.

---

15 Case C-270/12.

16 See a comment on the possible options regarding the CJEU's behaviour: Everson, 'European Agencies', p. 50.

17 J. Barcz, *Unia Europejska na rozstajach. Traktat z Lizbony. Dynamika i główne kierunki reformy ustrojowej*, Warszawa 2010, pp. 175 ff.

18 See Dubowski, *Zasada*, pp. 102 ff., 111.

They are obliged to take part in this under the provisions of Article 13(2) TEU. Although this provision concerns the EU institutions specified in detail in Article 13(1) TEU, its broad interpretation is accepted in the doctrine[19]. It is, therefore, assumed that it also applies to other EU bodies and organisational units that are considered to be a part of the European administration. Consequently, also regulatory agencies, being entities, the status of which, as well as the scope of their competencies, are not set out directly in the Treaties, are obliged to respect the competence divisions in the EU's institutional structure and to strengthen their mutual cooperation[20].

The principle of institutional balance does not mean that all EU institutions are equal. Following Cezary Mik's interpretation, we can say that there is a peculiar arrangement of their mutual relations[21]. Institutional balance mandates the maintenance of a state of *equilibrium*, which can be preserved through respect for competency catalogues of particular institutions[22]. This is maintained when individual institutions have a necessary degree of independence in carrying out their tasks: they cannot unconditionally transfer their powers to other entities and they respect the competences of other institutions[23]. The institutional autonomy of EU bodies can also be seen as a separate principle of the EU system which, in this understanding, is closely linked to the principle of institutional balance and contributes to its implementation, although it constitutes a separate assumption about the functioning of the EU structure[24].

Yet balancing or keeping an *equilibrium* between the positions of individual institutions in the EU system is not an easy task. According to Gerard Conway, the main difficulty stems from a lack of clear criteria for determining the use of this concept. Balancing contains a significant subjective component as it involves an assessment of the interests of particular bodies. In this sense, it is a less transparent idea than the traditional concept of the tripartite separation of powers where the objective determinant of how particular bodies operate is the assignment of specific functions[25].

---

19 Michel, *Institutionelles Gleichgewicht*, p. 111; Weißgärber, *Die Legitimation*, p. 248.

20 See Hagen, *Ist die EU*, p. 156.

21 See C. Mik, *Europejskie prawo wspólnotowe. Zagadnienia teorii i praktyki*, Warszawa 2000, pp. 122 ff.

22 Galster, Łachacz, 'Kilka uwag', p. 64.

23 See Majone, 'Delegation', p. 327; Dubowski, *Zasada*, p. 124.

24 Mik, *Europejskie prawo wspólnotowe*, p. 124.

25 Conway, 'Recovering', p. 319.

d) Fitting the EU Regulatory Agencies into the Institutional Balance

Maintaining balance is particularly difficult if we look at the EU's institutional system in a broader perspective, not only through the prism of the main EU institutions specified in Article 13(1) TEU. For years regulatory agencies have been perceived, not least by the European Commission, as a potential threat to the delicate institutional balance. This was noticeable e.g. when the EFSA was established. As has been pointed out earlier, this agency was granted risk assessment tasks in the food market. Management tasks were to remain with the Commission, indeed, this was partly in order to avoid upsetting the institutional balance in the EU system. This position began to change gradually. This was reflected e.g. in the granting of decision-making powers to the ECHA. A major breakthrough was the establishment in 2011 of the ESAs, which, not only in terms of the number of assigned tasks but also their nature, deviated from the existing institutional solutions developed within the delegation of competences by the Commission[26].

The creation of regulatory agencies, especially those with increasingly wide powers, has long been seen as a "hard case" of institution building in the EU multilevel setting[27]. They are, as was demonstrated in the examples selected, permanent bodies with well-developed structures, their own personnel and budget. The process of creating them is lengthy and requires arduous negotiations. Therefore, assuming that EU regulatory agencies can be seen as "a heavy public law organisation form", it is difficult to expect that their powers will remain limited and will not involve any autonomous decision making[28]. Besides, it is not easy to separate the tasks of risk assessment and risk management in practice. Similarly, expert analysis of certain developments cannot always be clearly separated from diagnosis stemming from political calculation[29].

The cautious stance of the Commission should be stressed in this context once again. For several decades, the Commission's Legal Service has strictly

---

26 See Curtin, Dehousse, 'European Union Agencies', pp. 197 ff.; A. Neergaard, 'European Supervisory Authorities – A New Model for the Exercise of Powers in the European Union', *Euredia*, No. 4, 2009, pp. 603 ff.

27 M. Egeberg *et al.*, 'The EU's Subordinated Agency Administration and the Rise of Executive Power at European Level', in: M.W. Bauer, J. Trondal (ed.), *The Palgrave Handbook of the European Administrative System*, Basingstoke/New York 2015, p. 329.

28 See Curtin, Dehousse, 'European Union Agencies', p. 194; van Gestel, van Golen, 'Enforcement', p. 771.

29 See H.C.H. Hofmann, A. Morini, 'The Pluralisation of EU Executive – Constitutional Aspects of "Agencification"', *European Law Review*, Vol. 37, No. 4, 2012, p. 422.

ensured that the institutional balance was maintained in accordance with the assumptions of the *Meroni* case law. The literature refers to a dispute between the traditionalists represented e.g. by the Legal Service and the reformers from other Directorates-General interested in adapting institutional solutions to the rapid development of the internal market[30]. The main idea that guided the "traditionalists" was to maintain the *status quo*, or the strong position of the European Commission. This stance meant maintaining the unity and integrity of the executive function at the European level[31]. Indeed, the executive function had long been concentrated within the Commission's institutional structures. Over time, by way of exception, some executive powers were given to the Council and other Treaty-based entities, such as the European Central Bank or the Court of Auditors[32].

A change in the perception of the executive function at the European level has also been reflected in the Commission's evolving attitude towards regulatory agencies. Today, the coherence of the European executive apparatus means that regulatory agencies are involved in implementing legislation. They are also an inherent part of the European executive system and, at least theoretically, they fit into the EU's institutional balance[33]. Transferring specific tasks within the EU structure, in this context, is described as "delegation to agencies as an institutional practice"[34]. What needs to be remembered, however, is that the delegation of powers by the Commission to regulatory agencies is still perceived as a second-best alternative in cases when the Commission itself is unable to obtain the Council's approval for extending its competences in a particular sector of the internal market[35].

The Council plays a balancing role in the process of "agencification" of the European administrative space. This means that it actively participates in

---

30 See Majone, 'Delegation', p. 329.

31 See S. Griller, A. Orator, '*Meroni* Revisited – Empowering European Agencies between Efficiency and Legitimacy', *NewGov. New Modes of Governance Project*, No. 4, 2007, p. 8.

32 See Hofmann, Morini, 'The Pluralisation', p. 419.

33 *Cf.* E. Heims, *Building EU Regulatory Capacity: The Work of Under-Resourced Agencies in the European Union*, Cham 2019, pp. 27 ff.; M. Simoncini, *Administrative Regulation Beyond the Non-Delegation Doctrine. A Study on EU Agencies*, Oxford/Portland 2018, pp. 32 ff.

34 Hofmann, Morini, 'The Pluralisation', p. 425.

35 See also Egeberg *et al.*, 'The EU's Subordinated', p. 341; R. Dehousse, 'Delegation of Powers in the European Union: The Need for a Multi-Principals Model', *West European Politics*, Vol. 31, No. 4, 2008, p. 796.

the process of shaping the catalogues of tasks for these bodies, ensures intergovernmental management mechanisms in agencies, and their integration with national authorities, in a given sector within cooperation networks[36]. Since the mid-1990s, the role of the European Parliament in the processes of defining the position of regulatory agencies has also increased. This is mainly related to a change in practice when it comes to the choice of a legal basis for establishing these bodies. The provisions which are currently selected guarantee the Parliament's co-deciding role in the ordinary legislative procedure[37].

Therefore, it can be said, on the one hand, that on account of being a significant component of the European administration within the meaning of Article 298 TFEU, regulatory agencies actively participate in the processes of balancing the competences of individual EU institutions[38]. On the other hand, since they are created as a result of the delegation of specific powers, they are themselves a product of competition for the sake of gaining influence. This plays out between these particular authorities, and the agencies are also a product of compromises resulting from the currently existing institutional order[39].

2. The *Meroni* Non-Delegation Doctrine

a) Delegation of Competencies

aa) Understanding the Term "Delegation"

The phenomenon of delegation of competencies is regarded as one of the foundations of liberal democracy. In simple terms, it means the transfer of specific powers between at least two entities where one of them should have strong democratic legitimacy in an ideal theoretical model. Such empowerment is

36 Vos, 'Agencies', p. 127.

37 See Chapter 7.

38 "The institutional balance of powers will not be upset so long as a shift of power is accompanied by reinforcing or re-balancing the existing institutions […]. This means that already under the current Treaty provisions, discretionary powers could be delegated to agencies provided that this be accompanied by a strengthening or re-balancing of existing institutions and functions", see E. Vos, 'Agencies and the European Union', in: T. Zwart, L. Verhey (ed.), *Agencies in European and Comparative Perspective*, Antwerpen 2003, pp. 131 ff.

39 Egeberg *et al.*, 'The EU's Subordinated', p. 342.

obtained by particular decision-makers in democratic elections[40]. Delegation of competencies involves entrusting, moving, transferring, ceding or designating specific tasks and functions. Such a delegation of powers takes place in countries with democratic systems according to specific procedures usually provided for explicitly in their constitutions. Apart from the normative component, politically determined considerations and choices are an inherent part of this process[41].

In the modern world, where different forms of international cooperation are developed, "international delegation" is increasingly observed. According to Eli Salzberger and Stefan Voigt, this process takes place when "rulemaking powers are exercised by a body that is not entirely under the control of domestic constitutional organs. A government might participate in the creation of an international organisation to which legislative power is delegated, but will not be the only actor that has a 'say' in the modification and interpretation of its statutes"[42]. The delegation of powers in this case is most likely when the body to which powers are delegated, for example, a particular international institution, enjoys high prestige. This legitimises the transfer of competencies, especially in the eyes of the electorate. Participation in international structures that have great authority in the international environment increases the popularity of decision-makers who seek to take part in such integration forums.

Theories on delegation focus on the interactions between the abovementioned subject of delegation, i.e. the actor that receives powers, and the delegating subject, i.e. the one that transfers these powers[43]. In the context of independent agencies, both at the national and European levels, references are made to a principal-agent relationship, as was mentioned before. Two scenarios are taken into consideration in this case: in its external dimension, there can be a delegation of specific powers by a country or a group of countries to an international institution; and in its internal dimension, it can be the delegation of competencies between two

40 "Elected politicians can choose to decide themselves or to delegate competence. Delegation can occur in constitutional stage, but is most common in the post-constitutional stage. Furthermore, domestic delegation can be distinguished from international delegation", see E.M. Salzberger, S. Voigt, 'On the Delegation of Powers: With Special Emphasis on Central and Eastern Europe', *Constitutional Political Economy*, Vol. 13, No. 1, 2002, p. 25.

41 *Ibid.*, p. 27; Ruszkowski, *Ponadnarodowość*, p. 113.

42 Salzberger, Voigt, 'On the Delegation', p. 28.

43 J. Bendor *et al.*, 'Theories of Delegation', *Annual Review of Political Science*, Vol. 4, 2001, pp. 236 ff.; F. Franchino, 'Delegating Powers in the European Community', *British Journal of Political Science*, Vol. 34, No. 2, 2004, pp. 270 ff.

public administration entities – the delegating authority, e.g. a ministry, and the authority that receives tasks, e.g. an independent agency[44]. Delegation of specific tasks is a form of decentralisation and deconcentration of administrative competence[45]. Delegating often involves relationships of the agent's dependence on, or even hierarchical subordination, to the principal. It is, therefore, of a conditional nature, meaning it may involve certain caveats and control mechanisms[46]. Moreover, delegation of competences, both in the external and internal dimension, is selective. Transfers involve tasks that cannot properly be performed by the delegating subject or cases when performing them entails excessive costs. An additional reason is the desire to delegate powers in areas that require the expertise of professional bodies that are free from direct pressures of a political nature[47].

Taking into account the material criterion, or the nature of delegated competencies, we can identify regulatory, implementing and legislative delegation. In the first case, it is about the powers that regulate particular sectors of the market. In this understanding, regulation primarily means shaping sector-specific policies[48]. In the second case, delegation involves transferring tasks related to executing and applying specific provisions. In the third case, delegated competences are of a legislative nature, meaning that they involve the adoption of legal acts[49].

Another division takes into account subjects that participate in delegating. In this context, one can identify primary and secondary delegation. Primary

44 See B. Eberlein, E. Grande, 'Beyond Delegation: Transnational Regulatory Regimes and the EU Regulatory State', *Journal of European Public Policy*, Vol. 12, No. 1, 2005, p. 91.

45 See M. Chamon, 'EU Agencies: Does the *Meroni* Doctrine Make Sense?', *Maastricht Journal of European and Comparative Law*, Vol. 17, No. 3, 2010, p. 286.

46 Particularly in the case of international institutions, delegation of powers comes with a range of safeguards. Therefore, we can only agree with the remark expressed in the EU context: "Actors are competence maximisers – that is, they will seek to ensure that policy will be enacted through procedures which maximise their own degree of control over the process of policy-making, and not through procedures where they have little or no control. As a result, in policy arguments, they will press for the widespread use of procedures that favour their own interests, and for less frequent use [and, where possible, the alteration or abandonment] of those procedures that do not", C.-F. Bergström *et al.*, 'Legislate or Delegate? Bargaining over Implementation and Legislative Authority in the EU', *West European Politics*, Vol. 30, No. 2, 2007, p. 342.

47 *Ibid.*, pp. 342–344.

48 More E. Mathieu, *Regulatory Delegation in the European Union: Networks, Committees and Agencies*, London 2016, pp. 2 ff.

49 *Ibid.*, pp. 25 ff.; Ruszkowski, *Ponadnarodowość*, p. 121.

delegation means transferring competencies "for the first time", by countries to supranational institutions[50]. Secondary delegation, on the other hand, takes place at the supranational level, or within authorities and bodies established in a particular international organisation. It is, therefore, a kind of redistribution of competencies originally assigned to these organisations by the voluntary decision of the member states or acquired in the integration process also by way of free decisions made by its participants.

One variety of secondary delegation is the transfer of powers between EU institutions and regulatory agencies. As Janusz Ruszkowski rightly points out, primary delegation is undertaken voluntarily by democratically elected, majoritarian institutions in the member states, where tasks are delegated to the supranational level, which mainly includes bodies that have not been democratically elected and so their rulemaking powers are of a technocratic nature. Secondary delegation, on the other hand, takes place only within supranational and international structures. It is also voluntary, but delegation occurs between authorities that are not democratically elected and bodies established under provisions and decisions contained in secondary legislation. As Ruszkowski concludes, "redistribution occurs outside the democratic process"[51].

bb) Delegation of Powers to Administrative Bodies

The traditional understanding of the position of the authorities in democratic systems envisages a clear division between legislative and executive tasks. The former should, in principle, be assigned to entities directly accountable to the electorate. According to a concept used in administrative sciences, the so-called transmission-belt model, there is a hierarchical order of legal acts in democratic systems[52]. Legislative acts adopted by the legislature, the actions of which are

---

50 After the entry into force of the Treaty of Lisbon, competencies between the EU and the member states are divided into the Union's exclusive powers, shared powers and the EU's implied powers to carry out activities designed to support, coordinate or complement the activities of the member states. See Barcz, *Unia Europejska*, pp. 108–109, 138–139. See also C. Mik, 'Powierzenie UE władzy przez państwa członkowskie i jego podstawowe konsekwencje prawne', in: Kranz (ed.), *Suwerenność*, pp. 83 ff.

51 Ruszkowski, *Ponadnarodowość*, p. 125. See also A. Menon, S. Waetherill, 'Legitimacy, Accountability and Delegation in the European Union', in: A. Arnull, D. Wincott (ed.), *Accountability and Legitimacy in the European Union*, Oxford/New York 2002, p. 119.

52 R. van Gestel, 'Primacy of the European Legislature? Delegated Rule-Making and the Decline of the "Transmission Belt" Theory', *The Theory and Practice of Legislation*, Vol. 2, No. 1, 2014, pp. 34 ff.; M. Weimer, G. Pisani, 'Expertise as Justification: The Contested Legitimation of the EU "Risk Administration"', in: M. Weimer, A. de Ruijter (ed.),

directly legitimised by voters, take precedence over norms issued by executive bodies. The "transmission belt" makes it possible, therefore, for a particular electorate to grant authority to a specific legislative body. "Secondary legislation", elaborated by public administration bodies, is controversial on account of it drifting away from this electorate in the process of "transmitting" powers – this is particularly the case with regulatory tasks. Therefore, specific delegation of legislative competences to executive bodies must have a legal basis and involve the identification of adequate control mechanisms. Autonomous regulatory agencies are only supposed to participate in the process of implementing legislation. In principle, it should also be forbidden to delegate discretionary powers to executive bodies[53]. In the European normative order, Article 290 TFEU is the legal basis for delegating the power to adopt non-legislative acts of general-application to the Commission as well as to supplement or amend certain non-essential elements of the legislative acts. The Commission is the only addressee of such a delegation; thus it is assumed that Article 290 TFEU constitutes a safeguard against delegation of legislative powers to EU agencies[54].

In institutionally complex supranational governance systems, such as the European Union, a "drift" away from voters is much more clearly seen than in legal systems at a nation-state level. Secondary delegation within the EU institutional system in the case of regulatory agencies is "horizontal", which means the "sub-delegation" of powers associated with shaping sector-specific policies by the European Commission to EU agencies under a Treaty-based authorisation and procedures delineated in the agencies' founding regulations[55]. A rapid growth of the agency system in recent years confirms the thesis formulated in the literature more than ten years ago that the Commission has adopted a strategy of supporting "extensive delegation" of powers as a part of weakening the control by the member states[56]. In such a system, EU agencies become instruments

---

Regulating Risks in the European Union. The Co-production of Expert and Executive Power, Oxford/Portland 2017, pp. 170 ff.

53 For more about the theoretical and legal basis for transferring powers to regulatory agencies, see R.B. Stewart, 'The Reformation of American Administrative Law', *Harvard Law Review*, Vol. 88, No. 8, 1975, pp. 1673, 1675; Franchino, 'Delegating', p. 274; Everson, 'The European System', p. 316.

54 See C. Ohler, 'Anmerkung zu EuGH, Urteil *v.* 22.1.2014, Rs. C-270/12', *Juristenzeitung*, Vol. 69, No. 5, 2014, p. 251. More also Mathieu, *Regulatory Delegation*, pp. 165 ff.

55 H.C.H. Hofmann, 'Agency Design in the European Union', *Windsor Yearbook of Access to Justice*, Vol. 28, No. 2, 2010, pp. 313 ff.

56 Bergström *et al.*, 'Legislate or Delegate?', p. 343.

facilitating the centralisation of regulatory functions at the EU level[57]. It is worth remembering that implementing powers, in principle, remains the remit of the member states. It is possible to delegate executive powers to the Commission and, in exceptional cases, also to the Council only on the basis of the norms explicitly elaborated in the Treaties, or according to Article 291(2) TFEU on the basis of legally binding Union acts for which uniform conditions for implementation are needed[58].

The process of sub-delegating powers can be identified with the abovementioned prediction by Majone about the birth of a "regulatory state". Such a creation should not be equated with the traditionally understood nation state, but with these supranational structures. Delegation of regulatory tasks results from the development of international cooperation. Regulation, in this context, is a development that occurs as part of the broader phenomenon of Europeanisation of legal and institutional space. Regulation of sector-specific policies at the supranational level is supposed to be more effective within the integrated internal market than the activities of the nation states[59].

One could ask in this context, why do the member states accept the proceeding evolution of the EU administration according to that model? The motives that drive states to enter into such forms of cooperation are of a functional nature and they are directly associated with the potential benefits that are expected to outweigh the costs of a particular delegation. An assumption is made, in this context, about the greater exclusiveness of international expert bodies and that consequently they are also apolitical to a greater extent[60]. Regulatory tasks are mostly performed by such technocratic agencies. They are independent of direct pressure from the potential electorate or parliamentary opposition. They are also not linked directly to the term limits of bodies operating in the administrative systems of the individual member states. Member states remain the primary delegators as they have the abovementioned "competence-competence", meaning that they enjoy a presumption of competence, while institutions at the

57 Trondal, Jeppesen, 'Images', p. 424.

58 Weißgärber, *Die Legitimation*, p. 245.

59 See Trondal, Jeppesen, 'Images', pp. 421 ff.; G. Majone, 'Regulatory Legitimacy', in: G. Majone (ed.), *Regulatory State*, London/New York 1996, p. 287; Eberlein, Grande, 'Beyond Delegation', p. 92.

60 Hofmann, 'Agency Design', p. 312, van Gestel, 'Primacy', p. 34; Vos, 'Agencies', pp. 114 ff.

supranational level operate only within explicitly specified powers entrusted to them by the member states[61].

When it comes to the secondary delegation of powers to EU regulatory agencies, the main driver for the member states and the EU institutions is the desire to meet the challenges associated with the de-centralised implementation of European law. The member states, within their own administrative structures and their own legislative procedures, ensure the implementation of European legislation into national legal systems. This is done in two ways: either on the basis of directly applicable European laws (primary law, regulations, directly applicable directives) or on the basis of the transposition of European law into national legal systems (primarily through directives). This state of affairs stems from Treaty provisions. Two principles, which have already been mentioned, are of fundamental importance: the principle of conferred powers (Article 5(2) TEU) and the principle of subsidiarity (Article 5(3) TEU). The direct legal basis, in turn, is Article 291(1) TFEU, according to which member states "shall adopt all measures of national law necessary to implement legally binding Union acts". The term "to implement" should be understood broadly, for it includes not only legislative acts, but also acts of administrative bodies[62]. The idea of de-central implementation of European law is called "federalism in the execution of laws" (Germ. *Vollzugsföderalismus*)[63] in the German legal doctrine, in reference to models taken from German law.

Coherent implementation of legal norms, in an integrated system, that are in accordance with the assumptions of de-central implementation requires a high level of coordination between the member states, their administrative offices and common integrated institutions. This coordination of activities is ensured by various bodies, such as comitology committees or regulatory networks[64]. Regulatory agencies have, indeed, been the most common form of cooperation

---

61 J. Ruszkowski, 'Pierwotne i wtórne delegowanie kompetencji w wielopoziomowym systemie zarządzania Unii Europejskiej', *Rocznik Integracji Europejskiej*, No. 6, 2012, p. 50.

62 M. Ruffert, 'Art. 291 AEUV', in: Calliess, Ruffert (ed.), *EUV/AEUV*, p. 2487.

63 G. Sydow, *Verwaltungskooperation in der Europäischen Union. Zur horizontalen und vertikalen Zusammenarbeit der europäischen Verwaltungen am Beispiel des Produktzulassungsrechts*, Tübingen 2004, p. 1; K. Lenaerts, 'Constitutionalism and the Many Faces of Federalism', *The American Journal of Comparative Law*, Vol. 38, No. 2, 1990, pp. 232 ff.

64 Concerning delegation within comitology, see Bergström *et al.*, 'Legislate or Delegate?', pp. 341 ff.

in the past several years. This has happened in connection with a rapid development of the integration process and, consequently, the intensification of activities within the internal market[65].

Delegation of powers seeks to create a network system to coordinate the process of the implementation of law. It is a response to growing challenges associated with European integration, which, in the view of Renaud Dehousse, "is an unprecedented attempt to build a form of continental order without recreating the hierarchical power structure of states"[66]. It is much easier for EU regulatory agencies than for national bodies to meet the challenges that involve obtaining information necessary to coordinate the European process of law implementation. This corresponds to the classic thesis repeated in analyses of delegating powers in different administrative models. The claim assumes that "delegating to informed agent is optimal for uninformed principal" and at the same time "informational asymmetries between principal and agent [are] central to delegation"[67]. This means that delegation of tasks becomes a routine mechanism, perceived as a "natural choice" where there is a lack of expertise necessary to perform them[68].

b) Case Law

aa) Meroni Case

The trend to intensively delegate tasks to regulatory agencies has only been seen, nonetheless, in the past several years. Previously, the possibility of secondary delegation of powers from the level of Community institutions to independent agencies was approached with considerable caution. This attitude towards the creation of regulatory agencies resulted primarily from the so-called *Meroni* doctrine, which can be called a non-delegation doctrine[69]. It limited the "sprawl" of agency structures for many years. The non-delegation doctrine emerged following judgments given by the Court of Justice in 1958[70]. In its rulings from

65 Hofmann, 'A European Regulatory Union', pp. 461 ff.
66 Dehousse, 'Delegation', p. 794.
67 Bendor *et al.*, 'Theories', pp. 240, 248.
68 *Ibid.*, pp. 258 ff.
69 More M. Simoncini, *Administrative Regulation*, pp. 7 ff.
70 Cases C-9/56 and C-10/56, *Meroni & Co. v. High Authority of the European Coal and Steel Community*, [13.6.1958] ECR 133 and 157. Meroni filed two lawsuits which are based on similar facts and the judgments concerning them largely correspond to each other. The Court ruled that a delegation cannot be presumed on the basis of the facts figured in the case 9/56. That is why the most authors refer to this case in the various

more than half a century ago, the Court defined the criteria allowing for the delegation of competencies by Community authorities to other, non-treaty-based institutions.

The situation to which the Court of Justice referred at the time had little in common with today's EU agencies. The case about which the Court made a decision concerned a complaint by the Italian steel company Meroni against a decision that was an order for payment to the so-called Imported Ferrous Scrap Equalisation Fund (Fr. *Caisse de Péréquation des Ferrailles Importées*). This Fund and the Joint Bureau of Ferrous Scrap Consumers (Fr. *Office Commun des Consommateurs de Ferraille*) were so-called Brussels Agencies, bodies comprising reputable private steel companies operating as *sociétés coopératives* under Belgian private law. The High Authority, a body that was the predecessor of the European Commission, entrusted them with administrative tasks relating to the fulfilment of company obligations resulting from the obligatory ferrous scrap equalisation system. The Brussels Agencies were supposed to operate "under the responsibility of the High Authority"[71]. The transfer of competencies took place under Article 53 of the Treaty establishing the European Coal and Steel Community. When Meroni failed to comply with the recommendations of the Brussels Agencies on the required payment to the Fund, the matter was referred to the High Authority, which issued a binding decision ordering the payment to be made[72].

Meroni argued in its complaint that the High Authority was not empowered to delegate powers, because this was not explicitly provided for in the Treaty. Moreover, the High Authority had delegated the competences conferred on it in the Treaty to "non-Treaty" bodies, but failed to link them to the conditions set out for itself in the Treaty provisions. This would have meant that the High Authority had transferred broader powers to the other bodies than those it enjoyed under

---

studies concerning the EU agencies. See Chamon, *EU Agencies*, p. 177; Griller, Orator, '*Meroni* Revisited', p. 5; R. Priebe, *Entscheidungsbefugnisse vertragsfremder Einrichtungen im Europäischen Gemeinschaftsrecht*, Baden-Baden 1979, p. 34; M. Simoncini, 'The Erosion of the *Meroni* Doctrine. The Case of the European Aviation Safety Agency', *European Public Law*, Vol. 21, No. 2, 2015, pp. 309 ff.

71 Article 1(2) of the High Authority Decisions No. 22/54 [26.3.1954, OJ 1954, 286] and No. 14/55 [26.3.1955, OJ 1955, 685].

72 See M. Scholten, *The Political Accountability of EU and US Independent Regulatory Agencies*, Leiden/Boston 2014, p. 82.

the Treaties itself. The applicant also accused the High Authority of delegating specific competences to bodies that were not competent to exercise them[73].

The Court of Justice found that, while delegation was illegal in the case examined, the delegation of powers to subsidiary bodies "which have a distinct legal personality" was admissible[74]. This determination was based on the premise that the contested decision was issued under a delegation that was incompatible with the Treaty establishing the European Coal and Steel Community, which was in force at the time. The Court concluded that the High Authority had delegated broad decision-making discretion to "non-Treaty" bodies, i.e. the Brussels Agencies. The Court considered this discretion to be contrary to the Treaty. In order for the delegation of powers to third parties, described in German scholarship as bodies "outside the Treaties" or "not foreseen under the Treaties" ("non-Treaty" institutions)[75], to be admissible, specific conditions must be met. First and foremost, it is only permitted when it is "necessary for the performance of the tasks set out in" respective articles and "compatible with" the Treaty's provisions[76]. Therefore, there must be a legal basis for delegating competencies and the basis for this should be clearly specified. The delegating authority must delegate specific powers *expressis verbis*[77]. Moreover, the delegating authority, in accordance with the Latin maxim *nemo plus iuris transferre potest quam ipse habet*, cannot transfer more powers than it has itself under Treaty provisions[78]. The institution that receives specific powers is bound by the same obligations and conditions as the delegating authority would have been if it had exercised them itself[79]. This concerns e.g. information obligations. The Court considered

73 Case 9/56, pp. 138 ff., 145 ff. More Weismann, *European Agencies*, p. 22; Simoncini, 'The Erosion', pp. 310 ff.

74 Case 9/56, p. 151.

75 See Chapter 1.

76 Case 9/56, p. 151.

77 The Court stated it unequivocally: "Any procedure for assessment by a body on its own authority and for provisional estimates must be subject to precise rules so as to exclude any arbitrary decisions and to render it possible to review the data used. A delegation of powers cannot be presumed and even when empowered to delegate its powers the delegating authority must take an express decision transferring them. There is no legal basis for the Brussels agencies' assessment on their own authority or for the notification of provisional debts and for this reason also the decision of 24 October 1956, which is an enforceable decision in respect of obligations arising from a procedure lacking any legal foundation, must be annulled", *ibid.*

78 *Ibid.*, p. 150.

79 *Ibid.*, pp. 149–150.

that both the High Authority and the Imported Ferrous Scrap Equalisation Fund had inadequately informed Meroni about the method of calculating fees[80].

The Court also specified what types of tasks could be delegated to the Brussels Agencies. The types of delegated tasks depend on the effects entailed by the legal act delegating the tasks. On the one hand, the Court identified "clearly defined executive powers the exercise of which can be subject to strict review in the light of objective criteria determined by the delegating authority" [81]. On the other hand, it noted the existence of "discretionary power(s), implying a wide margin of discretion which may, according to the use which is made of it, make possible the execution of actual economic policy"[82]. In connection with this distinction, the Court concluded that: "a delegation of the first kind cannot appreciably alter the consequences involved in the exercise of the powers concerned, whereas a delegation of the second kind, since it replaces the choices of the delegator by the choices of the delegatee, brings about an actual transfer of responsibility"[83]. Therefore, only strictly defined executive powers can be delegated. Delegation of competences implying discretion was ruled out as it would upset the "balance of powers" enshrined in the Treaty provisions which specify the division of tasks between authorities as well as relevant control procedures[84]. The Court stated this explicitly: "[a] delegation of powers [...] which implies a wide margin of discretion [...] cannot be considered as compatible with the requirements of the Treaty"[85]. This statement is unequivocal and categorical, and it is also commonly considered as the core of the *Meroni* doctrine[86]. Hence, it is inadmissible to delegate powers that would involve policy-making discretion[87].

---

80 "No information has been published, either by the High Authority or by the Brussels Agencies, so as to inform those to be charged of the methods whereby their obligations had been worked out or of the facts on which the calculations were based", *ibid.*, p. 144. Christoph Görisch writes in this context about transparency conditions necessary to comply with the requirements for the democratic functioning of public institutions (Germ. *Transparenzanforderungen*). See Görisch, *Demokratische Verwaltung*, p. 379.

81 Case 9/56, p. 152.

82 *Ibid.*

83 *Ibid.*

84 *Ibid.*

85 *Ibid.*, p. 154.

86 Chamon, *EU Agencies*, p. 204.

87 Scholten, *The Political Accountability*, p. 82.

The main assumptions of the non-delegation doctrine usually function in the legal literature within the following catalogue[88]:

(1) The Commission cannot delegate wider powers than it itself has.
(2) Delegation can only involve strictly executive powers.
(3) It is inadmissible to delegate discretionary powers, i.e. bodies which are delegated particular powers by the Commission do not enjoy discretion.
(4) The exercise of delegated powers is subject to the same conditions that apply to the delegating authority.
(5) Delegation of powers is carried out under the Commission's control and responsibility.
(6) The institutional balance cannot be upset, i.e. among other things, one authority, for example the Commission, cannot encroach onto the remit of other institutions.

In the following decades, the Court occasionally referred to the criteria formulated in the *Meroni* case, but focused primarily on the nature of delegated powers and their necessary judicial review[89]. One of the major judgments, which tightened the *Meroni* doctrine in the context of the possible delegation of legislative tasks, was the 1981 judgment in the *Romano* case[90]. The Court at the time prohibited the Community legislature from entrusting bodies other than the Commission with competencies to adopt "act(s) having the force of law". The injunction concerned transferring powers to entities with no direct anchorage in the Treaties[91]. Even though the Court did not explicitly invoke the principle of

---

88 See also K. Lenaerts, 'Regulating the Regulatory Process: "Delegation of Powers" in the European Community', *European Law Review*, Vol. 18, No. 1, 1993, pp. 23 ff.; K. Lenearts *et al.* (ed.), *Constitutional Law of the European Union*, London 2005, pp. 620 ff.; Vos, 'Agencies', p. 130; Hummer, 'Von der Agentur', p. 99; Kietz, von Ondarza, 'Sicherheit', p. 13; T. Tridimas, 'Community Agencies, Competition Law and ESCB Initiatives on Securities Clearing and Settlement', *Yearbook of European Law*, Vol. 28, No. 1, 2009, pp. 241–243.

89 See B. Holznagel, P. Schumacher, 'Die politische Unabhängigkeit der Bundesnetzagentur', in: Gramlich, Manger-Nestler (ed.), *Europäisierte Regulierungsstrukturen*, pp. 49 ff.; Hagen, *Ist die EU*, pp. 159 ff.; C. Koenig *et al.*, 'Do We Really Need a European Agency for Market Regulation?', *Intereconomics*, Vol. 43, No. 4, 2008, p. 230.

90 Case 98/80 *Giuseppe Romano v. Institut National d'Assurance Maladie-Invalidité*, [14.5.1981] ECR 1241, para 20.

91 See D. Adamski, 'The *ESMA* Doctrine: A Constitutional Revolution and the Economics of Delegation', *European Law Review*, Vol. 39, No. 6, 2014, p. 814; Skowron, 'Agencje', p. 47; C. Manger-Nestler, 'EU-Agenturen als Ausdruck des europäischen Demokartiemangels?', *Zeitschrift für europarechtliche Studien*, Vol. 18, No. 3, 2015, pp. 331 ff.

institutional balance in the *Romano* judgment, it is often considered as a confirmation of the *Meroni* doctrine[92].

bb) "Free Discretion" in EU Regulatory Agencies' Decision Making

The underlying assumption of the *Meroni* doctrine involves the banning of transferring actual decision-making responsibility to bodies "outside the Treaties". In German literature, the term "free discretion" (Germ. *freies Ermessen*) is used in this context. In principle, according to a restrictive interpretation of the *Meroni* doctrine, such discretion in decision making is ruled out. However, considering that the creation of regulatory agencies is a serious step that fundamentally changes the institutional structure in a particular sector of the internal market, it is difficult to imagine such bodies having no discretion regarding matters falling within their scope of competence[93]. Such judgments (Germ. *Beurteilung*), however, should be strictly technical and result directly from the expert nature of a particular agency[94]. While tasks entrusted to agencies in the 1990s were, indeed, limited to technical expertise, the evolution of these bodies in the 2000s and the creation of such entities as the ESAs or ACER led to a rapid expansion of the understanding of specialised support[95].

In the latest agencies, classified as the so-called fourth generation, this includes decision-making competences set out explicitly in founding regulations. Their catalogue is often extended by complementary regulations for specific market sectors, as it was in the case of the ESMA described below. In addition, as was pointed out by Martin Shapiro in the second half of the 1990s, informational tasks often also have policy implications[96]. This particularly concerns sensitive areas of the market where agencies operate. It is enough to mention, for example, aviation, maritime and rail safety, trade in chemicals, food and medicines as well as environmental protection. In virtually every area where European regulatory agencies

---

92 van Cleynenbreugel, '*Meroni*', p. 82.

93 Takis Tridimas goes as far as to write that "the setting up of an agency makes sense only if it can take initiatives and exercise real powers of decision-making", T. Tridimas, 'Financial Supervision and Agency Power: Reflections on ESMA', in: N. Nic Shuibhne, L.W. Gormley (ed.), *From Single Market to Economic Union. Essays in Memory of John A. Usher*, Oxford 2012, p. 59.

94 See B. Holznagel, P. Schumacher, 'Funktionelle Unabhängigkeit und demokratische Legitimation europäischer Regulierungsagenturen', in: D. Joost *et al.* (ed.), *Festschrift für Franz Jürgen Säcker zum 70. Geburtstag*, München 2011, pp. 751 ff.; Görisch, *Demokratische Verwaltung*, p. 378.

95 Steger, *Zur Verselbstständigung*, pp. 58 ff.

96 Shapiro, 'The Problems', pp. 281 ff.

operate, the information they prepare can have an impact on specific policy actions and not only those at a regional level. When they are connected by a network of links to other entities in a particular market sector, such as e.g. EFSA, their opinion also often affects the behaviour of other international organisations or third countries[97].

Consequently, in practice it is difficult to imagine that the prohibition of agencies having delegated competences involving "discretion" could be viable in the current EU institutional system. It should be assumed instead that "political choices" in the narrow, specialised remit of a particular agency are a part of its everyday duties[98]. For this reason, control and legitimacy mechanisms used in relation to agency activity take on special importance.

c) Assessment of the *Meroni* Non-Delegation Doctrine

The *Meroni* doctrine became a symbol of the processes of evolution of the EU administration with particular consideration to the role of regulatory agencies. There are few studies concerning these bodies that do not refer, even briefly, to the 1958 judgments[99]. Interestingly, despite many comments about the need to update the doctrine, it is difficult to find opinions suggesting it should be rejected altogether[100]. The concept, created on the basis of the judgments from the 1950s, caused a decades-long "shock" and "traumatic impasse" blocking most initiatives involving the development of European administration[101]. Even back in the 1970s, some authors rightly called the iron discipline in complying with the *Meroni* doctrine "dogmatic paralysis"[102]. Hardly anyone expected at the time that European integration would become as wide-ranging as it is today. Even less could the Court's judges have predicted that their rulings would leave a deep mark on the institutionalisation of European administration.

---

97 Groenleer, Gabbi, 'Regulatory Agencies', pp. 484 ff.

98 See Weismann, *European Agencies*, p. 27; Fischer-Appelt, *Agenturen*, p. 109; M. Everson, E. Vos, 'European Agencies: What About the Institutional Balance?', in: A. Łazowski, S. Blockmans (ed.) *Research Handbook of EU Institutional Law*, Cheltenham/Northampton 2016, pp. 139 ff.

99 There are even opinions about many alternative "*Meroni* doctrines" depending on a particular interpretation of the Court's judgments. See Chamon, *EU Agencies*, pp. 187–192.

100 See J.-P. Schneider, 'A Common Framework for Decentralised EU Agencies and the *Meroni* Doctrine', *Administrative Law Review*, Vol. 61, Special Edition, 2009, pp. 37 ff.

101 P. Karpenstein, 'Die Entwicklung des Gemeinschaftsrechts', *Europarecht*, No. 4, 1975, p. 358; J. Kühling, 'Die Zukunft des Europäischen Agentur(un)wesens – oder: Wer hat Angst vor *Meroni*', *Europäische Zeitschrift für Wirtschaftsrecht*, Vol. 19, No. 5, 2008, p. 129; Griller, Orator, '*Meroni* Revisited', p. 6.

102 See Priebe, *Entscheidungsbefugnisse*, pp. 16 ff.; Hummer, 'Von der Agentur', p. 100.

For several decades from the 1970s to the early twenty first century, the *Meroni* doctrine constituted a sort of leitmotif in the discussion about regulatory agencies, both in the scientific debate and the political debate prompted by the European Commission. As mentioned above, depending on the current sentiment in the Commission itself, it has exhibited various attitudes towards the expansion of the European agency system. For a long time the tenor of the non-delegation doctrine also reflected the sentiment in the member states. They were afraid that regulatory agencies could develop into a competitor when it came to carrying out administrative tasks reserved for national authorities. The assumptions of the *Meroni* doctrine, therefore, often served as a "cover" for political motives and wariness towards the delegation or division of powers[103]. Hence, the question that accompanied the creation of regulatory agencies for years was whether to delegate various kinds of powers to those bodies. Over the past several years, this question has been undergoing a major transformation. Even though officially the *Meroni* doctrine has not disappeared from the legal discourse, there is no doubt that delegation of growing powers to new agencies and the broadening of the mandates of existing ones has become a *fait accompli.* Nonetheless, the question that should be asked is how to delegate these competences in compliance with primary law[104].

The *Meroni* doctrine has many flaws that primarily involve the fictionality of its restrictive application in relation to regulatory agencies[105]. A lot of arguments are put forward in this context. Those of a legal nature mainly concern changes in the Treaty law. The *Meroni* judgment dealt with a completely different legal situation than that within which EU agencies operate nowadays. The changes introduced by the Treaty of Lisbon institutionalised these bodies as a part of the independent EU administrative apparatus. Thus, they are not bodies established under private law, as was in the case of the Brussels Agencies examined in 1958, which had specific powers conferred onto them by the High Authority within

---

103 See Tridimas, 'Financial Supervision', p. 63.

104 T. Hustedt *et al.*, *Verwaltungsstrukturen*, p. 157.

105 "Over the years agencies have accumulated powers within their funding regulations that appear to exceed the strictly circumscribed executive powers stipulated by the Court in *Meroni*. [...] In practice the EU is host to a very particular paradox whereby EU institutions, in particular the Commission, stress that the delegation of powers to agencies will involve only narrowly circumscribed powers, yet, in a legislative reality, pursue a seemingly fare more indulgent attitude", Everson, Vos, 'European Agencies', p. 144. See also Pawlik, *Das REACH-System*, p. 20.

the ECSC system, but components of the EU administration, subject to the European Commission's control, and established under secondary legislation[106].

Regulatory agencies not only function within a different legal framework, but also in a substantially altered factual situation. The process of integrating European structures since the late 1950s has changed so dramatically that we can metaphorically speak of centuries rather than decades. Supranational sector-specific regulation is a fact and the agencies are one of its main pillars. Hence, practical arguments have for years focused on developing a more dynamic interpretation of the *Meroni* doctrine. It is not only about putting it in line with the growth of the agency system thus far, which has already occurred, and there is nothing to indicate a possible "reversal" in this regard, but also allowing for further evolution of the European administration. This evolution should proceed depending on functional needs, but also with respect to the fundamental normative principles underpinning the EU's institutional system[107]. One can agree with the view of Damien Geradin and Nicholas Petit "that the creation of European regulatory agencies [...] allow[s] the EC institutions to focus on their core [legislative] competencies and thus improve the institutional balance of the EU"[108]. There is little doubt that the harmonisation and implementation of European law in particular sectors of the internal market could not have taken place without delegation of powers to subsidiary bodies such as agencies. We can read about the invaluable benefits of expert support in countless studies devoted to specific areas of agency activity[109]. We should instead consider "inscribing" increasingly detailed decision-making and "semi-regulatory" powers into the concepts of institutional balance. The expectations for an updated *Meroni* doctrine and an adaptation of its understanding to the actual competences of today's regulatory agencies has been expressed in the past several years at almost every opportunity

---

106 See M. Ruffert, 'Die neue Unabhängigkeit: Zur demokratischen Legitimation von Agenturen im europäischen Verwaltungsrecht', in: P.-C. Müller-Graff *et al.* (ed.), *Europäisches Recht zwischen Bewährung und Wandel. Festschrift für Dieter H. Scheuing*, Baden-Baden 2011, pp. 403 ff.; Koenig *et al.*, 'Do We', p. 231.

107 See also Curtin, Dehousse, 'European Union Agencies', pp. 203 ff.; Everson, 'European Agencies', p. 53; S. Griller, A. Orator, 'Empowering European Agencies or How to Tame the Sorcerer's Apprentice', *NewGov Policy Brief*, No. 22, 2008, p. 3.

108 Geradin, Petit, 'The Development', p. 31.

109 E.g. extensively in the context of the advantages of the European system of chemical substance registration: Pawlik, *Das REACH-System*, pp. 145–191. Michelle Everson goes as far as to write in this context that "we could no longer govern the EU without agencies", 'European Agencies', p. 53.

in the context of the position and functioning of these bodies[110]. The CJEU responded to these expectations more than four years ago, in January 2014, in the *Short selling* case.

3. Reinterpretation of the Concept of Delegating Powers to Regulatory Agencies

a) The *Short Selling* Case

aa) The ESMA Intervention Powers

Despite the relatively short time that has passed since the 2014 judgment, one can get the impression, considering the number of publications, that the reinterpretation of the *Meroni* doctrine by the Court of Justice is equally important for the agency system as the *Meroni* doctrine itself[111]. Some authors, shortly after the judgment was issued, wondered in their comments whether we should speak explicitly about the *ESMA* doctrine[112]. Such statements seem to be, however, a bit exaggerated. That is because, contrary to expectations, the Court did not make a "revolutionary" change in the understanding of the existing rules for delegating tasks to EU agencies. Perhaps even the term "reinterpretation" (used in the title of this subchapter) promises more than one can actually infer from

110 See also Chamon, 'EU Agencies: Does the *Meroni*', pp. 281 ff.; Häde, 'Jenseits', pp. 663 ff.; Sölter, *Rechtsgrundlagen*, pp. 77 ff.; Wittinger, 'Europäische Satelliten', p. 620; Manger-Nestler, 'EU-Agenturen', p. 330; Kühling 'Die Zukunft', p. 129; Smulders, Eisele, 'Reflections', p. 118.

111 See e.g. in addition to comments to the *Short selling* judgment cited elsewhere: C. Manger-Nestler, 'Lehren aus dem Leerverkauf? Zum Verbot von Leervrkäufen durch ESMA', *Zeitschrift für das Privatrecht der Europäischen Union*, Vol. 11, No. 3, 2014, pp. 141 ff.; H. Marjosola, 'Bridging the Constitutional Gap in EU Executive Rule-Making: The Court of Justice Approves Legislative Conferral of Intervention Powers to European Securities Markets Authority', *European Constitutional Law Review*, Vol. 10, No. 3, 2014, pp. 500 ff.; S. Gabbi, 'The Principle of Institutional (Un)Balance after Lisbon. Case Note: C-270/12', *European Journal of Risk Regulation*, Vol. 5, No. 2, 2014, pp. 263 ff.; G. Lo Shiavo, 'A Judicial Re-Thinking on the Delegation of Powers to European Agencies under EU Law? Comment on Case C-270/12 UK *v.* Council and Parliament', *German Law Journal*, Vol. 16, No. 2, 2015, pp. 320 ff.

112 Adamski, 'The *ESMA* Doctrine', pp. 829 ff.; M. Scholten, M. van Rijsbergen, 'The *ESMA-Short Selling* Case. Erecting a New Delegation Doctrine in the EU upon the *Meroni-Romano* Remnants', *Legal Issues of Economic Integration*, Vol. 41, No. 4, 2014, pp. 390 ff.

the Court's position in the *Short selling* case. Not only did the CJEU not reject the assumptions adopted sixty years earlier in the *Meroni* case, but it even explicitly confirmed their continuous validity[113]. The "reinterpretation" found in the title primarily involves the conclusion that while delegation should remain within the framework set out in the *Meroni* case, what needs to be taken into account is the different nature of regulatory agencies compared to the Brussels Agencies that the 1958 judgment concerned. The former are not private law entities, but a permanent component of the European administration governed by EU law[114].

As has already been mentioned in the context of choosing the legal basis for the establishment of agencies, the United Kingdom filed a complaint with the Court concerning the "intervention powers in exceptional circumstances" conferred on the European Securities and Markets Authority under Article 28 of Regulation No. 236/2012[115]. The intervention powers specified in Article 28(1) of Regulation No. 236/2012 were subject to a number of specific safeguard clauses. The ESMA can make decisions under Article 28(1) only when: (1) there is a threat to the orderly functioning and integrity of financial markets or to the stability of the whole or part of the financial system in the Union, (2) there are cross-border implications of the ongoing developments, and (3) competent national authorities have failed to act or the measures they have taken do not adequately address the threat[116].

Moreover, ESMA should take into account the extent of protection against the threat to financial markets provided by the measures that need to be taken, consider whether the instruments used create a risk of regulatory arbitrage and whether by decreasing their efficiency or reducing liquidity, they disrupt the orderly functioning of financial markets[117]. All of these requirements must be met cumulatively. Measures adopted by ESMA, if they are not renewed, expire

113 For criticism on this issue, see M. Ruffert, 'Rechtsgrundlagen und Rechtsetzungsbefugnisse von Agenturen', *Juristische Schulung*, Vol. 54, No. 3, 2014, p. 280.

114 Everson, Vos, *European Agencies*, p. 144; Gabbi, 'The Principle', p. 263.

115 The powers are consistent with the ESMA's competences conferred on it back in the 2011 regulation establishing it (No. 1095/2010) in Article 9(5). The provision states that in certain situations "the Authority may temporarily prohibit or restrict certain financial activities". About the controversies related to Article 9 of Regulation No. 1095/2010 see Kohtamäki, *Die Reform*, pp. 195 ff.

116 Article 28(2) of Regulation No. 236/2012. See Gabbi, 'The Principle', p. 260.

117 Article 28(3) of Regulation No. 236/2012.

after three months[118]. They prevail over any previous measures adopted by national authorities[119].

It is noteworthy that Article 28 of Regulation No. 236/2012 grants ESMA some discretion that is not expressed in the founding Regulation No. 1095/2010. It was established after lengthy negotiations in 2010 that the Council was the only authority empowered to adopt a decision, in appropriate cases, determining the existence of an emergency situation[120], i.e. one whose development jeopardises the orderly functioning and integrity of financial markets or the stability of the whole or part of the financial system in the Union[121]. According to Article 18(2) of Regulation No. 1095/2010, ESMA can initiate such a decision, but it is not empowered to make a final assessment to determine the existence of a situation jeopardising the integrity and stability of EU financial markets. The crisis situation in Article 28(2) lit. a of Regulation No. 236/2012 is defined in the same way as in Article 18(1) of Regulation No. 1095/2010. Therefore, there is an impression of inconsistency. For unknown reasons, it was decided that only in the case of a short selling ban for legal and natural persons does ESMA have the right to independently assess whether a crisis situation exists and is empowered to intervene, even though according to the regulations establishing the European Supervisory Authorities (e.g. No. 1095/2010) a decision by the Council is necessary to determine that there is a risk of a financial crisis[122]. It is difficult to predict how the Court would, in practice, have assessed a ban issued by the ESMA without the Council's earlier announcement of a crisis situation[123].

bb) The ESMA Ruling

In its complaint, the United Kingdom pointed to four reasons for the unlawfulness of Article 28 of Regulation No. 236/2012. First, it is contrary to the fundamental principle established by the Court of Justice in the *Meroni* judgment, which involves the injunction to delegate discretionary powers. Second, ESMA is empowered under Article 28 to adopt binding measures of general application

---

118 Article 28(10) of Regulation No. 236/2012.
119 Article 28(11) of Regulation No. 236/2012.
120 Article 18(2) of Regulation No 1095/2010.
121 Article 18(1) of Regulation No 1095/2010.
122 Article 18(2) is worded identically in Regulations No. 1095/2010 (ESMA), No. 1094/2010 (EIOPA), No. 1093/2010 (EBA).
123 See e.g. Article 29 of Regulation No. 236/2012. Extensively about these inconsistencies see Ohler, 'Anmerkung', p. 250.

("quasi-legislative acts") contrary to the Court's decision in the *Romano* case. Third, Article 28 confers on ESMA the right to adopt non-legislative acts of general application, whereas according to Articles 290 and 291 TFEU, the Council is not empowered to delegate such powers to a mere agency outside of these provisions. And fourth, an interpretation that Article 28 empowers ESMA to take individual measures directed at natural or legal persons would contravene Article 114 TFEU[124]. The fourth argument and the Court's opinion in this respect have been presented as part of an examination of the legal basis cited for the establishment of regulatory agencies[125].

Contrary to the opinion of the Advocate General, the CJEU decided to dismiss the British complaint. The Court primarily focused on the arguments regarding the scope of competences conferred on the ESMA. It devoted less attention to the more important issue for the development of agency structures, i.e. the question whether the powers conferred on ESMA are compatible with primary law, including Article 114 TFEU.

As was mentioned above, the judgment in Case 9/56 (*Meroni*) formulated the framework for an admissible delegation of powers. The Court concluded that such a delegation must involve clearly defined executive powers rather than "discretionary power(s), implying a wide margin of discretion, which may, according to the use which is made of it, make possible the execution of actual economic policy"[126]. A shift of discretionary powers, which implies discretion for the authority exercising them, brings about an "actual transfer of responsibility". The Court, when characterising the *Meroni* judgments in its ruling from 22 January 2014, made it clear that they concerned a private entity while ESMA "is a European Union entity, created by the EU legislature"[127]. It is, therefore, a part of the EU administration within the meaning of Article 298(1) TFEU.

This is, nevertheless, not the only reason why the delegation limitations delineated in the *Meroni* case do not apply to the powers conferred on ESMA under Article 28 of Regulation No. 236/2012. First, the provision does not confer on it, in the Court's opinion, any autonomous power that goes beyond the bounds of the regulatory framework established by founding Regulation No. 1095/2010[128]. Second, the exercise of the powers under Article 28 is circumscribed by various

124 *Ibid.*

125 See Chapter 1.

126 Quote from Case 270/12, para 41.

127 Case 270/12, para 43.

128 *Ibid.*, para 44.

conditions and criteria that clearly define the agency's scope of activity[129]. Third, the measures from Article 28 (1) are strictly confined to the ESMA's competences set out in Article 9(5) of its founding Regulation No. 1095/2010. The provision empowers the agency to ban or restrict some types of financial activity in specific situations[130]. And fourth, ESMA consults with the European Systemic Risk Board pursuant to Article 28(4) and (5) of Regulation No. 236/2012 and with other authorities, if necessary, before taking action and also regularly reviews the measures adopted[131].

Therefore, in the CJEU's opinion, the powers conferred under Article 28 of Regulation No. 236/2012 are "precisely delineated and amenable to judicial review in the light of the objectives established by the delegating authority". This is not a "very large measure of discretion" as the applicant claimed. According to the Court's opinion, they comply with the requirements laid down in the *Meroni* judgments – the first plea raised in the complaint was, therefore, considered unfounded[132].

However, a question could be asked concerning whether the powers of the European Securities and Markets Authority are limited solely to factual assessments of a technical nature as the Court would have it[133]. It is easy to imagine that, in the event of a crisis, what will primarily matter will be political influence and various *ad hoc* coalition groups formed in the ESMA's main decision-making body – the Board of Supervisors[134] – comprising heads of national supervisory institutions representing financial markets with similar interests. It is hard to assume that motivations resulting from natural political interests will be completely excluded and decisions about banning or restricting short selling will be purely technical, and quasi-automatic – dependent only on legal arguments. This is confirmed by the type of chaotic situation, described earlier, when it comes to determining the existence of a crisis situation. It is not clear whether measures taken by ESMA without the Council's decision about the emergence of such a situation, in accordance with Article 18(2) of Regulation No. 1095/2010 (as well as Regulations Nos. 1093/2010 and 1094/2010), should be recognised as

129 *Ibid.*, paras 45–48.

130 *Ibid.*, para 49.

131 *Ibid.*, para 50.

132 *Ibid.*, paras 53–55. See M. Chamon, 'Granting Powers to EU Decentralised Agencies Three Years Following *Short-Selling*', *ERA Forum*, Published Online in September 2017, p. 3.

133 Case 270/12, para 52.

134 Articles 40–44 of Regulation No. 1095/2010.

valid. And if so, then why is it that only ESMA, excluding the other European Supervisory Authorities (EBA and EIOPA), would be empowered to make independent assessments on whether there is a threat to the orderly functioning and integrity of the financial markets and the stability of the whole, or part, of the financial system in the Union[135].

The Court, referring to the claim that ESMA is empowered under Article 28 of Regulation No. 236/2012 to adopt binding measures of general application ("quasi-legislative acts") contrary to the Court's judgment in the *Romano* case, concluded that the institutional framework created by the Treaty of Lisbon clearly permits the EU institutions and organisational units, thus also regulatory agencies, to adopt acts of general application[136]. Justifying this assertion, the Court pointed explicitly to Articles 263(1) and 277 TFEU. The first one guarantees legal protection against acts of EU institutions or organisational units intended to produce legal effects vis-à-vis third parties. It mentions reviewing the legality of such legislative acts by the Court rather than their potential classification as "quasi-legislative acts". Moreover, many lawyers consider Article 263 TFEU to be insufficient legal protection in relation to legal acts adopted by regulatory agencies[137]. Article 277 TFEU is more precise in this context as it mentions "acts of general application adopted by an institution, body, office or agency of the Union", thus also regulatory agencies. However, it is difficult to recognise Article 277 TFEU as a basis which empowers such bodies to adopt binding normative acts of general application[138].

In the Court's opinion, it cannot be inferred from the *Romano* judgment that delegation of powers to an institution such as ESMA is governed by conditions other than those described in the *Meroni* judgments. As the Court's assessment did not show that powers resulting from Article 28 of Regulation No 236/2012 are at odds with them, the applicant's second plea was dismissed[139].

The United Kingdom's third plea involved powers to adopt delegated acts governed by Article 290 TFEU, and powers to adopt executive acts governed by Article 291 TFEU. These provisions define delegation of such powers to the

---

135 See Article 28(2) lit. a of Regulation No. 236/2012 and Article 18(1) of Regulation No. 1095/2010.

136 Case 270/12, paras 63–65.

137 See Everson, 'European Agencies', p. 52; M. Chamon, 'EU Agencies between *Meroni* and *Romano* or the Devil and the Deep Blue Sea', *Common Market Law Review*, Vol. 48, No. 4, 2011, pp. 1070 ff.

138 See extensive discussion of this issue in Ohler, 'Anmerkung', pp. 250 ff.

139 Case C-270/12, paras 66–68.

Commission[140]. They do not refer to direct delegation to regulatory agencies. Already in its founding regulation, ESMA, like EBA and EIOPA, received some competences to adopt the so-called regulatory technical standards, which have the form of delegated acts within the meaning of Article 290 TFEU as well as the so-called implementing technical standards, developed by way of executive acts within the meaning of Article 291 TFEU[141]. However, in both these instances the Commission is the recipient of delegation to adopt regulatory and implementing technical standards. These powers, conferred on the supervisory agencies in the reform process of 2009–2011, immediately aroused some controversy as the agencies obtained a relatively independent role in adopting both types of standards. The Commission performs consultative functions, it only has a limited right to introduce changes in draft acts, and it can submit such drafts on its own only when the supervisory agencies fail to act. These competencies have already sparked a discussion on whether such a limited role of the Commission reflects the spirit of Articles 290 and 291 TFEU[142]. In the case of Article 28(1) of Regulation No. 236/2012, ESMA has even greater discretion. In this provision, it would be the recipient of the delegation of such powers. Moreover, there is no obligation for the adopted measures to be approved by the Commission, unlike in the case of regulatory and implementing technical standards.

The justification provided by the Court is surprising. It stated that, despite the Treaties not containing any provision to the effect that powers to adopt non-legislative acts of general application may be conferred on an organisational unit such as a regulatory agency, a number of TFEU provisions presuppose that such a possibility exists[143]. Moreover, Article 28 gives ESMA "decision-making powers in an area which requires the deployment of specific technical and professional expertise" which is probably supposed to justify the admissibility of delegating such competences[144]. This explanation is all the more surprising when compared

140 There is already extensive literature about these powers, see e.g. J. Mendes, 'Delegated and Implementing Rule Making: Proceduralisation and Constitutional Design', *European Law Journal*, Vol. 19, No. 1, 2013, pp. 22 ff.; S. Peers, M. Costa, 'Accountability for Delegated and Implementing Acts after the Treaty of Lisbon', *European Law Journal*, Vol. 18, No. 3, 2012, pp. 427 ff.

141 Articles 10–14 of Regulation No. 1095/2010 govern regulatory technical standards. Article 15 of Regulation No. 1095/2010 governs implementing technical standards.

142 See Ohler, 'Die Einheitlichkeit', p. 444; Busuioc, 'Rule-Making', pp. 115 ff.

143 The Court referred here to Articles 263 and 277 TFEU, already mentioned in reference to the second plea, as well as Articles 265 and 267 TFEU. See Case 270/12, paras 79–80.

144 *Ibid.*, para 82.

to the complex requirements in Article 290 TFEU that must be met when powers to adopt delegated acts are delegated to the Commission. Yet the last argument is the most surprising. It implies that while intervention competences in Article 28 do not correspond to any situations defined in Articles 290 and 291 TFEU, this provision should not be considered in isolation[145]. It should be seen through the prism of other regulations and as part of an entire system of mechanisms designed to provide protection against adverse developments that threaten the financial stability and market confidence in the EU[146]. Therefore, Article 28 of Regulation No. 236/2012 does not undermine the system created by Articles 290 and 291 TFEU, because the intervention powers it provides for are necessary to prevent market collapses[147]. In practice this kind of explanation means that the actual demand for certain interventionist actions in a crisis situation, in this case involving a ban or restrictions on short selling, is put above the existing Treaty framework.

This position of the Court is a logical consequence of the steps taken in the last several years towards further, intensive institutionalisation of cooperation within the EU system. Many authors who have followed this process for more than two decades have commented on the Court's judgment as a reasonably natural and logical result of the activities of EU agencies. In their view, taking into account the political determinants resulting from the undermined financial stability in the European markets, it would have been a more surprising solution if the Court had agreed with the British case and rejected the possibility of conferring intervention powers on ESMA[148].

b) Regulatory Agencies as a Permanent Component of the European Executive Order

Regardless of how we understand the CJEU's motives, one can get the impression that the judgment on the ESMA's intervention powers confirms what specialists have long noticed: that the ever growing decision-making competences of regulatory agencies barely fall within the existing framework of primary law. Another noteworthy item in the described judgment is the Court's relatively liberal attitude to the *Meroni* doctrine. It opens the way for a new interpretation of the term

---

145 Chamon, 'Granting', p. 5.

146 Case 270/12, paras 83–85. Extensively about the CJEU's reasoning in this respect: Ruffert, 'Rechtsgrundlagen', p. 281.

147 Case 270/12, paras 85–86.

148 Everson, Vos, 'European Agencies', p. 147.

“discretionary powers”. Matthias Ruffert puts it directly when he comments that this attitude paves the way for further expansion of the agency system[149].

Taking into account the principle of institutional balance in the European Union, one has to wonder whether such an expansion of the European executive order, observed for more than a decade, does not significantly upset this. The development of executive bodies in supranational structures poses an exceptional challenge. It is a long-lasting process that usually involves the slow evolution of existing bodies. A close relationship with the EU legislature is an inherent part of it. Regulatory agencies, assisting the Commission in preparing various draft legislation, participate in the legislative process[150]. In addition to that, as has been mentioned already several times, agencies have practical influence on the implementation of European law in the member states. Their existence at the EU level is primarily associated with facilitating the coherent transposition of EU legislation into national legal systems.

The argumentation put forward by the CJEU in 2014, which invoked the *Meroni* doctrine does not correspond to the challenges faced by the EU administration as integration advances, for example, in rapidly changing financial markets. In this context Ruffert goes as far as to write about the anachronism of the Court, which seems to be oblivious to the development of primary law and the changes introduced by the Treaty of Lisbon, such as Article 10(1) TEU or Article 298(1) TFEU which place regulatory agencies in the European institutional system more precisely than the *Meroni* non-delegation doctrine[151]. The former provision concerns the principle of representative democracy, which puts certain limits on the creation of bodies of this kind[152]. The latter, as already mentioned, introduces the term of independent European administration with agencies as its component.

Yet the evolution of the role of agencies in European executive mechanisms can also be examined from another angle – seeing them not as upsetting the balance, but as a special way of shaping the *equilibrium* within the EU “executive order”. Balancing the position of the European Commission is of particular importance here, because it remains the central authority coordinating the agency system and, as an authority formally delegating tasks, it also exercises

149 Ruffert, ‘Rechtsgrundlagen’, p. 281. Also Chamon: “To a great extent, the Court’s ruling in *Short selling* may be read as a drafting manual for the Commission and legislature when they contemplate granting further powers to EU agencies”, ‘Granting’, p. 4.
150 See also Hofmann, Morini, ‘The Pluralisation’, pp. 429 ff.
151 Ruffert, ‘Rechtsgrundlagen’, p. 281.
152 For more about this principle see Chapter 4.

control over individual entities in the European administration. Nonetheless, agencies can also perform a balancing function in the context of exercising powers previously unseen at the pan-European level. Their balancing function relies on their extensive independence while maintaining close relationships with the Commission and regulatory authorities in the member states. If agencies were completely independent and exercised their powers in isolation from the European Commission's supervision and intergovernmental cooperation mechanisms, there would be a risk of open competition between the delegating entities and recipients of this delegation. In the case of agencies, the Commission has largely succeeded in maintaining this fragile *equilibrium*[153].

A problem commented on in the legal literature in view of the *Short selling* case can be invoked in this context. It concerns the issue of the framework for delegated legislation created by the Treaty of Lisbon in Articles 290 and 291 TFEU[154]. Agencies were not identified in primary law as bodies to which powers could be delegated. This raises legitimate doubts in the context of systematisation of the legislation issued by the European administration, particularly when the powers of the European Supervisory Authorities to develop draft implementing and regulatory technical standards are taken into consideration. This specific situation, which can be described as a "non-position of agencies within the scheme of delegation", is perplexing given the actual demand for regulatory legislation issued by agencies[155]. Functions assigned to particular bodies of this kind confirm this aspect. Apart from the ESAs, it is enough to mention e.g. the authorisation powers of ECHA[156]. Omitting agencies in the Treaty provisions related to delegated legislation has significant consequences. First, it means that the catalogue of legislation functioning in the European executive order is not identical with the catalogue formulated in the normative framework introduced by the Treaty of Lisbon. Second, the omission of agencies in this specific case means an indirect denial of the actual situation, i.e. the special role of these bodies in the European pluralistic administrative space, where their semi-legislative powers are a significant element of decentralised implementation of European law[157].

What justifies this state of affairs is concern about the possible weakening of the position of the Commission as a delegating authority because it could

---

153 Chamon, 'EU Agencies: Does the *Meroni*', p. 287.

154 J. Pelkmans, M. Simoncini, 'Mellowing *Meroni*: How ESMA Can Help Build the Single Market', *CEPS Commentary*, 18.2.2014; Marjosola, 'Bridging', pp. 503, 511.

155 Everson, Vos, 'European Agencies', p. 148; Chamon, 'The Empowerment', p. 393.

156 See Scholten, v. Rijsbergen, 'The *ESMA*', p. 398.

157 Everson, Vos, 'European Agencies', pp. 149 ff.; Ruffert, 'Rechtsgrundlagen', p. 281.

lose its competencies. This concern is accompanied by the conviction that the strengthening of European cooperation can be properly carried out only by the activities of strong Treaty institutions[158]. One needs to remember in this context, however, that as sector-specific policies develop, the Europeanisation of these powers can be observed in most cases, rather than their delegation by the Commission to third parties. This means that tasks previously assigned to the authorities of the member states, or ones that were hitherto non-existent, are performed at the supranational level. Merijn Chamon describes this phenomenon as a "conferral of powers" which is not subject to the assumptions defined for sub-delegation[159]. This process can be called Europeanisation in the institutional dimension – i.e. a natural consequence of the Europeanisation of law[160]. In turn, this actually means a strengthening rather than a weakening of EU institutions.

Moreover, agencies are a kind of safeguard against the choice of "national paths" in the process of adapting the main assumptions of EU sectoral policies. They also constitute an instrument for harmonising institutional structures within national administrative systems[161]. On account of this, they are also a typical example of a departure from democratic mechanisms of "representative accountability" in the EU institutional system in favour of new management instruments based on expertise, transparency and deliberation[162]. Such technocratic management is a key feature of the European executive order. Traditional government, understood primarily as administration in the confined framework of the state system, is virtually impossible anymore in today's world. The reason for this is the processes of internationalisation of many areas of social life that have been intensifying since the late 1990s. Not only do we see processes of standardisation, synchronisation and homogenisation of practices, customs and rules of conduct in the integrated EU internal market. There is also a "transformation in the spatial organisation of social relations and transactions" and a disruption of the traditional links between specific places and the social space[163].

---

158 Priebe, *Entscheidungsbefugnisse*, p. 19.

159 Chamon, *EU Agencies*, p. 195.

160 H.C.H. Hofmann, 'Mapping the European Administrative Space', in: Curtin, Egeberg (ed.), *Towards*, p. 24; N. Jääskinen, 'Europeanisation of National Law: A Legal-Theoretical Analysis', *European Law Review*, Vol. 40, No. 5, 2015, pp. 671–678.

161 Egeberg *et al.*, 'The EU's Subordinated', pp. 331, 341.

162 Everson, 'The European System', p. 317.

163 D. Held *et al.*, *Global Transformations. Politics, Economics and Culture*, Stanford 1999, p. 16; Bieleń, *Polityka*, p. 190.

Concentration of regulatory and executive tasks at the supranational level is a prime example of this. For more than a decade we have seen attempts to create a compromise model between the ever-wider areas of activity of the EU institutions and efforts by the member states to halt the process of erosion of their executive competences in particular sectors of the market[164]. There are even observations that "the more powers are delegated to European agencies, the less room there is left for sovereign (unilateral) actions by member states"[165]. Regardless of how we assess this state of affairs, the "pluralistic executive" order is a special model of European management that does not exist on this scale and in this form in any other international order. Such a model of governance, therefore, constitutes a unique challenge in the context of searching for theoretical justifications for legitimising the activities of bodies operating within administrative structures.

---

164 See D. Riedel, 'Die Europäische Agentur für Flugsicherheit im System der Gemeinschaftsagenturen', in: E. Schmidt-Aßmann, B. Schöndorf-Haubold (ed.), *Der europäischer Verwaltungsverbund. Formen und Verfahren der Verwaltungszusammenarbeit in der EU*, Tübingen 2005, p. 119.

165 Adamski, 'The *ESMA* Doctrine', p. 812.

Part II Conceptualising the Legitimacy of EU Regulatory Agencies

4 The Cognitive and Explanatory Aspects

1. Defining Legitimacy

a) Examining the Term's Etymology

The term legitimacy originates from the Latin word *legitimus*, meaning "in conformity with the law, justified, rightful, appropriate, proper"[1]. One of its variants is the medieval Latin word *legitimitas*. That term meant "in conformity with customs"[2]. The origins of the term can also be traced to the word *lex*, meaning "law, rule, regulation"[3]. Different aspects of legitimacy may be emphasised. On the one hand, it is about a dynamic process that is historically determined and is constantly evolving. The objective of this process is to empower an authority or a certain legal system. On the other hand, the term refers to an already achieved state of rightfulness of certain rules, or mechanisms of exercising power[4].

This dichotomy is represented by two terms in many European languages. The process of seeking rightfulness, or efforts aimed at empowerment, is referred to as *Legitimation* in German and *légitimation* in French. An achieved rightfulness as a stable and constant state is *Legitimität* in German and *légitimité* in French. The two terms "legitimation" and "legitimacy" also exist in English, but the semantic distinction has been blurred in English-language literature, hence, the term "legitimacy" is used more often. It is applied both to the processual dimension and to describe an achieved state[5]. Therefore, synonyms of legitimacy include such words as "rightfulness", "legality", "empowerment", "legitimisation" and "justification"[6]. Legitimacy is not of an absolute nature, meaning it should

---

1 Kumaniecki (ed.), *Słownik*, p. 289.

2 T. Kubin, *Legitymizacja systemu instytucjonalnego Unii Europejskiej*, Katowice 2014, p. 28.

3 Kumaniecki (ed.), *Słownik*, p. 291.

4 T. Kownacki, *Legitymizowanie systemu politycznego Unii Europejskiej*, Warszawa 2014, p. 51.

5 The term "processual" will be understood in this book as relating to, or involving the study of processes rather than discrete events. About problems connected with defining this term, see C. Horan, J. Finch, 'The Temporal and Processual Dimensions of Practice for Enhancing Knowledge Exchange', *Dublin Institute of Technology Conference Papers*, No. 9, 2011.

6 See P. Gonod, 'Legitimacy in Administrative Law: Reform and Reconstruction', in: M. Ruffert (ed.), *Legitimacy in European Administrative Law: Reform and Reconstruction*, Groningen 2011, p. 3.

not be understood in absolute terms – that you have it or not. It is more appropriate to perceive legitimacy as a gradable property, because it can be strengthened or weakened in certain situations. Moreover, not all the elements of one legitimised political system have to be equally legitimate or rightful[7].

In the case of the issues analysed, legitimacy will be of a processual nature[8]. EU regulatory agencies are yet to achieve a state of full rightfulness or legality as is demonstrated by the frequent discussions on their legitimacy in legal doctrine. The complicated theoretical constructions developed by lawyers and political scientists that refer to mechanisms of accountability and instruments of acquiring social acceptance prove that it is uncertain that a complete justification for the activity of these bodies can be provided. Therefore, elements justifying the assignment of particular competences are sought, in terms of how the agencies act and function. The conviction that there is a purpose to the existence and activity of agencies is of fundamental importance for them, but also for the European Commission, which has used them as its expert support for years. This corresponds to the popular thesis, in the context of legitimacy, that a state of rightfulness is desired by both entities exercising power, and entities subordinated to it. Legitimacy is an intellectual construct. Every social group "needs to devise and conceive a rightfulness it attributes to the authority"[9]. The multitude of theoretical concepts formulated in the context of the decision-making mechanisms developed within the European Union's institutional system stem from a fashion in research. Interest in these issues is usually opportunistic[10].

This state of affairs results from the fundamental character of the question of why a particular entity has the right to exercise power and why it should deserve respect and obedience. Considerations on these issues date back to the time of Cicero. In this context, justifications for the "rightful" exercise of power have been sought for centuries. Concepts of legitimised, or empowered, authority have been created by philosophers such as Saint Thomas Aquinas, Henry de Bracton, Marsilius of Padua, Francisco Suárez, Theodore Beza, Niccolò Machiavelli, Jean Bodin, Thomas Hobbes, Hugo Grotius and John Locke. The traditional understanding of the legitimacy of authority, to which the abovementioned thinkers referred, holds that power can be exercised by those who meet certain

---

7 J. Caillosse, 'Legitimacy in Administrative Law? A French Perspective', in: Ruffert (ed.), *Legitimacy*, p. 13; Kubin, *Legitymizacja*, p. 36.

8 See Orator, *Möglichkeiten*, p. 333.

9 B. Baczko, *Wyobrażenia społeczne. Szkice o nadziei i pamięci zbiorowej*, Warszawa 1994, p. 40.

10 T. Biernat, *Legitymizacja władzy politycznej. Elementy teorii*, Toruń 1999, p. 8.

conditions – of divine origin, or compliance with the laws of nature, the laws of history, or age-old tradition[11].

b) Max Weber's Theory

However, for the modern understanding of legitimacy, French and German thought from the turn of the nineteenth and twentieth centuries is of greatest importance. The outstanding French lawyers François Gény and Léon Duguit as well as the German lawyer and sociologist Max Weber should be mentioned here. The latter became the "father" of empirical theories about the legitimacy of authority. His concepts constitute a cornerstone of modern considerations about legitimising the activities of bureaucratic systems. There are hardly any studies in social sciences on the issues of the legitimacy of the activities carried out by the state and its administrative structures that do not include references to the concepts created by Weber[12]. This widespread use of his concepts is a result of him placing the hierarchically organised "living machine" (Germ. *lebende Maschine*) of bureaucracy at the centre of his analysis[13]. The bureaucratic organisation of the administrative apparatus allows for a clear division of tasks and specialisations, and also hierarchical subordination of individual entities. This has an impact on the level of obedience that is necessary for the effective performance of the competencies assigned to them. In modern systems, in Weber's view, power materialises through administration (Germ. *Verwaltung*). This assertion is particularly relevant today in the deeply integrated structures of the "European Composite Administration"[14].

Weber identified three "ideal types" of legitimate authority (Germ. *Herrschaft*): legal (rational), traditional and charismatic. The "ideal types" are mental frameworks which are not a part of reality but reflect it, developed on the basis of empirical and historical analysis. According to Weber, they are not a hypothesis in themselves, but they do constitute a certain guideline in the process of building scientific hypotheses[15]. Legitimate authority rests on the foundation

---

11 See E. Peuker, *Bürokratie und Demokratie in Europa*, Tübingen 2011, p. 95; W. Sokół, *Legitymizacja systemów politycznych*, Lublin 1997, p. 16.

12 See Peuker, *Bürokratie*, Tübingen 2011, p. 196; W. Hennis, 'Legitimität. Zu einer Kategorie der bürgerlichen Gesellschaft', in: P. Graf Kielmansegg (ed.), *Legitimationsprobleme politischer Systeme*, Opladen 1976, p. 15.

13 M. Weber, *Wirtschaft und Gesellschaft. Grudriß der verstehenden Soziologie*, Tübingen 1972, pp. 129 ff.

14 More Peuker, *Bürokratie*, p. 197; W. Weiß, *Der Europäische Verwaltungsverbund. Grundfragen, Kennzeichen, Herausforderungen*, Berlin 2010, pp. 165 ff.

15 Peuker, *Bürokratie*, p. 200.

of the legality of a particular normative order. Obedience is not to people, but to principles and rules of conduct. Decision-makers exercise power under specific legal procedures. They are also bound by laws which shape the relationship between the ruled and the rulers. An abstract normative order, binding for everyone, is therefore the foundation of legal authority. Legal norms are changeable, but adjustments have to be made in accordance with existing legal rules and procedures.

Traditional authority is based on belief in the sanctity of tradition and customs that have always existed. In this "ideal type", the legitimacy of rulers is derived from their authority. Its foundation is respect. Charismatic authority, on the other hand, is based on the extraordinary talents, personality and the special charm of decision-makers. Typical examples of this authority, in Weber's view, include the power of prophets, war heroes or great demagogues. Obedience results from observance of norms established by decision-makers endowed with special abilities. According to Weber, the three ideal variants are not found in their pure form in the real world. Legitimacy is a result of elements taken from individual "ideal types". From the point of view of these considerations, the most important of them is legal (rational) authority, considered by Weber himself as the most modern method of legitimising power[16].

c) Legitimising Public Administration

In common understanding, legitimacy of administration involves empowerment of particular bodies authorised to take specific actions associated with the implementation of laws. The model of formal "legal rationality" formulated by Weber is of fundamental importance. It is even recognised in legal doctrine as a sort of "bureaucratic paradigm" which determined thinking about modern public administration in the twentieth century. The eminent Italian administrative law scholars Santi Romano and Sabino Cassese wrote in this context about a myth or fetish. They used these terms in reference to the principle of the legality of public administration, which is derived from Weber's theoretical considerations[17].

As for the legitimacy of administration, this term should be understood in two dimensions. First, it is about legitimising the activities of bodies involved

---

16 See Peuker, *Bürokratie*, p. 208; Kubin, *Legitymizacja*, p. 40.

17 See also J. Ponce Sole, 'The History of Legitimate Administration in Europe', in: Ruffert (ed.), *Legitimacy*, p. 158; S. Romano, *Fragmentos de un diccionario jurídico*, Buenos Aires 1964, pp. 225 ff., S. Cassese, 'New Paths for Administrative Law: A Manifesto', *International Journal of Constitutional Law*, Vol. 10, No. 3, 2012, pp. 608, 612.

in public administration. In this context, "legitimacy of administrative power" is important. Second, administrative law must be "legitimised" as well. In this context, the legitimacy of legal norms in that area is examined. Both dimensions are interdependent. It is impossible for recognised, rightful and legitimate public administration bodies to exist without appropriate procedures and legal norms. It is also difficult to imagine the applicability of administrative legislation that would be formulated and enforced by bodies lacking legitimacy[18]. Therefore, we can say that the conditions for obtaining legitimacy in the administrative domain are met if "people have confidence in administrative processes and they respect and accept decisions of public authorities, even though they may disagree with some individual determinations"[19].

There are also many terms used to specify the scope of meaning. For example, democratic and participative legitimacy are mentioned. The former highlights a "chain of legitimisation" that allows the identification of the entity which legitimises decision-makers to exercise power. In democratic systems, this entity is the nation (Lat. *demos*). At the other end of the "chain", there are representatives elected by the people or the nation. Such a mechanism of legitimising authority is not easy to apply in practice for public administration systems. The key would be to maintain a clear hierarchy, allowing for tracking mechanisms of delegating competencies[20]; mechanisms that would make it possible to find the subject delegating the right to exercise power, i.e. the electorate, within the "chain of legitimisation". Since it is not always possible to maintain a clear hierarchy in modern, extensive administrative systems, alternative ways to justify rulemaking powers are needed. They refer to the expertise and professional experience of the staff of particular administrative bodies[21].

In the other case – participative legitimacy – is about "opening" the public administration to citizens. Terms such as "self-management" or "joint management", designed to indicate citizen involvement in decision-making, are used in this context. It is not only about direct participation, e.g. deciding in the form of referendums. Such solutions are not possible in most modern countries for practical reasons. Rather, it is about citizen participation in various consultative or advisory bodies. The general public is supposed to be able to exercise

---

18 Caillosse, 'Legitimacy', p. 17.

19 A. Le Sueur, 'People as "Users" and "Citizens". The Quest for Legitimacy in British Public Administration', in: Ruffert (ed.), *Legitimacy*, p. 30.

20 See Groß, 'Unabhängige EU-Agenturen', p. 1088.

21 Gonod, 'Legitimacy', p. 4.

control over rulemaking activities[22]. The technocratic factor, involving the expert dimension of administrative bureaucracy, is strengthened by the social factor. This is also fostered by strategies, such as that of New Public Management, which envisages public administration reform in pursuit of efficiency, transparency and responsibility. An important role is played here by various advocacy groups or think tanks, but also the media, primarily the Internet[23].

Democratic legitimacy involves the mechanics of the entire political system in contemporary countries. Participative legitimacy, on the other hand, is more "fragmentary". It concerns individual sectors of administrative activity and involves the tasks of specific bodies. Moreover, it is just one of the mechanisms of democratic legitimacy, and it complements the others[24]. The assumption underpinning the modern understanding of public administration legitimacy is that its activities are representative and effective. Every authority must take into account the views and interests of the society that it works for and represents. Administration must therefore be open to the social impact of its actions. It must also be efficient. This means that it needs to operate smoothly, and respond adequately, to social needs within a short period of time[25].

d) Legitimacy within the International Frames

Efficency is also of importance for supranational structures such as the European Union. The specific character of rulemaking mechanisms in the international environment should be taken into account. There is no authoritative government there. No entity has a monopoly on using legal coercion[26]. These are features of the state system that allow for the distribution of wealth within particular social groups. The international environment, on the other hand, is an autonomous sphere of social life to which regularities seen in domestic politics cannot be applied. Divisions and contradictions are stronger there than inside individual countries and the decisions of international institutions are nowhere near as enforceable as state decisions. Therefore, when using the term "power" in the context of functioning mechanisms of such institutional systems as the European

---

22 P. Rosanvallon, *La contre-démocratie. La politique à l'âge de la défiance*, Paris 2006, p. 38.

23 *Ibid.*, p. 71.

24 Gonod, 'Legitimacy', p. 5.

25 F. Hayes-Renshaw, *The Role of the Council*, in: S.S. Andersen, K.A. Eliassen (ed.), *The European Union: How Democratic Is It?*, London 1996, p. 144.

26 *Ultima ratio* of the political authority, the use or threat of coercion, is present in every relationship of authority in a state system. See Biernat, *Legitymizacja władzy*, p. 76.

Union, we need to remember that the international environment is not a uniform whole, but a large and complex set of various actors within a "polyarchic" system of dependencies, i.e. one involving many powerful actors[27].

This is reflected in the development of the "global legal order". An "outpouring" of international organisations in the twentieth century led to the creation of many parallel systems of regulation in particular areas of international cooperation. Trade, finance, the environment, fishing, agriculture, food, telecommunications, intellectual property or nuclear energy could be mentioned here. This list is illustrative, for we can only agree with the statement by Cassese that nowadays "there is no realm of human activity wholly untouched by ultra-state or global rules"[28]. The "global legal order" is of a plural nature; therefore it lacks the coherence characteristic of state legal frameworks. There is no hierarchical structure of the system of law sources either. As harmonisation of laws advances internationally and interdependencies between authorities at different levels increase, it is becoming more and more difficult to separate what is "domestic/national" from what is "integrated/European/global". Cassese wrote in this context about a "grey area" or what is in between, what goes beyond the traditionally understood normative and institutional order[29].

We need to bear this in mind when analysing the three classic dimensions of legitimacy. The first one means legitimisation, justification and explanation of authority as well as applicable legal norms. The second one is associated with achieving the desired state of stability, or social order, resulting from the legitimacy of mechanisms of exercising power. The third dimension of legitimacy means perceiving it as an asset. In this context, legitimacy means authority earned by decision-makers, or compliance with existing rules of conduct. In this understanding, it as a form of approval for authority[30]. Thus, legitimacy includes elements such as legality, normative justification and a concrete form of approval for authority. Power is legitimised: (1) when it is legal, meaning it is acquired and exercised in accordance with certain rules of conduct, (2) when legal norms constituting the source of power are socially accepted and (3) when the position

---

27 See Bieleń, *Polityka*, pp. 14 ff.

28 S. Cassese, 'Administrative Law without a State? The Challenge of Global Regulation', *New York University Journal of International Law and Politics*, Vol. 37, No. 4, 2005, p. 671.

29 *Ibid.*, pp. 673, 683 ff.

30 T. Biernat, 'Legitymizacja procesu legislacyjnego', in: A. Preisner (ed.), *Prawowitość czy zgodność z prawem. Legitymizacja władzy w państwach demokratycznych*, Wrocław 2010, p. 177.

of the authority is confirmed by support, acquiescence or recognition on the part of the subordinates[31]. From the legal perspective, the first of these dimensions, involving legal acquisition and exercise of power, is the most important one. Legitimacy of "political authority" is, in this case, central for the functioning of the political system. From this point of view, the principle of institutional balance and the separation of powers, as well as the procedures used for exercising them and the control mechanisms applied to the rulers are paramount[32].

The issues of legalism and legitimacy of authority are discussed as part of a consideration of Weber's concept of legitimacy. Legal authority rests on a legal and procedural basis. The legal and procedural legality of power is one of the elements of legitimacy. It does not mean, however, that "legitimacy" and "legality" are synonyms. According to Jacques Caillosse, it is conceivable that concern about meeting the requirements of democratic legitimacy may drive administration bodies, in specific situations, to act on the border of legality[33]. Therefore, we can assume, following Tadeusz Biernat, that democratic procedures for creating authorities are not, on their own, a sufficient source of legitimacy[34]. In this understanding, the term legitimacy can be broken down into two parts. On the one hand, justification, or identifying the legal sources and basis for exercising power, is important. On the other hand, it is crucial to explain authority, and include references to the axiological domain associated with a certain catalogue of values[35].

It is usually assumed here that diverse social groups share a unified axiological attitude to reality. Empowerment of authority, in this case, comes from a uniform system of values[36]. Democratic legitimacy, understood this way, differs from the legitimacy of authority in authoritarian systems. In the first case, pluralism of ideas as well as political groups is required and the support of the majority of society expressed through democratic electoral procedures is of fundamental importance. In the other case, there is a "monopolistic belief system" and authority is legitimised through the mobilisation of society. This type of "mass-mobilisation" requires the creation of a rigorous system of surveillance and

31 D. Beetham, *The Legitimation of Power*, Basingstoke/New York 2013, pp. 3–24.

32 See J. Kranz, 'Deficyt demokracji w Unii Europejskiej?', *Sprawy Międzynarodowe*, No. 3, 2012, pp. 7 ff.

33 Caillosse, 'Legitimacy', pp. 12 ff.

34 Biernat, 'Legitymizacja', p. 179.

35 See P. Rosanvallon, *La légitimité démocratique. Impartialité, réflexivité, proximité*, Paris 2008, p. 19.

36 Biernat, *Legitymizacja władzy*, pp. 82 ff., 109; Kubin, *Legitymizacja*, p. 34.

repression that is designed to guarantee strong support for a particular group exercising power. Such legitimacy often comes in the aftermath of a revolution or the overthrow of the previous regime. The strength of collective beliefs, rather than democratic choice, plays the main role in such a case[37].

As for the issues analysed, what matters is democratic legitimacy. European Union member states are liberal democracies where the legitimacy of authority is intertwined with democratic values. These are interdependent phenomena[38]. Hence, a conviction has been expressed, since the outset of the process of institutionalisation of European integration, that common European institutions should act democratically. This is supposed to determine their legitimacy. This thought can be expressed in a simple conclusion: the more democracy at the supranational level, the stronger the legitimacy of the activities of EU institutions[39]. Within rulemaking mechanisms in supranational structures, specific organisational, institutional and legal solutions are developed that affect the lives of citizens in the member states in many ways.

Membership of such European supranational structures is connected with the desire to share a common catalogue of values and beliefs. This catalogue includes the values that form the basic principles of democracy which constitute the foundation of the democratic nation state. In the axiological realm, therefore, there is a convergence of mechanisms of legitimacy at the level of the supranational system and within the state order. A problem emerges at the normative or procedural level. The expansion of the European bureaucratic apparatus involves little citizen influence on the decisions taken within its structures. Unified institutions, the normative system and decision-making mechanisms are subject to limitations on their legitimacy; therefore it is much harder to obtain widespread social acceptance for them. This is caused by an array of determinants of psychological, ideological, emotional, mental and cultural natures[40]. Thus, many complementary concepts have been created and they will be further discussed in the next chapters. They are meant to constitute a theoretical explanation for the undoubted deficiencies in the legitimation of the activities of the European administration.

---

37 See also Beetham, *The Legitimation*, pp. 238 ff.

38 Kubin, *Legitymizacja*, p. 50.

39 See J. Blondel *et al.*, *People and Parliament in the European Union. Participation, Democracy, and Legitimacy*, Oxford 1998, p. 4.

40 Biernat, *Legitymizacja władzy*, p. 196.

2. Theorising Legitimacy

a) The Role of Theoretical Explanations

The term "theories of legitimacy" is often used, in the literature, in reference to concepts justifying the existence and functioning of specific bodies. In the case of EU regulatory agencies, whose establishment and scope of competences are not expressly laid down in primary law, the demand for such theories is particularly high. Hence, for at least twenty years, European lawyers, with particular consideration given to German legal doctrine, have been attempting to create complex theoretical explanations with respect to the process of "agencification" of the European administrative space[41]. It is worth considering whether such efforts can already be called a mature theory of legitimacy.

Demand for specific theoretical explanations is a feature of all scientific research. It is related to the basic tasks of developing scientific knowledge[42]. They boil down to three main functions, or objectives, for which a particular scientific discipline is used. Firstly, there is the descriptive function, meaning the use of a particular conceptual apparatus to describe reality. Individual conceptual categories should be of a special nature associated with the specificities of the developments analysed. Secondly, there is an explanatory function that involves defining certain regularities concerning the observed developments. It is about seeking answers to the question of why certain processes and phenomena develop in particular ways[43]. The descriptive function means the necessity of creating "scientific laws" which, however, are of a different nature in the humanities than in the sciences. Defining specific dependencies between analysed variables is not of an absolute nature. Hence the references to the "soft" dimension of the scientific laws that are formulated in the humanities[44]. Thirdly and finally, science should also perform a prognostic function. This means that scientific knowledge should make it possible to predict future developments on the basis of previously defined regularities. In the academic domain of the humanities, such as legal studies or political science, such forecasting is only possible over relatively short

41 For an overview of these concepts, see A. Meine, *Legitimität weiter denken?*, Würzburg 2012, pp. 54–67.

42 J. Stewart *et al.*, 'What is Theory?', *Journal of European Industrial Training*, Vol. 35, No. 3, 2011, p. 222.

43 *Ibid.*

44 See N. Vareman, 'Norms and Descriptions', *Decision Analysis*, Vol. 5, No. 2, 2008, pp. 89 ff.

periods of time. This is due to the volatility of reality[45]. This conclusion applies, for example, to the European integration process, which has evolved rapidly for more than half a century. Thus, theses and forecasts built on the basis of events in the late 1950s, the 1960s and the 1970s no longer apply to the current state of affairs.

In connection with the indicated functions of science, an integral part of any scientific discipline is to create appropriate theoretical foundations. It is believed that the more mature a scientific discipline is, the better developed are the theories it provides. However, the very term "theory" is not unambiguous. It has its roots in the Greek word *theōría* which means "contemplation", "intellectual view", "speculation" or "hypothesis"[46]. In contemporary understanding, the term refers to a result obtained by using the processes of observation and logical thinking. Taking into account the methodological perspective, it is a set of laws, assertions and hypotheses concerning a particular area of knowledge[47]. Nonetheless, the term depends on the context which determines its meaning. Therefore, in various research disciplines and also when faced with a specific historical context, the term "theory" is defined in a variety of ways.

Thierry de Montbrial rightly noted, on the basis of his analysis of several definitions of the term "theory" taken from different scientific disciplines, that it is a phenomenon that consists of two basic dimensions. On the one hand, what matters is "a logical aspect", i.e. the need for formulated assertions to be verified by reasoning, and, on the other hand, these assertions need to be subjected to "experimental criticism". An integral part of a theory is, therefore, also "an interaction between ideas and facts"[48]. A special dichotomy "between lived experience and worded communication" is, thus, at the root of this phenomenon[49]. Observations that result from experience need to be put into words, phrases or statements as part of the process of logical thinking. In order for a set of assertions to be considered a mature theory, they cannot be too general. Moreover, it must

45 See A. Dybczyński, 'Stosunki międzynarodowe w perspektywie teoretycznej', in: T. Łoś-Nowak (ed.), *Współczesne stosunki międzynarodowe*, Wrocław 2008, p. 17 ff.

46 P. Case *et al.*, 'From *theoria* to Theory: Leadership without Contemplation', *Organization*, Vol. 19, No. 3, 2012, pp. 346 ff.

47 See J. Dyduch *et al.*, *Krytyczne wprowadzenie do teorii stosunków międzynarodowych*, Wrocław 2006, p. 9.

48 T. de Montbrial, *Action and Reaction in the World System. The Dynamics of Economic and Political Power*, Vancouver/Toronto 2013, pp. 135 ff.

49 Case *et al.*, 'From *theoria* to Theory', p. 349.

be possible to verify them by experiment. Also, they should have some, even if very limited, prognostic power[50].

b) Difficulties in Formulating a Mature Legitimacy Theory

We can only agree with de Montbrial's observation that attractive intellectual constructions of an ideological nature, which are popularised in various scientific disciplines, are not theories even if they aspire to be[51]. They stimulate the imagination, and encourage reflection and debate, but they contribute little to a particular scientific discipline's progress. They are more a useful explanation for the political actions of a variety of decision-makers. Theorising about the legitimacy of the activities of EU institutions unfortunately often takes the form of catchy intellectual constructions which may, on occasion, form the nucleus of deeper theoretical considerations. Nevertheless, they are not formalised theories. This term should be understood as "a coherent and intertwined system of hypotheses and deductions that act as an infinite set of statements issued by deduction"[52]. A theory is designed to allow for the synthesis of large amounts of information and make it possible, with this synthesis, to explain, interpret and forecast developments in a particular domain of research.

A question can nonetheless be asked in this context, whether it is possible to construct any objective theory on the issues of state and law in the humanities. The answer will be negative, because the perception of these issues is directly determined by a particular historical context, the impact of the environment or the research perspective that is adopted[53]. There is no way to separate the researcher from the particular environment that influences his or her analysis or from the views and patterns of perceiving reality developed in the long-lasting processes of upbringing and education. Thus, such theories, as well as the process of their creation, which can be called theorising, are not of an objective nature. These issues have long been analysed as part of German post-Kantian and post-Hegelian philosophy. One can, for example, mention the problem of isolating the experiencing subject from the experienced world in the concepts

---

50 See also Stewart *et al.*, 'What is Theory?', pp. 223 ff.

51 de Montbrial, *Action*, p. 136.

52 S. Auroux (ed.), *Encyclopédie phliosophique universelle. Les Notions philosophiques*, Paris 1990. Quote from de Montbrial, *Action*, p. 138.

53 A. Wielomski, 'Stosunki międzynarodowe a filozofia polityczna', in: W. Mich, J. Nowak (ed.), *Wokół teorii stosunków międzynarodowych*, Lublin 2012, p. 85.

of Edmund Husserl[54] or the theories of prejudices (Germ. *Vorurteile*) formulated by Hans-Georg Gadamer[55]. Ideological and cultural differences directly affect the shape of a particular theory. This issue can also be considered from the post-modern perspective. The American philosopher Richard Rorty drew attention to the mechanism of the susceptibility of knowledge to self-fulfilling prophecies. In Rorty's opinion, language, as a channel for the flow of information and a carrier of knowledge, actively participates in constructing reality[56]. This means that what is presented as a result of the explanatory function attributed to a particular field of science, is a subject of discovery and explanation only because it was created previously by the researcher. Objectivity should, therefore, be replaced with the observation that knowledge is created as a reflection of particular interests and needs[57].

When seeking theoretical justifications for the functioning of various bodies in the EU institutional system, it is impossible to construct a general theory that would be universally applicable in all cases. It is necessary to use adequate approximation allowing for the development of relevant detailed theories. This thought applies primarily to regulatory agencies, which, due to not having their status directly regulated in the Treaties, have become the inspiration for many specific justifications formulated by both lawyers and political scientists. Interestingly, the concepts of input and output legitimacy, usually applied in the analysis of legitimising agency activity, are used with similar commitment in both of these scientific disciplines. The perspectives of legal and political science do not differ much in this regard. We can talk in this context about a peculiar system of concepts that are used in many theories in the domain of sociology as well as legal and political science.

Yet, can the observations based on the data collected from empirical studies on particular regulatory agencies be called a "theory of legitimacy"? More accurately, they constitute a certain stage in a complex theorising process. In this context, it is worth recalling a remark made by the American organisational theorist Karl Weick, who stated, after studying the activities of international organisations, that "products of theorising process seldom emerge as full-blown

54 See T. Staehler, *Hegel, Husserl and the Phenomenology of Historical Worlds*, London/New York 2016, pp. 21–38.

55 See L.K. Schmidt, *The Epistemology of Hans-Georg Gadamer: An Analysis of the Legitimization of Vorurteile*, Frankfurt am Main 1987.

56 See also F.B. Farell, *Subjectivity, Realism and Postmodernism. The Recovery of the World in Recent Philosophy*, Cambridge/New York 1996, pp. 117–147.

57 Dyduch *et al.*, *Krytyczne wprowadzenie*, p. 75.

theories"[58]. Theoretical concepts created with regard to the activities of regulatory agencies are of a limited nature. They usually involve narrow issues associated with justifying the existence of these bodies. In the last several years, they have gained great popularity and are frequently repeated, unfortunately often without deeper reflection on their actual usefulness in the context of explaining the growth of the EU agency system.

It is not without reason, therefore, that the title of this book is "theorising legitimacy" rather than "theories of legitimacy". These are still, after all, only attempts to create theoretical justifications rather than mature theories of an abstract and general nature that would be applicable in many cases, irrespective of the sector of the market where a particular agency operates. This conclusion indeed applies not only to seeking legitimacy for the activities of EU regulatory agencies, but also to the entire European management system. Many of the concepts in the literature on the EU's democratic deficit explain little, despite their sophisticated, academic vocabulary. It is sometimes difficult to avoid the impression that they are a set of loosely connected ideas, often unreflectively reproduced in order to justify particular worldviews. Among these worldviews, the dominant one refers to the inevitability of the integration process, which is bound to intensify. This unfortunately means that the efficiency and effectiveness of the emerging institutional structures are more important than their legal status. On account of the fact that bodies, such as regulatory agencies, lack regulation of their functioning and establishment in primary law, there is a quest for doctrinal and theoretical justifications that could legitimise this questionable state of affairs.

A significant element of such justifications is the case law of the CJEU, which has for years, as pointed out above, consistently paved the way towards accepting the ever-stronger position of regulatory agencies. In this context, it is worth citing the opinion of the eminent expert on European law, Hans-W. Micklitz, who stated many years ago: "I will not hide my admiration for the wisdom of judges and their sense of 'realism and passion' in building the EU legal system, while I equally admit the moral right, even the necessity, of raising the question of legitimacy"[59]. In response to this decades-long question concerning the legitimacy of European administrative structures, a number of theoretical concepts have been formulated, mainly in German and English legal doctrine.

58 K.E. Weick, 'What Theory Is Not, Theorizing Is', *Administrative Science Quarterly*, Vol. 40, No. 3, 1995, p. 385.

59 H.-W. Micklitz, *The Politics of Judicial Co-operation in the EU. Sunday Trading, Equal Treatment and Good Faith*, Cambridge 2005, p. 2.

Unfortunately, in the case of such thought constructions as input or output legitimacy, "theories" usually involve the reproduction of specific thought patterns[60]. The legitimacy of the existence of agencies is supposed to come primarily from various control mechanisms – from institutional oversight by the EU authorities and the member states, to the social control and judicial review of agency decisions. Authors tend to avoid formulating alternative theoretical concepts to complement the consistent pattern of justifications of agency activity, but it is hard to resist the impression that there is a need to dig deeper as the role of EU agencies increases. When analysing the powers of such institutions as ECHA, EBA or Frontex, the question arises as to whether consultative and control mechanisms sufficiently legitimise the activities of these bodies, which are "isolated" from ordinary citizens, while being often empowered to issue decisions that affect them directly.

This state of affairs is understandable when we take into consideration the secondariness of the legitimacy concepts developed with respect to supranational structures. The original subject of interest for researchers is the state. The legitimisation of the activities of state authorities for centuries has been the main area of intellectual reflection for specialists from different fields of social science – from law to philosophy and political science, to sociology, even psychology. Theoretical constructs formulated for supranational systems such as the European Union are, therefore, derived from existing theories of legitimacy, which were created in the context of the nation state[61].

3. Legitimacy *versus* Autonomy

a) Defining the Terms "Autonomy" and "Independence"

One can say that the legitimacy and autonomy of European administrative authorities are like an inseparable duo. Adequate legitimisation for the functioning of administrative bodies is necessary precisely in the case of their broad institutional autonomy. The greater the extent of independence, the greater the demand for a valid justification of the activity of an entity[62]. It is worth

60 For a broad perspective, see K.A. Wojtaszczyk (ed.), *Legitymizacja procesów integracji europejskiej*, Warszawa 2006.

61 Peuker, *Bürokratie*, p. 96.

62 See M. Ruffert, 'Verselbständigte Verwaltungseinheiten: Ein europäischer Megatrend im Vergleich', in: H.-H. Trute *et al.* (ed.), *Allgemeines Verwaltungsrecht – zur Tragfähigkeit eines Konzepts*, Tübingen 2008, p. 432.

considering, therefore, what the nature of the autonomy of administrative bodies is. Should it be understood synonymously with the term independence? Do any other words also reflect the scope of the meaning of this term? Are proposals put forward in the context of the autonomy of public administration bodies applicable to the European administration, which, according to the wording of Article 298(1) TFEU, has been assigned the attribute of independence by the EU legislature?

Assuming the accuracy of the dictionary definition, we can say that "autonomous" means self-reliance and independence in deciding about oneself[63]. Analysing the phenomenon of "autonomy" in the institutional context, one can say that it is a form of "self-governance", "self-regulation" or "self-direction"[64]. The term "independent" is usually regarded as synonymous. Independent, means not subordinated to anyone or anything, deciding about oneself, being capable of making decisions and managing one's actions responsibly, in a self-directed, free and sovereign way[65]. In the context of analysing the activities of administrative authorities, their possession of autonomy and independence is usually associated with impartiality, an apolitical nature, a lack of direct, hierarchical subordination to superior authorities and immunity to external influence[66].

In the case of EU regulatory agencies, there is no consistency in the terminology used to establish their position. The most common terms – "autonomy" and "independence" – are used interchangeably[67].

Some authors, like Miroslava Scholten, make a distinction, by referring the differences in meaning between autonomy and independence in the context of regulatory agencies to definitions used in international law with regard to countries and their autonomous areas. According to this understanding, a sovereign nation state is independent, or "not depending upon the authority of another, not in a position of subordination or subjection and not subject to external

63 D.B. Guralnik (ed.), *Webster's New World Dictionary of the American Language*, New York 1982, p. 42.

64 Groenleer, *The Autonomy*, p. 29.

65 Guralnik (ed.), *Webster's New World Dictionary*, p. 308.

66 See also M. Busuioc, M. Groenleer, 'The Theory and Practice of EU Agency Autonomy and Accountability: Early Day Expectations, Today's Realities and Future Perspectives', in: Everson *et al.* (ed.), *European Agencies*, pp. 180–183.

67 See L. Makhashvili, P. Stephenson, 'Differentiating Agency Independence: Perceptions from Inside the European Medicines Agency', *Journal of Contemporary European Research*, Vol. 9, No. 1, 2013, pp. 6 ff.

control or rule"[68], whereas an area, e.g. Catalonia, can enjoy autonomy within the Spanish nation state understood in a way as presented above. In this case, the "autonomous region depends upon the authority of some sort of central government, and is thus subject to external control or rule"[69]. In the view of Scholten, assuming this understanding of these terms means that independence is of an absolute nature – it exists or it does not. Independence in this context, by its very nature excludes any form of dependence, whereas autonomy is gradable and involves a number of control and supervisory mechanisms that imply dependence on a superior authority. It is because of its will that an agency enjoys a certain degree of autonomy[70].

This distinction in meanings, nonetheless, is not convincing in the light of the practical application of the terms "autonomy" and "independence" with respect to EU regulatory agencies. One can get the impression that in the literature about agencies, authors tend to prefer the term "autonomy", emphasising relationships between agencies and other actors that act as their political principals[71]. On the other hand, in normative acts, including the Treaties, the term "independence" or "independent" is used to establish the status of organisational units of the European administration[72]. This normative approach to independence both in primary and secondary law excludes Scholten's interpretation. That is because, when referring to Article 298(1) TFEU, which mentions an independent European administration, it is difficult to imagine that the EU legislature intended to exclude any form of dependence of European administration units[73].

---

68 M. Scholten, 'Independent, Hence Unaccountable? The Need for a Broader Debate on Accountability of the Executive', *Review of European Administrative Law*, Vol. 4, No. 1, 2011, p. 7.

69 *Ibid.*

70 Busuioc, Groenleer, 'The Theory', pp. 181 ff.

71 See Groenleer, *The Autonomy*, p. 29; E. Vos, 'European Agencies and the Composite EU Executive', in: Everson *et al.* (ed.), *European Agencies*, p. 36; Groß, *Die Legitimation*, pp. 101 ff.

72 M. Ruffert, 'Art. 298 AEUV', in: Calliess, Ruffert (ed.), *EUV/AEUV*, pp. 2520 ff.; Manger-Nestler, 'EU-Agenturen', p. 334.

73 The term "independent EU administration" appears in many statements of the EU authorities on the functioning of administrative structures. See European Parliament Resolution of 9.6.2016 for an Open, Efficient and Independent European Union Administration [2016/2610(RSP)]. For more about the development of the European administrative procedure, see E. Vos, 'EU Agencies and Independence', in: D. Ritleng (ed.), *Independence and Legitimacy in the Institutional System of the European Union*, Oxford 2016, pp. 214 ff.; R. Priebe, 'Agenturen der Europäischen Union – Europäische

Thus, while in state constitutional systems it is usually possible to clearly separate the scopes of meaning of terms such as "autonomy", "independence", "self-reliance", "separateness" or "sovereignty" [74], this clarity is missing in the case of EU agencies.

Terms like "autonomous", "independent" or "self-reliant" are attributive and relational. In the attributive meaning, these terms are perceived as a feature of a given entity related to its separateness. The feature is determined on the basis of its analysis or overview. In this understanding, the abovementioned adjectives are of a qualitative nature, describing the subject under consideration. The relational dimension, on the other hand, allows for discerning interactions between at least two entities or phenomena. "Autonomy", "independence" or "self-reliance" are perceived in this meaning in the broader context of a particular environment. Therefore, it is about e.g. independence from someone or something. Relationality, however, is expressed not only in deciding independently about oneself, but also as being accountable for one's actions to third parties. In this meaning, these terms are used to describe isolated components of reality[75].

In the case of the agency system, principal-agent relations are usually analysed, e.g. in the circumstances of nation-states: ministry – regulatory authority; in the European dimension: the Commission – agencies. Multilevel dependencies are also increasingly analysed due to numerous links between European institutions. In this case, "dual" or "double delegation" of tasks is mentioned[76]. National agencies are addressees of delegation both at the national and European level, cooperating with other "sister" authorities within regulatory networks. They operate in a "double hatted" manner in that they can be said to wear two hats, carrying out tasks in national and international administration processes. Thus, it can be said that not only are national ministries their principals, but also indirectly the European Commission, in the context of the decentralised implementation of the law[77]. An interesting phenomenon can therefore be seen

---

Verwaltung durch eigenständige Behörden', *Europäische Zeitschrift für Wirtschaftsrecht*, Vol. 26, No. 7, 2015, p. 270.

74 See W. Brzozowski, *Niezależność konstytucyjnego organu państwa i jego ochrona*, Warszawa 2016, pp. 31–48.

75 *Ibid.*, p. 29.

76 T. Bach *et al.*, 'The Differential Empowering Effects of Europeanization on the Autonomy of National Agencies', *Governance. An International Journal of Policy, Administration, and Institutions*, Vol. 28, No. 3, 2015, pp. 285, 288.

77 M. Egeberg, J. Trondal, 'Political Leadership and Bureaucratic Autonomy: Effects of Agencification', *Governance. An International Journal of Policy, Administration, and Institutions*, Vol. 22, No. 4, 2009, p. 686.

in the case of national regulatory agencies. Their dependence on two principals leads to increased independence in relation to each individually. This is particularly true in the context of self-empowerment of national regulatory agencies in their relations with individual ministries[78]. According to Tobias Bach and Eva Ruffing, who have been studying this phenomenon for several years, "the national agencies might gain autonomy if they become involved in European networks and [...] the European bureaucracy opens up considerable room for manoeuvre for national administrative actors"[79].

b) Understanding the Autonomous Position of EU Regulatory Agencies

Understanding of the independence, self-reliance or autonomy of administrative offices, including agencies both at the national and European level, is therefore, as a rule, of an attributive nature. These phenomena are always considered in the context of a given authority's interactions with its environment. The issues of status, mandate, remit or authority of a particular agency are always subject to analysis within a broader perspective as well as relationships with other actors in a particular administrative system. Most often, issues related to the independent or autonomous status of particular authorities are precisely defined in laws, including their constituent acts, such as e.g. founding regulations of regulatory agencies. It is then called legal or formal autonomy (Latin *de jure*) and it is reflected in behavioural or informal autonomy (Latin *de facto*), which is associated with the position of a particular body in a specific institutional system and directly results from the nature of its relationship with the administrative environment[80]. According to Wojciech Brzozowski, "independence is effected in relations between an independent authority and other entities, setting impassable barriers for the interference of these entities in a sphere excluded from their influence"[81]. Consequently, the full meaning of independence is revealed in the practice of the application of the law. In the case of EU regulatory agencies, this means that their autonomous position derives not only from their formal

78 T. Bach, E. Ruffing, 'Networking for Autonomy? National Agencies in European Networks', *Public Administration*, Vol. 91, No. 3, 2013, pp. 713 ff.

79 *Ibid.*, p. 715.

80 See M. Maggetti, K. Verhoest, 'Unexplored Aspects of Bureaucratic Autonomy: A State of the Field and Ways Forward', *International Review of Administrative Science*, Vol. 80, No. 2, 2014, p. 242.

81 Brzozowski, *Niezależność*, p. 30.

status enshrined in legal norms, but also arises from changes which take place in the rapidly evolving market environment and actual relations with the EU institutions, including above all the Commission[82].

One of the primary sources of the autonomous status of EU regulatory agencies was the choice of a deliberative design by the EU legislature. This forms the legal basis for the activity of a given body. In this context, relations between agencies and external entities are analysed within two areas; those concerning stakeholders/clients and those concerning political actors, which usually act as direct or indirect principals. In the case of stakeholders and clients, it is usually about actual autonomy, or resisting pressure from influential groups that lobby for solutions that favour them. In the case of the impact of political actors, it is both about normative autonomy, or legal safeguards against interference by political decision-makers, and the actual autonomy resulting from the ability to resist pressure applied by current political coalitions[83].

Agency autonomy, making it possible for them to act free from political pressure, is also a mechanism which ensures the credibility of their opinions and decisions over longer periods of time. Hence, it is believed that autonomy should be seen not only through the prism of the functionality of a particular agency, but also understood as an instrument of legitimacy, contributing to the strengthening of the position of the body[84]. Information is also a source of agency independence. It is assumed that disparities in knowledge about a particular agency's specific area of activity allow it to act more freely in relation to its principal, e.g. the European Commission which does not have such knowledge. In the deliberative European system, expertise held by particular agencies at the national and EU level is not only a result of specialist skills and experience of a particular authority's personnel, but also stems from complex interactions between these entities. Information is forwarded and exchanged. For this and other reasons, in some cooperation networks, there is a mechanism to include

82 See A. Wonka, B. Rittberger, 'How Independent are EU Agencies?', *RECON Online Working Paper*, No. 12, 2009, p. 2.

83 See also Groenleer, *The Autonomy*, p. 36; C. Ossege, 'Driven by Expertise and Insulation? The Autonomy of European Regulatory Agencies', *Politics and Governance*, Vol. 3, No. 1, 2015, pp. 103–105; Vos, 'European Agencies', p. 37; Egeberg, Trondal, 'Political Leadership', pp. 679 ff.

84 Bach, Ruffing, 'Networking', p. 716.

authorities in countries seeking EU membership in information exchange, so as to bridge any gaps in this area[85].

Some authors see the creation of European regulatory structures, with the participation of national authorities, where a coordinating role is usually played by EU agencies, as an important stage in the process of "liberation" of national agencies from the influence of the individual member states. Such inter-agency cooperation networks could be a way to transform intergovernmental cooperation into supranational activity under the auspices of EU regulatory agencies. In this context, it is important for EU agencies to be independent from the Council, and to work in close cooperation with the EU's main executive authority, the European Commission[86].

Both independence and autonomy, understood as decision-making discretion, are variable and gradable features of EU regulatory agencies. They are manifested with diverging intensity among various authorities, depending both on formally guaranteed procedures to regulate these relationships, and informal practices developed in mutual contacts. In theoretical analyses of institutional independence, it is pointed out that this phenomenon applies only to a specific section on a gradable scale. Below a certain threshold of guarantees that arise from the legal status of a particular authority and the resulting informal mechanisms, independence becomes superficial and in fact ceases to exist. However, the other extreme – absolute independence, understood as total insusceptibility to external influence – is in practice impossible to achieve in public administration[87]. Besides, "autonomy" is a relative phenomenon; therefore it should be analysed with respect to specific conditions and a particular context. This observation is clearly reflected in EU regulatory agencies, which in certain situations can enjoy greater autonomy than regulatory agencies of the member states operating in a particular sector of the market, but are much less independent when compared to similar authorities operating in the United States[88].

---

85 M. Busuioc and M. Groenleer write in this context about "networks of support", see Busuioc, Groenleer, 'The Theory', pp. 190 ff.

86 See E. Ongaro *et al.*, 'EU Agencies and the European Multi-Level Administrative System', in: E. Ongaro (ed.), *Multi-Level Governance: The Missing Linkages*, Bingley 2015, p. 90.

87 Brzozowski, *Niezależność*, p. 30; Groenleer, *The Autonomy*, pp. 30 ff.; Groß, *Die Legitimation*, p. 88; Busuioc, Groenleer, 'Wielders of Supranational Power?', p. 130.

88 Shapiro, 'The Problems', pp. 276 ff.; M. Wierzbowski, 'Współpraca niezależnych organów administracji publicznej', *Ruch Prawniczy, Ekonomiczny i Socjologiczny*, Vol. LXXVI, No. 2, 2014, p. 233.

c) Classifying the Autonomy of EU Regulatory Agencies

The independence of an institution is analysed in different dimensions of its functioning. Thus, it can refer to (1) the way in which tasks and competencies are carried out, (2) guarantees of existence in the administrative system, e.g. in terms of stable staff numbers, and (3) operating conditions for the authority. Consequently, interference in institutional autonomy, understood in this way means, on the one hand, co-shaping, modelling or distorting decisions of a particular entity, and on the other hand, it involves making determinations regarding its legal existence, also including the shape of its organisational structure, staffing procedures or internal delegation of tasks. Sources of interference can include both superior authorities that exercise control and supervision over a particular authority as well as authorities that are not in a relationship of hierarchical dependence[89].

Applying these theoretical findings to EU regulatory agencies, we can identify (1) decisional autonomy, also called policy autonomy, (2) managerial autonomy, which includes both financial autonomy and autonomy with regards to deciding about the use of personnel resources, and (3) legal autonomy.

Policy autonomy involves discretion in developing operating strategy and decision-making. In this case, it is about independence in defining the objectives and interests of a particular institution and the freedom, as far as the choice of appropriate instruments is concerned, to implement the assumptions planned. It is assumed that the more detailed the procedures are for the functioning of an authority, the less room there is for independence in formulating its programme of action[90]. Such decision-making autonomy also involves a prohibition on taking instructions, whether from EU institutions or the member states and other entities. In this context, it is assumed that agencies are neutral in the processes of co-shaping sectoral policies[91].

Managerial autonomy means freedom in two areas – deciding independently on financial resources and the staff employed. As for the first area, i.e. financial autonomy, it primarily involves conditions for acquiring and managing financial resources. EU regulatory agencies, which have the right to collect fees, are considered to be more independent than those funded only through the EU budget.

---

89 See Brzozowski, *Niezależność*, p. 31; Wonka, Rittberger, 'How Independent', pp. 3 ff.

90 Hansen-Nootbar, *Unabhängigkeit*, p. 33.

91 Weißgärber, *Die Legitimation*, p. 42; N. Font, 'Policy Properties and Political Influence in Post-Delegation: The Case of EU Agencies', *International Review of Administrative Sciences*, Vol. 81, No. 4, 2015, p. 774.

Most regulatory agencies receive more than half of their finances through direct budget allocation by the Commission, which undoubtedly contributes to their increased dependence on this EU institution[92]. The possibility to decide freely about financial resources includes the ability to take out loans or set fees for activities performed by the agency, e.g. as part of the authorisation procedures. As for the other area, i.e. staff management, what matters is independence in hiring, promoting and rewarding employees, freedom to set salary levels and being able to independently appoint executive personnel[93].

On the other hand, legal autonomy means independent functioning within the scope provided for in the normative framework. The starting point here is the separate legal personality of an entity. In the case of EU regulatory agencies, this is a feature that distinguishes them from many other independent organisational units operating in the EU institutional system. According to Merijn Chamon, conferring legal personality on agencies automatically means providing them with a certain degree of independence or operational autonomy[94]. A similar view is also expressed by Kirsten Weißgärber, who believes that singling out agencies as separate entities in the EU administrative system, which signifies their institutional and organisational distinctiveness, is reflected primarily in their status. Its basic element is that agencies are provided with legal personality[95]. Other authors, like Georg Hermes or Robert Uerpmann, emphasise, on the other hand, that legal personality alone is not a direct guarantee of independence. It constitutes a formal foundation that makes it possible to develop an autonomous position. It is, therefore, certainly a first step, but does not determine absolutely that a given entity is able to act independently[96]. Apart from formal status, an important role is played by the legal framework, e.g. procedures defining how much discretion an agency has in developing programmes of action, exercising particular powers and determining the organisational structure[97].

The division suggested is one of many functioning in the literature about agencies[98]. Looking at the independence of these bodies primarily through the

92 Ongaro *et al.*, 'EU Agencies', p. 100.

93 *Ibid.*, pp. 98–100.

94 Chamon, *EU Agencies*, pp. 13–15.

95 Weißgärber, *Die Legitimation*, p. 40. See also Fischer-Appelt, *Agenturen*, pp. 38 ff.

96 Hermes, 'Legitimationsprobleme', p. 464; Uerpmann, 'Mittelbare Gemeinschaftsverwaltung', pp. 568 ff.; Ruffert, 'Verselbstständigte Verwaltungseinheiten', p. 448.

97 Hermes, 'Legitimationsprobleme', pp. 464 ff.; Hansen-Nootbar, *Unabhängigkeit*, p. 32.

98 See Vos, 'EU Agencies', p. 216.

prism of their self-directed activity, we can, therefore, talk about things like institutional, budgetary and regulatory independence. In the first case, it refers to being separated within the existing institutional structure. In this way regulatory agencies are not a component of any EU authority[99]. Such separateness also means the possibility of shaping the organisational structure, while keeping the control mechanisms in the hands of both executive and legislative authorities. In the second case – budgetary independence – it is about the influence of other authorities on the material situation, including primarily the finances of an agency. It is important not only to provide it with appropriate funds, but also to monitor and possibly control planned expenditure. In the third case – regulatory independence – an agency's discretion in developing, implementing and enforcing proposed rules of conduct is analysed. This can include both legally binding instruments and non-legally binding opinions, guidelines and recommendations[100].

d) The Autonomy of EU Regulatory Agencies as an Important Legitimising Feature

Independence in decision-making or developing semi-legislative acts has been particularly controversial over the past decades, especially in the context of interpreting the *Meroni* doctrine. As the analysis carried out thus far indicates, the *Meroni* judgments have not stopped the growth of the agency system. However, agencies themselves would not have lived up to what was expected of them, primarily regarding the provision of reliable expert support, if they did not enjoy independence in making situational assessments and forming their own positions on the basis of those assessments[101]. From this point of view, the autonomy of agencies is not directly perceived as a balancing element between EU institutions, but as an appropriate response to regulatory challenges associated with rapid changes in particular sectors. "Monolithic bureaucracies" are

---

99 See C. Gaitanides, 'Kontrolle unabhängiger Institutionen der Europäischen Union', *Jahrbuch des öffentlichen Rechts der Gegenwart*, Vol. 61, 2013, p. 216.

100 R. Bismuth, 'The Independence of Domestic Financial Regulators: An Underestimated Structural Issue in International Financial Governance', *Goettingen Journal of International Law*, Vol. 2, No. 1, 2010, pp. 96–99; Wonka, Rittberger, 'How Independent', pp. 6 ff.

101 See Ruffert, 'Verselbständigte Verwaltungseinheiten', p. 443; Gaitanides, 'Kontrolle', p. 218.

unable to meet them[102]. The only way forward, therefore, is progressive specialisation, with the independence of established bodies being an inherent part of this[103].

Regardless of the dimension to be analysed, the autonomy of EU regulatory agencies is, therefore, closely connected with their expert background. Their independence is meant to underpin efforts to build trust in, and the authority of, competent and professional entities[104] and it is supposed to be understood as a model for action, enhancing the credibility of agency operations, rather than a goal in itself[105]. This assumption is best reflected by the autonomy of the agencies described in Chapter 2, such as ECHA or EFSA. Professional background plays a legitimising role in the existence of these bodies, but only on the assumption that they maintain their far-reaching independence. Interestingly, this impression persists even when open political pressure becomes obvious[106]. The conviction that it is necessary to maintain an independent position is connected with the desire to keep at a safe distance from the principals, primarily the European Commission. This authority, which under Article 17 TEU performs a managing role with respect to the European administration, has many informal ways of influencing agency decisions in addition to formal safeguards resulting from founding regulations. This influence is of a general nature, meaning it primarily involves political direction of agency operations in a particular market sector. Strictly technical decisions tend to be made by agencies having a higher degree of independence, which stems directly from their actual capabilities.

Statements affirming the independence of expert regulatory agencies have been repeatedly made by EU institutions in recent years. It suffices to recall the Commission's position from 2002: "The main advantage of using the agencies is that their decisions are based on purely technical evaluations of very high quality and are not influenced by political or contingent considerations"[107]. This position was reaffirmed in the "Common Approach", issued ten years later, which stated that "the independence of scientific experts should be fully ensured, *inter alia*

---

102 Bismuth, 'The Independence', p. 91.

103 "Classical *déformation professionelle*", or special perception of the surrounding reality through the prism of a narrow specialty, is mentioned in the literature in this context. See Shapiro, 'The Problems', p. 283.

104 See Gaitanides, 'Kontrolle', pp. 224, 227; Ossege, 'Driven', p. 102; Griller, Orator, 'Empowering', p. 4.

105 Manger-Nestler, 'EU-Agenturen', p. 334.

106 See also Ossege, 'Driven', pp. 105 ff.; Groenleer, 'Agency Autonomy', p. 256.

107 *The Operating Framework*, COM(2002) 718 final, p. 5.

by promoting the highest standards, setting sound selection criteria and promoting best practices"[108]. These words should be considered as a kind of a declaration due to the non-binding nature of the documents that contain it. One can conclude, on the basis of practical observations, that in many cases ensuring the far-reaching independence of experts is not possible. This is because of their ties to the European Commission, which is involved in agency work. It also allocates their budgets and has influence over the sector where a particular agency operates[109].

We can relate this to the concept put forward by Michel Foucault, whose philosophical deliberations in the second half of the twentieth century on the relationship between knowledge and power became an inspiration not only for the abovementioned postmodernism, but also for methodological considerations within the framework of critical theory[110]. Foucault noted that the way knowledge is produced is closely related to the way power is produced: therefore acquiring and owning knowledge makes it possible to exercise control in multilevel power structures[111]. Power is not distributed evenly. Access to information and data causes dependency on structures and relationships of hierarchical subordination. These kinds of interactions occur not only between different entities, but also inside those entities[112]. The advantage of having access to knowledge and information is, thus, felt not only e.g. between different administrative institutions, but also within them, between individual internal bodies, like the Executive Director and the Management Board within the agency's structure. This disparity is also true for agency staff. Those employed by an agency have a different scope of knowledge about its activities to the official personnel from the member states that participate in the work of the agency's MB as national

108 *Joint Statement and Common Approach*, 19.7.2012, p. 7.

109 C. Ossege, *European Regulatory Agencies in EU Decision-Making. Between Expertise and Influence*, Basingstoke/Hampshire 2016, p. 40. In some founding regulations (e.g. EMA, ESAs) independence of these agencies from the industry – pharmaceutical companies or financial institutions – was expressly specified. For more about this issue see Busuioc, Groenleer, 'The Theory', p. 181.

110 See also T. Wandel, 'The Power of Discourse: Michel Foucault and Critical Theory', *Cultural Values*, Vol. 5, No. 3, 2001, pp. 369 ff.

111 S. Wally, 'Konsequenzen einer Gerechtigkeit ohne Wahrheit', in: C.B. Wöhle *et al.* (ed.), *Rechtsphilosophie. Vom Grundlagenfach zur Transdisziplinarität in der Rechts-, Wirtschafts- und Sozialwissenschaften. Festschrift für Michael Fischer*, Frankfurt am Main 2010, p. 220.

112 See H.N. Weiler, 'Knowledge and Power. The New Politics of Higher Education', *Journal of Education Planning and Administration*, Vol. XXV, No. 3, 2011, pp. 209 ff.

representatives. According to an interpretation of Foucault's thought, in a world dominated by the knowledge-power relationship, hierarchical subordination resulting from a disparity in information distribution has a decisive influence on the authority, prestige and status of a particular entity[113].

Power, in Foucault's view, has a positive, creative character: "Power produces; it produces reality; it produces domains of objects and rituals of truth. The individual and the knowledge that may be gained of him belong to this production"[114]. Hence, power creates certain facts and gives them the attribute of veracity. According to this assumption, knowledge and power function in a relationship of "reciprocal legitimation"[115]. Knowledge legitimises power and power legitimises knowledge. Regulatory agencies are a model example of this relational legitimacy. European political decision-makers, or the supranational EU institutions and the member states, legitimise agencies to act. On the other hand, specific political decisions, both at the EU level and increasingly within national legal orders, are legitimised through reference to knowledge or expert support from independent technocratic bodies such as agencies[116].

4. Legitimacy *versus* Accountability

a) Controlling Independent EU Regulatory Agencies as a Legitimising Mechanism

Apart from "autonomy", an ever-present term in debate on instruments legitimising the activities of EU regulatory agencies is "accountability". Control mechanisms constitute something akin to "the other side of the coin" for what can be described as the independence or autonomy of public administration authorities. Ensuring their independent position was a *conditio sine qua non* for the creation of an agency apparatus in the EU structures. Agencies were designed to support the European Commission, which was unable to supply the increasing level of expertise needed to cope with regulatory issues in the internal market. This support was not only supposed to be highly specialised, but also, as mentioned before, politically neutral. Independence was, thus, an important condition to legitimise the existence of agencies. It turned out over time, however, that

113 *Ibid.*, p. 210.

114 M. Foucault, *Discipline and Punish: The Birth of the Prison*, New York 1979, p. 194.

115 Weiler, 'Knowledge', pp. 210 ff.

116 Similarly Vos, 'EU Agencies', p. 207.

in practice it is an obstacle to legitimising their existence. The legality of agencies "outside the Treaties" has been called into question as there are only weak control mechanisms in relation to them, whereas their independence is explicitly guaranteed[117].

The relationship between autonomy and accountability can more broadly refer to most administrative institutions, also those within intra-state systems. Matthias Ruffert points out, when analysing the British system, that problems of legitimacy for the activities of state administration are directly understood as problems of accountability[118]. In this case, the main mechanism of legitimacy is the accountability of administrative bodies to the parliament. For EU regulatory agencies, however, we should talk about many levels of accountability, which are a result of their participation in international and supranational structures[119].

On the one hand, therefore, it is about accountability to EU institutions, primarily the European Commission, the Parliament and the Council, but in this case, accountability to the European Parliament is a mechanism that is supposed to guarantee direct, election-based legitimacy. On the other hand, legitimacy obtained at the member state level results from the mandate of governments, which are legitimised to act on the basis of national constitutions[120]. In Ruffert's view, the control mechanisms applied by the Commission and involving its participation in e.g. procedures of appointing Executive Directors of individual agencies guarantee the so-called personal legitimacy (Germ. *personelle Legitimation*) of the agencies. Its level could correspond to the legitimation enjoyed by officials of the Commission itself. On the other hand, procedures detailing the functioning of agencies set out in their founding regulations form so-called factual legitimacy (Germ. *sachliche Legitimation*), which also primarily results from a number of safeguards against any arbitrariness of these bodies[121].

Both personal and factual legitimacy are typical instruments for justifying the activities of technocratic and non-majoritarian authorities. These justifications have been used for decades in the context of the European Commission. The professional expertise and specialist background of its personnel are supposed to be

---

117 See also Y. Papadopoulos, 'Accountability and Multi-Level Governance: More Accountability, Less Democracy?', *West European Politics*, Vol. 33, No. 5, 2010, pp. 1032 ff.; M. Costa, *The Accountability Gap in EU Law*, London/New York 2016, pp. 69 ff.

118 Ruffert, 'Verselbständigte Verwaltungseinheiten', p. 452.

119 E.g. Groß, *Die Legitimation*, pp. 100–102.

120 Costa, *The Accountability*, p. 71.

121 Ruffert, 'Verselbständigte Verwaltungseinheiten', p. 453.

the main element legitimising the European administration's right to act. In this context, an argument is advanced that separating regulatory agencies from the Commission, through the basic assumption of their institutional autonomy and decision-making independence, is inherently absurd. That is because agencies, like the Commission, are technocratic, expert entities. Thus, it means singling out institutions of a technical nature within exactly that kind of technical administrative apparatus[122]. The motives behind the creation of the European agency system have already been described. In addition to those referring to their functionality, they are mainly of a political nature.

There is no doubt that the desire to justify relationships between administrative authorities and political decision-makers lies at the heart of concepts regarding the accountability of public institutions such as regulatory agencies. Control, in this context, can be synonymously correlated with accountability[123]. It is meant to form an alternative to invoking mechanisms of direct election by citizens[124]. This generates a certain paradox. Administrative authorities, whose special role results from their independent expert opinion, are supposed to be subject to review. According to Busuioc "a body cannot be two opposite things at the same time: independent and controlled"[125]. And this is exactly what is expected from EU regulatory agencies which, due to the need to legitimise their activities, must be subject to control mechanisms while maintaining far-reaching independence in the process of developing professional opinions and recommendations[126].

b) Distinguishing between the Terms "Accountability" and "Control"

Even though the terms, "control" and "accountability", are used interchangeably in the literature on regulatory agencies, a clear distinction can be made in this regard. Its theoretical sources should be sought in Anglo-Saxon scholarship. "Control" is a term with a broader meaning. It entails interference in the process of exercising competencies as well as direct management of the decision-making process and influencing the behaviour of the controlled entity.

---

122 Shapiro, 'The Problems', p. 281.

123 M. Busuioc, 'Accountability, Control and Independence: The Case of European Agencies', *European Law Journal*, Vol. 15, No. 5, 2009, pp. 601 ff.

124 Groß, *Die Legitimation*, p. 102.

125 Busuioc, 'Accountability', p. 605.

126 On this issue see also M. Scholten, 'Independence *v.* Accountability: Proving the Negative Correlation', *Maastricht Journal of European and Comparative Law*, Vol. 21, No. 1, 2014, pp. 197 ff.

Similar terms include “steering” or “supervision”. Control instruments are intrusive and involve the intervention of an authorised controlling authority at all stages of agency activity[127].

Researchers identify *ex ante* and *ex post* control mechanisms in this context. The former signifies an initial means of verification, which involves a precise definition of the tasks and powers of the addressee of delegation. This prior control also means designating the scope of decision-making and institutional autonomy of the entity which has specific competencies conferred onto it in the process of tasks being delegated. In the case of EU regulatory agencies, such prior control mechanisms are set out in their founding regulations. They constitute the starting point for establishing the mandate of an agency and its scope of competences. *Ex post* control, on the other hand, means checking the execution of tasks that have already been performed and in this meaning it is a synonym of “accountability”[128].

The term “accountability” refers to mechanisms directly associated with being accountable for one’s actions, i.e. explaining, legitimising and justifying a particular activity. It occurs after certain tasks have been performed and when the process of exercising powers defined in normative acts has already been completed. “Accountability”, as a narrower term in its meaning, falls within the scope of “supervision”. However, the relationship does not go the other way. This is a result of a fundamental difference. Control means exercising powers over a subordinated entity. In the case of public administration authorities, on the other hand, accountability is connected with the mechanisms of delegating the competencies discussed above[129]. The delegating authority transfers some of its powers to the addressee of delegation. An assignment of tasks is followed by a shift of accountability: therefore direct control is excluded. The principal has the opportunity to monitor *ex ante* how the delegated tasks have been performed, whereas, the agency is obliged to implement them within their designated mandate. It must also inform, report, explain and agree to be assessed, in addition to bearing consequences with regard to the execution of the powers delegated to it[130].

---

127 Ongaro *et al.*, ‘EU Agencies’, p. 103.

128 See Busuioc, *European Agencies*, pp. 51 ff.

129 See also D. Curtin, ‘Holding (Quasi-) Autonomous EU Administrative Actors to Public Account’, *European Law Journal*, Vol. 13, No. 4, 2007, p. 525.

130 See also Busuioc, ‘Accountability’, p. 308; Scholten, ‘Independence’, pp. 198, 201; J. Supernat, ‘O pojęciu rozliczalności (*accountability*) administracji’, in: M. Duniewska, Z. Stahl (ed.), *Odpowiedzialność administracji i w administracji*, Warszawa 2013, pp. 35 ff.

In the Anglo-Saxon literature in the field of administrative sciences, there are many definitions of the term "accountability". The one suggested by Mark Bovens is quoted most often: "[In the] relationship between an actor and a forum, in which the actor has the obligation to explain and justify his or her conduct, the forum can pose questions and pass judgment, and the actor might face consequences"[131]. The emphasis is put here on interactions between the entity obliged to submit itself to a reviewing process and the entity checking the proper performance of the delegated tasks[132]. Johan P. Olsen looked at the term from another perspective. In his view, "accountability involves establishing facts and assigning causality and responsibility, formulating and applying normative standards for assessing conduct and reasons given, and building and applying capabilities for sanctioning inappropriate conduct"[133]. On the one hand, thanks to these processes "accountability" performs a legitimising role – it justifies and legitimates specific activities of a public administration authority and, on the other hand, the assessing mechanisms mentioned by Olsen in his definition also have a delegitimising function – naming and shaming improper conduct[134].

Similarly, as in the case of autonomy, normative (Latin *de jure*) and actual accountability (Latin *de facto*) can also be identified. The former involves establishing accountability mechanisms for regulatory agencies in their founding regulations and other – normative acts. In the latter, it is about how formal instruments, which guarantee that agencies are held accountable for actions undertaken are applied in practice. Actual accountability also extends to informal mechanisms stemming from unwritten arrangements[135].

131 M. Bovens, 'Analysing and Assessing Accountability: A Conceptual Framework', *European Law Journal*, Vol. 13, No. 4, 2007, p. 467.

132 A broad interpretation of the definition by Bovens: C. Harlow, R. Rawlings, 'Promoting Accountability in Multilevel Governance: A Network Approach', *European Law Journal*, Vol. 13, No. 4, 2007, p. 545.

133 J.P. Olsen, 'Democratic Order, Autonomy, and Accountability', *Governance. An International Journal of Policy, Administration, and Institutions*, Vol. 28, No. 4, 2015, p. 425.

134 *Ibid.*, p. 427.

135 Busuioc, Groenleer, 'The Theory', p. 192; J. Biela, Y. Papadopoulos, 'The Empirical Assessment of Agency Accountability: A Regime Approach and an Application to the German Bundesnetzagentur', *International Review of Administrative Sciences*, Vol. 80, No. 2, 2014, p. 362.

c) Internal and External Accountability of EU Regulatory Agencies

In the case of EU regulatory agencies, practical analyses of accountability and control mechanisms confirm the normative state. The European Commission has the greatest impact on agency activity[136]. On the basis of surveys conducted among the personnel of regulatory transport agencies (EASA, EMSA and ERA) and the European Commission Nuria Font writes about a "slight dominance" of the latter in agency decision-making bodies[137]. In this context, the issue of "accountability" of autonomous EU agencies can indeed be also viewed through the prism of interdependencies built between them and the Commission. Back in the 1990s, Shapiro pointed out that "EU independent agencies are 'independent' because they are (partially) independent of the Commission, not because they are independent of the normal partisan politics of the EU, that is, intergovernmental politics"[138].

As for different dimensions of agency accountability: managerial, political, judicial and financial accountability can be identified, among others. The first type involves the control of obligations performed in agency Management Boards. The second one concerns relationships between EU institutions. The third variation refers to the possibility of protection against instruments used by an agency through actions in Boards of Appeal that are inside the agency's structure or in the EU Court of Justice. These mechanisms are complemented with extra-judicial accountability that involves the handling of complaints relating to maladministration in EU institutions. This is the responsibility of the European Ombudsman. The fourth one involves reporting obligations, to institutions that monitor the financial policies of agencies (e.g. the Court of Auditors and the Commission's Internal Audit Service)[139].

Taking into account the entities to which agencies are accountable, we can identify the internal dimension, when it involves interactions with EU institutions, and the external dimension, when relationships occur between agencies and authorities in the member states. In this context, terms such as horizontal and vertical accountability are used respectively. However, there is no consistency in this case and some authors understand "horizontal accountability" as relationships

136 See Curtin, 'Holding', pp. 526–529.

137 Font, 'Policy Properties', p. 782.

138 Shapiro, 'The Problems', p. 281.

139 See also Busuioc, Groenleer, 'The Theory', pp. 193 ff.; J. Saurer, 'The Accountability of Supranational Administration: The Case of European Union Agencies', *American University International Law Review*, Vol. 24, No. 3, 2009, pp. 469–474.

with EU institutions[140] while others see it as day-to-day relationships between EU regulatory agencies and their "sister" agencies in the member states in "network accountability"[141]. The system of links in which they operate means that they are perceived as a part of the European administration network rather than fully autonomous entities operating independently on a supranational scale. The specific character of the European administration lies precisely in the creation of a common system of information exchange and support as well as instruments to coordinate the activities of many institutions[142]. This cooperation is a prerequisite for efficient management within the EU[143]; nonetheless, this complex system of interdependencies and accountability is opaque. The Treaty of Lisbon did not introduce a unified legal framework for mechanisms to control, supervise and monitor the work of agencies. Therefore, the assertion by Johannes Saurer stating that nowadays agency "accountability regimes are remarkably diverse" is accurate[144]. There are many differences resulting from the practice of particular agencies, their history and developed traditions, specific organisational culture, normative regulations and existing cooperation networks in a particular sector of the market.

This state of affairs is complicated even more as control instruments and "accountability" mechanisms for institutions of the European administration are included in an extensive catalogue of matters such as transparency, effectiveness, responsibility, openness, coherence and participation[145]. On the one hand, the multidimensionality and broad meaning of the terms analysed do not allow for the creation of a closed list of measures that would exhaust the attributes of "full accountability" of a particular entity, but, on the other hand, they make it possible to look at the mechanisms used in order to assess the functioning of agencies in a broader perspective. This broader perspective is necessary due to

140 Buess, 'Accountable and Under Control?', pp. 495 ff.

141 Saurer, 'The Accountability', pp. 475–479; Papadopoulos, 'Accountability', pp. 1034–1036.

142 More Maggetti, Verhoest, 'Unexplored Aspects', p. 245; Harlow, Rawlings, 'Promoting', pp. 542 ff.

143 See E. Schmidt-Aßmann, 'Introduction: European Composite Administration and the Role of European Administrative Law', in: O. Jansen, B. Schöndorf-Haubold (ed.), *The European Composite Administration*, Cambridge 2011, p. 4.

144 Saurer, 'The Accountability', p. 487. Also D. Curtin, 'Holding', p. 540.

145 *European Governance*, COM(2001) 428 final, p. 8; R. Coleman, 'Regulatory Agencies and the European Union', *Institute of Governance Public Policy and Social Research Working Paper*, No. 7, 2004, p. 10.

the growing competences of administrative authorities, not only domestically, but also increasingly in the international or supranational dimension.

A frequently quoted metaphor used in the title of the work by Frank Vibert "The Rise of the Unelected" has gained popularity in the literature. In his opinion, the expansion of technocratic administrative structures is associated with a transformation of the existing rules of the democratic separation of powers – "as the importance of the unelected rises, so the importance of the elected declines"[146]. Vibert makes this statement in reference to both states and the various cooperation platforms that they participate in, claiming that "the rise of the unelected is spread across the democratic world"[147]. This phenomenon, however, is particularly controversial in the supranational dimension. In the integrated European structures, it is difficult to talk about the traditional legitimacy of the activities of public authorities. In this case, extensive accountability, supervision or monitoring mechanisms performed at multiple levels and in relation to various entities would represent an equivalent of the legitimacy obtained from voters. But is this the right solution? Does the accountability of an agency to the EU institutions and the member states mean it obtains full legitimacy to act?

These questions have been asked in the literature for years and there are no clear answers to them. Some authors, like Groß, point out that it is indeed possible to legitimise the activity of administrative authorities at the supranational level through control and supervisory mechanisms. In his view, despite the fact that it is difficult to make a scientific assessment of the practical effectiveness of such measures, it is nonetheless the only solution in the case of European structures[148]. However, according to Groß, the prerequisite for the implementation of this concept is a clear legal situation, or else specifying precisely in the founding regulations what these control mechanisms are supposed to entail[149]. According to Eberhard Schmidt-Aßmann, one of the "fathers" of the German concept of "European Composite Administration", "legitimacy is to be differentiated from accountability and responsibility (which are translated into German as

146 F. Vibert, *The Rise of the Unelected: Democracy and the New Separation of Powers*, New York 2007, p. 2.

147 *Ibid.*, p. 1. See also Papadopoulos, 'Accountability', p. 1043.

148 Despite the difficulty in assessing such instruments from the legal perspective, there are many empirical analyses conducted by political scientists. See their overview Biela, Papadopoulos, 'The Empirical Assessment', pp. 364 ff.

149 See also Groß, *Die Legitimation*, pp. 102 ff.

Verantwortlichkeit or *Verantwortung*)"[150]. This view is shared by Sonja Puntscher Riekmann, who also separates these terms. She considers the phenomenon of "accountability" of EU institutions as a kind of fad in the quest for proper methods of legitimacy that has accompanied the process of European integration since its beginnings[151].

Control, assessment, supervisory and monitoring mechanisms are examples of the empowerment or legitimisation of the activity of administrative authorities, including EU regulatory agencies. They strengthen confidence in bureaucratic processes and they make it possible to obtain information about developments taking place that are hidden from the citizens of the member states. In this sense, "accountability is [...] a tool to shed light on the 'interstices of power' "[152]. However, control instruments alone are not enough to fully justify the existence and functioning of the European administration and the regulatory agencies that constitute its major component. Evidence for this is provided by efforts by researchers that are aimed at creating an accurate theory which, as well as being adequate for the current situation, could legitimise the development of the agency system in the European Union.

---

150 See E. Schmidt-Aßmann, 'Legitimacy and Accountability as a Basis for Administrative Organisation and Activity in Germany', in: Ruffert (ed.), *Legitimacy*, p. 51.

151 S. Puntscher Riekmann, 'In Search of Lost Norms: Is Accountability the Solution to the Legitimacy Problems of the European Union?', *Comparative European Politics*, Vol. 5, No. 1, 2007, pp. 121 ff. Similarly also Maggetti, Verhoest, 'Unexplored Aspects', pp. 249 ff., Bovens, 'Analysing', p. 453.

152 Puntscher Riekmann, 'In Search', p. 125.

5 Traditional Concepts of Legitimising the Activities of EU Regulatory Agencies

1. Searching for Democratic Legitimacy in the EU Institutional System

a) Legitimacy of International Organisations

Attempts to find an adequate concept of legitimacy for the activities of the European Communities and later the European Union have accompanied integration efforts since they started. These attempts form part of a corpus of theoretical concepts developed with respect to different forms of international cooperation. Both lawyers and political scientists have for years sought to come up with an antidote for the weak democratic legitimacy of international organisations and other forms of internationally developed cooperation[1]. Two main issues are stressed in this context. The legitimacy of activities in the international environment is, firstly, supposed to result from the increasing impact of international institutions on the legal systems of particular countries, and secondly, supposed to constitute a response to the "detachment" of decision-making processes from the citizens and their shift to the supranational level which is opaque from the voter's point of view.

In the case of international organisations, we can talk about the legitimacy resulting primarily from acknowledging that: "international organisations have legitimacy when other actors believe they do"[2]. Those "other actors" are mostly member states who, when joining international organisations, consciously agree to adopt a certain legal system and relinquish some of their rulemaking prerogatives in favour of common instruments. The will of sovereign countries is, therefore, the original source of legitimacy of international organisations. It is assumed that the legitimacy of international organisations is intersubjective. The term intersubjectivity comes from Weber[3]. In simple terms, it means that social phenomena are neither objective, i.e. independent from the perception

---

1 See also C.R. Kelly, 'Institutional Alliances and Derivative Legitimacy', *Michigan Journal of International Law*, Vol. 29, No. 4, 2008, pp. 612 ff.

2 *Ibid.*, p. 612. See also A. Moravcsik, 'In Defense of the Democratic Deficit: Reassessing Legitimacy in the European Union', *Journal of Common Market Studies*, Vol. 40, No. 4, 2002, pp. 603–624.

3 See N. Crossley, *Intersubjectivity. The Fabric of Social Becoming*, London 1996, pp. 87 ff.

of individual actors, nor subjective, i.e. resulting from the individual experience of those actors. The understanding of social phenomena is, thus, the result of beliefs, views or interpretations of more than one subject. The term intersubjectivity, therefore, refers to "collective understanding of reality developed in the course of continuous participation of actors in social practices"[4]. The conviction that the legitimacy of political systems is arbitrary is in accordance with Weber's concept, in which he uses the term "belief in legitimacy" (Germ. *Legitimitätsglaube*) in this context[5]. Thus, a political system obtains empowerment when it achieves acceptance and a proper level of compliance among the citizens who are subjected to it. Legitimacy to act is ensured when the society supports decision-makers, considering their performance of certain obligations as appropriate and compliant with applicable law[6].

Intersubjective perception of laws and rules of conduct in different social systems is one of the main elements of constructivist thought. As was mentioned in the context of the European Banking Authority, in the constructivist interpretation social norms are born in complex interactions between different actors at the intra-state and international levels, while co-shaping them at the same time. These interactions, in the opinion of Alexander Wendt, who is considered to be one of the creators of the constructivist paradigm, can take place in three scenarios: cooperation, indifference and competition. The nature of these relations depends on the meanings attributed to specific symbols, gestures and signals used for communication between subjects[7].

---

4 T. Widłak, 'Prawo a konstruktywizm w teorii stosunków międzynarodowych – możliwości interdyscyplinarnego zbliżenia', in: M. Zirk-Sadowski *et al.* (ed.), *Integracja zewnętrzna i wewnętrzna nauk prawnych*, Łódź 2014, p. 54. See J. Brunnée, S.J. Toope, 'Constructivism and International Law', in: J.L. Dunoff, M.A. Pollack (ed.), *Interdisciplinary Perspectives on International Law and International Relations: The State of the Art*, New York 2013, pp. 122 ff.

5 See Weber, *Wirtschaft*, pp. 16 ff. For more about this concept, see K. Gläser, *Über legitime Herrschaft. Grundlagen der Legitimitätstheorie*, Wiesbaden 2013, p. 23.

6 See also A. Wimmel, 'Theorizing the Democratic Legitimacy of European Governance: A Labyrinth with No Exit?', *Journal of European Integration*, Vol. 31, No. 2, 2009, p. 186; D. Gaus, 'The Dynamics of Legitimation. Why the Study of Political Legitimacy Needs More Realism', *ARENA Working Paper*, No. 8, 2011, pp. 2 ff.

7 See A. Wendt, 'Anarchy is What States Make of It: The Social Construction of Power Politics', *International Organization*, Vol. 46, No. 2, 1992, p. 400. For an extensive comment to Wendt's considerations, see A. Curanović, *Konstruktywizm*, in: R. Zięba *et al.* (ed.), *Teorie i podejścia badawcze w nauce o stosunkach międzynarodowych*, Warszawa 2015, pp. 108 ff.

There is no doubt that the main element legitimising the activities of international organisations and other mechanisms forming part of "Global Governance" is the law[8]. The law is founded in the will of the participating countries that adopt its norms and commit to implement them. Thus, democratic legitimacy is established through law[9]. In this context, it is worth citing the position of Gunther Teubner, one of the best-known contemporary German law theorists and sociologists who, referring to constructivist thought, believed that every legal system, especially if created within a particular international organisation, constitutes a separate social reality. Applicable legal norms in such a system bestow certain semantic features upon the behaviour of individuals and social groups. In Teubner's approach the external world is constructed through law[10]. Consequently, the system of international law becomes the foundation, and a constituent element of international relations as one of the many dimensions of social relations[11]. Thus, the sociological theory of law envisages a far-reaching autonomisation of law. The application of specific norms results directly from the inner features of a legal system. Following the constructivist interpretation, this system is legitimised on the basis of the relations between actors who identify with it through actively participating in it.

In a globalised world, the law loses some of its typical systemic attributes – particularly a clear hierarchy and its legitimisation by the nation-state[12]. A distinctive semantic code, developed within international organisations, becomes a point of reference. One of these specific supranational systems with well-developed "semantics" is the European Union. In its case, normative and institutional integration in detailed sectors of the internal market has reached an advanced level. Many concepts and formulations have been developed that

---

8 *Cf.* Herdegen, *Der Kampf*, pp. 87–94.

9 See M. Eifert, 'Legitimationsstrukturen internationaler Verwaltung', in: H.-H. Trute *et al.* (ed.), *Allgemeines Verwaltungsrecht - zur Tragfähigkeit eines Konzeptes*, Tübingen 2008, p. 312; Wimmel, 'Theorizing', p. 187.

10 See G. Teubner, 'How the Law Thinks. Towards a Constructivist Epistemology of Law', *Law and Society Review*, Vol. 23, No. 5, 1989, pp. 730, 740.

11 See Widłak, 'Prawo', p. 56.

12 Roberto Caranta aptly characterises this state: "The past century has shown that the dimension of most nation-states is insufficient to tackle very essential issues, leading to various form of supranational or regional integration for both military and economic purposes. Most of the institutional arrangements set up to meet these needs sit uncomfortably with the representative democratic structures that nation-states have given themselves", 'Democracy, Legitimacy and Accountability – Is There a Common European Theoretical Framework?', in: Ruffert (ed.), *Legitimacy*, p. 181.

have permanently entered the legal systems of member states, often acting as "indicators" in the understanding and interpretation of national laws.

b) Theorising Legitimacy of EU Institutions by Fritz Scharpf

A dichotomy proposed in the 1970s by the German lawyer and political scientist Fritz Scharpf has become one of the permanent semantic codes used in the analysis of the functioning of EU institutions[13]. He developed the theoretical concept of input-oriented legitimacy and output-oriented legitimacy. The former is supposed to be created when "entering" the system, the latter is outcome-based and placed at the opposite end, or at the "exit" from the system. This solution was inspired by a cybernetic model developed by the American mathematician and philosopher, Norbert Wiener[14].

Cybernetics, in very general terms, is the science that deals with organisation, as well as control and communication mechanisms in complex systems. These systems are both living organisms, like people and animals, and man-made objects, as well as social groups. Norbert Wiener believed that all these systems are characterised by "tangibility", and in the case of organised social groups, they are determined by the features of their individual participants. Systems receive inputs and send relevant outputs. Various systems function on the basis of many links between them. They send "input letters" and receive "output letters". In the cybernetic model, such exchange channels are called "information". In these "information channels", input impacts output and vice versa through feedback loops. Wiener called this phenomenon "feedback control circuits"[15]. One such "control circuit" is also a mechanism which provides legitimisation that is designed to justify actions undertaken within a certain system.

Another inspiration for Scharpf's creation of a theory of legitimacy, which is commonly used in relation to decision-making mechanisms in the European Union, was a theory of political systems developed by the Canadian political scientist, David Easton. He pointed out that the political behaviour of decision-makers forms part of a specific system. Such a political system functions in a

---

13 See F.W. Scharpf, *Demokratietheorie zwischen Utopie und Anpassung*, Konstanz 1970, pp. 21 ff.

14 See D. Kabat-Rudnicka, *Zasada federalna a integracja ponadnarodowa. Unia Europejska między federalizmem dualistycznym a kooperatywnym*, Kraków 2010, p. 207.

15 See N. Wiener, *Cybernetics or Control and Communication in the Animal and the Machine*, Cambridge 1985, pp. 155 ff.; D. Unwin, R. McAleese (ed.), *Encyclopedia of Educational Media Communications and Technology*, London/Basingstoke 1978, p. 267.

particular environment. Interactions between both dimensions – the system and the environment – were recognised by Easton as an input-output relationship. A political system is created in a process of conversion which processes the impulses that penetrate into it, constituting the input, into a measurable effect of its operation, which should be considered as the output. Only thanks to this continuous creative activity is the system able to survive[16].

Scharpf applied the division between input and output signals to processes legitimising European governance mechanisms. The concept he put forward has permanently entered the canon of research on these phenomena[17]. Interestingly, it has gained particular recognition in the context of analysing the activities of EU regulatory agencies. There are hardly any studies on justifying the role of EU agencies in the integrated European institutional system that do not cite Scharpf and his dichotomous division into mechanisms of legitimacy developed "at the input" and "at the output" of the system. It is usually assumed that traditional democratic legitimacy involves mechanisms "at the input" of the system. This means that input legitimacy is identical to representative legitimacy (government by the people, Germ. *Herrschaft durch das Volk*). This concerns democratic decision-making procedures at the supranational EU level, which should be implemented through the broadest possible representation of the citizens. In a way output legitimacy is a mirror image of broad social involvement in the form of input legitimacy. It is outcome-based and it is also called utilitarian or technocratic legitimacy. Its main component is the efficiency of decision-making procedures that involve specialised experts with greater knowledge than the general public. It is the government for the people (Germ. *Herrschaft für das Volk*)[18].

Scharpf perceived integration structures as a model political system in the vein of the models proposed by Easton[19]. In his opinion, what is crucial for

16 D. Easton, *The Political System. An Inquiry into the State of Political Science*, New York 1953, pp. 96–100. For an extensive discussion of this concept see E.F. Miller, 'David Easton's Political Theory', *Political Science Reviewer*, Vol. 1, 1971, pp. 198 ff.

17 See P. Bouwen, 'Business Interest Representation and Legitimate European Governance', in: S. Smismans (ed.), *Civil Society and Legitimate European Governance*, Cheltenham/Northampton 2006, p. 282; A. Glencross, 'Democratic Inputs *versus* Output-Oriented Governance: The ECB's Evolving Role and the New Architecture of Legitimacy in the EU', *Journal of Information and Organizational Sciences*, Vol. 5, No. 2, 2014, pp. 24 ff.

18 F.W. Scharpf, *Regieren in Europa. Effektiv und demokratisch?*, Frankfurt am Main 1999, pp. 16 ff.

19 See F.W. Scharpf, 'Die Euro-Rettung als Demokratieproblem', *DMS – Der moderne Staat. Zeitschrift für Public Policy, Recht und Management*, Vol. 6, No. 2, 2013, p. 279.

maintaining its continued existence and development is to keep a proper balance in input-output interactions. "Input" legitimacy, that is representative or parliamentary, needs to be, in Scharpf's concept, balanced by "output" legitimacy, meaning technocratic or utilitarian, which is the domain of unelected bodies. These two concepts go together. The authenticity that comes from citizens, who directly express their will, is complemented by the effectiveness that is derived from technocratic mechanisms[20].

This complementary nature, according to Scharpf, results from the deficiencies of representative mechanisms in the modern world. At a time of "mass media", which is frequently partisan, democratic participation, in itself, is not sufficient to bestow moral legitimacy on the choice of the majority. This majority, in fact, does not even have to be hostile towards particular minorities to infringe their rights or interests. According to Scharpf, the proper solution to reduce this threat is to achieve the ideal community proposed by Weber[21]. Trust developed within a given social group, resulting from a common history, culture and language, should form a basis for this. Weber called this trust a "belief in common values" (Germ. *Gemeinsamkeitsglauben*)[22].

Scharpf correctly predicted that, in spite of all their efforts, European integration structures would be unable to formulate the same sense of community as is characteristic for nation states. Hence, the strengthening of the European Parliament's position, which became a reality after the enactment of the Single European Act (1987), and the entry into force of the Treaties of Maastricht (1993) and Amsterdam (1999), did not clearly result in obtaining full legitimacy for Community decisions[23]. That is because, in the European dimension, the parliamentary majority has a lesser legitimising importance, precisely due to the lack of an institutionalised European identity[24]. It is one thing to have a sense of belonging to the European circle, understood as a system of certain values making up European civilization, and another thing to identify with the supranational institutional apparatus which obtains ever- broader competences affecting the lives of citizens. Consequently, the assertion by Scharpf formulated

---

20 Scharpf, *Regieren*, p. 12.

21 *Ibid*., p. 18.

22 See Weber, *Wirtschaft*, pp. 307 ff.

23 See M. Höreth, 'No Way Out for the Beast? The Unsolved Legitimacy Problem of European Governance', *Journal of European Public Policy*, Vol. 6, No. 2, 1999, p. 250; A.Z. Nowak, D. Milczarek (ed.), *Europeistyka w zarysie*, Warszawa 2006.

24 Scharpf, *Regieren*, p. 19; Wimmel 'Theorizing', p. 190.

twenty years ago that traditional representative democracy can exist in its full form only at the national level has not lost its validity[25].

Scharpf predicted that alternative methods of legitimising European governance structures would become necessary. He took a broad view of the output perspective, believing that it can include alternative instruments of legitimacy to the traditional democratic model. Therefore, some German authors hold the opinion that the technocratic (output) legitimacy proposed by Scharpf is not a variant of democratic legitimacy[26]. Government for the people derives its justification not from the will of citizens, but from the effectiveness of solutions to problems affecting larger communities. These are problems that cannot be tackled single-handedly, that are impossible to solve with grassroots initiatives and that do not submit to self-regulating market mechanisms. The only practical answer is institutional mechanisms, which (1) are specialised in their nature and imply limited membership, (2) are designed as permanent bodies, and (3) are intended to serve common interests[27].

In national systems, elements of representative legitimacy intertwine with elements of technocratic legitimacy in everyday political and administrative practices[28]. This does not cause much controversy and has for decades been considered to be a natural course of affairs in the context of the evolution of modern political systems and the need to adapt legitimising mechanisms to these changes. The situation looks different in the case of supranational structures. The clear advantage of output legitimacy means that the discussion about insufficient democratic justification for the activities of European institutions, particularly strictly technocratic bodies such as regulatory agencies, has not faded away[29].

---

25 Scharpf, *Regieren*, p. 20; Eifert, 'Legitimationsstrukturen', p. 317.

26 Peuker, *Bürokratie*, pp. 193 ff. Daniel Gaus, however, has a different opinion: "The distinction between input- and output-oriented legitimacy [...] refers to two different aspects of one and the same concept of democratic legitimacy", in: D. Gaus, 'Two Kinds of Democratic Legitimacy for the EU? Input- and Output-Oriented Legitimacy as a Case of Conceptual Misformation', Paper Presented at the Conference 'Democracy as Idea and Practice', 14–15.1.2010, p. 1.

27 Scharpf, *Regieren*, p. 20.

28 More F. Decker *et al.*, *Demokratie ohne Wähler? Neue Herausforderungen politischer Partizipation*, Bonn 2013, pp. 10 ff.; B. Majchrzak, *Problem delimitacji regulacji administracyjnoprawnej w systemie prawnym w świetle orzecznictwa Trybunału Konstytucyjnego*, Warszawa 2015.

29 See Gaus, 'Two Kinds', p. 2.

Scharpf aptly commented in the 1990s that creating theoretical constructions about legitimising the activities of EU bodies does not stop, or even modify, the activity of the European Union. In his opinion, European politics in the supranational dimension develops regardless of any attempts to justify it. What is interesting from the point of view of the academic debate is less important in the context of political practice[30].

c) Interpreting the Theoretical Concept of Fritz Scharpf

Other authors also approach intensive conceptualisation efforts to legitimise EU activities with some reserve. For example, Andreas Wimmel calls for conducting a "more sophisticated and more systematic analysis of a criticism of democracy and/or legitimacy" within the EU[31].

Daniel Gaus, on the other hand, claims that the division introduced by Scharpf is misleading and leads to "misformation" concerning the concept of democratic legitimacy[32]. He believes that the input-output division, in the context of studying the legitimacy of European institutions, is detached from practical observations and was introduced, in Scharpf's intent, from the beginning "as a typology of different standards by which contemporary normative democratic theories evaluate the worthiness of a political system"[33]. Therefore, "the distinction between input- and output-oriented legitimacy is an application of a systems-analytical view to the discourse of ideal theory meant to categorise different ideal arguments about democratic legitimacy"[34].

The interpretation of Gaus falls within the classic division of theories of legitimacy into those seeking justification for the exercise of power in law (normative legitimacy) and those seeking to empower the activities of rulers through social recognition (empirical legitimacy). A socially legitimised authority often has a normative justification that is derived from the law that is in force. And vice versa, social acceptance strengthens the acceptance of the activities of decision-makers resulting from law. According to Gaus, "it is commonly accepted to use input- and output-oriented legitimacy as normative standards for assessing [...] the EU's legitimacy without further ado"[35]. This means that both the variants of

30 Scharpf, *Regieren*, p. 21.
31 Wimmel, 'Theorizing', p. 196.
32 Gaus, 'Two Kinds', p. 2.
33 Gaus, 'The Dynamics', p. 7.
34 *Ibid.*
35 *Ibid.*, p. 6.

legitimacy introduced by Scharpf can be understood as normative theories. Such theories analyse the issues of exercising power through the prism of ethical and legal justifications. Not only is positive law important, but also specific customs and moral values attributed to particular actions. These are commonly respected rules of behaviour. As far as state systems are concerned, the point of reference, when it comes to searching for legitimacy understood in this way, is usually the constitution, whereas in the EU legal system, it is the Treaties. The legal and positive perspective is enhanced with references to values interpreted through the prism of natural law[36].

Following the interpretation by Gaus, one could get the impression that the most commonly reproduced vision of the EU institutions' legitimacy does not help to explain, or clearly describe, reality. Instead of complicated theoretical constructions, "the study of legitimacy needs an empirical turn that gives more attention to how ideas work in societal practice"[37]. If we were to apply the thesis to the earlier considerations about the functions of a theory, a similar conclusion could be made, and not only in the context of considerations by Scharpf, but also those of other authors who repeatedly modify his concepts. Theories of legitimacy constructed in the context of regulatory agencies and other actors involved in European governance not only describe reality with little clarity and hardly explain anything, but also in many cases make it impossible to provide a real forecast. Regardless of these difficulties, it is worth attempting to recap the theoretical approaches which have been selected. This will allow us to place regulatory agencies in a specific semantic context, without which, it is impossible to understand the continued existence and development of these institutions. Due to the weak "anchoring" of the agencies in primary law, theoretical justifications of their legitimacy are one of the pillars on which the EU agency system stands.

2. Democratic Deficit

a) Article 10 TEU as a Legal Basis for EU Representative Democracy

The starting point for further theoretical considerations is an attempt to answer the question of where to look for traditional democratic legitimacy and whether we can talk about empowerment understood this way in the supranational context at all. The appropriate legal basis for this pursuit is Article 10(1) TEU,

---

36 See also Peuker, *Bürokratie*, pp. 97–99; Kubin, *Legitymizacja*, pp. 42 ff.

37 Gaus, 'The Dynamics', p. 8.

which states explicitly that "the functioning of the Union shall be founded on representative democracy". Representative democracy in the Union, however, should be understood differently from that in national systems. In the opinion of Cezary Mik, it can be applied only incidentally in such a big body, e.g.: in the case of the elections to the European Parliament or in the case of the European Citizens' Initiative (Article 11(4) TEU)[38]. The meaning of representative democracy is defined in Article 10(2) TEU. Democracy within EU structures is of a dual nature[39]. Firstly, there is direct representation of citizens in the European Parliament. Secondly, there is representation of the member states (indirect democratic legitimacy). They are represented in the European Council by heads of state or governments, and in the Council of the EU (the Council) – by members of particular governments. These government representatives are democratically accountable to their national parliaments or their citizens[40].

In spite of clear Treaty provisions, the problem of a democratic deficit in the European Union, understood primarily as a lack of democratic legitimacy for the activities of its authorities and institutions operating in a multilevel governance system, has been widely discussed in legal and political science literature for several decades[41]. In simple terms, it is supposed to mean that e.g. the European Parliament and national parliaments, as bodies enjoying legitimacy from voters, or traditional democratic mandate, do not have enough influence on the EU decision-making process[42].

Due to the abundance of studies on these issues, it is neither possible nor advisable to cite all the arguments on this matter. They are not orderly and swing between two extremes as political sentiments shift[43]. On one side, there are those

---

38 C. Mik, 'Umocnienie legitymacji demokratycznej Unii Europejskiej', in: J. Barcz (ed.), *Traktat z Lizbony. Główne reformy ustrojowe Unii Europejskiej*, Warszawa 2008, p. 104.

39 *Ibid.*, p. 103; Görisch, *Demokratische Verwaltung*, p. 340; Groß, *Die Legitimation*, p. 80.

40 See M. Ruffert, 'Was ist Democratic Governance?', in: S. Botzem *et al.* (ed.), *Governance als Prozess. Koordinationsformen im Wandel*, Baden-Baden 2009, pp. 62 ff.

41 See Moravcsik, 'In Defense', pp. 603 ff.; A. Føllesdal, S. Hix, 'Why There is a Democratic Deficit in the EU: A Response to Majone and Moravcsik', *Journal of Common Markets Studies*, Vol. 44, No. 3, 2006, pp. 534 ff.; W. Jedlecka, *Legitymizacja prawa Unii Europejskiej. Legitymizacja demokratyczna czy cywilizacyjna?*, Łódź 2014, pp. 102 ff.; A. Føllesdal, 'Democracy and the European Union: Challenges', in: A. Føllesdal, P. Koslowski (ed.), *Democracy and the European Union*, Berlin 1997, pp. 2 ff.

42 J.M. Fiszer, 'Czy państwo demokratyczne może być wzorem dla przyszłej Unii Europejskiej', *Myśl Ekonomiczna i Polityczna*, Vol. 44, No. 1, 2014, p. 104.

43 More S. Piattoni, 'Representation as Delegation: A Basis for EU Democracy?', *Journal of European Public Policy*, Vol. 20, No. 2, 2013, p. 224.

who claim that the EU, as an international organisation, enjoys sufficient democratic legitimacy and realises the ideals of liberal democracy to the greatest extent possible[44]. On the other, there are voices saying that it is an undemocratic structure, which keeps drifting ever further away from democratic ideals as the integration process advances[45].

The European Union strives to create its own model of democracy stemming from the specific character of this international organisation. Difficulties in building such a model are inextricably linked to one specific issue, defined in the literature as the legitimacy crisis of European institutions[46]. It is assumed that due to the specific character of the European Union, democratic solutions developed in the political systems of the member states cannot be applied to its structures. Hence, the references to dualism when it comes to the functioning of democracy in EU structures – it not only takes the form of state-like representative democracy (with supranational specifics taken into account), but also procedural democracy, justified by so-called throughput legitimacy. The latter belongs to the alternative models of legitimacy. Empowerment to act that is understood in this way, results from the institutional determinants of the decision-making process – how particular decisions are made and who participates in making them – performs a legitimising role[47]. The activities of EU administration authorities are legitimised in many ways and the member states do not necessarily have to be the main source of empowerment of individual institutions in multilevel governance systems[48].

In this study, for the sake of clarifying the argumentation, a simple division of concepts relating to legitimacy has been adopted which is inspired by a proposal

---

44 Moravcsik, 'In Defense', pp. 605 ff.; G. Majone, 'From Regulatory State to a Democratic Default', *Journal of Common Market Studies*, Vol. 52, No. 6, 2014, pp. 1217 ff.

45 See e.g. H. Naßmacher, *Mehr Europa – weniger Demokratie*, München 2013, pp. 26 ff.; C. Gandrud, M. Hallerberg, 'Does Banking Union Worsen the EU's Democratic Deficit? The Need for Greater Supervisory Data Transparency', *Journal of Common Market Studies*, Vol. 53, No. 4, 2015, pp. 771 ff.

46 See M. Ruffert, 'Demokratie und Governance in Europa', in: Bauer *et al.*, *Demokratie*, Tübingen 2005, p. 319.

47 See also Wimmel, 'Theorizing', pp. 190 ff.; V.A. Schmidt, 'Democracy and Legitimacy in the European Union Revisited: Input, Output and "Throughput"', *Political Studies*, Vol. 61, No. 1, 2013, pp. 9, 18.

48 See M. Witkowska, 'Kryzys modelu demokracji w Unii Europejskiej – przyczyny, uwarunkowania, scenariusze rozwoju sytuacji', in: K.A. Wojtaszczyk, J. Nadolska (ed.), *Kryzysy w procesie integracji europejskiej i sposoby ich przezwyciężania*, Warszawa 2015, p. 121, Höreth, 'No Way Out', pp. 251 ff.

by Andreas Orator. He concluded that traditionally understood democracy should be sought for in theories based on "input" and involving things like citizen representation and participation. He placed the so-called alternative models of legitimacy in the "other" category of justifications for the activities of EU structures, including regulatory agencies. This includes the abovementioned output and throughput theories. Alternative approaches will be discussed in more detail in Chapter 6[49].

b) Democracy within the EU Institutional Structures

Multi-layered institutional systems such as the European Union differ considerably from intra-state systems. The European administrative network, where regulatory agencies operate, is the prime example. In such structures, typical features include the weakening of control mechanisms in a largely non-transparent decision-making process, in comparison to intra-state mechanisms and the weak accountability of relevant decision-makers and detachment from social expectations caused by the expansion of bureaucracy. In the case of the European Union, attention is drawn to the advantage of having executive authorities – the Council and the Commission – which are only marginally, and indirectly, subject to influence and control by national parliaments[50]. The strengthening of the executive at the expense of the legislature is a characteristic feature of the European integration process. It is not without reason that the European executive order is seen as the preferred model of EU governance. This executive apparatus, unlike the European Parliament, is not directly elected. Direct representation of voter interests is, thus, not possible in this case[51].

In this respect, the democratic deficit in the European Union is emphasised, or as Jerzy Kranz writes, unjustly and unnecessarily exaggerated[52]. The debate about the weaknesses of the democratic legitimacy of the Community structures has accompanied the European integration process from its beginnings. This stems from the basic motive of European integration, which was to bring national economies closer. "The founding fathers" of the European Communities, like Jean Monnet, put emphasis on the functional aspect of the structures which

49 Orator, *Möglichkeiten*, pp. 338–365, Witkowska, 'Kryzys', p. 151.

50 Føllesdal, Hix, 'Why', p. 535.

51 See M. Simoncini, 'Paradigms for EU Law and the Limits of Delegation. The Case of EU Agencies', *Perspectives on Federalism*, Vol. 9, No. 2, 2017, pp. 49 ff.

52 Kranz, 'Deficyt', p. 20. This view is shared e.g. by Majone. See 'From Regulatory State', p. 1218.

were to be created. The effectiveness of economic integration was of primary importance; therefore, many solutions were often implemented at the expense of democratic procedures[53]. In fact, this is hardly an isolated case when it comes to shaping different forms of international cooperation[54]. This is cause by a simple fact, namely: "Democracy is not a prime category in international relations, although contemporary international law is doing a great deal to develop and strengthen it"[55]. On account of this, Kranz is right when he concludes that the thesis of the democratic deficit in international organisations is misleading[56]. This is because we look for clear parallels with state systems, despite there being, by nature, obvious differences between international or supranational systems and state systems[57].

A problem which is frequently brought up in the case of the European Union is the lack of a European *demos*, or nation, which could legitimise the powers of supranational authorities in a similar way as in the case of a state system[58]. Democratic procedures as a method of creating authority and legitimising the decision-making process in an international organisation, even such a deeply integrated one as the European Union, have to look different than is the case of the individual member states. Hence, traditional democracy is replaced with fancy theoretical concepts such as "demoicracy" or "compound democracy"[59].

According to researchers who develop such concepts, arguments pointing to deficiencies of EU democracy, such as weak parliamentary structures, and the

---

53 See K. Mizera, 'Deficyt demokratyczny w Unii Europejskiej', *Folia Iuridica Wratislaviensis*, Vol. 3, No. 1, 2014, p. 90; T. Biernat, '"Deficyt demokracji" w strukturach Unii Europejskiej', in: T. Biernat, A. Siwik (ed.), *Demokracja. Teoria. Idee. Instytucje*, Toruń 2001, p. 33.

54 See J.H.H. Weiler, 'The Geology of International Law – Governance, Democracy and Legitimacy', *Zeitschrift für ausländisches öffentliches Recht und Völkerrecht*, Vol. 64, 2004, pp. 550 ff.

55 Kranz, 'Deficyt', pp. 10 ff.

56 *Ibid.*

57 See G. de Búrca, 'The Quest for Legitimacy in The European Union', *Modern Law Review*, Vol. 59, No. 3, 1996, pp. 352 ff.

58 Critically F.W. Scharpf, 'After the Crash: A Perspective on Multilevel European Democracy', *European Law Journal*, Vol. 21, No. 3, 2015, p. 395. See also Z. Rudnicki, 'Identity in a Differentiated Integration in Europe', in: S. Konopacki (ed.), *Europe in the Time of Crisis*, Łódź/Kraków 2014, pp. 57 ff.; A. Wielomski, M. Ziętek-Wielomska, *The Europe of Nations and Its Future. Nationalism, Euroscepticism, Natiocratism*, Warszawa 2017, pp. 15 ff.

59 Glencross, 'Democratic Inputs', p. 26.

lack of a political nation or the lack of a European citizenship that would make it possible to directly identify with the EU political system, are not convincing. The reason is simple – they cannot be applied to the European Union, because it is a different kind of entity. Instead of one nation, there are many. Thus, the EU is a "demoicracy", or a polity of multiple distinct peoples (Gr. *demoi*)[60].

The term was introduced into the academic debate in the 1990s by the Belgian philosopher Philippe van Parijs[61]. He took a critical view of the growth of EU institutions, pointing out that the integration structures still involve many "peoples", or societies of the member states. But the burden of accountability, along with the progressing integration of economies, should also be transferred to the common level rather than remain at the level of individual *demoi*. Van Parijs wrote explicitly about a necessary change: "A shift from *demoi-cracy* to *demos-cracy*, a shift from accountability to the separate peoples of Europe to accountability to the people of Europe as a whole"[62]. He believed that such a change was necessary not just because classic democracy would be, by its nature, better than "demoicracy". He held the opinion that "in the case of [...] redistribution under contemporary economic conditions, raising the scale of the democratic game [...] can be expected to lead to far better decisions, as far as the overall goal of social justice is concerned than those to which national governments would be driven by the interaction of economic and political mechanisms"[63]. Such an intensification of democratic involvement could be useful in shaping regulatory policies in many sectors of the internal market, not least due to their impact on the daily lives of millions of citizens in the member states. Instead, the Union has taken the opposite path of evolving towards "Eurocratic" structures.

Interestingly, the concept of "demoicracy" by van Parijs has been popularised in an altered form which is at odds with his postulates[64]. Many authors have recognised "demoicracy" as the only possible variant of functioning and deciding within the European Union. Europe will remain multinational. Consequently, the right model is one that creates participatory and deliberative mechanisms that will guarantee the broadest possible social participation in decision-making

---

60 F. Cheneval, F. Schimmelfennig, 'The Case for Demoicracy in the European Union', *Journal of Common Market Studies*, Vol. 51, No. 2, 2013, p. 334.

61 P. van Parijs, 'Should the European Union Become More Democratic?', in: Føllesdal, Koslowski (ed.), *Democracy*, pp. 287 ff.

62 *Ibid.*, pp. 298 ff.

63 *Ibid.*, p. 299.

64 See Cheneval, Schimmelfennig, 'The Case', pp. 334 ff.

processes[65]. This is also reflected in social surveys, in which less than fifteen per cent of citizens in the member states see themselves primarily as Europeans and, on the other hand, nearly forty per cent of respondents declare themselves as having solely a national identity[66].

Scharpf shares a similar narrative, pointing out that the EU is, and will remain, a "multinational empire" (Germ. *Vielvölker-Imperium*), where reaching broad transnational consensus is of primary importance[67]. He writes in this context about "consociational democracy" (Germ. *Konkordanz-Demokratie*)[68]. Within this model of democracy, the main governance pillar is the division of rulemaking competences between different participants (power sharing)[69]. A model that is akin to this concept is called "compound democracy" which envisages the creation of a "union of states and their citizens". One propagator of this concept is Sergio Fabbrini who believes that the seventy-year-long process of the integration of European countries has led to the development of a specific variant of democracy in the EU system, which is close to the one created in the United States. Through mutual "feedback" and interdependencies between them, states create a system which is something more than the democracies in nation-states[70].

---

65 Richard Bellamy writes about "republican intergovernmentalism" and "Union of Peoples". See R. Bellamy, 'An Ever Closer Union Among the Peoples of Europe: Republican Intergovernmentalism and Demoicratic Representation within the EU', *Journal of European Integration*, Vol. 35, No. 5, 2013, pp. 504 ff. See also K. Nicolaïdis, 'European Demoicracy and Its Crisis', *Journal of Common Market Studies*, Vol. 51, No. 2, 2013, pp. 351–369; J. Lacey, 'Conceptually Mapping the European Union: A Demoi-Cratic Analysis', *Journal of European Integration*, Vol. 38, No. 1, 2016, pp. 63 ff.

66 Cheneval, Schimmelfennig, 'The Case', p. 337.

67 Scharpf, 'Die Euro-Rettung', p. 281.

68 *Ibid.*

69 See also A. Pelinka, 'Die Europäische Union – eine Konkordanzdemokratie? Zur typologischen Verortung der EU', in: K.H. Schrenk, M. Soldner (ed.), *Analyse demokratischer Regierungssysteme. Festschrift für Wolfgang Ismayr zum 65. Geburtstag*, Wiesbaden 2010, pp. 83 ff.

70 S. Fabbrini, *Compound Democracies. Why the United States and Europe are Becoming Similar*, Oxford 2010, pp. 3, 45 ff. Critically about this concept S. Kröger, D. Friedrich, 'Democratic Representation in the EU: Two Kinds of Subjectivity', *Journal of European Public Policy*, Vol. 20, No. 2, 2013, pp. 172 ff. Extensively about different variants of democracy also in the international dimension D. Held, *Models of Democracy*, Stanford 2006, pp. 304, 306 ff.

3. Theories of Legitimacy Based on Representation

a) The German Concepts of Democratic Legitimacy

The most traditional view on governance mechanisms both in the national and international dimension is the concept of democratic legitimacy, which assumes that power is exercised by the people. Since direct democracy is impossible in contemporary political systems, an indirect variant of realising the will of the people through electoral mechanisms has been created[71]. Decisions of state authorities are lawful and they have democratic legitimacy, when those in power can cite the will of the people in an uninterrupted "chain of legitimation" (Germ. *Legitimationskette*). We can thus adopt the interpretation by Simona Piattoni that "[within] the electoral model of democracy, representation serves only the function of selecting those who will then decide"[72]. This means that delegation of particular tasks to administrative bodies takes place within the "chain of legitimation". The delegating bodies are entities directly empowered to perform their tasks through the democratic choice of citizens[73].

In this context German legal doctrine has developed the abovementioned concepts of personal legitimacy (Germ. *personelle Legitimation*) and factual legitimacy (Germ. *sachliche Legitimation*)[74]. In the state system, the strongest personal legitimacy is enjoyed by members of parliament, because they are directly elected by citizens. This legitimacy gets weaker as the "chain of appointment" of individual officials within the administrative apparatus becomes longer. The process of appointment should be clearly regulated by the legislature[75]. As personal legitimacy weakens in extensive administrative systems, factual legitimacy, which means binding decision-makers strictly and comprehensively by applicable law, must become stronger. They act only within the scope of the prerogatives laid down in normative acts empowering them to perform their tasks, and are subject to parliamentary control. This is consistent with the thought of Weber and

---

71 See Piattoni, 'Representation', p. 229.
72 Decker *et al.*, *Demokratie*, pp. 14 ff.
73 Hermes, 'Legitimationsprobleme', p. 467; Peuker, *Bürokratie*, p. 151.
74 They also exist with the same meaning as the concept of personal and organisational legitimacy (Germ. *organisatorisch-personelle Legitimation*) and the concept of accurate, objective and factually correct legitimacy (Germ. *sachlich-inhaltliche Legitimation*). See Weißgärber, *Die Legitimation*, pp. 109, 114.
75 *Cf.* C.D. Classen, *Demokratische Legitimation im offenen Rechtsstaat*, Tübingen 2009, p. 53.

his picture of the state administration functioning like a machine. In this understanding, the shaping of the "state will" takes place in bodies directly elected by the people, within a democratically legitimised legislature. The bureaucratic executive apparatus is only responsible for the implementation of what has been decided by the parliament[76].

It is assumed that in the state system the only rulemaking powers that must be legitimised are those involving specific decision-making independence. Non-legally binding consulting does not require empowerment in the way that was specified above. As Claus Classen rightly noted, the legitimacy of expert bodies is not, however, necessary when their professional support has no impact on the decisions made. If an expert judgement conditions or determines the activities of legitimate state authorities, then it also requires empowerment, or legitimacy[77]. This observation relates particularly to EU regulatory agencies, because their specialised consulting affects the functioning of administrative authorities not in a unitary administrative system of a particular member state, but throughout the Union. It does not really matter what powers a given agency has. As has already been mentioned several times, informational, supporting or monitoring tasks can also have a significant impact on the European decision-making process[78].

The idea of a "chain of legitimation" constitutes one of the main pillars of German constitutional law[79]. The abovementioned forms of legitimising the activities of public authorities are taken into account in this case. What matters here is not the type of legitimacy, but its effectiveness. In this context German legal doctrine mentions a sufficient (Germ. *hinreichendes Legitimationsniveau*) or definite level of legitimacy (Germ. *bestimmtes Legitimationsniveau*)[80]. Within the tripartition of power, different forms of state authority are legitimised in different ways. The goal is to balance mechanisms of personal and factual legitimacy. This is supposed to bring about the "minimum level of empowerment". That level, however, is difficult to define. Every case requires a careful analysis of instruments whose purpose is to compensate for any shortcomings whether in personal or factual legitimacy[81]. They are complemented by institutional and

---

76 See *ibid.*, p. 7.

77 *Ibid.*, pp. 53 ff.

78 Hermes, 'Legitimationsprobleme', pp. 474 ff.

79 See A. von Bogdandy, 'Globalization and Europe: How to Square Democracy, Globalization, and International Law', *European Journal of International Law*, Vol. 15, No. 5, 2004, p. 902.

80 Weißgärber, *Die Legitimation*, p. 104.

81 See *ibid.*, pp. 105–107.

functional legitimacy (Germ. *institutionell-funktionelle Legitimation*). This also falls within the traditional German concept of democratic legitimacy, which means that an authority's special function and place in the institutional structure are of major importance for justifying its activities. This form of legitimacy does not refer directly to the will of the people and it is not explicitly connected with the idea of its representation by rulemaking entities. One needs to remember, however, that the assignment of particular functions and a place in the institutional structure in democratic systems is done in the form of normative acts adopted by the legislature, which is directly legitimised through elections. This can strengthen institutional and functional legitimacy by explicitly enshrining the independent position of an entity in the constitution, primarily including its specifically defined decision-making autonomy[82]. Nevertheless, independent administrative bodies must not only act within a defined legal framework, but also must be subject to supervision and control by government authorities accountable to the parliament; conversely in the case of EU regulatory agencies, they are subject to the steering role of the European Commission[83].

b) Regulatory Legitimacy as a Modification of Representation-Based Legitimacy

Theories of legitimacy, which emphasise the role of the people as the only entity able to empower rulers to act on the basis of representation, as follows from the hitherto considerations, primarily apply to intra-state systems. Apart from the commonly used terms such as representative legitimacy, or input-oriented legitimacy, the "majoritarian model" of governance is also mentioned, in which, to quote Majone, "the main if not the only source of legitimacy is accountability to voters or to their elected representatives"[84]. In the case of such majoritarian bodies, or entities that obtain legitimacy to rule by the choice of the majority of citizens, a prerequisite for empowerment is to gain the trust of the minority. Such trust, in an ideal, theoretical model, is possible in coherent, homogeneous legal systems developed within independent nation states[85]. It is particularly difficult in international, or supranational, systems such as the European Union. Politicians face the complicated task of balancing the state's economic interests – important

82 *Ibid.*, pp. 107 ff.
83 See Hermes, 'Legitimationsprobleme', p. 468; Ruffert, 'Unabhängigkeit', pp. 404 ff.
84 Majone, 'Regulatory Legitimacy', p. 284.
85 See C.S. King, 'Economic Theories of Democratic Legitimacy and the Normative Role of an Ideal Consensus', *Politics, Philosophy & Economics*, Vol. 12, No. 2, 2013, p. 159.

especially in a crisis perspective, as was the case in recent years – with particularistic partisan interests dictated by the short-term, electoral perspective. In the face of ever-growing Eurosceptic sentiment, the desire to maintain social trust and strengthen one's electoral base can outweigh the long-term perspective involving e.g. maintaining financial stability in the European markets[86].

In the modern, globalised world, self-sufficiency is not possible in any area, including regulation. Legal systems at the national, international and supranational levels seamlessly integrate with each other[87]. On account of this, non-majoritarian entities increasingly stand alongside majoritarian ones. The former do not reflect a decision of the majority of the citizens. Quite the contrary – they usually build their authority on their elitism resulting from their unique expert insight, available only to the few who are particularly qualified to perform certain tasks and naturally cannot be elected by universal suffrage[88].

Even back in the 1990s, when the process of economic integration in the European markets was much less advanced than today, Majone explained empowerment of independent, non-majoritarian agencies and their involvement in the regulatory process. He wrote in this context about regulatory legitimacy. The non-majoritarian governance model could be a response to representation-based legitimacy in the realm of public administration, which requires increasingly narrow and specialised knowledge. It could provide protection for the minority from the tyranny of the ruling majority. Diffusion of power, which occurs in the process of delegating tasks to executive authorities endowed with regulatory tasks, is, in the view of Majone, a means of democratic control better suited to current circumstances than accountability to the voters[89].

This conclusion is formulated mainly in reference to the supranational perspective, e.g. the deeply integrated European structures, but it is also increasingly applied in the context of state systems. This claim is confirmed by German constitutional experts, including Georg Hermes, who believes that the "legitimising capability" of representative democracy is decreasing both at the European and

86 See Glencross, 'Democratic Inputs', pp. 25–32.

87 Armin von Bogdandy writes in this context about de-nationalization of national law, 'Globalization and Europe', p. 889.

88 See S. Borrás, T. Conzelmann, 'Democracy, Legitimacy and Soft Modes of Governance in the EU: The Empirical Turn', *Journal of European Integration*, Vol. 29, No. 5, 2007, pp. 541 ff.

89 *Cf.* Majone, 'Regulatory Legitimacy', p. 285; Caranta, 'Democracy', p. 184. See also J. Mendes, 'Discretion, Care and Public Interests in the EU Administration: Probing the Limits of Law', *Common Market Law Review*, Vol. 53, No. 2, 2016, p. 424.

national level[90]. The reason for this is the need to delegate tasks in increasingly complex administrative structures. The externalisation of functions to independent units, such as regulatory agencies, is the result of the limited capacity of the existing bodies, which are unable to handle the ever broader scope of competencies as the markets continue to develop and integrate[91]. In order to increase efficiency, concepts are sought to strengthen the traditional input-oriented model of legitimacy. Political science literature mentions an evolution of the concept of legitimisation in this context and the gradual supplementation, or even the replacement, of traditional representative democratic legitimacy with participatory legitimacy. The latter would fall within the model of output legitimacy, the main assumption of which is, indeed, an emphasis on the effectiveness and impact on the outcomes[92].

c) Functional Representation

An interesting variant combining both these concepts is legitimisation of the political system through functional representation. According to this idea, representation of citizens in public authorities is not merely based on universal suffrage, but it also must involve selecting their representatives indirectly on the basis of functional criteria[93]. A special background, affiliation with certain organisations or representing particular social groups is essential in this case. Such representatives are usually selected by relevant institutions, e.g. labour unions, consumer organisations, academia etc. in order to represent the social and economic interests of a specific group, e.g. employers, employees, cooperatives, small and medium-sized entrepreneurs etc. in a particular public administrative body. This model of representation is supposed to strengthen the empowerment of administrative entities. According to Corinna Wolff, "functional representation has the potential to enhance democracy by increasing both the quality and the quantity of input"[94].

---

90 Hermes, 'Legitimationsprobleme', p. 470. See also G. Lübbe-Wolff, 'Europäisches und nationales Verfassungsrecht', in: H. Dreier *et al.*, *Berichte und Diskussionen auf der Tagung der Deutschen Staatsrechtslehrer in Leipzig vom 4. bis 6. Oktober 2000*, Berlin 2001, pp. 265 ff.

91 Terms such as "overloaded government" or "ungovernability of society" appear in the literature in this context. See C. Wolff, *Functional Representation and Democracy in the EU. The European Commission and Social NGOs*, Colchester 2013, p. 56.

92 *Ibid.*, p. 57.

93 See Caranta, 'Democracy', pp. 184 ff., 194.

94 Wolff, *Functional Representation*, p. 59.

This variant of representation increases sensitivity to preferences of different stakeholders who do not always have a chance to elect their own representatives in general elections. This is one way of increasing the abovementioned trust of the minority in the rule of the majority. Observing the changes that modern democracies are undergoing makes it possible to conclude that "legitimate representation" does not necessarily have to involve the traditional election model. Representation can also, especially in supranational bodies, take a deliberative form. This deliberative representation means the involvement of the interested public and private parties from many environments in the co-decision process[95].

"Input", in the broad sense, therefore, concerns the management processes of how political decisions are made, what influences the creation of policies in various market sectors and how they are implemented. Legitimacy understood this way involves the possibility of societies influencing the authorities. Decision-makers seek social acceptance which is established when actions are undertaken in line with particular expectations, and the specific community to which they are addressed can identify with them[96]. In this procedural interpretation, the consent of countries operating within a particular international organisation significantly strengthens "input legitimacy". Interestingly, empirical studies conducted on the international cooperation in the field of environmental protection in the context of British and German societies prove that the issue of representative legitimacy, which as mentioned above can be identified with input legitimacy, is less important for citizens than the outcomes achieved by an international organisation[97]. These, in turn, should be identified with "output legitimacy". This does not mean, however, that the transparency of international governance mechanisms such as regulatory agencies or networks, the involvement of representatives of different social groups as part of deliberative representation or the direct reference to national parliaments in the "chain of legitimation" are irrelevant for citizens. These elements help to increase social trust and tolerance of voters towards the ever-growing influence of international bodies on national decision-making processes.

This is particularly significant in the case of the European Union, which is a supranational structure and impacts the legal systems of its member states to

95 See Caranta, 'Democracy', p. 193; Eifert, 'Legitimationsstrukturen', pp. 318 ff.; Ruffert, 'Demokratie', pp. 334, 346.

96 Kabat-Rudnicka, *Zasada federalna*, p. 209.

97 See T. Bernauer *et al.*, 'How Relevant are Input and Output Legitimacy in International Environmental Governance?', *NCCR Democracy Working Paper*, No. 94, 2016, pp. 2, 5. Similarly see also Hermes, 'Legitimationsprobleme', p. 480.

a much greater extent than classic international organisations. EU governance does not have democratic legitimacy similar to that of state mechanisms. The latter become empowered thanks to regularly held elections, parliamentary control, the rule of law and accountability before courts. Since it is difficult to establish similar mechanisms at the supranational level, as more and more integrated mechanisms of European governance are developed, a search has begun for solutions that would fall within the model of input legitimacy developed in intra-state solutions. EU representative legitimacy is underpinned by reference to the directly elected legislature, i.e. the European Parliament, and to national representation indirectly legitimised through the constitutional systems of the member states. The administrative apparatus led by the European Commission is technocratic in its nature and legitimised primarily on the basis of the outcomes of its work (output legitimacy). Following the interpretation by Colin Scott, maintaining a balance between democratic and technocratic governance is consistent with the dichotomy developed by Scharpf (input *versus* output)[98].

d) Searching for Representation-Based Legitimacy in the Context of EU Regulatory Agencies

This also corresponds to concepts formulated in relation to regulatory agencies which "can hardly be decoupled from their social and political environment"[99]. The justification for the mandate of EU agencies is complex. On the one hand, it contains formal arguments involving normative regulation of the scope of competencies and methods of operation of these bodies and, on the other hand, it is closely connected with building a network of interactions in a particular regulatory environment and the involvement of diverse social actors in agency work[100]. Adopting this perspective, we can say that participatory legitimacy constitutes an equivalent of traditional representative legitimacy. The ability of many actors

98 See C. Scott, 'Governing Without Law or Governing Without Government? New-ish Governance and the Legitimacy of the EU', *European Law Journal*, Vol. 15, No. 2, 2009, p. 171. See also Höreth, 'No Way Out', pp. 250 ff.

99 S. Borrás *et al.*, 'European Agencies and Input Legitimacy: EFSA, EMEA and EPO in Post-Delegation Phase', *Journal of European Integration*, Vol. 29, No. 5, 2007, p. 584.

100 *Ibid.*, p. 585. "Only if the 'ivory tower' is opened up and experts come to the 'agora' (meeting place) it is possible to find out what elements they provide to formulate and implement policy decisions, and how these elements are actually used", see A. Liberatore, S. Funtowicz, '"Democratising" Expertise, "Expertising" Democracy: What Does It Mean, And Why Bother?', *Science and Public Policy*, Vol. 30, No. 3, 2003, p. 147.

to participate in different consultative forums is supposed to replace the direct election of representatives acting in the name of social interests. This thesis is supported by a small number of studies about the justification of agency activities within the "chain of legitimation". Input legitimacy is cited e.g. by Susana Borrás who stresses that "agencies dealing with socially contested science are in need of input legitimacy and need to establish participatory networks in order to make their scientific assumptions socially and politically robust"[101]. According to this interpretation, input legitimacy is directly identified with the broad involvement of societies in the member states in regulatory procedures used in EU agencies. Hence, there is talk of "societal input", transparency and the importance of deliberative mechanisms. The concepts of input legitimacy, the key element of which is parliamentary control in the traditional understanding of representative democracy, are only of limited use in relation to EU regulatory agencies. Therefore, Borrás points out that "wider notions of input legitimacy are necessary, in combination with an increased robustness of the knowledge produced and conveyed by different types of stakeholders"[102].

In another study dedicated to input-oriented mechanisms of legitimacy, Miroslava Scholten points out in her introduction that this kind of legitimacy is "clearly problematic" in the context of regulatory agencies[103]. Their decision-making bodies, such as Executive Directors and Management Boards, are not elected[104]. We can even say that an "ordinary citizen" is unaware of the existence of the agency system and of the tasks that have been assigned to bodies operating within its framework. Therefore, while it is relatively easy to "get to know" the administrative apparatus in the member states, decentralised agencies remain an enigma. This is particularly controversial due to the "negative correlation between input and output legitimacy" mentioned by Scholten[105]. This negative correlation is by no means compensated for by output legitimacy, in the form of the efficiency, reliability and effectiveness of agencies.

Assertions regarding EU regulatory agencies are part of the considerations on democratic legitimacy at the transnational level. "Chains of legitimation" are in

---

101 Borrás *et al.*, 'European Agencies', p. 598.

102 *Ibid.*, pp. 598 ff. See also M. Poboży, 'Agencje zdecentralizowane i komitety komitologiczne w systemie instytucjonalnym UE – problem legitymizacji władzy', in: Witkowska, Wojtaszczyk (ed.), *Agencje*, pp. 135 ff.

103 M. Scholten, 'Democratic Input Legitimacy of IRAs: Proposing an Assessment Framework', *Utrecht Law Review*, Vol. 11, No. 2, 2015, p. 64.

104 See Griller, Orator, '*Meroni* Revisited', p. 12.

105 Scholten, 'Democratic Input', pp. 65 ff.

this case of an abstract nature. The distance from the original will of the voters is so large that it is difficult to talk about direct representation. Thus, in the view of Frank Nullmeier and Tanja Pritzlaff, it is necessary to create a complementary level of democratic legitimacy. In their understanding, one such enhancement of the weak "chains of legitimation" in the international system is specific political practice: "[…] Political order is legitimate only if and when the entire political process is taken into account – from the creation of institutions up to everyday acts of compliance. […] [The] legitimacy is a product of specific sets of political practices, not only a system of legal rules. It identifies the micro-level of political interaction as the decisive level at which the willingness of the citizens to comply with their obligations and the everyday implementation of decisions made by the political system co-occur"[106].

Nullmeier and Pritzlaff introduce an original definition of political practice that applies to the activity of EU regulatory agencies. They believe that decision-making practices at the transnational level should be perceived through the prisms of two phenomena. They called the first one "explicit normativity". This means legitimising the activities of international administration through direct reference to laws and formally binding rules of conduct. Law adopted in accordance with previously established rules legitimises the activities of particular international organisations: "A regulation gains its normative force through the act of referring to other, previously made regulations"[107]. Decision-making practice is justified on account of legal norms.

They called the other phenomenon "implicit normativity" which involves the interpretation of formal rules of conduct, or simply put, their application. This is closely related to the constructivist interpretation mentioned at the beginning of this chapter. "Implicit normativity" means the attribution of a specific, distinct understanding of norms and rules of conduct on the basis of its common recognition or an unarticulated agreement[108]. If we are to talk about democratic legitimacy in this case, the interpretation of norms must be inclusive, that is it must engage as many various actors involved in international cooperation as possible. They should be provided some discretion in shaping political practices. This discretion shapes part of so-called democratic self-determination and it means that we can talk about representative legitimacy in the transnational dimension only

106 F. Nullmeier, T. Pritzlaff, 'The Great Chain of Legitimacy: Justifying Transnational Legitimacy', *TranState Working Papers*, No. 123, 2010, pp. 4 ff.

107 *Ibid.*, p. 7.

108 *Ibid.*, p. 10.

if participating entities – different groups of stakeholders including individuals, the member states, intergovernmental cooperation forums and supranational institutions – are guaranteed a certain degree of influence on the interpretation and the implementation of the law[109]. From the philosophical point of view, the normative framework understood this way can be viewed through the prism of justification of political procedure. What matters, therefore, is whether the motives behind certain norms used in the political decision-making process are good from a moral standpoint[110].

109 *Ibid.*, p. 14.

110 See A. Buchanan, 'Political Legitimacy and Democracy', *Ethics*, Vol. 112, No. 4, 2002, p. 693; Gaus, 'Two Kinds', pp. 6 ff.; King, 'Economic Theories', p. 157.

6 Alternative Concepts of Legitimacy for the Activities of EU Regulatory Agencies

1. Social and Axiological Legitimacy

a) Legitimacy Resulting from Recognition

The problem of morality is raised not only in the context of justifying political procedures which follow from abiding by the law in force, but also with respect to alternative justifications for the activity of public administration bodies. As legal systems permeate each other in an integrating world, complicated theoretical concepts relating to the activities of independent authorities are applied not only to domestic administrative structures, but also increasingly to international administration and even supranational administration, as in the case of the EU. The issue of legitimising the activities of European administration has been discussed for years with varying intensity. The interest in the issue grows as existing institutions are granted new competencies, e.g. in the face of a crisis or another situation that requires immediate solutions or when new bodies are established as remedies for emerging difficulties in a particular sector of the internal market. Such events provide an impulse to create and develop non-majoritarian bodies that "draw a main part of their legitimacy from being outside the channels of direct democratic legitimation"[1]. Consequently, as has been indicated earlier, we typically see "[the] reassignment of political power from democratic institutions [...] to various non-elected bodies, which are not democratically accountable in the traditional sense by means of a chain of political delegation"[2]. They build their position on the foundation of their political neutrality and expertise.

These are the two pillars on which legitimacy resulting from recognition can be based. In simple terms, it is defined as the belief of the subordinates that those giving commands and taking decisions are entitled to their positions. Or, in other words, that it is the right authority, not only from the normative point of view, but also that of the ruled. Social and axiological legitimacy results from the citizens' acceptance of the way power is exercised in a particular political

---

1 D. Ritleng, 'Introduction', in: Ritleng (ed.), *Independence*, p. 11.

2 M. Maggetti, 'Legitimacy and Accountability of Independent Regulatory Agencies: A Critical Review', *Living Reviews in Democracy*, Vol. 2, 2010, p. 1.

structure. Both the organisation and the function of a particular structure are considered as the rightful ones by the interested social group. In Anglo-Saxon legal literature, as has already been mentioned, this type of legitimacy is often called empirical legitimacy. It is traditionally considered as complementary to normative legitimacy or one that follows from the laws-in-force[3].

A refusal to recognise a particular political system functioning in a particular systemic shape simultaneously means the rejection of the existing *status quo*. It is, therefore, assumed that challenging the way power is exercised leads to a social revolution and an "overhaul" of the existing balance of power and a new order is born as a result. While such changes can be dynamic and spontaneous, which has often been the case with major revolutions in history, the French Revolution to name but one, acquiring political, social and axiological legitimacy tends to be a lengthy process. Piotr Winczorek even pointed out that acquiring such legitimacy can take generations. In a situation of economic and political stability, some acceleration of this process can be seen, resulting from increased trust in a particular system. On the other hand, when its balance is upset and a power crisis occurs, public recognition is halted or even permanently withdrawn[4].

Taking into account the specific character of supranational structures, it can be said that the European Union, just like countries, also strives to complement classic normative legitimacy stemming from laws by seeking public recognition. Nowadays, public recognition rarely takes the form of a "collective demonstration of will" or the direct expression by particular social groups of their position, e.g. in a referendum or through street assemblies. Public recognition is usually manifested indirectly, through readiness to comply with what decision-makers decide, loyalty to existing organisational structures and the acceptance of political reasons presented at different levels of governance. For the stability of a particular political structure, especially one that goes beyond the framework of the state, it is important for power to be legitimised by commonly accepted social groups. One can mention here specific professional communities, comprised of experts in various fields and scientists, who help decision-making bodies to enhance their authority and reach the state of "spontaneous acquiescence" by the ruled, about which Antonio Gramsci wrote in the early twentieth century[5].

---

3 P. Winczorek, 'Legitymizacja władzy politycznej', *Państwo i Prawo*, Nos. 11–12, 1983, pp. 67–73; J. Steffek, 'The Output Legitimacy of International Organizations and the Global Public Interest', *International Theory*, Vol. 7, No. 2, 2015, pp. 265 ff.

4 Winczorek, 'Legitymizacja', p. 70.

5 See Q. Hoare, G. Nowell Smith (ed./transl.), *Selections from the Prison Notebooks of Antonio Gramsci*, London 1999, pp. 412–419; R. Dainotto, 'Notes on Q6§ 32. Gramsci

In his opinion, any group of decision-makers, regardless of the political form it operates in, has to look for additional legitimising elements beyond mere coercion. Such a basic additional element is, indeed, active acquiescence that leads to voluntary subordination to political power[6]. However, this state can only last as long as those in power are able to ensure progress and to improve the situation of as many of its recipients as possible. Decision-makers constitute a specific "caste" capable of organising political hegemony. As a rule, it is composed of people with specific predispositions and traits. They can be called the "local elite of managers and intellectuals"[7]. Gramsci related these considerations to colonial conquests and the systemic subjugation of particular territories e.g. in the form of administrative structures, by powers such as Great Britain or France[8].

By analogy, these ideas can be applied to the institutional structure of the European Union. A significant role in its shaping is played by the "Brussels pioneers of Europeanisation" who include the EU's bureaucratic personnel, the European administration, lobbyists, and cosmopolitan business and academic elites. According to Dietmar Schirmer, these groups create national awareness in their countries of origin in a specific way, based on the belief, which stems from their individual experiences, that Europe, understood in the context of EU structures, constitutes a whole. Law and common institutions are primarily supposed to be the foundation binding national systems within the Union, whereas the distinct identity of the European bureaucratic class is based on a sense of elitism and a common bond resulting from participation in building the EU system[9]. It can be considered a kind of legitimising identity and one that is shaped and supported by the European administrative apparatus in order to strengthen and justify its dominant role in particular areas. The aim here is usually to strengthen influence in creating sectoral policies and developing regulatory mechanisms. Schirmer believes, following Gramsci's lead, that the EU's bureaucratic personnel, including employees of regulatory agencies, can indeed be compared to colonial officials sent from the metropolis to the empire's remote

---

and the Dalits', in: C. Zene (ed.), *The Political Philosophies of Antonio Gramsci and B.R. Ambedkar. Itineraries of Dalits and Subalterns*, London/New York 2013, p. 78.

6 Hoare, Nowell Smith, *Selections*, pp. 206 ff.

7 Dainotto, 'Notes', p. 77.

8 T. Brennan, 'Antonio Gramsci and the Postcolonial Theory: "Southernism"', *Diaspora. A Journal of Transnational Studies*, Vol. 10, No. 2, 2001, pp. 145 ff.

9 D. Schirmer, 'Kłopoty z tożsamością w Europie. Nowe ujęcie braku *demos*, zróżnicowania kulturowego i granic integracji', in: B. Markiewicz, R. Wonicki (ed.), *Kryzys tożsamości politycznej a proces integracji europejskiej*, Warszawa 2006, pp. 58 ff.

corners[10]. They were not only tasked with creating institutional and normative systems in territories subordinated to the metropolis, but they were also supposed to gain recognition for this imposed rule based on the foundation of shared values, ideas and perceptions. Acceptance was not meant to come directly from coercion, but it was supposed to be largely derived from identification with the emerging administrative and normative system.

This comparison may be considered questionable. Nonetheless one can agree with the claim that the EU's bureaucratic personnel, including employees of regulatory agencies or the Commission's Directorates-General, identify with the European Union, on the whole, to a greater extent than ordinary citizens and, thus, they become the driver of EU-wide solutions that are ultimately supposed to transcend national particularities[11]. In the case of bodies functioning in the EU institutional system, the belief in the rightfulness of the activities of institutions functioning within administrative structures is the result of the state of public awareness. This means that decision-makers, who claim that their authority is legitimate, must obtain public recognition justifying their activities. In order to achieve this objective, they are subject to comprehensive evaluation. Hence, what matters for this analysis of the legitimacy of EU regulatory agencies' activities is e.g. the way the European administration is organised, the competencies of officials and the substantive quality of expertise. If there is an impression in public perception, which is unshaken, that a particular institution performs its role adequately, and that its authority is built on the foundation of specialised knowledge, as well as its professionalism, it can be assumed that it will be recognised as rightful and legitimised to act[12].

b) The Role of Common Ideas and Values

Within social and axiological legitimacy, an important role is also played by ideas and values that constitute the justification for the activities of entities endowed with specific competencies. In the case of EU regulatory agencies, these ideas and values are primarily associated with the development of the internal market. Those include: stability, safety in various areas (e.g. food safety, safety of trade in

10 *Ibid.*, p. 61.

11 More S. Suvarierol *et al.*, 'Working for Europe? Socialization in the European Commission and Agencies of the European Union', *Public Administration*, Vol. 91, No. 4, 2013, pp. 911 ff.; S. Suvarierol, 'Everyday Cosmopolitanism in the European Commission', *Journal of Public Policy*, Vol. 18, No. 2, 2011, pp. 181 ff.

12 Winczorek, 'Legitymizacja', pp. 72 ff.

chemicals and medicines, safety of financial markets, security at borders), welfare, efficiency and economic growth. The argument of having "real knowledge" (Latin *argumentum ex scientia*) is of particular importance for the sake of gaining public recognition, especially in the case of non-majoritarian bodies such as regulatory agencies[13]. The term "real knowledge" should be understood as specialised, scientific knowledge resulting from experience. According to this approach, knowledge is the precondition for efficiency, which is expected to bring success and the achievement of the objectives pursued. In the case of EU regulatory agencies, success is often understood as achieving specific economic targets. The activity of a particular agency is assessed here through the prism of advancing the interests of individual players, including primarily the member states and the European Commission. Turning against such an authority, which is guided by "real knowledge", embodies the values attributed to it, and is also effective, can be considered irrational within the legitimacy model in question. In the case of newly created agencies, which are e.g. a response to a crisis, reference to public expectations has a legitimising function. Reforms bring freshness and hope for a change in the existing situation. Such feelings legitimise conferred competencies, at least at the initial phase of the existence of an authority established in order to restore stability in a particular sector of the market and to prevent future crises[14].

Recognition also falls within the constructivist vision of international law, which can be applied to interpretation of the EU legal and institutional system. Norms shaped at the international level are perceived as a "social phenomenon embedded in, and shaped by, practices, beliefs, ideas, and traditions that constitute the society of states"[15]. Every normative system is "immersed" in a specific social context. The social nature of law means the acceptance of the introduced regulatory frameworks. It is particularly important in the context of the rapidly advancing integration of the European internal market. Achieving such acceptance is possible only in social groups that are similar with regard to their cultural level. The creation and application of law requires a distinct type of practice, which can only be created within a community or a society sharing particular ideas and values[16]. This practice can be considered "a social activity that includes

13 *Ibid.*, p. 75; Liberatore, Funtowicz, '"Democratising"', pp. 146–149.

14 See A. Ruser, 'By the Markets, of the Markets, for the Markets? Technocratic Decision Making and the Hollowing Out of Democracy', *Global Policy*, Vol. 6, No. S1, 2015, pp. 83–87.

15 D.R. Schmidt, 'Peremptory Law, Global Order, and the Normative Boundaries of a Pluralistic World', *International Theory*, Vol. 8, No. 2, 2016, p. 270.

16 See P.G. Stillman, 'The Concept of Legitimacy', *Polity*, Vol. 7, No. 1, 1974, pp. 36, 40.

inter alia historically evolved institutions and traditions, tacit understandings of silent rules, shared points of reference, and the constructions of cognitive-symbolic structures"[17]. Therefore, there is consistency between social and legal forms of normativity. Both dimensions make it possible to determine "what constitutes a legitimate actor" and when his or her actions are rightful[18].

c) Shaping Justification for a Specific Institutional System in the Example of EU Regulatory Agencies

Compliance with specific legal norms in liberal democracies is based on public acceptance of the existing system. This acceptance stems from the recognition of a particular code of ethics as the right one. Christopher King defines this state of affairs as follows: "To have a duty to obey [...] means citizens are morally required to accept democratic outcomes as legitimate"[19]. We can talk, in this context, about a phenomenon of "justification" for a specific political order. King identified two models of this justification. The first one involves the belief of the ruled that decisions of the rulers are created on the basis of specialised knowledge. "Expert reliabilism" is mentioned in this case. The administrative authority that prepares specific solutions in a particular sector of the market has knowledge and information that other entities do not have and, therefore, it is reliable. Nevertheless, explicit empowerment to act does not follow from the recognition of its expertise alone. It is derived from the belief of the ruled that it is necessary to comply with the recommendations of the rulers in accordance with socially accepted procedures, this second model is so-called duty reliabilism[20].

A political system can, therefore, be legitimised on the basis of socially recognised necessity. This concept refers to the thought of the abovementioned Easton who considered the community's faith in the rightness of the system to be one of the foundations of its legitimacy. Easton identified three types of

17 Schmidt, 'Peremptory Law', p. 271.

18 C. Reus-Smit, 'The Constitutional Structure of International Society and the Nature of Fundamental Institutions', *International Organization*, Vol. 51, No. 4, 1997, p. 566. This view is shared by Christopher S. King who rightly pointed out that legitimacy of political authority in contemporary liberal democracies is based on moral and procedural grounds, 'Problems in the Theory of Democratic Authority', *Ethical Theory and Moral Practice. An International Forum*, Vol. 15, No. 4, 2012, p. 432.

19 *Ibid.*, p. 433.

20 For an extensive write-up on this issue while indicating the problems associated with both models, see *ibid.*, pp. 435–438.

legitimacy referring to public recognition[21]. First – ideological legitimacy. A particular society considers some values and principles right, making them the foundation and binder of a particular political system. Faith in the rightness of specific ideas becomes the main source of the legitimacy of authority. Citizens express their expectations and needs through their choice of specific values and norms, which they consider to be right, appropriate, or morally acceptable. This way, they actively support a particular political system. Adopting the constructivist vision, one can say that they co-shape it through their acceptance and assumption of specific meanings for proposed values and norms. Elites exercising power can exploit this state of affairs, playing on social sentiments in order to secure support for the solutions they prefer[22].

The second type of recognition of authority proposed by Easton is structural legitimacy, which is a solution close to the abovementioned procedural legitimacy and falls within duty reliabilism. The source of this type of legitimacy is the acceptance of the norms underpinning a particular political system by the ruled. The rulers are legitimised to act if they have gained power in accordance with the established rules and are guided by them in their conduct. These variants are complemented by the third type, that is personal legitimacy, which involves the belief in the society that certain people, with specific traits and desired skills, knowledge and experience, have the right to make decisions. Their decisions will be the "right" ones[23]. According to Easton, people have a natural need to believe in the validity and rightfulness of the system in which they function[24].

In the case of EU regulatory agencies, a crucial role in recognising their activity as being rightful is played by their reputation, which should be understood as the way that the agencies present themselves in the European administrative space and how they are perceived by its other participants. Building authority is a significant element of how administrative bodies function: "A strong reputation […] is the source of bureaucratic power, allowing agencies to

---

21 D. Easton, *A Systems Analysis of Political Life*, New York 1965, pp. 286–310. See also J.G. Gunnell, 'The Reconstitution of Political Theory: David Easton, Behavioralism, and the Long Road to System', *Journal of the History of the Behavioral Sciences*, Vol. 49, No. 2, 2013, pp. 199 ff.

22 See also E.N. Muller, 'Correlates and Consequences of Beliefs in the Legitimacy of Regime Structures', *Midwest Journal of Political Science*, Vol. 14, No. 3, 1970, pp. 398 ff.

23 This classification was inspired by Weber's concepts. More about similarities between Easton and Weber in theoretic modelling of political reality: Gunnell, 'The Reconstitution', pp. 205 ff.

24 See Muller, 'Correlates', pp. 392, 409; Kownacki, *Legitymizowanie*, pp. 56 ff.

foster their autonomy, build alliances, enlist political support, and, ultimately, help to ensure their survival"[25]. In the case of such bodies, the belief of a particular social group in the "unique capacities, roles and obligations" attributed to them is of key importance as far as legitimising their activities is concerned. Society, i.e. the addressees of the decisions formulated by public authorities, can be described as an "audience". This audience recognises the high status of a particular agency, on the basis of its special authority and prestige in a specific institutional structure[26].

In the case of EU regulatory agencies, attaining such a high position is particularly difficult, because the addressee is not a single, specific social group. There are many addressees, from business communities directly involved in a particular agency's area of activity, to consumers and public administration representatives from the member states as well as EU and national policymakers[27]. This "networking", which is distinct for the activity of agencies and stems from their activity in the European multilevel governance, is also reflected in the complicated process of seeking social and ideological acceptance for their activities not from one addressee, but from many "networks of audiences"[28]. Obtaining such acceptance is of vital importance for the existence and development of agencies in the EU political system.

2. Technocratic Legitimacy

a) Placing the Concept of Technocratic Legitimacy into Existing Theoretical Classifications

In the case of EU regulatory agencies, acceptance for their existence and activity is primarily associated with the recognition of the outcomes of their work. Hence, as stated in the previous chapter, the main mechanism for

25 M. Busuioc, M. Lodge, 'The Reputational Basis of Public Accountability', *Governance. An International Journal of Policy, Administration, and Institutions*, Vol. 29, No. 2, 2016, p. 250.

26 *Ibid.*, p. 251.

27 See C. Landfried, 'Beyond Technocratic Governance: The Case of Biotechnology', *European Law Journal*, Vol. 3, No. 3, 1997, pp. 256 ff.; M. Wood, 'Mapping EU Agencies as Political Entrepreneurs', *European Journal of Political Research*, Published Online in August 2017, pp. 1 ff.

28 See M. Busuioc, M. Lodge, 'Reputation and Accountability Relationships: Managing Accountability Expectations through Reputation', *Public Administration Review*, Vol. 77, No. 1, 2017, pp. 92 ff.

accomplishing this goal is so-called output based legitimacy. In this study, the contribution of agencies to the development of the internal market and mechanisms of European governance that determines the empowerment of their activities will be understood in a broad manner. As has been clarified in Chapter 5 from the many variations of legitimising the activities of the European administration, we chose the classification by the Austrian lawyer, Andreas Orator. He clearly contrasted the traditional models of representative legitimacy, which constitute the input in the European institutional system, with alternative models, such as technocracy, transparency, participation and deliberation[29].

His classification will be modified for the needs of this analysis. Technocratic legitimacy should be juxtaposed with other major methods of empowerment: social and axiological legitimacy mentioned in the previous point as well as normative legitimacy. As for the first one – social and axiological legitimacy – it should be noted that what matters for recognising agency activities as appropriate, right and legitimate is, indeed, their expert, or technocratic, character. In the other case – normative legitimacy – what matters is the legal framework. In the context of the activities and functioning of regulatory agencies, this legal framework should mainly be identified as being the founding regulations and other acts of secondary legislation.

Technocratic legitimacy means obtaining public acceptance for the activities undertaken by expert bodies on the basis of the recognition of their special authority[30]. This results from the fact that the personnel of these bodies have knowledge that is not only unavailable to "ordinary" citizens, but also to other institutional entities. However, for technocratic bodies, including EU regulatory agencies, to be able to obtain public acceptance, and thus the legitimacy to perform their functions, different mechanisms of legitimacy must be used. The first of them is ensuring effectiveness and efficiency. The second consists of including as many interested parties as possible in consultation processes regarding the activities planned by the agency. The third is transparency, which needs to be maintained both in the creation of the institutional structure of such a body, as

---

29 Orator, *Möglichkeiten*, pp. 348–369.

30 This is a thought commonly emphasised e.g. in the administrative law literature: "Any public body has to guard its legitimacy in the eyes of the public", A. Schout, F. Pereyra, 'The Institutionalization of EU Agencies: Agencies as 'Mini Commissions'", *Public Administration*, Vol. 89, No. 2, 2011, p. 422.

well as in the normative definition of its competences and the control of their performance[31].

These alternative models fall within the output-oriented concept of legitimacy, according to the dichotomous division by Scharpf. This legitimacy results from the ideals that refer to the thought of Abraham Lincoln who spoke in his famous 1863 Gettysburg Address about "government for the people"[32]. Delegation of powers to public administration authorities is justified by the functionality and utility of such solutions and it is directly connected with the capability of these institutions to respond to citizen needs and problems. Hence, such terms to characterise the form of activity of regulatory agencies as "non-majoritarian", "efficiency-oriented" and "expertise-based" are juxtaposed almost synonymously[33]. The models that justify the existence and functioning of the EU administration on the basis of the main features of its activity, such as participation, effectiveness, transparency or social dialogue, fall within "experimentalist" methods of legitimising the European compound executive order[34]. The "experimentalist" character of legitimising the activities of public administration authorities comes in this case, not from a hierarchical structure that enables the process of delegating competencies to be tracked, but from a variety of coordinating, steering and control mechanisms[35].

The basic idea that accompanied the growth of the agency system involved the desire to ensure the high level of expertise that was necessary in the face of intensified regulatory activities in the integrated market. One needs to remember here that agencies were created in diverse domains, signified by varying levels of Europeanisation[36]. Just over a decade ago, they were considered one of the main

---

31 See also O. Perez, 'Can Experts Be Trusted and What Can Be Done About It? Insights from Biases and Heuristics Literature', in: A. Alemanno, A.-L. Sibony (ed.), *Nudge and the Law. A European Perspective*, Oxford/Portland 2015, pp. 115–119.

32 A. Lincoln, *The Gettysburg Address*, 19.11.1863, http://historytools.davidjvoelker.com/sources/lincoln-gettysburg.pdf (20.3.2018).

33 See S. Griller, A. Orator, 'Everything under Control? The "Way Forward" for European Agencies in the Footsteps of the *Meroni* Doctrine', *European Law Review*, Vol. 35, No. 1, 2010, p. 21.

34 C.F. Sabel, J. Zeitlin, 'Learning From Difference: The New Architecture of Experimentalist Governance in the EU', *European Law Journal*, Vol. 14, No. 3, 2008, pp. 273 ff.; D. Curtin, M. Egeberg, 'Tradition and Innovation: Europe's Accumulated Executive Order', in: Curtin, Egeberg (ed.), *Towards*, pp. 9–13.

35 Orator, *Möglichkeiten*, pp. 347 ff.

36 More R. Hauser, Z. Niewiadomski, A. Wróbel (ed.), *System prawa administracyjnego. Europeizacja prawa administracyjnego*, Warszawa 2014.

innovations in the European governance system, the primary objective of which was to depoliticise and professionalise European decision-making processes. Over time it turned out that they fitted into the existing patterns of European technocracy. They are symptoms of the evolutionary development of the EU level administration rather than a revolutionary breakthrough, or a reform that could significantly modify the existing state of affairs[37].

Discourse between experts is often based on informal rules, and is carried out in airtight isolation from mechanisms involving the citizens who make a majoritarian choice. Thus, it should not be surprising that the technocracy which is equated with the term "Eurocracy", i.e. EU bureaucracy, evokes doubts and justified concerns over a shift of competences to bodies that are excluded from citizen's oversight, but nevertheless shape socially important decisions[38]. Joseph Weiler put it aptly: "Legitimacy, powerfully skewed [towards] results and away from process, based mostly on outputs, and only to a limited degree on inputs, is a weak legitimacy [at best], and sometimes none at all"[39].

Despite that, the technocratic argument based on an assumption that could be called a false "founding myth" – the belief that expert management can be clearly separated from political influence – became the foundation of the theories of legitimacy applied to EU regulatory agencies[40]. Interestingly, the use of justifications involving specialised knowledge is considered e.g. in European legal studies literature as an important complementary element of democratic legitimacy[41]. This is also evidenced by Treaty arrangements, including above all the repeatedly mentioned Article 298(1) TFEU, which stress the importance of an open, efficient and independent European administration. Studies that are not directly related to the process of European integration, in turn, emphasise a different interpretation[42]. Governance carried out by specialists is considered to be elitist, and detached from the democratic influence of citizens. Thus, for example, in the administrative systems of the Nordic states, various balancing

---

37 For more about the institutionalisation of the agency system, see Schout, Pereyra, 'The Institutionalization', pp. 421, 430.

38 "The [...] deliberation involving experts is tantamount to a supranational or transgovernmental conspiracy against democracy", Sabel, Zeitlin, 'Learning', pp. 273, 276.

39 Weiler, 'The Geology', p. 562. See also Griller, Orator, 'Everything', p. 22.

40 Orator, *Möglichkeiten*, pp. 348–353.

41 *Ibid.*

42 See E. Bertsou, G. Pastorella, 'Technocratic Attitudes: A Citizen's Perspective of Expert Decision-Making', *West European Politics*, Vol. 40, No. 2, 2017, pp. 431 ff.

mechanisms have been developed which can be called "public support for expert decision making"[43]. This primarily signifies mechanisms which involve the inclusion of different social groups in administrative activities, as well as maintaining their comprehensibility and transparency.

b) Understanding the Term "Technocracy"

However, before we analyse these particular instruments of legitimacy, it is worth focusing on the phenomenon of "technocracy" itself. This constitutes the starting point for understanding the functioning, not only of regulatory agencies, but also the entire EU administrative system. This term tends to be juxtaposed with others of similar meanings, such as "expertocracy", "expert democracy", "epistocracy", "evidence-based decision making", or referring to Plato's vision – the "rule of the wise"[44]. All of these terms point to an elite group of decision-makers who are particularly entitled to govern, mainly on account of their specialised knowledge.

Knowledge, skills and experience are of a legitimising nature. And while technocracy, understood as elitist rule, is seemingly the opposite of democracy, interpreted as the rule of the majority, in common understanding within most of the societies in the member states these phenomena are by no means mutually exclusive[45]. Legal mechanisms are supposed to ensure broad public participation in electing authorities and also guarantee that experts in particular administrative bodies will act in accordance with applicable laws and with openness to citizens' needs.

It is worth noting here that the idea of balancing technocratic and democratic elements in modern political systems is not new. It was introduced back in the first half of the twentieth century by the Austrian economist Joseph Schumpeter. He understood technocratic governance, with modern bureaucracy at its core, as a "necessary complement" (Germ. *unvermeidliche Ergänzung*) to any democratic system[46]. Educated officials, aware of their responsibilities are a necessary

43 L. Rapeli, 'Public Support for Expert Decision-Making: Evidence from Finland', *Politics*, Vol. 36, No. 2, 2016, p. 143.

44 *Ibid.*

45 See surveys in Finland in: *ibid.*, pp. 145–149; or in Spain in: J. Font *et al.*, 'Participation, Representation and Expertise: Citizen Preferences for Political Decision-Making Process', *Political Studies*, Vol. 63, No. S1, 2015, pp. 154 ff. More also Bertsou, Pastorella, 'Technocratic Attitudes', p. 433.

46 See J.A. Schumpeter, *The Theory of Economic Development. An Inquiry into Profits, Capital, Credit, Interest, and the Business Cycle*, New Brunswick/London 1980, pp. 33, 85 ff.

element of the process of the professionalisation of democratic structures. To fulfil their role, and to carry out important functions for the state and its citizens, according to Schumpeter, they must be professional. He emphasised that we cannot count on voters to be fully rational as their decisions are short-sighted and determined by temporary preferences. Therefore, the effectiveness of the state apparatus must directly rely on its professional nature[47].

The role of bureaucracy in the development of modern societies was also emphasised by Weber. He envisaged the functioning of bureaucratic institutions within specific legal procedures, selection of officials on the basis of the criterion of knowledge and skills, (Germ. *Herrschaft kraft Wissen*) as well as the neutrality of the administration. This is ensured by prohibiting employees of public authorities from obtaining any personal benefits. In Weber's ideal type, bureaucratic management is the most rational variant of governance (Germ. *Zweckrationalität*)[48]. That is because, in this approach, bureaucracy is the most advanced and efficient form of administration. Yet in Weber's understanding, officials are not decision-makers but rather executors of orders. Leadership functions should be performed by politicians, whereas the bureaucracy should be treated as an effective tool in governance processes[49].

These concepts contributed to the creation of a specific image of a technocrat. In common understanding, he or she is usually a government official, party activist, or bureaucrat who, due to his or her expertise and professional experience, has the right to decide about the fate of citizens, e.g. by drafting and issuing decisions, orders, recommendations and opinions. This meaning of "technocracy" usually has negative connotations and involves perceiving bureaucracy as a "soulless machine" in which an individual person is an insignificant element[50]. Law established by technocrats is incomprehensible and inaccessible for the ordinary citizen who is at the mercy of "bureaucratic whims"[51]. This Kafkaesque

47 See also Orator, *Möglichkeiten*, p. 349; H.P. Widmaier, *Demokratische Sozialpolitik. Zur Radikalisierung des Demokratieprinzips*, Tübingen 1999, p. 63.

48 M. Weber, 'Parlament und Regierung im neugeordneten Deutschland', in: M. Weber, *Gesammelte Politische Schriften*, Tübingen 1988, pp. 352 ff. See also Landfried, 'Beyond', p. 257.

49 J.G. Gunnell, 'The Technocratic Image and the Theory of Technocracy', *Technology and Culture*, Vol. 23, No. 3, 1982, p. 395; Widmaier, *Demokratische Sozialpolitik*, p. 51.

50 See M. Shapiro, '"Deliberative", "Independent" Technocracy *v.* Democratic Politics: Will the Globe Echo the EU?', *Law and Contemporary Problems*, Vol. 68, Nos. 3–4, 2005, p. 344.

51 Extensively E. Pauer, 'Die Mobilisierung der Ingenieure in der Zwischenkriegszeit: Von der Technokratie zum "wissenschaftsgeleiteten Industrialismus" (kagakushugi kôgyô)',

vision is identified with the process of the "vulgarisation" of the fundamental meaning of the term "technocracy"[52].

The original interpretation of the term was developed in the 1920s in the United States and metaphorically meant the "reign" or "rule" of people with technical background, usually engineers. They were supposed to direct, lead and coordinate social activity in the domains of industry and economy. It was a somewhat utopian vision of modern society associated with a belief in technological progress and the distinguished supervisory predispositions of elites endowed with technical knowledge. This was connected with an American worldview underpinned by faith in humanity's ability to tame nature with the aid of technological achievements[53].

In the France of the 1930s, the term "technocracy" was modified and took on the meaning that has been popularised in modern times in most of the EU member states. The term then began to be equated with a specific sort of elite bureaucracy which has administrative and supervisory tasks. Its elite nature is supposed to result from the exceptional specialist background of the officials, which guarantees their effectiveness and high level of professionalism. Technical rationality was supposed to replace corrupt politicians and archaic management instruments that did not correspond to the rapid changes in the economy[54].

From here, it is just a step to the abovementioned "vulgarisation" of the term, and a negative perception of the bureaucratic machine, whose expansion reached proportions on a national and international scale, in the second half of the twentieth century that had never been seen before in the history of mankind. Elitism is usually associated with being unresponsive to the practical needs of citizens and being unable to understand their situation. Technocracy is seen as implementing top-down, heavy-handed solutions which are not necessarily appropriate for dealing with the problems which ordinary people face. Such arguments are raised e.g. by critics of the European integration process who point to the rapid growth of EU bureaucracy, the enormous costs that it entails

---

Nachrichten der Gesellschaft für Natur- und Völkerkunde Ostasiens, Nos. 175–176, 2004, pp. 93 ff.

52 See S. Willeke, *Die Technokratiebewegung in Nordamerika und Deutschland zwischen den Weltkriegen. Eine vergleichende Analyse*, Frankfurt am Main 1995, pp. 21 ff.

53 Such concepts were inspired by the considerations of economists Thorstein Veblen, Frederick W. Taylor and James Burnham. More Gunnell, 'The Technocratic Image', p. 393.

54 Pauer, 'Die Mobilisierung', p. 94; J. DeSario, S. Langton, 'Citizen Participation and Technocracy', *Policy Studies Review*, Vol. 3, No. 2, 1984, pp. 223 ff.

and the questionable effectiveness of the ideas which it has put forward to overcome the mounting number of crises that the EU has faced in recent years[55].

Nonetheless, various arguments have been advanced by proponents of such technocratic administrative structures e.g. in the United States in the 1970s and 1980s[56]. In their opinion, new areas of the state's regulatory policy necessitated the creation of institutions which could combine competences in the terms of expertise in particular industries, and also in the fields of distribution, trade and other comprehensive services which are required in rapidly developing markets. On account of these beliefs, strong federal regulatory agencies were created in the United States. The growth of European administration in this context is only a weak echo of the processes which took place in the U.S. in the second half of the twentieth century and that led to the creation of a "technostructure" in the administration[57].

c) Technocratic EU Regulatory Agencies

Experts in the EU regulatory agencies play a key role in formulating scientific opinions as well as the authorisation of decisions that are based on them and which have a decisive influence on the final shape of the draft legislative acts for particular sectors of the market prepared by the European Commission and the regulatory committees that support it. Although regulatory agencies, in principle, do not have actual norm-setting powers, they are important players in the EU decision-making process in the context of shaping detailed regulations. Their influence is evidenced by the Commission's respect for the recommendations of individual agencies, citing these in unchanged wording in almost all instances[58].

The basic argument for the Commission's respect for the decisions made by EU regulatory agencies is the high quality of the professional documents that they prepare, which are expected to contribute to increased regulatory quality in the entire system of EU legislation. Thus, the central component legitimising agencies to act is their scientific expertise and autonomy[59]. EU

---

55 See also G. Pastorella, 'Technocratic Governments in Europe: Getting the Critique Right', *Political Studies*, Vol. 64, No. 4, 2016, pp. 948 ff.

56 See DeSario, Langton, 'Citizen Participation', pp. 225–227.

57 *Ibid.*, p. 226.

58 Eighty per cent of the surveyed officials from EU regulatory agencies say that their influence on the wording of specific sectoral regulations, e.g. in the field of trade in chemicals, pharmaceuticals or on food safety issues is very high or high. See Ossege, *European Regulatory Agencies*, pp. 151 ff.; Wood, 'Mapping', pp. 3–5.

59 *Cf.* Pastorella, 'Technocratic Governments', p. 956.

officials, including those among the personnel who are directly recruited for regulatory agencies, tend to enjoy a wider margin of autonomy than their counterparts in national administration authorities. This occurs due to their disconnection from domestic political determinants related e.g. to their party affiliations as well as because they function in a slightly different institutional structure, which is signified by a different role of the parliament than in the state systems[60].

3. Legitimising Mechanisms

a) Efficacy

In the case of European governance, the most common legitimising argument is "effective or efficient problem solving". The efficacy of the EU administration often plays a bigger role in public discourse than the level of the democratisation of decision-making processes[61]. Also in the case of regulatory agencies, these two phenomena are juxtaposed in academic discourse and balancing "between democracy and efficiency" is emphasised[62].

Efficacy constitutes the core of the concept of output-oriented legitimacy. In simple terms, it amounts to the trivial assertion that the legitimising element is the success of a specific political system, the institutions that operate in it, including administrative authorities, and the policies pursued. What matters, therefore, is the "quality of the output" a given political system provides. The concept developed by Scharpf referred explicitly to the necessity to meet common social needs (Germ. *Gemeinwohl*), or in other words – the public interest, through institutional and normative solutions[63]. Therefore, "output" in

---

60 See M.W. Bauer, 'Tolerant, If Personal Goals Remain Unharmed: Explaining Supranational Bureaucrats' Attitudes to Organizational Change', *Governance. An International Journal of Policy, Administration, and Institutions*, Vol. 25, No. 3, 2012, pp. 486 ff.

61 Steffek, 'The Output Legitmacy', p. 266. Although converse trends also seen, more K.-O. Lindgren, T. Persson, 'Input and Output Legitimacy: Synergy or Trade-off? Empirical Evidence from an EU Survey?', *Journal of European Public Policy*, Vol. 17, No. 4, 2010, p. 449.

62 Griller, Orator, 'Everything', p. 21.

63 Jens Steffek describes in detail the terminological differences between the terms used by Scharpf and those used in the contemporary Anglo-Saxon political science literature, 'The Output Legitmacy', p. 267.

the interpretation popularised in reference to the EU institutional system can be identified with tangible benefits that are achievable within its framework[64].

This vision is rather distant from the original, which was a political system model created by Easton. Benefits that individual members of a community receive as the outputs of the functioning of a given system do not play a legitimising role. They are a kind of "specific support" which should not be identified with "diffuse support". This "diffuse support" is created on the foundation of a belief in the system as well as recognising its legitimacy and validity. According to Jens Steffek, the separation between the outputs resulting from the functioning of the system and the trust in its legitimacy falls within the classic concept by Weber, who rejected the possibility of basing legitimacy on the foundation of "personal advantages" accruing to the ruled[65].

In the cases of administrative authorities, including the EU regulatory agencies, it is believed that "[they] may be judged effective if [they] discharge [their] administrative and operational functions pursuant to [their] mission and pursue the mission for which [they were] enabled and conceived by [their] stakeholders"[66]. According to this perspective, what matters is the public interest that accompanies the establishment of a specific EU regulatory agency and control over its activities, primarily in the context of juxtaposing the outcomes and costs of the initiatives undertaken. What is emphasised in administration science is that a clear institutional structure, a rationally constructed catalogue of competencies and the inclusion of a particular authority in comprehensive, systemic, organisational and functional solutions, are of key importance for the performance of administrative authorities. Referring to the Weberian tradition, one can recognise here that efficient administration needs to be developed with respect for the rule of law, recognition of the equality of everyone before the law and maintaining the neutrality and impartiality of public authorities[67].

Due to the arguments long voiced in the press that EU agencies generate fewer benefits than costs, their institutional structure is not well-regarded and there is a belief that these bodies duplicate the competencies and tasks of existing organisations. Because of this a decision was taken to conduct research to

64 See also S. Kröger, 'The End of Democracy as We Know It? The Legitimacy Deficits of Bureaucratic Social Policy Governance', *Journal of European Integration*, Vol. 29, No. 5, 2007, p. 567; Stillman, 'The Concept', pp. 48 ff.

65 Steffek, 'The Output Legitmacy', p. 268; Easton, *A Systems Analysis*, p. 382.

66 L. Recascino Wise, 'On the Need for a Composite Theory of Bureaucratic Behavior', *Public Administration Review*, Vol. 64, No. 6, 2004, p. 670.

67 *Ibid.*, p. 672.

counteract this perception[68]. One significant report, formulated at the request of the Budgetary Affairs Committee of the European Parliament, was an analysis entitled "Cost of Non-Agencies with Relevance to the Internal Market"[69]. It addressed the issues of the savings for the member states and the European Union due to the existence of EU regulatory agencies. It examined e.g. what costs would be incurred by national regulatory institutions if they had to take over the tasks of the existing EU regulatory agencies. A direct inspiration for the creation of this report was the European Commission's Communication envisaging a small (approx. one per cent a year), gradual reduction in financial resources provided to agencies and, thus, also reductions in personnel[70]. In order to meet the challenges related to the growth of new agencies and the expansion of those broadening their competences, such as Frontex, the Commission proposed the creation of a "redeployment pool" funded by contributions from all the agencies[71].

Regulatory agencies currently have a budget of 1.2 billion euros and cost 0.8 % of the EU's annual budget. According to calculations made for the EU Agencies Network, they cost each citizen of the EU member states only 2.35 euros a year[72]. Therefore, they are supposed to constitute good value for European taxpayers. The argument of economies of scale is put forward in this context: performing certain tasks in a consolidated and coordinated manner at the European level is supposed to be more cost-effective, and also more efficient than performing the same functions repeatedly in all the member states. In addition to generating savings, economies of scale, theoretically, are also produced by the greater level of specialisation of the personnel resulting from their narrower selection within uniform recruitment mechanisms in one institution – instead of dozens scattered across the entire EU[73].

---

68 E.g. O. Grimm, 'Exzessive Kosten bei EU Agenturen', *Die Presse* of 11.5.2012; A. Gabriel, O. Grimm, 'Das nebulose Geschäft der EU-Agenturen', *Die Presse* of 29.3.2012.

69 J. Malan *et al.*, 'The Cost of Non-Agencies with Relevance to the Internal Market', *European Parliament. Policy Department: Budgetary Affairs. Study*, No. PE 572.702, 2016.

70 European Commission, 'Programming of Human and Financial Resources for Decentralised Agencies 2014–2020', COM(2013) 519 final, 10.7.2013.

71 *Ibid.*, p. 6.

72 EU Agencies Network, *The EU Agencies Working for You*, Luxembourg 2016, p. 4, https://euagencies.eu/sites/default/files/eu_agencies_brochure_2017.pdf (20.3.2018).

73 EU Agencies Network, *Position Paper of the EU Agencies Network*, Document Prepared for the Annual Exchange of Views between EU Agencies and European Parliament Committee on Budgets, http://www.europarl.europa.eu/meetdocs/2014_2019/documents/budg/dv/2014_euagenciespositionpa

b) Inclusiveness

Due to the specificity of the integration process, the ideal type of legitimacy of power, i.e. the one achieved through elections, may be understood in its conventional sense. The possibility of recreating mechanisms of representative democracy at the EU level is considered to be unrealistic, premature, even utopian[74]. The European Parliament's control over institutions operating in the EU system is different from that in the case of parliamentary control within a state. Due to the deficiencies of classic, parliamentary control mechanisms, it is necessary to create a more comprehensive, complex concept[75]. Representative legitimacy is, thus, modified and replaced with participatory and deliberative legitimacy. These variants imply strengthening of mechanisms favouring the broadest possible involvement of various social groups and mobilising them into the discourse. Bringing entities interested in the activity of particular regulatory agencies into the consultation process is equated with an alternative vision of the traditionally understood social input into European decision-making processes. However, there are also voices saying that such specific transnational deliberative democracy cannot involve direct citizen influence on the decision-making process in specialised bodies. The obstacle is primarily their expert character, which makes it impossible to engage non-experts[76].

Therefore, inclusiveness will primarily mean the functioning of EU regulatory agencies in a transnational network involved in the process of implementing regulations for specific market sectors. Apart from EU agencies, national regulatory authorities, ministries from the member states, DGs of the European Commission, comitology committees, private enterprises interested in the legislative process in

---

per2015_/2014_euagenciespositionpaper2015_en.pdf (20.3.2018). The main objective of the EU Agencies Network has been to increase the performance of the agency system and to raise the level of coordination. For this purpose, the agencies announced in 2015 the creation of joint mechanisms in the fields of (1) shared services and capabilities, (2) cooperation with EU key institutions: such as the European Parliament, Commission and Council, and (3) outward communication. The effectiveness of agency activities is, therefore, to be strengthened through the joint initiatives for the coordinated use of resources of all the institutions of this kind (e.g. in the areas of IT, policies, procedures, transfer of knowledge etc.), coherent presentation of their positions in the EU institutional system and informing the public about their intentions in a thoughtful way. See also Chapter 1.

74 Lindgren, Persson, 'Input and Output', p. 451.

75 See Orator, *Möglichkeiten*, p. 345.

76 See Kröger, 'The End', pp. 568–570.

a particular sector of the internal market, non-governmental organisations, academic centres, research institutes etc. operate in this network[77]. Cooperation within such networks is direct, i.e. it allows different entities to present their positions by way of free reasoning, with as little external pressure and as few binding guidelines as possible. The legitimacy of the decisions, taken in such forums, results from the same process of deliberation, the possibility of communicating and arguing with other participants, and thereby influencing their opinions.[78].

The key element of the deliberative decision making process is that it usually results in an agreement acceptable for all of its participants. In the case of the EU administration, including regulatory agencies, what also matters, besides reaching compromises, is the open expression of the competing positions, frank exchanges of views and the free flow of information between the debaters. Compromise solutions are often temporary and they constitute the starting point for further discussion and more changes in the complex EU regulatory system[79]. The inclusion of different entities in the process of consultation, which has a significant impact on the decisions that are to be made, is a modification of the dichotomous division between input- and output-oriented theories of legitimacy. So-called throughput legitimacy is achieved this way. The functioning of the European administration is justified through procedural guarantees for the active participation of the broadest possible range of stakeholders in the processes of creating sectoral regulations[80]. Throughput legitimacy is thus perceived as a modern form of empowering European management in its processual dimension: "[It] is judged in terms of the efficacy, accountability and transparency of the EU's governance process along with [its] inclusiveness and openness to consultation with the people"[81].

Therefore, participation in the discourse within the EU institutional structures is of importance in the process of legitimisation. An argument frequently raised

---

77 See Curtin, Egeberg, 'Tradition', pp. 12 ff.

78 The very idea of deliberative democracy has been a subject of scientific debate for several decades. The most famous concepts were created by Jürgen Habermas and John Rawls. See T. McCarthy, 'Kantian Constructivism and Reconstructivism: Rawls and Habermas in Dialogue', *Ethics*, Vol. 105, No. 1, 1994, pp. 44–63.

79 See Sabel, Zeitlin, 'Learning', p. 274; T. Bach *et al.*, 'Transnational Bureaucratic Politics: An Institutional Rivalry Perspective on EU Network Governance', *Public Administration*, Vol. 94, No. 1, 2016, pp. 11 ff.

80 See also I. Iusmen, J. Boswell, 'The Dilemmas of Pursuing "Throughput Legitimacy" through Participatory Mechanisms', *West European Politics*, Vol. 40, No. 2, 2017, pp. 462 ff.

81 Schmidt, 'Democracy', pp. 2, 18.

in relation to technocratic governance is the abovementioned elitism of expert bodies that excludes public dialogue concerning the shape of specific policies[82]. In practice, this argument is not useful with respect to international expert forums such as EU regulatory agencies. Decision-making mechanisms in these bodies are deliberative and oriented towards solving specific problems. This is characteristic for so-called epistemic communities, i.e. platforms of cooperation between professionals who build mutual contacts primarily on the basis of specialisation in a particular field. Interactions between experts in a given field are based on mutual trust and there is no hierarchical dependence. These relations are also built irrespective of one's nationality or political affiliation[83]. Admittedly, in expert cooperation networks where EU agencies and authorities from the member states participate, there is rivalry and competition for influence and roles in local markets. In particular, competition plays out between national agencies and EU regulatory agencies[84].

These natural developments, which are related to the protection of national interests, do not change the overall picture regarding the efforts of EU agencies to ensure their broadest possible participation in various cooperative forums. This understanding of participation is also reflected in the international legal system. Inclusiveness, therefore, involves respect for the same rules, understood both as a code of certain ethical values and a normative system, which in the case of the European Union includes primary and secondary law[85]. The normative framework for these mechanisms is formed primarily by Article 11 TEU in connection with Article 298 TFEU. Article 11(1) TEU mentions endowing citizens and representative associations with the opportunity to express and publicly exchange their views in all areas of the EU's actions. According to Article 11(2) TEU, in turn, the EU institutions must maintain an open, transparent and systematic dialogue with representative associations and civil society. These provisions are also strengthened

82 See Pastorella, 'Technocratic Governments', p. 954.

83 Ossege, *European Regulatory Agencies*, p. 2.

84 The best example to confirm this claim is the rivalry between national food safety authorities and EFSA. See Bach *et al.*, 'Transnational Bureaucratic Politics', p. 16; Shapiro, '"Deliberative", "Independent" Technocracy', p. 348. More about mutual influence between European and the national levels: E. Mathieu, 'When Europeanization Feeds Back into EU Governance: EU Legislation, National Regulatory Agencies, and EU Regulatory Networks', *Public Administration*, Vol. 94, No. 1, 2016, pp. 28 ff.

85 See A. von Bogdandy, 'Codes of Conduct and the Legitimacy of International Law', in: R. Wolfrum, V. Röben (ed.), *Legitimacy in International Law*, Berlin/Heidelberg/New York 2008, pp. 306 ff.

by paragraph 3 of the same article, which emphasises the role of the European Commission in the creation of a consultative platform with all the interested parties in order to ensure that the Union's actions are coherent and transparent[86].

Expert networks are, therefore, obliged by Treaty law to join an institutionalised dialogue with many stakeholders operating in a particular sector of the market. "Associative democracy" is the term used in this context, where participation of different entities in the consultation process concerning the proposed solutions is expected to help increase acceptance of them, and strengthen the legitimacy of institutions undertaking these specific actions. This is also a kind of modern modification of classic representative democracy taking into account the legal perspective. Article 10(1) TEU should be interpreted in this light. European representative democracy, due to the specific character of the EU system, needs to be strengthened and complemented by methods of involving citizens other than the electoral mechanism. In this context examples of "post-parliamentary democracy" or even "post-national" democracy are seen; where broad social participation is supposed to go beyond the usual procedures enabling social activity within intra-state systems[87].

Experimental governance involving regulatory agencies constitutes part of a theoretical model which Charles Sabel and Jonathan Zeitlin called "directly deliberative democracy". A characteristic feature of this model is the participation of many actors in decision-making processes, with varying capabilities of influencing others, diverse experience and objectives as well as a different perspective when it comes to regulation and solving particular issues in specific sectors of the market. Therefore, "deliberative polyarchy is a machine for learning from diversity, thereby transforming an obstacle to closer integration into an asset for achieving it"[88].

This model of governance and communication can also be found in the individual member states. Nonetheless, real development has occurred in the international environment. The main properties of polycentric regulatory regimes, where deliberation plays a key role, include fragmentation, complexity and interdependence between cooperating participants. Due to these features, they face the problem of dilution of individual roles and responsibilities, particularly in terms of setting objectives, formulating standards of conduct, and monitoring how instruments

86 See M. Ruffert, 'Art. 11 EUV', in: Calliess, Ruffert (ed.), *EUV/AEUV*, pp. 186 ff.

87 See Orator, *Möglichkeiten*, p. 354; C. Lord, D. Beetham, 'Legitimizing the EU: Is There a "Post-Parliamentary Basis" for Its Legitimization', *Journal of Common Market Studies*, Vol. 39, No. 3, 2001, pp. 445 ff.

88 Sabel, Zeitlin, 'Learning', p. 276.

are implemented[89]. Despite the Commission's efforts and its clearly specified position in the Treaties, when it comes to the coordination and management of the EU administrative system, the authorship of individual sectoral solutions is not always clear[90]. As has been mentioned before, due to the specialist nature of the issues that the European Commission is confronted with, in the regulatory process, its own administrative apparatus is often unable to draw up a relevant opinion or recommendation or indeed, draft a normative act by itself. One can say without much exaggeration that in the polycentric EU regulatory system, agencies play a key role[91].

c) Transparency

One of the most characteristic features of the development of control mechanisms used in relation to administrative bodies is the introduction of the obligation to be transparent in their work[92]. This is to be achieved e.g. by public consultations or the involvement of stakeholder groups in the administration's activities[93]. Public institutions are obliged to report on their activities not only under the formal orders laid down in specific legal acts, but often also as part of informal, established practices[94]. Their main objective may be to build trust, strengthen their authority or to restore stability in a particular market sector, especially when a crisis situation has occurred earlier[95].

---

89 See J. Black, 'Constructing and Contesting Legitimacy and Accountability in Polycentric Regulatory Regimes', *Regulation & Governance*, Vol. 2, No. 2, 2008, pp. 137, 140, 143.

90 Critically on this issue, see Shapiro, '"Deliberative", "Independent" Technocracy', pp. 346 ff.

91 See also Bach *et al.*, 'Transnational Bureaucratic Politics', pp. 14–16.

92 In May 2015 the European Commission published its new "Better Regulation" Agenda. It is designed to ensure that EU laws are prepared and implemented in a transparent manner. See the European Commission's Communication: *Better Regulation for Better Results. An EU Agenda*, COM(2015) 215 final, 19.5.2015. *Cf.* M. Eliantonio, A. Spendzharova, 'The European Union's New "Better Regulation" Agenda: Between Procedures and Politics', *European Journal of Law Reform*, Vol. 19, Nos. 1–2, 2017, pp. 3 ff. In connection with the trends in all major fields of international law, see A. Peters, 'The Transparency Turn of International Law', *Chinese Journal of Global Governance*, Vol. 1, No. 1, 2015, pp. 3 ff.

93 In the context of regulatory agencies, see Pérez-Durán, 'Political and Stakeholder's Ties', pp. 10 ff.

94 See D. Curtin, A.J. Meijer, 'Does Transparency Strengthen Legitimacy? A Critical Analysis of European Union Policy Documents', *Information Polity*, No. 11, 2006, pp. 111 ff.

95 Busuioc and Lodge point out that "such efforts are increasingly visible among EU regulators and range from the release of [raw] safety data, including clinical trial reports

Nevertheless, the mechanism of maintaining openness, transparency and clarity in the activities of public administration should be viewed from another perspective. Besides the obligation incumbent on European administration authorities to act in a transparent way, what also matters is the right of member state nationals to have access to public information. In this understanding, transparency of the activities of regulatory agencies and other EU organisational units is a necessary condition for the attainment of objectives regarding accountability for the tasks performed[96].

This is also directly reflected in primary law. In Article 15(1) TFEU, it was emphasised that "in order to promote good governance and ensure the participation of civil society, the Union's institutions, bodies, offices and agencies shall conduct their work as openly as possible". Transparency of the functioning of European administration in line with the models from the Nordic countries is also specified in Article 15(3) TFEU, where any citizen of the Union and any natural or legal person residing or having its registered office in one of the member states is guaranteed a right of access to documents of the Union's institutions, bodies and organisational units. Any limitations of this right must involve protection of public or private interests in accordance with the provisions of regulations adopted through the ordinary legislative procedure. What is also emphasised in Article 15(3) TFEU is that all the EU institutions, bodies and organisational units must ensure that their proceedings are transparent. In order to accomplish that, they have to develop appropriate internal procedures to regulate access to the documents that they prepare[97].

Transparency of the activities of public administration bodies constitutes an important element strengthening the legitimacy of decision-makers[98]. While the idea itself is not new, dating back at least to the early nineteenth century, it took the dynamic growth of state administrative structures and international

---

[e.g. EMA] to proactive public overviews of regulatory interactions with industry [e.g. EBA] or public consultations on a unprecedented opening up of the scientific process, including allowing for unsolicited input in all phases of the internal decision-making process [e.g. EFSA]", 'Reputation', p. 95.

96 Kröger, 'The End', p. 570.

97 See S.J. Lea, *Transparency in European Union Governance: The Misdirection of Europe's Legitimacy Enterprise*, Ph.D. Thesis, University of Shefield. Department of Law, September 2016, pp. 63, 78.

98 See also J. de Fine Licht *et al.*, 'When Does Transparency Generate Legitimacy? Experimenting on a Context-Bound Relationship', *Governance. An International Journal of Policy, Administration, and Institutions*, Vol. 27, No. 1, 2014, pp. 112–115.

cooperation in the second half of the twentieth century to make it one of the foundations of good governance and a part of fundamental human rights[99]. Acting with openness is supposed to prevent corruption, help improve the performance of public institutions and better advance public interest. Empirical research indicates, however, that this assumption is not always correct. This is particularly true when a political system is immature and lacks adequate legal safeguards to make it possible to actually achieve desired objectives regarding the transparency of the work of administrative authorities[100].

In the case of EU regulatory agencies, the policy of openness and transparency of action has been stressed for several years. The European Commission is the main advocate of these postulates, realising that an expansion of the agency system is impossible without securing broader public acceptance of the growing administrative apparatus[101]. Transparency of agency activities is meant to allow all interested parties to better understand the motives accompanying specific decisions, and thus strengthen the legitimacy of both agencies themselves and the expertise which they provide[102].

4. Normative Legitimacy

It is not without reason that this chapter concludes with an analysis of normative legitimacy. It is a counterweight to social and axiological legitimacy, which in the case of regulatory agencies is directly associated with technocratic legitimacy and mechanisms designed to strengthen it, such as performance, participation, deliberation and transparency of activities. It is worth citing a simple definition of normative legitimacy proposed by Allen Buchanan and Robert Keohane: "To say that an institution is legitimate in the normative sense is to assert that it has the right to rule – where ruling is promulgating rules and attempting to secure compliance with them by attaching costs to noncompliance and/or benefits to compliance"[103]. This means that an entity gains normative legitimacy when it

---

99 See M. Bauhr, M. Grimes, 'Indignation or Resignation: The Implications of Transparency for Societal Accountability', *Governance. An International Journal of Policy, Administration, and Institutions*, Vol. 27, No. 2, 2014, pp. 291 ff.

100 *Ibid.*, p. 294.

101 See Curtin, Meijer, 'Does Transparency', p. 117; *Joint Statement and Common Approach*, 19.7.2012, pp. 11–13.

102 de Fine Licht *et al.*, 'When', p. 114.

103 A. Buchanan, R.O. Keohane, 'The Legitimacy of Global Governance', in: Wolfrum, Röben (ed.), *Legitimacy*, p. 25.

abides by certain norms. These norms can be of different natures. The main role is played by those that can be considered "constitutional" which primarily means norms of positive law that nowadays include, besides formalised, legally binding norms, also "soft law" and non-legal, generalised written norms. In addition to this dimension, there are also the so-called justice claims. They represent what is customarily or informally considered to be just and right in a particular political system[104].

An interesting view of normative legitimacy is presented by Weiler who believes that it should not be explicitly identified with the legality of a particular system: "There are illegal measures which are considered, normatively […] as legitimate, and legal measures which are considered illegitimate"[105]. He introduced the term "telos legitimacy", which he considered to be a synonym of "political messianism", into the theoretical deliberations on legitimacy in the EU institutional system. In this approach, normative framework should be understood more broadly. It no longer only means law in the formalised sense, but also the system of values, ideas and beliefs which have a legitimising effect in a "normative" way on a political system. "Telos" means "purpose" in Greek. Interpreting the concept by Weiler, one can say that the mechanism of legitimacy in the case of EU administration would be the faith of EU member state nationals in some special objective, mission, or the political destiny of the European institutions. The justification for their activities comes not only from their democratic election, performance and effectiveness, but also from their "messianic visions" of the special role of the EU system in the development of European societies. One can mention "implied normativity" in this context, which could consist of such things as the confidence of the member states in economic success, or as neoliberals would have it – absolute gains achieved by all the participants in the integration process[106].

It is difficult to avoid the impression that in the case of EU regulatory agencies, which have a weak level of normative legitimacy when it comes to the regulation of their status in primary law, a significant role is indeed played by a "messianic" belief in the superiority of regulatory solutions over those proposed individually in the member states. From a lawyer's point of view, however, this is

104 See Black, 'Constructing', p. 146.

105 J.H.H. Weiler, 'In the Face of Crisis: Input Legitimacy, Output Legitimacy and the Political Messianism of European Integration', *Journal of European Integration*, Vol. 34, No. 7, 2012, p. 827.

106 *Ibid.*, pp. 831–833. See also Chapter 1.

not enough, because the functioning of agencies should be "constitutionally" regulated in order to settle their status in the Treaties. Agencies fall within the abovementioned provisions concerning the functioning of European administration (Article 11 TEU, Article 15 TFEU, Article 298 TFEU) and those concerning "delegated" legislation (Article 290 and Article 291 TFEU), but their founding regulations remain the main normative reference point for their functioning. They set out in detail the agencies' tasks, and mechanisms of accountability for the actions that they undertake.

The European Union, due to the nature of its legislation, which is created with the significant involvement of regulatory agencies, has factual sovereignty. This is signified by the principle of primacy and the direct effect of EU law. Due to the specific character of sovereignty within an international organisation, we should distinguish between rules concerning sources of power, which are of primary importance in the case of state systems, and rules that determine the methods of exercising EU power. In the search for the legitimacy of the functioning of the EU institutional system, therefore, not only political scientists and sociologists but also lawyers increasingly focus on the "mechanics of power" rather than its normatively regulated sources[107]. With such an emphasis, an increasingly important question is whether EU institutions take into consideration the "will of the people" in the legislative process, including the involvement of social groups which have an interest in it. Nonetheless, the issue of whether and to what extent this will become a source of EU power is fading into the background[108].

Consequently, it is increasingly pointed out that statehood legitimacy does not have to conflict with supranational legitimacy. The former is indeed based on the "will of the people" expressed through electoral democracy, the latter is based on "public reason". In this case, what matters is "the nature of reasons for [the supranational authorities'] norms", but also "[the] connection between authority and the addressees of these norms"[109].

In the context of EU legislation, the argument is raised that a major shortcoming of the norm-setting process is indeed the absence of a proper, public evaluation of regulatory initiatives, both *ex ante* and *ex post*. This primarily concerns specialist regulations in the areas where regulatory agencies operate.

---

107 Mik, 'Umocnienie', p. 101.

108 See T. Dubowski, A. Piekutowska, 'Legitymizacja władzy Unii Europejskiej – wybrane aspekty instytucjonalno-proceduralne', *Przegląd Politologiczny*, No. 4, 2013, p. 110.

109 See W. Sadurski, 'Supranational Public Reason: On Legitimacy of Supranational Norm-Producing Authorities', *Global Constitutionalism*, Vol. 4, No. 3, 2015, pp. 399, 418 ff.

A lack of consistency and so-called joined-up-thinking in this respect are highlighted. One set of actors participates in the process of evaluating regulatory initiatives in the preceding phase, while another one assesses the effects of introduced regulations[110]. This undoubtedly diminishes the utility of institutions coordinating regulatory activities in particular sectors of the internal market and it thus weakens both output-oriented legitimacy as well as that resulting from the public acceptance of the normative framework.

110 See also M. Quigley, E. Stokes, 'Nudging and Evidence-Based Policy in Europe: Problems of Normative Legitimacy and Effectiveness', in: Alemanno, Sibony (ed.), *Nudge and the Law*, pp. 78 ff.

Part III Empirical Implications of Theoretical Models

7 Input-Oriented Legitimacy of EU Regulatory Agencies as Public Institutions

1. Democratic Governance and EU Regulatory Agencies

EU regulatory agencies are perceived as a typical example of technocratic governance. Hence, the first thought that accompanies an analysis of the legitimisation of the activities of these bodies is associated with their effectiveness, efficiency and usefulness from the point of view of the member states. It is, therefore, a model transposition of Lincoln's idea of "government for the people" mentioned in the previous chapter. However, from a legal perspective, what matters is a model which assumes political participation by the people[1]. "Input" oriented concepts of legitimacy envisage decision-making procedures having a democratic character. In such an ideal model, all the citizens should have equal opportunities to influence public decision-making processes[2]. How, then, can these assumptions, which emphasise democratic choice of the representatives who are authorised to make law within majoritarian institutions, be related to EU regulatory agencies?

Their activities do not fall within the processes of wealth redistribution that should be vested in democratically elected authorities. As their name indicates, their activity is carrying out regulatory tasks whose main objective is to mitigate market failure. This involves intervention mechanisms usually applied by the state. In the case of the European Union, responsibility for regulating many sectors is transferred to the level of enhanced intergovernmental cooperation, that is, the transnational level. Such integrated regulatory policies require expertise, effectiveness, and networked structures that allow quick and effective contact between experts[3].

An essential element of the functioning of regulatory agencies is their autonomy. It constitutes the main argument in the discourse about the credibility

---

1 See Schmidt, 'Democracy', p. 5; R. Grzeszczak, 'Legitymizacja demokratyczna Unii Europejskiej', in: Kranz, *Suwerenność*, pp. 208–212.

2 Such an understanding of "democratic input" is presented e.g. by R. Bellamy, 'Democracy without Democracy? Can the EU's Democratic "Outputs" be Separated from the Democratic "Inputs" Provided by Competitive Parties and Majority Rule?', *Journal of European Public Policy*, Vol. 17, No. 1, 2010, pp. 3–7.

3 *Ibid.*, p. 8; J. Biela, 'What Deficit? Legitimacy and Accountability of Regulatory Agencies', Paper Prepared for the 42nd ECPR Joint Session, 10–15.4.2014, pp. 3, 9.

and the commitment of regulatory agencies to solving complex problems in the long run[4] and, at the same time, it is assumed that there are extensive normative safeguards that constrain the arbitrariness of these bodies[5]. These safeguards are much more transparent in the legal systems of member states than in the EU. Regulatory authorities are not only subject to direct control by the popularly elected institutions, but they are also monitored in a formalised manner and through various informal instruments by institutions that delegate specific powers to them. Relationships of dependence, control and subordination are clearly visible in the intra-state perspective. An additional safeguard is the general public, which pays more attention to the activities of the national administration than those of little known EU agencies scattered across different member states[6]. In the case of the EU administration, this direct public interest is often missing. Control mechanisms, on the other hand, are of a complex, multilevel nature and engage various entities[7].

In this context, an argument is often made that echoes the postulates put forward by Majone. Namely, the EU, as a "regulatory state", by nature, does not fit the classic mechanisms of parliamentary empowerment: "[It is] delivering policies which can only be made efficiently by experts and independent organs, traditional forms of accountability cannot be reproduced in this framework"[8]. The problem of weak democratic legitimacy, conventionally understood by comparison with direct electoral mechanisms, concerns the European Union as a whole rather than just its individual administrative bodies, such as e.g. regulatory

4 Scholten, 'Democratic Input', pp. 64 ff.; S. Gabbi, 'Independent Scientific Advice: Comparing Policies on Conflicts of Interest in the EU and the US', *European Journal of Risk Regulation*, Vol. 2, No. 2, 2011, p. 214.

5 "Administrative law is a well-known instrument for controlling regulatory agencies in the European Union and beyond", T. Gehring, 'Deliberative Regulation through European Union Agencies and Other Network Structures?', in: Busuioc *et al.* (ed.), *The Agency Phenomenon*, p. 111. More also M. Shapiro, 'The Institutionalization of European Administrative Space', in: A. Stone Sweet *et al.* (ed.), *The Institutionalization of Europe*, Oxford 2001, pp. 94 ff.

6 Bellamy, 'Democracy', p. 10.

7 See Bouwen, 'Business Interest', pp. 280–282, 288; D. Coen, 'Business-Regulatory Relations: Learning to Play Regulatory Games in European Utility Markets', *Governance. An International Journal of Policy, Administration, and Institutions*, Vol. 18, No. 3, 2005, pp. 377, 394 ff.; Gehring, 'Deliberative Regulation', pp. 105–109.

8 P. Magnette, 'Democracy in the European Union: Why and How to Combine Representation and Participation', in: Smismans (ed.), *Civil Society*, pp. 24 ff.

agencies[9]. Therefore, researchers dealing with the integration process have, for several decades, consistently pointed out that "the EU's legitimacy still rests primarily on national democracies, which accept and indirectly shape European policies"[10].

For this reason, it seems apt to conclude that the classic liberal theory of legitimacy does not always apply to technocratic forms of governance in the EU. It recognises certain "regimes" as legitimate, i.e. empowered to act, when they involve broad public participation in decision-making processes as well as when they enjoy high levels of support among those who are ruled. An indispensable complement of such legitimacy in the EU is, as indicated in the previous chapter, namely, recognition-based legitimacy that fits within the Weberian tradition. This is legitimacy based on the belief that a particular social order can be considered as legitimate when its validity is recognised by at least a part of the society while other citizens are unable to offer an alternative model of governance. In this context, an important legitimising role is played by the law[11].

The case of EU regulatory agencies confirms the thesis of Robert Dahl, an American democracy theorist, that extensive delegation of competencies can become so complex and distant from the original sources of legitimacy that in practice it eludes the assumptions of conventionally understood democratic mechanisms. In his opinion, these trends are characteristic for international organisations which are derived from the will of their member states and where decision-making processes tend to be independent from direct public influence or participation. Defining democracy "as a system of popular control over governmental policies and decisions", Dahl concludes that no international organisation, including the deeply integrated European Union, is, or can be, a classic liberal democracy[12].

---

9 See T. Kubin, 'Legitymizacja systemu instytucjonalnego Unii Europejskiej jako organizacji międzynarodowej *sui generis*', *Politeja*, No. 6(45), 2016, pp. 147 ff.

10 Magnette, 'Democracy', p. 24. That is why the European Commission in its "Better Regulation" Agenda pledges to listen more carefully to citizens and stakeholders, see Eliantonio, Spendzharova, 'The European Union's New "Better Regulation"', pp. 9–11. *Cf. Better Regulation for Better Results*, COM(2015) 215 final, pp. 4 ff.

11 See J. Kostrubiec, 'W kręgu problematyki prawnej legitymizacji władzy', *Studia Iuridica Lublinensia*, No. 1, 2003, pp. 98–100; C.A. Thomas, 'The Concept of Legitimacy and International Law', *LSE Law, Society and Economy Working Papers*, No. 12, 2013, pp. 14, 19 ff.

12 See R.A. Dahl, 'Can International Organizations be Democratic? A Skeptic's View', in: I. Shapiro, C. Hacker-Cordón (ed.), *Democracy's Edges*, Cambridge 1999, pp. 20–31. See also Herdegen, *Der Kampf*, pp. 240 ff.

Despite such repeatedly reproduced theoretical assertions[13], the member states have not ceased their efforts to make the democratic legitimacy of Community institutions a reality. Since the first democratic elections to the European Parliament in 1979, its position has been consistently strengthened in successive Treaties as the only authority with direct empowerment to act which has been obtained from voters (according to Article 14(2) TEU)[14]. This strengthening mainly involves conferring on the European Parliament greater powers in the legislative process, primarily within the co-decision procedure, as well as broadening its control competencies over the European Commission[15]. It needs to be remembered, however, that despite these efforts the European Parliament, is not an equivalent of the national parliaments. This stems from the difficulties in implementing the idea of representation of citizen interests in the supranational context. First, elections to the European Parliament do not generate as much interest among citizens in member states as national elections. This is due to its geographical as well as political remoteness when it comes to debating problems which are important for citizens. Second, these elections, due to the complexity of the EU system, do not give voters the same opportunities to influence the political character of decision-making bodies as in those which exist in the case of national legal systems[16].

Irrespective of these difficulties at the institutional and normative level, the member states implement democratic principles which constitute one of the main pillars of the integration process[17]. The Treaty of Lisbon sanctioned this state of affairs in Title II of the Treaty on European Union "Provisions on Democratic Principles". Articles 9 to 12 TEU govern the democratic functioning of EU institutions, including regulatory agencies, and thus form part of the

---

13 See also Y. Mény, 'Can Europe be Democratic? Is It Feasible? Is It Necessary? Is the Present Situation Sustainable?', *Fordham International Law Journal*, Vol. 34, No. 5, 2011, pp. 1301–1303; A. von Bogdandy, 'The European Lesson for International Democracy: The Significance of Articles 9–12 EU Treaty for International Organizations', *European Journal of International Law*, Vol. 23, No. 2, 2012, p. 316.

14 See W. Kluth, 'Art. 14 EUV', in: Calliess, Ruffert (ed.), *EUV/AEUV*, pp. 236 ff.

15 See V. Cuesta-Lopez, 'The Lisbon's Treaty Provisions on Democratic Principles: A Legal Framework for Participatory Democracy', *European Public Law*, Vol. 16, No. 1, 2010, pp. 123 ff.

16 See also Lindgren, Persson, 'Input", p. 451; Kröger, Friedrich, 'Democratic Representation', pp. 177 ff.; A. Warleigh, *Democracy and the European Union. Theory, Practice and Reform*, London 2003, pp. 77–91.

17 See Naßmacher, *Mehr Europa*, pp. 125–128.

tradition, developed since the 1980s, of perceiving democracy as a legal principle in European structures[18]. Víctor Cuesta-Lopez calls this set of provisions a "heterogenous title" which incorporates such principles as political equality (Article 9 TEU), representation and participation (Article 10 TEU), good governance, openness and transparency of the activities of EU institutions (Article 11 TEU)[19]. An important complement of this catalogue is Article 12 TEU which stresses the role of national parliaments which "contribute actively to the good functioning of the Union".

The combination created in this manner is expected to become a response to the difficulties in applying classic democratic legitimacy governed by constitutional provisions of the individual member states at the supranational level. Democratic justification in national legal orders, according to the German constitutional law tradition, results from the reference to the "subject of legitimacy" (Germ. *Legitimationssubjekt*) which empowers a particular authority – "object of legitimacy" (Germ. *Legitimationsobjekt*) to act[20]. For the state, the "subject of legitimacy" is the nation, which is the source of legitimacy for decision-makers who express a demand for it (Germ. *Legitimationsbedarf*), as it is necessary to justify their activity. In the abovementioned Title II, there is no explicit provision specifying the subject and object of legitimacy in such a clear manner, as is the case, for example, in the German constitution[21]. That is because the EU institutional system is legitimised by many nations and from the legal perspective it falls within broader normative empowerment than reference to "government of the people" (Germ. *staatliche Volksherrschaft*) understood in the context of the state[22].

This is clearly reflected in the repeatedly mentioned Article 10 TEU. The first paragraph of the article defines the basis for the EU's functioning as a representative democracy. It means that not only is the EU itself to be understood as similar to the liberal democracy developed within states, but also the way it operates,

18 See A. von Bogdandy, 'A Disputed Idea Becomes Law: Remarks on European Democracy as a Legal Principle', in: B. Kohler-Koch, B. Rittberger (ed.), *Debating the Democratic Legitimacy of the European Union*, Lanham 2007, p. 34.

19 Cuesta-Lopez, 'The Lisbon's Treaty', p. 127.

20 See e.g. Thomas, 'The Concept of Legitimacy', pp. 20–24.

21 See Article 20(2) German Basic Law: "All state authority is derived from the people. It shall be exercised by the people through elections and other votes and through specific legislative, executive and judicial bodies".

22 See e.g. Groß, *Die Legitimation*, pp. 80–85; Weißgärber, *Die Legitimation*, p. 200; Orator, *Möglichkeiten*, p. 334; Chamon, *EU Agencies*, pp. 54–57; Mény, 'Can Europe be Democratic?', pp. 1293 ff.

including the workings of European public administration, which should be seen as democratic. Article 10(2) TEU points to the complex nature of democratic legitimacy. On the one hand, it mentions empowerment through direct elections to the European Parliament. The sources of legitimacy here are the citizens of the European Union. On the other hand, the operation of the EU institutional system is legitimised through the member states. In this case, the sources of empowerment are the voters in the member states who elect decision-makers at the national level[23]. It is worth emphasising at this point that the European legislature, both in the previous legal situation (Article 6 TEC) and after the changes introduced by the Treaty of Lisbon, chose not to define representative democracy[24]. In the new Article 10(1) TEU it was emphasised that the functioning of the EU system should be democratic, therefore, stressing the "active" side of the existence of European institutions. Such an interpretation of this provision falls within the systemic interpretation of the norms contained in Title II TEU.

A comprehensive analysis of Treaty law makes it possible to conclude that in the case of EU authorities and institutions we can talk about functional legitimacy. Since the European Union is not a state, it does not have to, and it cannot, as has been already mentioned in the second part of this study, reproduce national models of legitimacy, which, additionally, often differ[25]. Hence, the emphasis is put on the functional aspect. Nonetheless, this understanding of legitimacy should not be identified only with output-oriented legitimacy. It is a broader approach which is not only associated with the efficiency or effectiveness of the EU administration. The term "outcome-based legitimacy" is used in legal literature[26]. What is also significant in this context is the credibility and purposefulness of the activities of independent administrative authorities such as regulatory agencies. The functional justification is associated with the necessity to implement European law with the involvement of autonomous administrative bodies at the supranational level which have a chance of retaining some independence in relation to the member states. They need to maintain their operational freedom. This is necessary in order to achieve common objectives[27]. Functional legitimacy, however, is not a negation of traditional democratic legitimacy, but rather a special modification

23 See Chapter 5.

24 See Bogdandy, 'A Disputed Idea', p. 35; Weißgärber, *Die Legitimation*, p. 203.

25 See T. Stein, 'Demokratische Legitimierung auf supranationaler und internationaler Ebene', *Zeitschrift für ausländisches öffentliches Recht und Völkerrecht*, Vol. 64, 2004, p. 564.

26 Thomas, 'The Concept of Legitimacy', p. 27.

27 See also Groß, *Die Legitimation*, pp. 91–93.

of it resulting from the specific character of the integration process[28]. Groß rightly points out that legal barriers are the main constraint on the arbitrariness of regulatory agencies. These institutions should not act using their own discretion. The starting point is Article 298 TFEU and the specific founding regulations, which define the scope of activity of every EU regulatory agency[29].

2. Legitimising Mechanisms in Practice

a) Authorisation

aa) Institutional Dimension

According to the complex justifications for the legitimacy of the European administration, there are hardly any direct links between the represented and the representatives, or between citizens in the member states, who are the original source of empowerment, and the EU regulatory agencies, the activities of which, constitute the subject of empowerment. Both directors and board members of individual agencies are not directly elected. Directors are usually selected in complicated recruitment procedures that foresee the involvement of the European Commission therein. Despite the assumptions contained in the "Common Approach", which are aimed at aligning the mechanisms for electing members of decision-making bodies, the procedures for appointing directors in individual agencies vary significantly. The model solution proposed in the "Common Approach" would mean selecting the director of the agency's board from among the candidates put forward by the European Commission on a "shortlist". Candidates who are included in this list should be selected in accordance with transparent, open rules for the recruitment of high-level officials[30]. Nonetheless, the assumptions set out in the "Common Approach" do not comprehensively modernise the existing provisions in individual founding regulations[31].

---

28 This thought was expressed back in the 1970s by the German lawyer, Hans Peter Ipsen, who pointed to the purpose-oriented nature of European integration which should be understood through the functional prism in the context of solving specific problems (Germ. *Zweckverband funktioneller Integration*). See H.P. Ipsen, *Europäisches Gemeinschaftsrecht*, Tübingen 1972, pp. 1044 ff.; S. Oeter, 'Europäische Integration als Konstitutionalisierungs prozeß', *Zeitschrift für ausländisches öffentliches Recht und Völkerrecht*, Vol. 59, 1999, p. 904.

29 Groß, *Die Legitimation*, p. 93.

30 *Joint Statement and Common Approach*, 19.7.2012, p. 6.

31 Paraphrasing the words of Curtin and Dehousse, one can say that in the case of regulatory agencies, both in the organisational and competence dimension, there is no such thing as a single model, 'European Union Agencies', pp. 193 ff.

This raises major doubts from the point of view of their democratic legitimacy – particularly in the context of "democratic input" in the development and the activities of these bodies. This is significant for the subject matter of these considerations. As has been pointed out in Chapter 1, founding regulations provide for the involvement of various EU institutions, primarily the Commission and the European Parliament, in the selection of officials for managerial positions in regulatory agencies. Since there are no adequate Treaty norms to define the establishment and functioning of agencies in the EU institutional system, legitimate questions are raised about the proper empowerment of such selection procedures and possible abuse of public power by the agencies[32].

Similar conclusions are drawn regarding the elections for the agency boards. They usually comprise representatives of national regulatory authorities alongside representatives of the Commission and other EU institutions[33]. Thus, in this case, it is difficult to speak about citizens of the member states having any significant influence on the shape of such decision-making bodies and it is therefore assumed that, in the institutional context, the authorisation for the functioning of agencies is of an indirect nature[34]. What necessitates the search for alternative variants to traditionally understood democratic legitimacy is the impossibility of creating a clear "chain of legitimation" within an international organisation that would make it possible to clearly construct a relationship of dependence between the principal and the agent, i.e. the parties within the relationship of delegation of specific powers[35]. One such variant is to create control and supervisory instruments which may be used to hold European institutions accountable for the actions they have undertaken[36].

---

32 Scholten, 'Democratic Input', p. 72. The possibilities of EU citizens to influence EU lawmaking processes remain as they were, irrespective of the European Commission's political initiatives (such as the "Better Regulation" Agenda). See A. Alemanno, 'How Much Better is Better Regulation? Assessing the Impact of the Better Regulation Package on the European Union. A Research Agenda', *European Journal of Risk Regulation*, Vol. 6, No. 3, 2015, pp. 344 ff.

33 See the variant set out in the "Common Approach": *Joint Statement and Common Approach*, 19.7.2012, p. 5.

34 Scholten, 'Democratic Input', p. 72.

35 See Kröger, Friedrich, 'Democratic Representation', pp. 172 ff.; Gehring, 'Deliberative Regulation', p. 107.

36 See Peuker, *Bürokratie*, p. 172; Biela, 'What Deficit?', p. 8.

bb) Instrumental Dimension

Authorisation of EU Regulatory Agencies

Taking into account these considerations, it is important to identify specific examples of such instruments, primarily those mechanisms developed between regulatory agencies and the European Parliament. Due to the specific character of the European administration, there can neither be democratic selection of representatives within the agency bodies, nor a clear delegation of powers to the bodies assembled that way[37]. Thus, adopting the definition by Scholten, we can say that in the case of EU regulatory agencies the source of democratic input legitimacy consists of authorisation, safeguards and accountability[38]. In this analysis, these elements will be considered as democratic input in the context of the subject's perspective, i.e. in relation to the subject of legitimacy, namely a public institution, specifically – an EU regulatory agency.

Authorisation of regulatory agencies primarily means the creation of relevant normative foundations that are related to the establishment of a particular regulatory agency. In this context, Scholten points to the issue of the possible involvement of the general public in the process of establishing such an institution. What is also important, is the possible influence of citizens on the creation of decision-making bodies within these agencies. In the case of European agencies, both of these dimensions are present to a limited extent.

These developments can be considered as a part of the idea of "responsiveness" which has been developed in the literature on instruments of accountability in public administration. This means that administrative authorities act in accordance with the public will, and in response to public demand[39]. However, when taking into account the independence of regulatory agencies, full "responsiveness" is not desirable. Submitting to public opinion could compromise the normative safeguards contained in founding regulations, which explicitly

37 See Maggetti, 'Legitimacy', p. 2; P. Craig, 'Legitimacy in Administrative Law: European Union', in: Ruffert (ed.), *Legitimacy*, p. 200.

38 Scholten, 'Democratic Input', p. 68. Miroslava Scholten also relates the abovementioned legitimacy triad to procedures concerning the functioning of agencies and the ways of shaping decision-making processes in these bodies. Nonetheless, when one adopts the modified classification which was outlined in Chapter 5, this perspective falls within the category defined as throughput-oriented legitimacy. See Iusmen, Boswell, 'The Dilemmas', pp. 461 ff.

39 D. Curtin *et al.*, 'Positioning Accountability in European Governance: An Introduction', *West European Politics*, Vol. 33, No. 5, 2010, p. 938.

guarantee the independence of the agencies. In consequence, this could undermine the autonomous status of these bodies. This risk constitutes one of the main arguments for expanding the technocratic agency system[40].

When referring to the four agencies selected, which were analysed in Chapter 2, we can identify the most important elements of formal empowerment that may be considered to be the authorisation for these public institutions. EFSA and ECHA are typical expert agencies[41]. What one can say about both of them is that their main mission is to provide scientific advice, as well as scientific and technical support, on matters related to legislation and shaping of policies in relevant sectors of the market (food safety and trade in chemicals)[42]. The mandate of Frontex, as an operational agency, was formulated in a slightly different way. Its basic element, according to Article 1 of Regulation 2016/1624, is to ensure integrated European border management at the EU's external borders. To this end, Frontex facilitates the application of existing and future EU measures relating to the management of the external borders and it contributes to the continuous and uniform application of Union law[43]. EBA, due to its broad scope of competencies and the complexity of the tasks that have been assigned to it, also has a mandate to act in a more sophisticated way than the three agencies mentioned above. The EU legislature emphasised its mode of functioning within the European System of Financial Supervision[44] and also divided its numerous tasks aimed at preserving the financial stability and safety in the European integrated banking market into several groups. Thus, EBA's tasks include contributing to the establishment of common regulatory and supervisory standards and practices, facilitating contacts between national banking supervision authorities, ensuring the proper flow of information relating to the situation in the banking markets of the member states and also monitoring and observing, in addition to elaborating guidelines and recommendations in this regard[45].

---

40 See Biela, 'What Deficit?', p. 10.

41 Their mandate was set out in Article 22 of Regulation No. 178/2002 and Article 77 of Regulation No. 1907/2006 respectively.

42 See also G. Abels, A. Kobusch, 'Regulation of Food Safety in the EU: Changing Patterns of Multi-Level Governance', Paper Presented at the Conference of the ECPR Standing Group on Regulatory Governance, June 2010, pp. 4 ff.; Pawlik, *Das REACH-System*, pp. 115 ff.

43 Article 6(2) and (3) of Regulation No. 2016/1624; see Barner-Gaedicke, *FRONTEX*, pp. 39 ff.

44 Article 2 of Regulation No. 1093/2010.

45 Article 8 of Regulation No. 1093/2010; see Weismann, *European Agencies*, pp. 121 ff.

The powers of the abovementioned agencies, in accordance with the ideas of functional legitimacy, fall within the broad definition of regulatory competencies. Therefore, they are primarily meant to contribute to realising the idea of an integrated market[46]. In this sense, tasks related to advising, collecting information, and monitoring, as well as drafting recommendations, guidelines, opinions and regulatory standards, i.e. strengthening the cooperation between authorities in the member states and other stakeholders, are understood as being regulatory powers[47].

Informational and Advisory Powers

The assignment of informational, supporting, advisory and coordinating powers to the abovementioned agencies is an important element in advancing the calls to make participatory and deliberative democracy a reality in accordance with Article 10(3) and 11 TEU. Almost all EU regulatory agencies have these kinds of powers, but in the case of the four agencies mentioned above, they play a special role in the creation of effective multilevel governance and regulation structures[48]. As Emilia Korkea-aho and Päivi Leino rightly note: "Information is not a mere commodity, which companies trade in pursuit of regulatory compliance, but a tool through which these agencies govern. In such a setting, information is a critically important topic when evaluating the legitimacy and effectiveness of EU agency governance"[49]. The information collected by agencies as well as the recommendations, guidelines, opinions and other expert documents that they draft are primarily addressed to the European Commission. However, in accordance with the idea of the broad, participatory authorisation of the activities of EU regulatory agencies, founding regulations provide for the possibility of other entities obtaining their expert support[50].

---

46 See V. Hatzopoulos, 'Hard to Soft: Governance in the EU Internal Market', *Cambridge Yearbook of European Legal Studies*, Vol. 15, 2013, p. 127.

47 Scholten, 'Democratic Input', p. 70.

48 See also N. Chowdhury, R.A. Wessel, 'Conceptualising Multilevel Regulation in the EU: A Legal Translation of Multilevel Governance?', *European Law Journal*, Vol. 18, No. 3, 2012, pp. 338 ff.

49 E. Korkea-aho, P. Leino, 'Who Owns the Information Held by EU Agencies? Weed Killers, Commercially Sensitive Information and Transparent and Participatory Governance', *Common Market Law Review*, Vol. 54, No. 4, 2017, p. 1065.

50 See S. Vaughan, 'Differentiation and Dysfunction: An Exploration of Post-Legislative Guidance Practices in 14 EU Agencies', *Cambridge Yearbook of European Legal Studies*, Vol. 17, 2015, pp. 72 ff.

The European Parliament, as well as the member states, can request EFSA to issue a scientific opinion[51]. ECHA also provides scientific and technical guidance to entrepreneurs and authorities in the member states, particularly in the area of writing chemical safety reports and informing the public about the dangers associated with particular chemicals[52]. Frontex monitors migratory flows and on that basis it prepares general risk analyses which are submitted to the European Parliament and the Council, as well as to the Commission[53]. As part of its coordination of border management, the agency also submits vulnerability assessments to the member states concerned, which include information about the availability of technical equipment, capabilities, resources and the infrastructure necessary for effective border control[54]. EBA, where appropriate, issues guidelines and recommendations addressed to competent authorities in the member states as well as to financial institutions[55]. With a view to building a European banking supervision culture as well as consistent supervisory practices, it provides opinions to competent authorities, promotes bilateral and multilateral exchanges of information between various entities in the European banking market, reviews the application of technical standards as well as conducting appropriate training to bring national banking systems closer together[56].

The guidelines, recommendations and opinions prepared by regulatory agencies are usually treated as soft law[57]. But the simple, dichotomous division into "hard" and "soft law" turns out to be not entirely precise, particularly in the context of this agency activity. Therefore, Steven Vaughan has suggested a new term "hybrid law" that more accurately reflects modern trends in European governance. In his opinion, in the case of "European Composite Administration", which implies multilevel law implementation and the involvement of multiple

---

51 Article 29(1) of Regulation No. 178/2002.

52 Article 77(2) of Regulation No. 1907/2006. *Cf.* J. Scott, 'In Legal Limbo: Post-Legislative Guidance as a Challenge for European Administrative Law', *Common Market Law Review*, Vol. 48, No. 2, 2011, p. 342.

53 Article 11 of Regulation No. 2016/1624.

54 Article 13(2) and (5) of Regulation No. 2016/1624.

55 Article 16(1) of Regulation No. 1093/2010.

56 Article 29 of Regulation No. 1093/2010. On agency opinions: Busuioc, 'Blurred Areas', pp. 391 ff.; Chalmers, 'Food for Thought', p. 540; Bronckers, van Gerven, 'Legal Remedies', pp. 1830 ff.; Barner-Gaedicke, *FRONTEX*, pp. 68 ff.; Weismann, *European Agencies*, pp. 146–148.

57 *Cf.* L. Senden, *Soft Law in European Community Law*, Oxford/Portland 2004, pp. 26 ff.; J. Schwarze, '*Soft Law* im Recht der Europäischen Union', *Europarecht*, No. 1, 2011, pp. 4–6.

actors at different levels – national, intergovernmental and supranational[58] – we should speak of a "hybrid world of post-legislative guidance"[59]. The term "soft law" is, on the other hand, "both over- and under-inclusive in its capacity to capture changes in law and governance"[60]. This particularly concerns the regulatory instruments developed by agencies as part of so-called post-legislative guidance practice. These very "post-legislative codes and guidance", i.e. guidelines, recommendations and opinions drafted by these bodies, directly influence the process of European law implementation and specific actions of competent national authorities.

Consequently, it is difficult to clearly determine what their binding force is. Classifying them as "soft law" would mean that formally they have no specific legal force. However, considering this phenomenon, which is characteristic for the internal market, of a "blurring of authorship" of legally binding final documents such as regulatory ones as well as implementing technical standards for the financial sectors or marketing authorisations for medicines, officially issued by the Commission but in fact developed by the European Supervisory Authorities and the European Medicines Agency respectively, we can conclude that a new "hybrid" model of legal norms is indeed taking shape[61]. This model is consistent with the process of transforming public power within the "post-national order" where sovereign powers, including those involving the implementation of law are shifted to the level of integrated structures falling outside the administrative system of a single state. In practice this means that both

58 Tanja Börzel rightly points out here that this governance model means that primarily public actors are involved in the decision-making process. In her opinion, "network governance" understood as common inclusion of private entities in the EU process of developing and implementing policies in various market sectors is a kind of myth which is not supported by facts. Their influence is limited and primarily means consultations and informing rather than actual co-decision, 'European Governance: Negotiation and Competition in the Shadow of Hierarchy', *Journal of Common Market Studies*, Vol. 48, No. 2, 2010, pp. 194 ff., 206.

59 Vaughan, 'Differentiation and Dysfunction', p. 70.

60 K.A. Armstrong, 'New Governance and the European Union: An Empirical and Conceptual Critique', *Queen Mary University of London. School of Law Legal Studies Research Paper*, No. 135, 2013, p. 4.

61 *Ibid.*, pp. 17, 28 ff.; M. Kopeć, 'Wspólnotowe *soft law* jako przejaw europeizacji prawa farmaceutycznego', in: I. Lipowicz (ed.), *Europeizacja administracji publicznej*, Warszawa 2008, pp. 349 ff. According to Steven Vaughan, "self-authored guidance issued by EU agencies is a classic example of hybrid law", 'Differentiation and Dysfunction', p. 71.

authorisation instruments and accountability mechanisms have to be transnational in the case of supranational institutions as well[62].

EU regulatory agencies support the flow of information between market participants[63] and act as specific centres to coordinate the activities of many actors in a specific regulatory sector. Information flow and sharing data are important for the development of a particular sector of the internal market. They constitute a significant mechanism that strengthens the limited representative democracy which exists within the European Union. Important measures of authorisation include operational transparency as well as informing the public about the activities of individual agencies. "Public authorisation", resulting from the openness of the public administration authorities, forms one of the main components of the system of control over EU institutions[64]. This is particularly important in view of the assertion that a "cloak of 'expertise'" often conceals the actual decision-making entity in the case of these agencies. This consideration not only determines the actions of the European Commission and other EU authorities in a specific area, but also influences public authorities in the member states as well as private entities such as financial institutions[65]. Even though powers to issue guidelines, recommendations or opinions are explicitly laid down in founding regulations, these powers usually raise reasonable concerns, particularly in the light of the questionable democratic legitimacy of EU agencies[66].

---

62 "The problem for the accountability of all forms of governance that operate beyond the nation state". See Curtin *et al.*, 'Positioning Accountability', pp. 932 ff.; 938. Matthias Ruffert also writes about other legislative mechanisms in such supranational orders which elude the traditional understanding of "rule-making", 'The Many Faces of Rule-Making in the EU', in: E. Fahey (ed.), *The Actors of Postnational Rule-Making. Contemporary Challenges of European and International Law*, Oxon 2016, pp. 47 ff.

63 For more on the doubts regarding the management of information that is significant from the point of view of individual sectors of the internal market, see Korkea-aho, Leino, 'Who Owns the Information', pp. 1059 ff.

64 See D. Adamski, *Prawo do informacji o działaniach władz publicznych Unii Europejskiej*, Warszawa 2011, pp. 17 ff.

65 See D. Chalmers *et al.*, *European Union Law: Cases and Materials*, Cambridge 2010, pp. 66 ff. Thomas Gehring comments on the development of European governance structures in a similar fashion: "Scientific and technological assessment panels establish a protected niche for the deliberative validation of relevant matters of truth and set the agenda for the ensuing political decision process", 'Deliberative Regulation', p. 112.

66 See W. Weiß, 'Dezentrale Agenturen in der EU-Rechtsetzung', *Europarecht*, No. 6, 2016, pp. 631 ff.

One noteworthy example may be found in the powers of the European Aviation Safety Agency (EASA) and the process of preparing the draft Commission proposals concerning the basic principles, applicability and essential requirements for implementing rules in the field of certification of the airworthiness of aircraft and permitting the use of specific technical parts[67]. Although these draft proposals are not legally binding, they are in fact implemented by relevant authorities in the member states, thus it is said they have a "*de facto* binding legal force"[68].

The powers of EBA and the other two European Supervisory Authorities – ESMA and EIOPA can be considered to be other examples, because they issue guidelines and recommendations in accordance with a strengthened procedure of "act or explain"[69], meaning that it is necessary for authorities in the member states to justify any failure to comply with these instruments, as well as for the financial institutions to inform the relevant agency if they do comply. Both the authorities in the member states and financial institutions are obliged to make every possible effort to comply with these guidelines and recommendations[70]. One special case is technical standards, which are issued by the Commission, but the drafts of which, according to Article 10 and 15 of Regulation No. 1093/2010, are prepared by EBA and similarly its counterparts in other sectors of the financial market. After the introduction of the Single Supervisory Mechanism, standards developed by EBA are also binding for the European Central Bank[71].

Also other agencies, e.g. the European Medicines Agency, shape specific actions of both authorities in the member states and private entities as part of their expert activity. EMA issues opinions regarding applications for marketing authorisation for medicinal products intended for human use. On the basis of these opinions, the Commission publishes decisions that are compatible with the position of EMA[72]. It is assumed, in this context, that the Commission

67 Article 19 of Regulation No. 216/2008.

68 Sölter, *Rechtsgrundlagen*, p. 60; A. Peters, 'Soft Law as a New Mode of Governance', in: U. Diedrichs *et al.* (ed.), *The Dynamics of Change in EU Governance*, Cheltenham/ Northampton 2011, pp. 25 ff.

69 In the case of EBA, Article 16 of Regulation No. 1093/2010.

70 Article 16(3) of Regulation No. 1093/2010.

71 See Ruffert, 'The Many Faces of Rule-Making', pp. 52 ff.

72 Articles 5–13 of Regulation No. 726/2004. *Cf.* Dehousse, 'Delegation', p. 799; T. Cook, *Pharmaceuticals Biotechnology and the Law*, Croydon 2016, pp. 343, 494; Gehring, 'Deliberative Regulation', pp. 113–116. About the historical development of the authorisation system for medicines in the European market, see J.S. Gardner, 'The European Agency for the Evaluation of Medicines and European Regulation of

performs only an administrative function – i.e. of the authority that formally issues a decision. Nonetheless, the substantive authority in this regard is EMA, which actually makes decisions to authorise the marketing of innovative medicinal products within the EU. In the case of generic, less complex medicines that are the equivalents of original medicines, national procedures based on the principles of decentralisation and mutual recognition by the member states take effect[73]. It is also pointed out here that when expert tasks are performed especially by agencies such as EMA, ECHA, EFSA or EBA, collecting specific information and then publishing or sharing it as part of open consultations, can lead to interference in the legal status of individual actors operating in a particular sector of the market[74]. In the case of companies from the medical, chemical, food or financial industries, this primarily concerns the disclosure of data that can be used by potential competitors, whereas in the case of natural persons, it can also concern possible infringements of their fundamental rights[75].

Coordinating Powers

Coordination of the functioning of different entities within cooperative networks is considered as one of the most important elements authorising the operation of agencies. Through deliberation and participation, which is expressed not only in negotiations and discussions on topics that are important for sectoral policies, but also in training, exchanges of officials and the organisation of IT systems, a seemingly democratic platform of agreement is constituted. The

---

Pharmaceuticals', *European Law Journal*, Vol. 2, No. 1, 1996, pp. 53 ff.; M. Górka, 'Rola Europejskiej Agencji Oceny Produktów Leczniczych w procedurze dopuszczania leków do obrotu w Unii Europejskiej', *Kwartalnik Prawa Publicznego*, Vol. 1, No. 2, 2001, pp. 138 ff.

73 See Cook, *Pharmaceuticals*, p. 583; Landscheidt, 'Der Sitzwechsel', pp. 7 ff. For an example of Polish regulations on trade in medicinal products, see M. Krekora, M. Świerczyński, E. Traple, *Prawo farmaceutyczne*, Warszawa 2012, pp. 392 ff. See also M. Świerczyński, 'Second Medical Use Patents and the Substitution of Medical Products', *Zeszyty Naukowe UJ. Prace z prawa własności intelektualnej*, No. 3, 2017, pp. 64 ff.

74 In the case of EMA and ECHA, data on individual product applications should be understood as commercially sensitive information and for this reason it is not made fully public. In particular, the information on the production process is classified. See Article 63(1) and Article 14(11) of Regulation No. 726/2004. See Ossege, *European Regulatory Agencies*, p. 122; Makhashvili, Stephenson, 'Differentiating', pp. 12 ff.

75 See Sölter, *Rechtsgrundlagen*, p. 62; Michel, *Institutionelles Gleichgewicht*, p. 145; Korkea-aho, Leino, 'Who Owns the Information', pp. 1062 ff.

misleading nature of the "democratic input" comes in this case from the fact that the participants of such a network are elitist and that the influence of external private entities, such as consumer organisations, on the final formulation of specific regulations is illusory[76]. From the legal perspective, the coordinating activities of the agencies should be, on the one hand, seen as instruments of informal influence on entities which operate in a specific sector and, on the other hand, as legally binding mechanisms which oblige these entities to behave in certain ways. All of the agencies that were referred to in Chapter 2 have such an informal set of instruments at their disposal.

Informal actions often obtain normative authorisation through a specific provision in the founding regulation that requires certain public institutions to cooperate under the auspices of a particular regulatory agency. This is the case with e.g. EFSA, which, according to Article 36 of Regulation No. 178/2002, promotes the networking of organisations operating in the fields within its mission. Competent authorities from the member states function within the network and EFSA can entrust them with specific tasks, primarily involving participation in preparatory work in the process of formulating scientific opinions. In the case of ECHA, the important authority which coordinates cooperation between competent authorities in the member states, is the Enforcement Forum which, according to Article 77(4) of Regulation No. 1907/2006, spreads good practice in the area of trade in chemicals. It coordinates harmonised enforcement projects and exchange of inspectors as well as cooperating with enterprises and other stakeholders, including international organisations[77]. Likewise, in the case of Frontex, Article 9 of Regulation No. 2016/1624 lays down obligations for the agency, and national authorities responsible for border management, including coastguards, to the extent that they carry out border control tasks and cooperate in good faith[78].

---

76 See Börzel, 'European Governance', p. 203. Although agencies officially emphasise that they take into consideration the opinions of stakeholders voiced within the consultation process that accompanies the drafting of guidance documents. See e.g. ECHA, Scott, 'In Legal Limbo', p. 347.

77 See Korkea-aho, 'Effects', pp. 763 ff.

78 More about the role of EU regulatory agencies in the process of network building within the European administrative space, see M.P. Schwind, *Netzwerke im Europäischen Verwaltungsrecht. Ein Beitrag zu Theorie und Dogmatik der Behördenkooperation*, Tübingen 2017, pp. 297 ff.

Coordination obligations have been established much more broadly in the case of EBA. This agency, in addition to the tasks mentioned above[79], can also issue legally binding decisions, which can be addressed to financial institutions and regulatory authorities in the member states and that take precedence over decisions adopted earlier by competent national authorities on a given matter. Therefore, in this context, we can speak of formalised instruments that determine the binding coordination of activities in the case of e.g. breaches of Union law, acting in emergency situations or the settlement of disagreements between competent authorities in cross-border situations[80].

b) Safeguards

Safeguards, according to Scholten's interpretation, mean the legal guarantees that determine the circumstances which allow elected authorities to initiate the establishment of EU regulatory agencies. This involves authorities such as the European Parliament with particular obligations that determine the conditions under which another body of this kind can be established. In the EU system, the European Commission initiates the process of creating agencies more frequently than do the member states. They tend to prefer cooperation, within sectoral regulatory networks, that is less institutionalised, since they strive to protect their national interests[81].

There is no doubt that a Treaty provision which could elaborate the specific conditions indicating the opportunities for creating EU regulatory agencies as well as determining the limits of delegation within the EU administrative system would constitute a major argument in favour of strengthening the democratic legitimacy of these bodies. These kinds of safeguards are found in national legal systems where the circumstances, under which a new regulatory agency can be created, are precisely determined by local legislation[82].

However, since there are no indications that such regulations will be included in the Treaties in the near future, some suggestions on this issue can be sought

79 See Article 29 of Regulation No. 1093/2010 which stipulates that EBA contributes to developing a common supervisory culture and consistent supervisory practices, as well as ensuring uniform procedures and consistent approaches throughout the EU. According to Article 31 of Regulation No. 1093/2010, in turn, the agency fulfils a coordination role between competent authorities in the member states.

80 See Articles 17–19 of Regulation No. 1093/2010; Sölter, *Rechtsgrundlagen*, pp. 65–69.

81 Scholten, 'Democratic Input', p. 72.

82 *Ibid.*

in the non-legally binding "Common Approach". It states that, "the decision to create a new agency should be based on objective impact assessments of all relevant opinions"[83]. According to the provisions of this document, founding regulations should contain sunset and review clauses in order to guarantee that the functioning of a particular agency is reviewed after a specific period of time. Moreover, the "Common Approach" recognised the possibility of merging agencies, the competencies of which overlap, as well as the possibility of closing them down if they underperform[84]. As part of implementing the assumptions of the "Common Approach", the Commission created a "startup toolkit" in 2014, which has been, henceforth, constantly updated and made available to DGs and individual agencies. This "toolkit" identifies the most important conditions that must be met when a new agency is established and which was given practical expression during the process of creating the Single Resolution Board – an EU agency functioning within the Banking Union[85].

Normative safeguards for the activities of the public administration authorities fall within the classic concept of rule of law and constitute one of the basic mechanisms used to legitimise the functioning of the state apparatus. In accordance with the assumptions of this concept, which constitutes a significant element of the European tradition of liberal democracy, citizens are protected from any arbitrary actions of state authorities. This is because such authorities, including the government, are subject to law[86]. In this context, a major safeguard is the principle of tripartition of power and the system of checks and balances involving the mutual balancing and control between the most important state institutions. In the case of the EU, these safeguards have become modified. In the horizontal dimension, there is the principle of institutional balance, mentioned in Chapter 3 and the judicial control performed by the CJEU.

The vertical dimension, on the other hand, concerns relations between EU agencies and the member states. It involves the principle of subsidiarity and the EU only being active within the competences conferred upon it[87]. What is worth noting here is that the centralised application of European law, which means that

83 *Joint Statement and Common Approach*, 19.7.2012, p. 3.

84 *Ibid.*

85 *Report from the Commission*, COM(2015) 179 final, p. 3.

86 A different perspective with respect to American federalism: B.R. Clark, 'Putting the Safeguards Back Into the Political Safeguards of Federalism', *Texas Law Review*, Vol. 80, No. 2, 2001, pp. 330 ff.

87 See also Scientific Council for Government Policy, *Rediscovering Europe in the Netherlands*, WRR Rapporten, Amsterdam 2007, pp. 91–118.

EU bodies are able to issue individual acts. This has, for decades, been considered a solution that should only be used in exceptional circumstances. The main obstacle to the centralisation of executive functions at the EU level has, indeed, been the principle of subsidiarity. Irena Lipowicz writes, in the context of the growth of the agency system, about the adverse modification of the principle of subsidiarity. In her opinion, we can even speak of an erosion of this principle. The main reason for this is the right of some agencies to issue individual decisions addressed to the authorities in the member states, as well as to private entities, including natural persons and enterprises. These decisions are issued by technocratic institutions – the European Commission and its satellite agency system. A complementary argument that points to the weakening of the principle of subsidiarity is the introduction of complex deliberative and participatory elements in the European decision-making processes. As a result, the clear line of separation between what is national and what is European becomes blurred[88].

The horizontal and vertical safeguards are meant to perform a protective function. This is not only about protecting individuals from any arbitrariness of supranational institutions in addition to the EU's administrative apparatus, such as regulatory agencies, the decisions of which can increasingly oblige citizens to exhibit particular behaviours, but it is also about protection within the mutual relations between authorities at the national and European levels[89]. These safeguards are particularly important in the case of such agencies as ECHA, EFSA, EMA, ESMA, EIOPA or EBA, which create hybrid law. The opinions, guidelines and recommendations of these agencies shape a comprehensive system of "non-legislative rules" which has a multidimensional impact on private and public entities within the member states.

Thus, in parallel with national legal systems, it is also necessary within the EU to have procedural safeguards in order to protect individuals and private institutions against any arbitrariness of regulatory agencies. According to such an approach, administrative procedures that determine the scope of competences and the capabilities of a particular agency are the source of legitimacy for such a body[90]. Nonetheless, one should keep in mind that procedural safeguards which "afford democratic legitimisation to agency guidance [should not cause]

88 See I. Lipowicz, 'Europeizacja i modernizacja. Administracyjnoprawne aspekty zmian polskiej administracji publicznej', in: Lipowicz (ed.), *Europeizacja*, pp. 19 ff. See also Schwind, *Netzwerke*, p. 281.

89 Scientific Council, *Rediscovering Europe*, p. 92.

90 *Cf.* J. Mantel, 'Procedural Safeguards for Agency Guidance: A Source of Legitimacy for Administrative State', *Administrative Law Review*, Vol. 61, No. 2, 2009, pp. 357 ff.

undue harm to administrative efficiency"[91]. A basic procedural safeguard, of this sort, for regulatory agencies is the control of the European Commission, which authorises their activities and builds their authority by approving the documents which they draft. Therefore, the Commission also plays a legitimising role, acting, according to Article 17(1) TEU, as both the supervisor and the coordinator of administrative activities in the EU[92].

c) Accountability to the European Parliament

The provision of adequate instruments to ensure the accountability of regulatory agencies for decisions which have been made is commonly recognised as the main element of their legitimacy in the institutional system, both at the state and supranational levels. In the EU, this takes place within a model based on trust between the institutions conferring certain powers on the agency (according to a fiduciary mode of delegation)[93]. The main reason for the development of such checks is the desire to ensure proper performance of the tasks conferred and to prevent abuse of power in decision-making processes. The law is also an important safeguard in this case – i.e. specific provisions indicating the abovementioned authorisation of an agency's activities. The concept of "accountability", therefore, also includes the term "responsibility" which is understood as a guarantee that behaviour of decision-makers is consistent with applicable law[94].

Accountability to the European Parliament comes to the fore among numerous security controls that have been the subject of separate monographs and that play a secondary role from the point of view of these considerations[95]. This is significant, since it is one of the main elements of "democratic input" in the case of EU regulatory agencies. While the European Parliament can be considered as "an imperfect repository of democratic legitimacy at the European level"[96], it constitutes the most perfect solution which refers directly to the "will" of the member state nationals among those which exist in the European institutional system[97].

---

91 *Ibid.*, pp. 405 ff.

92 Groß, 'Unabhängige EU-Agenturen', p. 1093. See also Chapter 8.

93 Maggetti, 'Legitimacy', p. 4.

94 See Biela, 'What Deficit?', p. 7.

95 See more references to political, financial and judicial accountability Scholten, *The Political Accountability*, pp. 67 ff.; Busuioc, *European Agencies*, pp. 114 ff.

96 Curtin, Dehousse, 'European Union Agencies', p. 201.

97 Scholten goes as far as to write about the exceptional empowerment on an international scale – in connection with the direct election of MEPs by citizens of so many

The European Parliament is also an institution that for years has been elaborating formal and informal instruments of control over the European agency system. In the beginning one of the main motives for such efforts was the desire to counterbalance the influence of the European Commission. Facing the birth of the "European composite executive", functioning under the auspices of the Commission, which was surrounded by its satellite agency system, the European Parliament took steps to balance the powers vested in the technocratic institutions of the European administration[98]. Admittedly, the European Parliament had recognised the desirability of creating decentralised bodies to strengthen the European administrative system since the 1970s. Nonetheless, it remained sceptical about effective balancing of powers between the executive and the legislative branches in the face of a shift of ever-broader competencies to the former. These concerns were particularly related to the possible scenario of limiting the European Parliament's competencies, especially regarding control over the Commission's activities and issues related to budget adoption[99].

Interestingly, the Parliament has evolved over time from its original role of an authority which was sceptical in its assessment of the agency system to an entity advocating even broader competencies for some already powerful agencies, as was the case e.g. during the process of creating ECHA, EBA, ESMA and EIOPA[100].

---

countries, therefore the European Parliament is "a unique institution" not only in the European backyard, but also in comparison with other organisations worldwide. See Scholten, *The Political Accountability*, pp. 31 ff. See also F. Trauner, 'The European Parliament and Agency Control in the Area of Freedom, Security and Justice', *West European Politics*, Vol. 35, No. 4, 2012, p. 785.

98 See Busuioc, *European Agencies*, pp. 3 ff.; Hofmann, 'Mapping', p. 671. It is worth noting here that the European Parliament was one of the first actors to highlight the dangers of an expansion of the agency system. The so-called 'Herman Report' emphasised in 1999 that "agencification" of the European administrative space can lead to a breakup of the executive power into an apparatus centralised around the Commission and agencies without effective public control. See European Parliament (Committee on Institutional Affairs), *Report on Improvement in the Functioning of the Institutions without Modifications of the Treaties* ['The Herman Report'], Rapporteur: F. Herman, 26.3.1999, PE 229.072/fin. More C. Lord, 'The European Parliament and the Legitimation of Agencification', *Journal of European Public Policy*, Vol. 18, No. 6, 2011, p. 912.

99 See Chamon, *EU Agencies*, p. 126; R.D. Kelemen, 'The Politics of "Eurocratic" Structure and New European Agencies', *West European Politics*, Vol. 25, No. 4, 2002, p. 104.

100 About ECHA see Lord, 'The European Parliament', pp. 914, 919 ff.; about the process of establishing EBA, ESMA and EIOPA see Kohtamäki, *Die Reform*, pp. 106 ff.

The Parliament has at the same time become an advocate of streamlining the functioning of regulatory agencies through its engagement in the development of the "Common Approach". This involvement was a result of the Parliament making efforts, over several years, to introduce changes in the system of supervision, reporting and financing of the agencies[101].

The increased role of the European Parliament was reflected in the abandonment of the consultation procedure with respect to the establishment of regulatory agencies under Article 308 EC (now Article 352 TFEU) in favour of the co-decision procedure characteristic for so-called material norms of competence, i.e. detailed Treaty provisions chosen as a necessary legal basis for the creation of new bodies of this kind. Since the second half of the 1990s the more intensive inclusion of the European Parliament in the process of shaping the agency system has led to a growing interest in these institutions, which have gradually become a subject of public debate[102].

For more than a decade it has been assumed that the European Parliament has applied *ex ante* control measures involving this influence within the co-decision procedure on the final shape of a particular agency. The European Parliament's amendments to the Commission's proposals relating to the establishment of a specific EU regulatory agency usually concern its tasks, powers and the composition of its main decision-making bodies[103]. This was the case with e.g. EEA where the Parliament suggested its participation in the selection process of the agency's director and pushed to secure the right to remove him or her in certain circumstances, and also sought to have four representatives on the agency's

---

101 See e.g. European Parliament (Committee on Budgets), *Working Document on a Meeting with the Decentralised Agencies on the PDB for 2008*, Rapporteurs: J. Haug, K. Virrankoski, 23.5.2007, PE388.642v01-00; European Parliament (Committee on Budgetary Control), Report on Financial Management and Control of EU Agencies; Rapporteur: C. Fjellner, 19.3.2009, PE418.394v02-00; European Parliament (Committee on Constitutional Affairs), *Report on Strategy for the Future Settlement of the Institutional Aspects of Regulatory Agencies*, Rapporteur: G. Papastamkos, 17.9.2008, 2008/2103 (INI), PE407.635v02-00. According to Christopher Lord, the European Parliament has over the years developed a system of assumptions concerning regulatory agencies the introduction of which ensures that it has better control and greater influence on these bodies: Lord, 'The European Parliament', pp. 909 ff.

102 *Cf.* Chapter 1. See T. Bach, J. Fleischer, 'The Parliamentary Accountability of European Union and National Agencies', in: Busuioc *et al.* (ed.), *The Agency Phenomenon*, pp. 152–155, 161.

103 F. Jacobs, 'EU Agencies and the European Parliament', in: Everson *et al.* (ed.), *EU Agencies*, p. 202.

board[104]. In the end, the Parliament succeeded in placing two of its representatives onto the EEA's decision-making body[105]. The Parliament presented similar demands during the establishment of EMA, where it also proposed a provision on the Parliament's approval of the agency's director and an equal number of the Commission's and the Parliament's representatives on the agency's board[106]. In this case, a candidate nominated by the board is obliged to answer questions from MEPs. Two representatives of both the Commission and the European Parliament were also successfully included on the EMA's board[107]. In the case of EFSA, in turn, the Parliament suggested e.g. a formal hearing for the candidate for the post of agency director[108]. It was finally settled that a candidate for this position selected by the EFSA's board should make a statement before the Parliament and answer questions by MEPs[109].

Among the mechanisms which fall into the remit of the system's capabilities for holding agencies accountable for undertaken actions (*ex post*), the competencies of the European Parliament come to the fore as an authority that co-decides together with the Council on the shape of the EU budget which funds agencies under the provisions of Article 314 TFEU. The Parliament adopts the budget and controls its implementation (Article 318 TFEU) as well as gives a discharge to the Commission in respect of its implementation under Article 319 TFEU. Most EU regulatory agencies are funded solely with the amount specified in the EU general budget. Some of them, like ECHA, ESMA or EMA, also finance their activity with the fees that they collect. Relevant committees of the European Parliament: the Committee on Budgets and the Committee on Budgetary Control actively participate both in the creation of the financial plan for agencies as well as in monitoring the implementation of their budget. Every year, both of these committees, along with representatives of individual agencies, discuss specific issues related to annual budget expenditure at tripartite meetings. Existing

104 See Amendments Nos. 48, 52, and 53 of the European Parliament, OJ 1990 C 68/50.
105 Article 8(1) of Regulation (EC) No. 401/2009 of 23.4.2009 on the European Environment Agency (EEA) and the European Environment Information and Observation Network, OJ 2009, L 126/13.
106 See Amendments Nos. 85, 88, and 168 of the European Parliament, OJ 1991 C 183/145.
107 Article 64(1) and 65(1) of Regulation No. 726/2004. These provisions were introduced in the regulation modifying the functioning of EMA. They were not originally included. See Busuioc, *EU Agencies*, p. 122; Jacobs, 'EU Agencies', p. 207.
108 See Amendment No. 107 of the European Parliament, OJ 2002 C 53E/47.
109 Article 26(1) of Regulation No. 178/2002. More about these and other examples Chamon, *EU Agencies*, pp. 126–130.

funding and implementation of financial plans are subject to evaluation. The European Parliament is the only institution which can block agency funding[110]. Another control mechanism in this regard is the obligation of individual agencies to produce annual reports on their activities and related costs, which is provided for in most founding regulations (e.g. annual reports, annual activity reports, and hearings)[111].

Costs are one of the main flashpoints surrounding the debate on the agency system. Many MEPs explicitly call for reducing the number of agencies due to the costly expansion of this bureaucratic apparatus. They point to the possibility of merging some agencies as well as the option of moving them to a single location in order to increase savings in this area[112]. This position was reflected in the "Common Approach" which set out general guidelines on rational budgeting for individual agencies as well as the amount of fees that are payable to self-financed or partially self-financed agencies[113]. It was also emphasised that changes introduced in the legislative process should be reflected in increased funding for such bodies and also later as the catalogue of tasks of a particular agency broadens. The role of the European Parliament was stressed here as a legislative authority involved both in the process of modifying the Commission's proposals during agency creation and the process of shaping the EU budget[114].

Apart from the financial issues, which are significant for the creation and functioning of any agency, in the past decade or so the European Parliament has also gained influence on issues related to the composition of the main decision-making bodies within individual agencies. The Parliament can control their activities, as the Parliament's representatives are on some of the agencies' boards. It can also conduct "hearings" of candidates for the post of director as well as the directors themselves. The Parliament has also greatly strengthened its position in the EU institutional system by way of controlling budget implementation and monitoring the functioning of individual agencies by way of analysing their day-to-day performance. In this way it has become a special guarantor of the transparency and effectiveness of these technocratic bodies.

---

110 Bach, Fleischer, 'The Parliamentary Accountability', pp. 161, 167; Lord, 'The European Parliament', p. 914.

111 See Busuioc, *European Agencies*, pp. 116, 118 ff.

112 See e.g. Raport ECR Policy Group on Budgets, 'Efficiency and Subsidiarity. Guidelines on Reforming EU Budgetary Policy', https://ecrgroup.eu/files/ECR_BUDGETS_BROCHURE__english.pdf (20.3.2018), pp. 20, 22.

113 *Joint Statement and Common Approach*, 19.7.2012, p. 10.

114 *Ibid.*, p. 11; European Commission's Analytical Fiche No. 32, 2010, *Parliament Role*.

In addition to the abovementioned committees, which are involved in drawing up the EU budget, issues related to EU regulatory agencies are handled also by committees responsible for specific market sectors and coordination of a coherent position on the development of regulatory policies on behalf of the Parliament[115]. Specific agencies designate a contact person, who provides necessary information to a relevant parliamentary committee, to which the agency has been assigned, on the functioning of the agency represented and its specific regulatory intentions[116]. A more general position is taken by the Constitutional Affairs Committee, a body interested in maintaining institutional balance between EU institutions. This is a committee which, therefore, perceives agencies in the broader perspective of their constitutional status, directly related to the gradual strengthening of the EU executive[117].

Parliamentarians on these specialist committees have greater knowledge, which allows them to ask substantive questions during hearings of agencies' officials. The specialised knowledge of EU regulatory agencies, in this case, constitutes a significant barrier to broad participation in parliamentary debates[118]. On the other hand, it is worth emphasising the ties between agencies and parliamentary committees that involve professional support for committees coming from agency expertise. This includes various studies, reports, reviews, data collections, briefing notes and scientific opinions, which are important advisory instruments actively utilised by the European Parliament[119].

In addition to the obligations concerning information, involving e.g. advising, reporting and agency officials making appearances before MEPs, the Parliament also has the right to apply control measures which are used, not only in relation to agencies, but also to other institutions in the EU system. These instruments include written questions[120], reports, parliamentary visits,

115 For instance, The Committee on Transport and Tourism, the Committee on Environment, Public Health and Food Safety, and the Committee on Legal Affairs.

116 See Orator, *Möglichkeiten*, p. 423.

117 See Jacobs, *EU Agencies*, p. 203.

118 In this context, it is worth quoting the apt remark by Busuioc: "With regard to the lack of technical expertise in the agency's field of operation, the fact that high-level political forum are deficient in such knowledge is not surprising. To a large extent, it is to be expected, given the inherent tension between representation and expertise", Busuioc, *European Agencies*, p. 127.

119 Jacobs, *EU Agencies*, pp. 204, 210.

120 See an extensive analysis on this issue: N. Font, I. Pérez Durán, 'The European Parliament Oversight of EU Agencies through Written Questions', *Journal of European Public Policy*, Vol. 23, No. 9, 2016, pp. 1350 ff.

special committees and committees of inquiry. Interestingly, some of these mechanisms are explicitly used following the request of an agency itself[121]. This stems from the desire to increase the transparency of actions and to strengthen ties with the European Parliament[122]. That is because agencies also use the Parliament as a kind of hedge against the excessive influence of the Commission on their decision-making procedures and institutional structures.

A particularly controversial issue was the appointment of representatives of the European Parliament, or the legislature, to agencies' boards, which are a significant part of the European executive[123]. In this context, the Commission argued that the Parliament's objectivity in its performance of control tasks was undermined by direct participation in agency decision-making bodies[124]. Nonetheless, this measure can indeed be seen as a hedge against the Commission's dominance and part of a broader opening of agencies to the public. A similar role is played by the Parliament's inclusion in the process of selecting candidates for directorships of individual agencies. Public hearings during the Parliament's sessions and consultations on specific persons foster transparency and awareness of agency activities[125].

Regulatory agencies usually strive for good relations with the European Parliament. This is caused not only by the existential issues related to the Parliament's influence on the shape of agency finances, but also by the desire to strengthen their legitimacy to act. Institutional acceptance on the part of the Parliament plays an important role in building trust towards agencies as well as in shaping their position within the European administration.

Summing up the considerations so far, one can say that the European Parliament has the most rational attitude towards regulatory agencies among all EU institutions. Its pragmatic stance, which is referred to in this context, stems from a realistic assessment of the opportunities that agencies offer as well as of the costs that they generate[126].

---

121 Busuioc, *European Agencies*, pp. 120, 125, 129.
122 See Trauner, 'The European Parliament', p. 787.
123 The Parliament's representatives sit on boards of six agencies. See Chapter 1.
124 See Orator, *Möglichkeiten*, p. 414.
125 Jacobs, *EU Agencies*, pp. 203 ff.
126 Chamon, *EU Agencies*, p. 130.

d) Accountability to the Member States

Regardless of the control mechanisms used by the European Parliament, various mechanisms for making regulatory agencies accountable have been developed by the member states. Besides that, they also have a legitimising nature and according to Article 10(2) TEU they fall within the realm of safeguards which guarantee "democratic input". The leading role in this respect is played by the Council which is the authority involved in the process of establishing regulatory agencies. Its legislative role is mentioned, in this context, either by co-deciding together with the European Parliament or by shaping founding regulations of particular agencies on its own[127]. In this context, the Council has a great influence on the status of an agency and its tasks, which is best demonstrated by the heated debates which take place during the process of establishing specific powers of EBA, ESMA and EIOPA at the meetings of the ECOFIN Council[128].

The Council is also involved in the drafting of the EU budget and consequently has powers of control over agencies with regard to shaping and implementing their financial plans. It also receives annual reports on budgetary and financial management along with an opinion from the board of a particular agency[129]. As well as this, it has the greatest influence on agencies in the area of the common security and defence policy, which have not been included in this analysis. Those are explicitly called "Council agencies" and they are based on close intergovernmental cooperation under the auspices of the Council[130]. The agencies of the former I pillar, which are covered by these considerations, are subject to the Council's control primarily through information and reporting obligations. Most founding regulations make it necessary to submit annual reports and work programmes[131].

---

127 EUROPOL and CEPOL were created under independent decisions of the Council. See European Commission's Analytical Fiche No. 33, 2010, *Council Role*.

128 Among the particularly controversial competencies were the ones relating to emergency situations that were specified in Article 18(2) of the founding regulations of these agencies. The Council did not agree to empower the agencies to issue decisions which were in such cases directly addressed to financial institutions as well as modified the solution put forward by the Commission, proposing agency recommendations addressed to national financial supervision authorities. See Chapter 3. *Cf.* Kohtamäki, *Die Reform*, p. 107.

129 Analytical Fiche No. 33.

130 See also Busuioc, *European Agencies*, pp. 139 ff.

131 For instance FRA. More Orator, *Möglichkeiten*, p. 424.

An interesting example is EASA, the director of which, can be invited to report on its tasks not only by the European Parliament, but also by the Council[132]. Accountability to the Council was also explicitly stated in Regulation No. 1093/2010, which established EBA[133]. Also in this case, the agency chairperson, or his or her deputy, can be invited by both the Parliament and the Council to make a relevant statement[134]. An article specifying the agency's accountability to the Council and the Parliament was also included in the new regulation defining the functioning of Frontex[135]. The Frontex director can also be invited by the European Parliament and the Council to report on the realisation of his or her tasks[136]. In the case of ECHA, the Council appoints members of the board nominated by the member states[137]. The Council also appoints EFSA's board members in consultation with the European Parliament from a list drawn up by the Commission[138].

Another safeguard is the inclusion of national parliaments in the process of monitoring the activities of the European administration. Mechanisms of this kind function mostly in relation to agencies of the former II and III pillar, such as Europol or Eurojust (Article 12(c) TEU). As regards the agencies from the former I pillar, there are no such specified control mechanisms that could provide for the involvement of the parliaments of the member states in assessing and monitoring the work of individual agencies. Undoubtedly, an interesting solution could be to create "accountability networks" that would entail the coordinated involvement of committees from national parliaments and the European Parliament in the process of supervising technocratic agencies at the EU level[139].

The abovementioned safeguards, which involve control by the Parliament and the Council are external mechanisms. They are complemented by internalised instruments in the institutional structures of the agencies. This primarily entails control by the member states through the participation of representatives of national regulatory authorities in the work of the boards of the individual agencies. In some founding regulations, like in the regulation that established

132 Article 38(2) of Regulation No. 216/2008.
133 See Recital 10 and Article 3 of Regulation No. 1093/2010.
134 Article 50(1) of Regulation No. 1093/2010.
135 Article 7 of Regulation No. 2016/1624.
136 Article 68(2) of Regulation No. 2016/1624.
137 Article 79(1) of Regulation No. 1907/2006.
138 Article 25(1) of Regulation No. 178/2002.
139 See Orator, *Möglichkeiten*, p. 426.

EASA, it was explicitly stated that "Member States should be represented within the Management Board in order to control the functions of Agency effectively"[140].

Agency boards, due to their composition, which is dominated by national representatives, are perceived as a type of representation of national interests[141]. Consequently, they often become forums that allow for lobbying in favour of specific solutions, especially by representatives of the most powerful national regulatory authorities in particular market sectors[142]. Participation in the work of boards, which is enshrined in founding regulations, constitutes a formal expression of the influence of member states on the work of these bodies[143]. This is complemented by informal influence, as the member states fill expert positions in various scientific committees and consultative networks which function inside agencies themselves and under their auspices[144].

In connection with this, the literature also points to close links between boards and the Council which, while itself being representative of member states at the EU level, perceives the boards as an important platform on which to agree on common positions regarding significant market policies, as well as an important mechanism of integration[145]. In this context, it is worth mentioning the position of the European Commission in the early 2000s when it advocated shifting away from national representation in agency boards in favour of creating these bodies solely on the basis of expertise[146]. However, such a solution could mean abandoning mechanisms of "vertical accountability" which play a key role from the point of view of maintaining a balance in the EU administrative

---

140 See Recital 23 of Regulation No. 216/2008. See also J. Saurer, 'Supranational Governance and Networked Accountability Structures: Member State Oversight of EU Agencies', *European Journal of Risk Regulation*, Vol. 2, No. 1, 2011, pp. 53 ff.

141 Kohtamäki, 'Realizacja interesu narodowego', pp. 138–141.

142 See also Busuioc, 'European Agencies and Their Boards', pp. 724 ff.

143 Empirical studies conducted by Buess on selected agencies prove that in most cases (EMA being an exception) representatives of national ministries and regulatory agencies are bound by instructions. See M. Buess, 'European Union Agencies' Vertical Relationships with the Member States: Domestic Sources of Accountability?', *Journal of European Integration*, Vol. 36, No. 5, 2014, pp. 518, 520.

144 More M. Egeberg, J. Trondal, 'EU-level Agencies: New Executive Centre Formation or Vehicles for National Control?', *Journal of European Public Policy*, Vol. 18, No. 6, 2011, pp. 870 ff.

145 Saurer, 'Supranational Governance', p. 54.

146 The idea was already implemented, as mentioned in the first part of this study, in the case of EFSA. See Article 25 of Regulation No. 178/2002.

system and implementing democratic principles within the EU. Such "vertical accountability" also constitutes one of the most important "substitutes for direct input legitimacy"[147]. It is, therefore, particularly important especially since the agency system is complex in its nature and it is signified by a multitude of principals – hence the term "multi-principal" is used in reference to the nature of relationships between agencies as well as various entities which directly and indirectly delegate specific tasks and powers to them[148].

Such principals are, thus, primarily the EU authorities: the European Commission, the European Parliament and the Council. Relationships with them are horizontal and involve intra-EU mechanisms of control, supervision and accountability. Apart from that, the member states are also principals directly, and they share their powers in those sectors of the market that are vital for their national economies, such as trade in pharmaceuticals or financial supervision. Going beyond the EU system is, therefore, only possible within the vertical dimension of contacts with the member states – primarily through contacts with their regulatory authorities. This constitutes one of the foundations of the activity of agencies. It is also impossible not to notice that the participation of the member states in agency bodies is necessary due to the shifting of ever broader powers, which were previously the prerogative of national authorities or even non-existent in this form at all, to the integrated, EU-wide level[149]. This entails natural consequences related to the desire to influence the shape of final decisions which are not made at a national level.

Hence, there is no doubt that indirect delegation of such powers to the Commission's "satellite" regulatory agencies "taken out" of its administrative apparatus was a safer solution for the member states than transferring similar competences to the Commission itself and its Directorates-General[150]. Mechanisms of control and influence used directly by the member states within an agency's institutional structure constitute, thus, an important additional safeguard and undoubtedly contribute to the enhancement of the legitimacy of these bodies. The main element strengthening the empowerment of agencies is, indeed, providing them with the possibility of vertically influencing the decision-making

147 See Buess, 'European Union Agencies' Vertical Relationships', p. 510.

148 For example Scholten, *The Political Accountability*, p. 323.

149 Buess, 'European Union', p. 512.

150 See R.D. Kelemen, A.D. Tarrant, 'The Political Foundations of the Eurocracy', *West European Politics*, Vol. 34, No. 5, 2011, pp. 928 ff.

process. Separating agencies from the member states and leaving them only under horizontal supervision as part of their relationships with EU authorities could seriously weaken their position and undermine acceptance of their activities by national regulatory authorities. Contacts with them constitute the core activity of all EU regulatory agencies.

8 EU Regulatory Agencies' Legitimacy in Transition: Output *versus* Throughput

1. Searching for the Legitimate Bureaucracy

a) Procedural Justice within the Technocratic Structures

Establishing specific institutions in today's international reality involves lengthy debates, negotiations, and consultations aimed at finding compromise solutions. This stems from the voluntary nature of joining and creating institutions focused on cementing cooperation between countries in the international environment. Sovereign states, of their own free will, without consent and authorisation coming from other entities, undertake international activity in a binding manner and they bear responsibility for their actions. Therefore, states have so-called treaty capacity, the right to create active and passive legation, as well as the right to establish and join international organisations[1]. The institutional shape of an organisation is a result of the compromise between states that declare their will to cooperate in a specific organisational framework.

In this context, in academic literature "voluntary policy transfer" is identified. It is a result of the rivalry between individual participants. Specific organisational solutions are related to so-called procedural interests. This means that certain procedures and institutional frameworks serve to advance the national interests of specific players, e.g. countries with the status of world power and small and medium-sized countries[2]. The choice of an institutional solution in the form of the establishment of an independent, decentralised European Union agency is always a result of compromise not only between the member states, but also within the EU institutional structure.

Multilevel, technocratic, or – in other words – bureaucratic, cooperation between various entities takes place in almost every sector of the internal market. The main reason for institutionalising cooperation and deepening the integration process, which is increasingly expressed in the expansion of European bureaucratic structures, is a belief in the special capabilities of such bodies as EU regulatory agencies. It is assumed that, due to the involvement

---

1 See A. Łazowski, A. Zawidzka-Łojek, *Prawo międzynarodowe publiczne*, Warszawa 2011, pp. 125, 135, 145; M. Muszyński, *Państwo w prawie międzynarodowym. Istota, rodzaje, atrybuty*, Bielsko-Biała 2011, pp. 179 ff.; Bieleń, *Polityka*, pp. 97 ff.

2 See C. Roederer-Rynning, C. Daugbjerg, 'Power Learning', pp. 315–317.

of eminent specialists with particular expertise stemming from education and experience, these agencies are in a position to respond more effectively to the ever more rapidly changing market challenges being faced in today's world than elected bodies. This line of reasoning is complemented by a growing need to search for supranational, common solutions that approximate and coordinate national efforts. In the EU narrative, it is a natural consequence of an integration process, which is supposed to basically rule out acting on one's own without taking common values and ideals into account. Recognising certain values as paramount for the existence, survival and development of societies is a characteristic feature of liberal democracies. Transferring these ideals to the supranational level involves the need to take the distinct character of such integrated structures into account[3].

Observing the evolution of the contemporary political systems, Wojciech Sadurski developed the concept of "pure procedural democracy" in reference to John Rawls's concept of "pure procedural justice"[4]. According to Sadurski, there can be no assurance that values which are a component of a specific democratic procedure, understood primarily as a specific set of norms, will, indeed, be realised within the functioning of a particular political system[5]. This assertion is particularly pertinent in the context of the evolution of the European bureaucracy. It is meant to be technocratic, i.e. expert in the modern sense, and, therefore, it obtains empowerment on the basis of the measurable effects of its actions – in a way it balances democratic electoral mechanisms. To quote the American researcher Bruce Gilley, who has examined the issue of legitimacy of bureaucratic bodies for years, we can see democracy and technocracy as "distinctive approaches to justice that need to be protected from the domination of the other"[6].

---

3 See also C. Harlow, R. Rawlings, *Process and Procedure in EU Administration*, Oxford/Portland 2014, pp. 93–96, 265.

4 See M. Gustafsson, 'On Rawls's Distinction between Perfect and Imperfect Procedural Justice', *Philosophy of the Social Sciences*, Vol. 34, No. 2, 2004, pp. 300 ff.

5 See W. Sadurski, 'Law's Legitimacy and "Democracy-Plus"', *Oxford Journal of Legal Studies*, Vol. 26, No. 2, 2006, p. 379.

6 B. Gilley, 'Technocracy and Democracy as Spheres of Justice in Public Policy', *Policy Sciences*, Vol. 50, No. 1, 2017, pp. 9 ff. Similarly Christina Ribbhagen: "[...] The tensions between technocracy and democracy should be understood as the tension between a technocratic and a democratic mode of reasoning or justification", *Technocracy within Representative Democracy. Technocratic Reasoning and Justification among Bureaucrats and Politicians*, Ph.D. Thesis, University of Gothenburg. Department of Political Science, February 2013, pp. 16 ff.

The belief in the technocratic legitimacy of administrative authorities has its source in the idea of separating politics from administration that originates from American administration science[7]. This idea underwent a gradual transformation when it was realised that the basic activities of bureaucratic administrative authorities involve a specific allocation of values and redistribution of certain goods. The technical, or technocratic, dimension of this activity is, therefore, contrary to the original concept of "government by independent experts", as well as often being political in nature. As administrative structures expanded rapidly in the twentieth century, it turned out that public administration not only acts as an executor of legislation adopted by elected legislative bodies, but it also increasingly obtains "discretionary power". This power should be understood as direct influence on the implementation of certain normative acts in a particular way or altering their wording through specific administrative activities. Therefore, "bureaucracy helps to define the will of the state" and thus becomes a political actor[8]. While these developments are to a greater or lesser degree acceptable in frameworks within the state, they raise significant controversies at the supranational dimension.

b) Technocracy *versus* Democracy

The fundamental question that arises in this context is whether administrative processes, being the opposite of democratic processes, can shape public policy also in the pan-European dimension. For many decades, the answer to this question has been affirmative. We can speak about a particular acceleration in the last twenty years or so, when the agency system became a permanent component of the institutional landscape. A question can be asked, therefore, concerning what the main element legitimising the existence and activity of the technocratic EU bureaucracy is. Referring to the Weberian concept in the case of technocratic legitimacy, i.e. one that focuses on the outcomes and performance of administrative authorities, which has been discussed in the second part of this monograph, we should speak of charismatic empowerment[9]. Acceptance of bureaucratic

7 W. Wilson, 'The Study of Public Administration', *Political Science Quarterly*, Vol. 2, No. 2, 1887, pp. 197 ff. See also J. Supernat, 'Teoria polityki biurokratycznej', in: J. Supernat (ed.), *Między tradycją a przyszłością w nauce prawa administracyjnego*, Wrocław 2009, pp. 689 ff.

8 *Ibid.*, p. 691.

9 See E. Ongaro, 'Administrative Reforms in the European Commission and the Neo-Weberian Model', in: Bauer, Trondal (ed.), *The Palgrave Handbook*, pp. 108 ff.

activities, including those of the "Eurocracy" that are transferred to the supranational level, results directly from recognition which is based on confidence and belief in the special knowledge as well as the predispositions of officials with particular rulemaking prerogatives. They are not only executors of orders within increasingly longer "chains of delegation" in extensive, integrated administrative systems. Referring to the thought which Woodrow Wilson expressed more than one hundred years ago, "the administrator should have, and does have, a will of his own in the choice of means for accomplishing his work. He is not and ought not to be a mere passive instrument"[10].

The bureaucratic machine appears in the considerations of mid-twentieth century U.S. administration theorists as an embodiment of the will of the state. Researchers such as Dwight Waldo, Robert K. Merton or William H. Whyte asked questions e.g. about justifying bureaucratic behaviour and the way in which the process of redistributing power from elected authorities to administrative authorities in specific organisational structures takes place[11]. The basic element justifying the existence and functioning of administration, which is directly identified with bureaucracy, is belief in its important public mission. It is, therefore, assumed that administrative bodies pursue the public interest. Their activity is supposed to be underpinned by law enacted by the legislature.

Delegation of powers is perceived as a processual and relational phenomenon. This means that every bureaucracy should be seen through the prism of a particular organisational structure. What matters is relationships of dependence, cooperation and subordination between individual players operating within this structure. In the case of the EU agency system, we should not only think about the complex relationships with administrative authorities in the member states, as well as control mechanisms exercised by the European Parliament and the Council, but above all about the agencies' special dependence on the European Commission. Institutions such as national and European regulatory agencies are also marked by high developmental dynamics, which mean that their place and status in a particular administrative system are not static. They change not only in a formal manner, i.e. through modifications in specific legal acts defining the normative framework for powers and the responsibilities of a particular body,

10 Wilson, 'The Study', p. 212. More B.J. Cook, *Bureaucracy and Self-Government. Reconsidering the Role of Public Administration in American Politics*, Baltimore/London 1996, pp. 91 ff.

11 For an overview of their theories see Supernat, 'Teoria polityki', pp. 692–695.

but also through the evolution of informal behaviours that underpin the functioning of such entities[12].

It is, therefore, emphasised in studies of bureaucracy that the activities of such bodies are not only determined by law. Irrespective of the interpretation of the EU Court of Justice in the *Meroni* and *Short selling* cases, there is a common view that a certain degree of discretion is necessary for the administration to function effectively. This means that the informal element plays a complementary role in relation to the normative framework. However, as Eduardo Chiti rightly points out, "the discretionary nature of the action carried out by the new (post-crisis) EU administrations is not openly recognised, but somehow hidden or camouflaged, as a consequence of a restrictive interpretation of the constitutional framework governing the adoption of EU administrative measures"[13]. In his view, in such a situation, there can be no effectiveness or efficiency of regulatory agencies. The lack of official recognition of their competencies which are often directly related to political choices and making actual decisions on specific solutions results in a weakening of the output-oriented legitimacy of regulatory agencies. They are not, and in the current stage of European integration they cannot be, merely technical advisory bodies. Besides, there is no way to determine the clear boundaries between technical and political decisions, or to clearly separate what can be classified as policy-making from technical measures[14].

Adopting the interpretation by James Q. Wilson, one of the leading U.S. specialists in studies of public administration, the primary motive for bureaucratic activities is to achieve the objectives that have been set out. These objectives are not always explicitly determined by law. They are often of a political nature and they are also determined by current events which evoke specific responses from the administrative authorities. Objectives are also defined by the expectations of different groups of stakeholders outside a particular administrative system as well as by entities coexisting in this system. Thus, it involves various recipients of decisions and actions developed by specific bureaucratic bodies. In the case of EU regulatory agencies, there is a variety of such "recipients": from EU institutions and authorities in the member states to different private and

12 See J. Pierre, B.G. Peters, 'From a Club to a Bureaucracy: JAA, EASA, and European Aviation Regulation', *Journal of European Public Policy*, Vol. 16, No. 3, 2009, pp. 338–343.

13 Chiti, 'In the Aftermath of the Crisis', p. 313.

14 See *ibid.*, p. 314.

public actors operating in a particular sector of the market. Objectives are, thus, modified by the needs and interests of various internal and external entities[15].

We can speak of a sort of feedback in this context. On the one hand, recipients of decisions issued by public institutions expect these bodies to demonstrate a high level of credibility, which is based on expertise and professionalism. They should also ensure that clear relationships exist between all market participants, and guarantee opportunities for effective business decision-making, while maintaining low transaction costs[16]. On the other hand, an essential condition for the survival and development of technocratic institutions such as EU regulatory agencies is the desire to legitimise their activities by market participants. In this case, the pillar of legitimacy obtained is the acceptance and recognition of actions and decisions of public administration authorities, even if they are informal and legally non-binding. A good example is the aviation market and opinions issued by EASA. According to Jon Pierre and B. Guy Peters, "compliance in this context refers to accepting or submitting to rules less because of potential sanction but more as a result of legitimacy of the institution and the appropriateness of the rules"[17]. There is a similar case with agencies such as EMA, EFSA, ECHA or EBA. Their narrow specialisation determines a special degree of initiation, both among the recipients of the actions of these agencies and within the bureaucratic apparatus of the agency in particular. Mutual trust between a public institution and the recipient of a decision is important. This issue takes on even greater importance in complex structures, where recipients operate transnationally and public institutions are international or even supranational. In this case, regulatory capacity is much more than a catalogue of normatively regulated powers. The formal-legal authority of a bureaucratic institution is strengthened as part of interactions with other entities. The relational dimension, therefore, has a significant legitimising importance[18].

---

15 See J.Q. Wilson, *Bureaucracy: What Government Agencies Do and Why They Do It*, New York 2000, pp. 14 ff.; D.A. Hyman, W.E. Kovacic, 'Why Who Does What Matters: Governmental Design and Agency Performance', *George Washington Law Review*, Vol. 82, No. 5, 2014, pp. 1463 ff. In the context of regulatory agencies, see S. Wilks, I. Bartle, 'The Unanticipated Consequences of Creating Independent Competition Agencies', in: M. Thatcher, A. Stone Sweet (ed.), *The Politics of Delegation*, London 2003, p. 148.

16 D.C. North, *Institutions, Institutional Change and Economic Performance*, Cambridge 1990, pp. 50–58. See also Ribbhagen, *Technocracy*, pp. 20 ff.

17 J. Pierre, B.G. Peters, 'From a Club', pp. 340 ff.

18 *Ibid.*

Concerns among observers increase when informal elements related to the functioning of these very narrow groups of those who are "initiated" become ever more important in the face of weakening mechanisms of democratic control[19]. The crisis that affected the global financial markets in 2008–2010 triggered accurate assertions about a drift away from democratic procedures towards "more appropriate", "more efficient", theoretically independent expert panels[20]. Rationalisation of decision making, which stems directly from the belief in "administrative rationality", is mentioned in this context[21] and it is considered to be a pan-European phenomenon. It turns out that, even as the memory of the effects of the turmoil in the financial markets slowly fades away, its unfading echo is a tendency to search for technocratic solutions. Output, i.e. the efficiency, effectiveness, or functionality of specific institutional and normative solutions, is becoming the main mechanism legitimising the existence of executive authorities[22].

The last decade is clearly marked by the significant strengthening of the role of the executive at the expense of the other two authorities – the legislature and the judiciary. Expert governments in Greece and Italy, EU-wide systemic solutions such as ESFS or the Banking Union, prove that technocracy is doing better and better, gaining ever stronger support at the level of European decision-makers[23]. On the other hand, public confidence in supranational bodies has significantly

19 *Cf.* Chiti, 'In the Aftermath of the Crisis', pp. 313 ff.; S. Alonso, ' "You Can Vote but You Cannot Choose": Democracy and the Sovereign Debt Crisis in the Eurozone', *Estudio Working Paper*, No. 282, 2014, pp. 3–6.

20 See A. Ruser, 'Der (in)diskrete Charme der Technokratie. Wirtschaftskrisen, Staatskrisen und die Entdemokratisierung von Entscheidungsstrukturen', in: M. Lehmann, M. Tyrell (ed.), *Komplexe Freiheit. Wie ist die Demokratie möglich?*, Wiesbaden 2017, pp. 203 ff.

21 More Ruser, 'By the Markets', p. 85; M.A. Centeno, 'The New Leviathan: The Dynamics and Limits of Technocracy', *Theory and Society*, Vol. 22, No. 3, 1993, p. 308; C. Harlow, R. Rawlings, *Process*, p. 39.

22 More extensively about the role of regulatory agencies in crisis situations, see J. Jordana *et al.*, 'European Transboundary Crises and EU Agencies: Examining Board Members' Attitudes Towards Crisis Involvement', *IBEI Working Papers*, No. 55, 2018, pp. 2 ff.

23 "[…] The EU and its political actors have rapidly identified in the EU administrative machinery and instrument of integration, or at least, an instrument to avoid disintegration", Chiti, 'In the Aftermath of the Crisis', p. 312. See also Ongaro, 'Administrative Reforms', p. 113; C. Hillgruber, *Weniger ist mehr – Plädoyer für eine Begrenzung der Kompetenzen der EU zwecks Wiederherstellung einer föderalen Balance*, in: S. Kadelbach (ed.), *Die Europäische Union am Scheideweg: mehr oder weniger Europa?*, Baden-Baden 2015, pp. 29 ff.

decreased in the face of transboundary crises. One of the reasons, indeed, was that advisory expert bodies shaped controversial political solutions designed to break the economic and financial deadlock at a great distance from citizens. Voices questioning the legitimacy of transferring rulemaking powers to the EU level in order to introduce solutions aimed at restoring financial stability in the European markets were clearly heard in numerous member states. Often the grounds for raising objections varied diametrically depending on the country. Germany opposed the creation of "packages of anti-crisis measures" that were supposed to rescue the weakest countries in the Monetary Union which were at risk of bankruptcy, including, above all, Greece. The latter, in turn, objected to the tough conditions under which the member states decided to extend their financial assistance for it in 2010[24].

Belief in free-market mechanisms, and the progressive deregulation which has stemmed from it, has led to a weakening of the role of the member states as guarantors of financial stability, considered as a public good that is of importance for national economies. The financial crisis of recent years, thus, became the proverbial "zero hour" which determined a "new opening" when it comes to regulatory policy in many sectors of the market, not only the financial sector[25]. This development has become an important incentive to strengthen the role of the European Commission and its satellite system in the form of regulatory agencies, the powers of which have hardly been reduced at all or, indeed, progressively decentralised, as the European nomenclature would suggest[26]. On the contrary, what is actually taking place is a progressive institutionalisation and entrenchment of this system.

---

24 See Ruser, 'Der (in)diskrete Charme', p. 212; I. Sánchez-Cuenca, 'From a Deficit of Democracy to a Technocratic Order. The Postcrisis Debate on Europe', *Annual Review of Political Science*, Vol. 20, 2017, pp. 352 ff.

25 See A. Boin *et al.*, 'Managing Tranboundary Crises: The Emergence of European Union Capacity', *Journal of Contingencies and Crisis Management*, Vol. 22, No. 3, 2014, pp. 131 ff.

26 See also Ruser, 'By the Markets', p. 87; M. Ferrera, 'Social Europe and Its Components in the Midst of the Crisis: A Conclusion', *West European Politics*, Vol. 37, No. 4, 2014, pp. 834, 836; J. Pollak, S. Puntscher Riekmann, 'European Administration: Centralisation and Fragmentation as Means of Polity-Building?', in: Curtin, Egeberg (ed.), *Towards*, pp. 137–140.

2. Legitimising Technocracy through Technocratic Control

a) Accountability to the European Commission

Already back in the late 1980s it was predicted that technocracy would become "a new type of organisational control structure" and rapidly developing administrative systems would undergo "polarisation into 'expert' and 'non-expert' sectors"[27]. This development has shifted from the individual member states to the level of the European system. We see a process of gradual interpenetration of the tasks of state and European bureaucratic authorities in the area of transposition, administration and public enforcement of law. The central role in this process is played by government officials, external agencies and non-governmental organisations[28]. EU regulatory agencies have become a missing element, which, in the process of the rapidly growing role of European-level legislation, was supposed to fill "the institutional vacuum" between the shared, and member-state, levels of government[29].

A question arises in this context, which has for years accompanied the evolution of the European multilevel governance system: who watches over the "watchdogs"?[30] The "watchdogs" are, indeed, those technocratic bodies that increasingly determine the process of the transposition of the law. They have significant obligations with regard to control, supervision, monitoring and coordination. Nonetheless, who is their main "controller"? The answer to this question is simple, but controversial in a way, and it was pointed out several years ago by David Kelemen, on the eve of the dynamic expansion of the European agency system. The actual controller and "principal" is also a technocratic body with questionable democratic legitimacy – the European Commission[31]. This is

27 See B.H. Burris, 'Technocratic Organization and Control', *Organization Studies*, Vol. 10, No. 1, 1989, pp. 2 ff. In this study, the terms technocracy and bureaucracy are used synonymously. However, some researchers consider technocrats as representatives of the "expert sector" of bureaucracy understood as the entire administrative system. See Centeno, 'The New Leviathan', p. 310.

28 See Ferrera, 'Social Europe', p. 834; Hyman, Kovacic, 'Why', p. 1451.

29 More J. Trondal, *An Emergent European Executive Order*, New York 2010, p. 129; D.R. Kelemen, *The Rules of Federalism: Institutions and Regulatory Politics in the EU and Beyond*, Cambridge/Massachusetts 2004, pp. 171 ff.

30 R. Dehousse, 'Misfits: EU Law and the Transformation of European Governance', *Jean Monnet Working Paper*, No. 2, 2002.

31 Kelemen, 'The Politics', pp. 95, 98; M. Scholten, M. van Rijsbergen, 'The Limits of Agencification in the European Union', *German Law Journal*, Vol. 15, No. 7, 2014,

confirmed by numerous empirical studies that point to many informal opportunities for the Commission to influence agencies, which are treated by individual DGs as an administrative system that may have the nature of a satellite in the apparatus of the Commission itself, but it is also an important supplement of this body[32]. While in EU rhetoric, relations between the Commission and the agencies are perceived through the prism of their partnership[33], in practice we should, instead talk about a parental relationship, where the role of a parent who scolds a disobedient child when it is necessary is played by the European Commission[34]. However, this state of affairs, which is confirmed by numerous studies in the fields of management and political science, does not correspond to the interpretation put forward by lawyers[35]. They refer to Article 298(1) TFEU and provisions in individual founding regulations, stressing the need to ensure independent European administration. The institutional and functional autonomy of agencies would rule out direct control by the Commission[36].

Many measures applied by the Commission are explicitly specified in founding regulations, such as the presence of the Commission's representatives on boards of individual agencies, its influence on the selection of agency directors or the necessity for opinions and other soft law acts drafted by agencies to be approved by the Commission. Instruments guaranteed normatively are also developed by the Commission in informal ways, e.g. by exerting influence on the boards'

p. 1225. A different view is taken by the authors of an empirical analysis of administrative legitimacy of EU institutions, including the Commission. In their opinion, efforts to include the contributions of various social groups in the European decision-making process as well as the work of the Commission, offset the weaknesses of input-oriented legitimacy. See Z. Murdoch *et al.*, 'Administrative Legitimacy and the Democratic Deficit of the European Union', *Journal of European Public Policy*, Vol. 25, No. 3, 2018, pp. 389 ff.

32 For example Groenleer, *The Autonomy*, pp. 23 ff.; Busuioc, *European Agencies*, p. 161; Font, 'Institutional Rules', pp. 2 ff. See also Jarle Trondal's studies into the intensity of contacts between agencies and individual DGs. They show that these interactions are quite frequent, particularly with the DG from the relevant market sector, Trondal, *An Emergent*, pp. 138, 158.

33 See European Commission's Analytical Fiche No. 31 (*Commission Role*), 2010.

34 N.M. Vestlund, 'Exploring the EU Commission-Agency Relationship: Partnership or Parenthood?', in: Bauer, Trondal (ed.), *The Palgrave Handbook*, pp. 349 ff.

35 For instance M. Egeberg *et al.*, 'The Quest for Order: Unravelling the Relationship between the European Commission and European Union Agencies', *Journal of European Public Policy*, Vol. 22, No. 5, pp. 611 ff.

36 See Weißgärber, *Die Legitimation*, p. 296.

decision-making processes, during discussions preceding final votes, which are designed to "thrash out" compromise positions[37]. Not without importance is also the Commission's influence on establishing the budget and the expenditure allocated to agencies[38]. This raises some concerns about their dependence on the Commission.

In the case of the legitimacy of regulatory agencies in the EU institutional system, this state of affairs would undermine their full empowerment. That is because the legitimacy of EU agencies is supposed to stem from their independence from EU institutions, including the Commission[39]. Empirical studies indicate, however, "that the Commission has more actual control over agencies than can be inferred from formal provisions"[40]. This view is also shared by Michelle Everson and Christian Joerges, specialists who have long analysed the European agency system. According to them, "European agencies are far from being independent instances. [...] They remain firmly ensconced within the institutional umbrella of the Commission"[41]. This is also confirmed by the political actions of particular presidents of the Commission, including Barroso, who aimed to "presidentialise" and coordinate the activities of European bureaucracy more intensively under the "political guidance" provided by the Commission[42]. This vision of a strong European Commission as the main decision-making body reflected the neofunctionalist concepts which lay at the foundation of the European integration process[43]. What can be said, therefore, is that the Commission has been, and remains, the main political actor in relations with EU regulatory agencies[44].

---

37 Font, 'Institutional Rules', pp. 9 ff.

38 Busuioc, *European Agencies*, p. 158; Trondal, *An Emergent*, p. 157.

39 See Trondal, *An Emergent*, p. 133; M. Szapiro, 'The Framework for European Regulatory Agencies: A Balance between Accountability and Autonomy', Paper Presented at the 3rd ECPR Conference, 8–11.9.2005, p. 4.

40 Egeberg *et al.*, 'EU Subordinated', p. 330.

41 M. Everson, C. Joerges, 'Re-Conceptualising Europeanisation as a Public Law of Collisions: Comitology, Agencies and an Interactive Public Adjudication', in: H.C.H. Hofmann, A.H. Türk (ed.), *EU Administrative Governance*, Cheltenham/Northampton 2006, p. 529.

42 See Trondal, *An Emergent*, p. 149; S. Kurpas *et al.*, 'The European Commission after Enlargement: Does More Add Up to Less?', *CEPS Special Report*, February 2008, p. 32.

43 See also P. Craig, 'Integration, Democracy and Legitimacy', in: P. Craig, G. de Búrca (ed.), *The Evolution of EU Law*, Oxford 2013, pp. 14 ff.

44 "Most EU agencies are vertically specialised outside the Commission, although they may be *de facto* integral components of the Commission when measured by their

The functioning of the Commission itself and its evolution is still best illustrated by its influence with regard to the European administrative space. The only concern in this area should be the effectiveness and the efficiency of administrative authorities, in contrast with the "political space". The Commission, however, performs both administrative and political tasks[45]. The latter sphere of activity has been reduced, in comparison to the administrative and supervisory activity as European integration has advanced, but it has not disappeared. This is best illustrated by the Commission's role e.g. in the shaping of the EU budget[46]. The Commission has also undergone a transformation when it comes to its character as an institution in common structures. In the 1950s, it was a typical example of a technocratic body in an international organisation. Today, it is the principal executive body of the European Union similar in its organisational structure and tasks to nation state authorities[47]. This does not, however, change its technocratic nature. The European administrative system is relatively young in comparison to its national counterparts. As it is still *in statu nascendi*, the relationships between its components are not yet fully developed[48].

b) The Scope of the European Commission's Supervision over EU Regulatory Agencies

On account of this, the issues of relations between EU regulatory agencies and the Commission are a subject of research and discussion. Lawyers disagree about the scope of supervision over regulatory agencies that has been assigned to the Commission in the Treaties. There is no doubt that, according to Article 17(1) TEU, the Commission is the central authority in the EU administrative system. According to the wording of this provision, the Commission should (1) "ensure the application of the Treaties, and of measures adopted by the institutions

---

activity and by actors' perceptions"; "EU agencies are actually less under the control of national governments and more under the control of the Commission", Egeberg *et al.*, 'The Quest', pp. 611, 613.

45 The establishment of the agency system as such was also an attempt to "depoliticise" the Commission. See Kelemen, Tarrant, 'The Political Foundations', p. 924.

46 See also M. Cini, 'The European Commission – Politics and Administration', in: Bauer, Trondal (ed.), *The Palgrave Handbook*, pp. 130–138.

47 See Vestlund, 'Exploring', p. 350; Curtin, Egeberg, 'Tradition', pp. 4–13. Lawyers, however, emphasise only a conditional similarity between the European Commission and the government in a state system. See Ruffert, 'Die neue Unabhängigkeit', p. 405; Craig, 'Integration', p. 15.

48 Similarly Chiti, 'In the Aftermath of the Crisis', p. 313.

pursuant to them", (2) "oversee the application of Union law under the control of the CJEU" and (3) "exercise coordinating, executive and management functions, as laid down in the Treaties". Article 17(1) TEU is recognised as a guarantee of general management, supervisory and control competencies assigned to the European Commission.

In German-language legal literature, the term "general Union supervision" (Germ. *allgemeine Unionsaufsicht*) appears in this context. However, according to most German specialists, the Commission's general control power over regulatory agencies follows neither from the wording of Article 17(1) TEU nor the principle of institutional balance[49]. Thus, the Commission does not formally have, under primary law, the competence to exercise "professional supervision" (Germ. *Fachaufsicht*) over these bodies. This term should be understood as the ability of the Commission to formulate direct, substantive guidelines and recommendations with respect to the specific actions and soft law acts drafted by agencies[50]. Such powers could follow from specific norms in founding regulations, but usually – even in the case of agencies as powerful as ESAs – such direct provisions are missing[51]. Regardless of the lack of formal rules when it comes to professional supervision of agencies, in practice the Commission is, indeed, the main body in the process of sectoral rulemaking.

Empirical studies carried out by Christoph Ossege prove that in the case of agencies such as ECHA, EMA and EFSA, we can speak of a medium or low degree of rulemaking autonomy. While in most cases the Commission approves strictly scientific documents drafted by research committees and panels of individual agencies without much alteration[52], the issuing of new procedures, the codification of a particular sector or interpreting of existing norms are elaborated by agencies in close cooperation with the Commission. The guiding idea of the European regulatory bureaucracy is to coordinate the efforts of the institutions involved. Hence, it is a natural mechanism used by the Commission to consult with experts from the agency committees of a scientific nature (e.g.: in

---

49 See Augsberg, 'Agencification', p. 136; M. Führ, '§ 58 Chemikalienrecht', in: D. Ehlers *et al.* (ed.), *Besonderes Verwaltungsrecht*, Bd. 2, Heidelberg 2013, p. 1018.

50 Ruffert, 'Verselbständigte Verwaltungseinheiten', p. 447; M. van Rijsbergen, 'On the Enforceability of EU Agencies' Soft Law at the National Level: The Case of the European Securities and Markets Authority', *Utrecht Law Review*, Vol. 10, No. 5, 2014, p. 117.

51 See Ruffert, 'Die Unabhängigkeit', p. 406; Hermes, 'Legitimationsprobleme', p. 463; Lübbe-Wolff, 'Europäisches und nationales Verwaltungsrecht', p. 270.

52 See Gaitanides, 'Kontrolle', p. 216; Wittinger, 'Europäische Satelliten', p. 625.

EFSA: Panel on Genetically Modified Organisms, GMO; in EMA: Committee for Medicinal Products for Human Use, CHMP) and search for common positions[53].

Interventions are of a procedural nature. They do not restrict the freedom of expert bodies to formulate drafts requiring expertise. Nonetheless, they influence the final normative shape of the resulting documents. According to the opinions of officials from agencies such as EFSA, EMA or ECHA, these bodies often operate just like internal organisational units in the Commission's administrative apparatus[54]. In most cases, agencies voluntarily fall within the Commission's legislative policy domain, often asking their "parent" DG for a legal interpretation of a particular situation in advance. This attachment to the Commission's legal advice is particularly strong in the first years of an agency's operation, i.e. before it reaches maturity and confidence in formulating its own judgments in the area of specific regulatory policies. Moreover, the agency system includes institutions with greater authority and consequently greater regulatory autonomy, like EFSA, which has over the years established its position as a body with a high degree of professionalism as well as agencies which are in the process of building such a position, like ECHA[55].

Primary law, in the abovementioned Article 17(1) sentence 2 and 3 TEU, establishes the role of the European Commission as the "guardian of the Treaties". As a rule, it is assumed in legal doctrine that this provision should be understood broadly, i.e. recognised as ensuring so-called legal supervision (Germ. *Rechtsaufsicht*) over regulatory agencies as well[56]. Thus, in this interpretation legal supervision results directly from primary law and does not require additional norms in founding regulations. Normative safeguards formulated explicitly in founding regulations only give a specific form to this Treaty formula. Such obligations, derived from founding regulations, consist of drafting annual reports and reports on the execution of the budget[57]. Formal mechanisms are complemented with informal instruments to ensure coherent European rulemaking, such as regular meetings between representatives of dedicated

---

53 Ossege, *European Regulatory Agencies*, pp. 91, 93, 95.

54 Egeberg *et al.*, 'The Quest', p. 611.

55 See also Ossege, *European Regulatory Agencies*, pp. 91 ff.

56 See Koch, *Externalisierungspolitik*, pp. 101, 103, 135; Ruffert, 'Die Unabhängigkeit', p. 406.

57 "[The] agencies must follow the Commission's budgetary and financing provisions as well as adept the staff regulations of Officials of the European Communities", Vestlund, 'Exploring', p. 353.

organisational units dealing with legal tasks and legal staff from "partner" DGs or directly the European Commission's Legal Service[58].

Despite this state of affairs, which confirms that the Commission exercises legal supervision over regulatory agencies, there are voices saying that this is inadmissible from the point of view of a formal interpretation of primary law. Kirstin Weißgärber argues in this context that Article 17(1) sentence 2 TEU is not a norm that assigns specific powers to the Commission (Germ. *Befugniszuweisungsnorm*). This provision only assigns general groups of tasks to the Commission (Germ. *Aufgabenzuweisungsnorm*). Therefore, the admissibility of legal supervision should also depend on additional provisions in founding regulations authorising such supervision. According to Weißgärber, the Commission, EU regulatory agencies and regulatory authorities in the member states are equal partners with no relationship of dependence or subordination towards one another[59]. While this interpretation can be attractive from the point of view of a restrictive linguistic interpretation of Article 17(1) TEU, it has little in common with reality. Practical studies confirm a close and strong relationship between the Commission and agencies, which is, as mentioned above, more like a "parent/child" relationship than a "partner" relationship. It involves legal supervision, irrespective of how the particular powers, in this respect, are specified in the founding regulations. The actual state of affairs regarding the European Commission's relationship with regulatory agencies thus fits in with the idea of centralising the EU's executive power, which has been developed for at least two decades[60].

This does not change the fact that agencies function in an environment marked by complex dependencies that are hardly comparable with the hierarchical subordination seen in a nation-state administrative system. Therefore, an important element of the functioning of agencies in EU institutional structures is mutual trust. Due to their professionalism and authority, some agencies enjoy high legitimacy for their activities in European structures[61]. In such cases, the

---

58 See Ossege, *European Regulatory Agencies*, p. 98. More than eighty per cent of the surveyed officials from EU regulatory agencies confirm that these bodies operate on the foundation of regular meetings with the Commission's representatives which deal with the current agenda, the agency budget, or work plans. See Egeberg *et al.*, 'The Quest', p. 622.

59 Weißgärber, *Die Legitimation*, pp. 296, 298.

60 See Egeberg *et al.*, 'The Quest', pp. 619–624, Vestlund, 'Exploring', p. 361.

61 See also A. Nowicka, 'Metoda zarządzania przez rezultaty w agencjach UE jako sposób efektywnego zarządzania publicznego', in: M. Sadowski, P. Szymaniec (ed.), *Prace z*

Commission is less frequently a party that directly controls or intervenes in the wording of specific documents created by a particular regulatory body. Quoting a remark of one of the EFSA officials surveyed, it can be said that while this agency formally does not have significant powers, in practice, as a result of the prestige it enjoys, it is strong and it relieves the Commission, in numerous cases, of the task of preparing guidelines which then are approved without any major reservations or amendments[62].

3. Administrative Culture as a Form of the "Throughput" Legitimacy

An interesting legitimising element, which is rarely noticed in academic literature, is the distinct administrative style of a particular regulatory agency which is a result of its "anchoring" in a selected sector of the internal market[63]. Administrative style should be understood as a component of an administrative culture practised by a particular public institution. Administrative culture can be seen as a procedural framework, an institutional structure of administrative authorities and mechanisms of information flow between them[64]. Thus, it forms part of the broader culture of a particular social group – alongside its legal and economic dimension. The administrative culture of the integrated EU institutional structures exhibits many characteristic features seen not only in administrative cultures of the individual member states, but also in other large international organisations. It is not simply a conglomerate resulting from the combination of many national models.

Over the decades of progressing European integration, something of a model of a specific "legal community" (Germ. *Rechtsgemeinschaft*) has been established which, apart from adopting features characteristic for the administrative

---

teorii i historii prawa oraz administracji publicznej, Wrocław 2012, pp. 124 ff.; Gabbi, 'Independent', pp. 216 ff.

62 "Formally, we are extremely weak. In practice, however, we are stronger, since we build on this trust – in the end the Commission is happy if they do not have to care of the issue", Ossege, *European Regulatory Agencies*, p. 100.

63 An analysis of this issue in a comparative approach has so far only been conducted by C. Knill, S. Grohs, 'Administrative Styles of EU Institutions', in: Bauer, Trondal (ed.), *The Palgrave Handbook*, pp. 93 ff.

64 See K.-P. Sommermann, 'Die Entwicklung europäischer Verwaltungskultur', in: M. J. Montoro Chiner *et al.*, *Les administracions en perspectiva europea*, Barcelona 2012, pp. 58 ff.

systems of the individual member states, has also managed to develop its own procedures, or institutional models[65]. The prime example are the EU regulatory agencies, which have actively participated in the formulation of the EU administrative culture for at least two decades. It is not, however, a monolith, it consists of many components, which include the administrative styles of institutions that form a particular bureaucratic apparatus. In depth analyses of national-level public administration find that individual public administration authorities, depending on the specific sector of the economy, are seen to develop their own *esprit de corps*[66]. This observation can also be applied to EU regulatory agencies, even the European Commission itself, which, "as the key executive institution of the EU", has not developed a single, coherent administrative style[67].

Administrative styles are "standard operating procedures of administrative behaviour and decision making"[68]. In the case of EU institutions, due to the regulatory nature of EU policies, three factors determining the style of a particular EU institution can be identified. The first thing which is considered is whether its actions are anticipative or reactive[69]. In the case of the regulatory agencies discussed in this study, we can speak of both variants of activity. It is also observed that fourth-generation agencies, i.e. those endowed with broader decision-making powers, like EBA, ESMA or EIOPA demonstrate more initiative in their actions which leads to them initiating policy developments "from the inside"[70]. This means that specific solution proposals come from the agency itself rather than e.g. a specialised Directorate-General of the European Commission. ESAs are also agencies with regulatory powers, which independently develop draft regulatory technical standards as well as ones referring to implementation. Similar regulatory competences are held e.g. by EMA or ECHA which play a key role in the European administrative order in the process of registering medicines or chemicals, and also, in the case of ECHA, identifying substances that pose a potential hazard (the procedure concerning SVHC)[71].

---

65 See also A. von Bogdandy, 'Beyond the *Rechtsgemeinschaft*, with Trust – Reframing the Concept of the European Rule of Law', *MPIL Research Paper Series*, No. 02, 2018, pp. 5 ff.

66 Sommermann, 'Die Entwicklung', pp. 57, 59.

67 Knill, Grohs, 'Administrative Styles', pp. 97 ff.

68 *Ibid.*, p. 94.

69 *Ibid.*, p. 95.

70 *Cf.* v. Rijsbergen, 'On the Enforceability', pp. 117–122.

71 See https://echa.europa.eu/substances-of-very-high-concern-identification-explained (20.3.2018). See also Busuioc, *European Agencies*, pp. 211 ff.

Thus, in the case of such agencies, we can speak of European "administrative rulemaking" which, however, functions within an "imperfect regulatory chain"[72]. This means deficiencies of multilevel governance systems, which, due to their complexity and multi-national nature, make it impossible to clearly divide duties and shape relations between all the subjects of administrative cooperation in a fully transparent manner[73]. This is a typical feature of the European administrative space, which forces EU institutions, especially the European Commission, to make further efforts to strengthen the common, coherent European executive system. The term "structural connectedness" appears in academic literature in this context – EU institutions and authorities in the member states, including "European agencies and their surroundings", are "structurally connected" and, thus, create an "EU institutional architecture"[74]. Nonetheless, the term "architecture" used by Nina M. Vestlund is misleading, because it implies some organisational and normative order, which in many cases is missing.

Second, one considers the way a particular European institution functions. Is it gradually evolving case-by-case, or can one see a comprehensive, logical strategy of its action[75]? In the case of the agencies that have been described, we can speak of multiannual strategies of action. Agencies draw up complex, annual and multiannual programmes where they specify their objectives and their basic assumptions in shaping policies for particular market sectors. Behaviours that are sudden reactions to emerging challenges occur relatively rarely and are directly linked to crisis situations. Since agencies have been created in many sectors, precisely as a protective mechanism to detect and tackle threats of a cross-border nature, their administrative style also includes powers to take action in emergency situations[76].

Third, administrative style is also determined by the ways decisions of a particular public institution are implemented. Intervening and mediating methods are identified in this respect[77]. Since the capacity to enforce the decisions undertaken is relatively weak in the case of regulatory agencies, they should be classified as

72 See Chiti, 'In the Aftermath of the Crisis', p. 314.

73 See also K. Tomaszewski, *Unia Europejska – w poszukiwaniu skutecznego mechanizmu zarządzania. Analiza krytyczna modelu teoretycznego Multi-Level Governance*, Toruń 2013, pp. 180 ff.

74 Vestlund, 'Exploring', p. 351.

75 Christoph Knill and Stephan Groll identify "incremental" and "synoptical" policy formulation styles in this context. See Knill, Grohs, 'Administrative Styles', p. 96.

76 See Boin *et al.*, 'Building', pp. 423 ff.

77 Knill, Grohs, 'Administrative Styles', p. 96.

part of the mediating administration. This is a consequence of the Treaty-based formation of the entire European administration conducted by the Commission, which "follows a pattern of negotiation and mediation rather than hierarchical intervention"[78]. The power to intervene is of an exceptional nature and has only been assigned to a few agencies. One can recall in this case the intervention competences of e.g. ESMA[79].

Most actions of the regulatory agencies arise out of negotiation methods that provide for the broadest possible inclusion of various stakeholders. As mentioned in Chapter 6, deliberative and participatory methods are meant to be the equivalent of traditionally understood democratic legitimacy. Thus, even a sort of "participatory administration" is identified in the context of the EU system[80]. In such a structure, legitimacy is supposed to be formulated through the inclusion of civil society[81]. This is confirmed by the results of surveys conducted among agency officials as well as studies on the founding regulations. Around eighty per cent of all agencies involve various non-state stakeholders, e.g. NGOs, trade unions, firms and industry associations, in their work[82].

There are many mechanisms aimed at including interested parties in the work of a particular agency, among others, public consultations which can concern documents produced by agencies, e.g. in the case of EFSA these are consultations on draft scientific opinions[83]. Representatives of stakeholders can sit on agency boards. Moreover, some agencies, e.g. EBA, have formalised organisational units, such as the Banking Stakeholder Group,[84] which act as representatives

78 *Ibid.*, p. 103.

79 Article 28 of Regulation No. 236/2012. More P. van Cleynenbreugel, *Market Supervision in the European Union. Integrated Administration in Constitutional Context*, Leiden/Boston 2014, pp. 256 ff.

80 See C. Harlow, 'Civil Society Organisations and Participatory Administration: A Challenge to EU Administrative Law', in: Smismans (ed.), *Civil Society*, pp. 131 ff.; K. Bachmann, 'Deliberatywny supranacjonalizm', in: R. Kuźniar (ed.), *Porządek międzynarodowy u progu XXI wieku*, Warszawa 2005, pp. 437 ff.

81 See also M. Thiel, 'European Civil Society and the EU Fundamental Rights Agency: Creating Legitimacy through Civil Society Inclusion?', *Journal of European Integration*, Vol. 36, Vol. 5, 2014, pp. 441 ff.

82 S. Arras, C. Braun, 'Stakeholders Wanted! Why and How European Union Agencies Involve Non-State Stakeholders', *Journal of European Public Policy*, Vol. 25, No. 9, 2018, p. 1258.

83 Articles 22, 23, 28 and 29 of Regulation No. 178/2002.

84 Article 37 of Regulation No. 1093/2010.

of interested parties operating in a particular agency's area of activity[85]. Such formal organisational units in agencies have their status and tasks laid down in founding regulations and they regularly participate in agency work. Empirical studies indicate that agencies with broader powers, included in the third and fourth generation, have a greater number of consultative instruments than older-type agencies with informational powers, on account of their stronger need to legitimise their activities[86]. Regardless of the existing consultative mechanisms, it can hardly be concluded that "participatory administration" can fully replace democratic processes and related instruments of citizen influence on European policy-making.

In this context, it is appropriate to ask what the charm of technocracy is, since it moves decision-making bodies away from the citizen. In structures such as the European Union, the citizen completely loses sight of specific powers delegated to seemingly endless bureaucratic chains, which are comprehensible only for specialists. Technocracy's main advantage is the possibility of drafting appropriate, in theory politically neutral, effective responses to rapidly changing challenges. After reviewing the German-language literature on the growth of technocratic structures in Europe, Alexander Ruser reaches an appropriate conclusion: expert bodies are seen as ones that are able to quickly and logically respond to situations which require complex, professional and functional solutions. Nonetheless, their legitimacy is limited as it is confined to a particular normative, as well as institutional system, and is determined by its specific interests and goals. This change of perspective stems from a loss of acceptance of the authority of specific expert bodies. It entails modifications of their rules of conduct, i.e. procedures that legitimise the existence of particular bureaucratic institutions. This leads to them losing of the empowerment necessary for their existence[87].

---

85 See also P. Iglesias Rodriguez, 'The Role of Interest Groups in EU Financial Regulation after the European Supervisory Authorities in the Financial Field: The Case of the Stakeholder Groups', *European Society of International Law Conference Paper*, No. 10, 2011, pp. 3 ff.; I. Bajakić, M.B. Beroš, 'Examining Agency Governance in the European Union Financial Sector – A Case-Study of ESMA', *Economic Research*, Vol. 30, No. 1, 2017, pp. 1743 ff.

86 Arras, Braun, 'Stakehoders', p. 1261; Pérez-Durán, 'Political', pp. 13 ff.

87 See Ruser, 'Der (in)diskrete Charme', pp. 213 ff. Similarly many years earlier: Szapiro, 'The Framework', pp. 3 ff.

Closing Remarks

The main purpose of this monograph was to conduct a legal analysis of the issue of the legitimacy of EU regulatory agencies. Among many studies devoted to EU regulatory agencies, there are hardly any critical analyses of the existing theories of legitimacy. These theories are often general and relate overall to the process of European integration or to the EU institutional system, without any particular regard to EU regulatory agencies. The theoretical justification of how these bodies function arouses little interest. This is explained by the actual state of affairs. Namely, as Andreas Wimmel rightly put it in the context of research into European multilevel governance, theorising on legitimacy of EU administration is like searching for the right way in a "labyrinth with no exit"[1].

Achieving democratic empowerment, akin to that which is attributed to public administration authorities in the member states, is not possible for EU regulatory agencies. This stems directly from the fact that they are naturally distant from citizens. The long chains of delegation, when it comes to transferring particular tasks to the level of supranational and intergovernmental cooperation, as well as specific operational areas of individual agencies, make them inaccessible for the uninitiated. The last fact means that even the opening of EU agencies to broader contacts with those potentially interested in recent years has been only a partial success, because these efforts remain targeted at stakeholders from a particular sector of the market or those who have been already "initiated". This type of agency "expertocracy" functions in specific networks of dependencies with private and public entities closely linked to a particular area of the internal market. These relationships are largely based on trust, informal contacts, the authority of the institutions that are involved, as well as the recognition of the professionalism of regulatory and decision-making bodies. The public empowerment that forms an important part of the deliberative institutionalism, which is characteristic for EU institutional structures is, therefore, a poor substitute for democratic legitimacy.

The beginnings of European integration involved little administrative support within the common European system. The increased involvement in the shaping of policies in many sectors of the internal market required the creation of an integrated administrative framework. That is because modern governance is associated with the necessity of building appropriate organisational structures

1 Wimmel, 'Theorizing', pp. 181 ff.

in order to enable consistent implementation of law enacted at the European level as well as control over implementation of common policies. One of the guiding ideas that drove European integration at its outset was maintaining the procedural and administrative autonomy of the member states in order to guarantee their full independence in the transposition of European law into national legal systems. Therefore, this integrated administrative framework means that many entities, at different levels, cooperate in the shaping and implementation of policies within individual market sectors.

The motto that guides the administrative apparatus of the European Union which functions under the aegis of the European Commission is attachment to three basic principles: cooperation, coordination and communication. The effectiveness and efficiency of the complex governance system which, in addition to EU regulatory agencies, includes various expert groups, comitology committees, lobbying groups, national regulatory authorities, interested private parties, representatives of academic and research communities and many others, is indeed ensured through these "three Cs"[2].

The decision-making process is dominated in many cases by technocrats as well as national groups of influence. Consequently, it is not always subject to sufficient control by democratically legitimised institutions such as the European Parliament[3]. Many authors gloss over it, concluding that in international or supranational structures the only mechanism of legitimacy can be the "output" or results achieved by common bodies[4]. Delegating certain powers to them is, indeed, motivated by a desire to secure political and economic benefits. This is done by the major players, which in the case of regulatory agencies, apart from the Commission, primarily include the member states, the Council and increasingly also the European Parliament. This body currently plays a significant role in negotiations concerning the specific founding regulations that establish new agencies.

This overview of the situation can also be reinterpreted by the attachment to the idea of administrative legitimacy. This is supposed to arise from the recognition and acceptance of the activities of certain public administration authorities. Recognition derives from confidence in the special professional background of officials and also their "service" in the name of the public interest. This is also connected with a belief in the legality of existing structures and their operation

2 See Harlow, Rawlings, *Process*, p. 323.
3 See also Craig, 'Integration', pp. 30 ff.
4 See e.g. Majone, 'The New European Agencies', pp. 262 ff.

within a legal framework that precisely defines the scope of the powers that have been conferred on them. According to this understanding of empowerment, "unelected bureaucrats" become representatives of society[5], but such concepts are not mature theories. They refer to theoretical efforts of researchers like Max Weber and serve to justify the functioning of administrative structures of a new type, which, not only in Weber's era or at the turn of the twentieth century, but also later at the outset of the European integration process in the 1950s and 1960s, would have been difficult to imagine. A rapid development of international cooperation led to the dynamic growth of intergovernmental and supranational institutions that receive their tasks as part of multi-step delegation from the state level.

A special situation occurs in the deeply integrated EU internal market where the emergence of a European administrative space, or "European Composite Administration" as German legal doctrine would have it, has been observed for several decades. These terms are meant to reflect the specific character of collaboration between administrative authorities in the member states and common institutions functioning in the EU institutional structure. Regulatory authorities at both levels have been modernised in recent decades in line with the assumptions of New Public Management. According to this concept, public administration institutions were supposed to operate in the manner of private organisations. In practice, it means operating according to free-market mechanisms, i.e. greater competitiveness, and profit and loss calculations, as well as evaluating the effectiveness and efficiency of the tasks performed. The main argument in favour of creating regulatory agencies both at the state and pan-European levels was to depoliticise the functioning of public administration, which was expected to act in a transparent, open and independent manner. In the case of the European administration, these assumptions were recognised in primary law after the changes introduced by the Treaty of Lisbon. Article 298(1) TFEU explicitly lists EU regulatory agencies along with other entities as part of an open, efficient and independent European administration. They are an important platform in which to work out common positions on major EU policies.

Not without importance in this context, is the issue of maintaining institutional balance in the EU system. Without doubt, both the Council and the European Parliament play an important role in the process of creating European agencies and, after they were created – in the processes of controlling the way they function. What is also significant is the role of the EU Court of Justice as

---

5 Murdoch *et al.*, 'Administrative Legitimacy', p. 391.

a judicial authority responsible for checking compliance with European law. Nevertheless, the European Commission remains the main institution coordinating the activities of the agency system and its relations with regulatory agencies have evolved. Initially perceived as potential competition within the European administrative system, they were recognised by the Commission over time, as an effective instrument for strengthening its capacity to coordinate the processes of the implementation of European law into national legal systems. Due to its independence, which is important for the process of developing expert judgements, it is assumed that the European Commission formally does not exercise professional supervision, or even, as some authors would have it, legal supervision over agencies[6]. In this interpretation, they are institutionally and functionally autonomous bodies acting on equal terms with the European Commission as independent "administrative centres" within the European administrative space.

This interpretation does not correspond to the actual state of affairs. Many empirical studies conducted by Scandinavian, German and Spanish political scientists point to a large, even growing involvement of the Commission in the work of individual agencies. This results directly from formal safeguards, primarily provisions contained in founding regulations, and other sectoral legal acts that broaden the existing powers of particular agencies, but also indirectly from primary law, including above all Article 17 TEU. This provision establishes the Commission's status as the "guardian of the Treaties", i.e. the main authority when it comes to management and administrative tasks in the European institutional system. Regulatory agencies are not EU institutions. Despite repeated proposals in the field of legal scholarship, they were not included in Article 13 TEU, which lists EU institutions.

Moreover, there are many non-formalised practices that strengthen the relationship between the Commission and regulatory agencies. The latter, due to their intensive contacts with individual Directorates-General, are even perceived as part of the Commission's bureaucratic apparatus. Their close mutual contacts are not unilaterally imposed by the Commission. They are derived to a large extent from a common desire to build a European administration on the foundation of consent, trust and understanding the positions of as many interested parties as possible. This is supposed to be a recipe for developing functional, efficient solutions that are satisfactory for various actors at different levels within the European administrative space. However, it does not change the fact that the increasingly powerful EU regulatory agencies are not fully independent bodies.

---

6 For example Weißgärber, *Die Legitimation*, pp. 296 ff.

They are in different relationships of dependence, primarily with the European Commission. The emergence of the European administrative space is an important stage in the process of European integration. It signifies the strengthening of supranational mechanisms, intensification of intergovernmental cooperation and advancing technocratisation of the European Union. In many cases, like the pharmaceutical market, financial supervision, registration of chemicals, aviation safety system etc., regulatory agencies become coordinators, and regulators with powers previously unseen at the common, EU level. Networks of administrative cooperation centred on these bodies, and connected via them to the European Commission, have been created.

This development of institutional structures raises reasonable doubts as to the empowerment of the activities of EU regulatory agencies. There are also concerns about a "desovereignisation" of states, which lose important powers in sectors that are vital for their national economies. Registration, control, regulatory or authorisation duties are transferred to common institutions which the member states can only influence to a limited extent, usually through their representatives on agency boards. The argument of increased efficiency and functionality of common administrative structures is convincing only to a limited degree in the face of an intensive integration of different sectors of the internal market. One has to recognise the fact that common institutions, supervisory mechanisms, and a coherent regulatory system which enables e.g. the creation of harmonised standards and practices, contribute to greater safety in deeply integrated markets, and guarantee faster economic growth.

According to neoliberal thought, in such a case we undoubtedly see absolute gains, or measurable benefits for all the participants in this type of cooperation. The thesis has been confirmed by a significant increase in safety in Europe, when it comes to trade in pharmaceuticals, chemicals, food and financial products, compared to previous years when the level of coordination of activities was much lower and a dominant role was played by the principle of minimum harmonisation. This left the member states a lot of leeway in the process of law transposition, and building their own systems of sectoral safeguards. Faced with the dilemma that usually crops up in crisis situations – which is more important: effectiveness, or a proper legal basis for new organisational solutions – it should be noted that the principle of "the end justifies the means" increasingly prevails. The proposed solutions have been adapted to the existing legal situation without much reflection over the need to modify it in the context of the actual evolution of the EU agency system.

Out of all the concepts of legitimacy used in relation to regulatory agencies which have been discussed and critically analysed, justifications that refer to normative stability are the most convincing. The authority of administrative bodies grows out of their anchoring in a specific legal system. The mere fact of their existence, which has already continued for several decades in the case of regulatory agencies, may foster a "familiarisation" with these bodies, but it legitimises their existence only to a limited extent.

Treaty law does not raise any formal obstacles to the creation of regulatory agencies. Article 5 TEU, which constitutes the foundation for the vertical division of competences between the EU and national levels, is not a formal block in quantitative or qualitative terms when it comes to building the agency system. Yet establishing a regulatory agency requires reference to a particular Treaty norm to constitute a proper legal basis. Article 352 TFEU, used in the first phases of "agencification", can play this role only to a limited extent. Due to the difficulties in finding appropriate material norms, suitable for use in the creation of agencies, the EU legislature increasingly cites Article 114 TFEU, which is controversial in the case of agencies. This norm, in its original interpretation, is limited to being a restrictive harmonisation clause for the internal market. Institutional solutions aimed at harmonising the implementation of EU sectoral provisions, by creating an institutional system in the form of regulatory agencies, required a modification of the legal interpretation of this article. This gradually happened through the decisions of the EU Court of Justice and culminated in the 2014 *Short selling* ruling, where the Court accepted a broad interpretation of Article 114 TFEU which made it actually possible to transfer decision-making and control powers to agencies.

To recap the considerations in this monograph, the following conclusions can be formulated:

(1) Regulatory agencies are a permanent component of the European administrative system. They constitute an important mechanism of coordination in the complex deliberative structures that form the European administrative space. They facilitate the creation of common interpretations of European law and the development of uniform practices. They play an important role in information flow between different market participants, perform monitoring, control and supervisory functions, and actively participate in training officials at various levels.

(2) Despite the recognition of regulatory agencies in the new normative framework after the changes introduced by the Treaty of Lisbon, the status, procedure of establishment, scope of competence and organisational model of these bodies have not been explicitly laid down in primary law. These issues have only been addressed in declarative, legally non-binding documents.

These include the 2012 "Common Approach", which is the result of many years of negotiations between the Commission, the Council and the European Parliament on creating a common framework for the chaotically expanding agency system.

(3) The above findings are in line with the less than optimistic conclusion that the normative legitimacy of EU regulatory agencies is not strong. Its enhancement is guaranteed by secondary law provisions, primarily norms in founding regulations, which are often born out of fierce debates between all the interested parties: the member states, the Council, the European Parliament and the Commission. The catalogue of powers is broadened through legal acts created for specific market sectors. Another important safeguard is the control function of the CJEU, which, under Article 263 TFEU, ensures protection against any arbitrariness of regulatory agencies. The Court also performs a significant function in legitimising the existence of agencies through case law. This has been seen since the 2006 *ENISA* ruling. It was confirmed in the *Short selling* ruling. Acceptance of institutional solutions of a technocratic nature, such as regulatory agencies, which are supposed to contribute to safeguarding stability in the internal market and its further intensive development, is noticeable.

(4) In many academic studies on regulatory agencies the legitimacy of their activities is linked to accountability for their performance. These two things should be clearly separated. The broad mechanisms of control that have been developed as the agency system has evolved are not a sufficient answer to questions about the legitimacy of the existence of these bodies. They constitute an important safeguard against actions of "unelected bureaucrats", but they cannot replace traditional mechanisms of legitimacy.

(5) In state systems, these traditional mechanisms of legitimacy are electoral mechanisms. In international structures, particularly deeply integrated ones such as in the European Union, belief in the possibility of creating common, "majoritarian" institutions is utopian. Hence the growth of bureaucratic, expert, technocratic structures which have become a response to the rapid development of the integrated market. "Non-majoritarian" bodies fit in with the idea of a European "regulatory state" that is underpinned by common law and implemented in a uniform, harmonised way. The European Union, and thus also its administration, are supposed to be rooted in the principle of the rule of law. The principle of institutional balance in the EU organisational structure is also an important legitimising element.

(6) Regulatory agencies function within complex networks of dependence in the European administrative space, where there are many influential

bodies. It is difficult to find examples of legally sanctioned coercion there, in contrast to mechanisms characteristic of state systems. It does not mean, however, that there are no coordinating or steering measures in the EU polyarchy. Interests of individual participants are "thrashed out" in multi-stage negotiations where the skills of individual players as well as their political and economic potential are important. A significant role is also played by normative safeguards, such as decision-making procedures defined in founding regulations. They can provide for the inclusion of certain groups of stakeholders, or holding public consultations. The choice of a particular form of decision-making by the agency board (e.g. unanimity, qualified majority, simple majority) also affects the possibility of influencing final decisions by individual participants.

(7) Regulatory agencies mainly create "soft law". It does not mean, however, that their decisions do not affect the legal systems of the member states. On the contrary, they play an increasing role in the process of creating normative frameworks in individual sectors of the market. The authority that ensures coherence of regulatory activities is the European Commission. It plays a significant role in the process of rulemaking which is carried out by EU agencies. A number of the control mechanisms used by the Commission are informal and aim at working out compromise solutions. These form part of a broader strategy, usually devised by the legal department of the Directorate-General operating in a particular sector of the market. Relationships with the Commission are therefore more parental than partner-like. Its close links to the satellite regulatory agencies play a significant legitimising role.

(8) Chains of delegation within the complex institutional structures of the European Union are much longer than in state systems. There is no clearly specified legitimising agent that would empower a particular body to act. The legitimising agent is not "the people", but various nations. The European Union itself is not a liberal democracy in the manner of state democracies. Rather, the point is that its functioning should be based on principles characteristic of representative democracies. Empowerment results not only from direct elections to the European Parliament, but also from legitimacy obtained through the member states, represented by democratically elected representatives. According to these assumptions, European administration should function in a democratic way, too. Authorisation, safeguards and accountability instruments are supposed to guarantee "democratic input".

(9) A complementary role to input-oriented legitimacy is played by output-oriented legitimacy. Empowerment is supposed to result from the specialist nature of the independent European administration. A certain paradox emerges in this context as independence must mean acting on one's own and having an autonomous position in relation to the EU authorities. Full autonomy would run counter to the assumptions of input-oriented legitimacy, which in the case of regulatory agencies is associated with the legitimating triad of authorisation, safeguards and accountability. An important element that binds both concepts – input- and output-oriented legitimacy – is procedural legitimacy (throughput). What matters here is the quality of procedures that define how a particular public administration authority functions. In the case of regulatory agencies, openness and transparency play a large role. They are associated with the idea of including the broadest possible groups of stakeholders in the processes of consultation and working out compromise solutions.

(10) There is no single theory of legitimacy that could be considered as universally applicable to the agency system as a whole. We should instead speak of a multiplicity of theoretical efforts to find answers to questions about the justifications given for the functioning of regulatory agencies in the EU institutional system. In many of the outlined theoretical concepts, which are yet to develop into mature theories of legitimacy, we can find descriptive and explanatory features. Demonstration of predictive ability, which is an important component of any theory is usually missing. This makes it impossible to include regulatory agencies in broader considerations on the development of the European Union as a whole. Authors who theorise on the legitimacy of regulatory agencies usually employ the dichotomous division into input and output legitimacy introduced by Fritz Scharpf. New elements, let alone critical arguments about the weak empowerment of European administration, appear rarely. Notwithstanding the contribution of EU agencies to the harmonisation of legal frameworks, and their coordination of the regulatory activities of many entities involved in multilevel governance, it must be concluded that their legitimacy should be strengthened. Setting out their status, and the way they are created explicitly in Treaty law, could be such a breakthrough.

Bibliography

Abels Gabriele, Kobusch Alexander, 'Regulation of Food Safety in the EU: Changing Patterns of Multi-Level Governance', Paper Presented at the Conference of the ECPR Standing Group on Regulatory Governance, June 2010; available at: https://papers.ssrn.com/sol3/papers.cfm?abstract_id=2131363 (20.3.2018).

Adamski Dariusz, *Prawo do informacji o działaniach władz publicznych Unii Europejskiej* [*The Right of Access to Information about the Activities of EU Public Sector Bodies*], C.H. Beck, Warszawa 2011.

Adamski Dariusz, 'The *ESMA* Doctrine: A Constitutional Revolution and the Economics of Delegation', *European Law Review*, Vol. 39, No. 6, 2014, pp. 812–834.

Alemanno Alberto, 'How Much Better is Better Regulation? Assessing the Impact of the Better Regulation Package on the European Union. A Research Agenda', *European Journal of Risk Regulation*, Vol. 6, No. 3, 2015, pp. 344–356.

Alemanno Alberto, 'The European Food Safety Authority at Five', *European Food and Feed Law Review*, Vol. 3, No. 1, 2008, pp. 2–29.

Alexander Kern, 'European Banking Union: A Legal and Institutional Analysis of the Single Supervisory Mechanism and the Single Resolution Mechanism', *European Law Review*, Vol. 40, No. 2, 2015, pp. 154–187.

Alonso Sonia, '"You Can Vote but You Cannot Choose": Democracy and the Sovereign Debt Crisis in the Eurozone', *Estudio Working Paper*, No. 282, 2014; available at: https://e-archivo.uc3m.es/bitstream/handle/10016/18315/IC3JM-2014-282.pdf (20.3.2018).

Amtenbrink Fabian, 'Institutionelle Aspekte der neuen europäischen Finanzmarktregulierung und -aufsicht', in: Gramlich Ludwig, Manger-Nestler Cornelia (ed.), *Europäisierte Regulierungsstrukturen und -netzwerke. Basis einer künftigen Infrastrukturvorsorge*, Nomos Verlag, Baden-Baden 2011, pp. 119–129.

Andoura Sami, Timmerman Peter, 'Governance of the EU: The Reform Debate on European Agencies Reignited', *EPIN Working Paper*, No. 19, 2008; available at: https://www.ceps.eu/system/files/book/1736.pdf (20.3.2018).

Appel Bernd *et al.* (ed.), 'EHEC-Ausbruch 2011. Aufklärung des Ausbruchs entlang der Lebensmittelkette', *Bundesinstitut für Riskobewertung. Wissenschaft*, No. 4, 2011; available at: http://www.bfr.bund.de/cm/350/ehec-ausbruch-2011-aufklaerung-des-ausbruchs-entlang-der-lebensmittelkette.pdf (20.3.2018).

Armstrong Kenneth A., 'New Governance and the European Union: An Empirical and Conceptual Critique', *Queen Mary University of London. School of Law*

Legal Studies Research Paper, No. 135, 2013; available at: https://papers.ssrn.com/sol3/papers.cfm?abstract_id=2244762 (20.3.2018).

Arras Sarah, Braun Caelesta, 'Stakeholders Wanted! Why and How European Union Agencies Involve Non-State Stakeholders', *Journal of European Public Policy*, Vol. 25, No. 9, 2018, pp. 1257–1275.

Augsberg Steffen, 'Agencification der Kommissionsverwaltung', *Europarecht*, Beiheft, No. 1, 2016, pp. 119–142.

Auroux Sylvain (ed.), *Encyclopédie phliosophique universelle. Les Notions philosophiques*, Presses Universitaires de France, Paris 1990.

Bach Tobias *et al.*, 'The Differential Empowering Effects of Europeanization on the Autonomy of National Agencies', *Governance. An International Journal of Policy, Administration, and Institutions*, Vol. 28, No. 3, 2015, pp. 285–304.

Bach Tobias *et al.*, 'Transnational Bureaucratic Politics: An Institutional Rivalry Perspective on EU Network Governance', *Public Administration*, Vol. 94, No. 1, 2016, pp. 9–24.

Bach Tobias, Fleischer Julia, 'The Parliamentary Accountability of European Union and National Agencies', in: Busuioc Madalina *et al.* (ed.), *The Agency Phenomenon in the European Union. Emergence, Institutionalisation and Everyday Decision-Making*, Manchester University Press, Manchester/New York 2014, pp. 152–171.

Bach Tobias, Ruffing Eva, 'Networking for Autonomy? National Agencies in European Networks', *Public Administration*, Vol. 91, No. 3, 2013, pp. 712–726.

Bachmann Klaus, 'Deliberatywny supranacjonalizm' ['Deliberative Supranationalism'], in: Kuźniar Roman (ed.), *Porządek międzynarodowy u progu XXI wieku* [*The International Order at the Threshold of the Twenty First Century*], WUW, Warszawa 2005, pp. 434–450.

Baczko Bronisław, *Wyobrażenia społeczne. Szkice o nadziei i pamięci zbiorowej* [*Social Imagery. Sketches about Hope and Collective Memory*], PWN, Warszawa 1994.

Bajakić Ivana, Beroš Marta B., 'Examining Agency Governance in the European Union Financial Sector – A Case-Study of ESMA', *Economic Research*, Vol. 30, No. 1, 2017, pp. 1743–1757.

Balint Tim *et al.*, 'Bureaucratic Change in the European Administrative Space: The Case of European Commission', in: Curtin Deirdre, Egeberg Morten (ed.), *Towards a New Executive Order in Europe*, Routledge, London/New York 2015, pp. 39–62.

Barbieri Dario, Ongaro Edoardo, 'EU Agencies: What is Common and What is Distinctive Compared with National-Level Public Agencies', *International Review of Administrative Science*, Vol. 74, No. 3, 2008, pp. 395–420.

Barcz Jan, 'Pojęcie suwerenności w świetle współzależności między sferą ponadnarodową a państwową' ['The Notion of Sovereignty in the Light of the Interaction between State- and Supranational Spheres'], in: Kranz Jerzy (ed.), *Suwerenność i ponadnarodowość a integracja europejska* [*Sovereignty and Transnationality and the European Integration*], Prawo i Praktyka Gospodarcza, Warszawa 2006, pp. 55–79.

Barcz Jan, *Unia Europejska na rozstajach. Traktat z Lizbony. Dynamika i główne kierunki reformy ustrojowej*, [*The European Union at the Crossroads. The Treaty of Lisbon. Dynamics and Main Directions of the Reform of the Political System*], EuroPrawo, Warszawa 2010.

Barcz Jan, Górka Maciej, Wyrozumska Anna, *Instytucje i prawo Unii Europejskiej* [*Institutions and Law of the European Union*], LexisNexis, Warszawa 2012.

Barner-Gaedicke Elisabeth, *FRONTEX – Ohne Kontrolle zur europäischen Grenzschutztruppe? Demokratische Kontrolle der Agentur FRONTEX*, Verlag Dr. Kovač, Hamburg 2017.

Barnett Michael, 'Social Constructivism', in: Baylis John *et al.* (ed.), *The Globalization of World Politics. An Introduction to International Relations*, Oxford University Press, New York 2011, pp. 148–165.

Bauer Michael W., 'Tolerant, If Personal Goals Remain Unharmed: Explaining Supranational Bureaucrats' Attitudes to Organizational Change', *Governance. An International Journal of Policy, Administration, and Institutions*, Vol. 25, No. 3, 2012, pp. 485–510.

Bauhr Monika, Grimes Marcia, 'Indignation or Resignation: The Implications of Transparency for Societal Accountability', *Governance. An International Journal of Policy, Administration, and Institutions*, Vol. 27, No. 2, 2014, pp. 291–320.

Bebr Gerhard, 'Case C-70/88, European Parliament *v.* Council, Judgment of the Court of Justice of 22 May 1990', *Common Market Law Review*, Vol. 28, No. 3, 1991, pp. 663–680.

Beetham David, *The Legitimation of Power*, Palgrave Macmillan, Basingstoke/New York 2013.

Bellamy Richard, 'An Ever Closer Union Among the Peoples of Europe: Republican Intergovernmentalism and Demoicratic Representation within the EU', *Journal of European Integration*, Vol. 35, No. 5, 2013, pp. 499–516.

Bellamy Richard, 'Democracy without Democracy? Can the EU's Democratic "Outputs" be Separated from the Democratic "Inputs" Provided by Competitive Parties and Majority Rule?', *Journal of European Public Policy*, Vol. 17, No. 1, 2010, pp. 2–19.

Bendor Jonathan *et al.*, 'Theories of Delegation', *Annual Review of Political Science*, Vol. 4, 2001, pp. 235–269.

Bergström Carl-Fredrik *et al.*, 'Legislate or Delegate? Bargaining over Implementation and Legislative Authority in the EU', *West European Politics*, Vol. 30, No. 2, 2007, pp. 338–366.

Bernauer Thomas *et al.*, 'How Relevant are Input and Output Legitimacy in International Environmental Governance?', *NCCR Democracy Working Paper*, No. 94, 2016; available at: http://www.nccr-democracy.uzh.ch/publications/workingpaper/pdf/wp_94.pdf (20.3.2018).

Beroš Marta B., 'Some Reflections on the Governance and Accountability of the Single Resolution Board', *TARN Working Paper*, No. 3, 2017; available at: https://papers.ssrn.com/sol3/papers.cfm?abstract_id=2940198 (20.3.2018).

Bertsou Eri, Pastorella Giulia, 'Technocratic Attitudes: A Citizen's Perspective of Expert Decision-Making', *West European Politics*, Vol. 40, No. 2, 2017, pp. 430–458.

Będkowski-Kozioł Michał, 'Status i zadania Europejskiej Agencji Kolejowej – stan obecny i perspektywy w świetle projektu IV pakietu kolejowego UE' ['Status and Tasks of the European Railway Agency – The Current Situation and Prospects for the Future in the Light of the Draft of the 4th EU Railway Package'], *Internetowy Kwartalnik Antymonopolowy i Regulacyjny*, No. 7(3), 2014, pp. 36–56.

Biela Jan, 'What Deficit? Legitimacy and Accountability of Regulatory Agencies', Paper Prepared for the 42nd ECPR Joint Session, 10–15.4.2014; available at: https://ecpr.eu/Filestore/PaperProposal/c294ff37-abb7-4aff-8583-868a1fa3b227.pdf (20.3.2018).

Biela Jan, Papadopoulos Yannis, 'The Empirical Assessment of Agency Accountability: A Regime Approach and an Application to the German Bundesnetzagentur', *International Review of Administrative Sciences*, Vol. 80, No. 2, 2014, pp. 362–381.

Bieleń Stanisław, *Polityka w stosunkach międzynarodowych* [*Politics in International Relations*], ASPRA-JR, Warszawa 2010.

Biernat Tadeusz, '"Deficyt demokracji" w strukturach Unii Europejskiej' ['"Democratic Deficit" in the EU Structures'], in: Biernat Tadeusz, Siwik Anna (ed.), *Demokracja. Teoria. Idee. Instytucje* [*Democracy. Theory. Ideas. Institutions*], Wydawnictwo Adam Marszałek, Toruń 2001, pp. 31–44.

Biernat Tadeusz, 'Legitymizacja procesu legislacyjnego'['Legitimisation of the Legislative Process'], in: Preisner Artur (ed.), *Prawowitość czy zgodność z prawem. Legitymizacja władzy w państwach demokratycznych* [*Legality or Lawfulness. The Legitimacy of Power in Democratic Countries*], Beta-druk, Wrocław 2010, pp. 173–194.

Biernat Tadeusz, *Legitymizacja władzy politycznej. Elementy teorii* [*Legitimacy of the Political Power. Theoretical Basics*], Wydawnictwo Adam Marszałek, Toruń 1999.

Bismuth Régis, 'The Federalisation of Financial Supervision in the US and the EU: A Historical Comparative Perspective', in: Andenas Mads, Deipenbrock Gudula (ed.), *Regulating and Supervising European Financial Markets. More Risks than Achievements*, Springer Verlag, Cham 2016, pp. 231–250.

Bismuth Régis, 'The Independence of Domestic Financial Regulators: An Underestimated Structural Issue in International Financial Governance', *Goettingen Journal of International Law*, Vol. 2, No. 1, 2010, pp. 93–110.

Black Julia, 'Constructing and Contesting Legitimacy and Accountability in Polycentric Regulatory Regimes', *Regulation & Governance*, Vol. 2, No. 2, 2008, pp. 137–164.

Blondel Jean *et al.*, *People and Parliament in the European Union. Participation, Democracy, and Legitimacy*, Clarendon Press, Oxford 1998.

Bogdandy v. Armin, 'A Disputed Idea Becomes Law: Remarks on European Democracy as a Legal Principle', in: Kohler-Koch Beate, Rittberger Berthold (ed.), *Debating the Democratic Legitimacy of the European Union*, Rowman & Littlefield Publishers, Lanham 2007, pp. 33–44.

Bogdandy v. Armin, 'Beyond the *Rechtsgemeinschaft*, with Trust – Reframing the Concept of the European Rule of Law', *MPIL Research Paper Series*, No. 02, 2018; available at: https://papers.ssrn.com/sol3/papers.cfm?abstract_id=3103691 (20.3.2018).

Bogdandy v. Armin, 'Codes of Conduct and the Legitimacy of International Law', in: Wolfrum Rüdiger, Röben Volker (ed.), *Legitimacy in International Law*, Springer Verlag, Berlin/Heidelberg/New York 2008, pp. 299–307.

Bogdandy v. Armin, 'Globalization and Europe: How to Square Democracy, Globalization, and International Law', *European Journal of International Law*, Vol. 15, No. 5, 2004, pp. 885–906.

Bogdandy v. Armin, 'The European Lesson for International Democracy: The Significance of Articles 9–12 EU Treaty for International Organizations', *European Journal of International Law*, Vol. 23, No. 2, 2012, pp. 315–334.

Bogdandy v. Armin, Bernstorff v. Jochen, 'The EU Fundamental Rights Agency within the European and International Human Rights Architecture: The Legal Framework and Some Unsettled Issues in a New Field of Administrative Law', *Common Market Law Review*, Vol. 46, No. 4, 2009, pp. 1035–1068.

Boin Arjen *et al.*, 'Building European Union Capacity to Manage Transboundary Crises: Network or Lead-Agency Model', *Regulation & Governance*, Vol. 8, No. 4, 2014, pp. 418–436.

Boin Arjen *et al.*, 'Managing Transboundary Crises: The Emergence of European Union Capacity', *Journal of Contingencies and Crisis Management*, Vol. 22, No. 3, 2014, pp. 131–142.

Borrás Susana, Conzelmann Thomas, 'Democracy, Legitimacy and Soft Modes of Governance in the EU: The Empirical Turn', *Journal of European Integration*, Vol. 29, No. 5, 2007, pp. 531–548.

Borrás Susana *et al.*, 'European Agencies and Input Legitimacy: EFSA, EMEA and EPO in Post-Delegation Phase', *Journal of European Integration*, Vol. 29, No. 5, 2007, pp. 583–600.

Bouwen Pieter, 'Business Interest Representation and Legitimate European Governance', in: Smismans Stijn (ed.), *Civil Society and Legitimate European Governance*, Edward Elgar Publishing, Cheltenham/Northampton 2006, pp. 277–296.

Bovens Mark, 'Analysing and Assessing Accountability: A Conceptual Framework', *European Law Journal*, Vol. 13, No. 4, 2007, pp. 447–468.

Börzel Tanja, 'European Governance: Negotiation and Competition in the Shadow of Hierarchy', *Journal of Common Market Studies*, Vol. 48, No. 2, 2010, pp. 191–219.

Brennan Timothy, 'Antonio Gramsci and the Postcolonial Theory: "Southernism"', *Diaspora. A Journal of Transnational Studies*, Vol. 10, No. 2, 2001, pp. 143–187.

Brenner Michael, 'Die Agenturen im Recht der Europäischen Union – Segen oder Fluch?', in: Ipsen Jörn, Stüer Bernhard (ed.), *Europa im Wandel. Festschrift für Hans-Werner Rengeling*, Carl Heymanns Verlag, Köln/München 2008, pp. 193–204.

Bronckers Marco, Gerven v. Yves, 'Legal Remedies under the EC's New Chemicals Legislation REACH: Testing a New Model of European Governance', *Common Market Law Review*, Vol. 46, No. 6, 2009, pp. 1823–1871.

Brunnée Jutta, Toope Stephen J., 'Constructivism and International Law', in: Dunoff Jeffrey L., Pollack Mark A. (ed.), *Interdisciplinary Perspectives on International Law and International Relations: The State of the Art*, Cambridge University Press, New York 2013, pp. 119–145.

Brzozowski Wojciech, *Niezależność konstytucyjnego organu państwa i jego ochrona* [*Independence and the Security of the State's Constitutional Structure*], Wydawnictwo Sejmowe, Warszawa 2016.

Buchanan Allen, 'Political Legitimacy and Democracy', *Ethics*, Vol. 112, No. 4, 2002, pp. 689–719.

Buchanan Allen, Keohane Robert O., 'The Legitimacy of Global Governance', in: Wolfrum Rüdiger, Röben Volker (ed.), *Legitimacy in International Law*, Springer Verlag, Berlin/Heidelberg/New York 2008, pp. 25–62.

Buess Michael, 'Accountable and Under Control? Explaining Governments' Selection of Management Board Representatives', *Journal of Common Market Studies*, Vol. 53, No. 3, 2015, pp. 493–508.

Buess Michael, 'European Union Agencies and Their Management Boards: An Assessment of Accountability and Demoi-Cratic Legitimacy', *Journal of European Public Policy*, Vol. 22, No. 1, 2015, pp. 94–111.

Buess Michael, 'European Union Agencies' Vertical Relationships with the Member States: Domestic Sources of Accountability?', *Journal of European Integration*, Vol. 36, No. 5, 2014, pp. 509–524.

Burris Beverly H., 'Technocratic Organization and Control', *Organization Studies*, Vol. 10, No. 1, 1989, pp. 1–22.

Busuioc Madalina, 'Accountability, Control and Independence: The Case of European Agencies', *European Law Journal*, Vol. 15, No. 5, 2009, pp. 599–615.

Busuioc Madalina, 'Blurred Areas of Responsibility: European Agencies' Scientific "Opinions" under Scrutiny', in: Ambrus Monika *et al.* (ed.), *The Role of "Experts" in International and European Decision-Making Processes. Advisors, Decision Makers or Irrelevant Actors*, Cambridge University Press, Cambridge 2014, pp. 383–402.

Busuioc Madalina, 'European Agencies and Their Boards: Promises and Pitfalls of Accountability Beyond Design', *Journal of European Public Policy*, Vol. 19, No. 5, 2012, pp. 719–736.

Busuioc Madalina, *European Agencies. Law and Practices of Accountability*, Oxford University Press, Oxford 2013.

Busuioc Madalina, 'Rule-Making by the European Financial Supervisory Authorities: Walking a Tight Rope', *European Law Journal*, Vol. 19, No. 1, 2013, pp. 111–125.

Busuioc Madalina *et al.*, 'Agency Growth Between Autonomy and Accountability: The European Police Office as a "Living Institution"', in: Rittberger Berthold, Wonka Arndt (ed.), *Agency Governance in the EU*, Routledge, London/New York 2012, pp. 70–89.

Busuioc Madalina *et al.*, 'The Phenomenon of European Union Agencies: Setting the Scene', in: Busuioc Madalina *et al.* (ed.), *The Agency Phenomenon in the European Union. Emergence, Institutionalisation and Everyday Decision-Making*, Manchester University Press, Manchester/New York 2014, pp. 3–16.

Busuioc Madalina, Groenleer Martijn, 'The Theory and Practice of EU Agency Autonomy and Accountability: Early Day Expectations, Today's Realities and Future Perspectives', in: Everson Michelle *et al.* (ed.), *European Agencies in between Institutions and Member States*, Wolters Kluwer, Alphen aan den Rijn 2014, pp. 175–200.

Busuioc Madalina, Groenleer Martijn, 'Wielders of Supranational Power? The Administrative Behaviour of the Heads of European Union Agencies', in: Busuioc Madalina *et al.* (ed.), *The Agency Phenomenon in the European Union.*

Emergence, Institutionalisation and Everyday Decision-Making, Manchester University Press, Manchester/New York 2014, pp. 128–151.

Busuioc Madalina, Lodge Martin, 'Reputation and Accountability Relationships: Managing Accountability Expectations through Reputation', *Public Administration Review*, Vol. 77, No. 1, 2017, pp. 91–100.

Busuioc Madalina, Lodge Martin, 'The Reputational Basis of Public Accountability', *Governance. An International Journal of Policy, Administration, and Institutions*, Vol. 29, No. 2, 2016, pp. 247–263.

Byrne David, 'The Genesis of EFSA and the First 10 Years of EU Food Law', in: Alemanno Alberto, Gabbi Simone (ed.), *Foundations of EU Food Law and Policy. Ten Years of the European Food Safety Authority*, Ashgate, Farnham/ Burlington 2014, pp. 17–28.

Caillosse Jacques, 'Legitimacy in Administrative Law? A French Perspective', in: Ruffert Matthias (ed.), *Legitimacy in European Administrative Law: Reform and Reconstruction*, Europa Law Publishing, Groningen 2011, pp. 9–26.

Calliess Christian, 'Art. 13 EUV', in: Calliess Christian, Ruffert Matthias (ed.), *EUV/AEUV. Das Verfassungsrecht der Europäischen Union mit Europäischer Grundrechtecharta. Kommentar*, C.H. Beck, München 2011, pp. 211–229.

Calliess Christian, 'Art. 5 AEUV', in: Calliess Christian, Ruffert Matthias (ed.), *EUV/AEUV. Das Verfassungsrecht der Europäischen Union mit Europäischer Grundrechtecharta. Kommentar*, C.H. Beck, München 2011, pp. 514–516.

Caranta Roberto, 'Democracy, Legitimacy and Accountability – Is There a Common European Theoretical Framework?', in: Ruffert Matthias (ed.), *Legitimacy in European Administrative Law: Reform and Reconstruction*, Europa Law Publishing, Groningen 2011, pp. 175–196.

Case Peter *et al.*, 'From *theoria* to Theory: Leadership without Contemplation', *Organization*, Vol. 19, No. 3, 2012, pp. 345–361.

Cassese Sabino, 'New Paths for Administrative Law: A Manifesto', *International Journal of Constitutional Law*, Vol. 10, No. 3, 2012, pp. 603–613.

Centeno Miguel A., 'The New Leviathan: The Dynamics and Limits of Technocracy', *Theory and Society*, Vol. 22, No. 3, 1993, pp. 307–335.

Chalmers Damian, '"Food for Thought": Reconciling European Risks and Traditional Ways of Life', *Modern Law Review*, Vol. 66, No. 4, 2003, pp. 532–562.

Chalmers Damian *et al.*, *European Union Law: Cases and Materials*, Cambridge University Press, Cambridge 2010.

Chamon Merijn, 'Agencification in the United States and Germany and What the EU Might Learn From It', *German Law Journal*, Vol. 17, No. 2, 2016, pp. 119–152.

Chamon Merijn, 'EU Agencies between *Meroni* and *Romano* or the Devil and the Deep Blue Sea', *Common Market Law Review*, Vol. 48, No. 4, 2011, pp. 1055–1075.

Chamon Merijn, 'EU Agencies: Does the *Meroni* Doctrine Make Sense?', *Maastricht Journal of European and Comparative Law*, Vol. 17, No. 3, 2010, pp. 281–317.

Chamon Merijn, *EU Agencies. Legal and Political Limits to the Transformation of the EU Administration*, Oxford University Press, Oxford/New York 2016.

Chamon Merijn, 'Granting Powers to EU Decentralised Agencies Three Years Following *Short-Selling*', *ERA Forum*, Published Online in September 2017, DOI: 10.1007/s12027-017-0486-z.

Chamon Merijn, 'The Empowerment of Agencies under *Meroni* Doctrine and Article 114 TFEU: Comment on United Kingdom *v.* Parliament and Council (*Short Selling*) and the Proposed Single Resolution Mechanism', *European Law Review*, Vol. 39, No. 3, 2014, pp. 380–403.

Cheneval Francis, Schimmelfennig Frank, 'The Case for Demoicracy in the European Union', *Journal of Common Market Studies*, Vol. 51, No. 2, 2013, pp. 334–350.

Chirulli Paola, de Lucia Luca, 'Specialised Adjudication in EU Administrative Law: The Boards of Appeal of EU Agencies', *European Law Review*, Vol. 40, No. 6, 2015, pp. 832–857.

Chiti Edoardo, 'An Important Part of the EU's Institutional Machinery: Features, Problems and Perspectives of European Agencies', *Common Market Law Review*, Vol. 46, No. 5, 2009, pp. 1395–1442.

Chiti Edoardo, 'European Agencies' Rulemaking: Powers, Procedures and Assessment', *European Law Journal*, Vol. 19, No. 1, 2013, pp. 93–110.

Chiti Edoardo, 'In the Aftermath of the Crisis – The EU Administrative System between Impediments and Momentum', *Cambridge Yearbook of European Legal Studies*, Vol. 17, 2015, pp. 311–333.

Chiti Edoardo, 'The Emergence of a Community Administration: The Case of European Agencies', *Common Market Law Review*, Vol. 37, No. 2, 2000, pp. 309–343.

Chiu Iris H.-Y., 'Macroprudential Supervision: Critically Examining the Developments in the UK, EU and Internationally', *Law and Financial Markets Review*, Vol. 6, No. 3, 2012, pp. 184–199.

Chiu Iris H.-Y., 'Power and Accountability in the EU Financial Regulatory Architecture: Examining Inter-Agency Relations, Agency Independence and Accountability', in: Andenas Mads, Deipenbrock Gudula (ed.), *Regulating and Supervising European Financial Markets. More Risks than Achievements*, Springer Verlag, Cham 2016, pp. 67–101.

Chowdhury Nupur, Wessel Ramses A., 'Conceptualising Multilevel Regulation in the EU: A Legal Translation of Multilevel Governance?', *European Law Journal*, Vol. 18, No. 3, 2012, pp. 335–357.

Christensen Jørgen G., Lehmann Nielsen Vibeke, 'Administrative Capacity, Structural Choice and the Creation of EU Agencies', *Journal of European Public Policy*, Vol. 17, No. 2, 2010, pp. 176–204.

Christensen Tom *et al.*, 'Still Fragmented Government or Reassertion of the Centre?', in: Christensen Tom, Lægreid Per (ed.), *Transcending New Public Management. The Transformation of Public Sector Reforms*, Ashgate, Aldershot 2007, pp. 17–42.

Christensen Tom, Lægreid Per, 'Introduction – Theoretical Approach and Research Questions', in: Christensen Tom, Lægreid Per (ed.), *Transcending New Public Management. The Transformation of Public Sector Reforms*, Ashgate, Aldershot 2007, pp. 1–16.

Christensen Tom, Lægreid Per, 'Regulatory Agencies – The Challenges of Balancing Agency Autonomy and Political Control', *Governance. An International Journal of Policy, Administration, and Institutions*, Vol. 20, No. 3, 2007, pp. 499–520.

Cini Michelle, 'The European Commission – Politics and Administration', in: Bauer Michael W., Trondal Jarle (ed.), *The Palgrave Handbook of the European Administrative System*, Palgrave Macmillan, Basingstoke/New York 2015, pp. 127–144.

Clark Bradford R., 'Putting the Safeguards Back Into the Political Safeguards of Federalism', *Texas Law Review*, Vol. 80, No. 2, 2001, pp. 327–342.

Classen Claus D., *Demokratische Legitimation im offenen Rechtsstaat*, Mohr Siebeck, Tübingen 2009.

Cleynenbreugel v. Pieter, *Market Supervision in the European Union. Integrated Administration in Constitutional Context*, Brill Nijhoff, Leiden/Boston 2014.

Cleynenbreugel v. Pieter, '*Meroni* Circumvented? Article 114 TFEU and EU Regulatory Agencies', *Maastricht Journal of European and Comparative Law*, Vol. 21, No. 1, 2014, pp. 64–88.

Coen David, 'Business-Regulatory Relations: Learning to Play Regulatory Games in European Utility Markets', *Governance. An International Journal of Policy, Administration, and Institutions*, Vol. 18, No. 3, 2005, pp. 375–398.

Coen David, Doyle Chris, 'Liberalisation of Utilities and Evolving European Regulation', *Economic Outlook*, Vol. 24, No. 3, 2000, pp. 18–26.

Coen David, Thatcher Mark, 'Network Governance and Multi-Level Delegation: European Networks of Regulatory Agencies', *Journal of Public Policy*, Vol. 28, No. 1, 2008, pp. 49–71.

Coen David, Thatcher Mark, 'Reshaping European Regulatory Space', *NewGov Policy Brief*, No. 28, 2008; available at: http://www.eu-newgov.org/database/PUBLIC/Policy_Briefs/NEWGOV_Policy_Brief_no28.pdf (20.3.2018).

Coleman Robert, 'Regulatory Agencies and the European Union', *Institute of Governance Public Policy and Social Research Working Paper*, No. 7, 2004, Queens University Belfast.

Coman-Kund Florin, *European Union Agencies as Global Actors. A Legal Study of the EASA, Frontex and Europol*, Routledge, Oxon/New York 2018.

Coman-Kund Florin, 'The International Dimension of the EU Agencies. Charting a Legal-Institutional "Twilight Zone"', *TARN Working Paper*, No. 5, 2017; available at: https://papers.ssrn.com/sol3/papers.cfm?abstract_id=2951184 (20.3.2018).

Conway Gerard, 'Recovering a Separation of Powers in the European Union', *European Law Journal*, Vol. 17, No. 3, 2011, pp. 304–322.

Cook Brian J., *Bureaucracy and Self-Government. Reconsidering the Role of Public Administration in American Politics*, John Hopkins University Press, Baltimore/London 1996.

Cook Trevor, *Pharmaceuticals Biotechnology and the Law*, LexisNexis, Croydon 2016.

Costa Marios, *The Accountability Gap in EU Law*, Routledge, London/New York 2016.

Craig Paul, 'Integration, Democracy and Legitimacy', in: Craig Paul, de Búrca Gráinne (ed.), *The Evolution of EU Law*, Oxford University Press, Oxford 2013, pp. 13–40.

Craig Paul, 'Legitimacy in Administrative Law: European Union', in: Ruffert Matthias (ed.), *Legitimacy in European Administrative Law: Reform and Reconstruction*, Europa Law Publishing, Groningen 2011, pp. 197–215.

Crossley Nick, *Intersubjectivity. The Fabric of Social Becoming*, Sage Publications, London 1996.

Cuesta-Lopez Víctor, 'The Lisbon's Treaty Provisions on Democratic Principles: A Legal Framework for Participatory Democracy', *European Public Law*, Vol. 16, No. 1, 2010, pp. 123–138.

Curanović Alicja, *Konstruktywizm* [*Constructivism*], in: Zięba Ryszard *et al.* (ed.), *Teorie i podejścia badawcze w nauce o stosunkach międzynarodowych* [*Theories and Research Approaches in the Studies on International Relations*], WDiNP UW, Warszawa 2015, pp. 107–125.

Curtin Deirdre, 'Delegation to EU Non-Majoritarian Agencies and Emerging Practices of Public Accountability', in: Geradin Damien *et al.* (ed.), *Regulation through Agencies in the EU: A New Paradigm of European Governance*, Edward Elgar Publishing, Cheltenham 2005, pp. 87–117.

Curtin Deirdre, 'Holding (Quasi-) Autonomous EU Administrative Actors to Public Account', *European Law Journal*, Vol. 13, No. 4, 2007, pp. 523–541.

Curtin Deirdre, Dehousse Renaud, 'European Union Agencies: Tipping the Balance?', in: Busuioc Madalina *et al.* (ed.), *The Agency Phenomenon in the European Union. Emergence, Institutionalisation and Everyday Decision-Making*, Manchester University Press, Manchester/New York 2014, pp. 193–205.

Curtin Deirdre, Egeberg Morten, 'Tradition and Innovation: Europe's Accumulated Executive Order', in: Curtin Deirdre, Egeberg Morten (ed.), *Towards a New Executive Order in Europe*, Routledge, London/New York 2015, pp. 1–23.

Curtin Deirdre *et al.*, 'Positioning Accountability in European Governance: An Introduction', *West European Politics*, Vol. 33, No. 5, 2010, pp. 929–945.

Curtin Deirdre, Meijer Albert J., 'Does Transparency Strengthen Legitimacy? A Critical Analysis of European Union Policy Documents', *Information Polity*, No. 11, 2006, pp. 109–122.

Czaputowicz Jacek, 'Sovereignty in Theories of European Integration and the Perspective of the Polish Constitutional Tribunal', *Yearbook of Polish European Studies*, Vol. 17, 2014, pp. 15–35.

Czaputowicz Jacek, 'Wprowadzenie. Potencjał konstruktywizmu w wyjaśnianiu integracji europejskiej' ['Introduction. The Potential of Constructivism for Explaining European Integration'], in: Czaputowicz Jacek (ed.), *Zastosowanie konstruktywizmu w studiach europejskich* [*Applying Construcivism in the European Studies*], WUW, Warszawa 2016, pp. 7–30.

Dahl Robert A., 'Can International Organizations be Democratic? A Skeptic's View', in: Shapiro Ian, Hacker-Cordón Casiano (ed.), *Democracy's Edges*, Cambridge University Press, Cambridge 1999, pp. 19–36.

Dainotto Roberto, 'Notes on Q6§ 32. Gramsci and the Dalits', in: Zene Cosimo (ed.), *The Political Philosophies of Antonio Gramsci and B.R. Ambedkar. Itineraries of Dalits and Subalterns*, Routledge, London/New York 2013, pp. 75–86.

Danwitz v. Thomas, 'Was ist eigentlich Regulierung?', *Die öffentliche Verwaltung. Zeitschrift für öffentliches Recht und Verwaltungswissenschaft*, Vol. 57, No. 23, 2004, pp. 977–985.

de Bellis Maurizia, 'Procedural Rule-Making of European Supervisory Agencies (ESAs). An Effective Tool for Legitimacy?', *TARN Working Paper*, No. 12, 2017; available at: https://papers.ssrn.com/sol3/papers.cfm?abstract_id=3030064 (20.3.2018).

de Búrca Gráinne, 'The Quest for Legitimacy in The European Union', *Modern Law Review*, Vol. 59, No. 3, 1996, pp. 349–376.

de Fine Licht Jenny *et al.*, 'When Does Transparency Generate Legitimacy? Experimenting on a Context-Bound Relationship', *Governance. An International Journal of Policy, Administration, and Institutions*, Vol. 27, No. 1, 2014, pp. 111–134.

de Montbrial Thierry, *Action and Reaction in the World System. The Dynamics of Economic and Political Power*, UBC Press, Vancouver/Toronto 2013.

de Morprugo Marco, 'The European Union as a Global Producer of Transnational Law of Risk Regulation: A Case Study on Chemical Regulation', *European Law Journal*, Vol. 19, No. 6, 2013, pp. 779–798.

Decker Frank *et al.*, *Demokratie ohne Wähler? Neue Herausforderungen politischer Partizipation*, Dietz, Bonn 2013.

Dehousse Renaud, 'Delegation of Powers in the European Union: The Need for a Multi-Principals Model', *West European Politics*, Vol. 31, No. 4, 2008, pp. 789–805.

Dehousse Renaud, 'Misfits: EU Law and the Transformation of European Governance', *Jean Monnet Working Paper*, No. 2, 2002; available at: https://jeanmonnetprogram.org/archive/papers/02/020201-01.html (20.3.2018).

DeSario Jack, Langton Stuart, 'Citizen Participation and Technocracy', *Policy Studies Review*, Vol. 3, No. 2, 1984, pp. 223–233.

DiMaggio Paul J., Powell Walter W., 'The Iron Cage Revisited: Institutional Isomorphism and Collective Rationality in Organizational Fields', in: Powell Walter W., DiMaggio Paul J. (ed.), *The New Institutionalism in Organizational Analysis*, University of Chicago Press, Chicago 1991, pp. 63–82.

Dragomir Larisa, *European Prudential Banking Regulation and Supervision. The Legal Dimension*, Routledge, London/New York 2010.

Dubowski Tomasz, *Zasada równowagi instytucjonalnej w prawie Unii Europejskiej* [*The Principle of Institutional Balance in EU Law*], EuroPrawo, Warszawa 2010.

Dubowski Tomasz, Piekutowska Agnieszka, 'Legitymizacja władzy Unii Europejskiej – wybrane aspekty instytucjonalno-proceduralne' ['Legitimacy of the EU Power – Selected Institutional and Procedural Aspects], *Przegląd Politologiczny*, No. 4, 2013, pp. 109–120.

Dumała Andrzej (ed.), *Agencje Unii Europejskiej* [*Agencies of the European Union*], UKIE, Warszawa 2002.

Dybczyński Andrzej, 'Stosunki międzynarodowe w perspektywie teoretycznej' ['A Theoretical Perspective on International Relations'], in: Łoś-Nowak Teresa (ed.), *Współczesne stosunki międzynarodowe* [*Contemporary International Relations*], WUWr, Wrocław 2008, pp. 15–24.

Dyduch Joanna *et al.*, *Krytyczne wprowadzenie do teorii stosunków międzynarodowych* [*Critical Introduction into the Theory of International Relations*], Arboretum, Wrocław 2006.

Easton David, *A Systems Analysis of Political Life*, John Wiley & Sons, New York 1965.

Easton David, *The Political System. An Inquiry into the State of Political Science*, Knopf, New York 1953.

Eberlein Burkard, Grande, Edgar, 'Beyond Delegation: Transnational Regulatory Regimes and the EU Regulatory State', *Journal of European Public Policy*, Vol. 12, No. 1, 2005, pp. 89–112.

Egeberg Morten *et al.*, 'Building Executive Power at the European Level: On the Role of European Union Agencies', in: Busuioc Madalina *et al.* (ed.), *The Agency Phenomenon in the European Union. Emergence, Institutionalisation and Everyday Decision-Making*, Manchester University Press, Manchester/New York 2014, pp. 19–41.

Egeberg Morten *et al.*, 'The EU's Subordinated Agency Administration and the Rise of Executive Power at European Level', in: Bauer Michael W., Trondal Jarle (ed.), *The Palgrave Handbook of the European Administrative System*, Palgrave Macmillan, Basingstoke/New York 2015, pp. 329–348.

Egeberg Morten *et al.*, 'The Quest for Order: Unravelling the Relationship between the European Commission and European Union Agencies', *Journal of European Public Policy*, Vol. 22, No. 5, pp. 609–629.

Egeberg Morten, Trondal Jarle, 'Agencification of the European Union Administration. Connecting the Dots', *TARN Working Paper*, No. 1, 2016; available at: https://papers.ssrn.com/sol3/papers.cfm?abstract_id=2754716 (20.3.2018).

Egeberg Morten, Trondal Jarle 'EU-level Agencies: New Executive Centre Formation or Vehicles for National Control?', *Journal of European Public Policy*, Vol. 18, No. 6, 2011, pp. 868–887.

Egeberg Morten, Trondal Jarle, 'National Agencies in the European Administrative Space: Government Driven, Commission Driven or Networked?', *Public Administration*, Vol. 87, No. 4, 2009, pp. 779–790.

Egeberg Morten, Trondal Jarle, 'Political Leadership and Bureaucratic Autonomy: Effects of Agencification', *Governance. An International Journal of Policy, Administration, and Institutions*, Vol. 22, No. 4, 2009, pp. 673–688.

Egeberg Morten, Trondal Jarle, 'Researching European Union Agencies: What Have We Learnt (and Where Do We Go from Here)?', *Journal of Common Market Studies*, Vol. 55, No. 4, 2017, pp. 675–690.

Ehnert Tanja, *The European Chemicals Agency. Beyond the Scope of the Meroni Doctrine?*, Graduate Theses' Series: Risk Regulation at International, European and National Level, Maastricht 2008; available at: https://www.steptoe.com/assets/attachments/3928.pdf (20.3.2018).

Eifert Martin, 'Legitimationsstrukturen internationaler Verwaltung', in: Trute Hans-Heinrich *et al.* (ed.), *Allgemeines Verwaltungsrecht - zur Tragfähigkeit eines Konzeptes*, Mohr Siebeck, Tübingen 2008, pp. 307–331.

Ekelund Helena, 'The Establishment of Frontex: A New Institutionalist Approach', *Journal of European Integration*, Vol. 36, No. 2, 2014, pp. 99–116.

Eliantonio Mariolina, Spendzharova Aneta, 'The European Union's New "Better Regulation" Agenda: Between Procedures and Politics', *European Journal of Law Reform*, Vol. 19, Nos. 1–2, 2017, pp. 3–15.

Ennser-Jedenastik Laurenz, 'The Politization of Regulatory Agencies: Between Partisan Influence and Formal Independence', *Journal of Public Administration Research and Theory*, Vol. 26, No. 3, 2016, pp. 507–518.

Everson Michelle, 'European Agencies: Barely Legal?', in: Everson Michelle *et al.* (ed.), *European Agencies in between Institutions and Member States*, Wolters Kluwer, Alphen aan den Rijn 2014, pp. 49–69.

Everson Michelle, 'Independent Agencies: Hierarchy Beaters?', *European Law Journal*, Vol. 1, No. 2, 1995, pp. 180–204.

Everson Michelle, 'The European System of Financial Supervision: A Technology of Expertise', in: Ambrus Monika *et al.* (ed.), *The Role of "Experts" in International and European Decision-Making Processes. Advisors, Decision Makers or Irrelevant Actors*, Cambridge University Press, Cambridge 2014, pp. 315–340.

Everson Michelle *et al.*, 'European Agencies in between Institutions and Member States', in: Everson Michelle *et al.* (ed.), *European Agencies in between Institutions and Member States*, Wolters Kluwer, Alphen aan den Rijn 2014, pp. 3–7.

Everson Michelle, Joerges Christian, 'Re-Conceptualising Europeanisation as a Public Law of Collisions: Comitology, Agencies and an Interactive Public Adjudication', in: Hofmann Herwig C.H., Türk Alexander H. (ed.), *EU Administrative Governance*, Edward Elgar Publishing, Cheltenham/Northampton 2006, pp. 512–540.

Everson Michelle, Majone Giandomenico, 'European Agencies within the Treaties of the European Union', in: Majone Giandomenico *et al.* (ed.), *The Role of Specialised Agencies in Decentralising EU Governance. Report Presented to the Commission*, Brussel 1999, pp. 18–80.

Everson Michelle, Vos Ellen, 'European Agencies: What About the Institutional Balance?', in: Łazowski Adam, Blockmans Steven (ed.), *Research Handbook of EU Institutional Law*, Edward Elgar Publishing, Cheltenham/Northampton 2016, pp. 139–151.

Fabbrini Sergio, *Compound Democracies. Why the United States and Europe are Becoming Similar*, Oxford University Press, Oxford 2010.

Fahey Elaine, 'Does the Emperor Have Financial Crisis Clothes. Reflections on the Legal Basis of the European Banking Authority', *Modern Law Review*, Vol. 74, No. 4, 2011, pp. 581–595.

Farell Frank B., *Subjectivity, Realism and Postmodernism. The Recovery of the World in Recent Philosophy*, Cambridge University Press, Cambridge/New York 1996.

Fedorowicz Magdalena, *Nadzór nad rynkiem finansowym Unii Europejskiej* [*Supervision of the EU Financial Market*], Difin, Warszawa 2013.

Fedorowicz Magdalena, 'Porównanie koncepcji normatywnych nowego europejskiego nadzoru finansowego oraz Europejskiego Systemu Banków Centralnych – wybrane zagadnienia' ['Comparison of the Normative Concepts of the New European Financial Supervisory Authority and the European System of Central Banks – Selected Issues'], *Studia Europejskie*, No. 2, 2011, pp. 49–68.

Ferran Eilís, 'The Existential Search of the European Banking Authority', *European Business Organization Law Review*, Vol. 17, No. 3, 2016, pp. 285–317.

Ferraro Francesca, de Capitani Emilio, 'The New European Border and Coast Guard: Yet Another "Half Way" EU Reform?', *ERA Forum*, Vol. 17, No. 3, 2016, pp. 385–398.

Ferrera Maurizio, 'Social Europe and Its Components in the Midst of the Crisis: A Conclusion', *West European Politics*, Vol. 37, No. 4, 2014, pp. 825–843.

Fischer-Appelt Dorothee, *Agenturen der Europäischen Gemeinschaft. Eine Studie zu Rechtsproblemen, Legitimation und Kontrolle europäischer Agenturen mit interdisziplinären und rechtsvergleichenden Bezügen*, Duncker & Humblot, Berlin 1999.

Fiszer Józef M., 'Czy państwo demokratyczne może być wzorem dla przyszłej Unii Europejskiej?' ['Can a Democratic State Be a Model for the Future Development of the European Union?'], *Myśl Ekonomiczna i Polityczna*, Vol. 44, No. 1, 2014, pp. 101–125.

Fleischer Julia, 'Die europäischen Agenturen als Diener Vieler Herren? Zur Steuerung und Rolle von EU-Agenturen', in: Jann Werner, Döhler Marian (Hrsg.), *Agencies in Westeuropa*, VS Verlag für Sozialwissenschaften, Wiesbaden 2007, pp. 212–252.

Fleischer Julia, 'European Agencies as Engines of Regulation? On Different Architectural Strategies of the Regulatory State', Paper Prepared for the 3rd ECPR Annual Conference, 8–10.9.2005; available at: http://regulation.upf.edu/ecpr-05-papers/jfleischer.pdf (20.3.2018).

Font Joan *et al.*, 'Participation, Representation and Expertise: Citizen Preferences for Political Decision-Making Process', *Political Studies*, Vol. 63, No. S1, 2015, pp. 153–172.

Font Nuria, 'Informal Rules and Institutional Balances on the Boards of EU Agencies', *Administration & Society*, Published Online in June 2015, DOI: 10.1177/0095399715588782.

Font Nuria, 'Policy Properties and Political Influence in Post-Delegation: The Case of EU Agencies', *International Review of Administrative Sciences*, Vol. 81, No. 4, 2015, pp. 773–792.

Font Nuria, Pérez Durán Ixchel, 'The European Parliament Oversight of EU Agencies through Written Questions', *Journal of European Public Policy*, Vol. 23, No. 9, 2016, pp. 1349–1366.

Foucault Michel, *Discipline and Punish: The Birth of the Prison*, Random House, New York 1979.

Føllesdal Andreas, 'Democracy and the European Union: Challenges', in: Føllesdal Andreas, Koslowski Peter (ed.), *Democracy and the European Union*, Springer Verlag, Berlin 1997, pp. 1–10.

Føllesdal Andreas, Hix Simon, 'Why There is a Democratic Deficit in the EU: A Response to Majone and Moravcsik', *Journal of Common Markets Studies*, Vol. 44, No. 3, 2006, pp. 533–562.

Franchino Fabio, 'Delegating Powers in the European Community', *British Journal of Political Science*, Vol. 34, No. 2, 2004, pp. 269–293.

Führ Martin, '§ 58 Chemikalienrecht', in: Ehlers Dirk *et al.* (ed.), *Besonderes Verwaltungsrecht*, Bd. 2, C.F. Müller, Heidelberg 2013, pp. 987–1029.

Fülbier Rolf U., 'Regulierung. Ökonomische Betrachtung eines allgegenwärtigen Phänomens', *Wirtschaftswissenschaftliches Studium*, Vol. 28, No. 9, 1999, pp. 468–473.

Gabbi Simone, 'Independent Scientific Advice: Comparing Policies on Conflicts of Interest in the EU and the US', *European Journal of Risk Regulation*, Vol. 2, No. 2, 2011, pp. 213–226.

Gabbi Simone, 'The Principle of Institutional (Un)Balance after Lisbon. Case Note: C-270/12', *European Journal of Risk Regulation*, Vol. 5, No. 2, 2014, pp. 259–266.

Gaitanides Charlotte, 'Kontrolle unabhängiger Institutionen der Europäischen Union', *Jahrbuch des öffentlichen Rechts der Gegenwart*, Vol. 61, 2013, pp. 213–227.

Galster Jan, 'Zasada równowagi instytucjonalnej w orzecznictwie Trybunału Sprawiedliwości Unii Europejskiej' ['The Principle of Institutional Balance in the Case Law of the Court of Justice of the European Union'], *Gdańskie Studia Prawnicze*, Vol. XXXI, 2014, pp. 109–120.

Galster Jan, Łachacz Olga, 'Kilka uwag o podziale władzy w Unii Europejskiej' ['Some Remarks on the Separation of Power within the EU'], *Studia Prawnoustrojowe*, No. 26, 2014, pp. 63–76.

Gandrud Christopher, Hallerberg Mark, 'Does Banking Union Worsen the EU's Democratic Deficit? The Need for Greater Supervisory Data Transparency', *Journal of Common Market Studies*, Vol. 53, No. 4, 2015, pp. 769–785.

Gardner John S., 'The European Agency for the Evaluation of Medicines and European Regulation of Pharmaceuticals', *European Law Journal*, Vol. 2, No. 1, 1996, pp. 48–82.

Gaus Daniel, 'The Dynamics of Legitimation. Why the Study of Political Legitimacy Needs More Realism', *ARENA Working Paper*, No. 8, 2011; available at: http://www.sv.uio.no/arena/english/research/publications/arena-working-papers/2011/wp-08-11.pdf (20.3.2018).

Gaus Daniel, 'Two Kinds of Democratic Legitimacy for the EU? Input- and Output-Oriented Legitimacy as a Case of Conceptual Misformation', Paper Presented at the Conference 'Democracy as Idea and Practice', 14–15.1.2010; available at: http://www.uio.no/english/research/interfaculty-research-areas/democracy/news-and-events/events/conferences/2010/papers/Gaus-TwoKindsOfDemocraticLegitimacy-2010.pdf (20.3.2018).

Gehring Thomas, 'Deliberative Regulation through European Union Agencies and Other Network Structures?', in: Busuioc Madalina *et al.* (ed.), *The Agency Phenomenon in the European Union. Emergence, Institutionalisation and Everyday Decision-Making*, Manchester University Press, Manchester/New York 2014, pp. 105–127.

Gehring Thomas, Krapohl Sebastian, 'Supranational Regulatory Agencies between Independence and Control: The EMEA and the Authorization of Pharmaceuticals in the European Single Market', *Journal of European Public Policy*, Vol. 14, No. 2, 2007, pp. 208–226.

Geradin Damien, 'The Development of European Regulatory Agencies: What the EU Should Learn from American Experience', *Columbia Journal of European Law*, Vol. 11, No. 1, 2004, pp. 1–52.

Geradin Damien, Petit Nicolas, 'The Development of Agencies at EU and National Levels: Conceptual Analysis and Proposals for Reform', *Jean Monnet Working Paper*, No. 1, 2004; available at: http://www.jeanmonnetprogram.org/archive/papers/04/040101.pdf (20.3.2018).

Gestel v. Rob, 'European Regulatory Agencies Adrift? Case-270/12 United Kingdom of Great Britain and Northern Irland *v.* European Parliament and Council of the European Union, Judgment of 22 January 2014', *Maastricht Journal of European and Comparative Law*, Vol. 21, No. 1, 2014, pp. 189–196.

Gestel v. Rob, 'Primacy of the European Legislature? Delegated Rule-Making and the Decline of the "Transmission Belt" Theory', *The Theory and Practice of Legislation*, Vol. 2, No. 1, 2014, pp. 33–59.

Gestel v. Rob, Golen v. Thomas, 'Enforcement by the New European Supervisory Agencies: Quis Custodiet Ipsos Custodes?', in: Purnhagen Kai Peter, Rott Peter (ed.), *Varieties of European Economic Law and Regulation: Liber Amicorum for Hans Micklitz*, Springer Verlag, New York 2014, pp. 757–780.

Gilardi Fabrizio, 'Policy Credibility and Delegation to Independent Regulatory Agencies: A Comparative Empirical Analysis', *Journal of European Public Policy*, Vol. 9, No. 6, 2002, pp. 873–893.

Gilley Bruce, 'Technocracy and Democracy as Spheres of Justice in Public Policy', *Policy Sciences*, Vol. 50, No. 1, 2017, pp. 9–22.

Gläser Karin, *Über legitime Herrschaft. Grundlagen der Legitimitätstheorie*, Springer Verlag, Wiesbaden 2013.

Glencross Andrew, 'Democratic Inputs *versus* Output-Oriented Governance: The ECB's Evolving Role and the New Architecture of Legitimacy in the EU', *Journal of Information and Organizational Sciences*, Vol. 5, No. 2, 2014, pp. 23–36.

Gonod Pascal, 'Legitimacy in Administrative Law: Reform and Reconstruction', in: Ruffert Matthias (ed.), *Legitimacy in European Administrative Law: Reform and Reconstruction*, Europa Law Publishing, Groningen 2011, pp. 2–7.

Görisch Christoph, *Demokratische Verwaltung durch Unionsagenturen*, Mohr Siebeck, Tübingen 2009.

Górka Maciej, 'Instytucje i organy UE' ['EU Institutions and Bodies'], in: Łazowski Adam, Zawidzka-Łojek Anna (ed.), *Instytucje i porządek prawny UE* [*Institutions and the Legal Order in the EU*], EuroPrawo, Warszawa 2015, pp. 59–102.

Górka Maciej, 'Rola Europejskiej Agencji Oceny Produktów Leczniczych w procedurze dopuszczania leków do obrotu w Unii Europejskiej' ['The Role of the European Agency for the Evaluation of Medicines within the EU Regulatory System for Authorising Medicinal Products'], *Kwartalnik Prawa Publicznego*, Vol. 1, No. 2, 2001, pp. 131–158.

Greta Marianna, Otto Jacek, *Proces decyzyjny i zarządczy w UE. Znaczenie systemu agencyjnego* [*The Decision-making and Governance Processes within the EU. The Role of the Agency System*], Wyd. PŁ, Łódź 2016.

Griller Stefan, Orator Andreas, 'Empowering European Agencies or How to Tame the Sorcerer's Apprentice', *NewGov Policy Brief*, No. 22, 2008; available at: http://www.eu-newgov.org/database/PUBLIC/Policy_Briefs/NEWGOV_Policy_Brief_no22.pdf (20.3.2018).

Griller Stefan, Orator Andreas, 'Everything under Control? The "Way Forward" for European Agencies in the Footsteps of the *Meroni* Doctrine', *European Law Review*, Vol. 35, No. 1, 2010, pp. 3–35.

Griller Stefan, Orator Andreas, '"Mapping the Jungle": A Legal Attempt to Classify European Agencies', *NewGov. New Modes of Governance Project*, No.

4, 2006; available at: http://www.eu-newgov.org/protected_pages/DELIV/D04 %20D32_Working_Paper_Mapping_the_Jungle.pdf (20.3.2018).

Griller Stefan, Orator Andreas, '*Meroni* Revisited – Empowering European Agencies between Efficiency and Legitimacy', *NewGov. New Modes of Governance Project*, No. 4, 2007; available at: http://www.eu-newgov.org/database/DELIV/D04D40_WP_Meroni_Revisited.pdf (20.3.2018).

Groenleer Martijn, 'Agency Autonomy Actually: Managerial Strategies, Legitimacy, and the Early Development of the European Union's Agencies for Drug and Food Safety Regulation', *International Public Management Journal*, Vol. 17, No. 2, 2014, pp. 255–292.

Groenleer Martijn, *The Autonomy of European Union Agencies. A Comparative Study of Institutional Development*, Eburon, Delft 2009.

Groenleer Martijn *et al.*, 'Regulatory Governance Through Agencies of the European Union? The Role of the European Agencies for Maritime and Aviation Safety in the Implementation of European Transport Legislation', *Journal of European Public Policy*, Vol. 17, No. 8, 2010, pp. 1212–1230.

Groenleer Martijn, Gabbi Simone, 'Regulatory Agencies of the European Union as International Actors. Legal Framework, Development over Time and Strategic Motives in the Case of the European Food Safety Authority', *European Journal of Risk Regulation*, Vol. 4, No. 4, 2013, pp. 479–492.

Groß Thomas, 'Die Kooperation zwischen europäischen Agenturen und nationalen Behörden', *Europarecht*, No. 1, 2005, pp. 54–68.

Groß Thomas, *Die Legitimation der polyzentralen EU-Verwaltung*, Mohr Siebeck, Tübingen 2015.

Groß Thomas, 'Unabhängige EU-Agenturen – eine Gefahr für die Demokratie?', *JuristenZeitung*, Vol. 67, No. 22, 2012, pp. 1087–1093.

Grosse Tomasz G., 'Kryzys integracji europejskiej w świetle koncepcji Arnolda Toynbee'go' ['The Crisis of the European Integration in the Light of Arnold Toynbee's Concept'], *Przegląd Zachodni*, No. 4(365), 2017, pp. 25–40.

Grzeszczak Robert, 'Legitymizacja demokratyczna Unii Europejskiej' ['Democratic Legitimacy of the EU'], in: Kranz Jerzy (ed.), *Suwerenność i ponadnarodowość a integracja europejska* [*Sovereignty versus Transnationality and the European Integration*], Prawo i Praktyka Gospodarcza, Warszawa 2006, pp. 207–242.

Grzeszczak Robert, 'Podział kompetencji w UE' ['The Division of Powers within the EU'], in: Łazowski Adam, Zawidzka-Łojek Anna (ed.), *Instytucje i porządek prawny UE* [*Institutions and the Legal Order in the EU*], EuroPrawo, Warszawa 2015, pp. 15–26.

Grzeszczak Robert, 'Prawo pierwotne UE' ['EU Primary Law'], in: Łazowski Adam, Zawidzka-Łojek Anna (ed.), *Instytucje i porządek prawny UE* [*Institutions and the Legal Order in the EU*], EuroPrawo, Warszawa 2015, pp. 109–127.

Gubbels-van Hal Ineke, Pelkmans Jacques, 'Is REACH Going Well?', *CEPS Policy Brief*, No. 198, 2009; available at: https://www.ceps.eu/publications/reach-going-well (20.3.2018).

Gunnell John G., 'The Reconstitution of Political Theory: David Easton, Behavioralism, and the Long Road to System', *Journal of the History of the Behavioral Sciences*, Vol. 49, No. 2, 2013, pp. 190–210.

Gunnell John G., 'The Technocratic Image and the Theory of Technocracy', *Technology and Culture*, Vol. 23, No. 3, 1982, pp. 392–416.

Guralnik David B. (ed.), *Webster's New World Dictionary of the American Language*, Warner Books, New York 1982.

Gustafsson Martin, 'On Rawls's Distinction between Perfect and Imperfect Procedural Justice', *Philosophy of the Social Sciences*, Vol. 34, No. 2, 2004, pp. 300–305.

Hagen Bożena, *Ist die EU für eine zentrale Versicherungsaufsicht bereit? Kompetenzrechtliche Untersuchung der institutionellen Dimension der Europäisierung der Versicherungsaufsicht*, DIKE Verlag, Zürich/St. Gallen 2014.

Hansen-Nootbaar Anna Christine, *Unabhängigkeit und Legitimation europäischer Agenturen*, Peter Lang, Frankfurt am Main 2013.

Harlow Carol, 'Civil Society Organisations and Participatory Administration: A Challenge to EU Administrative Law', in: Smismans Stijn (ed.), *Civil Society and Legitimate European Governance*, Edward Elgar Publishing, Cheltenham/Northampton 2006, pp. 115–140.

Harlow Carol, Rawlings Richard, *Process and Procedure in EU Administration*, Hart Publishing, Oxford/Portland 2014.

Harlow Carol, Rawlings Richard, 'Promoting Accountability in Multilevel Governance: A Network Approach', *European Law Journal*, Vol. 13, No. 4, 2007, pp. 542–562.

Hatzopoulos Vassillis, 'Hard to Soft: Governance in the EU Internal Market', *Cambridge Yearbook of European Legal Studies*, Vol. 15, 2013, pp. 101–137.

Hauser Roman, Niewiadomski Zygmunt, Wróbel Andrzej (ed.), *System prawa administracyjnego. Europeizacja prawa administracyjnego* [*System of Administrative Law. The Europeanisation of Administrative Law*], C.H. Beck, Warszawa 2014.

Hayes-Renshaw Fiona, *The Role of the Council*, in: Andersen Svein S., Eliassen Kjell A. (ed.), *The European Union: How Democratic Is It?*, Sage Publications, London 1996, pp. 143–164.

Häde Ulrich, 'Jenseits der Effizienz: Wer kontrolliert die Kontrolleure? Demokratische Verantwortlichkeit und rechtsstaatliche Kontrolle der europäischen Finanzaufsichtsbehörden', *Europäische Zeitschrift für Wirtschaftsrecht*, Vol. 22, No. 17, 2011, pp. 662–666.

Hänle Florian, *Die neue Europäische Finanzaufsicht. Kompetenzen der neuen Europäischen Wertpapier- und Marktaufsichtsbehörde (ESMA)*, Verlag Dr. Kovač, Hamburg 2012.

Heims Eva, *Building EU Regulatory Capacity: The Work of Under-Resourced Agencies in the European Union*, Springer Verlag, Cham 2019.

Held David, *Models of Democracy*, Stanford University Press, Stanford 2006.

Held David *et al.*, *Global Transformations. Politics, Economics and Culture*, Stanford University Press, Stanford 1999.

Hellebø Rykkja Lise, 'Independent Food Agencies – Restoring Confidence', *Policy and Society. An Interdisciplinary Journal of Policy Research*, Vol. 23, No. 4, 2004, pp. 125–148.

Hennis Wilhelm, 'Legitimität. Zu einer Kategorie der bürgerlichen Gesellschaft', in: Graf Kielmansegg Peter (ed.), *Legitimationsprobleme politischer Systeme*, Springer Verlag, Opladen 1976, pp. 9–38.

Herdegen Matthias, *Der Kampf um die Weltordnung. Eine strategische Betrachtung*, C.H. Beck, München 2019.

Hermes Georg, 'Legitimationsprobleme unabhängiger Behörden', in: Bauer Hartmut *et al.* (ed.), *Demokratie in Europa*, Mohr Siebeck, Tübingen 2005, pp. 457–488.

Heyvaert Veerle, 'The EU Chemicals Policy: Towards Inclusive Governance?', *LSE Law, Society and Economy Working Papers*, No. 7, 2008; available at: http://www.lse.ac.uk/law/working-paper-series/2007-08/WPS2008-07-Heyvaert.pdf (20.3.2018).

Hilf Meinhard, *Die Organisationsstruktur der Europäischen Gemeinschaften. Rechtliche Gestaltungsmöglichkeiten und Grenzen*, Springer Verlag, Berlin 1982.

Hillgruber Christian, *Weniger ist mehr – Plädoyer für eine Begrenzung der Kompetenzen der EU zwecks Wiederherstellung einer föderalen Balance*, in: Kadelbach Stefan (ed.), *Die Europäische Union am Scheideweg: mehr oder weniger Europa?*, Nomos Verlag, Baden-Baden 2015, pp. 29–48.

Hoare Quentin, Nowell Smith Geoffrey (ed./transl.), *Selections from the Prison Notebooks of Antonio Gramsci*, ElecBook, London 1999.

Hofmann Herwig C.H., 'A European Regulatory Union? The Role of Agencies and Standards', in: Koutrakos Panos, Snell Jukka (ed.), *Research Handbook on the Law of the EU's Internal Market*, Edward Elgar Publishing, Cheltenham 2017, pp. 460–478.

Hofmann Herwig C.H., 'Agency Design in the European Union', *Windsor Yearbook of Access to Justice*, Vol. 28, No. 2, 2010, pp. 309–323.

Hofmann Herwig C.H., 'Mapping the European Administrative Space', in: Curtin Deirdre, Egeberg Morten (ed.), *Towards a New Executive Order in Europe*, Routledge, London/New York 2015, pp. 24–38.

Hofmann Herwig C.H., Morini Alessandro, 'The Pluralisation of EU Executive – Constitutional Aspects of "Agencification"', *European Law Review*, Vol. 37, No. 4, 2012, pp. 419–443.

Holznagel Bernd, Schumacher Pascal, 'Die politische Unabhängigkeit der Bundesnetzagentur', in: Gramlich Ludwig, Manger-Nestler Cornelia (ed.), *Europäisierte Regulierungsstrukturen und -netzwerke. Basis einer künftigen Infrastrukturvorsorge*, Nomos Verlag, Baden-Baden 2011, pp. 37–53.

Holznagel Bernd, Schumacher Pascal, 'Funktionelle Unabhängigkeit und demokratische Legitimation europäischer Regulierungsagenturen', in: Joost Detlev *et al.* (ed.), *Festschrift für Franz Jürgen Säcker zum 70. Geburtstag*, C.H. Beck, München 2011, pp. 737–754.

Horan Conor, Finch John, 'The Temporal and Processual Dimensions of Practice for Enhancing Knowledge Exchange', *Dublin Institute of Technology Conference Papers*, No. 9, 2011; available at: https://arrow.dit.ie/cgi/viewcontent.cgi?article=1123&context=buschmarcon (20.3.2018).

Howell Elizabeth, 'The Evolution of ESMA and Direct Supervision: Are There Implications for EU Supervisory Governance?', *Common Market Law Review*, Vol. 54, No. 4, 2017, pp. 1027–1058.

Howlett Michael *et al.*, 'Streams and Stages: Reconciling Kingdon and Policy Process Theory', *European Journal of Political Research*, Vol. 54, No. 3, 2015, pp. 419–434.

Höreth Marcus, 'No Way Out for the Beast? The Unsolved Legitimacy Problem of European Governance', *Journal of European Public Policy*, Vol. 6, No. 2, 1999, pp. 249–268.

Höreth Marcus, 'The European Commission's White Paper on Governance: A "Tool-Kit" for Closing the Legitimacy Gap of EU Policymaking?', *ZEI Discussion Paper*, No. 94, 2001; available at: https://www.zei.uni-bonn.de/dateien/discussion-paper/dp_c94_hoereth.pdf (20.3.2018).

Hummer Waldemar, 'Von der „Agentur" zum „interinstitutionellen Amt"', in: Hammer Stefan *et al.* (ed.), *Demokratie und sozialer Rechtsstaat in Europa. Festschrift für Theo Öhlinger*, Facultas, Wien 2004, pp. 92–130.

Hurej Zbigniew, 'Zasada kompetencji przyznanych w prawie wspólnotowym a suwerenność państw członkowskich' ['The Principle of Conferral in the EU Law and the Sovereignty of the Member States'], *Acta Universitatis Wratislaviensis. Przegląd Prawa i Administracji*, Vol. 77, No. 3052, 2008, pp. 129–144.

Husar Holmes Maja, 'Validating the Relevance of Leadership in Public Administration', *International Journal of Organization Theory and Behavior*, Vol. 12, No. 2, 2009, pp. 254–265.

Hustedt Thurid *et al.*, *Verwaltungsstrukturen in der Europäischen Union. Kommission, Komitologie, Agenturen und Verwaltungsnetzwerke*, Springer Verlag, Wiesbaden 2014.

Hyman David A., Kovacic William E., 'Why Who Does What Matters: Governmental Design and Agency Performance', *George Washington Law Review*, Vol. 82, No. 5, 2014, pp. 1146–1516.

Iglesias Rodriguez Pablo, 'The Role of Interest Groups in EU Financial Regulation after the European Supervisory Authorities in the Financial Field: The Case of the Stakeholder Groups', *ESIL Law Conference Paper*, No. 10, 2011; available at: https://papers.ssrn.com/sol3/papers.cfm?abstract_id=1989917 (20.3.2018).

Inman Robert P., Rubinfeld Daniel L., 'Economics of Federalism', in: F. Parisi (ed.), *The Oxford Handbook of Law and Economics. Public Law and Legal Institutions*, Vol. 3, Oxford University Press, Oxford/New York 2017, pp. 84–105.

Ipsen Hans P., *Europäisches Gemeinschaftsrecht*, Mohr Siebeck, Tübingen 1972.

Iusmen Ingi, Boswell John, 'The Dilemmas of Pursuing "Throughput Legitimacy" through Participatory Mechanisms', *West European Politics*, Vol. 40, No. 2, 2017, pp. 459–478.

Jachtenfuchs Markus, 'Der Wandel des regulativen Mehrebenensystems der EU', *DMS – Der moderne Staat. Zeitschrift für Public Policy, Recht und Management*, Vol. 3, No. 1, 2010, pp. 109–124.

Jacobs Francis, 'EU Agencies and the European Parliament', in: Everson Michelle *et al.* (ed.), *European Agencies in between Institutions and Member States*, Wolters Kluwer, Alphen aan den Rijn 2014, pp. 201–228.

Jacqué Jean-Paul, 'The Principle of Institutional Balance', *Common Market Law Review*, Vol. 41, No. 2, 2004, pp. 383–391.

Jann Werner *et al.*, 'Best Practice in Governance of Agencies – A Comparative Study in View of Identifying Best Practice for Governing Agencies Carrying out Activities on Behalf of the European Union', *Study. Policy Department on Budgetary Affairs*, January 2008; available at: http://www.europarl.europa.eu/RegData/etudes/etudes/join/2008/392953/IPOL-JOIN_ET(2008)392953_EN.pdf (20.3.2018).

Jasinskaja-Lahti Inga, Laine Markus (ed.), 'Founding the European Chemicals Agency: The Perspectives of the Employees and the Authorities of the City of Helsinki', *City of Helsinki Urban Facts. Research Series*, No. 7, 2009; available at: https://www.hel.fi/hel2/tietokeskus/julkaisut/pdf/09_12_30_Tutkimuksia_7_Laine.pdf (20.3.2018).

Jaśkowski Marek, 'Miejsce podstawowych zasad ogólnych prawa wspólnotowego w hierarchii wspólnotowych źródeł prawa' ['General Principles of Community Law in the Hierarchy of Sources in European Community Law'], in: Mik Cezary (ed.), *Zasady ogólne prawa wspólnotowego* [*General Principles of Community Law*], TNOiK, Toruń 2007, S. 55–86.

Jääskinen Niilo, 'Europeanisation of National Law: A Legal-Theoretical Analysis', *European Law Review*, Vol. 40, No. 5, 2015, pp. 667–682.

Jedlecka Wioletta, *Legitymizacja prawa Unii Europejskiej. Legitymizacja demokratyczna czy cywilizacyjna?* [*Legitimisation of EU Law. Democratic versus Civilizational Legitimisation*], WUŁ, Łódź 2014.

Jordana Jacint *et al.*, 'European Transboundary Crises and EU Agencies: Examining Board Members' Attitudes Towards Crisis Involvement', *IBEI Working Papers*, No. 55, 2018; available at: https://www.ibei.org/european-transboundary-crises-and-eu-agencies-examining-board-members-attitudes-towards-crisis-involvement_94519.pdf (20.3.2018).

Jordana Jacint *et al.*, 'The Global Diffusion of Regulatory Agencies: Channels of Transfer and Stages of Diffusion', *Comparative Political Studies*, Vol. 44, No. 10, 2011, pp. 1343–1369.

Jordana Jacint, Triviño-Salazar Juan Carlos, 'European Union Agencies: A Transnational Logic?', *IBEI Working Papers*, No. 54, 2017; available at: https://www.ibei.org/european-union-agencies-a-transnational-logic_84276.pdf (20.3.2018).

Jurkowska-Zeidler Anna, 'Europejski System Gwarantowania Depozytów: Trzeci brakujący filar do dokończenia Unii Bankowej' ['European Deposit Insurance System: The Third Missing Pillar for Completing the Banking Union'], *Annales Universitatis Mariae Curie-Skłodowska. Lublin – Polonia. Sectio H*, Vol. L, No. 4, 2016, pp. 171–181.

Kabat-Rudnicka Danuta, *Zasada federalna a integracja ponadnarodowa. Unia Europejska między federalizmem dualistycznym a kooperatywnym* [*The Federal Principle and Supranational Integration. The EU between Dual and Cooperative Federalism*], Lettra-Graphic, Kraków 2010.

Kahl Arno, 'Europäische Agenturen im Lichte der dynamischen Verwaltungslehre', in: Arnold Konrad *et al.* (ed.), *Recht, Politik, Wirtschaft. Dynamische Perspektiven. Festschrift für Norbert Wimmer*, Springer Verlag, Wien/New York 2008, pp. 245–268.

Karpenstein Peter, 'Die Entwicklung des Gemeinschaftsrechts', *Europarecht*, No. 4, 1975, pp. 354–360.

Karska Elżbieta (ed.), *Globalne problemy ochrony praw człowieka* [*Global Problems with the Protection of Human Rights*], WPiA UKSW, Warszawa 2015.

Kämmerer Jörn A., Starski Paulina, 'Die Europäische Zentralbank in der Bankenunion oder: Vor Risiken und Nebenwirkungen wird gewarnt', *Zeitschrift für Gesetzgebung*, Vol. 28, No. 4, 2013, pp. 318–338.

Kelemen Daniel R., 'The Politics of "Eurocratic" Structure and New European Agencies', *West European Politics*, Vol. 25, No. 4, 2002, pp. 93–118.

Kelemen Daniel R., *The Rules of Federalism: Institutions and Regulatory Politics in the EU and Beyond*, Harvard University Press, Cambridge/Massachusetts 2004.

Kelemen Daniel R., Tarrant Andrew D., 'The Political Foundations of the Eurocracy', *West European Politics*, Vol. 34, No. 5, 2011, pp. 922–947.

Kelly Claire R., 'Institutional Alliances and Derivative Legitimacy', *Michigan Journal of International Law*, Vol. 29, No. 4, 2008, pp. 609–664.

Kenig-Witkowska Maria M., Łazowski Adam, Ostrihansky Rudolf, *Prawo instytucjonalne Unii Europejskiej* [*EU Institutional Law*], C.H. Beck, Warszawa 2017.

Kietz Daniela, Ondarza v. Nicolai, 'Sicherheit delegieren. EU-Agenturen in der inneren und äußeren Sicherheit', *SWP-Studie*, April 2016; available at: https://www.swp-berlin.org/fileadmin/contents/products/studien/2016S06_ktz_orz.pdf (20.3.2018).

Kilb Wolfgang, 'Europäische Agenturen und ihr Personal – die großen Unbekannten?', *Europäische Zeitschrift für Wirtschaftsrecht*, Vol. 17, No. 9, 2006, pp. 268–273.

King Christopher S., 'Economic Theories of Democratic Legitimacy and the Normative Role of an Ideal Consensus', *Politics, Philosophy & Economics*, Vol. 12, No. 2, 2013, pp. 156–178.

King Christopher S., 'Problems in the Theory of Democratic Authority', *Ethical Theory and Moral Practice. An International Forum*, Vol. 15, No. 4, 2012, pp. 431–448.

Kingdon John, *Agendas, Alternatives and Public Policies*, Pearson Education, Boston 2014.

Kirste Stephan, 'Das System der Europäischen Agenturen. Erläutert am Beispiel des Europäischen Innovations- und Technlogieinstituts', *Verwaltungsarchiv. Zeitschrift für Verwaltungslehre, Verwaltungsrecht und Verwaltungspolitik*, Vol. 102, No. 2, 2011, pp. 268–284.

Klika Christoph, 'The Implementation of the REACH Authorisation Procedure on Chemical Substances of Concern: What Kind of Legitimacy?', *Politics and Governance*, Vol. 3, No. 1, 2015, pp. 128–138.

Kluth Winfried, 'Art. 14 EUV', in: Calliess Christian, Ruffert Matthias (ed.), *EUV/AEUV. Das Verfassungsrecht der Europäischen Union mit Europäischer Grundrechtecharta. Kommentar*, C.H. Beck, München 2011, pp. 229–244.

Knight Derek J., 'Chemicals in the European Union. The European Chemicals Agency Experience', *Chemistry International*, Vol. 34, No. 6, 2012; available at: http://www.iupac.org/publications/ci/2012/3406/2_knight.html (20.3.2018).

Knill Christoph, Grohs Stephen, 'Administrative Styles of EU Institutions', in: Bauer Michael W., Trondal Jarle (ed.), *The Palgrave Handbook of the European Administrative System*, Palgrave Macmillan, Basingstoke/New York 2015, pp. 93–107.

Knio Karim, 'The Role of Experts and Financial Supervision in the European Union: The de Larosière Commission', in: Ambrus Monika *et al.* (ed.), *The Role of "Experts" in International and European Decision-Making Processes. Advisors, Decision Makers or Irrelevant Actors*, Cambridge University Press, Cambridge 2014, pp. 341–360.

Koch Michael H., *Externalisierungspolitik der Kommission. Zulässigkeit und Grenzen mittelbarer Gemeinschaftsverwaltung*, Nomos Verlag, Baden-Baden 2004.

Koch Michael H., 'Mittelbare Gemeinschaftsverwaltung in der Praxis', *Europäische Zeitschrift für Wirtschaftsrecht*, Vol. 16, No. 15, 2005, pp. 455–459.

Kocharov Anna, 'EFSA and Identification of Emerging Risks', *European Food and Feed Law Review*, Vol. 5, No. 3, 2010, pp. 144–155.

Koenig Christian *et al.*, 'Do We Really Need a European Agency for Market Regulation?', *Intereconomics*, Vol. 43, No. 4, 2008, pp. 226–235.

Kohtamäki Natalia, 'Autonomia instytucjonalna urzędów regulacyjnych Unii Europejskiej: przykład Europejskiej Agencji Bezpieczeństwa Lotniczego' ['Institutional Autonomy of EU Regulatory Agencies: The Case of the European Aviation Safety Agency'], *Internetowy Kwartalnik Antymonopolowy i Regulacyjny*, No. 2(5), 2016, pp. 56–69.

Kohtamäki Natalia, *Die Reform der Bankenaufsicht in der Europäischen Union*, Mohr Siebeck, Tübingen 2012.

Kohtamäki Natalia, 'Kultura organizacyjna w agencjach regulacyjnych Unii Europejskiej' ['Organisational Culture in the EU Regulatory Agencies'], *Polski Przegląd Stosunków Międzynarodowych*, No. 5, 2015, pp. 67–88.

Kohtamäki Natalia, 'Realizacja interesu narodowego w strukturach Unii Europejskiej na przykładzie autonomicznych agencji regulacyjnych' ['National Interests within the European Union: The Case of the Autonomous European Regulatory Agencies'], *Annales Universitatis Paedagogicae Cracoviensis. Studia Politologica*, Vol. XVII, No. 214, 2016, pp. 129–144.

Koop Christel, Lodge Martin, 'What is Regulation? An Interdisciplinary Concept Analysis', *Regulation & Governance*, Vol. 11, No. 1, 2017, pp. 95–108.

Kopeć Marcin, 'Wspólnotowe *soft law* jako przejaw europeizacji prawa farmaceutycznego' ['Community "Soft Law" as a Sign of Europeanisation in the Field of Pharmaceutical Law'], in: Lipowicz Irena (ed.), *Europeizacja administracji publicznej* [*Europeanisation of the Public Administration*], Wyd. UKSW, Warszawa 2008, pp. 246–259.

Korkea-aho Emilia, *Adjudicating New Governance: Deliberative Democracy in the European Union*, Routledge, Abingdon/New York 2015.

Korkea-aho Emilia, 'Effects of the EU Chemicals Regulation REACH in a Globalized Internal Market: FCD and FMB', *Common Market Law Review*, Vol. 53, No. 3, 2016, pp. 763–778.

Korkea-aho Emilia, Leino Päivi, 'Who Owns the Information Held by EU Agencies? Weed Killers, Commercially Sensitive Information and Transparent and Participatory Governance', *Common Market Law Review*, Vol. 54, No. 4, 2017, pp. 1059–1091.

Kosińska Anna M., 'The Role of the Fundamental Rights Agency in Irregular Migrant's Rights Protection', *Review of Comparative Law*, Vol. XVIII, 2013, pp. 93–105.

Kostrubiec Jarosław, 'W kręgu problematyki prawnej legitymizacji władzy' ['The Question of the Legal Legitimisation of Authority'], *Studia Iuridica Lublinensia*, No. 1, 2003, pp. 97–110.

Kownacki Tomasz, *Legitymizowanie systemu politycznego Unii Europejskiej* [*Legitimising the EU Political System*], Elipsa, Warszawa 2014.

Kranz Jerzy, 'Deficyt demokracji w Unii Europejskiej?' ['Democratic Deficit in the European Union?'], *Sprawy Międzynarodowe*, No. 3, 2012, pp. 5–25.

Kranz Jerzy, 'Kilka uwag o federalizmie i suwerenności w kontekście UE' ['Some Remarks on Federalism and Sovereignty in the Context of the EU'], *Sprawy Międzynarodowe*, No. 1, 2012, pp. 109–115.

Krapohl Sebastian, 'Credible Commitment in Non-Independent Regulatory Agencies: A Comparative Analysis of the European Agencies for Pharmaceuticals and Foodstuffs', *European Law Journal*, Vol. 10, No. 5, 2004, pp. 518–538.

Kreher Alexander, 'Agencies in the European Community – A Step Towards Administrative Integration in Europe', *Journal of European Public Policy*, Vol. 4, No. 2, 1997, pp. 225–245.

Krekora Magdalena, Świerczyński Marek, Traple Elżbieta, *Prawo farmaceutyczne* [*Pharmaceutical Law*], Wolters Kluwer, Warszawa 2012.

Kröger Sandra, 'The End of Democracy as We Know It? The Legitimacy Deficits of Bureaucratic Social Policy Governance', *Journal of European Integration*, Vol. 29, No. 5, 2007, pp. 565–582.

Kröger Sandra, Friedrich Dawid, 'Democratic Representation in the EU: Two Kinds of Subjectivity', *Journal of European Public Policy*, Vol. 20, No. 2, 2013, pp. 171–189.

Kubin Tomasz, *Legitymizacja systemu instytucjonalnego Unii Europejskiej* [*Legitimisation of the EU Institutional System*], Uniwersytet Śląski, Katowice 2014.

Kubin Tomasz, 'Legitymizacja systemu instytucjonalnego Unii Europejskiej jako organizacji międzynarodowej *sui generis*' ['Legitimisation of the Institutional System of the European Union as an International Organization *sui generis*'], *Politeja*, No. 6(45), 2016, pp. 145–169.

Kumaniecki Kazimierz (ed.), *Słownik łacińsko-polski* [*Latin-Polish Dictionary*], PWN, Warszawa 1983.

Kurpas Sebastian *et al.*, 'The European Commission after Enlargement: Does More Add Up to Less?', *CEPS Special Report*, February 2008; available at: https://www.ceps.eu/system/files/book/1620.pdf (20.3.2018).

Kuś Artur (ed.), *Prawo instytucjonalne Unii Europejskiej* [*EU Institutional Law*], Wyd. KUL, Lublin 2012.

Kühling Jürgen, 'Die Zukunft des Europäischen Agentur(un)wesens – oder: Wer hat Angst vor *Meroni*', *Europäische Zeitschrift für Wirtschaftsrecht*, Vol. 19, No. 5, 2008, p. 129.

Lacey Joseph, 'Conceptually Mapping the European Union: A Demoi-Cratic Analysis', *Journal of European Integration*, Vol. 38, No. 1, 2016, pp. 61–77.

Lamy Steven L., 'Contemporary Mainstream Approaches: Neo-Realism and Neo-Liberalism', in: Baylis John *et al.* (ed.), *The Globalization of World Politics. An Introduction to International Relations*, Oxford University Press, New York 2011, pp. 114–129.

Landfried Christine, 'Beyond Technocratic Governance: The Case of Biotechnology', *European Law Journal*, Vol. 3, No. 3, 1997, pp. 255–272.

Landscheidt Fabian, 'Der Sitzwechsel europäischer Agenturen am Beispiel der Europäischen Arzneimitelagentur im Rahmen des "Brexit"', *Zeitschrift für europarechtliche Studien*, Vol. 20, No. 1, 2017, pp. 3–22.

Laubinger Hans-Werner, 'Regulierungsrecht: Gibt's das – und wenn ja: wie viele?', *Verwaltungsblätter für Baden-Württemberg*, Vol. 31, No. 8, 2010, pp. 306–310.

Lawless James, 'EFSA under Pressure: Emerging Risks, Emergencies and Crises', in: Alemanno Alberto, Gabbi Simone (ed.), *Foundations of EU Food Law and Policy. Ten Years of the European Food Safety Authority*, Ashgate, Farnham/Burlington 2014, pp. 93–109.

Le Sueur Andrew, 'People as "Users" and "Citizens". The Quest for Legitimacy in British Public Administration', in: Ruffert Matthias (ed.), *Legitimacy in European Administrative Law: Reform and Reconstruction*, Europa Law Publishing, Groningen 2011, pp. 27–48.

Lea Stephen J., *Transparency in European Union Governance: The Misdirection of Europe's Legitimacy Enterprise*, Ph.D. Thesis, University of Shefield. Department of Law, September 2016; available at: http://etheses.whiterose.ac.uk/16758/ (20.3.2018).

Lehmann Matthias, Manger-Nestler Cornelia, 'Das neue europäische Finanzaufsichtssystem', *Zeitschrift für Bankrecht und Bankwirtschaft*, Vol. 23, No. 1, 2011, pp. 2–24.

Lenaerts Koen, 'Constitutionalism and the Many Faces of Federalism', *The American Journal of Comparative Law*, Vol. 38, No. 2, 1990, pp. 205–263.

Lenaerts Koen, 'Regulating the Regulatory Process: "Delegation of Powers" in the European Community', *European Law Review*, Vol. 18, No. 1, 1993, pp. 23–49.

Lenaerts Koen, 'Some Reflections on the Separation of Powers in the European Community', *Common Market Law Review*, Vol. 28, No. 1, 1991, pp. 11–35.

Lenearts Koen *et al.* (ed.), *Constitutional Law of the European Union*, Sweet & Maxwell, London 2005.

Léonard Sarah, 'EU Border Security and Migration into the European Union: Frontex and Securitisation through Practices', *European Security*, Vol. 19, No. 2, 2010, pp. 231–254.

Leschke Martin, 'Regulierungstheorie aus ökonomischer Sicht', in: Fehling Michael, Ruffert Matthias (ed.), *Regulierungsrecht*, Mohr Siebeck, Tübingen 2010, pp. 281–331.

Levi-Faur David, 'Regulatory Networks and Regulatory Agencification: Towards a Single European Regulatory Space', in: Rittberger Berthold, Wonka Arndt (ed.), *Agency Governance in the EU*, Routledge, London/New York 2012, pp. 32–51.

Levi-Faur David, 'The Global Diffusion of Regulatory Capitalism', *Annals of the American Academy of Political and Social Science*, Vol. 598, No. 1, 2005, pp. 12–32.

Liberatore Angela, Funtowicz Silvio, '"Democratising" Expertise, "Expertising" Democracy: What Does It Mean, and Why Bother?', *Science and Public Policy*, Vol. 30, No. 3, 2003, pp. 146–150.

Lindgren Karl-Oskar, Persson Thomas, 'Input and Output Legitimacy: Synergy or Trade-off? Empirical Evidence from an EU Survey?', *Journal of European Public Policy*, Vol. 17, No. 4, 2010, pp. 449–467.

Lipowicz Irena, 'Europeizacja administracji publicznej' ['Europeanisation of the Public Administration'], *Ruch Prawniczy, Ekonomiczny i Socjologiczny*, Vol. LXX, No. 1, 2008, pp. 7–17.

Lipowicz Irena, 'Europeizacja i modernizacja. Administracyjnoprawne aspekty zmian polskiej administracji publicznej' ['Europeanisation and Modernisation: Administrative and Legal Aspects of the Reform of the Polish Public

Administration'], in: Lipowicz Irena (ed.), *Europeizacja administracji publicznej* [*Europeanisation of the Public Administration*], Wyd. UKSW, Warszawa 2008, pp. 15–35.

Livonius v. Hilger, 'EuGH: Generalanwalt halt Art. 28 der EU-Leerverkauf-Verordnung für nichtig', *Recht der Finanzinstrumente*, No. 4, 2013, p. 339.

Lo Shiavo Gianni, 'A Judicial Re-Thinking on the Delegation of Powers to European Agencies under EU Law? Comment on Case C-270/12 UK *v.* Council and Parliament', *German Law Journal*, Vol. 16, No. 2, 2015, pp. 315–335.

Lo Schiavo Gianni, 'The European Supervisory Authorities: A True Evolutionary Step along the Process of European Financial Integration?', Conference Papers. Vilnius University, 2013, pp. 293–302.

Lodge Martin, 'Regulation, the Regulatory State and European Politics', *West European Politics*, Vol. 31, Nos. 1–2, 2008, pp. 280–301.

Lord Christopher, 'The European Parliament and the Legitimation of Agencification', *Journal of European Public Policy*, Vol. 18, No. 6, 2011, pp. 909–925.

Lord Christopher, Beetham David, 'Legitimizing the EU: Is There a "Post-Parliamentary Basis" for Its Legitimization', *Journal of Common Market Studies*, Vol. 39, No. 3, 2001, pp. 443–462.

Lübbe-Wolff Gertrude, 'Europäisches und nationales Verfassungsrecht', in: Dreier Horst *et al.*, *Berichte und Diskussionen auf der Tagung der Deutschen Staatsrechtslehrer in Leipzig vom 4. bis 6. Oktober 2000*, Walter de Gruyter, Berlin 2001, pp. 246–289.

Łazowski Adam, 'Charakter prawny i cele UE' ['The Legal Character and Goals of the EU'], in: Łazowski Adam, Zawidzka-Łojek Anna (ed.), *Instytucje i porządek prawny UE* [*Institutions and the Legal Order in the EU*], EuroPrawo, Warszawa 2015, pp. 3–10.

Łazowski Adam, Wessel Ramses A., 'The External Dimension of Withdrawal from the European Union', *Revue des Affaires Européennes*, No. 4, 2016, pp. 623–638.

Łazowski Adam, Zawidzka-Łojek Anna, *Prawo międzynarodowe publiczne* [*International Public Law*], C.H. Beck, Warszawa 2011.

Macedo Stephen, 'Against Majoritarianism: Democratic Values and Institutional Design', *Boston University Law Review*, Vol. 90, No. 2, 2010, pp. 1029–1042.

Maggetti Martino, 'Legitimacy and Accountability of Independent Regulatory Agencies: A Critical Review', *Living Reviews in Democracy*, Vol. 2, 2010, pp. 1–9.

Maggetti Martino, Gilardi Fabrizio, 'The Policy-Making Structure of European Regulatory Networks and the Domestic Adoption of Standards', in: Rittberger Berthold, Wonka Arndt (ed.), *Agency Governance in the EU*, Routledge, London/New York 2012, pp. 52–69.

Maggetti Martino, Verhoest Koen, 'Unexplored Aspects of Bureaucratic Autonomy: A State of the Field and Ways Forward', *International Review of Administrative Science*, Vol. 80, No. 2, 2014, pp. 239–256.

Magnette Paul, 'Democracy in the European Union: Why and How to Combine Representation and Participation', in: Smismans Stijn (ed.), *Civil Society and Legitimate European Governance*, Edward Elgar Publishing, Cheltenham/Northampton 2006, pp. 23–41.

Majchrzak Bartosz, *Problem delimitacji regulacji administracyjnoprawnej w systemie prawnym w świetle orzecznictwa Trybunału Konstytucyjnego* [*The Problem of Delimitation of Administrative Law in the Legal System in the Light of Selected Constitutional Law Decisions*], Wyd. UKSW, Warszawa 2015.

Majone Giandomenico, 'Delegation of Regulatory Powers in a Mixed Polity', *European Law Journal*, Vol. 8, No. 3, 2002, pp. 319–339.

Majone Giandomenico, 'From Regulatory State to a Democratic Default', *Journal of Common Market Studies*, Vol. 52, No. 6, 2014, pp. 1216–1223.

Majone Giandomenico, 'Regulatory Legitimacy', in: Majone Giandomenico (ed.), *Regulating Europe*, Routledge, London/New York 1996, pp. 284–301.

Majone Giandomenico, 'Temporal Consistency and Policy Credibility: Why Democracies Need Non-Majoritarian Institutions', *EUI Working Paper RSC*, No. 96/57, 1996; available at: http://cadmus.eui.eu/bitstream/handle/1814/1472/RSCAS_1996_57.pdf (20.3.2018).

Majone Giandomenico, 'The Credibility Crisis of Community Regulation', *Journal of Common Market Studies*, Vol. 38, No. 2, 2000, pp. 273–302.

Majone Giandomenico, 'The New European Agencies: Regulation by Information', *Journal of European Public Policy*, Vol. 4, No. 2, 1997, pp. 262–275.

Majone Giandomenico, 'The Rise of the Regulatory State in Western Europe', *West European Politics*, Vol. 17, No. 3, 1994, pp. 77–101.

Makhashvili Levan, Stephenson Paul, 'Differentiating Agency Independence: Perceptions from Inside the European Medicines Agency', *Journal of Contemporary European Research*, Vol. 9, No. 1, 2013, pp. 4–23.

Malan Jack *et al.*, 'The Cost of Non-Agencies with Relevance to the Internal Market', *European Parliament. Policy Department: Budgetary Affairs. Study*, No. PE 572.702, 2016; available at : http://www.europarl.europa.eu/RegData/etudes/STUD/2016/572702/IPOL_STU(2016)572702_EN.pdf (20.3.2018).

Maletić Isidora, 'Delegating Harmonization of the Internal Market in Case C-270/12 United Kingdom of Great Britain and Northern Irland *v.* European

Parliament and Council of the EU (Short Selling Ban), Judgment of 22 January 2014', *Yearbook of European Law*, Vol. 33, No. 1, 2014, pp. 501–517

Maletić Isidora, *The Law and Policy of Harmonisation in Europe's Internal Market*, Edward Elgar Publishing, Cheltenham/Northhampton 2013.

Manger-Nestler Cornelia, 'EU-Agenturen als Ausdruck des europäischen Demokratiemangels?', *Zeitschrift für europarechtliche Studien*, Vol. 18, No. 3, 2015, pp. 315–346.

Manger-Nestler Cornelia, 'Lehren aus dem Leerverkauf? Zum Verbot von Leerverkäufen durch ESMA', *Zeitschrift für das Privatrecht der Europäischen Union*, Vol. 11, No. 3, 2014, pp. 141–143.

Mantel Jessica, 'Procedural Safeguards for Agency Guidance: A Source of Legitimacy for Administrative State', *Administrative Law Review*, Vol. 61, No. 2, 2009, pp. 343–406.

March James G., Olsen Johan P., *Rediscovering Institutions. The Organizational Basis of Politics*, The Free Press, New York/London 1989.

Marchewka-Bartkowiak Kamilla, 'Agencje wykonawcze' ['Executive Agencies'], *Biuro Analiz Sejmowych. Infos. Zagadnienia społeczno-gospodarcze*, No. 17, 2011; available at: http://orka.sejm.gov.pl/wydbas.nsf/0/D16A32A470A32496C12578EA0042BBE4/%24File/Infos_109.pdf (20.3.2018).

Marjosola Heikki, 'Bridging the Constitutional Gap in EU Executive Rule-Making: The Court of Justice Approves Legislative Conferral of Intervention Powers to European Securities Markets Authority', *European Constitutional Law Review*, Vol. 10, No. 3, 2014, pp. 500–527.

Marjosola Heikki, 'Case C-270/12 – Stress Testing Constitutional Resilience of the Powers of EU Supervisory Authorities – A Critical Assessment of the Advocate General's Opinion', *EUI Working Papers LAW*, No. 2, 2014; available at: http://cadmus.eui.eu/handle/1814/29219 (20.3.2018).

Martens Maria, 'Executive Power in the Making: The Establishment of the European Chemicals Agency', in: Busuioc Madalina *et al.* (ed.), *The Agency Phenomenon in the European Union. Emergence, Institutionalisation and Everyday Decision-Making*, Manchester University Press, Manchester/New York 2014, pp. 42–62.

Martens Maria, 'Voice or Loyalty? The Evolution of the European Environment Agency (EEA)', *Journal of Common Market Studies*, Vol. 48, No. 4, 2010, pp. 881–901.

Mastenbroek Ellen *et al.*, 'Clawing Back Lost Powers? Parliamentary Scrutiny of the Transposition of EU Social Policy Directives in the Netherlands', *West European Politics*, Vol. 37, No. 4, 2014, pp. 750–768.

Mathieu Emmanuelle, *Regulatory Delegation in the European Union: Networks, Committees and Agencies*, Palgrave Macmillan, London 2016.

Mathieu Emmanuelle, 'When Europeanization Feeds Back into EU Governance: EU Legislation, National Regulatory Agencies, and EU Regulatory Networks', *Public Administration*, Vol. 94, No. 1, 2016, pp. 25–39.

Mayrhofer Michael, 'Europäische Agenturen: Organisation und Verfahren', in: Raschauer Nicolas (ed.), *Europäische Agenturen*, Jan Sramek Verlag, Salzburg 2012, pp. 41–64.

McCarthy Thomas, 'Kantian Constructivism and Reconstructivism: Rawls and Habermas in Dialogue', *Ethics*, Vol. 105, No. 1, 1994, pp. 44–63.

Mead Richard, Andrews G. Tim, *International Management. Culture and Beyond*, John Wiley & Sons, Chichester/Hoboken 2009.

Meerten v. Hans, Ottow Annetje, 'The Proposals for the European Supervisory Authorities (ESAs): The Right (Legal) Way Forward?', *Tijdschrift voor Financieel Recht*, No. 1/2, 2010, pp. 6–16.

Meine Anna, *Legitimität weiter denken?*, Ergon Verlag, Würzburg 2012.

Mendes Joana, 'Delegated and Implementing Rule Making: Proceduralisation and Constitutional Design', *European Law Journal*, Vol. 19, No. 1, 2013, pp. 22–41.

Mendes Joana, 'Discretion, Care and Public Interests in the EU Administration: Probing the Limits of Law', *Common Market Law Review*, Vol. 53, No. 2, 2016, pp. 419–452.

Menon Anand, Waetherill Stephen, 'Legitimacy, Accountability and Delegation in the European Union', in: Arnull Anthony, Wincott Daniel (ed.), *Accountability and Legitimacy in the European Union*, Oxford University Press, Oxford/New York 2002, pp. 113–131.

Mény Yves, 'Can Europe be Democratic? Is It Feasible? Is It Necessary? Is the Present Situation Sustainable?', *Fordham International Law Journal*, Vol. 34, No. 5, 2011, pp. 1287–1303.

Michel Katja, *Institutionelles Gleichgewicht und EU-Agenturen. Eine Analyse unter besonderer Berücksichtigung der European Banking Authority*, Duncker & Humblot, Berlin 2015.

Micklitz Hans-W., *The Politics of Judicial Co-operation in the EU*, Cambridge University Press, Cambridge 2005.

Mielczarek Grażyna, 'Rola systemu REACH w zarządzaniu chemikaliami' ['The Role of the REACH System in the Governance of Chemicals'], in: Lesiuk Adam (ed.), *Praktyka ochrony środowiska* [*Practices in the Field of Environmental Protection*], Wyd. UMCS, Lublin 2015, pp. 79–91.

Mik Cezary, *Europejskie prawo wspólnotowe. Zagadnienia teorii i praktyki* [*European Union Law. Theory and Practice*], C.H. Beck, Warszawa 2000.

Mik Cezary, 'Powierzenie UE władzy przez państwa członkowskie i jego podstawowe konsekwencje prawne' ['The Conferral of the European Union Power to the Member States's and Its Fundamental Legal Consequences'], in: Kranz Jerzy (ed.), *Suwerenność i ponadnarodowość a integracja europejska* [*Sovereignty versus Transnationality and the European Integration*], Prawo i Praktyka Gospodarcza, Warszawa 2006, pp. 80–147.

Mik Cezary, 'Umocnienie legitymacji demokratycznej Unii Europejskiej' ['Strengthening the Democratic Legitimacy of the European Union'], in: Barcz Jan (ed.), *Traktat z Lizbony. Główne reformy ustrojowe Unii Europejskiej* [*The Treaty of Lisbon. The Main Reforms of the EU Political System*], UKIE, Warszawa 2008, pp. 98–110.

Miller Eugene F., 'David Easton's Political Theory', *Political Science Reviewer*, Vol. 1, 1971, pp. 184–235.

Miller Vaughne, 'EU Agencies and Post-Brexit Options', *House of Commons Briefing Papers*, No. 7957, 2017; available at: http://researchbriefings.parliament.uk/ResearchBriefing/Summary/CBP-7957 (20.3.2018).

Mizera Kamila, 'Deficyt demokratyczny w Unii Europejskiej' ['The Democratic Deficit in the European Union'], *Folia Iuridica Wratislaviensis*, Vol. 3, No. 1, 2014, pp. 87–138.

Młodzik Ewelina, 'Założenia koncepcji New Public Management' ['The Assumptions of the Concept of "New Public Management"'], *Zeszyty Naukowe Uniwersytetu Szczecińskiego. Współczesne Problemy Ekonomiczne*, Vol. 858, No. 11, 2015, pp. 185–193.

Molinier Joël, 'L'élaboration d'un cadre commun aux agences de l'Union', in: Molinier Joël (ed.), *Les agences de l'Union européenne. Collection droit de l'Union européenne dirigée par Fabrice Picod*, Bruylant, Bruxelles 2011, pp. 221–246.

Moloney Niamh, 'EU Financial Market Regulation after the Global Financial Crisis: "More Europe" or More Risks?', *Common Market Law Review*, Vol. 47, No. 5, 2010, pp. 1317–1383.

Moloney Niamh, 'European Banking Union: Assessing Its Risks and Resilience', *Common Market Law Review*, Vol. 51, No. 6, 2014, pp. 1609–1670.

Moravcsik Andrew, 'In Defense of the Democratic Deficit: Reassessing Legitimacy in the European Union', *Journal of Common Market Studies*, Vol. 40, No. 4, 2002, pp. 603–624.

Moravcsik Andrew, 'Taking Preferences Seriously: A Liberal Theory of International Politics', *International Organization*, Vol. 51, No. 4, 1997, pp. 513–553.

Muller Edward N., 'Correlates and Consequences of Beliefs in the Legitimacy of Regime Structures', *Midwest Journal of Political Science*, Vol. 14, No. 3, 1970, pp. 392–412.

Murdoch Zuzana *et al.*, 'Administrative Legitimacy and the Democratic Deficit of the European Union', *Journal of European Public Policy*, Vol. 25, No. 3, 2018, pp. 389–408.

Musa Anamarija, 'Reforming the European Union Agency Governance: More Control, Greater Accountability', *Croatian and Comparative Public Administration*, Vol. 14, No. 2, 2014, pp. 317–353.

Muszyński Mariusz, *Państwo w prawie międzynarodowym. Istota, rodzaje, atrybuty* [The State in the International Public Law. Its Substance, Types and Attributes], Wydawnictwo Sto, Bielsko-Biała 2011.

Myklebust Trude, 'Form and Function of the ESRB. A Critical Analysis', in: Andenas Mads, Deipenbrock Gudula (ed.), *Regulating and Supervising European Financial Markets. More Risks than Achievements*, Springer Verlag, Cham 2016, pp. 43–66.

Naßmacher Hiltrud, *Mehr Europa – weniger Demokratie*, Oldenbourg Verlag, München 2013.

Navin-Jones Marcus, 'A Legal Review of EU Boards of Appeal in Particular the European Chemicals Agency Board of Appeal', *European Public Law*, Vol. 21, No. 1, 2015, pp. 143–168.

Neergaard Anders, 'European Supervisory Authorities – A New Model for the Exercise of Powers in the European Union', *Euredia*, No. 4, 2009, pp. 603–630.

Nicolaïdis Kalypso, 'European Demoicracy and Its Crisis', *Journal of Common Market Studies*, Vol. 51, No. 2, 2013, pp. 351–369.

Nieborak Tomasz, *Aspekty prawne funkcjonowania rynku finansowego Unii Europejskiej* [*Legal Issues of the Functioning of the EU Financial Market*], Difin, Warszawa 2008.

Niedźwiedź Monika, 'Rola agencji europejskich w strukturze instytucjonalnej Unii Europejskiej a postanowienia traktatu ustanawiającego Konstytucję dla Europy' ['The Role of European Agencies within the EU Institutional Structure *versus* the Provisions in the Treaty Establishing a Constitution for Europe'], in: Dudzik Sławomir (ed.), *Konstytucja dla Europy. Przyszły fundament Unii Europejskiej* [*The Constitution for Europe as a Future Foundation for the EU*], Zakamycze, Kraków 2005, pp. 301–320.

North Douglass C., *Institutions, Institutional Change and Economic Performance*, Cambridge University Press, Cambridge 1990.

Nowak Alojzy Z., Milczarek Dariusz (ed.), *Europeistyka w zarysie* [*European Studies: An Outline*], Polskie Wydawnictwo Ekonomiczne, Warszawa 2006.

Nowak-Far Artur, 'Jednolitość prawa unijnego a jego wielojęzyczność' ['The Coherence of the EU Law in the Context of Its Multilinguality'], in: Mik Cezary (ed.), *Unia Europejska. Zjednoczeni w różnorodności* [*The European Union: United in Diversity*], Wydawnictwo Sejmowe, Warszawa 2012, pp. 74–92.

Nowak-Far Artur, Michoński Arkadiusz, *Krajowa administracja w unijnym procesie podejmowania decyzji* [*National Administration within the EU Decision-Making Process*], ISP, Warszawa 2004.

Nowicka Aleksandra, 'Metoda zarządzania przez rezultaty w agencjach UE jako sposób efektywnego zarządzania publicznego' ['Effective Governance within the EU Regulatory Agencies as a Way of Good Public Governance'], in: Sadowski Mirosław, Szymaniec Piotr (ed.), *Prace z teorii i historii prawa oraz administracji publicznej* [*Studies in the Field of the Theory and History of Law and Public Administration*], WUWr, Wrocław 2012, pp. 121–133.

Nullmeier Frank, Pritzlaff Tanja, 'The Great Chain of Legitimacy: Justifying Transnational Legitimacy', *TranState Working Papers*, No. 123, 2010; available at: https://www.econstor.eu/bitstream/10419/36686/1/628599471.pdf (20.3.2018).

Oeter Stefan, 'Europäische Integration als Konstitutionalisierungsprozeß', *Zeitschrift für ausländisches öffentliches Recht und Völkerrecht*, Vol. 59, 1999, pp. 901–917.

Ohler Christoph, 'Anmerkung zu EuGH, Urteil *v.* 22.01.2014, Rs. C-270/12', *Juristenzeitung*, Vol. 69, No. 5, 2014, pp. 249–252.

Ohler Christoph, 'Back in Balance? The EU and the Challenges of International Financial Regulation', in: Kochenov Dimitry, Amtenbrink Fabian (ed.), *European Union's Shaping of the International Legal Order*, Cambridge University Press, New York 2014, pp. 285–305.

Ohler Christoph, 'Die Einheitlichkeit der europäischen Aufsichtsarchitektur und die Besonderheit der Versicherungswirtschaft', *Zeitschrift für die gesamte Versicherungswissenschaft*, Vol. 101, No. 4, 2012, pp. 431–445.

Ohler Christoph, 'Rechtmäßige Errichtung der Gemeinschaftsagentur ENISA', *Europäische Zeitschrift für Wirtschaftsrecht*, Vol. 17, No. 12, 2006, pp. 369–374.

Olsen Johan P., 'Democratic Order, Autonomy, and Accountability', *Governance. An International Journal of Policy, Administration, and Institutions*, Vol. 28, No. 4, 2015, pp. 425–440.

Ongaro, Edoardo, 'Administrative Reforms in the European Commission and the Neo-Weberian Model', in: Bauer Michael W., Trondal Jarle (ed.), *The Palgrave Handbook of the European Administrative System*, Palgrave Macmillan, Basingstoke/New York 2015, pp. 108–123.

Ongaro Edoardo *et al.*, 'EU Agencies and the European Multi-Level Administrative System', in: Ongaro Edoardo (ed.), *Multi-Level Governance: The Missing Linkages*, Emerald Group Publishing Limited, Bingley 2015, pp. 87–123.

Orator Andreas, *Möglichkeiten und Grenzen der Einrichtung von Unionsagenturen*, Mohr Siebeck, Tübingen 2017.

Ossege Christoph, 'Driven by Expertise and Insulation? The Autonomy of European Regulatory Agencies', *Politics and Governance*, Vol. 3, No. 1, 2015, pp. 101–113.

Ossege Christoph, *European Regulatory Agencies in EU Decision-Making. Between Expertise and Influence*, Palgrave Macmillan, Basingstoke/Hampshire 2016.

Ottow Annetje, 'The New Supervisory Architecture of the Financial Markets', in: Everson Michelle *et al.* (ed.), *European Agencies in between Institutions and Member States*, Wolters Kluwer, Alphen aan den Rijn 2014, pp. 123–143.

Pal Renata M., 'The Body of European Regulators for Electronic Communications and Its Influence on Polish Telecommunications Law', *Review of Comparative Law*, Vol. XXII, 2015, pp. 89–106.

Papadopoulos Yannis, 'Accountability and Multi-Level Governance: More Accountability, Less Democracy?', *West European Politics*, Vol. 33, No. 5, 2010, pp. 1030–1049.

Papastavridis Efthymios, '"Fortress Europe" and Frontex: Within or Without International Law?', *Nordic Journal of International Law*, Vol. 79, No. 1, 2010, pp. 75–111.

Parijs v. Philippe, 'Should the European Union Become More Democratic?', in: Føllesdal Andreas, Koslowski Peter (ed.), *Democracy and the European Union*, Springer Verlag, Berlin 1997, pp. 287–301.

Parisi Salvatore *et al.*, *Chemistry and Food Safety in the EU. The Rapid Alert System for Food and Feed (RASFF)*, Springer Verlag, Cham 2016.

Pastorella Giulia, 'Technocratic Governments in Europe: Getting the Critique Right', *Political Studies*, Vol. 64, No. 4, 2016, pp. 948–965.

Pauer Erich, 'Die Mobilisierung der Ingenieure in der Zwischenkriegszeit: Von der Technokratie zum "wissenschaftsgeleiteten Industrialismus" (kagakushugi kôgyô)', *Nachrichten der Gesellschaft für Natur- und Völkerkunde Ostasiens*, Nos. 175–176, 2004, pp. 93–128.

Paul Katharina T., 'The Europeanization of Food Safety: A Discourse-Analytical Approach', *Journal of European Public Policy*, Vol. 19, No. 4, 2012, pp. 549–566.

Pawlik Martin, *Das REACH-System und die Meroni-Doktrin. Ein imperfekter Quantensprung im Europäischen Verwaltungsverbund*, Nomos Verlag, Baden-Baden 2013.

Payne Jennifer, 'The Regulation of Short Selling and Its Reform in Europe', *European Business Organization Law Review*, Vol. 13, No. 3, 2012, pp. 413–440.

Peczenik Aleksander, *A Treatise of Legal Philosophy and General Jurisprudence. Scientia Juris: Legal Doctrine as Knowledge of Law and as a Source of Law*, Vol. 4, Springer Verlag, New York 2005.

Peers Steve, Costa Marios, 'Accountability for Delegated and Implementing Acts after the Treaty of Lisbon', *European Law Journal*, Vol. 18, No. 3, 2012, pp. 427–460.

Pelinka Anton, 'Die Europäische Union – eine Konkordanzdemokratie? Zur typologischen Verortung der EU', in: Schrenk Klemens H., Soldner Markus (ed.), *Analyse demokratischer Regierungssysteme. Festschrift für Wolfgang Ismayr zum 65. Geburtstag*, VS Verlag für Sozialwissenschaften, Wiesbaden 2010, pp. 83–92.

Pelkmans Jacques, Simoncini Marta, 'Mellowing *Meroni*: How ESMA Can Help Build the Single Market', *CEPS Commentary*, 18.2.2014; available at: https://www.ceps.eu/publications/mellowing-meroni-how-esma-can-help-build-single-market (20.3.2018).

Perez Oren, 'Can Experts Be Trusted and What Can Be Done About It? Insights from Biases and Heuristics Literature', in: Alemanno Alberto, Sibony Anne-Lise (ed.), *Nudge and the Law. A European Perspective*, Hart Publishing, Oxford/Portland 2015, pp. 115–138.

Pérez-Durán Ixchel, 'Political and Stakeholder's Ties in European Union Agencies', *Journal of European Public Policy*, Published Online in September 2017, DOI: 10.1080/13501763.2017.1375545.

Permanand Govin, Vos Ellen, 'Between Health and the Market: The Roles of the European Medicines Agency and European Food Safety Authority', *Maastricht Faculty of Law Working Paper*, No. 4, 2008; available at: https://papers.ssrn.com/sol3/papers.cfm?abstract_id=1337111 (20.3.2018).

Peters Anne, 'Soft Law as a New Mode of Governance', in: Diedrichs Udo *et al.* (ed.), *The Dynamics of Change in EU Governance*, Edward Elgar Publishing, Cheltenham/Northampton 2011, pp. 21–51.

Peters Anne, 'The Transparency Turn of International Law', *Chinese Journal of Global Governance*, Vol. 1, No. 1, 2015, pp. 3–15.

Peters Kerstin, 'Die geplante europäische Bankenunion – eine kritische Würdigung', *WM. Zeitschrift für Wirtschafts- und Bankrecht*, No. 9, 2014, pp. 396–404.

Peuker Enrico, *Bürokratie und Demokratie in Europa*, Mohr Siebeck, Tübingen 2011.

Piattoni Simona, 'Representation as Delegation: A Basis for EU Democracy?', *Journal of European Public Policy*, Vol. 20, No. 2, 2013, pp. 224–242.

Pierre Jon, Peters B. Guy, 'From a Club to a Bureaucracy: JAA, EASA, and European Aviation Regulation', *Journal of European Public Policy*, Vol. 16, No. 3, 2009, pp. 337–355.

Pintado Citlali, 'A Taxonomy of EFSA's Scientific Outputs', in: Alemanno Alberto, Gabbi Simone (ed.), *Foundations of EU Food Law and Policy. Ten Years of the European Food Safety Authority*, Ashgate, Farnham/Burlington 2014, pp. 29–45.

Poboży Monika, 'Agencje zdecentralizowane i komitety komitologiczne w systemie instytucjonalnym UE – problem legitymizacji władzy' ['Decentralised Agencies and Comitology Committees in the EU Institutional System – The Problem of Legitimising Power'], in: Witkowska Marta, Wojtaszczyk Konstanty A. (ed.), *Agencje, komitety i inne jednostki organizacyjne UE* [*Agencies, Committees and*

Other Organizational Bodies within the EU Institutional System], ASPRA-JR, Warszawa 2015, pp. 135–168.

Pollak Johannes, Puntscher Riekmann Sonja, 'European Administration: Centralisation and Fragmentation as Means of Polity-Building?', in: Curtin Deirdre, Egeberg Morten (ed.), *Towards a New Executive Order in Europe*, Routledge, London/New York 2015, pp. 133–150.

Pollak Johannes, Slominski Peter, 'Experimentalist but not Accountable Governance? The Role of Frontex in Managing the EU's External Borders', *West European Politics*, Vol. 32, No. 5, 2009, pp. 904–924.

Pollitt Christopher *et al.*, *Agencies. How Governments Do Things Through Semi-Autonomous Organizations*, Palgrave Macmillan, Basingstoke/Hampshire 2005.

Pollitt Christopher *et al.*, 'Agency Fever? Analysis of an International Policy Fashion', *Journal of Comparative Policy Analysis. Research and Practice*, Vol. 3, No. 3, 2001, pp. 271–290.

Ponce Sole Juli, 'The History of Legitimate Administration in Europe', in: Ruffert Matthias (ed.), *Legitimacy in European Administrative Law: Reform and Reconstruction*, Europa Law Publishing, Groningen 2011, pp. 153–173.

Półtorak Magdalena, 'EIGE jako przykład działalności wspierającej równe traktowanie kobiet i mężczyzn w UE' ['The EIGE as an Example of the Activities Supporting the Equal Treatment of Women and Men in the EU'], *Roczniki Administracji i Prawa*, Vol. XIV, 2014, pp. 57–73.

Priebe Reinhard, 'Agenturen der Europäischen Union – Europäische Verwaltung durch eigenständige Behörden', *Europäische Zeitschrift für Wirtschaftsrecht*, Vol. 26, No. 7, 2015, pp. 268–272.

Priebe Reinhard, *Entscheidungsbefugnisse vertragsfremder Einrichtungen im Europäischen Gemeinschaftsrecht*, Nomos Verlag, Baden-Baden 1979.

Puntscher Riekmann Sonja, 'In Search of Lost Norms: Is Accountability the Solution to the Legitimacy Problems of the European Union?', *Comparative European Politics*, Vol. 5, No. 1, 2007, pp. 121–137.

Quigley Muireann, Stokes Elen, 'Nudging and Evidence-Based Policy in Europe: Problems of Normative Legitimacy and Effectiveness', in: Alemanno Alberto, Sibony Anne-Lise (ed.), *Nudge and the Law. A European Perspective*, Hart Publishing, Oxford/Portland 2015, pp. 61–82.

Radaelli Claudio M., 'Policy Transfer in the European Union: Institutional Isomorphism as a Source of Legitimacy', *Governance. An International Journal of Policy, Administration, and Institutions*, Vol. 13, No. 1, 2000, pp. 25–43.

Randazzo Vinzenzo, 'Case C-217/04, United Kingdom *v.* European Parliament and Council of the European Union', *Common Market Law Review*, Vol. 44, No. 1, 2007, pp. 155–169.

Rapeli Lauri, 'Public Support for Expert Decision-Making: Evidence from Finland', *Politics*, Vol. 36, No. 2, 2016, pp. 142–152.

Recascino Wise Lois, 'On the Need for a Composite Theory of Bureaucratic Behavior', *Public Administration Review*, Vol. 64, No. 6, 2004, pp. 669–680.

Rehbinder Eckard, 'Die REACH-Verordnung – Entstehungsgeschichte, Zielsetzung, Anwendungsbereich, Hauptinhalte', in: Hendler Reinhard *et al.*, *Neues europäisches Chemikalienrecht (REACH)*, Erich Schmidt Verlag, Berlin 2008, pp. 35–74.

Reus-Smit Christian, 'The Constitutional Structure of International Society and the Nature of Fundamental Institutions', *International Organization*, Vol. 51, No. 4, 1997, pp. 555–589.

Ribbhagen Christina, *Technocracy within Representative Democracy. Technocratic Reasoning and Justification among Bureaucrats and Politicians*, Ph.D. Thesis, University of Gothenburg. Department of Political Science, February 2013; available at: https://gupea.ub.gu.se/bitstream/2077/32363/1/gupea_2077_32363_1.pdf (20.3.2018).

Riedel Daniel, 'Die Europäische Agentur für Flugsicherheit im System der Gemeinschaftsagenturen', in: Schmidt-Aßmann Eberhard, Schöndorf-Haubold Bettina (ed.), *Der europäischer Verwaltungsverbund. Formen und Verfahren der Verwaltungszusammenarbeit in der EU*, Mohr Siebeck, Tübingen 2005, pp. 103–125.

Riesz Thomas, 'Europäische Gesundheitsagenturen – zugleich ein Beitrag zum Europäischen Arzneimittelzulassungssystem', in: Raschauer Nicolas (ed.), *Europäische Agenturen*, Jan Sramek Verlag, Salzburg 2012, pp. 129–171.

Rijpma Jorrit, 'Frontex: Successful Blame Shifting of the Member States', *Analyses of the Elcano Royal Institute*, No. 69, 2010; available at: https://www.files.ethz.ch/isn/117232/ARI69-2010_Rijpma_Frontex_Memeber_State_European_Union.pdf (20.3.2018).

Rijpma Jorrit, 'Hybrid Agencification in the Area of Freedom, Security and Justice and Its Inherent Tensions: The Case of Frontex', in: Busuioc Madalina *et al.* (ed.), *The Agency Phenomenon in the European Union. Emergence, Institutionalisation and Everyday Decision-Making*, Manchester University Press, Manchester/New York 2014, pp. 84–102.

Rijsbergen v. Marloes, 'On the Enforceability of EU Agencies' Soft Law at the National Level: The Case of the European Securities and Markets Authority', *Utrecht Law Review*, Vol. 10, No. 5, 2014, pp. 116–131.

Ritleng Dominique, 'Introduction', in: Ritleng Dominique (ed.), *Independence and Legitimacy in the Institutional System of the European Union*, Oxford University Press, Oxford 2016, pp. 1–14.

Rittberger Berthold, Wonka Arndt, 'Introduction: Agency Governance in the European Union', in: Rittberger Berthold, Wonka Arndt (ed.), *Agency Governance in the EU*, Routledge, London/New York 2012, pp. 2–11.

Roederer-Rynning Christilla, Daugbjerg Carsten, 'Power Learning or Path Dependency? Investigating the Roots of the European Food Safety Authority', *Public Administration*, Vol. 88, No. 2, 2010, pp. 315–330.

Romano Santi, *Fragmentos de un diccionario jurídico*, Ediciones JuÍdicas Europa-América, Buenos Aires 1964.

Rosanvallon Pierre, *La contre-démocratie. La politique à l'âge de la défiance*, Le Seuil, Paris 2006.

Rosanvallon Pierre, *La légitimité démocratique. Impartialité, réflexivité, proximité*, Le Seuil, Paris 2008.

Rosenfeldt Herbert, 'The European Order and Coast Guard Rising: Recent Developments in the Light of EU Accountability Standards and Mechanisms', Paper Presented at the Refugee Law Initiative 2nd Annual Conference, London, June 2017; available at: https://papers.ssrn.com/sol3/papers.cfm?abstract_id=3021648 (20.3.2018).

Rossi Matthias, 'Art. 77 AEUV', in: Calliess Christian, Ruffert Matthias (ed.), *EUV/AEUV. Das Verfassungsrecht der Europäischen Union mit Europäischer Grundrechtecharta. Kommentar*, C.H. Beck, München 2011, pp. 2235–1088–1097.

Rossi Matthias, 'Art. 352 AEUV', in: Calliess Christian, Ruffert Matthias (ed.), *EUV/AEUV. Das Verfassungsrecht der Europäischen Union mit Europäischer Grundrechtecharta. Kommentar*, C.H. Beck, München 2011, pp. 2231–2756.

Rudnicki Zbigniew, 'Identity in a Differentiated Integration in Europe', in: Konopacki Stanisław (ed.), *Europe in the Time of Crisis*, WUJ, Łódź/Kraków 2014, pp. 57–70.

Ruffert Matthias, 'Art. 11 EUV', in: Calliess Christian, Ruffert Matthias (ed.), *EUV/AEUV. Das Verfassungsrecht der Europäischen Union mit Europäischer Grundrechtecharta. Kommentar*, C.H. Beck, München 2011, pp. 185–191.

Ruffert Matthias, 'Art. 249 AEUV', in: Calliess Christian, Ruffert Matthias (ed.), *EUV/AEUV. Das Verfassungsrecht der Europäischen Union mit Europäischer Grundrechtecharta. Kommentar*, C.H. Beck, München 2011, pp. 2235–2236.

Ruffert Matthias, 'Art. 291 AEUV', in: Calliess Christian, Ruffert Matthias (ed.), *EUV/AEUV. Das Verfassungsrecht der Europäischen Union mit Europäischer Grundrechtecharta. Kommentar*, C.H. Beck, München 2011, pp. 2486–2491.

Ruffert Matthias, 'Art. 298 AEUV', in: Calliess Christian, Ruffert Matthias (ed.), *EUV/AEUV. Das Verfassungsrecht der Europäischen Union mit Europäischer Grundrechtecharta. Kommentar*, C.H. Beck, München 2011, pp. 2518–2526.

Ruffert Matthias, 'Begriff', in: Fehling Michael, Ruffert Matthias (ed.), *Regulierungsrecht*, Mohr Siebeck, Tübingen 2010, pp. 332–362.

Ruffert Matthias, 'Demokratie und Governance in Europa', in: Bauer Hartmut *et al.* (ed.), *Demokratie in Europa*, Mohr Siebeck, Tübingen 2005, pp. 319–348.

Ruffert Matthias, 'Die neue Unabhängigkeit: Zur demokratischen Legitimation von Agenturen im europäischen Verwaltungsrecht', in: Müller-Graff Peter-Christian *et al.* (ed.), *Europäisches Recht zwischen Bewährung und Wandel. Festschrift für Dieter H. Scheuing*, Nomos Verlag, Baden-Baden 2011, pp. 399–414.

Ruffert Matthias, 'Rechtsgrundlagen und Rechtsetzungsbefugnisse von Agenturen', *Juristische Schulung*, Vol. 54, No. 3, 2014, pp. 279–281.

Ruffert Matthias, 'The Many Faces of Rule-Making in the EU', in: Fahey Elaine (ed.), *The Actors of Postnational Rule-Making. Contemporary Challenges of European and International Law*, Routledge, Oxon 2016, pp. 47–66.

Ruffert Matthias, 'Verselbständigte Verwaltungseinheiten: Ein europäischer Megatrend im Vergleich', in: Trute Hans-Heinrich *et al.* (ed.), *Allgemeines Verwaltungsrecht - zur Tragfähigkeit eines Konzepts*, Mohr Siebeck, Tübingen 2008, pp. 431–457.

Ruffert Matthias, 'Was ist Democratic Governance?', in: Botzem Sebastian *et al.* (ed.), *Governance als Prozess. Koordinationsformen im Wandel*, Nomos Verlag, Baden-Baden 2009, pp. 55–74.

Ruser Alexander, 'By the Markets, of the Markets, for the Markets? Technocratic Decision Making and the Hollowing Out of Democracy', *Global Policy*, Vol. 6, No. S1, 2015, pp. 83–92.

Ruser Alexander, 'Der (in)diskrete Charme der Technokratie. Wirtschaftskrisen, Staatskrisen und die Entdemokratisierung von Entscheidungsstrukturen', in: Lehmann Maren, Tyrell Marcell (ed.), *Komplexe Freiheit. Wie ist die Demokratie möglich?*, Springer Verlag, Wiesbaden 2017, pp. 203–217.

Ruszkowski Janusz, 'Pierwotne i wtórne delegowanie kompetencji w wielopoziomowym systemie zarządzania Unii Europejskiej' ['Primary and Secondary Delegation of Competencies within the EU-Multi-Governance-System'], *Rocznik Integracji Europejskiej*, No. 6, 2012, pp. 45–62.

Ruszkowski Janusz, *Ponadnarodowość w systemie politycznym Unii Europejskiej* [*Supranationality in the EU Political System*], Wolters Kluwer, Warszawa 2010.

Sabel Charles F., Zeitlin Jonathan, 'Learning From Difference: The New Architecture of Experimentalist Governance in the EU', *European Law Journal*, Vol. 14, No. 3, 2008, pp. 271–327.

Sadurski Wojciech, 'Law's Legitimacy and "Democracy-Plus"', *Oxford Journal of Legal Studies*, Vol. 26, No. 2, 2006, pp. 377–409.

Sadurski Wojciech, 'Supranational Public Reason: On Legitimacy of Supranational Norm-Producing Authorities', *Global Constitutionalism*, Vol. 4, No. 3, 2015, pp. 396–427.

Saerbeck Barbara, *Unabhängige europäische Regulierungsagenturen. Ihr Einflusspotenzial am Beispiel der Europäischen Umweltagentur*, Springer Verlag, Wiesbaden 2014.

Salzberger Eli M., Voigt Stefan, 'On the Delegation of Powers: With Special Emphasis on Central and Eastern Europe', *Constitutional Political Economy*, Vol. 13, No. 1, 2002, pp. 25–52.

Sánchez-Cuenca Ignacio, 'From a Deficit of Democracy to a Technocratic Order. The Postcrisis Debate on Europe', *Annual Review of Political Science*, Vol. 20, 2017, pp. 351–369.

Sander Peter, 'Europäische Agenturen: Rechtsgrundlagen in und sonstige Berührungspunkte mit dem primären Unionsrecht', in: Raschauer Nicolas (ed.), *Europäische Agenturen*, Jan Sramek Verlag, Salzburg 2012, pp. 1–39.

Santos Vara Juan, Sánchez-Tabernero Soledad R., 'In Deep Water: Towards a Greater Commitment for Human Rights in Sea Operations Coordinated by Frontex?', *European Journal of Migration and Law*, Vol. 18, No. 1, 2016, pp. 65–87.

Saurer Johannes, 'EU Agencies 2.0 – The New Constitution of Supranational Administration beyond the EU Commission', Paper Presented by the Comparative Administrative Law Conference, Yale Law School, April 2016; available at: https://law.yale.edu/system/files/area/conference/compadmin/compadmin16_saurer_euagencies.pdf (20.3.2018).

Saurer Johannes, 'Supranational Governance and Networked Accountability Structures: Member State Oversight of EU Agencies', *European Journal of Risk Regulation*, Vol. 2, No. 1, 2011, pp. 51–60.

Saurer Johannes, 'The Accountability of Supranational Administration: The Case of European Union Agencies', *American University International Law Review*, Vol. 24, No. 3, 2009, pp. 429–488.

Schammo Pierre, 'Actions and Inactions in the Investigation of Breaches of Union Law by the European Supervisory Authorities', *Common Market Law Review*, Vol. 55, No. 5, 2018, pp. 1423–1429.

Scharpf Fritz W., 'After the Crash: A Perspective on Multilevel European Democracy', *European Law Journal*, Vol. 21, No. 3, 2015, pp. 384–405.

Scharpf Fritz W., *Demokratietheorie zwischen Utopie und Anpassung*, Universitätsverlag, Konstanz 1970.

Scharpf Fritz W., 'Die Euro-Rettung als Demokratieproblem', *DMS – Der moderne Staat. Zeitschrift für Public Policy, Recht und Management*, Vol. 6, No. 2, 2013, pp. 279–288.

Scharpf Fritz W., *Regieren in Europa. Effektiv und demokratisch?*, Campus Verlag, Frankfurt am Main 1999.

Schemmel Jakob, *Europäische Finanzmarktverwaltung. Dogmatik und Legitimation der Handlungsinstrumente von EBA, EIOPA und ESMA*, Mohr Siebeck, Tübingen 2018.

Schirmer Dietmar, 'Kłopoty z tożsamością w Europie. Nowe ujęcie braku *demos*, zróżnicowania kulturowego i granic integracji' ['Problems with Identity. New Perspectives in the Field of *Demos*' Deficit, Cultural Diversity and the Limits of Integration], in: Markiewicz Barbara, Wonicki Rafał (ed.), *Kryzys tożsamości politycznej a proces integracji europejskiej* [*Crisis of Political Identity versus the Process of the European Integration*], Scholar, Warszawa 2006, pp. 57–68.

Schlögl Martina, 'Europäische Agenturen im Umweltrecht. EUA und ECHA', in: Raschauer Nicolas (ed.), *Europäische Agenturen*, Jan Sramek Verlag, Salzburg 2012, pp. 173–208.

Schmidt Dennis R., 'Peremptory Law, Global Order, and the Normative Boundaries of a Pluralistic World', *International Theory*, Vol. 8, No. 2, 2016, pp. 262–296.

Schmidt Lawrence K., *The Epistemology of Hans-Georg Gadamer: An Analysis of the Legitimization of Vorurteile*, Peter Lang, Frankfurt am Main 1987.

Schmidt Vivien A., 'Democracy and Legitimacy in the European Union Revisited: Input, Output and "Throughput"', *Political Studies*, Vol. 61, No. 1, 2013, pp. 2–22.

Schmidt Vivien A., Radaelli Claudio M., 'Policy Change and Discourse in Europe: Conceptual and Methodological Issues', *West European Politics*, Vol. 27, No. 2, 2004, pp. 183–210.

Schmidt-Aßmann Eberhard, 'Introduction: European Composite Administration and the Role of European Administrative Law', in: Jansen Oswald, Schöndorf-Haubold Bettina (ed.), *The European Composite Administration*, Intersentia, Cambridge 2011, pp. 1–22.

Schmidt-Aßmann Eberhard, 'Legitimacy and Accountability as a Basis for Administrative Organisation and Activity in Germany', in: Ruffert Matthias (ed.), *Legitimacy in European Administrative Law: Reform and Reconstruction*, Europa Law Publishing, Groningen 2011, pp. 49–57.

Schneider Jens-Peter, 'A Common Framework for Decentralised EU Agencies and the *Meroni* Doctrine', *Administrative Law Review*, Vol. 61, Special Edition, 2009, pp. 29–44.

Schoenmaker Dirk, 'An Integrated Financial Framework for the Banking Union: Don't Forget Macro-Prudential Supervision', *European Commission Economic Papers*, No. 495, 2013; available at: http://ec.europa.eu/economy_finance/publications/economic_paper/2013/pdf/ecp495_en.pdf (20.3.2017).

Scholten Miroslava, 'Democratic Input Legitimacy of IRAs: Proposing an Assessment Framework', *Utrecht Law Review*, Vol. 11, No. 2, 2015, pp. 64–77.

Scholten Miroslava, 'Independence *v.* Accountability: Proving the Negative Correlation', *Maastricht Journal of European and Comparative Law*, Vol. 21, No. 1, 2014, pp. 197–204.

Scholten Miroslava, 'Independent, Hence Unaccountable? The Need for a Broader Debate on Accountability of the Executive', *Review of European Administrative Law*, Vol. 4, No. 1, 2011, pp. 5–44.

Scholten Miroslava, 'Mind the Trend! Enforcement of EU Law Has Been Moving to "Brussels"', *Journal of European Public Policy*, Vol. 24, No. 9, 2017, pp. 1348–1366.

Scholten Miroslava, 'The Newly Released "Common Approach" on EU Agencies: Going Forward or Standing Still?', *The Columbia Journal of European Law Online*, Vol. 19, No. 1, 2012; available at: https://papers.ssrn.com/sol3/papers.cfm?abstract_id=2236240 (20.3.2018).

Scholten Miroslava, *The Political Accountability of EU and US Independent Regulatory Agencies*, Brill Nijhoff, Leiden/Boston 2014.

Scholten Miroslava, Ottow Annetje, 'Institutional Design of Enforcement in the EU: The Case of Financial Markets', *Utrecht Law Review*, Vol. 10, No. 5, 2014, pp. 80–91.

Scholten Miroslava, Rijsbergen v. Marloes, 'The *ESMA-Short Selling* Case. Erecting a New Delegation Doctrine in the EU upon the *Meroni-Romano* Remnants', *Legal Issues of Economic Integration*, Vol. 41, No. 4, 2014, pp. 389–406.

Scholten Miroslava, Rijsbergen v. Marloes, 'The Limits of Agencification in the European Union', *German Law Journal*, Vol. 15, No. 7, 2014, pp. 1223–1256.

Schout Adriaan, 'Assessing the Added Value of an EU Agency for Aviation Safety', *Journal of Public Policy*, Vol. 31, No. 3, 2011, pp. 363–384.

Schout Adriaan, 'Inspecting Aviation Safety in the EU: EASA as Administrative Innovation?', in: Vos Ellen (ed.), *European Risk Governance – Its Science, Its Inclusiveness and Its Effectiveness*, CONNEX/MZES, Mannheim 2008, pp. 257–294.

Schout Adriaan, Jordan Andrew, 'The European Union's Governance Ambitions and Its Administrative Capacities', *Journal of European Public Policy*, Vol. 15, No. 7, 2008, pp. 957–974.

Schout Adriaan, Pereyra Fabian, 'The Institutionalization of EU Agencies: Agencies as 'Mini Commissions'", *Public Administration*, Vol. 89, No. 2, 2011, pp. 418–432.

Schumpeter Joseph A., *The Theory of Economic Development. An Inquiry into Profits, Capital, Credit, Interest, and the Business Cycle*, Transactions Publishers, New Brunswick/London 1980.

Schwarze Jürgen, '*Soft Law* im Recht der Europäischen Union', *Europarecht*, No. 1, 2011, pp. 3–18.

Schwind Manuel P., *Netzwerke im Europäischen Verwaltungsrecht. Ein Beitrag zu Theorie und Dogmatik der Behördenkooperation*, Mohr Siebeck, Tübingen 2017.

Scientific Council for Government Policy, *Rediscovering Europe in the Netherlands*, WRR Rapporten, Amsterdam University Press, Amsterdam 2007.

Scott Colin, 'Agencies for European Regulatory Governance: A Regimes Approach', in: Geradin Damien *et al.* (ed.), *Regulation through Agencies in the EU: A New Paradigm of European Governance*, Edward Elgar Publishing, Cheltenham 2005, pp. 67–87.

Scott Colin, 'Governing Without Law or Governing Without Government? New-ish Governance and the Legitimacy of the EU', *European Law Journal*, Vol. 15, No. 2, 2009, pp. 160–173.

Scott Joanne, 'In Legal Limbo: Post-Legislative Guidance as a Challenge for European Administrative Law', *Common Market Law Review*, Vol. 48, No. 2, 2011, pp. 329–355.

Selznick Philip, 'Focusing Organizational Research and Regulation', in: Noll Roger G. (ed.), *Regulatory Policy and the Social Sciences*, University of California Press, Berkeley 1985, S. 363–367.

Senden Linda, *Soft Law in European Community Law*, Hart Publishing, Oxford/Portland 2004.

Shapiro Martin, '"Deliberative", "Independent" Technocracy *v.* Democratic Politics: Will the Globe Echo the EU?', *Law and Contemporary Problems*, Vol. 68, Nos. 3–4, 2005, pp. 341–356.

Shapiro Martin, 'The Institutionalization of European Administrative Space', in: Stone Sweet Alec *et al.* (ed.), *The Institutionalization of Europe*, Oxford University Press, Oxford 2001, pp. 94–112.

Shapiro Martin, 'The Problems of Independent Agencies in the United States and the European Union', *Journal of European Public Policy*, Vol. 4, No. 2, 1997, pp. 276–291.

Shirvani Foroud, 'New Public Management und europäische Agenturen: Transparenzfragen bei der Modernisierung der Verwaltungsorganisation', *Die öffentliche Verwaltung. Zeitschrift für öffentliches Recht und Verwaltungswissenschaft*, Vol. 61, No. 1, 2008, pp. 1–10.

Siegel Thorsten, *Entscheidungsfindung im Verwaltungsverbund*, Mohr Siebeck, Tübingen 2009.

Silano Vittorio, 'EFSA's Science Strategy: Taking Stock and Looking Ahead', in: Alemanno Alberto, Gabbi Simone (ed.), *Foundations of EU Food Law and Policy. Ten Years of the European Food Safety Authority*, Ashgate, Farnham/Burlington 2014, pp. 23–28.

Simoncini Marta, *Administrative Regulation Beyond the Non-Delegation Doctrine. A Study on EU Agencies*, Hart Publishing, Oxford/Portland 2018.

Simoncini Marta, 'Legal Boundaries of European Supervisory Authorities in the Financial Markets: Tensions in the Development of True Regulatory Agencies', *Yearbook of European Law*, Vol. 34, No. 1, 2015, pp. 319–350.

Simoncini, Marta, 'Paradigms for EU Law and the Limits of Delegation. The Case of EU Agencies', *Perspectives on Federalism*, Vol. 9, No. 2, 2017, pp. 47–71.

Simoncini, Marta, 'The Erosion of the *Meroni* Doctrine. The Case of the European Aviation Safety Agency', *European Public Law*, Vol. 21, No. 2, 2015, pp. 309–342.

Skowron Magdalena, 'Agencje i urzędy europejskie w orzecznictwie TS' ['Agencies and Offices in the European Case Law'], *Europejski Przegląd Sądowy*, No. 9, 2014, pp. 43–48.

Smulders Ben, Eisele Katharina, 'Reflections on the Institutional Balance, the Community Method and the Interplay between Jurisdictions after the Lisbon', *Yearbook of European Law*, Vol. 31, No. 1, 2012, pp. 112–127.

Sokół Wojciech, *Legitymizacja systemów politycznych* [*Legitimising Political Systems*], Wyd. UMCS, Lublin 1997.

Somermann Karl-Peter, 'Die Entwicklung europäischer Verwaltungskultur', in: Montoro Chiner María J. *et al.* (ed.), *Les administracions en perspectiva europea*, Escola d'Administració Pública de Catalunya, Barcelona 2012, pp. 57–74.

Sowels Nicholas, 'The Role of Finance in the UK's Relationship with the European Union', in: Tournier-Sol Karine, Gifford Chris (ed.), *The UK Challenge to Europeanization: The Persistence of British Euroscepticism*, Palgrave Macmillan, Basingstoke/Hampshire 2015, pp. 210–231.

Sölter Nicolas, *Rechtsgrundlagen europäischer Agenturen im Verhältnis vertikaler Gewaltenteilung*, Duncker & Humblot, Berlin 2017.

Spendzharova Aneta, 'Becoming a Powerful Regulator. ESMA in European Financial Sector Governance', *TARN Working Paper*, No. 8, 2017; available at: https://papers.ssrn.com/sol3/papers.cfm?abstract_id=2965429 (20.3.2018).

Staehler Tanja, *Hegel, Husserl and the Phenomenology of Historical Worlds*, Rowman & Littlefield International, London/New York 2016.

Steffek Jens, 'The Output Legitimacy of International Organizations and the Global Public Interest', *International Theory*, Vol. 7, No. 2, 2015, pp. 263–293.

Steger Martin A., *Zur Verselbständigung von Unionsagenturen. Eine Untersuchung am Beispiel der Energie-Agentur ACER und ihrer Mitwirkung beim Erlass tertiären Unionsrechts*, Nomos Verlag, Baden-Baden 2015.

Stein Thorsten, 'Demokratische Legitimierung auf supranationaler und internationaler Ebene', *Zeitschrift für ausländisches öffentliches Recht und Völkerrecht*, Vol. 64, 2004, pp. 563–570.

Stewart Jim *et al.*, 'What is Theory?', *Journal of European Industrial Training*, Vol. 35, No. 3, 2011, pp. 221–229.

Stewart Richard B., 'The Reformation of American Administrative Law', *Harvard Law Review*, Vol. 88, No. 8, 1975, pp. 1669–1813.

Stillman Peter G., 'The Concept of Legitimacy', *Polity*, Vol. 7, No. 1, 1974, pp. 32–56.

Stokes Elen, Vaughan Steven, 'Great Expectations: Reviewing 50 Years of Chemicals Legislation in the EU', *Journal of Environmental Law*, Vol. 25, No. 3, 2013, pp. 411–435.

Storr Stefan, 'Rechtsschutz gegen Regulierungsmaßnahmen in der Europäischen Union', in: Gramlich Ludwig, Manger-Nestler Cornelia (ed.), *Europäisierte Regulierungsstrukturen und -netzwerke. Basis einer künftigen Infrastrukturvorsorge*, Nomos Verlag, Baden-Baden 2011, pp. 107–118.

Sulikowski Adam, 'Prawa a ideologia. Prawa jednostki z perspektywy krytycznej myśli prawniczej i socjologicznej' ['Law and Ideology. Individual Rights from the Perspective of Critical Legal and Sociological Thought'], *Roczniki Nauk Społecznych*, Vol. 7(43), No. 4, 2015, pp. 17–32.

Supernat Jerzy, 'Agencje europejskie' ['European Agencies'], in: Ura Elżbieta *et al.* (ed.), *Rola i znaczenie zarządzania kryzysowego w systemie bezpieczeństwa państwa* [*The Role of the Crisis Management in the Security System of the State*], Wyd. UR, Rzeszów 2013, pp. 79–97.

Supernat Jerzy, 'O pojęciu rozliczalności (*accountability*) administracji' ['On the Concept of Accountability of the Administration'], in: Duniewska Małgorzata, Stahl Zofia (ed.), *Odpowiedzialność administracji i w administracji* [*Accountability of and within the Administration*], Wolters Kluwer, Warszawa 2013, pp. 35–41.

Supernat Jerzy, 'Teoria polityki biurokratycznej' ['The Theory of Bureaucratic Politicy'], in: Supernat Jerzy (ed.), *Między tradycją a przyszłością w nauce prawa administracyjnego* [*Between Tradition and Future in the Studies of Public Administration*], WUWr, Wrocław 2009, pp. 689–698.

Surdej Aleksander, 'Rola wyspecjalizowanych agencji w funkcjonowaniu UE: Stan obecny i kierunki rozwoju' ['The Role of Specialised Agencies in the Functioning of the EU: Current State and Development Trends'], *Zeszyty Naukowe AEK*, No. 654, 2004, pp. 87–102.

Suvarierol Semin, 'Everyday Cosmopolitanism in the European Commission', *Journal of Public Policy*, Vol. 18, No. 2, 2011, pp. 181–200.

Suvarierol Semin *et al.*, 'Working for Europe? Socialization in the European Commission and Agencies of the European Union', *Public Administration*, Vol. 91, No. 4, 2013, pp. 908–927.

Sydow Gernot, *Verwaltungskooperation in der Europäischen Union. Zur horizontalen und vertikalen Zusammenarbeit der europäischen Verwaltungen am Beispiel des Produktzulassungsrechts*, Mohr Siebeck, Tübingen 2004.

Szapiro Manuel, 'The Framework for European Regulatory Agencies: A Balance between Accountability and Autonomy', Paper Presented at the 3rd ECPR Conference, 8–11.9.2005; available at: http://regulation.upf.edu/ecpr-05-papers/mszapiro.pdf (20.3.2018).

Szydło Marek, *Prawo konkurencji a regulacja sektorowa* [*Comptetition Law and Sectoral Regulation*], Wolters Kluwer, Warszawa 2010.

Szydło Marek, *Regulacja sektorów infrastrukturalnych jako rodzaj funkcji państwa wobec gospodarki* [*Regulation of Infrastructure Sectors as a Kind of Function of the State in Relation to the Economy*], Wydawnictwo Prawo i Praktyka Gospodarcza, Warszawa 2005.

Świerczyński Marek, 'Second Medical Use Patents and the Substitution of Medical Products', *Zeszyty Naukowe UJ. Prace z prawa własności intelektualnej*, No. 3, 2017, pp. 64–75.

Šefčovič Maroš, 'Ein Ordnungsrahmen für die dezentralisierten Agenturen der EU', *Europäische Zeitschrift für Wirtschaftsrecht*, Vol. 23, No. 21, 2012, pp. 801–802.

Talbot Colin, 'The Agency Idea. Sometimes Old, Sometimes New, Sometimes Borrowed, Sometimes Untrue', in: Pollitt Christopher, Talbot Colin (ed.), *Unbundled Government. A Critical Analysis of the Global Trend to Agencies, Quangos and Contractualisation*, Routledge, London/New York 2004, pp. 3–21.

Tammikko Teemu, 'The New Frontex and the Future of Schengen. A Brick Fortress, or a Castle Made of Sand?', *FIIA Briefing Paper*, No. 219, 2017; available at: http://www.fiia.fi/en/publication/677/the_new_frontex_and_the_future_of_schengen/ (20.3.2018).

Teubner Gunther, 'How the Law Thinks. Towards a Constructivist Epistemology of Law', *Law and Society Review*, Vol. 23, No. 5, 1989, pp. 727–758.

Thatcher Mark, 'European Regulation', in: Richardson Jeremy (ed.), *European Union: Power and Policy Making*, Routledge, London 2001, pp. 303–320.

Thatcher Mark, 'The Creation of European Regulatory Agencies and its Limits: A Comparative Analysis of European Delegation', in: Rittberger Berthold, Wonka Arndt (ed.), *Agency Governance in the EU*, Routledge, London/New York 2012, pp. 12–31.

Thatcher Mark, 'The Third Force? Independent Regulatory Agencies and Elected Politicians in Europe', *Governance. An International Journal of Policy, Administration, and Institutions*, Vol. 18, No. 3, 2005, pp. 347–373.

Thatcher Mark, Stone Sweet Alec, 'Theory and Practice of Delegation to Non-Majoritarian Institutions', *West European Politics*, Vol. 25, No. 1, 2002, pp. 1–22.

Thiel Markus, 'European Civil Society and the EU Fundamental Rights Agency: Creating Legitimacy through Civil Society Inclusion?', *Journal of European Integration*, Vol. 36, No. 5, 2014, pp. 435–451.

Thomas Chris A., 'The Concept of Legitimacy and International Law', *LSE Law, Society and Economy Working Papers*, No. 12, 2013; available at: https://papers.ssrn.com/sol3/papers.cfm?abstract_id=2265503 (20.3.2018).

Toggenburg Gabriel N., 'Die EU-Grundrechteagentur: Satellit oder Leitstern?', *SWP-Aktuell*, No. 8, 2007; available at: https://www.swp-berlin.org/fileadmin/contents/products/aktuell/2007A08_toggenburg_ks.pdf (20.3.2018).

Tomaszewski Krzysztof, *Unia Europejska – w poszukiwaniu skutecznego mechanizmu zarządzania. Analiza krytyczna modelu teoretycznego Multi-Level Governance* [*The European Union – Searching for the Effective Governance Model. Critical Analysis of the Theoretical 'Multi-Level Governance' Model*], Adam Marszałek, Toruń 2013.

Trauner Florian, 'The European Parliament and Agency Control in the Area of Freedom, Security and Justice', *West European Politics*, Vol. 35, No. 4, 2012, pp. 784–802.

Tridimas Takis, 'Community Agencies, Competition Law and ESCB Initiatives on Securities Clearing and Settlement', *Yearbook of European Law*, Vol. 28, No. 1, 2009, pp. 216–307.

Tridimas Takis, 'Financial Supervision and Agency Power: Reflections on ESMA', in: Nic Shuibhne Niamh, Gormley Lawrence W. (ed.), *From Single Market to Economic Union. Essays in Memory of John A. Usher*, Oxford University Press, Oxford 2012, pp. 55–83.

Trondal Jarle, *An Emergent European Executive Order*, Oxford University Press, New York 2010.

Trondal Jarle, Jeppesen Lene, 'Images of Agency Governance in the European Union', *West European Politics*, Vol. 31, No. 3, 2008, pp. 417–441.

Trubalska Justyna, 'Wielowymiarowe zarządzanie granicami zewnętrznymi Unii Europejskiej' ['Multi-Dimensional Governance in the Field of External Border Management'], *Przegląd Geopolityczny*, Vol. 19, 2017, pp. 104–113.

Tsagas Georgina, 'The Regulatory Powers of the European Supervisory Authorities: Constitutional, Political and Functional Considerations', in: Andenas Mads, Deipenbrock Gudula (ed.), *Regulating and Supervising European Financial Markets. More Risks than Achievements*, Springer Verlag, Cham 2016, pp. 101–138.

Tuominen Tomi, 'The European Banking Union: A Shift in the Internal Market Paradigm?', *Common Market Law Review*, Vol. 54, No. 5, 2017, pp. 1359–1380.

Uerpmann Robert, 'Mittelbare Gemeinschaftsverwaltung durch gemeinschaftsgeschaffene juristische Personen des öffentlichen Rechts', *Archiv des öffentlichen Rechts*, Vol. 125, No. 4, 2000, pp. 551–586.

Ugur Mehmet, 'Regulatory Quality and Performance in EU Network Industries: Evidence on Telecommunications, Gas and Electricity', *Journal of Public Policy*, Vol. 29, No. 3, 2009, pp. 347–370.

Unwin Derick, McAleese Ray (ed.), *Encyclopedia of Educational Media Communications and Technology*, Palgrave Macmillan, London/Basingstoke 1978.

Utzinger André, 'Thomas Hobbes' "Leviathan". Anatomie eines Staats-Wesens', in: Michel Paul (ed.), *Spinnenfuß und Krötenbauch. Genese und Symbolik von Kompositwesen*, Pano Verlag, Zürich 2013, pp. 279–316.

Vareman Niklas, 'Norms and Descriptions', *Decision Analysis*, Vol. 5, No. 2, 2008, pp. 88–99.

Vasile Sergiu A., 'The European Union Refugee Crisis. A General Description of the Phenomenon and Its Implications on Long-Term Architecture of the European Legislation', *Journal of Criminal Investigations*, No. 2, 2015, pp. 119–125.

Vasile Sergiu A., Călugărită Andreea, 'European Agencies, Institutions and Bodies Engaged in Border Security in the Face of Illegal Migration Flows', *Journal of Criminal Investigations*, No. 1, 2012, pp. 193–200.

Vaughan Steven, 'Differentiation and Dysfunction: An Exploration of Post-Legislative Guidance Practices EU Agencies', *Cambridge Yearbook of European Legal Studies*, Vol. 17, 2015, pp. 66–91.

Vestlund Nina M., 'Exploring the EU Commission-Agency Relationship: Partnership or Parenthood?', in: Bauer Michael W., Trondal Jarle (ed.), *The Palgrave Handbook of the European Administrative System*, Palgrave Macmillan, Basingstoke/New York 2015, pp. 349–365.

Vetter Rainer, 'Die Kompetenzen der Gemeinschaft zur Gründung von unabhängigen europäischen Agenturen', *Die Öffentliche Verwaltung. Zeitschrift für öffentliches Recht und Verwaltungswissenschaft*, Vol. 58, No. 17, 2005, pp. 721–731.

Vibert Frank, *The Rise of the Unelected: Democracy and the New Separation of Powers*, Cambridge University Press, New York 2007.

Vos Ellen, 'Agencies and the European Union', in: Zwart Tom, Verhey Luc (ed.), *Agencies in European and Comparative Perspective*, Intersentia, Antwerpen 2003, pp. 113–147.

Vos Ellen, 'EU Agencies and Independence', in: Ritleng Dominique (ed.), *Independence and Legitimacy in the Institutional System of the European Union*, Oxford University Press, Oxford 2016, pp. 206–227.

Vos Ellen, 'European Agencies and the Composite EU Executive', in: Everson Michelle *et al.* (ed.), *European Agencies in between Institutions and Member States*, Wolters Kluwer, Alphen aan den Rijn 2014, pp. 11–47.

Vos Ellen, 'Independence, Accountability and Transparency of European Regulatory Agencies', in: Geradin Damien *et al.* (ed.), *Regulation through*

Agencies in the EU: A New Paradigm of European Governance, Edward Elgar Publishing, Cheltenham 2005, pp. 120–140.

Vos Ellen, 'Reforming the European Commission: What Role to Play for EU Agencies?', *Common Market Law Review*, Vol. 37, No. 5, 2000, pp. 1113–1134.

Vos Ellen, 'Responding the Catastrophe: Towards a New Architecture for EU Food Safety Regulation', in: Sabel Charles F., Zeitlin Jonathan (ed.), *Experimentalist Governance in the European Union: Towards a New Architecture*, Oxford University Press, Oxford 2010, pp. 151–178.

Wally Stefan, 'Konsequenzen einer Gerechtigkeit ohne Wahrheit', in: Wöhle Claudia B. *et al.* (ed.), *Rechtsphilosophie. Vom Grundlagenfach zur Transdisziplinarität in der Rechts-, Wirtschafts- und Sozialwissenschaften. Festschrift für Michael Fischer*, Peter Lang, Frankfurt am Main 2010, pp. 217–230.

Wandel Torbjörn, 'The Power of Discourse: Michel Foucault and Critical Theory', *Cultural Values*, Vol. 5, No. 3, 2001, pp. 368–382.

Warleigh Alex, *Democracy and the European Union. Theory, Practice and Reform*, Sage Publications, London 2003.

Weber Max, *Wirtschaft und Gesellschaft. Grundriß der verstehenden Soziologie*, Mohr Siebeck, Tübingen 1972.

Weber Max, 'Parlament und Regierung im neugeordneten Deutschland', in: Weber Max (ed.), *Gesammelte Politische Schriften*, Mohr Siebeck, Tübingen 1988, pp. 306–443.

Weick Karl E., 'What Theory Is Not, Theorizing Is', *Administrative Science Quarterly*, Vol. 40, No. 3, 1995, pp. 385–390.

Weidenfeld Werner, 'Europa in der Krise – die strategischen Perspektiven', in: Hilpold Peter, Steinmair Walter (ed.), *Neue europäische Finanzarchitektur. Die Reform der WWU*, Springer Verlag, Berlin/Heidelberg 2014, pp. 83–87.

Weiler Hans N., 'Knowledge and Power. The New Politics of Higher Education', *Journal of Education Planning and Administration*, Vol. XXV, No. 3, 2011, pp. 205–221.

Weiler Joseph H.H., 'In the Face of Crisis: Input Legitimacy, Output Legitimacy and the Political Messianism of European Integration', *Journal of European Integration*, Vol. 34, No. 7, 2012, pp. 825–841.

Weiler Joseph H.H., 'The Geology of International Law – Governance, Democracy and Legitimacy', *Zeitschrift für ausländisches öffentliches Recht und Völkerrecht*, Vol. 64, 2004, pp. 547–562.

Weimer Maria, Pisani Gaia, 'Expertise as Justification: The Contested Legitimation of the EU "Risk Administration"', in: Weimer Marta, de Ruijter Anniek (ed.), *Regulating Risks in the European Union. The Co-production of Expert and Executive Power*, Hart Publishing, Oxford/Portland 2017, pp. 167–192.

Weismann Paul, *European Agencies and Risk Governance in EU Financial Market Law*, Routledge, Oxon 2016.

Weiß Wolfgang, 'Agencies *versus* Networks: From Divide to Convergence in the Administrative Governance in the EU', *Administrative Law Review*, Vol. 61, Special Edition, 2009, pp. 45–70.

Weiß Wolfgang, *Der Europäische Verwaltungsverbund. Grundfragen, Kennzeichen, Herausforderungen*, Duncker & Humblot, Berlin 2010.

Weiß Wolfgang, 'Dezentrale Agenturen in der EU-Rechtsetzung', *Europarecht*, No. 6, 2016, pp. 631–665.

Weißgärber Kirsten, *Die Legitimation unabhängiger europäischer und nationaler Agenturen*, Nomos Verlag, Baden-Baden 2016.

Wendt Alexander, 'Anarchy is What States Make of It: The Social Construction of Power Politics', *International Organization*, Vol. 46, No. 2, 1992, pp. 391–425.

Wettestad Jørgen, 'Do New EU Agencies Mean Decreased National Powers? The Case of Chemicals and Norway', *FNI Report*, No. 14, 2014; available at: https://www.fni.no/getfile.php/132089/Filer/Publikasjoner/FNI-R1414.pdf (20.3.2017).

Węc Janusz J., 'Proces konstytuowania Unii Bankowej. Geneza, podstawy prawna, cele i zasady działania' ['The Process of Establishing the Banking Union: Origins, Legal Foundations, Objectives and Operating Principles'], *Rocznik Integracji Europejskiej*, No. 8, 2014, pp. 33–47.

Widłak Tomasz, 'Prawo a konstruktywizm w teorii stosunków międzynarodowych – możliwości interdyscyplinarnego zbliżenia' ['Law and Constructivism in the Theory of International Relations - Opportunities for Interdisciplinary Approximation'], in: Zirk-Sadowski Marek *et al.* (ed.), *Integracja zewnętrzna i wewnętrzna nauk prawnych* [*External and Internal Integration of Legal Sciences*], WUŁ, Łódź 2014, pp. 51–63.

Widmaier Hans P., *Demokratische Sozialpolitik. Zur Radikalisierung des Demokratieprinzips*, Mohr Siebeck, Tübingen 1999.

Wielomski Adam, 'Stosunki międzynarodowe a filozofia polityczna' ['International Relations and Political Philosophy'], in: Mich Włodzimierz, Nowak Jakub (ed.), *Wokół teorii stosunków międzynarodowych* [*Discussions on the Theory of International Relations*], Wyd. UMCS, Lublin 2012, pp. 83–100.

Wielomski Adam, Ziętek-Wielomska Magdalena, *The Europe of Nations and Its Future. Nationalism, Euroscepticism, Natiocratism*, KZ-M, Warszawa 2017.

Wieloński Michał, 'Prawny wymiar funkcjonowania agencji, komitetów i innych jednostek organizacyjnych. Wnioski na przyszłość' ['The Legal Dimension of the Functioning of Agencies, Committees and other Bodies within the EU System. Conclusions for the Future'], in: Witkowska Marta, Wojtaszczyk Konstanty A.

(ed.), *Agencje, komitety i inne jednostki organizacyjne UE* [*Agencies, Committees and Other Organizational Bodies within the EU Institutional System*], ASPRA-JR, Warszawa 2015, pp. 31–64.

Wiener Norbert, *Cybernetics or Control and Communication in the Animal and the Machine*, MIT Press, Cambridge 1985.

Wierzbowski Marek, 'Współpraca niezależnych organów administracji publicznej' ['Co-operation between Independent Bodies of the Public Administration'], *Ruch Prawniczy, Ekonomiczny i Socjologiczny*, Vol. LXXVI, No. 2, 2014, pp. 231–235.

Wilks Stephen, 'Agencies, Networks, Discourses and the Trajectory of European Competition Enforcement', *European Competition Journal*, Vol. 3, No. 2, 2007, pp. 437–464.

Wilks Stephen, Bartle Ian, 'The Unanticipated Consequences of Creating Independent Competition Agencies', in: Thatcher Mark, Stone Sweet Alec (ed.), *The Politics of Delegation*, Frank Cass, London 2003, pp. 148–172.

Wilks Stephen, McGowan Lee, 'Disarming the Commission: The Debate over a European Cartel Office', *Journal of Common Market Studies*, Vol. 32, No. 2, 1995, pp. 259–273.

Willeke Stefan, *Die Technokratiebewegung in Nordamerika und Deutschland zwischen den Weltkriegen. Eine vergleichende Analyse*, Peter Lang, Frankfurt am Main 1995.

Wilson James Q., *Bureaucracy. What Government Agencies Do and Why They Do It*, Basic Books, New York 2000.

Wilson Woodrow, 'The Study of Public Administration', *Political Science Quarterly*, Vol. 2, No. 2, 1887, pp. 197–222.

Wimmel Andreas, 'Theorizing the Democratic Legitimacy of European Governance: A Labyrinth with No Exit?', *Journal of European Integration*, Vol. 31, No. 2, 2009, pp. 181–199.

Winczorek Piotr, 'Legitymizacja władzy politycznej' ['Legitimisation of Political Power'], *Państwo i Prawo*, Nos. 11–12, 1983, pp. 65–76.

Winter Gerd, 'Kompetenzverteilung und Legitimation in der Europäischen Mehrebenenverwaltung', *Europarecht*, No. 2, 2005, pp. 255–276.

Witkowska Marta, 'Kryzys modelu demokracji w Unii Europejskiej – przyczyny, uwarunkowania, scenariusze rozwoju sytuacji' ['The Crisis of the Model of Democracy in the EU – Causes, Determinants and Scenarios for the Future'], in: Wojtaszczyk Konstanty A., Nadolska Jadwiga (ed.), *Kryzysy w procesie integracji europejskiej i sposoby ich przezwyciężania* [*Crises in the Process of European Integration and Ways to Overcome Them*], ASPRA-JR, Warszawa 2015, pp. 119–160.

Wittinger Michaela, '"Europäische Satelliten": Anmerkungen zum Europäischen Agentur(un)wesen und zur Vereinbarkeit Europäischer Agenturen mit dem Gemeinschaftsrecht', *Europarecht*, No. 5, 2008, pp. 609–626.

Wojtaszczyk Konstanty A., 'Agencje w systemie UE. Typologia oraz podstawy teoretyczno-metodologiczne prowadzenia badań' ['Agencies in the EU System. Typology and Theoretical Aspects of Current Research'], in: Witkowska Marta, Wojtaszczyk Konstanty A. (ed.), *Agencje, komitety i inne jednostki organizacyjne UE* [*Agencies, Committees and Other Organisational Bodies within the EU Institutional System*], ASPRA-JR, Warszawa 2015, pp. 11–30.

Wojtaszczyk Konstanty A. (ed.), *Legitymizacja procesów integracji europejskiej* [*Legitimising the Processes of European Integration*], ASPRA-JR, Warszawa 2006.

Wolff Corinna, *Functional Representation and Democracy in the EU. The European Commission and Social NGOs*, ECPR Press, Colchester 2013.

Wolff Sarah, Schout Adriaan, 'Frontex as Agency: More of the Same?', *Perspectives on European Politics and Society*, Vol. 14, No. 3, 2013, pp. 305–324.

Wonka Arndt, Rittberger Berthold, 'Credibility, Complexity and Uncertainty: Explaining the Institutional Independence of 29 EU Agencies', *West European Politics*, Vol. 33, No. 4, 2010, pp. 730–752.

Wonka Arndt, Rittberger Berthold, 'How Independent are EU Agencies?', *RECON Online Working Paper*, No. 12, 2009; available at: http://www.mzes.uni-mannheim.de/d7/en/publications/report/how-independent-are-eu-agencies (20.3.2018).

Wood Matthew, 'Mapping EU Agencies as Political Entrepreneurs', *European Journal of Political Research*, Published Online in August 2017, DOI:10.1111/1475-6765.12232.

Wörner Thorsten, *Rechtlich weiche Verhaltenssteuerungsformen Europäischer Agenturen als Bewährungsprobe der Rechtsunion*, Mohr Siebeck, Tübingen 2017.

Yataganas Xénophon A., 'Delegation of Regulatory Authority in the European Union. The Relevance of the American Model of Independent Agencies', *Jean Monnet Working Paper*, No. 3, 2001; available at: https://infoeuropa.eurocid.pt/files/database/000036001-000037000/000036463.pdf (20.3.2017).

Yuratich David, 'Artcile 13(2) TEU: Institutional Balance, Sincere Co-operation, and Non-Domination During Lawmaking', *German Law Journal*, Vol. 18, No. 1, 2017, pp. 99–125.

Zaun Natascha, *EU Asylum Policies. The Power of Strong Regulating States*, Palgrave Macmillan, Cham 2017.

Zieliński Marek, 'Agencje Unii Europejskiej' ['EU Agencies'], in: Grzeszczak Robert, Szczerba-Zawada Aleksandra (ed.), *Prawo administracyjne Unii*

Europejskiej [*Administrative Law of the European Union*], EuroPrawo, Warszawa 2016, pp. 163–174.

Zieliński Marek, 'Agencje wykonawcze UE' ['EU Executive Agencies'], *Europejski Przegląd Sądowy*, No. 6, 2014, pp. 15–19.

Zieliński Marek, 'Porozumienie dotyczące siedziby agencji Unii Europejskiej Frontex w Polsce. Aspekty konstytucyjne' ['The Agreement on the Seat of the EU Agency Frontex in Poland: Constitutional Aspects'], *Przegląd Sejmowy*, Vol. XXIV, No. 1(132), 2016, pp. 53–63.

Zito Anthony R., 'European Agencies as Agents of Governance and EU Learning', *Journal of European Public Policy*, Vol. 16, No. 8, 2009, pp. 1224–1243.

Index

www.ingramcontent.com/pod-product-compliance
Ingram Content Group UK Ltd.
Pitfield, Milton Keynes, MK11 3LW, UK
UKHW021830100926
8556IPUK00004B/258

9 783631 748619